BY DAVID KIPEN

The Schreiber Theory: A Radical Rewrite of American Film History

TRANSLATOR

The Dialogue of the Dogs by Miguel de Cervantes

EDITOR

Dear Los Angeles: The City in Diaries and Letters, 1542 to 2018

California in the 1930s: The WPA Guide to the Golden State

San Diego in the 1930s: The WPA Guide to America's Finest City

Los Angeles in the 1930s: The WPA Guide to the City of Angels

San Francisco in the 1930s: The WPA Guide to the City by the Bay

Dear California

THE GOLDEN STATE IN DIARIES AND LETTERS

EDITED BY David Kipen

REDWOOD PRESS
Stanford, California

Redwood Press
Stanford, California

Library of Congress Cataloging-in-Publication Data

Names: Kipen, David, editor.
Title: Dear California : the golden state in diaries and letters / edited by David Kipen.
Other titles: Golden State in diaries and letters
Description: Stanford, California : Redwood Press, [2023] | Includes index.
Identifiers: LCCN 2022060466 (print) | LCCN 2022060467 (ebook) | ISBN 9781503614697 (cloth) | ISBN 9781503637054 (ebook)
Subjects: LCSH: California—History—Anecdotes. | California—Quotations, maxims, etc. | LCGFT: Anecdotes | Quotations
Classification: LCC F861.6 .D44 2023 (print) | LCC F861.6 (ebook) | DDC 979.4—dc23/eng/20221228
LC record available at https://lccn.loc.gov/2022060466
LC ebook record available at https://lccn.loc.gov/2022060467

Cover design: Aufuldish & Warinner
Cover photograph: Unsplash / Gerson Repreza
Text design: Elliott Beard
Typeset by Newgen in Warnock Pro Regular 10/14

To everyone whose first answer,
when asked, out of state,
where they're from,
is
"California"

and for my beloved brothers,
Howard Matthew Kipen
and
Laurence Daniel Kipen,
sons of California both,

for my adored nieces,
Sydney Laskin Kipen
and
Carly Laskin Kipen,
granddaughters of California,

and for my wife,
Colleen Marie Jaurretche,
my Mexican-British-Basque-Ojibwe
California girl

Know that, on the right side of the Indies, there is an island called California, very near to the Terrestrial Paradise...all of gold...
—*The Adventures of Esplandián*
by **GARCI RODRÍGUEZ DE MONTALVO**, 1510

"This," said the barber, "is *The Adventures of Esplandián...*

"Here, mistress housekeeper," said the cleric, "open that window, and toss it into the paddock, where it shall serve as kindling for the bonfire..."
—*Don Quijote*
by **MIGUEL DE CERVANTES DE SAAVEDRA**, 1605

CONTENTS

PREFACE

Imagine no Californian ever died. That was always the promise, wasn't it? Move to California and live forever? *Now* imagine that everybody who ever visited California had never left. Not so farfetched. People have been cashing in their return tickets here since the very first steamship made landfall.

Finally, imagine all those Californians above—the natives, the non-natives, and the gone-natives alike—all talking together across the centuries, and never shutting up.

Mark Twain hitting on Joan Didion. Zora Neale Hurston cheering up Sylvia Plath. Gaspar de Portolá comparing road trips with Sally Ride. Ambrose Bierce and Oscar "Zeta" Acosta postponing their ill-fated trips to Mexico. That's just some of the hubbub audible in the pages that follow.

Welcome, then, to *Dear California: The Golden State in Diaries and Letters*—a commonplace book for an uncommon place. If you've encountered this book's progenitor, *Dear Los Angeles*, you have some idea what you're in for. If you're new to the *Dear* franchise—do two books make a franchise?—then thank you for hopping on board, or at least considering it.

On first looking into *Dear California*, your first reaction might well be, what's with the hiccupping, date-by-date structure? Why not just march out all these California diary and letter excerpts (plus a few irresistible scraps of columnizing, tweets, blogs, and speeches) in straightforward chronology, like *Bartlett's Familiar Quotations* does? Who ever heard of a book that inches forward each day, only to ratchet back overnight, just as far or farther? Is this a daybook or the myth of Sisyphus?

It wasn't my idea. Teresa Carpenter's delightful *New York Diaries* provided the general structure, and I added letters to diaries to help round out the picture. Mercifully, most Californians don't keep diaries, or keep their letters. If they did, we'd be here all century.

Another inevitable question to address is what got in and what didn't. You could spend a lifetime in California libraries and archives and barely scratch the surface of what's available. The only constraints would be publisher patience and authorial liquidity. Within these parameters, my criteria for including an entry were basically 1) relevance to California and 2) undefinable, indefensible editorial prerogative.

Mostly I liked these entries because they told me something about my state. For reasons not always easy to quantify, they played off each other in quirky, quarky, covalent ways. Some underscored how far we've come, some how far we still have to go. Ultimately, though, the entries had a hard time getting in if they didn't make me laugh, or tick me off, or choke me up.

A shamefaced word here about those who didn't make the cut often enough, i.e., poor people, minorities, women, and all the other Californians who've lived some fascinating but tantalizingly unrecorded lives. California's own Tillie Olsen famously wrote that "literary history and the present are dark with silences." Historical reasons exist for many of the silences in this book. So, probably, do careless, myopic ones on my part. Those omitted might or might not have cared that this book stints them, but I do, and I apologize for it.

That's why I'm not done yet. Every day, dumpster-loads of family diaries and letters wind up in landfills. Descendants cherrypick the antiques for estate sales and, regretfully or not, consign the rest to oblivion. Executors of California, I implore you: Have pity on the social historians (and beach-combing pseudo-historians) of the future. Half-assed temporary preservation is easier than ever. Haul out your *bubbe's* Saratoga trunk. Open up your *abuelita's* closet. Read some of those yellowed notebook pages, those bundled love letters, even some of that "Sent Mail." Snap pictures of at least a good example or two. If you don't have anywhere else to donate them, email me a transcription at DearCA@sup.org. I'll be working to launch an initiative that'll give your history a home. If you've shelled out for *Dear California*, it's the least I can do.

Finally, what, if anything, might *Dear California* be telling us about the fate of the Golden State at this even more fraught than usual moment in our history? We're all used to seeing California described in the popular imagination as golden one year and tarnished the next, but at least these opinions used to take turns. Nowadays, in reputable publications on the very same day, you can see California characterized by fairly smart people as either the idea laboratory of the future or a sclerotic, debt-burdened dream of the past. There's no consensus; there's barely a trustworthy *census* anymore.

Whenever the Romans felt similarly unmoored, they liked to practice something called the *sortes virgilianae*, or *Virgilian divination*. They'd stick a finger in a copy of Virgil's *Aeneid* and try to divine the poet's advice from the first line they landed on. Unfortunately, if we're trying to figure out whether California is really going to hell or not, a sentence like "Aeneas plowed the plains of brine with prows of bronze" may not get us very far. Something closer to home is in order. In lieu of Virgil, we might try more of a *sortes Californiensis*—a kind of Golden State, diary-and-letter-derived I Ching. (Call it the "*¡Ay, chingón!*")

Sticking a finger in *Dear California* on an arbitrary date, then, what might we find? To remove even the possibility of somehow gaming the result, let's pick a date that I don't know without looking it up. For example, Virgil's birthday is, I find, October 15. As a real-time experiment, what if we ask *Dear California* for that date to say something profound about the Golden State itself?

Turning to October 15 in search of priceless wisdom about California, we find . . . we find that we *really* should've picked another day. On that date in 1863, alas, per the landscape architect and writer Frederick Law Olmsted, the divination isn't promising: his patch of California "is a desolate country," he writes. In the next paragraph, in case we missed the point, he even calls it "detestable."

So what's a Californian to do now, when even the *sortes Californiensis* conspires against us? Luckily, every Californian knows the answer, or their ancestors did. If not, they wouldn't be here. Whether they got here by plane, by car, by clipper ship or land bridge from Asia, all Californians know what you do when all the entrails spell out "Run for your lives!":

You turn the page. You start a new year . . .

Dear California

BEFORE THE BEGINNING

Turtle was gone a long time. He was gone six years; and when he came up, he was covered with green slime, he had been down so long. When he reached the top of the water, the only earth he had was a very little under his nails: the rest had all washed away.

Earth-Initiate took with his right hand a stone knife from under his left armpit, and carefully scraped the earth from under Turtle's nails. He put the earth in the palm of his hand, and rolled it about till it was round; it was as large as a small pebble. He laid it on the stern of the raft. By and by he went to look at it: it had not grown at all. The third time that he went to look at it, it had grown so that it could not be spanned by the arms.

The fourth time he looked, it was as big as the world, the raft was aground, and all around were mountains as far as he could see. The raft came ashore at Tadoiko [in Butte County, near Durham], and the place can be seen today . . .

THE CREATION STORY OF TURTLE ISLAND (MAIDU)

JANUARY 1

1795

. . . on January 1, 1795 . . . pagan parents presented a child, which was three months old . . . The parents were from the rancheria of Cajatse . . .

SANTA BARBARA MISSION RECORDS

1847

We pray the God of mercy to deliver us from our present Calamity if it be his Holy will Amen. Commenc'd Snowing last night . . . sun peeps out at times provisions getting scant . . . **PATRICK BREEN**, *Donner Party diarist*

1847

. . . [Commodore Stockton] with his staff passed the night at the Ranch—and report says had a fine supper . . .

JOHN S. GRIFFIN, MD, *Mexican-American War surgeon*

1848

This indenture made *the first Day of January* [italics mine] in the year of our Lord One thousand Eight hundred and fourty eight between Pulpuli and Gesu, Chiefs. Colule and Sole, Alcaldes of the Yalesumney tribe . . . and John A. Sutter and James W. Marshall . . .

the Yalesumney tribe . . . doth rent and lease unto Sutter and Marshall the following described track of Land for the term of twenty years, beginning at the mouth of a small creek known by the Indian name of Pumpumul where said creek empties into the south branch of the American fork . . . [and] grant to the said Sutter and Marshall . . . the right to erect a saw mill . . . [and] open such mines and work the same as the said aforsaid tract of land may contain . . .

the said Sutter & Marshall doth bind themselves . . . to pay on the first day of January each year one hundred and fifty dollars [and] to give quiet and peaceable possession of the aforesaid premises unto the said Pulpuli,

Gesu, Colule and Sole their heirs and assigns[,] they paying the said Sutter and Marshall a reasonable price for the mill . . .

In witness whereof the said parties of the first and second part set their names and seals. Done this *the fourth day of February* [italics mine] in the year of our Lord one thousand Eight hundred and fourty eight . . .

Done in the presence and with my aprobation

JOHANN AUGUSTUS SUTTER, *Sub-Indian Agent,*
backdating his lease on the gold discovery site

1906

New Year's day was celebrated here as usual: noisy crowd at Van Ness and Fillmore, shouting, men in a state of joy, strangers wishing each other Happy New Year and giving each other long, warm handshakes. Everybody has had a good dinner, everybody is happy, but as it is San Francisco, there has to be, from time to time, some little scuffle with pistol shots.

Just nine months since everything burned and they dance to a different tune! San Franciscans are built of galvanized iron, or something just as hard but more elastic . . .   *linguist, writer* **JAIME DE ANGULO**

1944

. . . saw *Song of Bernadette*—and Otto stayed the night here. Hope next year will be as nice.   *actress* **KAY FRANCIS**

1969

Dear Mom, Dad, Scot & Paul
Hi again hope you had a Happy New Year. I got to stay here on base, what fun. I figure if I can't drink I won't celebrate the New Year that's all there is to it . . .

Say Paul if its okay with you people could you come down and get me out of here this Saturday . . .   **PRIVATE JAMES CHARLES VANDEVENTER**
at boot camp in San Diego,
killed five months later in Quang Tri

1971

. . . [President Nixon] was very upset by a report in the sports section today that the Stanford football team was running around their hotel in sandals and shorts and that their quarterback had enjoyed posing for pictures with the topless dancers from San Francisco. The story was trying to make them out as being good guys because of this, and sneering at Ohio State as squares because they were wearing neckties and blazers. The P said for the first time he was going to root for the Midwest team in the Rose Bowl.

H. R. HALDEMAN, *White House chief of staff*

1988

. . . I have written an awful lot about death—at times I have thought I must be getting monotonous, but then I think of Emily D who seemed to write ONLY well about death, so I suppose it's a good large subject, about which there's an awful lot to be said. I have rather few friends left, but a greatly increased wardrobe. That seems to be the legacy of AIDS, the survivors do end up with heaps of shirts!

. . . I shall be 60 in a year and a half! Amazing, I think. Not that I look any younger than I am. I'm just so surprised that I'm almost there already. The years do flash by like a strobe light don't they . . .   *poet* **THOM GUNN**

JANUARY 2

1931

We were to take Hearst's special train, leaving Los Angeles at eight o'clock in the evening . . .

Soon we passed herds of buffalo, striped zebra, deer and antelope, exotic birds that looked like white ostriches. Abruptly, in the distance, at the top of a tree-spotted mountain, we caught sight of a vast, sparkling white castle in Spain. It was right out of a fairy story. 'Gosh,' I said . . .

Indoors, the mob crowded the assembly-room and waited for midnight. We drank champagne, tried to be hilarious, exchanged kisses all round. But the party was so large that many of the guests remained strangers one to the other. Bells ringing, sirens going off and a whining moan in the distance announced that the New Year was in. Marion [Davies] had sudden spurts of energy, did a Charleston, shook her hands frenziedly, then hurried out of the room to consult with Hearst. Gradually, all hopes of an orgy disappeared. We dwindled to bed.   *couturier* **CECIL BEATON**

1942

TOR HOUSE. CARMEL. CALIFORNIA

[Our son] Garth got down from the gold mine where he is in charge of the ore reduction mill,—70 mi up in the mts. above Bakersfield—down a terrific mt. road in a big truck. He is still held there by deep snow & doesnt know when he can get up again with his load of dynamite & drums of gasoline. You can imagine how little we like his slithering over these roads with such a load . . .

We've had much excitement here, blackouts & airplanes, supposedly enemy ones, a partial evacuation, much organization of citizen defense etc. People behaved very well mostly, a few hysterical ones had to be soothed . . .

writer **UNA KUSTER JEFFERS**, *to publisher Bennett Cerf*

JANUARY 3

1543

Passing the winter on the island of La Posesión [San Miguel Island], on the 3d of the month of January, 1543, Juan Rodriguez Cabrillo . . . departed from this life, as the result of a fall which he suffered on said island when they were there before, from which he broke an arm near the shoulder. He left as captain the chief pilot, who was one Bartolomé Ferrelo, a native of the Levant . . .   **CAPT. BARTOLOMÉ FERRELO**

1863

WEAVERVILLE

I have been looking over my journal that I keep for the year past and I find that there have been forty one births, eleven marriages and 19 deaths in town. The lowest reading of the thermometer was on January 31st, 10° above zero; the highest, August 3d, 102° above . . .

I hope the War will be prosecuted and I am willing to do my part toward prosecuting it, to the end, till the South is conquered, annihilated, made a desert of, if need be. I would accept no terms of peace but unconditional surrender—come back into the Union as you are without any compromise or yielding on the part of the free States, if it takes five years to do it. I want the programme carried out—them's my sentiments and that is the platform of the Union Party in California.   *forty-niner* **FRANKLIN A. BUCK**

JANUARY 4

1928

It is precisely a week ago that we suffered a fright with Miguelito. He was crossing the street nearby when he was hit by a car. Even though it was not serious, it wasn't without consequences, for the car passed over him and dragged him a good stretch. It seems that perhaps he will come out of it with only slight bruises and contusions that have kept him in bed for a couple of days. He now gets around with a bit of a limp, somewhat like don Cuco.

Lola did go through a terrible ordeal. Since I wasn't there when it all happened, she went out to see what was going on and there she found only his shoes and was told that her boy had been carried away dead and had been taken to the hospital. And so she returned with his shoes in hand and with her heart in pieces. We immediately telephoned to find out which hospital they had taken him to so we could go see him when a man arrived with him very much alive . . .   **DOLORES VENEGAS**, *to family in Mexico*

1928

I wish I could see you. It has been many years since we saw each other. We are very happy because dad has a store, and . . . when I was going to buy tortillas I was struck by a car that dragged me about 10 blocks. My dad is thinking how we can return and be together again with my aunt Anita and with all of you.   **JOSÉ MIGUEL VENEGAS**, *to family in Mexico*

1930

Carmel is not so much an art colony as it is a work of art. The secret of its charm can be summarized briefly: the land is lovely. Its effects are startling—and unforgettable . . .

The present fascination of Carmel owes much to the presence of Robinson Jeffers . . . His Carmel "retreat" is now a thing of the past. Neighbors crowd in about Tor House, and a huge highway is crawling north along the coast and will some day pass within a stone's throw of his door. Los Angeles "realtors" are already at Cambria, a few miles down the coast, and are even now gazing on Carmel like the lady feasting her eyes on the Roan Stallion. It is unforgettable. Carmel has become a splendid experience in the lives of many western artists and they will view its desecration with unspeakable horror.
historian **CAREY MCWILLIAMS**

JANUARY 5

1776

The method which the fathers observe in the conversion is not to oblige anyone to become a Christian, admitting only those who voluntarily offer themselves, and this they do in the following manner: Since these Indians are accustomed to live in the fields and the hills like beasts, the fathers require that if they wish to be Christians they shall no longer go to the forest, but must live in the mission, and if they leave the Ranchería, as they call the little village of huts and houses of the Indians, they will go to seek them and will punish them. With this they begin to catechize the heathen who voluntarily come, teaching them to make the sign of the cross and other things necessary, and if they persevere in the catechism for two or three months and in the same frame of mind, when they are instructed they proceed to baptise them.

If any Indian wishes to go to the mountain to see his relatives or to hunt acorns, they give him permission for a specified number of days. As a rule they do not fail to return, and sometimes they come bringing some heathen relative, who remains for the catechism, either through the example of the others or attracted by the pozole, which they like better than their herbs and the foods of the mountain; and so these Indians are usually caught by the mouth.

Father **PEDRO FONT**

1942

At around four, the doorbell rang. It was two neatly dressed Americans about thirty years of age. They said, "There is something we want to ask Aoki."

. . . I called Sachiko and told her, "Go get Father from Mr. Onodera's place."

Sachiko said, "Okay." And in her cheerful way as usual, she took off, walking like she was jumping sideways, so I hurriedly ran down the front stone steps and caught up with her and in rapid Japanese told her, "They are FBI. Father is going to be investigated, so keep that in mind." She said, "What?" And the little girl's face that was always shining white with health suddenly went pale and turned blue, and with tears in her eyes, she took off running!

After a short while, my husband came home; and with my husband, we sat at a table facing the two Americans.

The two Americans rose slightly and said, "This is who we are." And they opened their coat and showed us their FBI badges and let loose their first arrow of questions.

author, internee **AOKI HISA**

JANUARY 6

1931

Here in Pasadena it is like Paradise. Always sunshine and clear air, gardens with palms and pepper trees and friendly people who smile at one and ask for autographs.   *physicist* **ALBERT EINSTEIN**

1993

Dear Miss Manners,

Last April you very kindly agreed to be my etiquette consultant. I need your advice rather urgently. To explain: I've just got a FAX machine, and have been sending out lots of letters on it. One of my sisters in England also has FAX (much to my amazement) so naturally I sent her one straight away. I was surprised that she didn't answer by return—hers came the next day. However, she did say that she was in London when mine arrived, hence delay. Which brings me to the point: What is an answer "by return" in the case of FAX?

For a letter, it's simple; one should answer if possible by return of post. From California, where I live, to England letters take a minimum of 4 days, often much longer, so one is fairly safe in allowing a week or so before answering. One has had it dinned into one since childhood that if you get a letter from somebody, you should answer within a week—or max. two weeks. Anything later requires an apology, or rather an excuse even if untrue ("awfully sorry for late answer—I just got back from Alaska/Timbuctoo/etc," depending on lateness).

With FAX, should one answer within the hour? Or even 15 minutes, given the speediness of transmittal?

Perhaps every new technology requires some re-thinking of the correct response. For example, telegrams (which you are probably too young to remember) almost always had bad news; as they were jolly expensive, the answer was simple, such as "Desperately sorry. Mitford," only 3 words. Or if it was just a broken limb, not a death: "Rotten luck. Mitford." Again, only 3 words; ample, at a shilling a word.

Eagerly awaiting your response. It's now about 1:30 p.m., Wednesday. I'm sitting by my FAX machine.   *author, journalist, activist* **JESSICA MITFORD**

2017

We did see wild swans on Rte. 20 from Grass Valley to Marysville. Jackie said we would. Their heads were tucked under their wings and they were floating in the rice paddies near Marysville. It was an easier ride than the route north, when I almost turned around and went home. White-knuckled on the I-5 in pouring rain, arguing with Lloyd about how to use the car's heating system . . .

Today is Epiphany, day of Claire's birth. We met her just-birthed on the same trip north when we last saw Uncle Herb, then 103. The oldest and the youngest. Herb was of the last survivors of the SF Earthquake. His mother carried him down the stairs outside. He was three. Claire is 13 and first-born of a new generation . . .

Bumped into Janet Fitch in front of Gingergrass, the Vietnamese noodle place . . .   *writer* **LOUISE STEINMAN**

JANUARY 7

1851

That a war of extermination will continue to be waged between the races until the Indian race becomes extinct must be expected. While we cannot anticipate this result but with painful regret, the inevitable destiny of the race is beyond the power or wisdom of man to avert. **GOV. PETER BURNETT**

1853

[John Bowman] will plant the first nursery in Santa Cruz on our land and besides make us a family garden . . . he brought with him some young pine trees and set them around the house . . .   *teacher* **GEORGIANA KIRBY**

1934

. . . I now intend to start my trip up the coast the first week in February. I feel the need of doing some first-hand work. I hope the February allotment reaches me in time for an early start, before I have to pay more rent.

I have been having some interesting and valuable experiences here in San Francisco. I cherish them, for I know that there will never be another period in my life like this . . .   *vanished adventurer* **EVERETT RUESS**,
to his father

JANUARY 8

1847

Friday 8ᵗʰfine morning wind E froze hard last night very cold this morning Mʳˢ. Reid & company came back this morning could not find their way on the other side of the Mountain they have nothing but hides to live on Martha is to stay here . . . may God relieve us all from this difficulty if it his Holy will *Amen*   **PATRICK BREEN**

1847

As we approached the river the Enemy appeared in great force . . . We advanced steadily—the Dragoons and Cyane's Marines supporting the two guns which were in the advance— two large guns . . .

We exchanged shots here with the enemy—and dismounted one or two of their guns— One of the guns that dismounted [,] a gun of the enemy—was fired & armed by Commodore Stockton.—After firing a few shots from the first bank we made a rush at the second. The plain between the points must have been two hundred and fifty yards broad—Across this we charged under the full fire from the Enemy . . . We continued to charge at the hill, topped it & ran our friends the Mexicans clearly out of the field . . .

JOHN S. GRIFFIN, MD, *at the Battle of San Gabriel*

1969

. . . they took us inside to this little room behind Jim's garage. It's really cool—completely red lights and all! We talked a bit more and then they started blowing [smoking pot].

Je fait aussi, et Kathy aussi ["I did, and Kathy did too," in high-school French].   *San Francisco teenager* **NIKKI LASTRETO**, *later cannabis* **CEO**

2008

. . . it's Kaiser Permanente. It's an HMO mundo we inhabit (digo, those of us even lucky enough to *have* health coverage), so I won't know anything for up to ten days, can you believe it?   *writer* **SUSANA CHÁVEZ-SILVERMAN**

JANUARY 9

1847

Continues fine freezing hard at night this a beatiful morning . . . virginias toes frozen alittle snow settleing   **PATRICK BREEN**, *in an entry where the day's deaths of two native Californian vaqueros go unmentioned*

1847

. . . This morning a Mexican came galloping up with a white flag—this man we found to be [Lorenzo] Soto—a californian who had been sent out by the commodore some days before—he reported that Fremont was at San Fernando within eight leagues of the Pueblo . . .

When we first left camp we saw but few of the enemy in sight—although he had encamped within a mile of us in the evening—As we proceeded—we saw him—in considerable force on our right flank—we exchanged shots with our artillery—What damage we did to him we know not. The only hurt we sustained, was one mule—one ox wounded one of our men, a sailor shot himself in the foot . . . Capt Gilispie & Capt Rowan were hit by spent balls . . .

The enemy drew up at some distance—out of gun shot . . . threatening our right rear—& left front—finally they made the rush, and got most terribly peppered . . .   **JOHN S. GRIFFIN, MD**, *at the Battle of La Mesa*

1850

SACRAMENTO

. . . I had put Mary quietly to bed and was resting myself for a minute or two before undressing for the night, when I heard quick footsteps without, and Mr. A-'s voice saying hastily to my husband who stood at the door, "The water's coming in." The reply expressed doubt; but A's voice continued very emphatically, "O, yes, I am sure, I have just been to the 'sloo,' and the water is flowing over the banks fast. See, come this way—to this low spot—and you will soon find yourself stepping in water. There, watch a minute, don't you see it rising on your boot?"

. . . The waves dashed against the sides of the house, shaking and rocking it so that there seemed great danger of it capsizing. The noise of wind and waves made sleep, for some hours, impossible to me; and as I lay there in the darkness I tried to prepare myself to seize Mary and cling to whatever might be uppermost, in case the house careened . . .

pioneer, teacher, writer **SARAH ROYCE,**
mother of Josiah Royce [q.v.]

1890

Rode on a burro, first time. Liked it.   *novelist* **CHARLOTTE PERKINS GILMAN**

1956

Reported at 9.30 am for third day at Colombia lot. Shot more scenes on the picture. Today did 'Rock Around The Clock' and 'Rudy's Rock'. That makes 5 songs so far we've done in the picture. So far the picture is going great. This is a big break for us. Keeping my fingers crossed. To bed early and up at them tomorrow at 7.30 am.   *rocker* **BILL HALEY**

2022

Arrived on campus yesterday evening and took my rapid COVID test. The guy giving me instructions says, "If you test positive, just raise your hand." I thought, "Sir, if I test positive I'm taking a flying leap from that window over there—why else would you be holding this on the top floor?" I was directed to a place at one of many long tables set up in rows around a conference room. It was dead quiet. Something about the word "test" just invokes silence in students, despite this particular one not necessitating it at all. I opened the box in front of me, which included an extensive sheet of fold-out instructions, but I looked around and noticed that nobody else had theirs out. Not wanting to foolishly open mine and look like an imbecile tourist on the side of the road in Yosemite, I disregarded the map of test instructions. Instead I had to rely on the very pared-down version that was on a laminated sheet a little ways away from me.

Rather involved, was this test. You had to swab your nose, then swirl the Q-tip in this tube, then squeeze the tube while turning the Q-tip, then cap the tube and squeeze four drops onto the test sample. As I waited for my result, I looked around. I wasn't very impressed with what I saw. Behind me, a poor girl who hadn't caught on that it was taboo to open the instructions had the massive paper folded out in front of her as she navigated to what I can only assume was Loserville. When the 15 minutes had passed, I looked down at my test and was thrilled to discover I could forgo the window and exit the building by the stairs.   *UCLA art major* **SAMIA SAAD**

JANUARY 10

1872

Dear Emerson,

Here is a sheaflet of winter wheat, ripe & mellow from fields of snow—a plume of Libocedrus golden with staminate cones—It will give you a tingle of beauty, & I will be glad.

Would you were here to sing our Yosemite snowbound—to bathe in these fountain lights—to warm in these fountain loves. What prayers push my pen for your coming, but I must hush them all back for our roads are deep blocked with snowbloom.

naturalist **JOHN MUIR** *to Ralph Waldo Emerson*

1888

The boy is growing and talks now remarkably well. He remarked the other day—when told to be careful or he would break his neck—"I don't want to break my neck—I wouldn't break it for any 'mount of money."

Mary had quite a sore throat—& the other night Ruth & I kept both babies all night. We had a circus—had to take both in bed—at the same time. The boy [Gen. George S. Patton, Jr.] is fearful as a bed-fellow. I had just as soon sleep with a mule   **COL. GEORGE PATTON, SR.**

1968

Only [Hell's Angel] I ever had, tho tattooed scores of em. Dint want any more.

writer, sex-research subject **SAMUEL STEWARD**, *tattooist to the Angels*

1969

. . . I can honestly say that in this 4 day school week I changed so much it is unbelievable. I guess I finally proved to myself what kind of girl I am. That was pretty fast considering I just decided to start "finding myself" about 1½ weeks ago!   **NIKKI LASTRETO**

JANUARY 11

1847

I have been engaged all day arranging my Hospital. I have not heard any thing that is going on, everything seems quiet, the citizens of the place do not so far as I can discover manifest very friendly feelings—Nothing heard from Fremont, last night there was a devil of a row among the men, liquor the cause of it all—although every precaution had been taken. An Indian was found dead this morning—how killed I do not know.

JOHN S. GRIFFIN, MD

1847

Emerging from the hills, the advance party to which I was attached met two Californians, bareheaded, riding in great haste. They stated that they were from the mission of San Fernando; that the Californian forces had met the American forces under the command of General Kearny and Commodore Stockton, and had been defeated after two days' fighting; and that the Americans had yesterday marched into Los Angeles . . .   EDWIN BRYANT

1847

Saw the dead bodies of the two Indian boys.   JAMES REED,

regarding a pair of Donner Party guides
killed by another member of the company

1933

I have just consumed a stack of wheats & a mug of mocha in this place [The Brown Derby restaurant]. The weather is very hot: yesterday went out in a motor boat from Balboa harbour. Have lectured three times & addressed several classes; have driven a Ford and got stuck in a snow drift. The trees are full of oranges.   *poet* T.S. ELIOT

1944

Otto called at 12—furious—having checked Mocambo! Well, that's that!

KAY FRANCIS

JANUARY 12

1847

Snows fast yet new snow about 3 feet deep wind S:W no sign of Clearing off

PATRICK BREEN

1847

This morning two Californian officers, accompanied by Tortaria Pico, who marched with us from San Luis Obispo, came to the mission to treat for

peace. A consultation was held and terms were suggested, and, as I understand, partly agreed upon, but not concluded.   **EDWIN BRYANT,**
witness to the Treaty of Cahuenga

1847

. . . in virtue of the aforesaid articles, equal rights and privileges are vouch-
safed to every citizen of California, as are enjoyed by the citizens of the
United States of North America.   **DOÑA BERNARDA RUÍZ DE RODRÍGUEZ,**
amending the Treaty of Cahuenga

1850

"A beautiful country, romantic scenery, excellent harbor, a fine climate and
plenty of game. This is the place for me in the winter season," thinks I as I
came on deck and looked around on the morning after we anchored.

"It's the most degraded, immoral, uncivilized and dirty place that can be
imagined, and the sooner we are away from here the better for us," were my
after thoughts five minutes after being landed on shore!

The city is laid out in squares, and from the highest hills, makes a splendid appearance, as not only are there many fine looking buildings, which
shew well at a distance, but also hundreds of tents of all sizes and descriptions, and of various colors, squads of which scattered around on the hill
sides, fill up the valleys, and shew to great advantage. A beautiful view of
the bay and surrounding scenery may here be taken, the entrance to the
harbor at the westward, and that of the Bay of San Pablo at the northward,
while directly beneath lay crowds of shipping shewing flags of all nations a
miniature forest of boats pulling here and there, discharging cargo, steamers running to and fro, and all the peculiar business-like appearance of any
large Atlantic or European city. Such is San Francisco now. What it formerly
has been, what it was only one year since, we all know, and (as with every
other new country) what it eventually will be still remains to be proved.
ISAAC W. BAKER, *arriving at San Francisco*

1982

[The] big news is we found the land!

20 acres of very hilly but beautiful Mendocino land . . . A handmade yurt
which will do nicely for my studio. Two structures that can be used as cabins
until we build our house. We plan to build our house way up on the knoll
with a sweeping view of lower hills, ponds, trees and grapes—vineyards way
in the distance.

Sellers are two 6oish lesbian women. Very nice. Decent. One a potter . . .

ALICE WALKER

JANUARY 13

1847

We continued our march, and encamped near a deserted rancho at the foot of Couenga plain. Soon after we halted, the Californian peace-commissioners appeared, and the terms of peace and capitulation were finally agreed upon and signed by the respective parties . . .   EDWIN BRYANT

1847

snowing fast wind N.W Snow higher than the Shanty . . .   PATRICK BREEN

JANUARY 14

1930

Amelia Earhart . . . is the most amazing person—just as tremendous as [Charles], I think . . . She has the clarity of mind, impersonal eye, coolness of temperament, balance of a scientist. Aside from that, I like her.

I am sitting with my back to the radiator and the table in front of me, just as I always did in college. They don't expect cold out here and the rain is the dismalest, coldest, penetratingest rain—worse than Northampton Sunday rains . . .   ANNE MORROW LINDBERGH

1988

I love tripe in all its many forms and this minute am full of a big bowl of homemade menudo . . .   *writer, novelist* M. F. K. FISHER

JANUARY 15

1971

This morning the sheets are twisted and the pillows lie on the floor. Perhaps I shall get up and drive over the mountains to find myself sitting in a field of clover...   *L.A. Free Press columnist* **LIZA WILLIAMS**

1990

dearest Decca and Bob:
I have wanted to get in touch with you long before this, but things have not been going too well. Tomorrow I am to have three or four teeth extracted, as they have become infected due to the fall in the street so many weeks ago. I do want to see you both so much and hope you will be able to make it to The Redwoods soon. It has not been a happy beginning of the year, darkened by my beloved Beckett's death. Three weeks before, he wrote his last letter to me, just two lines: "Feeling too poorly to write. Sixty years of love, Sam." He was younger than I and should not have died.

May 1990 bring you much happiness. Twenty-seven years of love

novelist **KAY BOYLE**

2009

Dear President Elect and Michelle Obama,
. . . For the last 40 years, I have been immersed in a grassroots food revolution that I believe will make a tremendous difference to the health, security, and values of all Americans. Local, affordable, nutritious food should be a right for everyone and not just a privilege for a few . . .

Of course, I cannot forget the vision I have had since 1993 of a beautiful vegetable garden on the White House lawn. It would demonstrate to the nation and to the world our priority of stewardship of the land—a true *victory* garden!

With great admiration and hope,   **ALICE WATERS**

JANUARY 16

1933

I don't like California much: no country, only scenery.

T.S. ELIOT, *to Lady Ottoline Morrell*

1940

. . . you would be giving me the greatest help of all if you can find out why I am in the doghouse . . .

Once [Budd Schulberg] told me that, while the story of an official blacklist is a legend, there is a kind of cabal that goes on between producers around a backgammon table, and I have an idea that some such sinister finger is upon me. I know also that if a man stays away from pictures deliberately like I did from March to July he is forgotten, or else people think there's something the matter with him . . .

This vague sense of competence unused and abilities unwanted is rather destructive to the morale . . .

Ever your friend,   *novelist* **F. SCOTT FITZGERALD**, *to Leland Hayward*

1965

MGM wants to make a movie around the January 3rd article in the New York Times, and I've given a tentative consent. I am working up a step out-line of the material now, and my director, Jeffrey Hayden (who, incidentally, is married to the actress Eva Marie Saint), is most enthusiastic. There's a lot of quick money in the project, though every mirror I look in I expect to see Scott Fitzgerald's weary ghost looking back. But so far I haven't seen him . . .

All yours,
Jim
8950 Balboa Boulevard
Northridge, California   *poet, novelist* **JAMES DICKEY**, *to Donald Hall*

JANUARY 17

1882

. . . my *Atlantic* has not arrived—& if you will believe it, I can't buy one in this place . . .

Whoever will come & and live a year on this coast, can make a book of romance which will live: It is a tropic of color and song. It is real pain to have to skim over it flying, as I do. –   *writer* **HELEN HUNT JACKSON**,
soon the author of Ramona, *to her editor*

1944

WILLIAM ANDREWS CLARK MEMORIAL LIBRARY

. . . I wish you could see this place. It's a gem, set in a 5-acre walled garden. I have 4 librarians, 3 gardeners & 1 janitor-bookbinder under me . . . Clark spent a million bucks on this building—all bronze & English oak, marble & travertine—in beautiful taste. I squat in my panelled office, my hoofs buried in an Oriental rug, & toss the flotsam & jetsam over my left shoulder into a $200 hand-carved oak waste-basket . . .

A wonderfully quiet restful place, about 12 miles downtown from the campus. Admission only by card. I look forward to the time when I can show you the place. Next year I'll try to spend a day a week here—a sort of idyllic retreat from the busy campus library . . .

Finally to return to the University as somebody to have authority & to be responsible only to the President whose full confidence I have, this is what I cherish. I put in 5-1/2 years of penal servitude & did not sour. Now I am sweet as a nut. I race through detail work like a mouse through cheese . . .

I wish I could visit you. Perhaps in the late spring I might take to the road & vagabond my way up. I will have 2 weeks off before starting at the University library.

And how wonderful a few women can make life! Sometimes you never even talk with them, or see them up close . . . Only the quick vision of a lovely body & carriage, how exciting to the imagination! And going up into the hills for holly, breaking through the forest of dead mustard stalks & tall dry grasses. Say, a man & woman going into the hills for holly & becoming lovers for the first time, in the bedded dry grass under the berried toyon tree, up above the valley, secret, hidden, hot & ardent. Stories to write, Bill—I teem with them. And latterly it will not matter whether they actually happened to me or not. That is the freedom I am striving toward.

Affectionately,   *UCLA Librarian, author*

LAWRENCE CLARK POWELL, *to the poet William Everson*

1952

There has never been a violin like the Red Diamond.

As long as men make records of these things, the strange Stradivarius violin that went to sea will be recalled for all its incredible mystery . . .

Only last Jan. 11, a shipment of rare Cremona violins, including several Stradivari, went down with the Flying Enterprise off the coast of England . . .

But the Red Diamond, lost five days later, was saved in a fantastic series of accidental choices of man.

It had been tossed from the arms of violinist Sascha Jacobsen by swirling waters as he sought to leave his stranded automobile on Pacific Coast Highway at Sunset Blvd. for high ground only 15 feet away . . .

Jacobson called for help. Two men nearby leaped into the torrent to pull him to safety.

They watched, silently, as the Red Diamond floated swiftly out to sea. The loss was told in the nation's press. A world of music was shocked, resigned to another art treasure lost.

Then came an incredible series of accidents.

Had there been a tennis appointment for Atty. Frederic H. Sturdy on the following day at the Bel-Air Bay Club, he might not have decided to walk alone along the beach.

When he reached the water's edge he might have walked South. And when he finally passed what appeared to be a piece of discarded, water-logged luggage on the sand, he was tempted to ignore it.

Instead he carried the mud-filled baggage to the clubhouse, where associates promptly dubbed it "the thing."

He left the package in the locker room and drove home. The car radio was on and [he heard a] news broadcast telling of the Red Diamond's loss . . .

unsigned **L.A. TIMES** *item*

1960

I am, of course, the Robert Rich who wrote the original story and screenplay of a simple—if not simple-minded—little film called *The Brave One*, for which young Rich was awarded an Oscar. He hasn't got it yet, and neither have I. However, it's just as well, for although those statues look like gold, I'm told they're nothing but pot-metal inside . . .

[The] only woman I ever married is still at my side. She brings in extra money as a photographer, so we eat well and love each other rather more than we did on that day twenty-two years ago when each confronted the other, with justifiable suspicion . . .

screenwriter, novelist **DALTON TRUMBO,** *to an editor*

1994

Big earthquake . . . The tallest bookcase flew apart, broke a window. Books everywhere. Made my way outside; car alarms wailing, lots of people in the dark streets . . .   *singer-songwriter* **WARREN ZEVON**

JANUARY 18

1866

In poesy California will advance to the front—to the head of the nation, at a single stride! . . . We cannot bear to see things done in a mild and unassuming way, here; we delight in dash, boldness, startling effects. We take no pride in anything we do unless it be something that will knock the wind out of the world for a moment and make it stand appalled before us. We like to hear the nations say, "There is no mistaking where that thunderbolt hails from—that's California, all over!"

novelist, essayist, publisher, entrepreneur **MARK TWAIN**

1879

608 BUSH STREET, SAN FRANCISCO, CAL.

Any time between eight and half past nine in the morning, a slender gentleman in an ulster, with a volume buttoned into the breast of it, may be observed leaving No. 608 Bush and descending Powell with an active step. The gentleman is R.L.S.; the volume relates to Benjamin Franklin, on whom he meditates one of his charming essays. He descends Powell, crosses Market, and descends in Sixth on a Branch of the original Pine Street Coffee House . . .

[He] seats himself at a table covered with waxcloth; and a pampered menial, of high Dutch extraction and indeed as yet only partially extracted, lays before him a cup of coffee, a roll and a pat of butter, all, to quote the deity, very good. A while ago, R.L.S. used to find the supply of butter insufficient; but he has now learned the art to exactitude, and butter and roll expire at the same moment . . .

Half an hour later, the inhabitants of Bush Street observe the same slender gentleman armed, like George Washington, with his little hatchet, splitting kindling and breaking coal for his fire . . .

Thenceforth, for from three to four hours, he is engaged darkly with an inkbottle. Yet he is not blacking his boots, for the only pair that he possesses are innocent of lustre and wear the natural hue of the material turned up with caked and venerable slush. The youngest child of his landlady remarks several times a day as this strange occupant enters or quits the house: 'Dere's de author.' Can it be that this bright-haired innocent has found the true clue to the mystery? The Being in question is, at least, poor enough to belong to that honourable craft . . . *novelist, essayist* **ROBERT LOUIS STEVENSON**

2005

At this moment, I'm sitting in the car parked at my favorite meditation spot. It is a viewpoint off Marina del Rey—just south of the Venice Beach canals . . .

My husband is napping in the reclining passenger's seat. We ate my picnic dinner of egg-salad sandwiches and lemon cake minutes ago. Marvin Gaye is lilting "sexual feelings/healings" on the soft-jazz radio station . . . A young blonde trots behind a shaggy brick-red dog half her height as the pier-side lamps come on.

Geez, Truong, I'm old enough to remember this city's last gas-lit street lamps, and the lamplighter who came around on his truck, with ladder, to light them—that street Santa Barbara has been renamed Martin Luther King, Jr. Blvd. (MLK), and all the old landmarks, including Wrigley Field (a mini-version of the original) and my great Aunt and Uncle's home are vanished . . .

Their old neighborhood is not far from Magic Johnson's Shopping Center and Theatre complex, and many Black and Latino immigrants are displacing the Afro-American population that replaced the Whites who fled after the Baldwin Hills Dam burst, back in 1963.

The year I graduated high school, 1964, I took a bus ride into that chic neighborhood. Mr. Newsom, my White English teacher and debate coach lived off Stocker, one of its classier avenues. It was a clean, well-kept neighborhood, then, but notorious for racial and officer involved incidents. I was 17-years-old, big at 5'9" and 200 pounds, but I was terrified that something might happen to me. Mr. Newsom had invited a handful of his best speech-and-debate students to hang out that afternoon. My nervousness about the trip was so great it has blotted out the visit, leaving only the residue of fear, which extended to my return bus ride home. I was so anxious to get back to my neighborhood, I left the leather-bound caddy I was carrying on the bus stop bench. In it were five plays that I had painstakingly written by hand, under the spell of Eugene O'Neill and Arthur Miller. They were my only copies. I didn't realize that they were lost until I got home, and didn't have the money for return fare to hunt for them, and couldn't ask my mother, exhausted from her day's labor at the sweatshop, spending hours bent over a power sewing machine.

The young White man who would become my first husband was waiting for me when I got home. He paid our fares as we returned to hunt for the caddy. It was not to be found. As he escorted me back home it couldn't have escaped him that he had made another favorable impression.

poet, essayist **WANDA COLEMAN**, *to* **TRUONG TRAN**

JANUARY 19

1929

The book has the charm of your earlier ones, with more power, I think; and if anyone dares to say that it has peaks and valleys: all the better, so have the Alps.   *poet* **ROBINSON JEFFERS,** *to Edna St. Vincent Millay*

1971

Your review filled me with joy, as your earlier letter did. I have been able to encourage other writers, but never until now have the tables been turned so blessedly on me. To you I can confess that I left the academic world to write popular fiction in the hope of coming back by underground tunnels and devious ways into the light again, dripping with darkness. You encourage me to think that there was some strange merit in this romantic plan.

novelist **ROSS MACDONALD,** *to Eudora Welty*

2021

SANTA CRUZ

Pretty incredible to see so many individual fires popping up in the Santa Cruz Mountains in mid-January . . .   **DANIEL SWAIN,** *meteorologist*

JANUARY 20

1868

My Dear Mary:—By my drinking to excess, and gambling also, I have involved myself to the amount of about three thousand dollars which I have borrowed from time to time from friends and acquaintances [under] the promise to return the same the following day, which I have often failed to do. To such [an extent] have I gone in this way that I am now ashamed to meet my fellow man on the street; besides that, I have deeply wronged you as a husband, by spending my money instead of maintaining you as it becomes a husband to do. Though you have [never] complained of my miserable conduct, you nevertheless have suffered too much. I therefore, to save you from farther disgrace and trouble, being that I cannot maintain you respectably, I shall end this state of thing this very morning . . .

If I write these few lines, it is to set you [right] before this wicked world, to keep slander from blaming you in [any] manner whatever. Now, my dear beloved, I hope that you will pardon me . . . It is time to part, God bless you, and may you be happy yet, your husband Damien Marchesseault.

Mayor **DAMIEN MARCHESSEAULT**, *his suicide note*

1905
Arrived in Los Angeles. On the way passed through San Bernardino, where we observed our first glimpse of beautiful orange and lemon groves against a background of snow-clad mountains. The country is like a garden. Arrived in Los Angeles about 8:30 and drove to the Westminster. Clanging trolley cars drove us away in a half-hour, determined to go right to Coronado. Waited in Station. Saw dying consumptive woman. Ride to San Diego was charming. High hills covered with fresh green grass. Sheep grazing. Old mission.

novelist **ZANE GREY**

2018
"Girls just wanna have fun-damental human rights," "I've seen better cabinets at Ikea," "We are girlcotting this presidency," and "Donald Trump uses Comic Sans" were a few of my favorite posters at the women's march in downtown LA. Everyone was fired up, empowered, and sick of Donald Trump's s**t. The rally was full of positive energy and support for women of all races, religions, sexualities, classes, and origins. The speakers discussed political and social rights, and there was live music! After, my friend and I walked through downtown to buy plants. I bought a little air plant in a glass container. As an environmental science major, I should really be better at not killing plants, but honestly I always forget to water them. My little air plant, that I named Sheldon, only needs to be watered once every two weeks though, so I should be able to keep the little guy alive for awhile. Plus, everytime I water him I'll remember the women's march. This country definitely isn't perfect, but there are a lot of great people here that I trust to keep the country growing.

JULIA CAMPBELL, *student*

JANUARY 21

1861
That portion of our party which went to the Lighthouse had the good fortune to see the shot from a boat . . . and the chase, first up, then down the coast. In their excitement, they thought the run was four miles. Capt. C,

who was the lucky shot, says not more than three-fourths of a mile, when the flurry ended in death; he brought in the whale that same night. Often, however, it sinks and does not rise . . .

Both these companies employ chiefly Indian hands, at $15 per month. The work is measurably light, and the Indians well content with this pay, better than they can get at any other kind of employment.

Capt. Packard considers that he has done well, but thinks the large number of ships that will come here next season on hearing of the success of his venture will seriously interfere with the proceeds of those who operate on land and will soon destroy the whales.   *Judge* **BENJAMIN HAYES**

1993

Dearest M.,

I was SO distraught at missing yr phone call day before Inaugural. Dink rang, said you'd been trying to reach me-it was the one day in history when the blasted answering machine was on the blink.

Forward to the Main Event. Of course we knew it wld be magnifique—but hadn't realized just HOW marvellous, what a peak experience, it wld be. We've taped it (natch) & played it over & over; and today the whole poem was in the SF Chronicle.

When you read it over the phone for "shape," sort of in embryo, I cld see that it was going to be YOUR stride, a total Maya production. Absolutely & unequivocably smashing . . . .

Yr loving Decca   **JESSICA MITFORD**, *to Maya Angelou*

2000

. . . messenger arrived with my birthday present: a signed, numbered "Finnegans Wake" fragment from 1930. Okay!   **WARREN ZEVON**

JANUARY 22

1860

WEAVERVILLE

I believe from what I read in the papers that they will work this slavery excitement up to a civil war by and by. Whenever you get at it and divide North and South on your side of the mountains[,] we shall secede, with the Rocky Mountains for a line and form an Empire on the Pacific, with Washington

Territory, Oregon and California and we shall annex all of this side of Mexico. We should have a fine country. We don't care a straw whether you dissolve the Union or not. We just wish that the Republicans and Democrats in the Capital would get into a fight and kill each other all off like the Kilkenny cats. Perhaps that would settle the hash.   **FRANKLIN A. BUCK**

1885

I hope you have read my story *Ramona* and become converted by it (if you needed conversion) on the Indian question. I have, in this book, flung my last weapon! If this does not tell, I know nothing more to do. In my *Century of Dishonor* I tried to attack people's consciences directly, and they would not listen. Now I have sugared my pill, and it remains to be seen if it will go down.   **HELEN HUNT JACKSON**, *to her editor*

1934

CARMEL

I would like, if possible, to see the jacket blurb before it is printed, as we must be careful to offend neither Negroes or whites—on the blurb!

poet, playwright **LANGSTON HUGHES**

JANUARY 23

1930

Of all the Christbitten places and businesses in the two hemispheres this one is the last curly kink on the pig's tail. And that's without prejudice to D. W. Griffith. I like him and think he's good. But, Jesus, the movies!

poet, playwright **STEPHEN VINCENT BENET**

1946

[TO] THE PRESIDENT,

THE WHITE HOUSE.

SIR: The undersigned were appointed by Executive order . . . to ascertain and report the facts relating to the attack made by Japanese armed forces upon the Territory of Hwaii on December 7, 1941 . . .

[The] acting Secretary of War [instructed us] to investigate the conduct of Colonel Theodore Wyman, Jr. as District Engineer in the Hawaiian Department as his activities had affected Pearl Harbor . . . The record shows that Wyman, as a Captain going to duty as a District Engineer at Los Angeles, was an able and steady officer, devoted to his professional duties and to the government's interest, with a forceful disposition.

While at Los Angeles [Wyman] fell into the company of Hans Wilhelm Rohl, German alien, whose contracting firm that became the successful bidder on a contract to build a breakwater at Los Angeles. This contract was under the administration and jurisdiction of Wyman . . .

Rohl was a man-about-town in Los Angeles and had become increasingly prominent in the night life and social activities of Los Angeles and Hollywood. His personal habits in connection with extreme drinking and with "party girls" of the community, his extravagant methods of living and his disregard of the domestic and social proprieties of a responsible person increased as the years went by, but they were already well developed at the time of his initial associations with Wyman, who was introduced by him into new and more extravagant methods of living. Rohl evidently introduced Wyman, or at least influenced him to join in extravagant and disgraceful parties as Rohl's house guest in Los Angeles hotels, and in heavy drinking over considerable periods. Trips on Rohl's yacht were expensive and lavish . . .   **THE ROBERTS COMMISSION,** *investigating Wyman and Rohl's substandard Hawaiian airstrips*

1987

While driving through Beverly Hills with Julie today, saw an RTD bus pulled over next to some park. The driver was outside practicing his golf swing *with a club.* Only in Beverly Hills.   *writer* **CAROLYN KELLOGG**

1991

LAST HOUSE, GLEN ELLEN, CALIFORNIA

Transcendental is the word. I don't believe in all this stuff about grief because I think we grieve forever, but that goes for love too, fortunately for us all.

Love,   **M. F. K. FISHER,** *to Lawrence Clark Powell*

JANUARY 24

1848

This day some kind of mettle was found in the tail race that looks like goald first discovered by James Martial, the boss of the Mill.

HENRY WILLIAM BIGLER,

laborer, Mormon missionary, soldier of the Mexican War

1969

Santa Barbara is Nixonville with a vengeance and the English Department is completely dominated by avowed fascists . . .   *poet* KENNETH REXROTH

2009

. . . mis dreams. Bubbling up, también—con el tarry viscosity and regularity de ese *glug glug glug* que se escucha at the La Brea Tar Pits—from the primeval swamp *sine qua non*: el subconsciente. My dream/journal. Working on, working *out* tantas cosas.   SUSANA CHÁVEZ-SILVERMAN

JANUARY 25

1962

2457 FOLSOM ST.

BOYLE HEIGHTS

I wish I had time to tell you some of my latest dreams . . . I hope you dig this, man!!! I am going to try this on my own . . . by the time I get to Hanford I may be forced to take a hard look at the situation and decide to latch on to the dear old paycheck for all its worth and continue here in the little office and really enjoy it. What I need is an accomplice to go along with me . . . .

union leader CÉSAR CHÁVEZ, *to his mentor Fred Ross*

2021

Participated in a theater event yesterday, in my own home, in my office, with a total stranger 3000 miles away. There was also a robot voice involved, asking questions of each of us on the phone. One of us was A the other B, like in a Paul Auster novel . . . We were asked to recall one thing from childhood we would never forget. I told him about how I was sure I'd poisoned

Bobby Rotstein by telling him to take our playdough cookies home, ask his mother Ethel to bake them, and then eat them. Which he did . . .

I walked through the neighborhood, through the path in the sunny meadow where all these families had come out to bask out of their bunkers, with their children. father setting up fantastic kites. over the hill to the home of Gabriel Garcia, a young artist (UCLA grad) who is living in the little house behind his parents' place in the hood. And he's been curating these intimate art exhibits in the back yard . . .

I was really tickled that in one day I could walk to see some interesting art, and have a theater experience without driving across town or getting dressed up or not having to talk to folks you really don't want to talk to at an art opening. just looking on the positive side of lockdown.

tomorrow is the day to try and get our vaccinations at Dodger Stadium. I've heard from one to two to three to five hours wait. just so they don't run out.

                                                                  LOUISE STEINMAN

JANUARY 26

1871

. . . I steal from sleep. I have written nothing by daylight for over a year.

                                  poet **INA COOLBRITH**, *to Charles Warren Stoddard*

1904

I left St. Paul last Friday amidst ice and snow —14 degrees below zero and the first thing I saw in the railway station when I got here was a notice to say that for 11 dollars return people could take their children to see "real ice and snow." Here there are palm trees and pepper trees and one walks about without a coat.   **W. B. YEATS**

JANUARY 27

1977

To whom it may concern, I am a PhD candidate in astrophysics at Stanford University, and am interested in the space shuttle program. Please send me the forms necessary to apply as a 'mission specialist' candidate. Thank you,

teacher, astronaut **SALLY RIDE**

2018

Dear Family Friends and whoever reads this,

I really didn't want it to come down to this but it was something that I felt I had to do. Living in Newport Beach is like living in a bubble. So much pressure is put on kids to do good, and a lot of kids make mistakes. One slip up makes a kid feel like the smallest person in the world. You are looked at as a loser if you don't go to college or if you get a certain GPA or test score. All anyone talks about is how great they are or how great their kid is. It's all about how great I am. It's never about the other kid. The kid who maybe does not play a sport, have a 4.0+ GPA, but displays great character . . .

To me the school of Corona del Mar is not a public school. It is treated like a private school. So much pressure is placed on the students to do well that I couldn't do it anymore. There is never a moment to brake. Finals have pressured me immensely, along with a lot of other people. I want you to know that my parents were not the reason for this. My parents actually don't put almost any stress on me at all. It is purely the school. Nobody can understand what people might be going through. Be nice to everyone . . . If there is a kid out there who is alone it never hurts to sit with them or ask them how they're doing . . .

[Playing] baseball gave me the most joy that I ever had. Baseball was a daily relaxing time where I could just go out and have fun with my friends. Thanks for giving me the opportunity. Live and play everyday like it's your last because you never know when you will be done forever. Thanks to all for the memories . . .

I hope you will understand what I'm trying to convey to you. The stress put on me led me to this point. Make changes.

teenager **PATRICK TURNER** *(2001–2018)*

JANUARY 28

1848

[James] Marshall arrived in the evening, it was raining very heavy, but he told me he came on important business. After we was alone in a private Room he showed me the first Specimens of Gold, that is he was not certain if it was Gold or not, but he thought it might be; immediately I made the proof and found that it was Gold. I told him even that most of all is 23 Carat Gold; he wished that I should come up with him immediately . . .

JOHANN AUGUST SUTTER

1850

. . . Uncle John says it is not such a dreadful thing to come to California, and when the railroad is finished I should not be surprised to see you and Father out for a visit. Would it not be funny if you were yet to see this golden land? . . .

This is a changing world . . . *pioneer* **MARGARET DEWITT**,
to her mother-in-law

1947

. . . In my youth could never have dreamed that I would spend my latter days as an American on this palm-grown coast. . . .

[During] the past two and a half years I have been occupied with a novel—or whatever the thing should be called—which I hope to complete within a few days and which is something so utterly German that I have the greatest fears concerning its translatability . . . **THOMAS MANN**,
at work on Doktor Faustus

1973

Dawn is coming up in San Francisco now: 6:09 A.M. I can hear the rumble of early morning buses under my window at the Seal Rock Inn . . . this is the end of the line, for buses and everything else, the western edge of America. From my desk I can see the dark jagged hump of "Seal Rock" looming out of the ocean in the grey morning light. About two hundred seals have been barking out there most of the night. Staying in this place with the windows open is like living next to a dog pound. Last night we had a huge paranoid poodle up here in the room, and the dumb bastard went totally out of control when the seals started barking, racing around the room like a chicken hearing a pack of wolves outside the window, howling & whining, leaping up on the bed & scattering my book-galley pages all over the floor, knocking the phone off the hook, upsetting the gin bottles, trashing my carefully organized stacks of campaign photographs . . .

That dog will not enter this room again. He came in with the book-editor, who went away about six hours ago with thirteen finished chapters—the bloody product of fifty-five consecutive hours of sleepless, foodless, high-speed editing. But there was no other way to get the thing done. I am not an easy person to work with, in terms of deadlines . . .

What I would like to preserve here is a kind of high-speed cinematic reel-record of what the campaign was like at the time, not what the whole thing boiled down to or how it fits into history. There will be no shortage of books covering that end . . .

Meanwhile, my room at the Seal Rock Inn is filling up with people who seem on the verge of hysteria at the sight of me still sitting here wasting time on a rambling introduction, with the final chapter still unwritten the presses scheduled to start rolling in twenty-four hours . . . but unless somebody shows up pretty soon, with extremely powerful speed, there might not *be* any Final Chapter . . .   *reporter, novelist* **HUNTER S. THOMPSON,**

at work on Fear and Loathing on the Campaign Trail

JANUARY 29

1904

"Thursday Club May Present Poet Yates"   **THE SACRAMENTO BEE**

1904

. . . All well but am a bit hoarse.   **W. B. YEATS**

1928

Writing is next to impossible—what with the purling of fountains, the drawling of mockingbirds, the roaring of surf, the blazing of movie stars, the barking of dogs, the midnight shakings of geraniums, the cruising of warships, etc., etc. . . .

The peculiar mixtures of piety and utter abandon in this welter of cults, ages, occupations, etc., out here make it a good deal like Bedlam. Retired schoolmarms from Iowa, Kansas and all the corn-and-wheat belt along with millions of hobbling Methuselahs, alfalfa-fringed and querulous, side by

side with crowds of ambitious but none-too-successful strumpets of movie-
dom, quite good to look at . . .

Our house, a large U with patio and fountain, rambles all over the place,
and is almost vertical to the observatory on Mt. Wilson. Plenty of roses, ca-
mellias, oleanders, acacias, etc., as well as a good wine-cellar. I've just been
interrupted by the butler bringing in a makeshift for champagne, composed
of carbonated apple-juice with a sling of gin; so all attempts at epistolary
consecutivety are hereby and henceforth abandoned!   *poet* **HART CRANE**

1947

My country, California, is a pure wonder, and according to my taste, it is
more trees than humans. 500 trees for each human.

poet **GABRIELA MISTRAL**, *Nobel laureate in Literature*

1958

HALF MOON BAY, CALIFORNIA

Today I am thirty-one years old, which isn't nearly old enough. I still feel like
a child. A gifted child, of course, but still a child.

The pot boils: *Brave Cowboy* appears in England, as a paperback reprint
in the drugstores and finally is sold (for $7,500) to Kirk Douglas, movie actor.
Unbelievable. Exasperating and unbelievable, yet there was the contract,
there's the check, and did I make any attempt at any point to queer the deal?
I did not.

Stanford and my writing fellowship: another fellowship like this and I'll
claim bankruptcy . . .

Ginsberg's *Howl*, the best poem written in America by an American since—
well, since Pearl Harbor. (So far as I know.) Yes, a beautifully shaggy little book.
Wild and shaggy, and also highly accurate: "Moloch whose heart is a cannibal
dynamo," etc. Very touching. My wife hates it, of course, just as everyone else
I know does. They're all so superior to that kind of thing, you know. After all,
they imply, Ginsberg is no poet—only a kid. (Like Chatterton? Rimbaud?) Only
a crazy, hopped-up kid. . . . But in America, that means nothing. We all mature
slow and late, if at all, in this country . . .

Paradise: Any thunderstorms in Paradise? Any buzzards? cactus? flash
floods? Any violence, mountains, sand dunes, scorpions? No? Then keep it.

Liberal friends look down their noses, but should they? There is much of
value in the Mormon feeling for decentralization and home rule . . . 3.2 beer,
however, is unforgivable . . .   *novelist, essayist* **ED ABBEY**

JANUARY 30

1904

SAN FRANCISCO

It is very hot here—I have sat all afternoon without coat or waistcoat with the window wide open. Yesterday I spoke at two colleges among palm trees & there was an orange tree by the hotel where I slept.   **W. B. YEATS**

1977

I must end it. There's no hope left. I'll be at peace. No one had anything to do with this. My decision totally.   **FREDDIE PRINZE**, *his suicide note*

1985

1216 COLE STREET

SAN FRANCISCO, CALIF. 94117

USA

. . . I am not coming to England this year after all . . . everybody will probably be annoyed with me—but it can't be helped. Under Reagan—or rather in his second term—the sexual bigotry that is usually not far beneath the surface of any immigration official at airports and 'points of entry' has indeed surfaced, and immigration is giving a hard time to foreign homosexuals entering the country. Worse than hard time, I should say—turning them back. So I would run the risk of not being able to get back here, my own home. There is nothing to worry about if I don't leave the country and then try to get back in, but there is if I do! So I have decided to wait until there is some test case that gets things decided in the courts (I hope I don't have to wait until there is a new president), but have no wish to be a martyr and the subject of the test case. Wouldn't be able to afford the lawyers, anyway   **THOM GUNN**

JANUARY 31

1915

Poet laureate! I? May the Lord forfend. Why, the dear good Friends do not realize that the opposition would not leave me a fig leaf, much less a laurel!

INA COOLBRITH, *California Poet Laureate for the next 13 years*

1930

. . . [L.A.'s Manual Arts High School] is still boresome but i have settled myself to its rules and the ringing bells so i have not been in trouble lately, this term i am going to go but one half day the rest i will spend reading and working here at home . . . i have started doing some thing with clay and have found a bit of encouragement from my teacher, my drawing i will tell you frankly is rotten it seems to lack freedom and rhythm it is cold and lifeless, it isn't worth the postage to send it. i think there should be an advancement soon . . . i feel i will make an artist of some kind i have never proven to myself nor any body else that i have it in me.

this so called happy part of one's life youth to me is a bit of damnable hell if i could come to some conclusion about my self and life perhaps then i could see something to work for. my mind blazes up with some illusion for a couple of weeks then it smoalters down to a bit of nothing . . .

we have gotten up a group and have arranged for a furnace where we can have our stuff fired, we will give the owner a commission for the firing and glazing, there is chance of my making a little book money . . . .

painter JACKSON POLLOCK, to his brother

1931

. . . We never miss an opportunity to acquire culture. We take the humanities in ponderous gulps. We attend lectures. We become linguists . . . Practically all of us own a book, and most of us, if necessary, can read it also . . . .

[We] have been so engaged in self-defense that we have never thought to look into the back yards of our attackers. The graveyard of rotten novels, over-rated poetry, and intolerable stage plays is filled as amply as the crypt reserved for miserable films: and the number of our artistic successes will stack up rather well beside yours.   **DALTON TRUMBO**,

in an open letter about Hollywood to critic George Jean Nathan

1980

The other day I saw a set of Parkman in a bookshop. If I thought that you were interested in the early history of North America, the French-Indian wars, I'd send it to you. These are most exciting books. I'd read them myself if I had the time. I did read *The Oregon Trail* once and parts of the book on the Pontiac. I'd be awfully glad to hear from you.

Love,   **SAUL BELLOW**, *in Pasadena, to his son*

1994

A very brilliant and gallant millionaire I know who made a fortune from computers, Jerry, moved a couple of years ago to a chalet in Sun Valley, which he believed would be a better place to raise his child and live with his wife than horrible L.A. with all its bad publicity in reality and fiction. However, recently I saw him at one of those Sunday brunches I often go to and asked, "Jerry, you're here on business?"

"I'm not here on business," he said. "We moved back."

"You're back?" I said. "You moved back?"

"Yes," he said. "My brain died. I need action."

. . . In a few months, when all this this all settles down, what people will realize is that this weird new subway they built to take people to downtown LA held up so well we hardly heard it mentioned. Perhaps people in Los Angeles will finally become good citizens taking the Metro Rail . . .

EVE BABITZ

FEBRUARY 1

1906

Beloved H.—

. . . You've seen this wonderful spot [Stanford], so I needn't describe it. It is really a miracle; and so simple the life and so benign the elements, that for a young ambitious professor who wishes to leave his mark on Pacific civilization while it is most plastic, or for any one who wants to teach and work under the most perfect conditions for eight or nine months, and who is able to get to the East, or Europe, for the remaining three, I can't imagine anything finer. It is Utopian. Perfection of weather. Cold nights, though above freezing. Fire pleasant until 10 o'clock A.M., then unpleasant. In short, the "simple life" with all the essential higher elements thrown in as communal possessions. The drawback is, of course, the great surrounding human vacuum—the historic silence fairly rings in your ears when you listen—and the social insipidity. I'm glad I came, and with God's blessing I may pull through. One calendar month is over, anyway. Do you know aught of G. K. Chesterton? I've just read his "Heretics." A tremendously strong writer and true thinker, despite his mannerism of paradox. Wells's "Kipps" is good. Good-bye. Of course you're breathing the fog of London while I am bathed in warmest lucency. Keep well. Your loving,

W. J.   *philosopher* **WILLIAM JAMES**, *to his brother Henry*

1970

Kin wanted to take me to the Glide Methodist Chapel for their Sunday morning service. This not the usual manner of worship. It was in fact a mixture of the Negro revivalist and a hippie service, the congregation mainly very clean, laundered hippies, Negroes, and the young who come for a pleasant "work-out," a "get together" in a Christian frame of mind, aided by every modern device, including a psychedelic screen show above the altar on which every sort of picture was shown from a close-up of a girl's tongue, on which an acid pill was poised, to media shots and the information that

Eichmann was still alive. The place was gradually jam-packed with hundreds standing at the back of the hall, and the aisles filled with squatters. A rock group started to play, Negro voices joined in, the gaiety was contagious, and the entire congregation started clapping in rhythm . . .

Jesus Christ was referred to as Our Director, lyrics by Dylan were sung, and a song from Hair recited. The volume of music became unbelievable. For one and a half hours a condition of euphoria was sustained . . .

[We] all linked up arms and swayed from side to side, and when after this catharsis of jazzed-up emotion we left the building, the Rev. Cecil Williams kissed each member of the congregation. The Rev. Cecil has a smash hit on his hands. This is the way religion is going. It gives the churchgoer a real reason to feel good.   **CECIL BEATON**

1970

. . . I got a call from David Hilliard on a Friday. He said "we've got this cat Jean Genet here, he's willing to speak for us, we'd like to have a fundraiser at your house on Sunday." . . .

David & a few other Panthers arrived early, and stationed themselves in a row on a large sofa in the sitting-room. Cat Genet . . . spoke eloquently and passionately about racism in the United States and his reason for coming to speak in support of the Panthers, all excellently translated by the Ramparts interpreter . . .

Somebody got up from the floor (actually sitting on the floor, with myriad others) . . . he asked a rather stupid question along the lines of "M. Genet—what do you think we should do?" So Genet, quite rightly in my view, launched into a furious attack against the questioner. "I'm from France, this is YOUR country, and YOU ask ME how to counteract racism in America? Asinine! That's YOUR job . . . "

Dan Siegel, who was also sitting on the floor, got up with hands upraised saying "Cool it" or some such phrase. Or perhaps he didn't say anything. In any case, David Hilliard saw his hand-gesture as a threat. He picked up an empty half-gallon jug & tossed it at Dan—or prepared to toss it. Luckily for all, some-how the weapon slipped out of his hand and fell on the head of Michael Mc-Clure's little daughter, who ran shrieking to her daddy . . . it hit her square on the forehead . . . As M. McClure said afterwards, "It's always the children who get hurt in wars" (my paraphrase as I haven't got a text for this true statement).

Now it was my turn to mount the stepladder to say something along the lines of Thank you all for coming . . . I led them all away, & walked down with J. Genet—who had clearly loved the whole evening, compounded as it was with race & violence, his favorite subjects.   **JESSICA MITFORD**

2012

We don't build services to make money; we make money to build better services.   *businessman* **MARK ZUCKERBERG**,
on an SEC form before Facebook's IPO

FEBRUARY 2

1848

*TREATY OF PEACE, FRIENDSHIP, LIMITS, AND SETTLEMENT
BETWEEN THE UNITED STATES OF AMERICA AND THE UNITED
MEXICAN STATES CONCLUDED AT GUADALUPE HIDALGO*

The boundary line between the two Republics shall commence in the Gulf of Mexico, three leagues from land, opposite the mouth of the Rio Grande, otherwise called Rio Bravo del Norte . . . thence across the Rio Colorado, following the division line between Upper and Lower California, to the Pacific Ocean . . .

[The] Government of the United States engages to pay to that of the Mexican Republic the sum of fifteen millions of dollars . . . in the gold or silver coin of Mexico . . . together with interest on the same at the rate of six per centum per annum . . .

In faith whereof we, the respective Plenipotentiaries, have signed this treaty of peace, friendship, limits, and settlement, and have hereunto affixed our seals respectively. Done in quintuplicate, at the city of Guadalupe Hidalgo, on the second day of February, in the year of our Lord one thousand eight hundred and forty-eight.   *Treaty of Guadalupe Hidalgo,
nine days after the discovery of gold*

1854

HUMBOLDT COUNTY

. . . We can look out to sea as far as the eye can extend. There are four villages on the bay. One at the outlet, Humbolt Point is the name, where there are probably not more than 50 inhabitants. What they depend upon for support I don't know. They are probably persons who supposed that it would be the point for a City and they would realize a California fortune by the rise of lots . . . From there they pack provisions to the gold mines, and return with the dust . . .   *Captain* **ULYSSES S. GRANT**

1942

My husband and I went to the Alien Registration Office. There were four policemen on guard. It is only a little after opening hour of eight, but there are many people there. There are Germans and Italians, but Japanese make up the majority . . .   **AOKI HISA**

1948

Dear Harry:

I have received a notice, presumably from you as treasurer of the Guild, warning that I am now in jeopardy of being placed in bad standing for non-payment of dues.

Please be informed that my contract with M-G-M has been abrogated, my work has been proscribed and that I myself have been banned from employment in my profession until such time as I perform an act of political purification hitherto characteristic of Fascist states.

I am sure you understand the situation in which I find myself, since you may take credit for being one of its architects by reason of your advocacy of the same political test for Guild officership which the producers have taken over as a test for employment.

In consequence, my income has ceased and I have no money with which to pay dues . . . I am therefore obliged to go into bad standing.

Attached herewith my card.
Cordially,
[unsigned]
Lazy T Ranch
Frazier Park California   **DALTON TRUMBO**

FEBRUARY 3

1911

The bear flag is hereby selected and adopted as the state flag of California. . . . The said bear flag shall consist of a flag of a length equal to one and one-half the width thereof . . . there shall appear in the white field in the upper left-hand corner a single red star, and at the bottom of the white field the words 'California Republic,' and in the center of the white field a California grizzly bear upon a grass plat, in the position of walking toward the left of the said field; said bear shall be dark brown in color and in length, equal to one-third of the length of said flag. **CALIFORNIA LEGISLATURE**

1939

[San Francisco] is a large, terrific, beautiful city and Treasure Island is the most beautiful Island you ever saw and our theatre is a dream and all three hit me simultaneously. **HALLIE FLANAGAN**, *director,*
Federal Theatre Project

1949

[Neal Cassady's] California was a long sunny place of railroads, grapes, pinochle games in cabooses, women in towns like Tracy or Watsonville, Chinese & Mexican restaurants behind the tracks, great stretches of land—hot, sweaty, important—And moreover, he is a true Californian, in the sense that everybody in California is like a broken-down movie actor, i.e., handsome, decadent, Casanova-ish, where all the women really love to try various beds. In Frisco, particularly, Neal fits in with the special California type . . . where perfect strangers talk to you most intimately on the street. California is as if a land of lonely & exiled & eccentric lovers come to foregather, like birds. Everyone is debauched, completely (somehow.) And there is that old-fashioned look of the land, & the towns, (not in L.A., but on up) still reminiscent of the Golden American West we think of. The nights are "unbearably romantic" . . . & sadder than the East's. [MORE ANON] *novelist* **JACK KEROUAC**

FEBRUARY 4

1859

The Chinese are now celebrating New Year and the crackle of firecrackers is constant as at vintage time. But they ignite hundreds and thousands at once; it is their favorite amusement. If only you could take a pleasure trip to see us here someday; Papa would greatly amuse himself by walking in the streets! I have long since known my way well in the streets, where I as a housewife have to shop. To market is about as far as Schonungen, but the way seems much shorter because of the pretty and diverse shops and the many people one meets. I am no longer astounded whether I meet a Chinese with a long braid swinging against the shop or a German; one adjusts quickly.

Today, or tomorrow rather, a young man goes back who arrived here first with us, probably with too high hopes. People think it is as easy to settle themselves here as it was 10 years ago and when they are not instantly taken in tow by Dame Fortune they are too easily disheartened . . .

pioneer EVA HOFMANN GUNDLACH

1966

3405 OCEAN DRIVE

MANHATTAN BEACH, CALIFORNIA 90266

. . . I am as usual half out of my skull trying to figure out how to juggle more material than I can cope with before the money runs out and I have to start in on potboilers again. If you know of a good dictionary of American slang for the period 1876-1888 that's still in print I'd appreciate it. I am trying to make do with Wentworth & Flexner, but they don't really give you a clear notion of who used what words under what circumstances. But then I ask myself, who gives a shit anyway? What's the point of being historically accurate, nobody's going to notice one way or another. A sticky question, one I've puzzled for a long time, how much you have a right to make up out of your own head . . .

novelist, essayist THOMAS PYNCHON

FEBRUARY 5

1850

. . . I went to Mass; after which witnessed the burial of an Indian who had died the day before. The corpse was interred beneath the floor of the Church . . .

The whole scene, "American" by the side of "Mexican," (to adopt the language of the day), Indian and white, trader and penitent, gayety, bustle and confusion on the one side and religious solemnity on the other, was singular to me. A beggar at the door, as we sallied out, at the conclusion of the service, struck my attention, although I did not understand the language in which he now chanted and again prayed, as many in passing placed their alms in his hand.

Judge BENJAMIN HAYES

1893

ANGWIN, IN NAPA COUNTY

My dear Blanche,

My health is very good now, and Leigh and I take long walks. And after the rains we look for Indian arrow-heads in the plowed fields and on the gravel bars of the creek. My collection is now great; but I fear I shall tire of the fad before completing it. One in the country must have a fad or die of dejection and oxidation of the faculties. How happy is he who can make a fad of his work!

By the way, my New York publishers (The United States Book Company) have failed, owing me a pot of money, of which I shall probably get nothing. I'm beginning to cherish an impertinent curiosity to know what Heaven means to do to me next . . .   *writer* **AMBROSE BIERCE**

1914

Goodie! Getting so interested I can't sleep!

writer **CHARMIAN KITTREDGE LONDON**,

on scoring a book deal

1942

Since I have written anti-Nazi literature from the year 1922 on, I had to leave Germany in October 1932. My Berlin house was raided by the Nazis in February 1933. On August 23, 1933, I was expatriated by the Nazi government, and all my possessions were confiscated. Goebbels himself announced my expatriation over the radio and declared me one of the most ardent enemies of the Nazis. Nearly all Nazi-leaders and Hitler himself attacked me as an enemy of the Nazi Reich in their articles and broadcasts.

My anti-Nazi novels have been translated into many languages and have been published in millions of copies all over the world, in this country in about half a million. My anti-Nazi pictures are shown in many countries, and in this country too. Leading American newspapers considered my literary activity as an efficient weapon in the struggle against Nazism.

Therefore I cannot feel myself to be an enemy alien.

historical novelist, refugee **LION FEUCHTWANGER**

FEBRUARY 6

1947

Arrived at Pasadena at 9 am and were met by a car from MGM. We drove for a long time down autobahns and boulevards full of vacant lots and filling stations and nondescript buildings and palm trees with a warm hazy light. It was more like Egypt—the suburbs of Cairo or Alexandria—than anything in Europe. We arrived at the Bel Air Hotel—very Egyptian with a hint of Addis Ababa in the smell of the blue gums . . .

We unpacked, sent great quantities of clothes to the laundry, bathed and lunched. A well-planned little restaurant, good cooking. We drank a good local wine, Masson's Pinot Noir. We were the only people in the room drinking. Two tables of women with absurd hats. Rested. At 6 sharp we were called on by the two producers Gordon and McGuinness, who were preceded with fine bunches of flowers—with their shy wives. We sat in our bedroom and drank. Conversation difficult. Bed early, after dining without appetite in the restaurant, and slept badly; woke in pain.   *novelist* **EVELYN WAUGH**

2009

Lloyd's Uncle Herb died, obit in NYT. 106, one of last survivors of the 1906 San Francisco earthquake. Less than a month after he celebrated his birthday with a big party at a steakhouse in Daly City. Way to go, Uncle Herb! Still working as a grocer (stocking dented cans) at Andronico's, more likely holding court in the corner . . .

Everyone came out to see Uncle Herb. Smoked cigars into his 90's, and every year on the anniversary of the earthquake, he was driven down Market Street in a Model T Ford, with a beautiful woman on either side of him. He loved it. Told whoever asked that the secret to a long life was "wild women and good liquor." Herb worked stocking shelves and greeting customers until last month. He took BART and the bus to work. "You're not going to get an earthquake every day," he told AP. "So we celebrate the one that we had. It was a beautiful earthquake, if you want to look at it in the glorious way."

. . . I loved going for corn beef on rye with hot cabbage at Uncle Herb's favorite Irish lunch joint, down the hill from his apt in Daly City. He always wore a cardigan sweater, we always walked there. The heavy dust in his apartment which he couldn't see anymore. His story about going to the movie theater on Market Street as a young teen, sitting next to a girl in the dark and how he put his arm around her. She let him. Walking her home to her house, even met her mother. Stayed for a meal. A nice Jewish girl. He never called her again. He eventually married Ciel, who was Catholic. And

Ciel was his Orthodox Jewish mother's favorite daughter-in-law. "I wonder where that girl is now," he said to us when we last visited. that girl at the movie theater. Back in 1915? He was still thinking about her now, at age 104?

LOUISE STEINMAN

FEBRUARY 7

1924

To My Honorable Mother, Greetings:
Your daughter has come to America. I have been ill for several months and have not yet recovered . . . The man, Huey Yow, who brought me to California, compelled me to pay him one thousand dollars. I have already done so . . .

Your daughter's condition is very tragic, even when she is sick, she must practice prostitution (literally, do business with her own flesh and skin). Daughter is not angry with you. It seems to be just my fate . . .

After I have earned money by living this life of prostitution, I will return to China and become a Buddhist nun . . . If, having earned money for my mother, I am able to expiate my sin also by becoming a nun, I shall be grateful to my mother. By accomplishing these two things I shall have attained all the requirements of complete filial piety.

If people treat me kindly, I shall be kind to them. Since I have not done evil to others, why should others do evil to me? At home, a daughter should be obedient to her parents; after marriage to her husband; after the death of her husband, to her son. These are the three great obediences . . .

Now I may be somebody's daughter, but some day I may be somebody's mother.

WONG AH SO, to her mother in Fresno

1938

I don't know whether I could write a decent book now. That is the greatest fear of all. I'm working at it but I can't tell. Something is poisoned in me. You pages—ten of you—you are the dribble cup—you are the cloth to wipe up the vomit . . .

It is so hard to know anything. So impossible to trust oneself. Even to know what there is to trust. My will is low. I must build my will again. And I can do it even as I have done before. The time passes. The thoughts race.

novelist, screenwriter JOHN STEINBECK,
beginning The Grapes of Wrath

1955

Here we are having a really good time. The only drawback is that the Foundation is at the bottom of a rather deep California canyon, so that we have sunlight only about 7 hours a day. On the other hand, we have good company . . .

The great thing hereabouts (we are on the outskirts of Los Angeles) is the astonishing architecture that has been springing up in the last 15 years. A young art critic who knows you, Langsner by name, told me that you were here a few years ago . . . But when I said you should come here again, he said, "Yes," but that you might be bewildered; and I think he meant that there is such richness and variety in the building that you might not be able to generalize about it. But I don't think Gladys and I can be wrong in feeling it is remarkable—original and varied to a degree. Sunset Boulevard (which leads here) is lined with most beautiful houses, and one feels here a tremendous vitality that makes it seem to be the architectural laboratory of our time. Everyone seems to be prosperous—the city is growing at the rate of 50,000 a year—and there are swarms of architects, from the son of F. Lloyd Wright, who built some of the cottages in our canyon, to men from the Bauhaus, etc.—Would you care to get the New Yorker to send you out to survey it all? as they commissioned you to write about London? I should think you ought to see the recent developments here, if, as I suppose, you haven't seen them. (Incidentally, we have seen no "smog" at all.)

Meanwhile, we have been taken about to see the "celebrities," and I think we are to see Stravinsky and A. Huxley next week. Also Upton Sinclair, who lives near by. The Biddles took us to see old Lion Feuchtwanger whom, with his wife, we much liked, and who has an astonishing library of 25,000 books (Shakespeare first folio, Spinoza's books with his annotations, complete Goethe, Schiller, first editions, etc., etc., etc.) [Edward] G. Robinson has shown us his wonderful collection of French pictures. We had an afternoon with Frederic March at the Paramount studios—and saw him acting, also Danny Kaye acting—also Rosalind Russell . . . Such a whirl!

critic **VAN WYCK BROOKS**, *to Lewis Mumford*

FEBRUARY 8

1844

Sacramento Valley has been sighted! We are slowly working our way through the snow. Sleds and snowshoes make such a good track that the horses, without packs, will probably get across. The men are now the pack horses. It was impossible to sleep last night; all the blankets and hides could not keep a person warm. During the day it is beautiful. The Indians here live almost entirely on fir seeds, which are savory and oily. Mice and rats are choice morsels. The guide stole some things and decamped, leaving bow and arrows behind. We had to abandon the cannon a few days ago.

CHARLES PREUSS, *expeditionary photographer*

1921

I do not like Berkeley. It is shrubs and shingles, and cold. Ugh! It is cold!

INA COOLBRITH

1944

On Friday at Salka's for tea . . . there was only this sportily dressed woman who was vaguely familiar. I had only noticed that Salka told her our names, but not vice versa, from which I inferred that she must be so famous that she expected us to know who she was anyway. It was only after having this thought that I recognized her as Garbo. She was pleasant and friendly, and stayed for a long time—whereas she normally leaves, out of an almost pathological shyness, any social gathering at which she encounters new faces. She is beautiful . . . very affected and probably not especially intellectual, to put it discreetly—comes across as someone who makes a great effort to live up, at least somewhat, to her own nimbus. Ali Baba waited in the car. He cropped up in the conversation, and Ms. Garbo, who loves Afghans, requested that he be brought in. Now, Salka has three dogs of her own, two highly nervous setters and an enormous German shepherd that had just bitten Ms. Garbo (it bites everyone). But the three monsters were locked away. So Ali was then allowed in. He smelled his colleagues, stormed about like mad—I had never seen him so beside himself—and suddenly, before we knew it, he had lifted his little leg by a bookshelf and made his mark upon a book by Osa Johnson—in the presence of the supposedly most beautiful woman in the world. . . .

philosopher **THEODOR ADORNO**

FEBRUARY 9

1931

... They keep writers in little coops out here, on the movie lots, and sometimes it is months before the writers can find out who hired them and why. I was supposed to be writing a picture for Will Rogers, but they changed the plot on me five times in nine days, so I went away, and they didn't even know I had gone away for some time—that was with the Fox Film Corporation—but they were very nice financially: they didn't want what I did, but they paid me $5000 for something I hadn't done. There is a kind of an idea around there that I am still working for them, in some quarters, I believe. Then I went into Paramount one day to sell the movie rights of an old novel of mine, and it seems they got the idea I was working there, so they paid me some money too, and I went on a vacation after that; and now I don't think I have a job, but I don't know, because no one knows anything about anything at all in Hollywood.

But it seems to me that the proper system here is to find out where all the pay windows of all the different studios are, and go around them every now and then and ask if there's a check, and act a little surprised if there isn't; after while maybe there will be . . .   *novelist* **P. G. WODEHOUSE**

1989

... We went up the Bucklin Trail. Walked up a ways. Nothing in bloom but did see 2 or 3 violets, a few "footprints of spring"—Bob loves that name, keeps saying it over and over . . .

One red maid, one milk maid and one wild iris. Birds: hawks and the most amazing thing happened: we were walking along and observed a small thrush on the path ahead. He was really fuzzy and we watched a long time. Then he began hopping up the path ahead of Bob as if he had a perfect notion of where he was going. John the Baptist thrush. Hop hop hop! Bob bob bob! He went ahead. And he stayed on that trail a good 15 minutes ahead of us, stopping only occasionally to eat a little speck of something.

Feeling much less devastated about Linda. I "saw" this a.m. how her soul was taken. She really was prepared & it filled with light & then she left it. The it.   *poet* **BRENDA HILLMAN**

FEBRUARY 10

1770

When these natives . . . noticed how small our numbers were . . . [the] fight was on . . .

[He] darted into my hut, spouting so much blood at the mouth and from his temples, that I had hardly time to absolve him and help him to meet his end . . . Still the exchange of shots—bullets and arrows—went on. There were only four on our side against more than 20 on theirs. And there I was with the dead man, thinking it most probable I would soon have to follow him . . . [They] all fled. And I believe none of them were killed; therefore they can all yet be baptized . . .   *Father* **JUNÍPERO SERRA**

1929

. . . drove to Oakland and to "The Heights" to find Joaquin Miller's home, which I had not seen for thirty-six years. I could not have found it alone, so dense is the forest that has sprung up around it. The room in which he received me in those days seemed smaller and there was only a rusty pipe to remind me of his shower . . . I came away with a sense of dismay that in so short a time Joaquin's remains should be so few and so ratty.

novelist **HAMLIN GARLAND**

FEBRUARY 11

1931

Do a group of stories about Los Angelesians in the manner of Joyce's "Dubliners."   **CAREY MCWILLIAMS**

1962

2533 HILLEGASS

BERKELEY 4, CAL.

Dear Tim, I forgot, in my last letter, to answer your question about Tantra . . . LSD and the mushrooms shd be used, it seems to me, in the context of this basic Tantrik idea of the yoga of total awareness, leading to enlightenment within the world of everyday experience which of course becomes the world of miracle and beauty and divine mystery . . .

Yours,

Aldous   *novelist, essayist* **ALDOUS HUXLEY,** *to Timothy Leary*

FEBRUARY 12

1903

With the money I shall receive from the serial publication of this story, the title of which is *The Call of the Wild*, I expect to do two things. (1), pay off some of my debts. (2)—Take what is left, engage cabin passage in a sailing vessel for the South Seas, take a typewriter, plenty of paper & ink and the plot for my sea story [*The Sea-Wolf*, 1904] along, and thus get the sea atmosphere on which I have during the last several years gone stale.

novelist **JACK LONDON**, *to his publisher*

1965

We have an opportunity, like "Gulliver's Travels" of a century or more ago, to combine spectacle-excitement for a mass group along with meaningful drama and something of substance and pride . . .

For the first time I think I see our particular and peculiar medium exactly for what it is. It has been and can be very good—and if someone proves to me they want me to try for that level, I gladly will. On the other hand, without that proof, I intend to aim for safe copies and parallels of existing successes—settle for doing it just two or three percent better than the next guy so that job and profits are always there, and I eat dinner every night at 6:00 p.m. with the children and have two days at home out of every seven to play horseshoes and putter in the garden . . .

Star Trek creator **GENE RODDENBERRY**, *to his agent*

1986

Jackson [Browne] told me he'd moved—sounds pretty upscale. I asked, "Are you embarrassed?" He said he was—I said "Good."

WARREN ZEVON

FEBRUARY 13

1844

The meat train did not arrive this evening, and I gave Godey leave to kill our little dog, (Tlamath,) which he prepared in Indian fashion; scorching off the hair, and washing the skin with soap and snow, and then cutting it up into pieces, which were laid on the snow. Shortly afterwards, the sleigh arrived with a supply of horse meat; and we had to-night an extraordinary dinner—pea soup, mule, and dog.   *pathfinder* **JOHN C. FRÉMONT**

1844

The second victim was my poor Jack, because he was the fattest mule. Last night we received a sledful of his meat, but I did not eat any of it and do not intend to.

. . . Just now the situation is this: Frémont has gone with four men to work on the trail. I am lying in the kitchen hole on my buffalo hide near the fire to prevent things from burning. On the fire are two pots and a tea kettle. In one pot are peas and pieces of the meat of my Jack; in the smaller pot is half of the dog. When the others return, everything will be tender. Then we shall bake bread, with sugar instead of salt (so far we have not had this in our mess), make a pot of good coffee, and start the meal. If you want me to tell you about my internal condition, I must say that my stomach is in a bad state . . .

I know of nothing else to record at present. Hence I shall give the dog a little more water and begin to read Byron's Don Juan.   **CHARLES PREUSS**

FEBRUARY 14

1949

. . . It is beginning to look like television may soon kill not only the theater and the movies but radio, books, magazines, newspapers, and finally articulate speech and all the processes of ratiocination. Talk of the barbarian invasions—the fifth century was nothing to the 20th.

We had Grace and Edwin [Hubble] staying with us for three days last week. Both in good form, and Edwin full of enthusiasm over the first photographs taken by the two-hundred-inch telescope. The thing does all that was hoped for it, and the first sample shot revealed two entirely new and unsuspected kinds of nebulae, with faint images of nebulae going on and on in undiminished numbers to 1 billion light years into space . . .

ALDOUS HUXLEY, *to Anita Loos*

1978

Francis called me this evening. He said he got the valentine I sent him. He said he didn't believe in valentines but that he wanted me to know that my notes were really good, that he always knew I had talent.

He said he is really getting scared.

He said he had been working very long hours. He is screening an assembly of the film in ten days.   *filmmaker, artist, writer* **ELEANOR COPPOLA**

1987

Today I sit on the library lawn in front of Doheny and it's cloudy and I'm cold in my cotton overalls and Tanya's t-shirt. I'm sitting on the green hunting jacket. I have a little cold. I have bruises from the Chili Peppers last night and I kind of have to pee. This is a very normal day. Maybe sometime I'll have a special Valentine's Day. Maybe it'll mean a lot to me. Maybe it's time to walk home.   **CAROLYN KELLOGG**

FEBRUARY 15

1898

If you were to enter upon a position where you had to remain each weekday from 9 a.m. to 10 p.m. with only *just* time off for lunch and dinner; and on Sunday from 10 to 4, with *no moment off*; if that meant steady work, without reading or resting, or writing, or *anything* but drudgery . . . would you feel like smiling or striking when you were congratulated on your position?

INA COOLBRITH, *to Charles Warren Stoddard*

1941

We got us a cabin in a two by four tourist court. Aircraft boom here make it hard to get shelter. Wont take kids hardly a tall. We househunted three days with no luck. Same old tale, How many kids? Sorry the owner's away. No kids. Awful sorry. The god dam silly way they look at you like you'd ought to take your kids off somewhere and tie a grinding stone around their neck and throw them in the river—and then you could pay twice as much as you ought to and rent you a house . . . Some kind of houses has got to be built for families with kids—the more kids, the bigger bargain you would get . . .

Los Angeles and southern California is thickly settled. This little station covers a strip about 100 miles in each direction. It is full of people that work and talk a working man's lingo, no matter what tongue or color . . . it might be better for me to step off out here and take a swing at her six times a week, and cover this country that's so newly settled and where there's a possible chance for alot of new things to get started.

Take it easy but take it,   *troubadour* **WOODY GUTHRIE**

1968

I am having a splendid hedonistic time here. My host . . . has a bosky garden on a hill (Mount Washington, in Highland Park) overlooking almost all of L.A., which provides an enormous light show every night. I am giving regular poetry readings with great vigor, and to my surprise I have become so lacking in nervousness that I am reading pretty well—certainly better than ever before. They are a bit trying, of course, as all work is, and can seriously interfere with drinking schedules. The night before my reading at UCLA I got as drunk as I ever have in my life—there was actually an hour of consciousness of which next day I remembered nothing at all. I woke up the next day surrounded by naked bodies and uniquely hungover. While I gave my reading I kept wondering whether any poet had ever thrown up on the stage during a poetry reading. Luckily I got through it all right. Anyway, days here start with bloody Marys.

We went to Jimi Hendryx, at the Shrine, which is quite a place . . .

- Stay safe.   **THOM GUNN**

1989

dear, dear Shawn:

I am not able to get any amount of my writing done because everything else in my daily life takes all my time and energy . . . So my doctor, Ian, and I have reached the conclusion that I must go to a "retirement home" as soon as possible. Ian found a very satisfactory place just ten minutes away from his studio in Marin . . .

This place in Kentfield is only $960 a month . . . and the long glass doors open upon a garden and acacia and redwood trees. I knew that Joan Baez's (senior) sister was in a senior home since two years, but it was sheer coincidence that she happened to be in this one . . .

Another startling coincidence at the moment is that Sam Beckett and I have the very same afflictions at the very same time. He is several years younger than I am and has been forced (against his will) to enter a retirement place with other "old crocks," as he describes it. He, too, has "pernicious anemia," arthritis, memory failure, and I am sending him a pair of those splendid Rockport shoes that enable me to walk without a cane . . .

KAY BOYLE

FEBRUARY 16

1844

My Jack has been entirely consumed; I have not eaten any of it. Today a horse will be killed, and since we have salt now, I shall eat with relish. Baking bread has come to an end; only a few handfuls of flour are left to give a little body to the horse meat and pea soup for a few more days. Frémont has such a good appetite that even between meals a piece is always kept ready for him on a roasting stick. Today he has gone with Jacob to reconnoiter toward the west . . .

CHARLES PREUSS

1844

February 16.—We had succeeded in getting our animals safely to the first grassy hill; and this morning I started with Jacob on a re-connoitring expedition beyond the mountain. We travelled along the crests of narrow ridges, extending down from the mountain in the direction of the valley, from which the snow was fast melting away. On the open spots was tolerably good grass; and I judged we should succeed in getting the camp down by way of these. Towards sun-down we discovered some icy spots in a deep hollow; and, descending the mountain, we encamped on the head water of a little creek, where at last the water found its way to the Pacific. The night was clear and very long. We heard the cries of some wild animals, which had been attracted by our fire, and a flock of geese passed over during the night. Even these strange sounds had something pleasant to our senses in this region of silence and desolation . . .

JOHN C. FRÉMONT

1850

DAWLYTOWN

The sight of a late newspaper is rare among us, and when one arrives in the mines it is read and reread, with all its advertisements even, and then it passes from hand to hand till little is left to entitle it to the distinction of being a newspaper. Suffice it then to say, that the package was most truly acceptable, and for which I thank you. When you next visit these diggings I shall be able to afford you something better for a breakfast than that of my self-praised battercake. I have made decided improvement in my culinary education since your sojourn with me at Mud Hill, having taken lessons from that old dame, Madame Necessity; and now, instead of confining my experiments in cooking to heavy griddle cakes, I have been elevated to the high dignity of breadbaker. I most truly hope to be able to give you specimens of my proficiency, at my cabin the coming spring . . .

[Where] was our gold?—echo answers, where! I did not see any, but I saw many places where it ought to be—my pocket, for instance.

newspaperman **ALONZO DELANO**

1986

Audre,

[If] I can contribute to this household in some way no matter how small, it will help thwart off some of that self-doubt that us strong Black amazons supposedly don't have, but as we know sits on the right shoulder constantly talking shit.

Girlfriend, your departure from this state was right on time. We have been hit by a storm that is unbelievable. Had it happened while you were here, we could have taken a row boat to our reading. Flash floods, mud slides, people being evacuated from their homes, power outages for hours and in some cases days, because the repair crews can't get in to fix the lines. Intense!

We had to bring the dogs in for fear of them being washed away . . .

Love, Pat

P.S. How do you cook beets?   *writer* **PAT PARKER**, *to Audre Lorde*

FEBRUARY 17

1954

Up to LA where I dig city again, to Woody Herman's band on marquee— Get off bus & down South Main St burdened with all pack and have jumbo beers for hot sun thirst—Go on down to SP railyards, singin, "An oldtime non-lovin hard-livin brake-man," buy wieners and wine in an Italian store, go to yards, inquire about Zipper. At redsun five all clerks go home, yard quiet—I light wood fire behind section shanty and cook dogs and eat oranges & cupcakes, smoke Bull Durham & rest—Chinese new year plap-plaps

nearby—at seven I get foolishly on Zipper caboose and talk to rear brake-
man as train is made up—BRAM! SLAM! Brakeman struggles to fix mantle
and lamp and start coal fire—conductor is Stormy Mason—doesn't bide my
papers, order me out of the caboose—train is underway to Santa Barbara
 . . . for first time in months, in cold rushing night air of California Golden
Coast, uncork wine & drink up—raw, bad, rotgut—but I warm and sing all
the way –   JACK KEROUAC

1999
In 1935 I made my way to the local WPA office in Oakland and asked for
an application. They told me they needed laborers to work on a project
near Lake Merritt, which included the present courthouse for the Superior
Court. I took what they offered, not informing them of what I had done
before. They put me out with a pick and shovel, and I dug ditches for one or
two days, along with other black male laborers . . .

When they found out I had college background and had just left the *Oakland Tribune*, they said, "You don't belong out here." They sent me to the Federal Writers Project at Bancroft Library on the campus of UC Berkeley . . .

There were roughly 30 people in our group, all very talented, and all lib-
erals. A couple of them had Ph.D's. Most of them had worked on small newspapers or trade papers. We did research work on the history of California,
because the library had the greatest collection of California history books
in the state . . .

It was a very unruly group. One of the first things they did was to form a
union, which I joined. We had the audacity to threaten to strike if we didn't
get higher wages. And this was welfare money: That's what seemed so amusing to me. The Federal Writers Project was the most rebellious unit in the
WPA, and got in disfavor all over the country.

The job only lasted about six months, because the funds ran out for that
particular project. I was the only black person in the group, and they accepted me as a colleague . . .   *newspaperman* THOMAS C. FLEMING

FEBRUARY 18
1844
Still in the old snow hole. The horses are now near by on a snow-free hill,
where grass is said to be rather plentiful. The sun is doing its part daily in

melting the snow. Frémont has not discovered very much, but it seems that we shall be able to pass several crests as soon as we have crossed the divide. The building of the path continues. The horse meat is all right as long as the salt holds out. My appetite has returned; I wish I had something better to satisfy it. Our latitude is 38° 41'. Good appetite, always in the free mountain air, only two meals, nothing but peas and horse meat—that does not seem to make sense. I wish I were at the market with a shopping basket. What wouldn't I buy!   **CHARLES PREUSS**

1939

It was a really gorgeous affair. The great Tower of the Sun gleaming, the elephant Towers blazing, the avenues gay with bands and fountains . . . leaping into the air. There was the theatre clean and shining and everything ready . . .   **HALLIE FLANAGAN**

1948

Since I do not intend to alter my behavior in the future, I'm afraid you'll just have to go on hating.   **DALTON TRUMBO**, *to a colleague*

1957

Well, we began shooting with a drama I've no doubt Orson planned. We rehearsed all day, lining up a dolly shot covering the entire first scene in Sanchez's apartment. We never turned a camera all morning or all afternoon, the studio brass gathering in the shadows in anxious little knots. By the time we began filming at a quarter to six, I know they'd written off the whole day. At seven-forty, Orson said, "OK, print. That's a wrap on this set. We're two days ahead of schedule." Twelve pages in one take, including inserts, two-shots, over-shoulders; the whole scene in one, moving through three rooms, with seven speaking parts.   **CHARLTON HESTON**

FEBRUARY 19

1847

19th at sundown reached the Cabins and found the people in great distress such as I never before wittnessed there having been twelve deaths and more expected every hour the sight of us appeared to put life into their emaciated frames . . .   *Donner Party diarist* **JOHN SINCLAIR**

1926

It's a pleasant wild coast. The roads are washed out a bit at present but they'll be in shape again, and we'll see splendid things down the coast and up the valley. The stonework I've done here with my hands might amuse you . . .

ROBINSON JEFFERS, *at work on Tor House*

1940

LOS ANGELES

This singular place is an odd haven in which to sit in the sun and read about the boarding of the [Nazi oil tanker] *Altmark*. Kaufman, Hart and Alice Miller, all of whom came out to see the opening, are all quitting their villas here today [at the Garden of Allah]. Rachmaninoff has the next one to mine and begins practicing every morning at dawn. Beyond him are the Charles Laughtons. Beyond them is Robert Benchley. Beyond him is Dorothy Parker. It's the kind of village you might look for down the rabbit-hole. That muted mutter from across the way is just Dame Mae Whitty, rehearsing as the nurse to the impending Juliet of Vivien Leigh and the Romeo of Larry Olivier. Down the street is the charming home of a small Jewish screenwriter who used to be my office boy. He has just bought a Reynolds. It's a mad world, my masters! And always was.

writer, actor ALEXANDER WOOLLCOTT

FEBRUARY 20

1861

. . . I climbed a high ridge, some two thousand feet above camp. Here a stratum of rock comes out filled with large shells in fine preservation. It rises in a ridge, ending in a precipice to the north. In places these fossil shells had been weathered out in immense numbers. The ridge was strewn with them, as thick as any seabeach I have ever seen . . .

Who shall tell how many centuries, how many decades of centuries, have elapsed since these rocks resounded to the roar of breakers, and these animals sported in their foam? I picked up a bone, cemented in the rock with the shells. A feeling of awe came over me. Around me rose rugged mountains; no human being was within miles of me to break the silence. And then I felt overwhelmed with the magnitude of the work ahead of me. I was at work alone in the field work of this great state, a territory larger than all New England and New York, complicated in its geology.

But the real soon roused me from reveries—I must get back. I was alone, far from camp—grizzlies might come out as the moon came up . . .

geographer, botanist **WILLIAM H. BREWER**

1870

MUD HILL, NEVADA COUNTY

Our usually quiet city has been excited of late over an article that appeared in the Daily Gazette, in which the editor compared the talent of the colored people of this place to that of the present Legislature of this State, and of course, the colored people took exception to it, not being willing to be classed with a traitorous set, and the editor of the Gazette was obliged to take back all he had said. *columnist* **JENNIE CARTER**

1960

Los Angeles is the American city, the impossible city **ITALO CALVINO**

FEBRUARY 21

1844

. . . Carson roused me this morning with an early fire, and we were all up long before day, in order to pass the snow fields before the sun should render the crust soft. We enjoyed this morning a scene, at sunrise, which even here was unusually glorious and beautiful. Immediately above the eastern mountains was repeated a cloud-formed mass of purple ranges, bordered with bright yellow gold; the peaks shot up into a narrow line of crimson cloud, above which the air was filled with a greenish orange; and over all was the singular beauty of the blue sky. **JOHN C. FRÉMONT**

1859

We, the undersigned residents of the State of California, and some of us citizens of the United States, previously citizens of the Republic of Mexico, respectfully say:

That during the war between the United States and Mexico the officers of the United States, as commandants of the land and sea forces, on several occasions offered and promised in the most solemn manner to the inhabitants of California, protection and security of their persons and their property and the annexation of the said state of California to the American Union, impressing upon them the great advantages to be derived from their being citizens of the United States . . .

When peace was established between the two nations by the Treaty of Guadalupe Hidalgo they joined in the general rejoicing with their new American fellow countrymen . . .

They heard with dismay of the appointment, by Act of Congress, of a commission with the right to examine all titles and confirm or disprove them, as their judgment considered equitable . . .

rancher, politician, Californio **ANTONIO MARÍA PICO**

FEBRUARY 22

1937

I happened to stray along Towne Street—a short street but interesting and colorful. It is there that the bums, the unemployed, the jetsam and flotsam hang out. In a small lot roped off a woman evangelist preached to benches filled with perhaps 60 men, old and young, stooped and beaten, of all races. She was fat, surely 40, and enthusiastic over the "saving of souls." She yelled: "Raise your hands, all of you who want to come to Christ and accept the Lord." Two responses. Sheepish grins and sly looks from some—they were waiting for one thing: the free meal . . .

Under a tall palm tree that reached approximately 25 feet into the sky stood a piano. Presently a woman drummed out a hymn and sang in a cracked, amateurish voice . . .

Down a little ways a little old man in a thread-bare suit, soiled with tobacco ashes, stood in the doorway of a garage. His eyes continually shifted up and down the street as if vigilant for the appearance of the police on the scene . . . .

He said . . . "These church people get you worked up, enthused—and then get your money. There are three reasons why people go to church: for social pleasures, business matters, and to go to heaven. Well heaven is supposed to be up past the sun and the sun is 73 million miles away. Who wants to go on that kind of a hike? . . . God gave life to everything; even the bed-bugs that bite you, you suckers. When you die you're dead. You'll get no body when you lose this one. Science proves that. When a thing dies it's dead. When Christ died he was dead." **WILLARD MOTLEY,** *novelist*

1948

NEW HELVETIA

SIR:

. . . I have taken the liberty of sending for your approval articles of agreement made by Mr. [James] Marshall and myself with the Yalesumney tribe of Indians. Should it meet with your approbation you would confer a special favour by sanctioning it . . . We have been at great expense in building and settling the place and would like to be protected in our title or claim for the term expressed in the Lease.

The settlement will be of great benefit to the Indians by protecting them against the wild tribes above them, furnishing them with food, clothing etc and teach them habits of industry. It will also be the means of settleing the lands at the base of the California mountains which are of a very superior quality by protecting the settlers against the Indians.

I have the honour to be very Respectfully you Obt Servt.

JOHANN AUGUSTUS SUTTER,

to Governor R. B. Mason

FEBRUARY 23

1965

[Where] would I come in? Just before Bunin, Ivan, *The Gentleman from San Francisco*? No? Well. Or Bulosan, Carlos? *America Is in the Heart.*

America is in the balls. America is in the factories. America is in the streets, hustling shines and newspapers, climbing down through skylights to the mother-blossom of the safes. I am the toilet paper wiped against America.　　　　　　　　　　　　　　*poet, novelist* **CHARLES BUKOWSKI**

1974

. . . i have read your letter many times

i do not know what to say. many mornings have come and gone people have came and went i have loved and i have cried many times. somehow, though, beneath it all it doesn't change—do you understand?

entrepreneur **STEVE JOBS**, *to his sweetheart,*

a day before his 19th birthday

1978

NAPA

Yesterday I was in San Francisco. I called Francis around one to make plans to meet in the city for dinner. He said he had just gotten an idea about a twist for the ending. Instead of Willard killing Kurtz and calling in the air strike, he was going to try it where Willard gets double-crossed. The air strike which was supposed to be his defense would be sent in to kill him, too. He was real excited. He said to call back later in the afternoon to make our plans. I had lunch, I did some shopping and waited around. I called back around four. He said he had everyone in there working and why didn't I just go back to Napa and he would come there in the evening when he got the editors all lined up with the new changes?

I got on the freeway, heading north. I felt a rush of emotion. I knew I would go home and wait, and he wouldn't come. I got more and more angry thinking about how my life is caught in so many moments of waiting . . .

ELEANOR COPPOLA

FEBRUARY 24

1844

The mules grew so hungry that they ate the tail of Fitzpatrick's horse, also parts of saddles, my bridle, etc.   **CHARLES PREUSS**

1967

I regret that I have been bad about writing . . . The truth is that I am in a kind of remoteness, or slump . . . I find myself rendered absolutely mute by the prospect of two or three uninterrupted weeks. I could not produce a page of Deathless Fisher if a gun were against my skull. Numb, dumb, dry as a crumb . . .   **M. F. K. FISHER,**

to New Yorker Paris columnist Janet Flanner

FEBRUARY 25

1866

[A] California critic knows it all, notwithstanding he may have been in the shoemaking business most of his life, or a plow-artist on a ranch.

MARK TWAIN

1942

. . . Secretary of Navy Knox announced that an enemy plane flying over Los Angeles was an error. On the other hand, the Department of the Army is saying an enemy reconnaissance plane definitely came. Both departments are publicly engaged in an absurd argument . . .

It seems the anti-aircraft rounds fired the night before were produced in the 1930s, and one third failed to explode. In the English-language newspaper, there were photos of these useless duds where they had come down on roads and people's yards.

AOKI HISA

1990

dearest Decca:

I want to thank you and Bob again for last evening. It was wonderful being with you both such a contrast to the prevailing state of mind at The Redwoods . . . Your flowers have transformed my room into a cheerful place, and I do appreciate your lavish gift of them . . . .

And I want to let everyone within listening distance know how Bob saved my career as a teacher when he hastened across the court-room that day, when I stood in my grey prison garb in the dock, and told the prosecutor that if I had to serve my thirty-one day sentence consecutively, in one whole piece, I would lose my job at the university. Against all odds, Bob succeeded in having me serve the sentence on week-ends. No book critic that I know of, and no biographer, could have that kind of magic in his blood and brain . . . The literary critic or biographer deals with personal prejudices and fantasies, while the doctor or lawyer has, by choice, acquired a broad framework in which to commit himself to all mankind . . .

Much love and many kisses, and again my thanks

KAY BOYLE

1999

Often I write with comedy records on: old Firesign Theater and Monty Python LPs, or lately CD reissues of Robert Klein albums from the '70s. Unfortunately, I don't know any comedy albums with Grammy Awards parodies. I watched the first two hours of this year's show, went out to see a band, then came back at 1 a.m. and ran the rest on tape.

"Jennifer, you look sick," Jimmy Smits said to Jennifer Lopez, his co-presenter. She did, too. Someone had done his best to make her look like Madonna, who was doing her best to look like Vampira. "I'll take that as a compliment," Lopez said. "Watching this show makes you question your own self-worth," my wife said, after the android Ricky Martin performed an acrobatic version of "Vuelve" without sweating. "This is so slick I feel like I need to take a bath. With soap. To get the oil off."

Looking like Papa Bear with Goldilocks in his stomach, George Lucas came on to present a segment on movie music. A montage ran: Judy Garland singing "Over the Rainbow," Kevin Bacon grinning in *Footloose*. For a few seconds a spark of life came through, but the film-to-film clips were so short, their focus so fuzzy, their color so faded, they canceled each other out. But it must have brought somebody in under budget.

Still, the Grammys have it all over the Oscars in self-congratulation . . . Oscar winners aren't humble: For a moment, they *rule*. You don't see any movie stars bending over like arthritics . . . to say "I want to thank God, and of course my manager," as if they're proud of their perspicacity in choosing both . . . .

To compare the Grammys with the show I went out to see would be a setup; comparing the Grammys with an abandoned car in the bad part of town would be a setup. What was interesting about the Scavengers—a reconstituted version of the Avengers, a San Francisco punk band that broke up 20 years ago—was that inside the nightclub there seemed to be no sense whatsoever that, simultaneously, a musical event attended to by a billion people (so one had been told) was even taking place . . .

A small blond woman next to me was singing every word of every song as well as the singer was; the guy in front of me, 5 feet 6, 250 pounds, a rolled '50s collar and a sweeping DA, slammed left and right without actually injuring anyone. I'd forgotten how much fun it is to get knocked around in a punk crowd—how much fun it is to push and shove without any ill will. Then I went home and fast-forwarded to Lauryn Hill: "Thanks to God for honoring me with this huge responsibility," she said, as if he'd taken time from his busy schedule to fix the balloting. But then, she talks to him, I don't.

critic GREIL MARCUS

FEBRUARY 26

1934

Dear Father and Mother,

I am burning all three candles as I listen to the magnificent music of Beethoven's Fifth Symphony. I am fairly well-established in my new room; it is better than the other, and I had a jolly time making it my own.

The city seemed senselessly hideous and squatted when I reentered it, after the clean spaciousness of green hills and blue seas . . .

EVERETT RUESS

1983

The area was heavily populated with members of the secret service wearing hearing aids and talking into their sleeves. Less numerous but more cheerful were the citizens of San Diego, some of whom were allowed on to the pier itself . . .

A 21-gun salute crashed out as the Britannia tied up. You couldn't help thinking that all the explosions might be setting a bad example, but, out on the water, the voices of dissent were limited to one small boat carrying the rubric "God Save the Queen from Nuclear Attack". This was easily countered on shore by such friendly messages as "Body Beautiful Car Wash says Welcome, Queen Elizabeth" . . .   *critic, poet, translator* **CLIVE JAMES**

FEBRUARY 27

1965

. . . I am squarer than ever now, running five miles a day in the warm California dawn, hunting and walking a lot. It is good; it is my way, and I shall never set foot on any other. Liquor was trying to finish me, so I finished it. Now the world is very clear and steady, and very deep in every direction.

JAMES DICKEY, *to Denise Levertov*

1983

On Sunday, the royal couple lunch with Mr and Mrs Walter Annenberg in Palm Springs.

Back at the Britannia, which had meanwhile moved north to Long Beach, [the Queen] changed clothes for the biggest event of the week, the jumbo dinner in Sound Stage 9 at 20th Century Fox . . . she voluntarily entered the limousine that would take her to break bread with Marie Osmond, the current Tarzan, the man who used to be Davy Crockett, and at least two of the Gabor sisters . . .

Fred Astaire was one of the younger luminaries present. Some of them had risen from the grave for the occasion but they had more in common than mere immortality. Gradually, it dawned that they were nearly all republicans. The democrats were at home, seething. When Nancy Reagan finally welcomed the royal couple, she was shaking hands with practically the only invitees who hadn't voted for her husband.

The royals were seated with the British film-star colony all along one side of a long table up on stage, like a Last Supper painted by Sir Joshua Reynolds . . .

In fact, she had been had. The evening was a pay-off for Ronald Reagan's financial backers, who would never have met the stars if the stars had not come to meet the Queen. Buckingham Palace had been hustled into bankrolling the next campaign wagon.   **CLIVE JAMES**

FEBRUARY 28

1844

When cooked all night, a mule head is a delicacy.   **CHARLES PREUSS**

1852

The site of Los Angeles is lovely, but the city is very ugly. Most of the houses are built of mud, some are plastered outside, and have a porch around them, looking neat and pretty as any house, but these are few and far between. We are surrounded almost by high green hills. Remove this and place here one of the pretty towns in the States, and I do not think there could be a more lovely spot.   *pioneer* **EMILY HAYES**

1983

But if the Queen felt manipulated she didn't show it. The rain was sufficient proof that not even the president could fix everything. It fell all night and on through the next day. Sections of California began dissolving into the sea. Up in the Sierra Madre at the British Home for old people, the lawn squished like spinach quiche. The media stood in it ankle deep while Her Majesty met an old lady in a wheelchair and received a quilt for Prince William.

CLIVE JAMES

FEBRUARY 29

1860

A report was brought from Eureka on Sunday morning, that during the night nearly all the Indians camping on Indian Island, including women and children, were killed by parties unknown. A few loaded canoes bringing the dead bodies to Union on their way to Mad river, where some of the victims belonged, confirmed the report. But when the facts were generally known, it appeared that out of some sixty or seventy killed on the Island, at least fifty or sixty were women and children. Neither age or sex had been spared. Little children and old women were mercilessly stabbed and their skulls crushed with axes. When the bodies were landed at Union, a more shocking and revolting spectacle never was exhibited to the eyes of a Christian and civilized people. Old women, wrinkled and decrepit, lay weltering in blood, their brains dashed out and dabbled with their long gray hair. Infants scarce a span long, with their faces cloven with hatchets and their bodies ghastly with wounds.

We gathered from the survivors that four or five white men attacked the ranches at about 4 o'clock in the morning, which statement is corroborated by people at Eureka who heard pistol shots at about that time, although no knowledge of the attack was public. With the Indians who lived on the Island, some thirty from the mouth of Mad river were staying, having attended a dance on the evening previous. They were all killed with the exception of some few who hid themselves during the massacre. No resistance was made, it is said, to the butchers who did the work, but as they ran or huddled together for protection like sheep, they were struck down with hatchets. Very little shooting was done, most of the bodies having wounds about the head. The bucks were mostly absent, which accounts for the predominance of female victims . . .

Indian Island is scarcely one mile from Eureka, the county seat of Humboldt county. With the exception of the conjectures that the Indians on the Island offer aid and assistance to the mountain Indians, they are peaceful and industrious, and seem to have perfect faith in the good will of the whites. Many of them are familiar to our citizens. 'Bill' of Mad river, a well known and rather intelligent fellow, has proven a faithful ally to the white men on several occasions and—has had his wife, mother, sister, two brothers and two little children, cruelly butchered by men of that race whom he had learned to respect and esteem . . .   *writer* **BRET HARTE**

1964

Dear César:

I received your penitent letter, much to my surprise, and as the natives say, "No hay fijón." . . . I think I am still ahead when it comes to losing tempers. Frankly, I did not give it a second thought, and please feel free to express your opinions as far as my work is concerned, even though they may not always be in praise, because as you know, I always work better under pressure and "guided instruction." You will further blow your top with the following:

I did not get to call or go to Sacramento today as planned: my baby sitter went home for the weekend at the request of her parents and as they say, you never miss the water till the well runs dry, and I find I am absolutely grounded. I thought I would be able to get away after the girls came from school, but a few unexpected callers took care of that. I had hoped to get to a phone and call Sacramento today to find out about the welfare cases. . . .

activist **DOLORES HUERTA**, *to César Chávez*

MARCH 1

1990

To write in the midst of grieving seems both monumental and sense-less . . . So much time and energy was devoted to Tom during the last two years of his illness that I did not prepare myself to be alone, to think of the future, to take care of myself . . .

It is cold here this morning, in this apartment, in this neighborhood that nobody can identify, sandwiched between the Castro to the west and the Mission to the east. Still cloudy out, waiting for a storm; they say it might rain all weekend. I spend too much time watching for storms, just looking out the window, scanning the horizon, but that is because wild weather is the only vector for my mood these rough days. The cat, Peggy, is here, keep-ing me company, curled up in the corner, near the little heater I keep going by the desk. This end of the apartment is always cold—all windows off the end of the kitchen, probably a porch at one time. But with the little heater going and a cup of lemon tea steaming beside me, it's cozy enough. On this cloudy, dark day, it's as silent as a forest and as good a time as any to begin this work.   *diarist* **PAUL REED**

1996

Siskel gave it a thumbs down, Ebert a thumbs up . . .

In the eight years that *Up Close & Personal* absorbed our attention, Joan and I separately wrote two novels (one each) and six nonfiction books. We worked on seven other scripts, two of which (*Hills Like White Elephants* and *Broken Trust*) have so far been produced. In magazines, Joan wrote about the Central Park Jogger, about two presidential campaigns, and about the economic and social dislocations in California brought about by the end of the Cold War and the concomitant downsizing of the defense industry; I reported at length about Rodney King, about the Los Angeles riots, and about the O. J. Simpson case, and wrote and narrated an hour-long PBS documentary on Los Angeles.

We also had a good time.   JOHN GREGORY DUNNE

2022

Uber driver taking me to Union Station said, "You know, I died for four to six minutes." And I'm sitting there going: When?? Like ten seconds ago when we were careening through that intersection?? Turns out it was a few years back. Then he asked me, "Do you know why I came back to life?" I said no. "Student loans," he said, "as long as I have student loans to pay, I can't die."

SAMIA SAAD

MARCH 2

1938

It's a real flood. And my worst sorrow is that we have no radio on hand and can't [hear] all the minute to minute news . . .

Santa Monica Canyon is flooded and Santa Monica cut off, as also Malibu Topango and Laurel and most of the canyon places. The lights have taken to going off too, and the radio broadcasts urgent requests for people to stay at home and not to use the telephone except for emergency calls. Neglecting which, when the rain [slows] down to a fine mist we tour out to see a movie, and a very bad one which I suppose serves us right. [There] are sandbags along the store fronts on Brand so the water must have topped the curbs and we hope Central—i.e. Lyons Storage—has better drainage luck, Edward's negative box being on the floor of the ground floor.

photographer, muse CHARIS WILSON

1983

When the Queen stepped down to meet female Mayor Feinstein, the rain magically ceased.

"She's smiling!" cried a local television front person. "That's a first!"

The merry mood intensified when the Queen checked into 46 rooms of the St Francis Hotel, because the media were staying there too, although only in one room each . . .

Nothing could now keep the San Francisco stopover from being a success, even if the water level at the Alviso sewage treatment plant went over 9ft and automatically dumped the raw effluent of a million people into the bay. **CLIVE JAMES**

MARCH 3

1935

[Montaigne] refused to be depressed by death, which is the inevitable end of us all.

FREMONT OLDER, *S.F. newspaperman, before dying mid-column*

1943

Darling Muv,

. . . We are living in a boarding house, there are also 2 marines, 3 boys aged 8, 6 & 3, & one girl about my age with the boy of 3. Mrs. Betts takes care of the Donk all day, & the D. loves it because she is boy-crazy & there are 3 boys here. It is very cheap, so I'm saving a lot of dough with which to buy furniture later on if I decide to stay here for good. So far I haven't seen much of San F as I've been working pretty hard . . .

I think it will be pretty nice out here . . . If I don't like it in San F. after a few months I may skeke off to Mexico. **JESSICA MITFORD**

MARCH 4

1921

CAMP KEARNEY, CALIFORNIA

Dear Lady—

I didn't intend doing this—writing you a second letter before I got an answer to my first—but that's the hell of being in love with a vamp, you do all sorts of things . . .

Love

Hammett

novelist **DASHIELL HAMMETT**

to his fiancée

1995

My car died today. I don't care. It's gone. I should have known that would happen. It was making all of these noises, but I just kept turning up the radio so I didn't have to hear them and worry. I can be like that with my health too—if I see something wrong with me, I just cover it up, keep going, and try not to think about it.   *columnist* **AMY ASBURY**

MARCH 5

1927

Arrived home. Mayor's office clogged with divorces. May have to get rid of some of them before we can have any new marriages.

humorist, movie actor, Beverly Hills mayor **WILL ROGERS**

1966

School is much better this semester. I taught worse than ever before last semester, but this semester I'm teaching better than ever before. Partly because in several ways I have an easier schedule, partly because two of the 3 courses I have taught before, partly because spring is always better than fall when I spend half the time lamenting about goldengrove unleaving and other such useless nostalgia. > Result is that I get more time for drinking > Result is I am happy > Result is I write poetry again.   **THOM GUNN**

MARCH 6

1854

In the Summer I will try and make an excursion out into the mines and in the fall another out on the immigrant trail. This will help pass off so much of the time. This seems to be a very healthy place; all here are enjoying excellent health. The post has been occupied now for about 14 months, by two Companies, and I believe there has been two deaths. One by accidentally shooting himself and the other by a limb from a tree falling on a man . . .

There is no news here only occasionally a disaster at sea. A few days since a steamer went down just inside the Columbia river bar; vessel with all on board except one lost. I am in a great hurry to get this ready for the Mail so I must bid you all good buy for the present. Give my love to your pa, ma, sisters and brother. Kiss our little boys for me. Talk to them a great deal about their pa. A thousand kisses for yourself dearest . . .

Adieu dear wife.

ULYS.

captain **ULYSSES S. GRANT**

1937

Los Angeles, present city of my adoption; it's so cosmopolitan. Everything can and does happen here—all people rub shoulders on Main Street: the Hawk-nosed Jew, the hurrying little Japanese lady, the big blonde Swede, the Mexican peon, beautiful-eyed senoritas, the inoffensive little Chinaman, the . . .

Los Angeles and especially Main Street is a show-case of the world, a barometer of appetites, natures, peoples.

A little Mexican boy of about 12 catches my eye. He is in a green smock and is shining a man's shoes in a barber shop. A shock of hair as black as sin falls over his forehead. His customer is reading a paper and our little amigo is engrossed in the back page. As he reads his eyes grow larger and larger, his mouth opens wider and wider, his polish rag moves faster and faster until it dances up over the shoe and onto his customer's pant-leg. I stood there watching him and laughed loud and long. Los Angeles does that to one. Often tonight I stood laughing crazily to myself. And people passing me gave me a wide berth and looked back at me, I wanted to cry out to them— "Oh native sons of California—oh fools!— look about you, look at your California and enjoy it as I do. Discover its romance and humor, its pathos and fascination. Retard your hurrying steps. Linger. Stroll. Poke about and become a discoverer. Discover your city and its people. Laugh with me as your heart leaps. Cry with me as it breaks . . .

WILLARD MOTLEY

1947

I go there two or three times a week, am on easy terms with the chief embalmer & next week am to lunch with DR HUBERT EATON [the founder] himself. It is an entirely unique place—the only thing in California that is not a copy of something else. It is wonderful literary raw material. Aldous [Huxley] flirted with it in After Many a Summer but only with the superficialities. I am at the heart of it. It will be a very good story. [. . .] Did you know that the cadaver was referred to as 'the loved one' at [Forest Lawn]? I have seen dozens of loved ones half painted before the bereaved family saw them.

EVELYN WAUGH

MARCH 7

1848

The first party of Mormons, employed by me left for washing and digging Gold and very soon all followed, and left me only the sick and the lame behind. And at this time I could say that every body left me from the Clerk to the Cook . . . The same thing was in every branch of business which I carried on at the time. I began to harvest my wheat, while others was digging and washing Gold, but even the Indians could not be keeped longer at Work. They was impatient to run to the mine, and other Indians had informed them of the Gold and its Value; and so I had to leave more than 2/3 of my harvest in the fields.   **JOHANN AUGUSTUS SUTTER**

1947

In the morning we cross the Golden Gate Bridge without any hope of returning. We've left San Francisco and we're headed off to an adventure on unknown routes . . . Our first stop is Sacramento, where we arrive at around ten o'clock. In this capital of California, I taste for the first time in America the poetry of dead cities . . . One expects to see old gentlemen in silk hats and women in crinolines descending the steps. We've left San Francisco behind, and here we are in Bruges or Aigues-Mortes. In Europe, the defunct capitals are eight centuries old; here, the capital is scarcely one century old. But it feels just as embalmed . . .

We go through a gold mining town that's now called Placerville, but its real name is Hangtown, and the inn has a sign depicting a tree where they used to hang murderers and thieves. This town is only half-dead, but others are entirely abandoned and are called ghost towns . . . I'm almost as moved as if I'd discovered Sleeping Beauty's castle at a bend in the road. This is really where those men lived whose legends enchanted my childhood, whose stories set me dreaming. Here—or in a nearby forest, but it amounts to the same thing—Charlie Chaplin made *The Gold Rush*. These landscapes— which I imagined through the screen and books and which existed on the fringes of the world, just like fairy-tale palaces or the painted heavens of Fra Angelico—now I've seen them with my own eyes.

We haven't seen a house in a long time. Suddenly there's a sign: "6,000 feet." I look at it, incredulous: we've barely been climbing since Sacramento. Seven thousand feet . . . It would take at least a day's walk to reach human habitation, and we haven't seen a single car . . .

I'm angry at myself . . . I looked at the map as if it reflected a world submissive to the reign of man, with distances convertible to hours and exact gallons of gas. This morning we were in San Francisco, it's true, and police officers directed traffic. No more officers, no more direction. We no longer need to obey, but nothing obeys us either. The needle on our gasoline gauge is dangerously close to zero . . .   *philosopher* **SIMONE DE BEAUVOIR**

MARCH 8

1856

. . . Equality is harmony, and thereon rests peace in the Republic. Disrupting equality through excess is out of tune and what was once sweet music becomes simply noise . . .   **FRANCISCO P. RAMÍREZ**, *journalist*

1995

A journal about keeping a journal. This could be dangerous, venturing into the private world of a writer and exposing a vein. But isn't that what journals are all about? . . .

I've read many types of journals. I've tried lots of ways to keep a journal. I don't have a favorite journal writer and some of the best material I've read is about keeping a journal—or as in Joan Didion's case, "On Keeping a Notebook" (from *Slouching to Bethlehem*). Because I farm, my field work is often woven into my journals. But do records on when the peaches first bloom or the grape shoots peek out at the spring sun or the early signs of worms in my peaches—do they belong in my journal?

Yes and no. They are part of what makes a journal important—a documentation of where you were and what you felt at a specific time and place. But do worms and metaphors belong on the same page? I've written some of my best stories about worms—but I keep a different type of farm journal in addition to my writing journal. No one said I couldn't have more than one.

farmer, writer **DAVID MAS MASUMOTO**

MARCH 9

1906

We arose early and took the train to Los Angeles at about seven o'clock in the morning . . . The train followed the coastline for some one hundred miles and I never took such a beautiful journey. There are two train routes from San Francisco to Los Angeles: one through central California, through the great San Joaquin (Uácin as it is pronounced here) Valley, and the other by the coast. On either side, we saw the little rabbits they call 'gophers' standing on their hind legs . . .   DOUGLAS HYDE, *Irish president*

1935

There is no hope here. There is nothing but life as incredible as the place, and to that life and to that place a human becomes inured because nature refuses to let outraged senses and sensations and muscles react after they have been shocked to their limit. Else we should go mad.

So I am growing used to impossible snow-capped mountains, outrageous trees and lush gardens, heaven-blessed atmosphere and evening air impossibly laden with perfume of jasmine and orange blossoms. It is unjust that there should be such beauty in such a childish hellhole.

novelist, disappointed screenwriter ERIC KNIGHT

1947

The Mount Whitney Range provides Hollywood with images of Switzerland, the Himalayas, and the Caucasus. A few steps away there's Africa with its sand dunes and the Australian bush. Miraculously, this false Tibet and this illusory Switzerland are authentic parts of the planet. And since art is made of lies, I don't see why you can't create views of Asia in Lone Pine. Of all the reproaches leveled at Hollywood, this one seems the most stupid.

SIMONE DE BEAUVOIR

1950

. . . there has been no decision yet on a name for 98. Wallmann asked if a reward were offered, and Perlman quipped, "One milligram of the first gram produced." I added, "Payable to you or your descendants." We talked briefly on some of the suggestions for names, such as lewisium (after Gilbert N. Lewis) or californium . . .   *physicist* GLENN T. SEABORG

MARCH 10

1903

PIEDMONT, CALIF.

I am glad you like the *Call of the Wild* . . . The whole history of this story has been very rapid. On my return from England I sat down to write it into a 4000 word yarn, but it got away from me & I was forced to expand it to its present length . . .

They have paid me three cents a word for the American serial rights. This was the money I intended dividing between my debts and my South Sea trip . . . I compromised matters and bought a sloop-yacht for San Francisco Bay. It is now hauled out & being fitted up. I shall live on it a great deal, and on it I shall write the greater part of my sea-novel. The sloop is old, but it is roomy & fast. I can stand upright in the cabin which is quite large. I'll send you a picture of her some time.

I did not like the title, *The Call of the Wild* . . . There is a good title somewhere, if we can only lay hold of it . . .   **JACK LONDON**

1920

Dear Comrade and fellow-worker Debs:

Just a short letter to let you know that you have a comrade who think[s] of you tho I be an I.W.W. and locked tight into a cold steal sell at Los Angeles Cal. Just for my loyalty to the cause of industrial socialism and for running Red International Books my bail is twenty five thousand dollars and I don't know just when my trial will be however I am not losing any sleep over it knowing as I do that there are no justice to be gotten from a capitalist court the enemy of the working class and here I am to face them not only as an IWW or Bolshevik but also as a yellow man from the far East where only real bad men can come from.

I am not well today my very life longs for a great big green world where I can breathe fresh air and bath into the warm light of the sun, I trust you are well and strong and will live to see the jail doors swing wide and we go marching on. I am giving this letter to a boy to mail for me who is going to get his freedom today. I hope he will mail it right away. I am yours always

J. W. NISHIDA, *bookseller, to Eugene V. Debs*

2018

Lancaster. Knocking on doors for Katie Hill. Lawn art. Or lack thereof. Lack of lawns. Tired people. Sleeping in on a Saturday. Still in their PJs their sweats their bathrobes. Tired faces. Hernia belt. Knocked over tricycle. Barking dogs. Lots of barking dogs. And beware dog signs. Or a knock only if you're Christian sign and yes, i knocked . . . they don't know enough about this scoundrel, his 100-plus NRA rating, his votes for the tax cut for billionaires, his plans to come after their Medicare and Social Security . . .

The grandma living with her son in the garage and her arm in a sling. The woman without front teeth. The 18 year old who wasn't sure he was interested in voting, hadn't registered. Barbara and I let him have it. He won't forget the two women standing in the rain in front of his house, soggy paper and fogged up glasses, telling him why his future depends on it.

The guy at the CA-25 office, nice guy named LaBomba . . . he explained that he was named for Patrice Lumumba, but it got spelled wrong on his birth certificate.   **LOUISE STEINMAN**

MARCH 11

1950

The fellows and I have decided to name element 98 "californium."

GLENN T. SEABORG

1966

Taix's manufactures a round, flat, hearth-baked sourdough bread. Cradle it on your chest, push it between your breasts, pull it apart and chew on its stretching crust, cheese, butter, taste it. A Mr. Felix makes German pumpernickel. Markets it in cellophane with his Victorian-perfect face on the label. Keep it in the fridge and eat it all week, full of grain, and dark sultry mountain-climbing taste, as though it were the last taste on earth.

I should like to sleep in a bed of Jewish doublewhipped cream cheese . . .

LIZA WILLIAMS

2020

Los Angeles will be lovely when they finish it.

Even though it had recently rained, this fenced-off drain soon to join the river with the grandiose name still had no water. The L.A. River and its little tributary were in pain, I had always believed, calling out for mercy.

But now, as I nudged my bicycle onto the path, I felt that I had found some element of the city that had been hidden from me. No car could come here. No images of this strange, sad spectacle would ever be sent out into the world. There would be no:

"Come to L.A.! Ride your bike by a river!" No one in their right mind would be here.

But it was almost beautiful. I should not have laughed at the L.A. River.

novelist **COLM TÓIBÍN**, *in "Tales from the L.A. River"*

MARCH 12

1850

Our town has been some three months infested with a gang of rowdies and gamblers who alike set law and order at defiance. They have rendered the place a very unsafe one for the peaceable inhabitants . . .

The native population, unaccustomed to our laws, if called on would certainly be led on into excesses that would arouse national hatreds and lead to far worse evils . . .

Already, in two instances, sectional fights where firearms have been used have taken place between Californians and Americans, and we know not the hour when the difficulties of 1846 may not be renewed.

STEPHEN CLARK FOSTER, *mayor, vigilante*

1921

. . . I have to supervise for Wright the construction of 19 houses and a commercial building with 40 shops—a $400,000 development. I am still not at home here yet and I have to get used to everything slowly. Later I will try to open my own office. There is enough building here.

architect **RUDOLF SCHINDLER**, *to Richard Neutra*

1930

Is it already the light of the Pacific? *artist* **HENRI MATISSE**,
riding the Super Chief into California

2007

Over the weekend, I went to NYC . . . My semi-canned response to open questions about how I like Los Angeles is to say (the truth) that I love my weird hilly neighborhood in the heart of the city, but that as far as the city at large goes traffic is out of control; that I am happier these days making my life tiny, geographically speaking; that I am so jealous of my friends in New York who walk their children to school and then keep walking to get to work. I can't remember if I told anyone what it is like to be stuck on the 10 freeway going east at 1 o'clock in the afternoon, not moving, my daughter, crying, strapped into what looks like a tiny dentist's chair in the back— "Hang on sweetheart, don't cry, it'll just be another forty-five minutes." On those days I think this is not a good place to live. (Obviously, it's the other days that keep me here.)

In New York, it was actually refreshing to be with so many different types of people sharing the trains, so much less isolated than driving in a personal bubble alone, barely moving . . .

It may have been inevitable, but twice I was offered the line about Los Angeles, "There is no there there." To which I snapped at one person, "If there was no there there I wouldn't live there." So, there. So much for polish . . .

I might have said (but didn't) "Actually there is a there there. There are many theres there." And so on. Perhaps I should have handed him a Blackberry, called up the LA blogs and sent him to the corner to read . . .

So I flew back to Burbank . . . Then I was free to drive back to the dark rolling hills in Echo Park, where most of the neighborhood was settling down for the night, my window down, my thoughts my own, my car my own.

writer JENNY BURMAN

MARCH 13

1852

The country is beautiful, but I suppose there is no comparison between it now and twenty years ago. The gentleman we visited has been here 22 years. He lives only a mile and a half from the Mission of San Gabriel. This Mission is almost in ruins. The large Church is yet in good repair, but most of the other buildings have fallen down. Twenty years ago, says Mr. White, it was in a flourishing condition, the country all around in cultivation, with several mills and fine orchards of all kinds of fruit . . . .

We rode over to it, and it made me sad to see it, after hearing what it had been only a few years since. We visited the orange orchard, a remnant of what it was, yet a pleasant sight, large trees hanging full of fruit, others just blooming and the air filled with the fragrance of the bloom. There are now only about fifty trees; a few years ago there were about five hundred.

EMILY HAYES

1921

Dear Nurse

I should have started this "Dear Mama," for quite a bit of your last letter was most motherly—the advice about being a good boy and taking the cure and so forth. It only fell short of being a maternal letter in that you didn't give me any advice about my underwear. Don't forget that next time.

I have been following your orders tho—a few weeks more of this life and I'll be ready to grow a pair of downy wings and a pair of blue eyes. But my check should arrive (God only knows if it will) this week. Tijuana is open again so I reckon I'll make a trip down there as soon as I've something in my pockets besides my hands.

Altho it is none of my business, I'm glad you are sticking to your resolution about keeping away from the patients after hours. Even if it only lasts a little while. This is the first time I ever felt that way about a woman; perhaps it's the first time I have ever really loved a woman. That sounds funny but it may be the truth . . .

And when you can't get along with the rest of the world, look me up. I'll let you walk all over me—I'd get a good view of the pretty legs while you were doing it.

Lots of love to the dearest small person in the world, and lots of thanks for her dear letters

S.D.H.

DASHIELL HAMMETT

1942

. . . Cha took mom, Shok, Betty to see pop at county jail, but refused admittance. At same time Cha went to get the approved tire application that pop had applied for. Pop's signature was needed before and after buying the tire. Cha got first signature in pop's cell, but when he returned afterwards for the second, pop was gone—left by bus for undisclosed destination . . .

diarist, internee **GEORGE FUJIMOTO, JR.**

1985

ANDERSON VALLEY

If you're sap enough to buy a book some whore of a paid reviewer recommends, you get what you deserve.

TIGER TIM HAWKINS,

aka "Wanda Tinasky"

MARCH 14

1942

I did not sleep a wink, and daybreak came. It is raining. It is a spiteful chilling rain, and around ten, even the wind joined in. I went to the California bank to change my husband's savings account over to the children's account. In the afternoon, my younger sister came with her child to express her condolences. I received a chicken last night from one of the callers, so we fried that and we had dinner together. In a disappointed voice, Sachiko said, "Father's not here."   **AOKI HISA**

1957

Slept late and satisfied and woke to play a little tennis, but no dailies. The main setup tonight was the damndest shot I've ever seen, and that includes our first day's work. After Joe Cotten had finished his cameo scene, we started working on the opening shot of the film: a complicated setup with the Chapman boom moving three blocks, angling down over buildings to inserts, through two pages of dialogue to a car blowing up as I kiss Janet. The sun came up at six and wrapped our night, but I think we got it. To bed at seven, feeling *great*.   **CHARLTON HESTON**

MARCH 15

1943

. . . I'm getting on pretty well, but a damn dull life though. I spent Saturday at a friends in the country, on a tremendous big roan Tennessee walking gelding, and feel better for it.

novelist **WILLIAM FAULKNER**, *to his agent*

1949

The Ides of March and your punk, puny . . . Caesar Cassady, is at another of his phony Rubicons . . .   *writer, muse* **NEAL CASSADY**,

to Allen Ginsberg

MARCH 16

1969

Dear Dr. Hayakawa:

Your letter of March 12th is before me. In this letter you suggest that we forget the incident which occurred on December 2nd, 1968. Your suggestion is inconceivable. The spectacle of a college president, his emotions completely out of control, violently attacking a privately owned vehicle on a public thoroughfare is not a sight that can be easily forgotten. Nor can I manage to forget the words you shouted at me at that time. The scene you created was a disgraceful one, of a kind that you are constantly condemning in public statements. But far graver than this, you were by your actions at that time attacking right of freedom of speech. The abridgement of that right you have enforced by any and all means that have been placed at your disposal. If I were to forget your firing of me on December 2nd, at a moment when you clearly had no conception of what you were saying, I would then have to forget your betrayal of the academic community since you accepted the office of Acting President of San Francisco State College . . .

I am more than willing to admit that my lack of courtesy in calling you Eichmann on December 2nd cannot be justified by the accuracy of that word. But there are moments when courtesy becomes a questionable shelter from the violence of reality . . .

Sincerely **KAY BOYLE**

1999

. . . I sent the story on Poco, and a few days later followed up with a phone call. "It's Cameron Crowe from San Diego." "Crazy." "Was the story OK?" You shuffled through some papers. "It's fine." It was that simple. My first story for Rolling Stone . . .

A long time ago, staying at your home in San Francisco, struggling with my first full-length feature, you gave me a piece of advice: Be informative, but also be personal. Write as if you were writing a letter to a friend. And so I have. Thank you, Ben.

Love,

Cameron from San Diego *filmmaker, journalist* **CAMERON CROWE**, *to Ben Fong-Torres*

2007

A couple of things I didn't know (or maybe forgot): Echo Park Lake has a clay bottom. It's a real lake, albeit one that's filled with tap water and rimmed with cement. Also, the lake is leaking. They are not sure where the leak is occurring, but water is leaving . . .   JENNY BURMAN

MARCH 17

1949

. . . I have a child. My life's blood she is, lovely and perfect—she wakes at this very moment, I stop to kiss her. SO. I live in the child for as long as is possible, that's my stand; after that: the world, you, saxophones . . .

NEAL CASSADY, *to Allen Ginsberg*

1964

I am luxuriously ensconced in a hotel on the Sunset Strip, with a view south over the whole of LA. The night view is very beautiful, a spill of jewels glittering in limpid air . . . This is the mad rich woman America; with the courage of her convictions, her rich madness.

novelist JOHN FOWLES

1995

Journals capture my ideas, my emotions, the smell of the mowed grasses, the taste of a wildflower lemon stalk, the images from the farmhouse porch on a cool spring morning. My farm journals do the same; they record my feelings about a spring storm on peach blossoms or the fear of invisible diseases growing on my grapes . . .

Writing and farming share a common tie—neither is done well by using formulas. Good stories are not based on recipes, a juicy peach cannot be grown by following "how to" books. Nor does technology automatically improve my work. Riveting characters and moving themes are not created by word processors and new software; bigger machines and new chemicals do not equate to better produce . . .

So I write and farm drawing from experiential knowledge. I need to dirty my hands to write about farm work. I need to feel the tightening of stomach muscles when a dark storm approaches in order to understand a sense of helplessness as I bow before nature.   DAVID MAS MASUMOTO

MARCH 18

1872

You cannot be content with last years baptism. 'Twas only a sprinkle. Come be immersed. Your hitherward affinities are not half satisfied. I can't understand the laws that control you to Concord. You are called of the Sierras . . .

Here we may more easily see God. I know smooth places on the mountains & you will never be wearied. You will have a tent & be warm every night in a sheltered grove or on the plushy bank of a glacier meadow . . . If Shakspeare were with us we would teach him how to get out of a mortal coil without shuffling . . .

I am glad you call me to your house. I will come, but first I have two or three years work to do here on glaciers & mt'n structure . . . I have a low opinion of mountain books, they are like Signal smokes to call attention, little more. No amount of engraving on language or wood will ever make a single soul to know these mountains. As well try to warm the naked & frost bitten by lectures on caloric, or painted fires. One days exposure will do more than cartloads of books. No photographers plate is so sensitive as those of the human soul provided only that they are pure . . .

Thanks for the books & for your generous words. Your time is precious & all the world wants it. My letters look for but little answer, only an electric tap or two of your busy pen to make me feel that we see each other. Let me hear soon concerning your coming.

Most cordially yrs   **JOHN MUIR,** *to Ralph Waldo Emerson*

1933

We are met on the landing by Mr Gaer of the San Francisco Forum . . . Vita is silent, looking to right and left in order to catch sight of an earthquake up a side street before it reaches us. She holds her bag tightly in one hand and me in the other in order to jump out quickly with her two possessions once the tremors begin. We reach the hotel. A facade of brick. Now Vita had been told especially that we must go to a steel and not brick hotel. The porter begins to take off our bags . . . I murmur feebly, 'Is this hotel built of steel?' 'Steel and brick,' they answer.

Dumb victims of an impending earth catastrophe, we enter the hotel. We are taken up to the thirteenth floor where there is a lovely view from a corner window. From there I observe the Pacific. Vita, however, has only observed that we are terribly far off from the ground. 'Isn't,' she says, 'this very high up?' Being a tactful man, and having a bad cold, I do not press the two points which have arisen in my consciousness. I do not say 'there is the Pacific' since that would have suggested stout Cortez and Vita at the moment is not feeling stout in the least. Nor do I suggest that it is very questionable whether in an earthquake it is better to be high up or low down. In the former case there is less to fall on top of one, in the latter case there is less distance for oneself, if it comes to the point, to fall.

I avoid these controversial topics and seize the telephone. 'Couldn't we have a room lower down?' We can have a room on the fifth floor if we want. I am thus robbed of my view of the Pacific Ocean, but we leave it at that, and the rooms are larger and nicer.   *diplomat* **HAROLD NICOLSON**

1975

. . . Drinking Driver's class . . . some, like me, stricken with blank-eyed boredom; a few dummies debating with the instructress to hear their own eloquence—we watched a movie of a man slicing up brains—a young girl's and an old alcoholic's. He sliced them up like loaves of bread and sure enough, the inside of the man's head was uglier. Finished reading "Breakfast of Champions" which was pleasant.   **WARREN ZEVON**

MARCH 19

1940

To: Zelda Fitzgerald

Dearest . . . Nothing has developed here. I write these Pat Hobby stories— and wait. I have a new idea now—a comedy series which will get me back into the big magazines—but my God I am a forgotten man. *Gatsby* had to be taken out of the Modern Library because it didn't sell, which was a blow. With dearest love always   **F. SCOTT FITZGERALD**

1971

We crouched under the lintel, here—here, he said, holding us close under the crossbeam—here is the safest place. The floor rocked and I longed, for the walls to fall away, fall away and leave for my eyes a landscape of suspended people each in his box, each in his moment. And we would look at each other across this encapsulated city and recognize each other . . .

          LIZA WILLIAMS

2017

Hello—thank you so much for considering our offer! My name is Eden and I've been appointed the family secretary. I wanted to introduce myself and my family to you so that you could put some faces to our offer. We are a family of four: me; my husband, Patrick; our five-year-old son, Dixon, who goes by Bean (it's his middle name, and began as his in utero nickname); and our 16-month-old daughter, Ginger . . . Patrick and I met as employees at Book Soup, and we were friends (even pen pals!) before we started dating . . .

But back to the main event: your beautiful house! As soon as we saw it, we loved it . . . We love the different seating areas: we could have dinner out there, or a party, or even host a movie night! . . . What we felt most strongly about your home is that our family could live there happily for many, many years. Patrick and I would love to raise our children in this house. It's clear that you have taken good care of your home. Should you accept our offer, we promise to carry on that tradition. Thank you so much for your time and consideration . . .   *novelist* **EDEN LEPUCKI**

MARCH 20

1925

. . . you might as well make up your mind that you will never live there again. It's worse than Pacific Grove. There is a gas station. Autos running up and down, traffic regulations, people in smart clothes, all kinds of shops on Ocean Avenue, two or three drug stores, a lunch counter (Leidig is putting up a cafeteria), etc. It's awful!   **JAIME DE ANGULO**, *on Carmel*

1928

I want to try adapting this stream-of-consciousness method, conveniently modified, to a detective story, carrying the reader along with the detective, showing him everything as it is found, giving him the detective's conclusions as they are reached, letting the solution break on both of them together . . .

If I can manage it, I want to do this one without any regard for magazines' thou-shalts and thou-shalt-nots. I hope to get it finished by late summer, in time to do another—a plot I've been waiting to get at for two years—before 1928 is dead.

I'm one of the few—if there are any more—people moderately literate who take the detective story seriously. I don't mean that I necessarily take my own or anybody else's seriously—but the detective story as a form. Some day somebody's going to make "literature" of it (Ford's *Good Soldier* wouldn't have need much altering to have been a detective story), and I'm selfish enough to have my hopes, however slight the evident justification may be. I have a long speech I usually make on the subject, all about the ground not having been scratched yet, and so on, but I won't bore you with it now. I want to thank you again for your interest in "Poisonville" [*Red Harvest*].

Sincerely yours,   **DASHIELL HAMMETT**, *to Blanche Knopf*

1933
PASATIEMPO, SANTA CRUZ

We stopped in Monterey at an antique shop kept by Mrs. Elkins, which is the house where [Robert Louis Stevenson] lived for a time. A lovely old wooden house . . .

Then on to Carmel; white sand and cypresses. These cypresses are spreading, like cedars, instead of being pointed, and grow nowhere else but on that strip of coast. They are very dark and gnarled and lovely, with the white sand beneath them and the sea twinkling beyond. We found Robinson Jeffers' house, very rugged, on the edge of the sea. A curiously Cornish effect; great rocks, a grey sea, and alyssum all over the place.

A notice-board on the gate says "Not at home," but an old lady in corduroy trousers who drives up at the same moment walks firmly in. Jeffers emerges, a tall, lean, handsome man in riding-breeches and a shirt with a Byronically open throat. Electric-blue eyes and greying hair. He is very taciturn, and very much aware of his good looks. He asks us in, but not very cordially. A dark untidy room roughly panelled in wood, with a window-seat overlooking the sea and lots of books . . .

writer, gardener **VITA SACKVILLE-WEST**

2020

. . . a lot of people are handling isolation by reading long novels, but I spend my regular life reading long novels. Instead I've been listening to music and staring into space. I listen to unending amounts of Led Zeppelin, especially "Physical Graffiti"—an album I've never liked . . . at around 6 o'clock I go into our tiny yard. Very carefully—the pleasure of doing a small task well—I roll a joint, then inhale from it once, albeit deeply. The sun softens into pink and gold diffusions of empathetic color over the palm trees, the rooftops . . .

novelist, critic **CHARLES FINCH**

MARCH 21

1923

Finally, by paying a fee of two and a half dollars I got a job through a commercial labor agency.

It was a pick-and-shovel, or "mucking" job in Hollywood Hills, where a syndicate of Los Angeles realtors were starting a new and exclusive subdivision called Hollywoodland, intended to appeal specially to movie stars, directors, oil millionaires, high-powered evangelists, wealthy widows, and divorcees from the East . . . It was the hardest work I have ever done . . .

I shoveled gravel into huge wheelbarrows, pushed the wheelbarrows and dumped them into trucks from a platform, and rolled boulders from underneath an overhanging wall of rock. . . . I was in constant terror that a rock might break off the wall and crush me. The quarry was lighted by huge incandescents which cast over the scene weird shadows of trees and moving men. The owls hooted in the holly bushes . . .

I became acquainted with some of my fellow workers, many of whom were I.W.W., or "Wobblies . . .   *writer* **LOUIS ADAMIC**,
working to pave Beachwood Canyon

1941

I'm fairly sure that in the long run it would turn out disastrously. But he remains the only exciting new mind I've met in the last year or so—remarkably brilliant—but it's all just too much trouble for now and i prefer to let things drift. Besides, it would be so damn much trouble to "hook" him properly . . .

film critic **PAULINE KAEL**,
deciding against a beau

2006

just setting up my twttr   *entrepreneur* **JACK DORSEY**

2010

Well, isn't this always the way? You can go weeks without a compelling reading around here, and then—WHAM—not one, but, of course, two fantastic readings on the same night . . .

For you guys way out east, Sam Lipsyte touches down briefly to discuss his new novel, *The Ask*, at Vromans.

Over here in the 310, Sheila Heti, author of TEV favorite *Ticknor*, appears at the Hammer Museum as part of the New American Writing series.

It makes the head spin. Flip a coin, get your passport stamped, but make sure you are at one of these. If you're not, I'll hear about it.

novelist **MARK SARVAS**,

in his blog, The Elegant Variation

MARCH 22

1903

. . . Last night 3 robbers attacked an electric car of the L.A. and S.M.- killed a passenger and wounded 4 or 5. They believe one of the malefactors was wounded. 15 or 20 shots were shot and the robbers fled without stealing anything. Clear day and agreeable.

Californio **DON JUAN BAUTISTA BANDINI**

2020

I am eight months pregnant and plan to start writing a new novel so I could get wrist deep before the baby comes but I can't really concentrate, and part of me wonders if it even makes sense to put in the effort. I write contemporary novels about Los Angeles, and I suspect the city will have changed dramatically by the end of all this, in unpredictable and possibly permanent ways.   *novelist* **STEPH CHA**

2020

The pandemic has worsened my insomnia, adding anxiety about health to the list of things my mind occupies itself with . . . I had a cup of rooibos tea, which is caffeine-free and rich in antioxidants; it's one of my trusted home remedies for insomnia. Then I read a little more of "The Bell Jar" and went to sleep. I dream that I was a decorative-art historian in Bahia, Brazil, and that I was showing museum visitors an antique Moroccan tea pot. It was the most restful dream I had all week. Then I woke up and remembered.

novelist **LAILA LALAMI**

MARCH 23

1892

SAN FRANCISCO

... The "opium house" is mostly a room with two levels of beds or bunks. We visited the largest. Two Chinese lay on each bunk. Most were smoking, some were already sleeping. From the little lamp with which the smokers light their pipes a weak, low light glowed through the smoky room. The faces of the smokers are dull. A fat old man lay in a corner on his back with an open mouth and a dead, expressionless face. His pipe had fallen down, his lamp had gone out, he seemed to be dreaming . . . .

This Chinatown is the most depraved and shameless collection of people that I know of and yet I had a moment of strange beauty. It happened in a temple, a joss house . . . Two large dragons sit like lurking shadows in the twilight on the balustrade, and beyond them, between the fantastic pillars, one looked out into the world beyond. Beneath, the city with its dark sea of roofs stretched far into the distance. A red light rose like a miasma from the hellish depths. Men and women in strange costumes wandered through the streets; dull noises as if coming from distant orgies echoed up to us. It was as if one leaned out over a Dantesque vision of all depravity, and all vices and all crimes, and then you looked upward and the sky arced across the city and land in deep clarity and the stars shone and the fog moved in like a herald of peace on the night wind, toward the land. I stood there a long time and could not pull myself away from the view . . .

diplomat, writer, art patron **COUNT HARRY KESSLER**

1903

... Bought a book for a diary in Los Angeles . . .

DON JUAN BAUTISTA BANDINI

1910

Leo N. Tolstoy,

Sir: Having written a book on the question of "Crime and Criminals," we found that our Investigations forced us to the conclusion that violence and brutality can beget only violence and brutality and that to attempt to suppress crime by such methods is but to make bad infinitely worse.

Asking ourselves who was most closely identified with this conclusion we were unanimously of the opinion that you had inculcated, above all others, year after year and decade after decade, the principles which examination of the facts in the case had driven us to adopt.

It is with the profoundest respect, therefore, that we have ventured to dedicate to you the accompanying volume, entitled, "Crime and Criminals."

We trust you will accept with it the assurance of our most affectionate regard extended across the seas to one whom we recognize as a master worker in a cause that knows no limitations of race or territorial boundaries.

With the deepest respect, we remain,   **GRIFFITH J. GRIFFITH**,

philanthropist, would-be uxoricide

1946

Count Sforza, the Italian liberal politician who was in Los Angeles a few years ago . . . told me Los Angeles is the best place in the world to live today, and I can believe it. Here I am. Where I can rent a house?

GABRIELA MISTRAL

1946

In flying in to Los Angeles, we had snow-capped mountains on either side of us and soft white billowy clouds underneath. It was really a beautiful sight. But the most impressive time to fly in to Los Angeles is at night, when all the lights are on and the city lies below you like a multi-colored heap of jewels.   *activist, columnist, First Lady* **ELEANOR ROOSEVELT**

MARCH 24

1905

HOTEL VAN NUYS LOS ANGELES, CAL.

Dearest Alice. Here I am, at last . . . I have now (9.45 a.m.) after a night in a clean bed, the sense of being in California, & though it seems as yet less exotic & romantic than I hoped, it is clearly very amusing & different, quite amiably & unexpectedly gay—quite another than the eastern note—& even in the large bustling hall of this (very excellent) hotel, where I write, intimations of climate, of a highly seductive order, are wafted in upon me. I presently go forth to assist, I trust, at their development, & at that of other pleasing phenomena. The light, in particular, seems most elegant & soignée . . .   *novelist* **HENRY JAMES**, *to his sister*

1931

I'm working this week at one of the most generous studios in Hollywood. Thirty or forty cents in stationery means practically nothing at all to this outfit. *"archy and mehitabel" creator* **DON MARQUIS**

MARCH 25

1915

LOS ANGELES

[It is] time to renew our Western covenant, to get our Western and civic pride aglow . . . There isn't anything South or North or East which we can't duplicate or excel here . . . *California "Dean of the Assembly,"*
great grandson of Thomas Jefferson and Sally Hemings,
FREDERICK MADISON ROBERTS

1933

We drive to Hollywood. We are taken into the luncheon room where there is a table with flowers and four directors. They are quiet cultured people not in the least the noisy boasting lot we had supposed. Gary Cooper comes to join us. He is like Paul Hyslop but with an arched eyebrow. The beginnings of a double chin and the hint of greying hair indicate that he may cease to be the *jeune premier*. Yet he is a nice shy quiet modest young man, devoid of any brains. They talk about the earthquakes—how frightened they were. About Charlie Chaplin, his moodiness, his affectations, his genius for mimicry. About the life of a film—not more than three years; the film which they thought was an innovation in 1930 now seems to them as old-fashioned as 1886. The stage-hands and property-men greet Gary Cooper with "lo Gary, how's life?' He is very nice to them. He then leaves us to look for a house with a huge fence where he can live in peace. **HAROLD NICOLSON**

1937

Took the steamer from Wilmington and had a pleasant crossing over the 26 miles of sea water from the mainland here on a choppy sea. Saw the mighty U.S. battleships lying at anchor and watched the sea gulls follow the ship. Met a man from "Ioway" on the boat and he told me of poor fishing at Santa Monica Beach, Los Angeles, where he had caught only 48 fish in an hour and a companion had landed a shark! **WILLARD MOTLEY**

2020

RIVERSIDE

This is the second week of no school in Riverside. On my long, narrow block, there are about 35 kids. Many of them are on the sidewalks, walking their parents, who are nervous. At night I watch two hours of "Gunsmoke," then an hour of "Gentefied." The sadness on those dirt roads and those L. A. sidewalks send me out back onto my porch, in the dark, to listen to the eerie silence without what I usually hear: the tubas and accordions of ranchera music, the booming bass of Tupac and laughter from the streets.

novelist, essayist **SUSAN STRAIGHT**

MARCH 26

1940

SAN FRANCISCO, CALIF.

Dear Bosie:

Oscar [Levant] came and went like a tornado, accompanied by his pregnant bride, and staying here at the Fairmont because I had suggested it. As it is extremely expensive he grew more bitter with every check he had to sign. My major triumph was seeing to it that his telephone call to Harpo, which he made from my room, was charged to his. At the concert his performance was truly incandescent. After he had finished the "Rhapsody" [*in Blue*, not the Second Rhapsody, composed in Los Angeles], Claudia Morgan and I joined him backstage and through the peep-hole we watched Monteux conduct the final Sibelius and Ravel numbers. With the concert finally over Oscar and I, heading for the green room, debouched into the corridor where a comely Miss with an autograph book was lying in wait. "Oh! Mr. Woollcott," she said, "may I have your autograph?" With a bellow of pain, Oscar left for New York.   **ALEXANDER WOOLLCOTT**, *to Charles Lederer*

1946

Yesterday afternoon, I drove out to the Junior Auxiliary Jewish Home for the Aged. This home is for both men and women. They have a small hospital, a very charming dining room and auditorium, a small synagogue, and pleasant living quarters.

The old Jewish people there seem to spend most of their time in prayer, and so it was fitting that they should hold their short but moving ceremonies of welcome to me in their synagogue. In these ceremonies, they remembered my husband as their friend . . .

I could not help being thankful that, in this country, these old people could find a sanctuary in their declining years. A happy contrast to the sad old people that I saw in a Jewish refugee camp in Germany.

ELEANOR ROOSEVELT

1968

. . . God, what I need is a man . . .   **OCTAVIA E. BUTLER**

2011

DAY ONE, Los Angeles

9:00 A.M. Arrived at LAX late last night . . .

5:00 P.M. . . . Funny how it takes coming to LA to see friends from New York . . .

8:15 P.M. . . . Erik is one of my all-time favorite artists. He is in the midst of installing a huge piece—a wall of lost-animal flyers—at MoCA for Jeffrey Deitch's much-buzzed-about hated/loved upcoming "Art on the Streets" exhibition . . .   *New York editor, parachutist*

KIM HASTREITER

2017

MARCH 27

1882

SAN FRANCISCO

[My] tour here is triumphal. I was four days in the train: at first grey, gaunt desolate plains, as colourless as waste land by the sea, with now and then scampering herds of bright red antelopes, and heavy shambling buffaloes, rather like Joe Knight in manner and appearance, and screaming vultures like gnats high up in the air, then up the Sierra Nevadas, the snow-capped mountains shining like shields of polished silver in that vault of blue flame we call the sky, and deep cañons full of pine trees, and so for four days, and at last from the chill winter of the mountains down into eternal summer here, groves of orange trees in fruit and flower, green fields, and purple hills, a very Italy, without its art.

There were 4,000 people waiting at the "depot" to see me, open carriage, four horses, an audience at my lecture of the most cultivated people in 'Frisco, charming folk. I lecture again here tonight, also twice next week; as you see I am really appreciated—by the cultured classes. The railway have offered me a special train and private car to go down the coast to Los Angeles—a sort of Naples here . . .

The women here are beautiful. Tonight I am escorted by the Mayor of the city through the Chinese quarter, to their theatre and joss houses and rooms, which will be most interesting . . .

playwright, poet, author **OSCAR WILDE**

1905

It presently appeared that [Henry James] had not been down to the beach, and "I want to see the Pacific," he said, and suggested that I accompany him thither. We took an electric car and went thundering down across the wide meadows, and while we talked nothing in the landscape escaped him. At last we turned the corner. "There is the Pacific," I said. He looked quickly round, and gazed, and his arms lifted. It was a very pleasant moment for me; I knew how he felt. "As when stout Cortez!" he murmured, after a moment. "I will be stout Cortez for the time!" . . .

We got out and walked along the shore. The tide was high but he wished to get down on the sands and we plowed our way along happily. "The light through those waves, just before they break!" he murmured, pausing to gaze. "Those gulls—how tame! The grace of those children bathing!" As we walked the light haze which partially veiled the sea cleared away and the strong blue line of the horizon became distinct. Ah, he was delighted. But he glanced somewhat painfully at the little bungalows crowding down to the shore. He gazed off at the ocean toward the west. Again and again he stopped, absorbing this feature of the scene or that . . .

We lunched at Playa del Rey on a bowl of soup and a piece of pumpkin pie . . . they have no pumpkin pies in Rye . . .   *writer* **JULIAN HAWTHORNE**

1933

CASA DEL MAR, SAN SIMEON

. . . your friends have boosted you as the champion and martyr of the Proletarian Revolution. Consequently your release would be the greatest misfortune that could happen to them. What use is a martyr when he no longer suffers? Also your release would be a political defeat for the dominant capitalist classes, for the police, and for the courts. The door that was locked on you is thus double-locked by your friends and triple-locked by your opponents . . .

I very greatly regret that my short stay on the west coast, and my fear of associating you with my own political views, which are much more extreme than yours, have prevented me from paying you a visit which would have been personally most interesting to me and would have varied prison routine to you for a moment.

Wishing you a speedy release, I remain, dear Mr Mooney,

Faithfully yours

playwright **GEORGE BERNARD SHAW,**

to accused Preparedness Day bomber Tom Mooney

1955

I'm really scared about Disneyland . . . So much I don't know and trying to design and not being sure I'm on the right track . . .

landscape architect **RUTH SHELLHORN**

2011

DAY TWO, 3:30 P.M. Race to the Fairfax "dreidel district" to meet up with Aussie David Jacob Kramer, the co-owner of the Family Bookstore, a cultural collective that guest-edited our March LA issue. Across from Canters Deli and its late-night Kibbutz [sic]room . . .

6:45 P.M . . . This party was as LA as it gets. Lots of leather-clad pole dancers, Nobu sushi chefs, and familiar faces. Ran into Fergie there whom I adore and have known since her early days as a *Paper Magazine* fanatic. It was her birthday, and my nephew was smitten when she kissed him hello. The Scissor Sisters performed, then dragged Fergie on to sing, who then dragged Kate Hudson on to sing. *So* LA . . .   **KIM HASTREITER**

MARCH 28

1933

My dear W.R.

Nobody will ever know what we two really wrote about the war.

Think of the articles we wrote which before the ink was dry were too late to print as the military and diplomatic situation changed from hour to hour like a kaleidoscope jolted by every cannon shot!

. . . Well, we both got into honorable trouble early in the war and kept in it to the end; so we have nothing to be ashamed of except our connexion with the human race, which was not just then doing itself much credit.

GEORGE BERNARD SHAW, *inscribing* What I Really Wrote About the War *to his host, William Randolph Hearst*

1933
SMOKE TREE RANCH, CALIFORNIA

We drive out into the desert past Palm Springs . . . To bed early. I do not sleep well as the desert air is too exciting. The coyotes howl in the hills.

HAROLD NICOLSON

1933
SMOKE TREE RANCH, SOUTH CALIFORNIA

I went to see the Huntington Library in Pasadena, and, observing that their collection of manuscripts had been brought so up to date as to include George Moore, asked them if they wouldn't like *A room of one's own* . . . Don't be too optimistic though, for as you know the Americans are very hard-hit just now . . .

After that I went back to San Francisco and then down to Los Angeles. Mr William Randolph Hearst asked us to stay at his ranch (250,000 acres, plus a Spanish Castle' which he removed bodily from a hill-top in Andalusia) and offered to send an aeroplane for us, but we were proud and refused, partly because it was 300 miles away and partly because Shaw was going to be there, and we thought we couldn't stand that . . .

[We] departed for Los Angeles. We just missed the earthquake; there was a little one while we were there, but we were both asleep and didn't notice it. Nature seems to have been pursuing us with vengeance ever since we left England: hurricanes in the Atlantic, blizzards in Chicago, earthquakes in California, a sand-storm here, and a meteor which lit up five states for half an hour and came to rest in Arizona. In spite of all this the climate of California is divine; an average temperature here of 80 in the shade, perpetual sunshine, and incredible wild flowers. I enclose a photograph of them just to annoy Leonard. It really is a photograph, although coloured. I mean, it really is like that.

Los Angeles is hell . . . The Americans have an unequalled genius for making everything hideous. Hollywood however is fun. It is pure fantasy— you never know what you will come on round the corner, whether half an ocean liner, or Trafalgar Square, or the facade of Grand Hotel, or a street in

Stratford-on-Avon with Malayan houris walking down it. We were taken round by Mr Gary Cooper . . .

A young lady rushed up to me in Pasadena and said she was writing a book about you and me. Isn't that nice for us? Would I give her an interview tell her our (yours and mine) views on Imagery? Fortunately I was able to say I had only just time to catch my train . . . .

And there were seals on the beaches, and humming-birds, and mocking-birds, and trees 5000 years old, and acres of cactus, like phallic symbols or else like prehistoric reptiles, and miles upon miles of orange groves,—Sunkist,—and such queer reversals of nature as plants that have to be taken up in November and put into cold storage because the winter is too hot for them. I doubt whether I shall ever recover from all this . . .

Your V.   **VITA SACKVILLE-WEST**, *to Virginia Woolf*

1946

Shall I tell you something perhaps a little surprising? I own a mountain. I bought it yesterday. I saw it for the first time day before yesterday. You know my constitutional foible for falling in love desperately at first sight. Apparently it works for mountains as well as for men . . .

I feel so sane and happy and quiet about it I must just be mad once for all. It is about five thousand feet up, perhaps a little less, a good road—for mountains—all the way, in a government reserve. There is a valley on my mountain, with two fine springs—I bought it for the air, and the view and the water (thirty thousand gallons a day, pure and cold).

My tract is eighty acres, but I have a man tunnelling the springs, the pipes were laid already, and when they are finished, the government grants me eighty acres more. It already has a little house and a little barn and some oddments like that on it, but I am going to build a rambling adobe business there later. I can have my own electricity with the water power, a swimming pool and a big irrigation reservoir. I am just telling you the practical things about it because I wouldn't dare to try to tell you how beautiful it is, and how, once having seen it, I could hardly leave it. . . .

I'm feeling awfully free, untrammelled and independent, darling. My elbow room extends thousands of miles in every direction. Even after three hours on my mountain, I come down being very critical of mere desert air, and the confined little lives going on down here . . .

One thing more—a government bombing range is near by—not too near I hope—so I can even sit in on the dress rehearsals for our destruction. Isn't that a splendid inducement?   *novelist* **KATHERINE ANNE PORTER**

2011

DAY THREE, 1:15 P.M. Walked (I swear) down Sunset (surreal) to meet
our colleague Sheri Timmons (from Levis) for a chopped-salad lunch at the
Chateau Marmont and were suddenly surrounded by recognizables: Zoe
Saldano [sic], Kate Bosworth, Chris Martin, and my favorite funny actress
Pamela Adlon from *Californication*. Oy. *So* LA . . .

As a native New Yorker, I can never wrap my head around the notion
of free fruit. I picked some lemons (why?) to bring back to New York with
me . . .

3:00 P.M. Headed in the Camry with Drew and Katie to check out the legendary Freecity Supershop which recently opened on Highland. (I'm feeling
a Highland moment happening lately in Los Angeles by the way.) . . . *So* LA.

KIM HASTREITER

MARCH 29

1933

We are aroused by bells ringing and have a huge and excellent breakfast in
the main cabin. V. walks south looking for flowers and I do ditto north. It
is very hot. The verbena is everywhere and there is a grey bush with orange
flowers. When we get near the oasis we are overpowered by the smell of
orange blossom.

At 6.15 the whole party gets into cars and on horses and drives to a
gorge some three miles away off the road. They light a fire over a grid and
cook steaks. Asparagus and coffee. We then sit round the camp-fire under
the rocks and the cowboys sing. There is one song—a lullaby to the young
cows which they call 'doeghies' or 'dôgies' and there is another one called
Out on that Utah trail. They have a real background of homesickness and
romance. One of the boys on the ranch called Bob comes and leans against
a rock and sings with the firelight on his fresh face. He sings Ole Man
River. It is very Walt Whitman. The moon dips behind the mountain and
the stars are warmed across the drifting smoke. Clara the maid comes and
sings her little songs. There is something rather splendid about that side
of American life. The way the servants mingle with the masters without
self-consciousness and with complete equality. Bob and Clara would have

giggled and felt awkward in England. We then return. A happy day in marvellous air.   **HAROLD NICOLSON**

1946

It must be ghastly in Germany, compared to that we really are in paradise, as incredible as that may seem.   **THEODOR ADORNO**

1979

L.A. is the ultimate expression of the capitalist system in spatial terms.

urbanist **AARON PALEY**

2011

DAY FOUR

11:05 A.M. Hop over with Drew and Jacob to Gagosian Gallery in Beverly Hills to catch the Gus Van Sant show as well as the Ed Ruscha garbage paintings. The guys were drooling over the Van Sant homoerotic boy paintings. They were just okay in my book and forty thousand dollars each. And the exhibition was sponsored by Gucci. (*So* LA) . . .

6:30 P.M. Head downstairs to the Standard pool to check out the setup . . . Everyone is running around. Madness . . . The party is full blast by eight. My posse arrives: . . . It's fun . . .

I breathe a sigh of relief, run upstairs, and pack, as we have to be at the airport at five A.M. the next morning to catch the first flight back to New York to be back in time to throw our East Coast "Beautiful People" party that night!   **KIM HASTREITER**

MARCH 30

1850

You remember Mr. Frank Ward, who lost his wife last summer. He has failed in business and it is said has lost every thing. This together with the loss of his wife has had a great effect upon him and (it is supposed in a moment of derangement) he attempted to kill himself with a pistol. The ball passed through his eye and lodged, I believe, in the opposite cheek bone. Strange to say, it did not kill him . . .   **MARGARET DEWITT**

1927

The shells I photographed were so marvelous one could not do other than something of interest. What I did may be only a beginning . . .

photographer **EDWARD WESTON**

1977

Back in LA. I read that Nunnally Johnson' has died at seventy-nine. I last saw him just before I left for Europe: he too had emphysema, though it's some consolation that he survived to such a splendid age. Nunnally was a laconic deep Southerner: his most famous one-liner was his comment on Jeeter Lester's family in Tobacco Road: 'Back where I come from, we'd have called them the Country Club set.'   *critic, playwright* **KENNETH TYNAN**

2008

SCENES FROM DUTTON'S FAREWELL

Nice to see the support but hard not to ask oneself—as many of us did as we stood around—whether if everyone present had regularly bought, you know, books if we'd all have to be here today.   **MARK SARVAS**

MARCH 31

1906

I went down to the wholesale district, to Lazarus & Milgan, to get an old historical pamphlet, "Historical Sketch of Los Angeles County," 1876 (known as Warner's). Got six copies, fifteen cents each. Someday this will be valuable Californiana.   *writer, gardener, bibliophile* **OLIVE PERCIVAL**

1913

The streptococci of learning have invaded the city's social system, and its list of mental improvement organizations defies tabulation. Among them are Shakespeare clubs, Browning clubs, Brahms clubs, Ibsen clubs, dramatic, literary, ethical and hygienic societies of all descriptions. The arms of Los Angeles go snaking round the neck of every second, third and tenth rate author, musician or rabble-rouser who enters the gates . . .

When they attempted to institute a tuberculin test for cattle they were defeated nearly two to one by the "medical freedomists." When the city board of health attempted to put down a recent epidemic of anterior poliomyelitis, again the loud cackling of the psychotherapists and their allied lodges thwarted simple quarantine measures. Vaccination in Los Angeles is looked upon as a murderous graft ...

On the other hand, the city numbers among its inhabitants a large number of civilized and well-to-do Easterners. These people are conversant with the works of Henry James. They eat their soup silently ...

And they have made Los Angeles nationally famous as a discriminating book-buying center ...

detective novelist, art critic **WILLARD HUNTINGTON WRIGHT**

1964

Marineland is built on a spare clifftop, a splendidly Roman place, a lovely circus tossed to the masses. Tiberius and Nero would have approved of the idea; and made it more 'interesting' by substituting sharks for dolphins, and living slaves for dead herrings ...

JOHN FOWLES

APRIL 1

1940

Here at the Fairmont I have rooms with a balcony that looks out over the bay and catches the morning sunlight at breakfast time. Larry Olivier and Vivien Leigh move today into the rooms below mine. They are here to rehearse *Romeo and Juliet*, which has its premiere at the Geary next Monday, and they are affably giving a Friday matinee so that I can see it . . .

I don't know what I told you about my performance in this play in Santa Barbara and Los Angeles, but I am a far better judge in such matters than anyone who could have reported to you, and you may take it from me that I was pretty lousy. It was at Fresno that I began to be comparatively good . . .

Porky   **ALEXANDER WOOLLCOTT**

1974

. . . For the second Monday in a row I have canceled a potentially jolly adventure with six dear friends: it is pouring rain again, the wettest warmest March in history, and the wine men are trembling (they are always trembling about something) that there will be late "black frosts" that will nip the buds. We were going to drive up to the top of the Lupine Field, a beautiful sight, and then up the Canyon to see the waterfall in full spate, and drink a glass of white wine and come back here for a hearty soup and Sonoma bread and baked apples. Last week I had already made the soup when we decided NO GO, so I ate it for the next five days. Today I decided to make it after the radio weather reports, so I only have to eat seven baked apples (I'll take a few up to the old foreman Joseph)! All of which proves that we are still Nature's children, I suppose . . . .

. . . and here Nature took over and there was a lengthy power shortage because of the rains, and I am fairly stymied without an electric typewriter. But I continue to feel saddened for you. It is an inevitable fact that one must lose touch gradually. But how wonderful that it has all been warm before! I really would freeze to death if I did not have the ashes still glowing in my heart. That is why friendships must be nurtured, no matter how deliberately. A lot of them die out naturally but some are forever . . .

Tell me when there may be a chance of another polka . . .

M. F. K. FISHER, *to James Beard*

APRIL 2

1931

FAIRMONT HOTEL, SAN FRANCISCO, CALIFORNIA

Mrs. Charles Wiener who lives here now . . . started me on my road in Red Cloud Nebraska, when I was ten years old. I suppose I got a kind of Hebrew complex at that age, and the grand Jews still seem to me the most magnificent people on earth. They simply get me, I'm theirs, I can't refuse anything.

novelist **WILLA CATHER**, *to Alfred A. Knopf,*
about the childhood neighbor who lent her books

1935

HOTEL VISTA DEL ARROYO AND BUNGALOWS

PASADENA, CALIFORNIA

My dear Thornton,

. . . Here we are in Hollywood, I have not gone on the lots and eaten in the green room but last night we did accept an invitation to meet the big directors and Charlie Chaplin, and it was a curious xperience, in Bilignin we will talk it all over but I am hoping that we will see you again before that, we probably will break our trip to New York at Chicago and spend the night with Bobsy and I am hoping that you will still be there and we will see you again but at any rate surely and entirely at Bilignin, we both love you so much, and please be all well and we will be all happy, lots and lots of love from us both

Always Gtrde.

novelist, librettist **GERTRUDE STEIN**,
to Thornton Wilder, after his nervous breakdown

1957

We finished work with a final dawn shot, of Orson's death, in an overturned chair on a dump heap, and then had a celebrant drink or two in the trailer.

Orson and I took along the last magnum of champagne and found a place still open to give us bacon and eggs to go with it. A hell of a picture to work on . . . I can't believe it won't be fine. It was wonderful to loaf tonight, all the same. We had steak and saw Orson's LADY FROM SHANGHAI on TV. It's good, but not as good as ours, I think.   **CHARLTON HESTON**

2020

I open Microsoft Word. I take a sip of coffee. I close Microsoft Word.

novelist **CHARLES YU**

APRIL 3

1966

Routine—got up just before 9:30 to watch Superman and Bulwinkle. Forgot to mention that in yesterday—cut the lawn. Today bathed, styled hair, got all ready to go to afro club. Club mostly boys. Nice, but while I could follow them easily, I was a damn weak voiced opposition. I apologized too much for calling Costa Rican, African. Made me look prej.

OCTAVIA E. BUTLER

1986

You see the problems and problems of writing a novel. You get all this stuff going and then figure out a way to make it make sense. It never was easy. But it does become more exciting as I get bolder about letting God or letting intuition, whichever you wanna call it., come in and fill out the empties and light up the corners and sand off the rough edges. Thinking this morning as I drove into Santa Cruz, towards Santa Cruz to be more accurate, on Hwy 35 then cutting over via Hwy 9. I was thinking about how it must feel to totally surrender; to let go with such faith and carelessness that you cannot help but land on your feet like a cat dropped from a hundred feet in the air . . .

Feels odd not having any journalism assignments hanging overhead at this very moment: miss those extra checks coming in. But it's book or bust at this point . . .   *poet, novelist, screenwriter* **AL YOUNG**

2020

As the Sports section dwindles, the Obituaries spread. We are nowhere near the Great War scheme where London papers printed columns of names, the losses. Still, today, there is a friend in the New York Times, Dr. John Murray, 92, an expert on pulmonary distress who died of the very condition he had helped define for other doctors. He was a grand guy, tall, handsome, humorous, usually in a bowtie. The obituary includes the observation that just before he went into his last coma John was asking the doctors in Paris about his blood oxygen levels.   *film critic, author* **DAVID THOMSON**

APRIL 4

1952

SAN FRANCISCO CALIFORNIA

Arriving at San Francisco, we found your 2 letters, & 2 cheques, & also a letter from the headmaster of Llewelyn's school saying he would be thrown out unless a £100 were paid by April 5 . . .

So (again) HELP. (On top of this, Caitlin had carefully arranged for some laundry to be sent on from New York to San Francisco. This cost 40 dollars.) I can just manage to get to Vancouver, & I'll leave Caitlin the fee for my S.F. State College reading which is tonight & which will be only 50 dollars. About other engagements: Is the date, on April 26, at the University of Chicago the same as that, on April 24, at the Northwestern University, Chicago? Or can't I read? It's summer here, not spring. Over 80. At Easter we go to Carmel & on to see Miller at Big Sur. We are both well . . .

Yours, Dylan   *poet* **DYLAN THOMAS**

1963

Dear diary: "You open this door with the key of imagination" Quoted from Rod Serling's T.L.Z. I'm living in a sort of twilight zone . . .

I cried today in spanish after standing infront of the class attempting to give a *lectura* summary. It was such a stupid human thing to do. . I don't know what to do about my personality (a fear of people and worms) I can't talk to people the way I want to. They nearly all see a difference in me. They talk to each other, then they talk to me. What's wrong?!! Also, is mother hiding? If so, why? I'm breaking through slowly . . .   **OCTAVIA E. BUTLER**

1968

Just before six, I heard that King has died. Oh fuck them all. How bloodhorny this'll make the killers on both sides.   **CHRISTOPHER ISHERWOOD**

1969

Time accomplishes for the poor what money does for the rich.

CÉSAR CHÁVEZ, *letter to the president*
of the California Grape and Tree Fruit League

APRIL 5

1905

California, on these terms, when all is said (Southern C. at least—which, however, the real C., I believe, much repudiates), has completely bowled me over—such a delicious difference from the rest of the U.S. do I find in it. (I speak of course all of nature and climate, fruits and flowers; for there is absolutely nothing else, and the sense of the shining social and human inane is utter.) The days have been mostly here of heavenly beauty, and the flowers, the wild flowers just now in particular, which fairly *rage*, with radiance, over the land, are worthy of some purer planet than this. I live on oranges and olives, fresh from the tree, and I lie awake nights to listen, on purpose, to the languid lisp of the Pacific, which my windows overhang . . .

It breaks my heart to have so stinted myself here—but it was inevitable, and no one had given me the least inkling that I should find California so sympathetic. It is strange and inconvenient, how little impression of anything anyone ever takes the trouble to give one before hand. I should like to stay here all April and May.

HENRY JAMES,
from Coronado, to his sister-in-law

1960

We are in Los Angeles where we found a charming house in a blooming canyon full of good butterflies. We live very quietly. My main occupation is a screenplay I am making, but I am also occupied in reading the proofs of my ONEGIN, the proofs of my SONG OF IGOR, and Dmitri's translation of my DAR [*The Gift*].

The screenplay [of *Lolita*] will keep me busy till August or September when we shall sail again for Europe. I feel happy and relaxed in lovely and serene Los Angeles . . .   *novelist* VLADIMIR NABOKOV, *to Edmund Wilson*

APRIL 6

1995

1216 COLE STREET, SAN FRANCISCO, CA 94117

. . . No, I never traced my cock on a blank page and mailed it, but once I did receive a letter containing an empty condom from a sex-buddy in S. California, asking me to return it, used. So I did. I like to oblige the handsome . . .

Well, I'm sure you'd be a hit in the escort service. What I wouldn't be able to stand about hustling would be that so many of the johns would be the last people you'd ever choose to have sex with. Still, I suppose you could just shut your eyes and think of America.

I finally made it with a guy I've been after for months. I think he must live in my favorite bar: he is good-looking, long-haired, sweet-natured, and sleeps in someone's truck. He has no job, appears to live on nothing (the occasional job, helping someone haul stuff, helping out at the bar). He is about 35, is slim though he lives largely on beer, and he doesn't appear to have a thought go through his head . . .

That's the only thing that has interested me lately, the rest has been teaching and constant rain. The back yard is lush and beautiful, it couldn't look better if I had weeded it . . .   THOM GUNN

APRIL 7

1942

Dear Tetsuzo,

I am going to miss you a great deal, as you must know. You have been one of my restorers-of-faith in the human spirit. I know that you will keep your courage and humor in the weeks and days that lie ahead, no matter what they may bring.

You said once that you were "afraid" of dissension among the Japanese. I have moments of being "afraid" of America. I want so much to have her live up to your unshaken belief in her, I want her to be just and democratic in her treatment not only of the Japanese Americans who are of course citizens, but of your father's generation.

You people who are going to Manzanar and the other camps can only help—as you have already—by proving your cooperation and loyalty, so thoroughly that even those who do not believe in your loyalty will have to

believe in it. And do not forget for a single moment that you have real friends who trust you to meet any situation that life may bring. You have stamina and strength.   *San Diego children's librarian* **CLARA E. BREED**,
to a camp-bound child

2020

Kitty's good friend Lorna dropped off a (sanitized) book today . . .
writer, editor **JACK MILES**

APRIL 8

1885

To the Board of Education—
Dear Sirs:
I see that you are going to make all sorts of excuses to keep my child out of the Public schools. Dear sirs, Will you please to tell me! Is it a disgrace to be born Chinese? Didn't God make us all!!!

. . . Her playmates are all caucasians ever since she could toddle around. If she is good enough to play with them, then is she not good enough to be in the same room and studie with them? You had better come and see for yourselves . . . It seems no matter how a Chinese may live and dress so long as you know they are Chinese, then they are hated as one. There is not any right or justice for them.

You have seen my husband and child. You told him it wasn't Mamie Tape you object to. If it were not Mamie Tape you object to, then why didn't you let her attend the school nearest her home! Instead of first making one pretense then another pretense of some kind to keep her out?

. . . May you Mr. Moulder, never be persecuted like the way you have persecuted little Mamie Tape. Mamie Tape will never attend any of the Chinese schools of your making! Never!!! . . . Just because she is of the Chinese descent, not because she doesn't dress like you, because she does—just because she is descended of Chinese parents. I guess she is more of a American then a good many of you that is going to prevent her being educated.
American activist **MARY TAPE**

1949

This afternoon I heard a lecture on "The function of art and the artist" by Anaïs Nin: she is very startling—pixie-like, other-worldly—small, finely built, dark hair, and much make-up which made her look very pale—large, questioning eyes—a marked accent which I could not label—her speech is over-precise—she shines and polishes every syllable with the very tip of her tongue and teeth—one feels that if one were to touch her, she would crumble into silver dust.   *essayist, novelist* **SUSAN SONTAG**

APRIL 9

1942

BERKELEY

Dear Mariko,

. . . It's quite likely that evacuation will take place in a matter of days. About 700 people have already gone to the Assembly Center in Santa Anita (move over Seabiscuit!) and the Federal Security Agency told me today that they expect to have the Bay Area cleared out immediately . . .

We are having quite a problem figuring out just what to take. There is still so much junk around and you know how the Japanese like to hang on to old things. Anyway, we will have to store a lot of it, since they will not allow us to take more than the barest of necessities . . .

All of the school authorities and my friends have been swell in this whole affair and sometimes I wonder where all this anti-Jap hatred is coming from. Of course, in times like this with so much at stake, people are bound to get a little hysterical and do things that they would not do under more rational considerations. Then the Japanese [Americans] really don't appreciate all that has been done for them because they don't get the information. However, you can be assured that they will be taken care of in a very humane manner . . .

So it's up to people like you who have gone out to prove to other Americans that we are Americans too (even if we have yellow fever faces!). It's hard on the old people, but for the Nisei it can be made an opportunity if they don't start getting to feel sorry for themselves and develop a persecutionist attitude . . .

S. F. Japanese Town certainly looks like a ghost town. All the stores are closed and the windows are bare except for a mass of "evacuation sale" signs. The junk dealers are having a roman holiday, since they can have their cake and eat it too. It works like this: They buy cheap from the Japanese leaving and sell dearly to the Okies coming in for defense work. Result, good profit . . .   *writer, internee* **CHARLES KIKUCHI**

1945

I never found the tar-pits in Los Angeles, but I had a dish of Spam with raisin sauce at the Thrifty Drug Store . . .   *writer* **JOHN CHEEVER**

1982

David [Hockney] was in a great state of excitement. He has invented a way of juxtaposing multiple Polaroid photographs as part of a subject (which may be a portrait, still life or landscape) so that they produce an effect of many superimposed images of the subject taken from different angles, as with cubism . . . He tells me that he has put into photography the dimension of passing through time which it lacks . . . .

People kept wandering in and out of the apartment the whole time I was there. David seemed utterly indifferent to them, neutral perhaps, welcoming them as spectators of his new photographs, and listeners to his new spiel about them. Usually David and I got up before anyone else, and David would say mildly: 'You would think that someone would have noticed there is no bread and no milk in the house' and I would accompany him to the store . . .

                                                   poet **STEPHEN SPENDER**

2021

In Piper's garden. Joshua Tree. My birthday retreat . . . Doves cooing. Ebullition of Lady Banksia roses . . .

Yesterday morning, we drove over rutted dirt roads to get to the Noah Purifoy Foundation, on the other side of the highway. We parked the Prius by the stucco house with the plaster horse heads, walked past the backwards WELCOME sign painted on old tires entered into artist Noah Purifoy's universe, a village of wonders and horrors built out of detritus; beauty accruing to a pile of old TV sets; a railroad of vacuum cleaners; a lyrical roller coaster of metal cafeteria trays. Where to go first . . .

Purifoy titled this piece, "From the Point of View of the Little People." Ten men tied together with wire. They stand some eight feet off the ground, positioned side by side on their cast-off plank, their scaffold. The wind ruffles their ragged cuffs, their pants sag in deep creases, their feet lifeless.

They've been standing there a long time. They are men only from waist-down, severed at the torso, no arms no shoulders no necks no heads. Their legs are sun-bleached, always exposed. Tired. They're from Money, Mississippi. Srebrenica. Babi Yar. San Juan Cotzal. Line them up. Drop the trap. Yank the rope. Aim the rifle. There they are. Always watching. Purifoy made the sculpture five years into his self-exile in the desert. He created it out of cast-offs; spare planks; pants from Goodwill or the dump; sneakers missing shoelaces, bedroom slippers with holes. He said he didn't care if these figures —or any of the works in his outdoor museum— got worn away over time. He wanted the wind, the sand, the insects, the sun to be partners in the work: fabric bleaching; wood rotting; old magazines disintegrating.

LOUISE STEINMAN

APRIL 10

1929

Yesterday Lincoln Steffens and wife called to see work, again two prints sold. He had already purchased a head of Diego,—a best seller: then as he was leaving I brought out an unmounted print of my new cypress root. He said, without hesitation, "Print me one of those." . . .

I'll have to get a secretary (a pretty one) to help out. She might answer a double purpose!

EDWARD WESTON

1937

1315 ANGELO DRIVE

BEVERLY HILLS, CAL.

Our favorite walk on the mountain is now barred, owing to rattlesnakes. This place is rather like La Frayére,—when you go out, you have to go either up a hill or down one, so that you can't stroll . . .

P. G. WODEHOUSE

APRIL 11

1939

I hope you like the watch; if not, we'll exchange it. In the meantime, please use it to help me count the minutes.

I adore you forever, darling.

P.S. Kiss the children for me, if you've had mumps. I love you.

poet **OGDEN NASH**

1940

Dearest Pie:

I go to cinema work tomorrow on a sort of half-pay, half-"spec" (speculation) business on my own story "Babylon Revisited." Which is to say Columbia advances me living money while I work and if it goes over in installments with the producer, the company, the releasing people, I get an increasing sum. At bottom we eat—at the top the deal is very promising.

Why I'm writing tonight is because I foresee three months of intensive toil. (I feel like a criminal who has been in a hideout, been caught, and has to go back to the Big House. I've been visited by my crooked doctor and my moll and Frances the Fence has protected me. Now the Big House—oh Jees them guards!) . . .   Dearest love,

Daddy

P.S. . . . if you have occasion to drive, I forgot to tell you that in the rain don't depress the clutch—use the brake only. And on hills—go down in the gear in which you'd have come up. I am moving in town to be near my work . . . .

F. SCOTT FITZGERALD, *to Scottie*

APRIL 12

1963

Dear diary: Mama woke me up this morning to tell me to wash my hair . . . How can I just sit and resign my body to such a life . . .

OCTAVIA E. BUTLER

1966

Volume 1 of the Diary is published!

. . . [*Los Angeles Times* book critic] Robert Kirsch confirmed my belief that if one goes deeply enough into the personal, one transcends it and reaches beyond the personal.

At the end of this Diary I feel I have accomplished what I hoped to accomplish: to reveal how personal errors influence the whole of history and that our real objective is to create a human being who will not go to war.

writer **ANAÏS NIN**

1995

Have lunch with Jodie Foster on the set of the film she is directing. One of the few attractions for me of living in LA is the sense of being in the centre of an industry. There's so much going on, so much energy, so much enthusiasm for making movies. In the end that's what got me down about England—it was so hard to get anything done. Here you just pop down the road and have a taco with Miss Foster . . .   *director* **MICHAEL APTED**

APRIL 13

1876

A general flare up in the office. Col. Peel, who was acting editor in the absence of Bassett, had a clash with the management and was relieved. The bone of contention was the newly appointed Board of Public Works and its support by the paper.

Hancock Johnson, the President of the company, then came to me and gave the editorial charge of the paper into my hands. I employed Hawley as city editor and went into the job with all the energy I could muster but not without some misgivings. This is my first experiment at real editorial work and the opportunity has been thrust upon me almost without a moment's notice . . .   **WILLIAM ANDREW SPALDING**, *L.A. newspaperman,*
embarking on his decades-long editorial career

1950

After stopping in the department office, I went up to the hill and dictated a response to a recent note that appeared in "Talk of the Town," a column in the April 1950 New Yorker. The New Yorker note read: New atoms are turning up with spectacular, if not downright alarming frequency nowadays, and the University of California at Berkeley, whose scientists have discovered elements 97 and 98, has christened them berkelium and californium, respectively. While unarguably suited to their place of birth, these names strike us as indicating a surprising lack of public relations foresight on the part of the university, located, as it is, in a state where publicity has flourished to a degree matched perhaps only by evangelism. California's busy scientists, will undoubtedly come up with another atom or two one of these days, and the university might as well have anticipated that. Now it has lost forever the chance of immortalizing itself in the atomic tables with some such sequence as universitium (97), ofium (98), californium (99), and berkelium (100).

The fellows got a kick out of this, and someone suggested that I reply with the following, addressed to Mr. Harold Ross, Editor: Talk of the Town missed the point in their comments on the naming of elements 97 and 98. We may have shown lack of confidence but not lack of foresight by naming these elements "berkelium" and "californium." By using these names first, we have forestalled the appalling possibility that, after naming 97 and 98 "universitium" and "ofium," some New Yorker might follow with the discovery of 99 and 100 and apply the names "newium" "yorkium."

Respectively yours, "Busy Scientists"   **GLENN T. SEABORG**

APRIL 14
1868

SAN FRANCISCO,

Please see that no reports or synopses (even the most meagre one) are made of my lecture. I must repeat, here & elsewhere . . . every point that appears in print must be left out—which is *ruinous* to me . . .

Your friend   **MARK TWAIN**,
to the dramatic editor of the Evening Bulletin

1931

Dearling,

What bad two days did my letters have to carry you through? You mean the street-cleaner's band wasn't at the station to greet you? And nobody gave you the keys to any cities?

. . . Last night I ran into Sid [Perelman] in the Brown Derby, brought him home with me, and wound up doing a little pimping for him. God knows I'm doing my best to keep celibacy from rearing its ugly head in Hollywood! But something's got to be done to keep the gals moderately content while I'm out of order . . .

Ovelay,

Dash

DASHIELL HAMMETT, *to Lillian Hellman*

1965

This is to record progress, physical mental and psionic toward my chosen goal. This is my first entry.   **OCTAVIA E. BUTLER**

APRIL 15

1865

Beloved Brethren! Overpowered with grief and sorrow at the terrible news which just at this moment was communicated to me, I am scarcely able to command my feelings, and to express before you the sad calamity that has befallen our beloved country. Who might believe! our revered President, Abraham Lincoln, the twice anointed High Priest in the sanctuary of our Republic, has fallen a bloody victim to treason and assassination, and is no more. He, who by the indomitable power of his energy, stood amidst us like a mighty giant, holding with his hands the tottering columns of our great. commonwealth, and planting them secure upon the solid basis of general freedom and humanity; his great mind full of wisdom, his great heart full of love, his whole being, a true type of the American liberal character . . .

[We] pray that He, in His infinite love, may graciously avert the dreadful consequences of this calamity, calm the passions of the people, so justly aroused at this atrocious crime, soothe the grief and sorrow so deeply cutting in the very heart of our nation, and speak to the Angel of Destruction: 'Enough!'   **RABBI ELKAN COHN**

1940

Taking Thoreau's *Journals* to the beach, for night reading.

Faithfully,   **LAWRENCE CLARK POWELL**, *to William Everson*

1968

4933 WORTSER AVENUE

SHERMAN OAKS, CALIF/ 91403

Dear Mr. Schulz,

Since the death of Martin Luther King, I've been asking myself what I can do to help change those conditions in our society which led to the assassination and which contribute to the vast sea of misunderstanding, fear, hate and violence.

As a suburban housewife; the mother of three children and a deeply concerned and active citizen, I am well aware of the very long and tortuous road ahead. I believe that it will be another generation before . . . open friendship, trust and mobility will be an accepted part of our lives.

In thinking over the areas of the mass media which are of tremendous importance in shaping the unconscious attitudes of our kids, I felt that something could be done through our comic strips and even in that violent jungle of horror is known as Children's Television.

You need no reassurances from me that *Peanuts* is one of the most adored, well-read and quoted parts of our literate society. In our family teenage Kathy has posters and sweatshirts . . . pencil holders and autograph books. Paul, who's 10 and our Charlie Brown Little Leaguer . . . has memorized every paper back book . . . has stationery, calendars, wall hangings and a Snoopy pillow. Three and a half year old Simon has his own Snoopy which he lives, loves, eats, paints, digs, bathes and sleeps with. My husband and I keep pertinent *Peanuts* cartoons on desks and bulletin boards as guards against pomposity. You see . . . we are a totally *Peanuts*-oriented family.

It occurred to me today that the introduction of Negro children into the group of Schulz characters could happen with a minimum of impact. The gentleness of the kids . . . even Lucy, is a perfect setting. The baseball games, kite-flying . . . Yes, even the Psychiatric Service cum Lemonade Stand would accommodate the idea smoothly.

Sitting alone in California suburbia makes it all seem so easy and logical. I'm sure one doesn't make radical changes in so important an institution without a lot of shock waves from syndicates, clients, etc. You have, however, stature and reputation which can withstand a great deal.

Lastly; should you consider the suggestion, I hope that the result will be more than one black child . . . Let them be as adorable as the others . . . But please . . . allow them a Lucy!

Sincerely,

MRS. HARRIET GLICKMAN, *citizen*

APRIL 16

1870

MUD HILL, NEVADA COUNTY

Mr. Editor,-The celebration here on the 12th was a decided success, and has done much to give influence to the colored people. Notwithstanding snow and mud in the morning, the Grass Valley folks were in time, and were met on the edge of the town by the Lincoln Club with music, and escorted to the Congregational Church . . .

At the church a procession was formed, which was something to be proud of here in the Sierras, headed by our band, which can't be beat. The school children, Lincoln Club, with their beautiful banner, citizens on foot and in carriages, marched through the principal streets, eliciting from many on the sidewalks, a hearty "God bless you," and "ain't this glorious" . . .

JENNIE CARTER

1945

Spoke this evening on station KFI, debating the Japanese question . . . Later received a threatening phone call from a man who gave his name as A.B Williams, 4975 Wilshire Blvd. Am noting this for the record.

CAREY MCWILLIAMS

APRIL 17

1885

The fact may as well be looked squarely in the face that consumption has an incurable hold upon me and that the end is not very far off . . .

dying San Francisco journalist **WILL FROST,**
sending his 11-year-old son, Robert,
to his parents in New England

1928

One fine day last week Henry, Brett, and I packed cameras, paints, lunch, and went to Santa Monica for work and outing. I had grown tired of 'still-life," of confinement,—I wanted air and soil. Santa Monica was chosen because of a fine group of sycamore trees . . .

I have printed another of the sycamore tree which I like without question. It is life at first hand . . .

Perhaps the most fun I have had lately has been in a swimming hole discovered by Cole and Neil. It was reminiscent of *Huckleberry Finn*, with bonfires, rafts and naked boys. Fed by fresh river water this hole gouged out by steam shovel is deep enough for diving, and much larger than the local swimming tanks. It is hidden from public gaze so no spinster can be horrified by naked boys and men.   **EDWARD WESTON**

APRIL 18

1906

I awoke to the city's destruction. Right away it was incredible, the violence of the 'quake. It started with a determination that left no doubt of its purpose. It pounced upon the earth like a bulldog.

. . . The motion seemed to be vertical with a rotary twist, like a French cook tossing a fish in a frying pan . . . I heard the roar of bricks coming down, and twisted girders, and at the same time saw a pale crescent moon in the green sky. The St. Francis Hotel was waving to and fro with a swing as violent and exaggerated as a tree in a tempest. Then the rear of my building, for three stories upward, fell. The mass struck a series of little wooden houses in the alley below. I saw them crash in like emptied eggs, the bricks passing through the roofs as though through tissue paper. I had this feeling of finality. This is death. Then curiosity took over. I had to see what had happened . . .

The streets were full of people, half-clad, dishevelled, but silent, absolutely silent, as if suddenly they had become speechless idiots. It went down Post Street towards the center of town, and in the morning's garish light I saw many men and women with gray faces. No one spoke. All of them had a singular hurt expression —not one of physical pain, but rather one of injured sensibilities, as if some trusted friend had suddenly wronged them, or as if someone had been rude to them . . .

JAMES HOPPER, *later state director for Northern California,*
Federal Writers' Project

1906

We learn of the collapse of a lodging house on Seventh and Howard Streets with about seventy-five occupants. A number of us hasten thither to help rescue the unfortunates. One dead man is already stretched out on the side-walk and his wife is bending over him greatly distressed. So complete is the wreck, so inextricable the mass, that an attempt to be of assistance is use-less. As though this is not horror enough, fire breaks out among the wreck-age to roast the poor wretches who are still alive. Leaving there we meet a poor mother piteously imploring for the rescue of her two babies who are among the entombed. *survivor* **EDWARD GRAFF**

1950

I am without the one thing in life that matters to me, which happens to be a small unhappy blonde in Laugharne, Carmarthenshire. Went to Hollywood, dined with Charlie Chaplin, saw Ivan Moffat, stayed with Christopher Isherwood, was ravingly miserable for you my true, my dear, my one, my precious love.

I LOVE YOU XXX   **DYLAN THOMAS**, *to his wife*

APRIL 19

1906

. . . the men were an inspiration. When they dropped, exhausted, in the gutters, somebody would always be there to pull them to their feet and help them to carry on. Their helmets were baked to their heads and their turn-out rig was peeling off their backs. More than one of the fire horses had collapsed in its harness. **JAMES HOPPER**

1906

Returning up Market Street, we saw many people near what had been jew-elry stores raking around in the street with their hands and picking up melted pieces of gold and silver. *survivor* **HELEN WILD**

1923

. . . I have never seen so many buildings going up all at one time. There are thousands in process in every direction I looked.

We rode back into the hills where they put their cars into their attics— literally—and have their stump of a house on the edge of the cliffs. Some of it was quite like Italy. A mad era of house building is on. How long it will continue is a question but I see no reason why it should not continue. The whole Middle West wants to come here. It is the only alternative to New York.

HAMLIN GARLAND

1958

SAN FRANCISCO

In my day at Berkeley I saw the campus, fixed up my schedule for teaching, arrange to take on a house, two Siamese cats, three lizards, and two cars, and recitals for Natasha. We pubcrawled a bit, and I was more or less greeted by some angry young San Francisco poets.   **STEPHEN SPENDER**

APRIL 20

1901

In the morning went to Los Angeles in the electric car . . . we went to O'Melveny's office in the Baker Block and we tried to arrange the business of lands in Sta Monica and San Vicente. Mr. Jones left the papers for O'Melveny to review them. O'Melveny said he had paid Arcadia's taxes in the amount of $14,000 . . .   **DON JUAN BAUTISTA BANDINI**

1934

Since January, and until a few weeks ago, I have been working on the Public Works of Art Project, So. Calif. region, with Merle, the director, as my boss. For the first time since my early twenties I have been on a salary. The weekly check, starting at $42.50 and finally because of shortage of funds reduced to $38.50, saved me during a very dull period . . .

I had two delightful adventures in Los Angeles; one a renewal with X., a memorable night; another with a most passionate, and pathetically repressed virgin. This adventure started just before I left and never reached fulfillment. I feel that if the time had been propitious, and with more time, the story would be different. X. on the other hand is most delightfully un-moral, pagan,—a grand person to love . . .   EDWARD WESTON

APRIL 21

1906

The future of the city—or rather what was left of San Francisco—was being decided here and now . . . The sight of their aged fire chief refusing to give up acted as a powerful spur. The firemen moved with new life . . .

JAMES HOPPER

1937

As to safety, no doubt [the letters] will be safer almost anywhere out of this region during the fire-season. The risk becomes worse hereabouts every year, because of the tindery dryness over a period of six or sometimes even eight months, and the god-damned carelessness of autoists, hunters and other to-bacco addicts—not to mention professional incendiaries. This is one reason (not the only one) why I have thought of quitting California. Of course, it is my native state, and I am attached to the scenery. But there is an increas-ing destruction and pollution of landscape beauties, and a growing influx of undesirable humans bringing with them filth and pestilence. Auburn, for example, has been ravaged this winter by a virulent species of measles some-times terminating in death and always serious: an epidemic which, I am con-vinced, can be blamed on the auto-tramps and their "trailers." California, it would seem, must serve as a kind of sink or cess-pool for the whole U.S . . . .

Apart from this, the local attitude toward art and literature is dis-couraging . . .   *novelist* CLARK ASHTON SMITH,

*mulling the safety of letters sent
by his late friend H.P. Lovecraft*

1944

You ask do I enjoy my retreat. Yes and no. Yes, because I am living with nature more and more, and this Big Sur country (where I have been now for two months) is truly tremendous. There are only about 25 people on this mail route. Back from the coast, over the mountains, there is an absolute emptiness. It is almost as forbidding as Tibet, and it fascinates me. I should like to go back in there and live for a time quite alone. But I would need a

horse and an axe and a few other things I have never used. I am a little terrified of it.

The other day I was offered a little house on a mountain—quite isolated—
difficult to get to on foot (and I have only my feet to use) but I am taking it. I
move in next week. My address remains the same. I shall have a taste of real
solitude. Certainly I miss everything else—terribly. But I consider myself
fortunate. And I am more and more at peace with myself. I don't know if
you realize it, but this is the country Robinson Jeffers writes about. He lives
in Carmel, but I gather he has walked and ridden all over this mysterious
region. I met him one day. A very strange person—almost like a wounded
animal—or a victim of shell shock . . .

novelist HENRY MILLER, to Anaïs Nin

APRIL 22

1906

To Miss Frances R. Morse

. . . We can now pose as experts on Earthquakes—pardon the egotistic form
of talking about the latter, but it makes it more real. The last thing Bakewell
said to me, while I was leaving Cambridge, was: "I hope they'll treat you to
a little bit of an earthquake while you're there. It's a pity you shouldn't have
that local experience." Well, when I lay in bed at about half-past five that
morning, wide-awake, and the room began to sway, my first thought was,
"Here's Bakewell's earthquake, after all"; and when it went crescendo and
reached fortissimo in less than half a minute, and the room was shaken like a
rat by a terrier, with the most vicious expression you can possibly imagine, it
was to my mind absolutely an *entity* that had been waiting all this time holding back its activity, but at last saying, "Now, *go* it!" and it was impossible not
to conceive it as animated by a will, so vicious was the temper displayed—
everything *down*, in the room, that could go down, bureaus, etc., etc., and
the shaking so rapid and vehement. All the while no fear, only admiration
for the way a wooden house could prove its elasticity, and glee over the viv-
idness of the manner in which such an "abstract idea" as "earthquake" could
verify itself into sensible reality. In a couple of minutes everybody was in
the street, and then we saw, what I hadn't suspected in my room, the extent
of the damage. Wooden houses almost all intact, but every chimney down

but one or two, and the higher University buildings largely piles of ruins. Gabble and babble, till at last automobiles brought the dreadful news from San Francisco.

I boarded the only train that went to the City . . . Was very glad I did; for the spectacle was memorable, of a whole population in the streets with what baggage they could rescue from their houses about to burn, while the flames and the explosions were steadily advancing and making everyone move far-ther. The fires most beautiful in the effulgent sunshine. Every vacant space was occupied by trunks and furniture and people, and thousands have been sitting by them now for four nights and will have to longer. The fire seems now controlled, but the city is practically wiped out (thank Heaven, as to much of its architecture!). The order has been wonderful, even the criminals struck solemn by the disaster . . .   **WILLIAM JAMES**

1906

Dolly and I walked to Golden Gate Park and saw hundreds of people camping there. The sign board just across the street from this end of the Panhandle is covered with notices for lost people and addresses of those who have moved or been driven out by fire or earthquake. This sign board is a block long.

All of the "tents" have the names and former addresses of their occupants written on the outside and there are notices all over the trees and bushes.

. . . Many horses have dropped dead from overwork but the tireless autos speed on . . .   **HELEN WILD**

1924

At that time in Watts there was an Italian man, named Simon Rodia—though some people said his name was Sabatino Rodella, and his neighbors called him Sam. He had a regular job as a tile setter, but on weekends and at nighttime, under lights he strung up, he was building something strange and mysterious and he'd been working on it since before my boy was born. Nobody knew what it was or what it was for. Around his small frame house he had made a low wall shaped like a ship and inside it he was constructing what looked like three masts, all different heights, shaped like upside-down ice cream cones.

First he would set up skeletons of metal and chicken wire, and plaster them over with concrete, then he'd cover that with fancy designs made of pieces of seashells and mirrors and things. He was always changing his ideas while he worked and tearing down what he wasn't satisfied with and starting over again, so pinnacles tall as a two-story building would rise up and dis-appear and rise again . . .

Mr. Rodia was usually cheerful and friendly while he worked, and sometimes, drinking that good red wine from a bottle, he rattled off about Amerigo Vespucci, Julius Caesar, Buffalo Bill and all kinds of things he read about in the old encyclopedia he had in his house . . . the local rowdies came around and taunted him and threw rocks and called him crazy, though Mr. Rodia didn't seem to pay them much mind . . .   *jazzman* **CHARLES MINGUS**

1944

. . . I have a considerable talent, perhaps as good as any coeval. But I am 46 now. So what I will mean soon by 'have' is 'had.'

WILLIAM FAULKNER, *to his agent*

APRIL 23

1937

FEDERAL WRITERS PROJECTS
751 SOUTH FIGUEROA ST.
LOS ANGELES, CALIF.
To Henry G. Alsberg, Director Federal Writers Projects, WPA
1734 New York Avenue, NW
Washington, D. C.

Dear Mr. Alsberg

May I not express to you my warmest congratulations and most sincere praise for the magnificent Washington Guide, a copy of which I received today from Mr. [James] Hopper. Every member of the Project joins me in this praise. We think it is marvelous.

This volume has brought home to us in a concrete way the value of our Project work. The appearance of the book here has had a stimulating influence on morale and has inspired in us renewed zeal to produce as fine a book for Los Angeles . . .

We are now editing and checking the copy and rewriting where we think it necessary. We are also sending out checking crews on the tours. If no untoward contingency delays us, we hope to have the pre-final copy ready for your inspection late in May or early in June. With kindest personal regards, I am

Sincerely yours,   *editor* **HUGH HARLAN**,

District Supervisor, Federal Writers Project

1941

The government, thank God, helps out farmers, but nobody cares about playwrights . . .   **LANGSTON HUGHES**

1961

By 2020, the Bay could be little more than a wide river. Berkeley would extend so far west that part of the city would be in San Francisco County.

journalist **ED SALZMAN**,
galvanizing the Save the Bay movement

APRIL 24

1942

. . . I asked my sister to tell me the situation in detail as soon as possible if she goes to Santa Anita. Are we going to be confined in a horse track? Until today, we had gone there as a family on a number of occasions to entertain visitors from Japan . . .

There may be many among the white people who say, "So what? Even horses, there are Arabian horses worth a hundred and fifty thousand dollars which is a lot more than you worthless Japanese . . . " But we are human beings. Humans are the lord of all primates. Just because we became enemy nationals, we didn't drop in rank to an animal. We have the pride of possessing mystical blood and spiritual depth of the East. Who would have thought that war, war between Japan and America, a war that was planned in a world we had no knowledge of even in our dreams, would get us involved this deeply and cause us to suffer?

. . . Evening, I heard Santa Anita stinks with the odor of dead horses, and Owens Valley is a place troubled by terrible whirlwinds of dust clouds.

AOKI HISA

1944

It is difficult to express just how much this means to me . . . Serious creative writing is an uphill grind against indifference, disapproval, antagonisms, and even destitution. Encouragement is seldom had from any source.

I can truthfully say that this is my first "break" in fifteen years of writing. I hope I will never look back.   *novelist* **CHESTER HIMES**,
upon receiving a Rosenwald Foundation grant

1966

The party for my book [*Been Down So Long It Looks Like Up to Me*] is being held this Sunday, Peter:

The Discovery Bookstore

241 Columbus

7p.m. (May 1)

Who knows, they may peddle a few . . .

novelist **RICHARD FARIÑA**, *a week before his death on April 30*

2020

I've lived in this old farmhouse for 32 years. Mine is a neighborhood of barter, where we trade oranges and avocados, fresh eggs and just-caught fish, clothes and tools. For these past two weeks, we've been trading groceries and tamales, and I give away books. I leave a bag on the fence slats, so we maintain distance. A mother and daughter stop at the fence, looking disconsolate. The daughter will graduate from high school with no ceremony, not sure if college will even open in the fall. On the porch, I find for her "Pearl Buck in China: Journey to the Good Earth."   **SUSAN STRAIGHT**

APRIL 25

1869

. . . The mother died. The father is a confirmed drunkard, and three children are without a protector—and this is an everyday occurrence in California. If the aching, breaking and broken hearts were weighed in the same scale with the gold, the gold would fly up light as air, while the hearts would weigh down! down!!   **JENNIE CARTER**

1906

We had quite a heavy earthquake shock this afternoon. . . . Over in the auto-garage near Jefferson Square, the soldiers dropped their guns and rushed pell-mell for the street. One of them tripped in the doorway and the others feel over him. . . . The papers try to make everything appear as cheerful as possible . . . Of course, all this is for the good of the future of San Francisco— if there is any—but it gives everyone outside a wrong impression which is, I suppose, exactly what is intended.

The Gompertz family across the street have a cracked gramophone which plays all of the favorites, such as *The Holy City, In the Shade of the Ole Apple Tree, Cavaliera Rusticana* and a few comic negro selections. A crowd of men in the street were laughing at what they said was the only amusement in San Francisco, sitting on a box in Hayes Valley listening to a gramophone. It's back to the woods for us . . .   **HELEN WILD**

1974

The friction that's been building with the studio for some time came to a head today. I never approved the original ending where my character survived the earthquake. They agreed to a change to accommodate my death in a futile, doomed effort to save my bitchy wife, which seems to me to lend some credibility to a basically implausible story. (An earthquake destroys the whole *city*, this guy with the mean wife and the neat girl friend escapes scot-free, wife killed, neat girl left alive for him while he rebuilds Los Angeles?) Anyway, they kept edging up on me about shooting an alternate ending. I've been at this trade too long not to know better than that. Script approval doesn't help you if you've shot it.   **CHARLTON HESTON**

APRIL 26

1908

SAN FRANCISCO

What is patriotism? Is it love of one's birthplace, the place of childhood's recollections and hopes, dreams and aspirations? Is it the place where, in childlike naiveté, we would watch the passing clouds, and wonder why we, too, could not float so swiftly? . . . In short, is it love for the spot, every inch representing dear and precious recollections of a happy, joyous and playful childhood? . . .

An army and navy represent the people's toys . . . The city of San Francisco spent one hundred thousand dollars for the entertainment of the fleet; Los Angeles, sixty thousand; Seattle and Tacoma, about one hundred thousand. Yes, two hundred and sixty thousand dollars were spent on fireworks, theater parties, and revelries, at a time when men, women, and children through the breadth and length of the country were starving in the streets; when thousands of unemployed were ready to sell their labor at any price.

What could not have been accomplished with such an enormous sum? But instead of bread and shelter, the children of those cities were taken to see the fleet, that it may remain, as one newspaper said, "a lasting memory for the child." A wonderful thing to remember, is it not? The implements of civilized slaughter. If the mind of the child is poisoned with such memories, what hope is there for a true realization of human brotherhood?

radical **EMMA GOLDMAN**

1928

Since the fleet with its 25,000 gobs has left for Hawaii I have had a chance to recognize the full inconsequence of this Pollyanna greasepaint pinkpoodle paradise.   **HART CRANE**

1945

San Francisco is as lively as a circus—the setting and the audience are much more amusing than the Conference performance . . . Nowhere could have been found in the world which is more of a contrast to the battered cities and tired people of Europe . . .

The Bay is a beautiful background, the sun shines perpetually, the streets are thronged, there are American sailors everywhere with their girls and this somehow adds to the musical comedy atmosphere. You expect them at any moment to break into song and dance, and the illusion is heightened because every shop and café wafts light music from thousands of radios. Colours too are of circus brightness, the flamboyant advertisements, the flags of all the Conference nations, the brilliant yellow taxis. This seems a technicolor world glossy with cheerful self-assurance. The people are full of curiosity about the Conference delegates. They crowd around them like the friendly, innocent Indians who crowded around the Spanish adventurers when they came to America and gaped at their armour and took their strings of coloured beads for real . . .

The exceptions are the Russians—they have stolen the show. People are impressed, excited, mystified and nervous about the Russians . . . They are painfully self-conscious, quiet, dignified—determined not to take a step which might make people laugh at the beautiful Soviet Union. The crowds throng outside the hotel to see Molotov . . . When he came into the initial plenary session he was followed by half-a-dozen husky gorillas from N.K.V.D. The town is full of stories about the Russians—that they have a warship laden with caviare in the harbour, etc., etc.

Meanwhile the local Hearst press conducts an unceasing campaign of anti-Russian mischief-making—doing their damnedest to start a new world war before this one is finished . . .   *Canadian diplomat* **CHARLES RITCHIE,** *attending the conference that created the United Nations*

APRIL 27

1871

CALISTOGA, CAL.

Last night, I read a lecture in San F.; & day after tomorrow should read a second, & perhaps still another, later . . . The city opens to us its Mercantile Library & its City Exchange, —one, rich with books; the other, with newspapers; & the roads & the points of attraction are Nature's chiefest brags. And if we were all young,—as some of us are not,— we might each of us claim his quarter-section of the Government, & plant grapes & oranges, & never come back to your east winds & cold summers,—only remembering to send home a few tickets of the Pacific Railroad to one or two or three pale natives of the Massachusetts Bay, & half-tickets to as many minors . . .

R. W. E.   *essayist, poet* **RALPH WALDO EMERSON**

1982

. . . One thing I've noticed is the two old canary palms that diagonally cut across a corner lot marking the entrance to Universal City. They were well placed. They marked out "gateway." The large billboard "Welcome to Universal City" in black and white was placed directly in front of them. It was very stupid. Considering how marvelously the two palm trees already said the same thing.

It was disturbing this morning to see a crane and crew of workers pulling one of the palm trees out of the ground.

And the other? . . .

It happens so quickly in L.A.   **AARON PALEY**

APRIL 28

1919

I never loved any place in my life as I do this and if anything happens that I don't make a go of it I believe that it would about break my heart.

novelist **EDGAR RICE BURROUGHS**

1945

Second meeting of the plenary session again in the Opera House with powerful klieg lights shining down from the balcony into the eyes of the delegates, dazzling and irritating them. The session is declared open by Stettinius who comes on to the dais chewing (whether gum or the remains of his lunch is a subject of speculation) . . .

He makes the worst impression on the delegates. He reads his speech in a laypreacher's voice husky with corny emotion. The Chilean Foreign Minister reads a tribute to Roosevelt which being translated consists of an elaborate metaphor (which gets completely out of control as he goes along) comparing Roosevelt to a tree whose foliage spreads over the world which is struck by what appears to be the lightning of death but is actually the lightning stroke of victory so that its blossoms, while they may seem to wither, are brighter than ever . . .   **CHARLES RITCHIE**

2006

8:05 p.m. Blogging live (more or less) from the Los Angeles Times Book Awards, a pleasantly cool Friday evening in Westwood. Walking up to Royce Hall, I happened to pass by as Joan Didion emerged from her town car. She is every bit the frail, petite wisp of legend. I also had the pleasure of bumping into my good pal Mr. Steve Wasserman, present in his famed seersucker. He received me graciously, as ever, and inquired after my cycling results, noting that I had been competing in the "Old Guys" category . . .

8:11 p.m. We're being treated to a multimedia presentation on the history of the Los Angeles Times. It's predictably self-congratulatory but the audience does seem to enjoy it. The Book Awards are 26 years old as of this evening.

8:14 p.m. LAT editor Dean Baquet takes the microphone. Gives a nice, elegant speech and introduces Kenneth Turan.

8:16 p.m. So odd to watch Turan, knowing that voice I know so well from NPR. He's introducing the judges reading down a fairly long category by category list. Too many names for a slow typist like me to catch. Now he introduces NEA chairman Dana Gioia, who has just called himself a "working class Latin kid from L.A." Interestingly, his cultural references so far have been film—Quentin Tarantino and Fritz Lang. But now he's reminiscing quite pleasantly about his reading youth at Hawthorne Public Library . . .

9:28 p.m. I'm fading and it's Biography time. Let's move it along, folks, we old types need our sleep. So the winner is *Matisse the Master* by Hilary Spurling, accepting by videotape. It's a lovely speech describing Matisse's love for American in general and California in particular.

9:38 p.m. Last award, the Robert Kirsch Award, their version of the Thalberg. We're getting a video presentation on winner Joan Didion. She's getting a well-deserved standing ovation. "I get a prize is from a paper I still read every morning . . . in New York." It's a brief but heartfelt speech, no more than three minutes and she's gone . . . **MARK SARVAS**

APRIL 29

1855

I preached this morning upon the destruction of Sodom and Gomorrah and had I wanted material for supposed scenes in those cities I could have found them in the very scenes now transpiring around me.

REV. JAMES WOODS

1992

. . . I approach a young man carefully pouring gasoline around the trunk of a chubby palm tree in downtown LA. The fuel soaks into the trunk as if the tree is thirsty, and as I watch its callused bark grows dark. The young man is concentrating; the round cheeks of his face are shiny as if he had anointed himself with oil before embarking on his task. But I know it's sweat. My own face is slick too. We are a block or two from Parker Center, LAPD headquarters. It is about 7:30 p.m. The sun is setting. Over half a day has passed since a Simi Valley jury acquitted four police officers charged with beating Rodney King . . .

The young man in front of me wedges newspaper into the cut fronds of the palm tree that form part of its trunk. He reaches for matches.

"Don't," I ask him. "Please." My voice sounds funny, small, cracked. He looks at me as if I am crazy. "Why not?" he asks.

"It's a tree," I say. "It didn't do anything. It's just a tree." I feel foolish, ashamed for worrying about a palm tree.

"Listen, lady," he says, leaning close. "It's not a real tree. It's a fake one. They're all fake." He swings his arms toward the city trees that stand at attention in their little plots of dirt. "They shouldn't be here. I'm taking this one out. Don't worry. It'll be all right."

He lights his newspaper and fire flames up the trunk like the backyard barbecues that, as a child, I drenched in lighter fluid. The tree will burn for a good long time. I move away but out of habit, I put my hands palms up, toward the fire, as if to gather the heat in, as if it is a campfire and not a burning palm tree.

"See," the young man tells me as he caps his gas can, "I told you it wasn't real. If it was real, it wouldn't burn. What's real doesn't burn." His logic seems to please him. He flashes me a smile and I realize just how young he is. I'm thirty-one. He's young. Sixteen. Fifteen. He's a kid . . .

As the crowd thins out, I notice I have company. Journalist Mike Davis scribbles nearby on a notepad, his crew-cut head bent low. Days later I'll read his account in the *L.A. Weekly* . . .

In our cars, heading west on the deserted 10 freeway, we see fires to the south and some to the north. I think of the kid lighting palm trees and his conviction that what's real doesn't burn.

My friend Anne puts something in my hand. "I found it," she says. "It was just lying there in the grass. So I picked it up."

It's cold and heavy. It's the metal letter "C" from Parker Center.

LISA ALVAREZ

2006

Steve Wasserman . . . elicited round after round of applause—including ours—pillorying, variously, Oprah, Bush and the evils of publishing in general. The panel was moderated by PW editor Bridget Kinsella . . .

SW shares a fascinating anecdote about his days at Times Books when, in a meeting with his editor, he was advised he could no longer acquire the 10,000-copy books but had to, instead, look for the 40-50,000 copy title. He pointed out that this required casting about for the "sure thing" and would have resulted in Random House's passing on two gold mine titles—*Midnight in the Garden of Good and Evil* and *Primary Colors*. From there he leaps to Oprah . . . naming her complicit in the creation of this confessional/recovery culture . . .

author JIM RULAND

APRIL 30

1896

Our last day in San Francisco was spent in visiting the "Thirteenth Semi-Annual Exhibition and Rose Show of the California State Floral Society"—roses, geraniums, pelargoniums, pansies (oh, so large), sweet peas in great variety and color, and large collections of each, contributed by amateurs and professionals. A collection of "historical" flowers of California attracted much attention. Among them was a bunch of roses, "Cloth of Gold," from the rose Sherman planted at Monterey . . .

Standing before a large collection of unnamed carnation seedlings, a member of the committee invited me to choose one that I admired most and to name it. There were mixtures of white and red, even a lavender one, but I selected a bright pink color and said to the lady, as to its name, "This is Shakespeare's birth month; I'll call it Shakespeare carnation," which name was accepted . . .   *travel writer* **LORRAINE IMMEN**

1942

Today is the day that we are going to get kicked out of Berkeley. It certainly is degrading. I am down here in the control station and I have nothing to do so I am jotting down these notes! The Army Lieutenant over there doesn't want any of the photographers to take pictures of these miserable people waiting for the Greyhound bus because he thinks that the American public might get a sympathetic attitude towards them.

I'm supposed to see my family at Tanforan as Jack told me to give the same family number. I wonder how it is going to be living with them as I haven't done this for years and years? I should have gone over to San Francisco and evacuated with them, but I had a last final to take. I understand that we are going to live in the horse stalls. I hope that the Army has the courtesy to remove the manure first . . .

Oh, oh, there goes a "thing" in slacks and she is taking pictures of that old Issei lady with a baby. She says she is the official photographer, but I think she ought to leave these people alone. The Nisei around here don't seem to be so sad. They look like they are going on a vacation. They are all gathered around the bulletin board to find out the exact date of their departure. "When are you leaving?" they are saying to one another. Some of those old Issei men must have gone on a binge last night because they smell like sake . . .

The Church people around here seem so nice and full of consideration saying, "Can we store your things?" "Do you need clothes?" "Sank you," the Issei smile even now though they are leaving with hearts full of sorrow . . . "The Japs are leaving, hurrah, hurrah!" some little kids are yelling down the street but everybody ignores them.

Well, I have to go up to the campus and get the results of my last exam and will barely be able to make it back here in time for the last bus. God, what a prospect to look forward to living among all those Japs!

CHARLES KIKUCHI,

encountering, like as not, Dorothea Lange

1963

. . . bigness is brutalizing the state; we are getting closer and closer to our Brave New World of border-to-border highways (I sometimes get the feeling that 90% of California's area is made up of freeways and parking lots; everybody has a car, including teenagers over 16), mass educational institutions that give out impressive statistics but don't educate (Harvey's largely illiterate classes; students whose exams i mark coming to me to find out not what they can learn but what they can do to get the magic A); and economic greediness encroaching on all of nature, which would be really a tragedy here, since Calif's natural assets are so unusually magnificent. After hearing so much about *Silent Spring*, I was really upset when I heard that the robin count was abnormally low in California this year . . . yesterday I saw a beautiful blue bird on the campus, which made me feel somewhat better . . .

Californians are a strange bunch, stranger the longer I live here . . . There is a strange lethargy and complacency about them; they live for the moment, in the sun (or fog), immersed in their own private and personal concerns— some of them would seem almost like mystics if they weren't so healthy and cheerful. I'm probably overgeneralizing . . .

In a recent article in *Esquire* about California, the author claims that there is something in the fog smog that acts as a soporific—she said that San Francisco escapes it because of the brisk wind, but that the East Bay cities such as Berkeley and Oakland get it full force. "Babies sleep till 10:30 in Oakland," as she put it. I really believe this must be true—though I've never been exactly the get-up-and-go type (in the morning, at least) I think I am sleepier than I used to be . . . Supposedly, Lost (Freudian?) Angeles is supposed to be the epitome of the California mystique—I am really looking forward with horror to seeing it . . .   *critic, essayist* **ELLEN WILLIS**

1995

An old neighbor drops by and shares his invention for drying grapes into raisins. My nine-year-old daughter drives the tractor by herself—my little girl is now big and strong enough to push down the clutch—a modern-day rite of passage for farm kids. We fertilize a young orchard as a family working together, we all have our jobs as we nourish life for the future. Raw ideas for good stories, like an artist's sketches.   **DAVID MAS MASUMOTO**

2006

Our final stop was a brief glimpse at the LA Lit panel, a glimpse made even briefer by my expiring laptop battery . . .

Jim Krusoe asks the question I've been asking—Do writers in Pennsylvania sit around in coffee shops talking about Pennsylvania literature?

Chris Abani: References things back to Hollywood's dominance which can overshadow LA's rich literary history.

Steve Erickson: Metaphorically and geographically, LA is as far as we can go. We fret about how the world is going to end here but we're very proprietary about that, too. Something about that conceit appeals to us, we'd find it galling to suggest the world might end somewhere else.

Michelle Huneven: Los Angeles used to be famous for chewing up the literary writer. But now there are a lot of literary writers in LA and it's become just another place to write . . .

JK: I asked it, I'm not supposed to answer it. And I actually thought this was a panel about *California* [italics mine] writing.   **MARK SARVAS**

MAY 1

1906

Routed out of bed at a quarter past five. Half an hour later Mrs. London and I were in the saddle. We rode miles over the surrounding country. An hour after the shock, from a high place in the mountains, we could see at the same time the smoke of burning San Francisco and of burning Santa Rosa. Caught a train to Santa Rosa—Santa Rosa got it worse than S.F. Then in the afternoon, Wednesday afternoon, we got into San Francisco and spent the whole night in the path of the flames—you bet, I saw it all.

JACK LONDON, *to a relative*

1906

Today I got . . . a piece of salt sea-lion. We cooked it but we didn't eat it. We were all looking at it rather suspiciously before it was cooked, but tried to feel happy and gay. It didn't work, though. And now it reposes peacefully in the bottom of an ash-can. . . . It was bad enough to endure the earthquake and the fire, but when it comes to trying to eat sea-lion doctored up with ocean water and rock salt, we quit.

HELEN WILD

1950

I do hope I can get me a book shop started this year.

KENNETH REXROTH, *to James Laughlin*

1981

I've always been above board with the press and I will talk now as I have always talked, from my heart . . .

tennis player, activist BILLIE JEAN KING,

coming out

MAY 2

1906

The Morgue is a wooden shack in the alley next to Hayes St. & near Laguna. The black wagons carrying the bodies, found as the ruins are cleared away, pass here continually. The number of dead is estimated as near 3,000. 1,500 bodies have been recovered so far.   **HELEN WILD**

1942

The searchlights go on in the evening and shine all night. We have to turn off our lights at ten and shut our radio at eight . . .

It's real cold in the night. I caught a cold the first night and I can't get rid of it . . . We have to get up early to eat or else they tell you to come back tomorrow morning. Goodby!   *writer, internee* **SANDIE SAITO**

1969

Finally inside, the regular Saturday night show patrons gone, we wandered down the aisles, more hellos, sliding into our seats, eating the imported chocolate bars Mike sold from a little pushcart in the lobby. Then Mike's disembodied voice over the microphone explaining things haltingly but with care, about the films, or places we should remember to go, like peace marches and poetry readings, and then, finally the films themselves . . .

LIZA WILLIAMS,

on Mike Getz's Cinema Theater in Los Angeles

1969

The knuckleball was fine tonight against Oakland—when it knuckled. When it didn't, it got hit for two home runs. That was in the first of three innings I pitched. One ball was completely still. It must have looked like a watermelon up there. Float like a watermelon, fly like a rocket . . . .

This afternoon Gary Bell and I hired a car and drove up to the Berkeley campus and walked around and listened to speeches—Arab kids arguing about the Arab-Israeli war, Black Panthers talking about Huey Newton and the usual little old ladies in tennis shoes talking about God. Compared with the way everybody was dressed Gary and I must have looked like a couple of narcs.

So some of these people look odd, but you have to think that anybody who goes through life thinking only of himself with the kinds of things that are going on in this country and Vietnam, well, he's the odd one. Gary and I are really the crazy ones. I mean, we're concerned about getting the Oakland Athletics out. We're concerned about making money in real estate, and about ourselves and our families. These kids, though, are genuinely concerned about what's going on around them. They're concerned about Vietnam, poor people, black people. They're concerned about the way things are and they're trying to change them. What are Gary and I doing besides watching?

So they wear long hair and sandals and have dirty feet. I can understand why. It's a badge, a sign they are different from people who don't care.

So I wanted to tell everybody, "Look, I'm with you, baby. I understand. Underneath my haircut I really understand that you're doing the right thing."

author, ballplayer **JIM BOUTON**

1988

I feel sorry for you. It is hard to know what to put in a biography . . . I appreciate more than I can say your instinctive need to walk in a gingerly way . . .

And I'm sorry about not sending my recipe for Ginger Snaps: just triple or quadruple the amount of ginger in Rombauer's recipe . . . They are wonderful for parties at the end of any long meal or drinking bout . . . in general, a good remedy for motion sickness, as well as a delicious cookie any time at all . . .

M. F. K. FISHER, *to eventual biographer Joan Reardon*

MAY 3

1931

The city and bay are overwhelming. What is especially fantastic is Chinatown. The Chinese are immensely sympathetic and never in my life have I seen such beautiful children as the Chinese ones. Yes, they are really extraordinary. I would love to steal one so that you could see for yourself. . . . it did make sense to come here, because it opened my eyes and I have seen an enormous number of new and beautiful things . . . .

I don't particularly like the gringo people . . . They are boring and they all have faces like unbaked rolls (especially the old women).

painter **FRIDA KAHLO**

1939

The *Times* carried quite a story about the flood, drout an' dust—bowlers a comin' to Calif in their rickety, rundown jalopies, their little handful of belongings, and' their children . . . only, says the *Times*, to dig into some of the Relief Gold . . .

Personal, I've been in Calif. 2 years—'cause the dust and the cold run me out of Texas . . . an' I ain't never applied for any kind of relief of any kind yet. An' for the past year I've averaged makin' less than $1 a day.

But before I'd make my livin' by a writin' articles that make fun of Hungry Folks, an' the Workin' Folks, I'd go on Relief.

Yrs Trly Woody   **WOODY GUTHRIE**

1960

So, in sum, I am more concerned than angry, more irritated than exhilarated, by what I see encroaching upon us everywhere today. Commercialism and quack intellectualism, the twin demons, the dual evils of our time as in every other time. To kick them both in the balls is my desire.

novelist **RAY BRADBURY**, *to Esther McCoy*

MAY 4

1883

If I could write a story that would do for the Indian the thousandth part what *Uncle Tom's Cabin* did for the Negro, I would be thankful for the rest of my life . . .   **HELEN HUNT JACKSON**

1927

May 4, 1927   Dutch Flats, to Rockwell Field, North Island
                     (Landed, because of fog, at 5:50 am)
                     Rockwell Field to Dutch Flats
                     Dutch Flats to Coronado Strand speed course to
                     Camp Kearney parade grounds (Tests)
                     Three test flights, starting with 38 gallons of gasoline
                     One test flight, with 71 gallons
                     One test flight, with 110 gallons
                     One test flight, with 150 gallons
                     One test flight, with 200 gallons
                     One test flight, with 250 gallons
                     One test flight, with 300 gallons

aviator **CHARLES LINDBERGH**,
testing The Spirit of St. Louis *outside San Diego*

1939

Let me be Los Angeles   *novelist* JAMES JOYCE, *in* Finnegans Wake

1995

. . . my story, "Snapshot, 1944," began when I found an old photograph of my uncle's funeral during the relocation of Japanese Americans from their homes during World War II.

The first line in my journal became the first line of the story, "I stare at the silent and still faces, expressions frozen in a snapshot." . . .

This story then took on a life of its own. From journal entry to the *LA Times* to now, a book entitled *Epitaph for a Peach, Four Seasons on My Family Farm*. Good things can happen with our journals.

DAVID MAS MASUMOTO

MAY 5

1852

To His Excellency Gov. Bigler

Sir: I am a Chinaman, a republican, and a lover of free institutions; am much attached to the principles of the government of the United States, and therefore take the liberty of addressing you as the chief of the government of this State . . . The effect of your late message has been thus far to prejudice the public mind against my people, to enable those who wait the opportunity to hunt them down, and rob them of the rewards of their toil . . . .

[We] would beg to remind you that when your nation was a wilderness, and the nation from which you sprung barbarous, we exercised most of the arts and virtues of civilized life; that we are possessed of a language and a literature, and that men skilled in science and the arts are numerous among us; that the productions of our manufactories, our sail, and workshops, form no small share of the commerce of the world; and that for centuries, colleges, schools, charitable institutions, asylums, and hospitals, have been as common as in your own land . . . .

And we beg to remark, that so far as the history of our race in California goes, it stamps with the test of truth the fact that we are not the degraded race you would make us. We came amongst you as mechanics or traders, and following every honorable business of life. You do not find us pursuing occu-

pations of degrading character, except you consider labor degrading, which I
am sure you do not; and if our countrymen save the proceeds of their industry from the tavern and the gambling house to spend it on farms or town lots
or on their families, surely you will admit that even these are virtues. You say
"you desire to see no change in the generous policy of this government as far
as regards Europeans." It is out of your power to say, however, in what way or
to whom the doctrines of the Constitution shall apply . . .

activist **SANG YUEN**

1906

You'll never have any idea of the disorder in San Francisco after the earthquake. The city was in a *state of siege*, under the orders of General Fulton.
The streets were guarded by soldiers. Naturally all kinds of thieves tried to
take advantage of the disaster to pillage the abandoned houses, and each
time they were caught in the act they were immediately shot. I *myself* saw
three killed like that.

The newspapers try to bluff, and talk of building San Francisco bigger
than ever. But I remain very skeptical . . .

JAIME DE ANGULO

1942

. . . My body is shivering and will not stop. I wonder if a nervous breakdown is like this. I cannot afford to become ill, but after moving to the hotel,
having to pay even more attention to my surroundings makes it even more
difficult to sleep, and I am troubled . . .

This kind of evacuation seemed like a spur of the moment thing, and I
felt I was being jerked around like a puppet. After five, six days, there probably won't be a single Japanese remaining in Los Angeles.

. . . We, who until war broke out, thought we would live in America for
the rest of our lives, became labeled as the enemy . . .

AOKI HISA

1953

. . . The Negro children of Sutter staring out of their cracked windows at the
tennis players in their white-white shorts chasing a white-white-white ball
across the courts of the California Tennis Club, a jet plane leaving a vapor
trail smudged across the blue sky like a sky writer who started a message
and then forgot it, springtime's young lovers parked at Land's End to enjoy
the view of each other, the grown-up kids who hang around Earle Swenson's
ice cream parlor at Union and Hyde and say, "Gee, thanks" (just like their

children) when Earle rewards them with a free sample, the unemployed guys in their dirty non-working clothes clustered on Howard Street to discuss their last meal and wonder where the next one is coming from . . . Oh, big-little town of wide views from dark alleys . . .

columnist **HERB CAEN**

MAY 6

1871

The valley here is quite level—like a table—running up each side to these perpendicular walls; it is made up of gravel, the debris of the mountains and is covered mostly with starveling scatted growth of grass and weeds and small bushes and a thin jungle of trees, oaks, and maples (as they seem) and pines and balsams; some of the pines are noble fellows; at other places there is more grass and meadow. Something at every turn impresses you with the greatness of the objects about you, especially the smallness of your companions as you see them walking about. Evidently, one's senses and instinctive judgments need readjusting here.

RALPH WALDO EMERSON

1943

We live our by now deeply habituated waiting-room days among our palms and lemon trees, in social concourse with the Franks, Werfels, Dieterles, Neumanns—always the same faces, and if occasionally an American countenance appears, it is as a rule so strangely blank and amiably stereotyped that one has had enough for quite some time to come . . .

I have made up my mind to give the war time for one more novel . . . The completion of the *Joseph* [*and His Brothers*] is already well in the past; it was finished in January . . .

Now I have something very different [*Doktor Faustus*] in mind, something rather uncanny, tending in the theological and demonological direction . . .

THOMAS MANN

1995

Sat through a screening of [*The Family Perez*] at the Academy. It was like an opening night in terms of the terror it induces. Hylda, my US agent, told me this will be the kindest audience the film will ever have. They all want to love it and they will . . . until the reviews come out, and then they'll know what to think.   *actor* **ALFRED MOLINA**

MAY 7

1903

This is the first time I have ever been to California, and I cannot say to you how much I have looked forward to making the trip. I can tell you now with absolute certainty that I will have enjoyed it to the full when I get through . . .

I have felt that the last five or six years have been steadily hastening the day when the Pacific will loom in the world's commerce as the Atlantic now looms . . .   **THEODORE ROOSEVELT**, *in Barstow*

1929

This is the most horrible, unreal place in the world, on a dreary curve of the coast, I have rheumatism dreadfully here, and never felt so down-and-out anywhere . . .

Oh, if only this dreadful thing had happened at home, in a human land, where mother would have had her lovely grandchildren to watch and work, where there were dear old friends, kind neighbors, memories, God. There is no God in California, no real life. Hollywood is the flower of all the flowers, the complete expression of it.   **WILLA CATHER**, *to Dorothy Canfield Fisher*

1992

. . . the intricate framework of the neighborhood collapsed for a few hours. Drawn out onto the streets by a particularly nasty bit of apartment-house arson—not by any means a rarity around here—a crowd coalesced, moved to the supermarkets and, barred from there, into the strip malls that line Vermont Avenue. From the stoop of my building, it seemed like a giant block party, a looters' bacchanalia of new tennis rackets and boom boxes, then of liberated rental tapes from the video store, plastic-wrapped clothes from the dry cleaner and fake palm trees from the furniture store. On Vermont itself, I saw thousands of people out on an illegal shopping spree, cheerfully helping one another maneuver a sofa or a heavy Barcalounger across the busy street. One tired-looking cop drank a cup of coffee and tried not to look anyone directly in the eye . . . [M]en stood rooftop sentry with Uzis, outlined

against the orange sky. It was the first time I can remember being comforted
by the sight of armed drug dealers . . .   JONATHAN GOLD

MAY 8

1871

Mr RW Emerson

. . . I was delighted at the thought of meeting you but have just learned that
you contemplate leaving the Valley in a day or two

Now Mr Emerson I do most cordially protest against your going away so
soon, & so also I am sure do all your instincts & affinities I trust that you
will not 'outweary their yearnings' Do not thus drift away with the mob
while the spirits of these rocks & waters hail you after long waiting as their
kinsman & persuade you to closer communion

But now if Fate or one of those mongrel & misshapen organizations
called parties compel you to leave for the present, I shall hope for some other
fullness of time to come for you.

If you will call at Mr Hutchings mill I will give you as many of Yosemite
& high Sierra plants as you wish as specimens.

I invite you [to] join me in a months worship with Nature in the high
temples of the great Sierra Crown beyond our holy Yosemite It will cost you
nothing save the time & very little of that for you will be mostly in Eternity . . .

With most cordial regards I am yours in Nature

                                                                 JOHN MUIR

1903

Stayed at home all day. Thought of going to Los Angeles to see the parade
for the Fiesta de las Flores and the arrival of President Roosevelt—the actual
president of the nation visiting these parts . . .

                                         DON JUAN BAUTISTA BANDINI

1903

I am not going to talk to you very long this morning, because I am too
much interested in your community. I want to see all I can see. We speak
often of the old pioneer days, and the wonderful feats of our countrymen in
those days, but we are living right in the middle of them now, only we are

living under pleasanter auspices. To think of the well-nigh incredible fact that all of this that I have been looking at—the city, the development of the country—that it has all occurred within twenty years; that twenty years has separated the sheep pasture from this city . . .

Yesterday and today I have been traveling through what is literally a garden of the Lord, in sight of the majestic and wonderful scenery of the mountains, going over this plain tilled by the hand of man as you have tilled it, that has blossomed like the rose—blossomed as I never dreamed in my life that the rose could blossom until I came here. Everywhere I have gone I have been greeted by the men who wear the button that shows that they belong to the Grand Army of the Republic, men who . . . as they fought, all, no matter from what State they came—as they fought all for the federal flag and the federal Union have come here from their original home to become Californians while remaining Americans. For, oh, my friends, the thing that has impressed me most here in this State of the West, this wonderful commonwealth that has grown up on the Pacific Slope, the thing that has impressed me most is that I am speaking to Americans just as I speak in any other section of the country! . . .

THEODORE ROOSEVELT, *in Pasadena*

1911

My dear Mary Austin:
There are poppies, fields of them, and there's a blue flower which sometimes blushes through the blush of red, which is lovely as any other conflict of emotions. And I have seen miles upon miles of such beauty. It is California— in the country. But I am here in a small city, and here the impression is one of roses, all sorts of roses, and in all shapes and conditions. They front the little houses, trimmed and prim, and then again they have got away and scramble all over the place. I saw one old neglected garden, where the roses had filled the whole yard and worked all up through all the trees till the whole place was a mess of loveliness. No doubt some gardener will some day come along and tame it all. He certainly will have to do something if he is to save the orange trees and the palms. But, as it stands, this place is the most winning argument for anarchy that I ever saw.

muckraker **LINCOLN STEFFENS**

1919

. . . We eat and sleep Tarzan . . . The dog is named Tarzan, the place is Tarzana . . . a guy bobbed up day before yesterday with the plan of a whole village he wished to plant in my front yard—school, city hall, banks, business houses, motion picture theater—and it was labelled City of Tarzana, which sounds like a steamboat.   **EDGAR RICE BURROUGHS**

MAY 9

1901

Went to Los Angeles to see the floral parade. It was very large and very pretty headed by the President and his Cabinet. There was an enormous crowd. I have never seen so many people in the city. In the afternoon came to the Soldiers Home as the President was due to come there. He arrived at 3 p.m. and after seeing the retired soldiers drill he went back to Los Angeles.

DON JUAN BAUTISTA BANDINI, *going to see President McKinley*

1968

WHITEHORN, CALIFORNIA

. . . This is a place you must get to know when you are out this way. Superb for a retreat . . .   *writer, monk, theologian* **THOMAS MERTON**

1979

More amazing, awful news . . . G—— is pregnant, W—— has been busted 3 or 4 times, their dad was shot through the head, probably by their stepmom. John isn't the greatest person in the world for Lisa, Dino got in a car accident. And I lost my homework.   *writer, scholar* **COLLEEN JAURRETCHE**

MAY 10

1903

The last weeks' travel I have really enjoyed . . . I have collected a variety of treasures, which I shall have to try to divide up equally among you children. One treasure, by the way, is a very small badger, which I named Josiah, and he is now called Josh for short. He is very cunning and I hold him in my arms and pet him. I hope he will grow up friendly—that is if the poor little fellow

lives to grow up at all. Dulany is taking excellent care of him, and we feed
him on milk and potatoes . . .   **THEODORE ROOSEVELT**, *to his son Kermit,*
from the Del Monte Hotel

1903

I wish you could have been with me today on Algonquin, for we had a perfectly lovely ride. Dr. Rixey and I were on two very handsome horses, with
Mexican saddles and bridles; the reins of very slender leather with silver
rings. The road led through pine and cypress forests and along the beach.
The surf was beating on the rocks in one place and right between two of the
rocks where I really did not see how anything could swim a seal appeared
and stood up on his tail half out of the foaming water and flapped his flip-
pers, and was as much at home as anything could be. Beautiful gulls flew
close to us all around, and cormorants swam along the breakers or walked
along the beach.

I have a number of treasures to divide among you children when I get
back. One of the treasures is Bill the Lizard. He is a little live lizard, called a
horned frog, very cunning, who lives in a small box. The little badger, Josh, is
very well and eats milk and potatoes. We took him out and gave him a run in
the sand today. So far he seems as friendly as possible. When he feels hungry
he squeals and the colored porters insist that he says "Du-la-ny, Du-la-ny,"
because Dulany is very good to him and takes care of him.

THEODORE ROOSEVELT, *to his son Archie,*
from the Del Monte Hotel

1903

I have been among the orange groves, where the trees have oranges growing
thick upon them, and there are more flowers than you have ever seen. I have
a gold top which I shall give you if mother thinks you can take care of it.
Perhaps I shall give you a silver bell instead. Whenever I see a little boy being
brought up by his father or mother to look at the procession as we pass by, I
think of you and Archie and feel very homesick . . .

THEODORE ROOSEVELT, *to his son Quentin,*
from the Del Monte Hotel

1951

Great news that Jack's finished ON THE ROAD, I trust in his writing . . . he
should create another and another work (like Proust) and then we'll have the
great American Novel . . .

Children, children, the pox of freedom and demander of money that siphons off luxury, but an enormous sponge to absorb your love and a bottomless pleasure pit into which I throw myself sometimes . . .

NEAL CASSADY, *to Allen Ginsberg*

MAY 11

1903

All of us ought to want to see nature preserved; and take a big tree whose architect has been the ages, anything that man does toward it may hurt it and cannot help it . . .

And see to it that you by your actions create the kind of public opinion which will put a stop to any destruction of or any marring of the wonderful and beautiful gifts that you have received from nature, that you ought to hand on as a precious heritage to your children and your children's children . . . **THEODORE ROOSEVELT**,

in what later become Henry Cowell Redwoods State Park

1939

. . . out here we have a strong progressive movement and I devote a great deal of time to it. Yet, although this new novel is about Hollywood, I found it impossible to include any of those activities in it. I made a desperate attempt before giving up. I tried to describe a meeting of the Anti-Nazi League, but it didn't fit and I had to substitute a whorehouse and a dirty film. The terrible sincere struggle of the League came out comic when I touched it and even libelous. Take the "mother" in Steinbeck's swell novel—I want to believe in her and yet inside of myself I honestly can't. When not writing a novel—say at a meeting we have out here to help the migratory worker—I do believe it and try to act on that belief. But at the typewriter by myself I can't . . .

novelist **NATHANAEL WEST**, *to a critic*

MAY 12

1863

We went up the canyon a few miles, then over a high ridge to Walker's Basin . . . We met in the basin a band of Indians, mostly women and children, the widows and orphans of the "braves" killed in the recent battles on Kern River. They were a hard looking set. On passing out of Walker's Basin we fell in with a man on foot, and we camped together on a stream. Company is desirable in a hostile Indian country, where, sleeping out, the lonely traveler is liable to be "picked off" in the night.   **WILLIAM H. BREWER**

1906

The fire had reached as far as Van Ness Avenue, two blocks from Green Street. It was our last hope, because Van Ness is a large artery, and if the fire had crossed over it, it would've finished off the city. Then a sort of rage seized me. For two days I had been pushed from house to house by the advancing fire. We were going to have to move on further. A line of soldiers guarded the approaches and didn't permit anyone to pass. I went to find the lieutenant to ask him to let me pass. "I want to volunteer to fight the fire."

"All right, let him go."

I got there. Most of the firemen were sitting on the road, looking stupidly at the fire. They could do no more. They had been fighting the flames, fighting, fighting, since the morning of the eighteenth, without food or sleep, and they were now exhausted, unable to stay on their feet, their faces black, their eyes red and drooping. Four or five volunteers like myself had just arrived. We were handed an enormous hose. Then I realized how hard the job of a fireman is! The hose was horribly heavy! It was a question of putting out the houses which were beginning to burn on the opposite side . . .

If they caught fire, that would be the end. On the other side was a neighborhood of narrow streets which would have burned like straw.

We wrapped wet woolen blankets around ourselves to protect us from the heat, and in spite of that sometimes we were obliged to get into the jet with our clothes to prevent them from catching fire! And we had to drag that long hose, which was so heavy! I was exhausted! We went into a house that was already beginning to burn and came out on the roof through a window. Finally after four hours of work the building opposite us collapsed. We were saved and we saved the entire district.

We looked at each other in silence and then let out a long "cheer" of joy. When we crossed back over the lines, people carried us in triumph! I've certainly had some adventures since I left home!

JAIME DE ANGULO, *to a colleague*

1911

As I was coming here this evening and reflected upon the name of this association, my thoughts naturally went back to that great man whose name you have adopted. And I asked myself, what would Jefferson say . . .

The great antiseptic in America is public information and public opinion. You can clarify and purify the worst things in life by simply letting the eyes of honest Americans have access to them . . .

Look at the other thing that is giving us trouble—it is simple another side of the same picture. Look at the corporations.

We are not hostile to corporations if corporations will prove that they are as much interested in the general welfare and the general development as we are . . . America is not jealous of wealth, but it is jealous of ill-gotten wealth. America is willing to give largess of infinite fortune to anybody who will serve her, but she is very chary, if she could have her own way, of giving fortunes to anybody who will impose upon her . . .

The alliance of these men with politics is the most demoralizing thing that could possibly descend upon any country. And it has descended upon us. Those are the things that need correction in our politics, and these are the things to which a man who acted in the Jeffersonian spirit would have to address himself.   *President* **WOODROW WILSON**

1943

I had lunch with Christopher [Isherwood] today. I invited him to lunch at the Brown Derby. I recognized him at once, just by instinct, and he does look just the way I imagine myself to look—it was funny.

I like him awfully, and I think he must have thought me rather schoolgirlish about his writing which I place with Chekhov's.

playwright **TENNESSEE WILLIAMS**

2006

Pierre and I drove all the way out to UCLA last night, for a much-anticipated concierto de Richard Thompson . . . Bueno, first off, nos tomó más de dos horas y media to get there. Según Mapquest, it should take fifty-two minutes, . . We could *never* afford Westwood, ni siquiera any other of the even semi-close-to-UCLA barrios en un sueldo cacadémico, no matter how "good" . . .

For the privilegio de vivir en el über-hip Westside, tendríamos que cough up . . .   **SUSANA CHÁVEZ-SILVERMAN**

MAY 13

1943

Yesterday, I had lunch with Tennessee Williams, the writer. He's a strange boy, small, plump and muscular, with a slight cast in one eye; full of amused malice. He has a job with Metro. He wanted to buy an autoglide to ride to work on. I tried to dissuade him, but he insisted. We went to a dealer's, and he suggested a very old junky machine which is obviously going to give trouble. **CHRISTOPHER ISHERWOOD**

1956

California reminds me of the popular American Protestant concept of heaven: there is always a reasonable flow of new arrivals; one meets many—not all—of one's friends; people spend a good deal of their time congratulating one another about the fact that they are there; discontent would be unthinkable; and the newcomer is slightly disconcerted to realize that now, the devil having been banished and virtue being triumphant, nothing terribly interesting can ever happen again . . .

These people practice what for centuries the philosophers have preached: they ask no questions; they, live, seemingly, for the day; they waste no energy or substance on the effort to understand life; they enjoy the physical experience of living; they enjoy the lighter forms of contact with an extremely indulgent and undemanding natural environment; their consciences are not troubled by the rumblings of what transpires beyond their horizon. If they are wise, surely the rest of us are fools.

historian, diplomat **GEORGE F. KENNAN**

1956

Darling Muv,

I got a job about a month ago and have been terrifically busy as a result. You can't think how I love going to work again after all this time . . . It's a very lowly kind of job, in the advertising department of a big San Francisco newspaper, and I only get $52.00 a week, which is supposed to go up to $75 after a year if I stick it out that long. My job is selling classified advts. Such a riotous thing happened after I'd been there a week. It's a closed shop (meaning all Union) and we belong to the Newspaper Guild. So one day the shop steward came round to me with the little monthly union paper, and said, "Your name is in here because you are one of the new employees; I know it's such a thrill to see one's name in print in a newspaper for the first time, so I thought I'd give this to you." I was inwardly roaring, do you remember how I was the first one in the family to be on posters?

JESSICA MITFORD, blacklisted,
reduced to working for the San Francisco Chronicle

2003

My name is Kevin Roderick. I am an author, a journalist, an Angeleno and wear assorted other labels. I suppose I'm also now a blogger . . . L.A. Observed is a logical step in my online evolution . . .

You can't be a serious consumer of L.A. news without registering at the LAT site, for instance. Submit bogus demographic data if it makes you feel better. I'm on the books as a 99-year-old woman with no income and an Alaska zip code at sites with the temerity to ask . . . .

I can't say yet how active this site will be. Let me know how you think it's going by email. If you don't want your email to show up on the page, say so. If you are rude and abusive I may use it anyway with suitable derision applied.

journalist, blogger **KEVIN RODERICK**

MAY 14

1856

Wednesday, May 14, at 5 P.M., I was in Commercial Street, a little below Montgomery. I had not noticed any pistol-shot, but I saw people running, and, as a matter of course, I ran. As I turned into Montgomery, I saw a man whom I knew.

"What is the matter?"—"Casey has shot [*Evening Bulletin* editor James King]"—and on we went, neither of us checking his speed.

A crowd was gathered at the Pacific Express Company's office, northwest corner of Montgomery and Washington. Many of the crowd knew me, and they made way for me to enter. I found Mr. King lying on the floor, with a bullet-hole just below the left clavicle. I saw that one or two physicians were already in attendance, and that my professional services were not needed; so I hurried out again, and ran up Washington Street, for I knew where the murderer would naturally have gone, that is, to the protection of his friend, the sheriff, David Scannell.

A carriage was standing at the entrance to Dunbar Alley, the rear of the police office. It was evidently about to start. I sprang on the step, and as I did so, Dave Scannell's pistol was thrust directly into my face. I looked in and saw Casey on the seat with Scannell, with his pistol pointed out of the opposite window. The driver started his horses and I was thrown to the ground, but was on my feet in an instant, and away with the crowd who were pursuing the carriage at full speed, yelling with every breath: "Hang him! Kill him!"

. . . Some one had touched me on the back: "The Vigilance Committee has organized." . . .   *doctor, ichthyologist* **WILLIAM ORVILLE AYRES**

1888

It is the easiest thing in the world to be drawn into the land fever. Real estate offices are as plentiful as bees on an August day. You pass along and you see some such sign as the following: "Bargain! For one day, Tract of land, Utopia, $25 to $100 per lot." This looks interesting; to buy a lot of land for $25 and sell it, perhaps, in a week or two for $50, titillates the mercenary palate. You are like a dull fly in the toils of an affable spider, with this difference, that, nine times out of ten, you take your turn at being the spider and someone else becomes the fly.

Undoubtedly Southern California is the garden spot of America, and judging from its past prosperity and progress it must hold a magnificent future. No one, even the most prejudiced, can dispute its advantages. The most stolid and lymphatic native must be stung into an appreciation of his country's resources and dream that he has reached that Biblical land flowing with milk and honey.   *travel writer* **HARRIET HARPER**

1935

This magnificent structure [the Griffith Observatory] will be of value not only to the scientists, but its greatest attraction will be to the masses of other citizens who will now have an opportunity to see how the universe is constructed.

physicist **ROBERT MILLIKAN**, *the same year Boulder Dam opened,*
soon to extinguish the stars over L.A. forever

1935

I finally offered my resignation. In typical Hollywood fashion it was rejected. I was fired two days later.   **ERIC KNIGHT**, *to a friend*

MAY 15

1934

LOS ANGELES

Some day I'll find out whether I'm an unusual specimen of humanity in that my instincts and reason are so inseparably one, with the reason ruling the instincts. Am I unusual or merely normal and healthy? Am I trying to impose my own peculiarities as a philosophical system? Am I unusually intelligent or merely unusually honest? I think this last. Unless—honesty is also a form of superior intelligence.   *novelist* **AYN RAND**

1950

It appears that any Monday I shall go to jail.   **DALTON TRUMBO**

MAY 16

1847

O Mary, I have not wrote you half of the truble we have had but I have Wrote you anuf to let you know now that you don't now what truble is but thank the Good god we have all got throw and the onely family that did not eat human flesh . . .   *Donner Party survivor* **VIRGINIA REED**

2011

. . . I leave an editorial meeting and take the 101 to the 5 to the 10 to Boyle Heights, en route to David Kipen's *Libros Schmibros*, "a community bookstore and lending library." It's pretty much the best bookstore in the world, not so much for its scope (its stock is superb, but it's an average-size storefront), but for its curation and spirit. Not only is every book in the shop one that any sane reader would covet, but if you happen to empty your pockets while you're there, you're free to borrow books you don't buy. Kipen is clearly some sort of a pinko, but if you can get your head around it—a store that lets you take out works of art on loan—the idea kind of grows on you. (If only someone would make so free and easy with the closely guarded spoils of the music business!) I plan on sending David's children to college by bankrupting myself in his store. Today's haul: some replacement Greil Marcuses, swanky hardbacks of Philip Roth's *The Counterlife* and *Our Gang*, Leonard Michaels's *Time Out of Mind*, Lewis Hyde's *Common as Air*, Daniel Fuchs's

The Golden West: Hollywood Stories. Also, a handsome copy of Elizabeth Bowen's *The Last September.* The rest I left, just because I was too embarrassed to ask for a dolly to carry it all to my car. (Edit—there's no store here! I'm making this up. Book lovers, stay away! David, I'll be back next week.) . . .

Dinner at Canter's Deli, on Fairfax. Those marvelously peculiar stained glass patternings on the ceiling. I see Rodney Bingenheimer, the Mayor of the Sunset Strip, in one of the booths. I thought Rodney was dead! I suspect he is. Still, that's him, eating a Danny Thomas.

novelist **MATTHEW SPECKTOR**,
at the Paris Review website, before Libros became a purely nonprofit lending library

MAY 17

1946

ANDERSON CREEK

BIG SUR

I told you I am getting a piece of property—a home. It came about strangely. It *is* almost impossible to get land or a house here. There was a neighbor on the hill where I lived, a Mrs. Wharton, who seemed to understand me—without reading the books . . .

. . . the spot itself is the very one I crave, the site which deeply satisfies me, and which I thought unobtainable. Sometimes I think, in offering me my dream, she is only teaching me another lesson. She says, for instance, in explaining her willingness to relinquish it, that it is now inside her, can't be lost . . .

So maybe to answer a question you put me recently, what I am about to learn is simply the meaning of home, the one thing I have never known. And when that becomes a part of me it won't matter where or how I live . . .

HENRY MILLER, *to Anaïs Nin*

1956

I'm out at Mill Valley trying to pull myself together . . . The city is all right, god knows very comfortable, a bit loose from an eastern sense—but easy—which has been a help to me. I have a small apt for $27.50, and have been doing odd jobs of typing, etc. People are very good to me, and I haven't really wanted for much of anything . . . am up to my ears in a perhaps impossible relation with Marthe Rexroth, who is very great—and god willing, we may make it. But you can think of how Kenneth takes it . . .

Anyhow, I give a reading Sunday, and think to take off for LA the coming week sometime, and then from there to Mexico City, with Marthe at best— and without if that's what has to happen . . .

I'm out here with Jack [Kerouac] now—he has just walked into town to get a fifth of port . . . You'll best get a sense of him as follows:

Fr/Canadian (Breton), about 5'8", a little stocky, from Lowell, Mass. He writes novels, a lot of them actually . . . Anyhow he is god knows a pleasure. Talks very little, listens a lot—could have been a wino, but isn't—likes to be by himself. One of those slightly red-faced quiet men. He went to Columbia on a football scholarship, was star football player on Lowell team . . . the prose is really, often, much more interesting, i.e., a curious light skipping and merging of images, a real continuity of changing impressions. . . . he has a beautiful will to endure whether or no he would think so. He manages . . .

All my love   *poet* **ROBERT CREELEY**

1961

JUDITH ANDERSON

CARPINTERIA CALIF

DON'T KNOW WHAT AN EMMY IS BUT CONGRATULATE YOU
LOVE   **ROBINSON JEFFERS**

MAY 18

1856

Mr. Coleman had demanded from Dave Scannell, the sheriff, the surrender to the Vigilance Committee of the persons of James P. Casey and Charles Cora. The sheriff hesitated, and then refused. Mr. Coleman's reply was: "Mr. Scannell, we give you five minutes and no more. If, at the end of that time, the two men are not surrendered, we shall take them by force; the doors of the jail will be blown open, and you will be taken, Mr. Scannell, as well as Casey and Cora." When about five seconds of the fifth minute remained, the door was opened . . .

Mr. Coleman and Mr. Doane came out, and between them walked James P. Casey. He must have known and felt that he was marching straight to the death he so richly deserved, but he showed no sign of weakness or emotion. His eyes were cast down, but his step was as firm as I ever saw it . . .

WILLIAM ORVILLE AYRES

1918

Came home. Spent the rest of the afternoon on the throne of China. I was constipated.   *dancer, choreographer* AGNES DE MILLE

1956

[*Howl*] is really built like a brick shithouse . . . The key phrase of method in Howl is "Hydrogen Jukebox" which tho quite senseless makes in context clear sense . . .

Jack Kerouac . . . is out here and is the Colossus unknown of U.S. Prose who taught me to write and has written more and better than anybody of my generation that I've ever heard of. Kerouac you may have heard of but any review of the situation here would be ultimately historically meaningless without him since he is the unmistakable fertile prolific Shakespearean genius—lives in a shack in Mill Valley with Gary Snyder. Cowley (Malcolm) is trying to peddle him in N.Y.C. now and can give you info. Kerouac invented and initiated my practice of speech-flow prosody.

I recount the above since anything you write will be irrelevant if you don't dig especially Kerouac—no shit, get info from Kenneth [Rexroth] or Louise Bogan who met him if you don't take my word . . .

I have written this in the Greyhound between loading busses and will send it on uncensored.

I've said nothing about the extraordinary influence of Bop music on rhythm and drugs on the observation of rhythm and mental processes—not enough time and out of paper.

Yours,   *poet* ALLEN GINSBERG, *to a fellow poet*

2011

Having somehow, miraculously, wrestled my six-year-old to sleep without a tranq gun, I settle in to watch *The Long Goodbye*. *Zeroville* research has led me to (re)discoveries new and old, from Gaspar Noé to The Germs, but few have set their hooks in me as deeply as Altman's Chandler. In part because I've always resisted Altman, having had the misfortune of first encountering *Nashville* and others on the small screen, where they make little sense. The sound-mixing alone just kills them. What once seemed muddled now reveals as sublime, however, and while *California Split* remains my dark horse favorite, *The Long Goodbye* is right with it. The dazed, dreamy, cat-hassled

Marlowe who shuffles through the first fifteen minutes of the film, the rancid canyon-and-colony atmospheres throughout. These things make me happier than words can say.   **MATTHEW SPECKTOR**

MAY 19

1903

SACRAMENTO, CAL.

I trust I need not tell you, my dear sir, how happy were the days in the Yosemite I owed to you, and how greatly I appreciated them. I shall never forget our three camps; the first in the solemn temple of the giant sequoias; the next in the snow storm among the silver firs near the brink of the cliff: and the third on the floor of the Yosemite, in the open valley fronting the stupendous rocky mass of El Capitan, with the falls thundering in the distance on either hand.

Good luck go with you always,   **THEODORE ROOSEVELT**, *to John Muir*

1947

PASADENA

... Dull mist hit the mountains but revealed the bunch-stemmed palms. The Chinese Theatre, against my intention, amused and charmed ...

novelist **E.M. FORSTER**

1961

New York is a real city—Los Angeles has no navel ...

playwright **BRENDAN BEHAN**

1968

My determination to eliminate RFK is becoming more and more of an unshakable obsession. RFK must die. RFK must be killed. Robert F. Kennedy must be assassinated ... Robert F. Kennedy must be assassinated before 5 June 68.   *assassin* **SIRHAN SIRHAN**

2004

The baskets are 10 feet high, with giant and very forgiving backboards. A couple of kids from the neighborhood start playing with a kickball at another hoop, and we invite them to join us instead. They are young, fifth-graders, so we split them up: Carlos plays on Steve's team and Matthew joins me. We play two games of two-on-two and one game of H-O-R-S-E. Matthew's third-grade brother, Justin, who can't quite throw a ball up to the basket yet, watches from the sidelines.

Talking to Carlos, I learn that his father also works at City Hall. I realize that Carlos Jr. is the son of a janitor I know, Carlos Sr., who has told me before that he lives in the neighborhood. I have an extra basketball at home, so I give Carlos my ball and walk home to dinner.   *Mayor* **ERIC GARCETTI**,

then a city councilman

MAY 20

1871

TRUCKEE

254 MILES EAST FROM S. FRANCISCO

We begun our homeward journey yesterday morning from San Francisco, & reviewed our landscapes of 4 weeks before. The forest has lost much of its pretension by our acquaintance with grander woods, but the country is everywhere rich in trees & endless flowers, & New England starved in comparison. Another main advantage is, that every day here is fair, if sometimes a wind a little raw & colder blows in the afternoon. The soil wants nothing nothing but water, which the lands call aloud for, & the immense herds of horses sheep & cattle are driven to the mountains as the earth dries. Steps begin to be taken to meet this want of the plains & cities, which the sierras that keep their snow tops all summer stand ever ready to supply . . .

One of my new acquaintances, Mr Peirce, a large owner & very intelligent much-travelled man, thinks California needs nothing but hard times & punishment to drive it to prudence & prosperity, the careless ways in which money is given & taken being a ruinous education to the young. Its immense prospective advantages only now beginning to be opened to mens eyes by the new Railroad are its nearness to Asia & S. America; & that with a port such as Constantinople, plainly a new centre like London, with immense advantages over that, is here. There is an awe & terror lying over this new garden—all empty as yet of any adequate people, yet with this assured future in American hands,—unequalled in climate & production. Chicago

& St Louis are toys to it in its assured felicity. I should think no young man would come back from it . . .

In Oaklands, & in Stockton, every house has its garden, & the wonderful vegetation aserts itself, & every house keeper is a botanist, with his agaves, figs, vines, & incomparable flowers. One feature is, in every yard, a windmill, which pumps all day & irrigates. In Stockton, an artesian well, over 1000 ft deep, which spouts up a fountain 17 ft high, & feeds all . . .

RALPH WALDO EMERSON

1903

Going through California, I have been struck with the prosperous and contented look of its people, and of course you are contented; I should be ashamed of you if you were not, living in such a State as this . . . The essential thing in any State is the character of the average man or woman, and I am proud to be your fellow-citizen, and to have men the type of people I have met in California.   President **THEODORE ROOSEVELT**,

in Hornbrook, Siskiyou County

1937

Through pristine San Clemente which I remember from Laguna days—all white bldgs. with red tile roofs—such an uncomfortable looking place—one rebel gas station has painted green bills on his windows and we bet the town council will soon see to him . . .

CHARIS WILSON

2020

I can't shake how badly I'm missing watching sports. On Sunday I finished "The Last Dance" . . . Watching this doc dovetailed with turning in the final draft of my next and probably last middle grade collaboration with Kobe Bryant, so the sense of loss when it was over was profound.

novelist **IVY POCHODA**

MAY 21

1871

LAKE TAHOE, CALIFORNIA.

. . . drove through several great streets, one of which was called the Chinese quarter, where are all the Chinese shops,—butchers and vegetable and flower-shops, and shoe-shops, and all the China-men dressed as they are in China, with long queues reaching almost to their feet, and in blue robes. But we drove on, and pretty soon came in sight of the Pacific Ocean . . .

. . . and not far in front of us a rocky island. The top of the rocks on it was covered with sea-birds which looked like ducks, but lower down we presently saw the sea-lions,—long creatures as large as bears, and much longer than bears. Some of them are twelve feet long, that is, if they could stand upright on their hind-feet they would be twice as tall as I am . . .

Now and then they roar loudly as if they would make more noise than the waves rushing up the rocks do and as if they wished to be heard by the people on the Cliff House balcony gazing at them through spy glasses. We talked loud but they did not seem to mind what we said about them I dont think they understand English . . . they had their young sea-lions with them, and had taught them how to swim. The Government of the State of California finding that fishermen killed the seals and sea-lions to get their oil have made a law that none of the sea-lions on the island near San Francisco shall be killed. So these are safe and waiting for you to come and see them one of these days . . .

Goodbye says Grandpapa   **RALPH WALDO EMERSON**

1937

Please know I am quite aware of the hazards. I want to do it because I want to do it. Women must try to do things as men have tried. When they fail, their failure must be but a challenge to others.   *aviatrix* **AMELIA EARHART,**

in a letter to her husband, G.P. Putnam,

before departing Oakland

1943

I think it is one of the funniest but most embarrassing things that ever happened to me, that I should be expected to produce a suitable vehicle for [Lana Turner] . . . I feel like an obstetrician required to successfully deliver a mastodon from a beaver.   **TENNESSEE WILLIAMS**

1992

I flew out of LA to give a lecture at SFSU, just as the violence was erupting. Before I left, a stranger knocked on our apt door: "It's starting!" Very painful to be separated from my city and my mate at that moment . . . .

Snakes are out in the park. Wanda's dog got bit by a baby rattler. Baby snakes, it turns out, are more dangerous because they have not learned to regulate their venom.

It's going to be a long hot summer in L.A.   **LOUISE STEINMAN**

MAY 22

1856

James P. Casey had been called on to plead in the usual form, to "Guilty, or not guilty," had had a full and fair trial; the jury had rendered their verdict, "Guilty of murder in the first degree"; and the sentence from the court, of death by hanging, was given in the customary words and form. The same was true in relation to Charles Cora. The execution of the sentence yet remained . . .

The traditional scaffold of death was projected at each of two windows of the upper story of the Vigilance Committee's rooms, and just as the funeral procession was leaving the church, Casey was led out on one of these platforms, and Cora on the other. The fatal cord was adjusted, and at a signal which no one on the outside saw or heard, the two murderers dropped into eternity.   **WILLIAM ORVILLE AYRES**

1915

SHASTA COUNTY

From the crater and crevasse were coming puffs of steam and ashes. Noises coming from the crater were heard that sounded like something dropping down in the bottom of the crater . . . Along the sides of the crater were small, round holes, where the steam was gushing out.   *ranger* **HARVEY ABBEY**,
just before the great Lassen Peak eruption

1971

I never could make anything work out right and now I'm betraying my friends. I can't make anything out of it—never could. I had great visions but never could bring them together with reality. I used it all up. It's gone . . . I went Southwest. Goodbye.   *poet* **LEW WELCH**,
his suicide note

2017

MADERA COUNTY

. . . at the exact geographic point of California's center, the North Fork History Group (NFHG) has replaced the bronze plaque stolen last November from the stone monument . . . though a valiant effort was made by Madera County Sheriff deputies and many community members, it was never recovered.   *historian* **GINA CLUGSTON**

MAY 23

1919

No one can imagine what this means to the young people of this part of the world nor what this institution will one day become.

UCLA vice president **ERNEST CARROLL MOORE**

1942

Saturday. Last night after I came home I heard a number of gun shots. Alice says (unofficial) that three boys were shot while trying to escape over the fence, one of whom is in the hospital. The administration won't take any moves to confirm or deny any of the stories so they continue to spread. This seems to be a shortsighted policy. There is no chance for the paper to bring such things out without being censored. They just won't allow us to take a definite policy on aims, except possibly Americanization. They are so afraid of radicalism. If it is being a radical to push American ideals and war effort among the Japanese without fear of stepping on toes, then we are radicals. The Japanese are really conservative and anything a little different is an indication of radicalism. They will have to get used to changes, because there will be many of them in the next few years. They will never go back to their old pre-war lives. If they cannot adjust themselves to changes, they are in for bitter disillusionment. I have hopes that they will, but the Americanization process will be slow. We can't expect anything else, I suppose, under the circumstances. Ever since Orientals have been in the U.S. they have had a difficult time. Denied citizenship and economic opportunities, it is not surprising that they have withdrawn and hung onto what they have brought with them. The cultural ties were stronger than the political ones. In a way it is a form of escapism . . . .   **CHARLES KIKUCHI**

1945

[The American delegation's] hearts are in the right place but . . . they dare not say so for fear of the Russians bolting the organisation. One incidental result of this line which the British and Americans may not contemplate is to increase the prestige of Russia . . .

The only American advisers I know are the State Department Team— shifty-eyed little Alger Hiss who has a professionally informal and friendly manner . . .   **CHARLES RITCHIE**

1949

I AM REBORN IN THE TIME RETOLD IN THIS NOTEBOOK . . . perhaps, the most important space of time—(important to whatever I will be as
a person)—I've known.   **SUSAN SONTAG**

MAY 24

1910

. . . I had a pleasant enough voyage and have pretty nearly got the "slosh" out
of my bones.

A bushel of letters awaits attention, besides a pair of lizards that i have
undertaken to domesticate. So good morning.

AMBROSE BIERCE, *to George Sterling*

1935

Schoenberg teaches me counterpoint now. And I am very happy because my
work seems to please him. Today he turned to the other two pupils and said:
You see, I don't even have to look at it (my exercises), I know they're right.
He is a teacher of great kindness and understanding and it is a rich comfort
that he gives . . .

And now—, Xenia. All I know is that she will be here early in June; that
there was a formal announcement (her sister's idea) in order that "showers"
might follow; and that I am, according to mother, as unprepared as if I were
living on the streets (Xenia knows this and says she will accept even starvation with me "gracefully") . . .

I ran into a lady who has a daughter. And she claims that although the
injections are necessary that they alone will not do the thing, that diet is
of supreme importance. She has taken the whole matter very scientifically.
Vitamins . . . Yeast. A vegetable juicer.   **JOHN CAGE**

MAY 25

1848

I think now from all this you can form some facts, and that you can mention
how thousands and thousands made their fortunes, from this Gold Discov-

ery produced through my industry and energy . . . and this folly saved not only the Mercantile World from Bankruptcy, but even our General Gov't. But for me it has turned out a folly . . . without having discovered the Gold, I would have become the richest wealthiest man on the Pacific Shore.

JOHANN AUGUST SUTTER

1888

. . . There is an old cathedral down in adobe town, the "Cathedral of the Queen of the Angels," where I rather like to find myself. It is built of adobe, and has no special architecture, being low and broad, with an ill-proportioned attempt at cruciform, and possessing an altogether familiar and undignified air, standing forth on Main street like some rotund, worldly abbot, brushing his skirts against the sordid stream of human life. Passing through a graveled yard, with a great wooden paintless cross set in its center, you find the side entrance. The door is always open; you pass inside and see a wooden floor, worn into little shelving hollows by the friction of faithful feet. It is the oldest looking, darkest, dingiest sort of a church imaginable, though built in 1823 . . .   **HARRIET HARPER**

1927

Dear Mr. Hearst:

Am just back from two days at San Simeon . . . Miss Worn was thinning the geranium-lantana border herself, so as to fix the idea in the gardener's eye. Also Mr. Meyberg was there, planning out the work for two of his most experienced workmen. The stone facing is going up and the work generally is being concentrated on, in the order of the program you approved. It is hard to hold everyone to this but by steady forcing it is working out.

The housekeeper is solving the "care of antiques" problem,—understands and cares about them, and also seems to get on well with the workmen involved.

The roses were at their prime, really most lovely, and I regret greatly you could not see them.

Things generally are in good shape.

Yours very truly,   *architect* **JULIA MORGAN**

1942

I have just about come to the conclusion that my destiny lies in hard work building up to one final everlasting explosion.   **CHESTER HIMES**

1997

COSTA MESA, CALIFORNIA

Today I also broke new ground when I was applauded *in the middle* of a 45-second solo . . .   *dancer* **DEBORAH BULL**

MAY 26

1852

This afternoon we discovered the nest of a hummingbird in our hole—the hole is about 30 feet square and perpendicular on the bank side where it is 12 or 14 ft. deep. Some roots project from near the top. On one of these—not as large as your little finger and shaded by other & larger roots above, which are covered with earth—the bird built its nest during our late absence. It is hatching and we shall not disturb it. While it left its nest for a half hour I pulled myself up by the large roots, sat on the shoulders of another man, and saw two eggs of the size of the end of your little finger & less than half an inch long. The nest is the size of a half hen's egg. The inside is not larger than mother's thimble . . .

I am now eating my supper—boiled potatoes, 10 cts. per pound; beef steaks (fresh every day), 18¢ pickles from Boston, in a glass jar holding a half gallon, 87 cts. the jar; bread, five loaves for 50¢, and we eat that amount daily; butter, $1.00 per pound. Poor butter, that none but a Mexican can eat, can be had for 50¢. Dried apples, 20¢ per lb. We usually have ham at 25¢ and some other trifles. You see it costs something to live in the land of gold.

deaf gold miner **EDMUND BOOTH**

1919

A few students were blowing horns about the campus & others were detonating anvils. Jubilation was in the air & I gave the word for an hour of it. They came from everywhere . . . with more shouting & cheering than they ever had in them before.   **ERNEST CARROLL MOORE**

1942

There's no satisfaction like giving satisfaction to one's employer . . . Satisfaction to yourself is fleeting, [in] spite of what the moralists say. And satisfaction to the public does not interest me . . .

Never did I love money more purely.

playwright, screenwriter, novelist **THORNTON WILDER**,
on working with Alfred Hitchcock

1992

Twenty-five years ago I tried to take my first trip to the United States. I went to the consulate and requested a visa. The form I had to fill out asked for, among other things, the following: *Are you planning to assassinate the president of the United States of America?* I was so modest at the time that I wasn't even planning to assassinate the president of Uruguay; but I responded: Yes. I was sure the question was a joke, inspired by my mentors Ambrose Bierce and Mark Twain.

The consulate denied my request. My response was a bad one. I didn't get it. Years have gone by and, if truth be told, I still don't get it. Please excuse me. I'm confusing this convention of North American booksellers with the confessional of my Catholic childhood. But to whom could a writer better confess himself than to a bookseller? . . .

Ah, the fog between Good and Evil. In the American press I see ads exhorting people to buy domestic products, buy American! But then I fail to understand why Japanese products that invade the U.S. market are bad, while U.S. products that invade Latin America are good.

And it's not only the question of products: let's imagine for a moment that Mexican marines invade Los Angeles, in order to protect Mexicans living there who are threatened by recent disturbances. Is this good or bad? . . .

EDUARDO GALEANO

MAY 27

1825

At twelve o'clock in the night, my father heard a great noise. He was sleeping at the time in a house here in the pueblo. He spoke to me—I was sleeping outside—and asked what the dreadful noise was. I responded that I did not know. He then said we should investigate. The river ran about one hundred varas from our house. I went to the bank, and discovered that it was a sea of water which was overflowing vegetable gardens, fences, trees, and whatever was before it. The water was running with great violence, making enormous waves. I warned my father immediately of the terrible danger in which we were. He remained there watching, and sent me without a moment's delay to inform the Commissioner of the pueblo, Sergeant Don Anastacio Carrillo, who was my first cousin . . .

My brothers and some of my father's servants were already running through the town warning the people. There was a moon almost as bright as the light of day. The sky was perfectly clear. Orders were given speedily for all the inhabitants of the town to move to a place of safety on the high land to the east. They did so, everyone loading family and belongings into carretas drawn by oxen which all had in the corrals near their homes, along with their cows and other animals. At daybreak I saw that the water in the old channel of the river was subsiding, and was running toward the other side of the narrow valley—which is where that river has its bed today. The channel changed . . .

Finally, the river emptied into the sea at San Pedro.

rancher, landowner, Californio **JOSÉ DEL CARMEN LUGO**

1861

We visited the old Mission of Carmelo, in the Carmelo Valle . . . It is now a complete ruin, entirely desolate, not a house is now inhabited. The principal buildings were built around a square, enclosing a court. We rode over a broken adobe wall into this court. Hundreds (literally) of squirrels scampered around to their holes in the old walls. We rode through an archway into and through several rooms, then rode into the church. The main entrance was quite fine, the stone doorway finely cut. The doors, of cedar, lay nearby on the ground.

The church is of stone, about 150 feet long on the inside, has two towers, and was built with more architectural taste than any we have seen before. About half of the roof had fallen in, the rest was good. The paintings and inscriptions on the walls were mostly obliterated. Cattle had free access to all parts; the broken font, finely carved in stone, lay in a corner; broken columns were strewn around where the altar was . . .

I dismounted, tied my mule to a broken pillar, climbed over the rubbish to the altar, and passed into the sacristy. There were the remains of an old shrine and niches for images. A dead pig lay beneath the finely carved font for holy water. I went into the next room, which had very thick walls—four and a half feet thick—and a single small window, barred with stout iron bars. Heavy stone steps led from here, through a passage in the thick wall, to the pulpit. As I started to ascend, a very large owl flew out of a nook. Thousands of birds, apparently, lived in nooks of the old deserted walls of the ruins . . .

[The] old garden was now a barley field, but there were many fine pear trees left, now full of young fruit. Roses bloomed luxuriantly in the deserted places, and geraniums flourished as rank weeds. So have passed away former wealth and power even in this new country . . . .

WILLIAM H. BREWER

1864

THREE YEARS LATER

. . . The drought is terrible. In this fertile valley there will not be over a quarter crop, and during the past four days' ride we have seen dead cattle by the hundreds. The hot air trembled over the plain, and occasionally a mirage seemed to promise cool weather ahead, only to vanish as we approached . . .

WILLIAM H. BREWER, *near San Jose*

1960

We want all the leisure that man has given us (in printing, in moviemaking, even in the typewriter, the bicycle, the curtain wall), but we want the machine to stop in the other fellow's case and handicraft-ism to prevail—and places to walk returned to us—hedgerows, the benches in Pershing Square. What serves the age and does the least damage to the spirit?

architecture critic **ESTHER MCCOY**, *to Ray Bradbury*

MAY 28

1851

. . . We arrived at the landing-place at five in the evening, and were taken in a carriage to Sonoma, a little village with four or five hundred inhabitants. The beautiful Sonoma Valley delighted me with its millions of flowers and the fresh healthy air that one breathes there. The land is very fertile, and Señor Vallejo produced in a small garden more than fifteen thousand pesos worth of wine . . .

archaeologist, discoverer of ancient Troy **HEINRICH SCHLIEMANN**

1933

. . . Sam Marx (head of writing department) asked me if I would like to write an original story, and I told him NO. Any original stories I have will go into books, not movies to be worked over by six or seven different writers after I've finished it. In other words, picture writing is nothing more than glorified newspaper work. And I had my fill of that in Atlanta. The only difference is that writers here work forty hours a week, and receive ten and twenty times as much pay. There are no regular hours for writers: just so long as 40 hours a week is got in. Most of them go to the studio about ten in the morning, take an hour or two for lunch and leave around 5:30. However, if one wishes, he can go at night and work, or anytime whatever. The studio is open all the time.

This country is no fit place to live, except for old people. There is no soil, nothing to put your feet on. I don't see how anything can take root here. And I would not be surprised to see the movie business blow up here some day. There is no stability. A magazine like Scribner's has a tradition behind it . . .

novelist **ERSKINE CALDWELL**,

six years before Scribner's magazine's final issue

1942

With lang, on the beach, thought about a hostage film (prompted by heydrich's execution in prague). there were two young people lying close together beside us under a big bath towel, the man on top of the woman at one point, with a child playing alongside. not far away stands a huge iron listening contraption with colossal wings which turns in an arc; a soldier sits behind it on a tractor seat, in shirtsleeves, but in front of one or two little buildings there is a sentry with a gun in full kit. huge petrol tankers glide silently down the asphalt coast road, and you can hear heavy gunfire beyond the bay.   *playwright, screenwriter* **BERTOLT BRECHT**,

developing the film Hangmen Also Die

MAY 29

1943

. . . Do you know Christopher Isherwood or like his work? I visited him last night at his monastery. He is going into one in Hollywood, of all places. It is a miniature copy, architecturally, of the Taj Mahal and when I entered about eight girls and three men, including one Hindu, were seated on cushions in a semi-circle about the fire-place, all with an absolutely expressionless silence . . . Isherwood suggested we go out for a walk. I cannot surmise his real attitude toward "the family"—he is English enough not to speak his mind very frankly—but I am wondering a little if he is not going to write a wonderful story of what is going on there . . .

TENNESSEE WILLIAMS, *to his publisher*

1947

BERKELEY.

Drove alone with Noel to the Golden Gate, we walked to the middle of the Bridge and I scraped off a piece of paint, memento of my Furthest West. Fog, beloved of the inhabitants. Dined in a Basque Restaurant well and cheaply $1.15 each . . .

The fog had cleared, Berkeley, Oakland, Richmond, all brilliant, St. F. fainter, the Gate Bridge winking red from its towers to warn the planes. Unless the atom is controlled all may vanish . . . **E.M. FORSTER**

1957

To ALL I LOVE:

Do not grieve for me. My nerves are all shot and for the last year I have been in agony day and night—except when I sleep with sleeping pills—and any peace I have by day is when I am drugged by pills.

I have had a wonderful life but it is over and my nerves get worse and I am afraid they will have to take me away. So please forgive me, all those I love and may God forgive me too, but I cannot bear the agony and it [is] best for everyone this way.

The future is just old age and illness and pain. Goodbye and thank you for all your love. I must have peace and this is the only way.

Jimmy *director* **JAMES WHALE**, *his suicide note*

2006

What makes this seem secure, whether or not it actually is?

MARK ZUCKERBERG, *in his notebook,*
toying with the release of Facebook beyond Harvard

MAY 30

1984

We have Allan (of Allan and Yoko) staying here as of the last few weeks. He has AIDS, kaposi sarcoma, is rather thin, and stays very tired. He will probably stay here quite a while, either till he gets a remission, or has to go to hospital, or dies. But it is a pleasure being a help to him: he is not self-pitying or pushily stoical—I must say I would like to act like him if I find myself with the condition. (As, after all, I well may.) . . .

I am at last getting round to weeding my yard, which is gorgeous this cloudless and fogless summer, just bursting with flowers and herbs and strawberries. I go regularly to the gym, and my ambition is to look like Popeye (old face on young body): I get a lot of pleasure from it anyway. Also I have come across a very fine Latin primer, and since I didn't really do very well with Catullus last year I have decided to relearn Latin from the start so that I can read the Latin poets with some ease. I learn most of it in the toilet, whenever I go there. Charlie tells me that one day I will sit down and read some Latin in a library and will start shitting from sheer association . . .

THOM GUNN

MAY 31

1889

FRISCO:

Dear Aunt Georgy: As is cold water in thirst so is good news from a far country. I felt very lonesome here in this big raging tearing city till I got your note and then the sky brightened. I read it in the street and on the spot took the cable-car—a contraption of the devil inasmuch as the motive power lies underground—and ran up many steep hills to Mrs. Carr . . .

She lives in a funny little house all of painted wood, (which is the custom in Frisco —and has refined —that is to say, unAmerican—daintiness about her). I am to give you all her love and tell you that America has hardened her and she can now watch a street accident or a shooting affray without emotion! I have up to date only seen a passing Chinaman stabbed in the eye. I was rather disgusted, but the populace did not mind. . . .

Now I must kite round the city and wallow in humanity and eat oysters and strawberry cream . . . I am up at the Bohemian Club for membership where I am likely to meet some amusing folk—have been interviewed by 4 reporters and described to an admiring world as a "handsome but bashful Englishman" . . .

Ever your nephew

Ruddy   *novelist, poet* **RUDYARD KIPLING**

1928

S. Francisco is fine, and life agreeable here. As I say, to everyone, if I leave S.F., I leave America. This is the only place I have found in the U.S. where Life is possible. . . .   *composer* **ERNEST BLOCH**

1938

Here is the diary of a book and it will be interesting to see how it works out. I have tried to keep diaries before but they don't work out because of the necessity to be honest . . . In this however, I shall try simply to keep a record of working days and the amount done in each and the success (as far as I can know it) of the day. Just now the work goes well. It is nearly the first of June. That means I have seven months to do this book and I should like to take them but I imagine five will be the limit. I have never taken long actually to do the writing. I want this one to be leisurely though. That is one of the reasons for the diary.   **JOHN STEINBECK**

1939

The tree outside is sad. It will die, I think.   *novelist* **MALCOLM LOWRY**

1949

The really important thing is not to reject anything—When I think how I wavered about actually coming up to Cal! That I actually considered not accepting this new experience!   **SUSAN SONTAG**

1970

. . . In the afternoon we went with David to Griffith Park, where there was a Gay-in. Only it wasn't very gay or very well attended. The police had been by, earlier, harassing them because they were distributing leaflets without a permit. Nobody got arrested but it scared a lot of people off . . .

Lee introduced to me an elderly man named Morris Kight who was wearing a silk dressing gown and a funny hat and who appeared to be directing the proceedings. He married two pairs of girls, explaining that this wasn't a marriage but a "mateship." We had to join hands and chant something about love. Kight also introduced me publicly and called on me to speak, so I said, in my aw-shucks voice, "I just came here because I'm with you and wanted to show it" . . .   **CHRISTOPHER ISHERWOOD**

JUNE 1

1863

SAN FRANCISCO, CALIF.

LICK HOUSE, S. F.

My Dear Mother & Sister

I rode down with a gentleman to the Ocean House, the other day, to see the sea-horses, and also to listen to the roar of the surf, and watch the ships drifting here, & there, and far away at sea. When I stood on the beach & let the surf wet my feet, I recollected doing the same thing on the shores of the Atlantic—& then I had a proper appreciation of the vastness of this country—for I had traveled from ocean to ocean across it, on land, with the exception of crossing Lake Erie—(and I wish I had gone around it.)

Sam   **MARK TWAIN**

1910

I have been hidden down here in Los Angeles for a month or two and have managed to get off a little book to Houghton Mifflin, which they propose to bring out as soon as possible. It is entitled "My First Summer in the Sierra." I also have another book nearly ready, made up of a lot of animal stories for boys, drawn from my experiences as a boy in Scotland and in the wild oak openings of Wisconsin . . . Next month I mean to bring together a lot of Yosemite material into a hand-book for travelers, which ought to have been written long ago.   **JOHN MUIR**

1939

One of the first sights I saw was four neat pretty high school girls sitting in a row on the cross seat of a city street car. They were a blonde, a Mexican girl, a colored girl and a Japanese girl. That was a very exact picture of Los Angeles. The city ranks second only to Mexico City in Mexican population and next to Harlem in Negro citizenry. There are 65,000 Japanese listed and the Filipinos also are well represented . . .

On a Los Angeles street car the passengers are one big family. This is particularly noticeable on the red cars. The conductor, who often doesn't even bother to wear his uniform, is a blend of official greeter, fare collector and friend. Of course a schedule exists but it is impolite to be too aware of one. Instead it seems that the motorman waits for a fairly full house before starting off. And he knows all his customers. If a passenger oversleeps or drinks a second cup of coffee, you read your morning paper until he arrives. Furthermore the conductor, before starting off, gets out and sights down the street. If a passenger is en route you wait for him and like it . . .

From all this it might be gathered that I don't like L.A. and hold it up, dressed in its jester costume, for popular amusement. Far from it. Los Angeles is in my blood. Of all the cities I have called home in my travels the City of Angels is my favorite. Only my home town has a stronger claim on my heart. The old jest of the gay nineties was that when Americans die they want to go to Paris. While I live I would like to live part of each year in Los Angeles. There I too can be a child, play in the sun, believe God created Paradise in California.   **WILLARD MOTLEY**

JUNE 2

1859

En route from the wharf to the hotel, the city spread out before my eyes like a panorama that was both animated and curious . . . First there was a run down shanty next to the most sumptuous residence; a wooden sidewalk with missing planks through which a passerby might disappear completely; other streets unpaved in many places, which only in the dry season then in effect would not be transformed into a veritable quagmire.

In the mixture of this luxury and decay, the inevitable consequence of the haste with which the city had been built, appear the most disparate and unusual costumes. First come the Americans in hurried rows, just as it suits a people who are at home. The French, English, Irish, Germans and Italians are mixed with the Americans and are distinguished from the latter by type or by language. Then comes a strange mixture of Mexicans, the dispossessed masters of California, proudly draped in their serapes; Chileans covered by their brightly colored ponchos; Chinese men in round bonnets and silk pants and Chinese women strangely dressed; finally Negroes, for the most part dressed in tatters picked up here and there, and who stroll by while singing and dawdling in the streets. Occasionally appears the strange figure of an Indian, newly arrived from the interior only to be swallowed up in the big city. This child of the desert, this descendant of the first owners of the land, stands in singular contrast with all the others by his copper or blackish skin and the ornaments he affects.

geologist, journalist **LOUIS LAURENT SIMONIN**

1860

BLACK POINT

The sea is my life. I have always gotten solid health in sea air & Mr. Frémont has found me here a "house by the sea" that is more beautiful than any Sea Dream that Tennyson or any poet ever fancied . . .

Mr. Frémont can I hope give himself a summer of comparative rest & be here most of the time. Then he will try to write his book. Until now it has been impossible for one head to think more than his has done . . .

When I knew I should never see Father again I turned my whole heart into this house and sometimes I think I magnetized Mr. Frémont into home life. He takes part in & likes all the details of our household—the children's plays & witticisms & lessons—he looks after our comforts, & is in fact head of the house . . .

It's so easy to take care of children when two help. I feel now as if we were a complete & compact family & really Mr. Frémont used to be only a guest— dearly loved & honored but not counted on for worse as well as better.

To him the palms
To us the shade –

Now we share & share and he is far happier for it. As for me you need no telling how satisfied my craving heart is.

You should take new life in here. The soft warm air joined to sea breeze makes it so different from the usual sea side weather. I have the prettiest little house you ever saw—furnished like a picture. I put my own experience into it & this is like Paris for beautiful things at most reasonable prices. The scenery is a combination of every beauty in nature. I am going to send you a photograph of the Point . . . *writer, ghostwriter* **JESSIE BENTON FRÉMONT**

1979

Out into Hollywood Boulevard. There is nothing of the breathtaking beauty of New York about this city. Low, flat, sprawling and laid-back—like a patient on a psychiatrist's couch . . . Two limousines arrive to take us to the Bruin Theatre in Westwood where *Brian* is to be 'sneak previewed'. At the theatre we find a full house and 1,000 people turned away. Meet the Warner's executives who are, understandably, grinning pleasurably.

It's a marvellous showing. Great laughs and applause on a scale we have not yet seen for *Brian*. At the end Eric leads the rush out—and gets into the wrong limousine—whilst Terry and I stand on the sidewalk and talk to one or two of the audience and those waiting—who are not of the tear-your-clothes-off fan type and want to talk quite unsensationally about the movie . . . Later in the evening TJ gets woken in his room by a present from Harry [Nilsson] in the shape of a Los Angeles naughty lady.

writer, actor, broadcaster, Python **MICHAEL PALIN**

JUNE 3

1942

. . . What do they think we are anyway? Oh well, I'm not going to school now. They're sure anxious to keep us dumb just like morons. Golly! All my plans of going to college and all that are all gone. All I could think of now is be a dumb ox and not ever graduate high school.

The food is getting better now (It's about time!) You know what happened? The other day district VI and VII all got diarrhea. 4:00 a.m. . . . Man, it looks as if the whole camp got sick with the food. They ran out of toilet paper too, right in the middle of the night. Boy! . . . Woo P.U.! . . .

SANDIE SAITO

1989

We drove to San Rafel. We were greeted graciously—Jerry Garcia was enthusiastic. After telling a Charles Ives anecdote & explaining Ornette Coleman's "harmonics" to me and talking about Dylan . . . Jerry dove right in playing fantastic stuff on "Transverse City." Between his amazing playing & boundless generosity-he played and recorded almost continuously all afternoon & evening-I finally understood The Grateful Dead's awesome popularity. It was a great time.   **WARREN ZEVON**

JUNE 4

1854

CALAVERAS COUNTY

We greedily devour the home *news,* which is generally from four to six weeks *old,* when we get it, and as for the advertisements, I always read them through from beginning to end; for I can always tell more about the doings in town by them than by half a dozen letters. I tell you, Friend Rock, you folks at home don't half know how to prize an old newspaper . . .

All sorts of improvements have been introduced in mining; the days of the "tin pan and sheath knife," are past and gone; the "cradle" is thrown aside, and the "long tom" is fast yielding to the "sluice." This is the grand leveller; by it banks and whole hillsides are fast disappearing down the gulches, creeks and rivers, and the old cradle "tailings" of '49 are considered among the richest of the auriferous soil. The rivers are dammed and turned, and by hundreds of long miles of canals, flumes and ditches, the water is brought into elevated flats, arroyas, and places where water never was seen except during the heaviest rains. A mountain is no protection at all to a gold deposit. If a big hill is suspected of containing any sort of a justifiable quantity of the "root of all evil," a few shrewd miners put their heads together, and directly immense excavations are made, enormous tunnels are run in and deep shafts are sunk. In all "hill diggings" many make their "piles," but where one makes a fortune fifty get "flat broke," owing to the expense incurred. Many are of the opinion that the mines are on the decline, and will soon be "worked out," and exhausted; but it is a *"quién sabe* case." I think it a moral impossibility to exhaust them, either in your day or mine. New placers are daily discovered, and the old diggings, by means of the all powerful sluice . . . are being washed over again with great profit. The "cream," certainly, has been skimmed off, and a "green one," just into the mines, stands rather of a poor chance even of making a living, unless he hires out . . .

We have been visited with an unusual quantity of thunder storms lately; the "poor Indian" shakes his head and lays it all to the presence of the pale-faced "Americano," who has introduced this extra quantity of thunder among the rest of his improvements.   **ALFRED DOTEN,** *newspaperman*

1926

HOTEL AMBASSADOR

Tell it not in Wardour Street, but I'm beginning to extract a certain sardonic amusement out of Hollywood. It takes itself so seriously, these days. And it's so self-centered that one sometimes wonders, as one sits in the Cocoanut Grove, whether there is such a place as New York, or Chicago, or indeed the United States.

So I've seen little of Los Angeles, which the unkind satirist claims to be so boastful a township that they had to christen the huge U.S. dirigible after it, because that was the only name they could give to the biggest gasbag in the world.   *novelist* **GILBERT FRANKAU**

1945

We drove out with Franklin [Pangborn] into the Valley. Not one house is appealing. The more we looked at the Valley the less we felt like living there. Decided to look only at hills.

actress, director, screenwriter **ALLA NAZIMOVA**

2010

Please ignore prior tweets, as that was someone pretending to be me:) This is actually me.   *businessman* **ELON MUSK**

2015

I'm teaching my daughter that the sun goes down each night because it's mad at her.   *actor* **RYAN REYNOLDS**

JUNE 5

1968

[We] can work together . . . the division, the violence, the disenchantment with our society—the division whether it's between white and black, between the poor and the more affluent or between the age groups in Vietnam . . . we can start to work together. We are a great country and a selfish country and a compassionate country and I intend to make that my basis for running.   *Sen.* **ROBERT FITZGERALD KENNEDY**

1968

The Ambassador, a venerable hotel miles away on Wilshire Boulevard, was the Senator Robert Kennedy headquarters and that was the place to be . . .

It was about eighteen minutes after midnight, a few of us strolled over to the swinging doors that gave on to the pantry. They had no glass peepholes but we'd soon hear the pleasant bustle of him coming through as the waiters and the coloured chef in his high hat and a bus boy or two waited to see him.

There was suddenly a banging repetition of a sound that, I don't know how to describe, not at all like shots, like somebody dropping a rack of trays. Half a dozen of us were startled enough to charge through the door, and it had just happened. It was a narrow lane he had to come through, for there were two long steam tables and somebody had stacked up against them those trellis fences with artificial leaves stuck on them, that they used to fence up the dance band off from the floor.

The only light was the blue light of three fluorescent tubes, slotted in the ceiling. But it was a howling jungle of cries and obscenities and flying limbs and two enormous men, Roosevelt Grier the football player and Rafer Johnson, I guess, the Olympic champion, piling on to a pair of blue jeans. There was a head on the floor, streaming blood, and somebody put a Kennedy boater hat under it and the blood trickled down like chocolate sauce on an iced cake.

There were flashlights by now and the button-eyes image of Ethel Kennedy turned to cinders. She was slapping a young man and he was saying, "Listen lady, I am hurt too" and down on the greasy floor was a huddle of clothes and staring out of it the face of Bobby Kennedy. Like the stone face of a child, lying on a cathedral tomb . . .

A dark woman nearby suddenly bounded to a table and beat it and howled like a wolf, "Stinking country, no no no no" . . .

writer, correspondent **ALISTAIR COOKE**, *in his "Letter to America"*

2018

Juan Romero has spent half a century trying to move on . . .

Romero, who recalled homes in Mexico with photos of the pope and of John F. Kennedy, badly wanted to meet a Kennedy. He told other busboys he'd do anything for them if they let him take a room service call from the candidate.

Romero and a waiter knocked at the door, then pushed two food carts into the room. Several people were present. Kennedy stood at a bay window, finished up a phone call and turned to the visitors.

"I remember staring at him with my mouth open, and I see him shaking the hand of a waiter and then reaching out to me. I remember him grabbing my hand and he gave me a two-handed shake," Romero said.

"He had piercing blue eyes, and he looked right at you. You knew he was looking at you and not through you . . . I remember walking out of that room . . . feeling 10 feet tall, feeling like an American." . . .

"At Seventh and Broadway, I remember sitting there on the bus, still looking at my hands and all the blood, not realizing what happened and hoping my mom would grab me by the leg and say, 'Wake up, you lazy bum.'

"What made me realize it was real was that a lady was sitting in front of me reading the newspaper. . . . I remember the lady showing me the picture and saying, 'This is you, isn't it?' That's when I first saw the picture, and I never wanted to see it again." . . .

Romero said he wanted to apologize to Kennedy and tell him he had tried his best to live a life of tolerance and humility . . .

When I visited him, he said that he had looked closely at the photos he'd tried for so many years to avoid.

"I saw a person in need," he told me, "and another person trying to help him." . . .

columnist **STEVE LOPEZ**

JUNE 6

1889

There is no other place like [San Francisco]. Reckless and roaring like nothing you ever saw. The men make money and "break up" with a rush that goes to your head. Everything is done on a large scale, even the coins are not small, two-bits is the smallest piece worthy the notice of a self-respecting citizen. But next to the ocean winds it is the reporter man that most takes you off your feet. Your soul is not your own, neither your secrets, your plans, your private ambitions, when they grapple you. It is knowing their Bohemian Club that makes you know San Francisco. High jinks and low jinks presided over by the Owl makes this body of men to hum.

RUDYARD KIPLING

1925

. . . One day of the week it rained all day and the Shriners sure did razz the Californians. Most of the natives couldn't understand why it should rain at this time of year, as it is very unusual . . . Others were standing on the policemen's boxes in the middle of the street in their bathing suits with fishing rods . . .

studio secretary **VALERIA BELLETTI**

1945

We were after all discussing the principles of the New World Order. The room was full of professional orators who were ravening to speak and speak again . . .

The representatives of the Colonial Powers were junior delegates (their chiefs were dining) who were frightened that any reference to 'justice' or 'human rights' might conceal a veiled attack on the colonial system. All afternoon and all evening until twelve o'clock at night we argued about the principles that must guide the conduct of men and nations. By eleven o'clock there were many haggard faces around the table. The room had got very hot and smelly—dozens of stout politicians sweating profusely in a confined space—outside the streetcars (and San Francisco is a great place for street-cars) rattled noisily and still the speeches went on. The Egyptian delegate was indefatigable in interpolations. He seemed to bounce to his feet on india-rubber buttocks . . .

[Thanks] to the knout, thanks to the ruthless, surgical operations of the Chairman, we finished our task in time. The committee was littered with punctured egos, and snubbed statesmen glowered at each other across the tables. The eminent political figures and distinguished jurists of half the world had been rated by the Chairman like schoolboys; but we had finished on time.
                                                                    CHARLES RITCHIE

1948

Up here in the breath-taking mountain spring, I can but feel a twinge of sympathy for all you money-grubbing bastards in Hollywood as you struggle against falling box office and recalcitrant studio treasuries. It's much simpler to borrow money and live graciously.
                                          DALTON TRUMBO, *to his attorney*

1967

We're hoping to leave here in about seven or eight days, depending mainly on the temper of our renter (erstwhile), to whom we have given summary notice after I found my whole goddam hill planted with marijuana. I don't give a damn what he does in his private life; what I object to is his practicing agriculture with neither lease nor license . . .

The difficulty is that the renter feels no sense of sin, and is sullen at the shortness of our notice, which in the circumstances couldn't be more than about three weeks. So he may stage a sit-down, and then what do we do? Arrive with the bailiff and set his furniture in the street? Alas. I doubt that we have deserved this, as landlords, but we had better learn to deal with it. I could turn over some carefully preserved evidence to the sheriff, but though if it got that far I might be pleased to see the sucker in jail, I'd have to stay here all summer testifying against him. Aren't you glad you live in a climate too arid to grow pot?   *novelist, environmentalist* **WALLACE STEGNER**,

to Malcolm Cowley

JUNE 7

1927

School. Made fire by friction.

GLENN T. SEABORG, *co-discoverer of plutonium*

1940

Here the term *fifth-column activities* is already so overworked as to be nauseating, and the air is full of spy scares and rumors of armed invasions. This noon we hear over the radio that the veterans of the last war are trying to raise a volunteer army of 100,000 men in Southern California to combat foreigners. It is sickening . . .

The siding is almost up, and the house looks fine and solid, although much yellower than we'd thought. It will darken with time. I hope we're here to see it when it's chocolate black.   **M. F. K. FISHER**

1943

At 12th and Central I came upon a scene that will long live in my memory. Police were swinging clubs and servicemen were fighting with civilians. Wholesale arrests were being made by the officers.

Four boys came out of a pool hall. They were wearing the zoot-suits that have become the symbol of a fighting flag. Police ordered them into arrest cars. One refused. He asked: "Why am I being arrested?" The police officer answered with three swift blows of the night-stick across the boy's head and he went down. As he sprawled, he was kicked in the face. Police had difficulty loading his body into the vehicle because he was one-legged and wore a wooden limb. Maybe the officer didn't know he was attacking a cripple.

At the next corner, a Mexican mother cried out, "Don't take my boy, he did nothing. He's only fifteen years old. Don't take him. "She was struck across the jaw with a night-stick and almost dropped the two and a half year old baby that was clinging in her arms . . .

Rushing back to the east side to make sure that things were quiet here, I came upon a band of servicemen making a systematic tour of East First

Street. They had just come out of a cocktail bar where four men were nursing bruises. Three autos loaded with Los Angeles policemen were on the scene but the soldiers were not molested. Farther down the street the men stopped a streetcar, forcing [the] motorman to open the door and proceeded to inspect the clothing of the male passengers. "We're looking for zoot-suits to burn," they shouted. Again the police did not interfere . . . Half a block away . . . I pleaded with the men of the local police substation to put a stop to these activities. "It is a matter for the military police," they said.

newspaperman **AL WAXMAN**

1944

The Allies have landed in France, and I am in Pasadena, working on Blake for the Viking Portable and writing on Dreiser! I feel sick with shame, useless and in total exile. Walking in the sun-drenched California streets on my way to the Huntington and its tinkle-tinkle "noiseless" typewriters, I confront the nothingness of my life here. The overbearing rich houses every side of me, the solemn little academic specialists each full of his "field" (sometimes called "my area"), the void in which I live. Thinking of tormented Mama and all the ghosts with which I wrestle, I cannot thrill to the Shakespeare Garden and my first taste of avocado. I was accompanied by an armed guard when I went downstairs at the Huntington to study the magnificent original of *Songs of Innocence and Experience*. The guard kept his hand on his holster all the time I was turning the pages in awe.

literary critic **ALFRED KAZIN**

2008

The Barnes & Noble gig is at noon—they want me to be there by 11:30 . . . I get ready and go down to fire up Mule. As always, he starts so quietly the only way I can tell he's running is that the dash lights come on . . .

actor **MIKE FARRELL**,
on his transcontinental book tour via an early hybrid car

JUNE 8

1937

Chan and Edward to Griffith Park . . . and they almost get hoosgowed because you cant photo in the park without a permit . . .   **CHARIS WILSON**

1942

Cast my absentee ballot today for the S. F. special elections. Voted yes on both measures to increase the bond debt for no special reason. The only reason I voted today was to protect my voting privileges for the important elections which will come up in the fall. The man elected at that time will shape the post war policies for the world. A special deputy came in and notarized our ballots. I counted about 630 Nisei voters in the room while I was there. Lily T. said that she was voting just to show the American Legion that we were interested in our franchise even in times like these. Grace S. said that she was voting because this was one way of showing our loyalty and interests in America. Taro W. voted because this was one privilege which he would fight to retain because it was a symbol of his Americanism. James O. cast his ballot because the JACL told him to. He didn't think it was worth anything anymore. Nobu T. thought that voting was one of the few civil rights left to us. The general opinion was that the Nisei should take advantage of his voting privilege in view of the fact that there were forces that want to take this right away from us . . .   **CHARLES KIKUCHI**

1944

I have a sort of Paradise here, as to scenery, but the work involved is almost too much. I live up a steep road, over a mile long, away from the highway. Three times a week the food and mail arrives, and I drag it up with the last ounce of energy in me. Coming down to get it I feel elated. Always think I am in the Andes, the view so magnificent. Often the ocean is hidden by thick layers of clouds or soapy mist or fog. But when I get back I have to go to the forest to look for dead limbs, haul it back, drag it, chop it, saw it, make a wood fire each meal—the chores are endless. I have about two hours for work and then I am not any too fresh. But it's a healthy life and I hope in time to get adjusted. It's just that I'm not used to heavy work, especially hauling and lifting . . .

I was just thinking today, learning of the invasion (which agitated me tremendously, especially for the French! of whom I expect great things, fire, vengeance, blood as never seen before!) how strange it is that it is now, at this great moment, just 30 years ago that you began the Diary—and now we are on the eve of seeing it printed. Thirty years! Could you ever have dreamed how it would end and come to light and at what a moment in history?

HENRY MILLER, *to Anaïs Nin*

1954

LOS ANGELES

One moment of tenderness and a year of nerves and intelligence, one moment of actual fleshly tenderness . . .

As of now I am 28, for the first time older than I dreamed of being. The beard a joke, my character with its childish core a tiring taste . . . I could dismiss the Allen with grim pleasure, yet I am saddled with myself . . .

ALLEN GINSBERG

JUNE 9

1955

I spent a few days in Hollywood (YMCA) on the way down: met Isherwood, who turned out to be one of the very few Men of Letters I have ever genuinely liked: he is a script writer for MGM, and took me round the studios, bringing me within a few feet of Lana Turner, and introducing me to a delightful and gorgeous twin of Pier Angeli, who has a part in a movie he has written and that was being filmed. This was all terribly interesting. Then in the evening Isherwood took me to meet a certain Gerald Heard, who has started a new religion called Vedanta (so far as I can see it consists of the thrills of a pseudo-mystical experience without the inconvenience of being a Buddhist or Christian) . . .   **THOM GUNN**

JUNE 10

1942

Thank you very much for your note. I am all right now, but so far, I've been ill for four days here. It's from the food, but the food is getting better.

Don't work too hard to end the semester! I really feel like a dope for not going to school. I miss it, believe it or not.

Sa-yo-nara is written: [Japanese characters]. Don't forget it now! Please write again.   **TOMOKO IKEDA**, *to a schoolfriend*

1969

Bonny Doon is a backwater of verdant hills and tall trees, almost inaccessible even with a stout car and a road map. For example, last night a skunk fell into our swimming pool and drowned—and I had to bury it . . . a small procession of me, carrying the deceased on a shovel, and clinging to it a live frog, and followed by one of our cats, deeply interested but bemused—a scene out of Three Men in a Boat. This, in Bonny Doon, is equivalent to a riot on-campus elsewhere . . .   *novelist* **ROBERT A. HEINLEIN**

1970

SOLEDAD PRISON

Dear Greg,

I went to Paso Robles. The very first time, it was like dying. Just to exist at all in the cage calls for some heavy psychic readjustments . . . It is the thing I've been running from all my life. When it caught up to me in 1957 I was fifteen years old and not very well equipped to deal with sudden changes. The Youth Authority joints are places that demand complete capitulation; one must cease to resist altogether or else . . .

In my early prison years . . . I read Jack London's "raw and naked, wild and free" military novels and dreamed of smashing my enemies entirely, overwhelming, vanquishing, crushing them completely, sinking my fangs into the hunter's neck and never, never letting go . . .

[A] brother came into the time tank to serve two days. The morning he was scheduled to leave I went back to his cell with a couple of sheets and asked him if he would aid me in an escape attempt. He dismissed me with one of those looks and a wave of the hand. I started tearing the sheet in strips, he watched. When I was finished he asked me, "What are you doin' with that sheet?" I replied, "I'm tearing it into these strips." "Why you doin' that?" "I'm making a rope." "What-chew gonna do with ah rope?" "Oh —I'm going to tie you up with it" . . .

I went out in his place . . .   *writer, inmate* **GEORGE JACKSON**

JUNE 11

1889

[SAN FRANCISCO] PALACE HOTEL:

[Please] look over a copy of the verses I sent to the Bohemian Club when they made me an honorary member. The totem of the club, which you will find throughout its rooms, is an owl. The piece runs:

> Men said, but here I know they lied,
> The owl was of a sullen clan
> Whose voice upon the lone hillside
> Forboded ill to mouse and man —
> A terror noiseless in the flight,
> A hooknosed hoodlum of the night.
>
> But I have found another breed,
> An owl of fine artistic feelings,
> A connoisseur of wine and weed
> Who flutters under frescoed ceilings
> Nor scorns to bid the passing guest
> Abide a season in his nest . . .
>
> A wanderer from East to West
> A vagrant under many skies,
> How shall a roving rhymster best
> Requite O owl thy courtesies?
> Accept in lieu of laboured stippling
> A simple "Thank you"
> signed,
> R. Kipling.

The Club is going to have it hung up and illuminated.   **RUDYARD KIPLING**

1939

. . . Rather horrible night with a picked up acquaintance Doug whose amorous advance made me sick at the stomach—Purity!—Oh God—It is dangerous to have ideals.   **TENNESSEE WILLIAMS**

1944

FRESNO, CALIF.

HAMMER FLD.

JAMES L. DICKEY T-180270 450TH AAFBU SQ T-1

Dear Folks,

I suppose you will be surprised to hear me say something good about the army for a change, but I am leading the best life I ever have (away from home, at least) and getting paid almost $300 a month for it. All we do is fly every night and go to a few lectures and classes, and the rest of the time is off. I just got back from San Francisco, where I stayed for a week. I was not able to get a train ticket, or I would have come home. As it is I don't think I'll be back for a while. When I was in San Francisco I was the guest of a girl (and what a girl) I met on the train coming out here. I'll tell you, Mom, they treated me like a king. They have a tremendous country estate, a swimming pool, and everything that I have always thought of very rich people having . . .

They wouldn't let me spend a cent of my own; all I had to do was casually drop a hint about "over seas" and they couldn't do enough for the "poor boy." Gwen and I went to Chinatown, the zoo, the aquarium, night clubs, bars, millions of places, all of them wonderful. I had on my night fighter flying jacket most of the time (with appropriate insignia, a buzzard sitting on a new moon with "radar" shooting out of his eyes and a cannon under his wing) and one kid even asked me for my autograph! Here, at last is one who can take Peg's place. Gwen and I are in love, Mom.

And its the real thing this time. Don't worry about us marrying, though. She wants to finish two more years at Bryn Mawr and I have the war to fight. I am in no danger at all. Flying at night is not dangerous, and I have fool-proof instruments that do all my thinking for me. I am flying all kinds of planes now. I may go into P-70's, P-61's, P-38's Bearfighters, Mosquitos or even the new jet job. Mostly we are flying P-70's and P-61's.

My love to all,

Jim   JAMES DICKEY

1969

. . . Hey! I have never criticized any Architects about their attitude toward California, ever. But I *do* criticize Eastern literary critics who, for the most part, neglected Chandler and Hammett when they were alive, and are now neglecting Macdonald.

As for myself, time and again, when I bump into New Yorkers they say, 'How can you *live* there in L.A.?! How can you *Create*? BULLSHIT!' . . .

My own director and producer of *Illustrated Man*, New Yorkers both, have never BEEN to Disneyland. Pure snobbism.

RAY BRADBURY, *to Esther McCoy*

JUNE 12

1770

I issued an invitation to all . . . to participate in the celebration of the first mass . . . Two processions from different directions converged . . . one from the Sea, and one from the land expedition . . . then we all made our way to a gigantic cross . . . After raising aloft the standard of the king of heaven, we unfurled the flag of our Catholic Monarch likewise . . . All the time the bells were ringing, and our rifles were being fired, and from the boat came the thunder of the big guns. Then we buried at the foot of the cross a dead sailor, a calker . . .

Father JUNÍPERO SERRA

1953

We had a wonderful first day, if that monster got what we pointed it at.

actor JOHN WAYNE, *to Jack Warner,*
after calling it a day on his first 3-D picture

1954

Pershing Sq.: Suddenly in the middle of downtown black ant traffic & little buildings, the little banana grove on the corner of Hill. There is this big block park on model of Mex town—except it has green flat rectangle of grass with benches all around in the sun—hardly any shape—and an outer perimeter for walking without benches, but you can sit on concrete steps—all the old types, something different from Bryant Park, because they all look respectable & there's no one young, all look clean & model with low palms all around & plantain leaves with bursts of tropic artichoke. Energy sprouting up on the sides—and a few high palms too.

ALLEN GINSBERG

JUNE 13

1936

A brief walk to the Pacific Ocean will sharpen the dullest writer's grammar and improve the finest stylist's rhetoric . . . anyone is privileged to appear in its presence without having to pay admission . . . It is there, the Pacific, and a brisk walk each morning to it is one of the things a good writer must perform . . .

There are several other rules, but they are boring. The most important rule, according to everybody, is to run like hell after the money. It helps to prolong the manufacture of automobiles . . .

The slickest rule of all, however, is: Don't write. I will gladly teach anyone the fundamentals of not writing. There is no cost, no obligation. You don't even have to clip a coupon. All you have to do is think it over carefully.

playwright, novelist **WILLIAM SAROYAN**

1946

2058 WATSONIA TERRACE

HOLLYWOOD

. . . Lunch in the patio is always quiet and pretty. This blessed minute— Monday morning, 17 June, 1946, at exactly five minutes after twelve noon, George is sunbathing on his terrace and he was doing the same thing yesterday and the day before and almost every day I have been here. As for me, I have lolled in perfect ease and accumulated new forces in what would be called here, in just ordinary conversation, mind you, my "psychic reservoir" whatever the hell that is. I feel enormously better, it has been a most charming visit, and I am having a hard time making up my mind to quit this lovely safe bed (seventeenth century Spanish with a high, wide and inordinately fancy painted headboard, all over flowers, red laquer and gilt . . . I love it.) and go home and Face Things again . . . But this time I can take it easier, which was what I couldn't do two weeks ago . . . It has all been lovely . . .

We have embarked upon an illicit lia—I find I can't spell it, but you-know-what. Well, Bernardine came to see us in our new love-nest and asked us what we had been doing and we said, "Playing records" and she asked "What, already?" or something of the sort, and beamed upon us gruesomely . . .

KATHERINE ANNE PORTER

JUNE 14

1882

Altogether this strange chasm in the mighty mass of granite mountains is really quite a large little world. Heads of department—legal, military, and medical, from various British colonies— stray members of foreign embassies, Oxford and Cambridge men on vacation tours, ecclesiastical authorities of all denominations, mighty hunters, actors, artists, farmers, miners, men who have lived through California's stormy days, when derringers and revolvers were the lawgivers,—these are but a sample of the mixed multitude who meet here with one object in common, and who, one and all, confess that their expectations are surpassed.

I know of no other "sight"—save the Taj Mahal—which so invariably exceeds the fancy-pictures of its pilgrims.

The worst of it is, that the majority of "*bonâfide* travellers," ignorant of the country, arrive here, having made their irrevocable plans, by the advice of coach-agents, on certain cut-and-dry calculations of time, which generally assume that three days in the valley is ample allowance. So they spend their three days rushing from point to point, missing half the finest scenes, and then resume their dust-coats, and rattle away again, with a general impression of fuss and exhaustion.

A most aggravating instance of such miscalculation was that of two English gentlemen who arrived a few days later, being bound to catch a particular steamer at San Francisco, discovered, on reaching the valley, that they had exactly two hours to remain in it, and must start by the afternoon coach. Like true Britons, they devoted their short visit to a refreshing bathe in the ice-cold waters of the Merced, followed by a hasty luncheon, and then bade a regretful farewell to the scenes they would so fain have explored at leisure.

travel writer **CONSTANCE FREDERICA GORDON-CUMMING,**

at Yosemite

1936

I had no more chance of changing Hollywood or stabbing one decent idea into its head than I have of moving these mountains around me by whistling to them to come to heel!

Now I sit in a shack, eight feet by eight, in the middle of an alfalfa field, and am completely happy and never think of films all day long. In our wide valley the mountains reach up, always changing in the light, on three sides. I cut hay and build a house. I irrigate land and make a living alone.

Let me tell you about my place. At night the oil lamp burns and the great Pullman trains go swinging past with people in them looking out. I always used to sit in trains and see a light in a shack and wonder who the person was. And now I know . . .

My dog learns quickly. She was a house dog. Now in a flash she becomes a country dog . . .

Now I am an honest man again. When I get a house built, alone, without help, my penance is over for the months I took money and did nothing in Hollywood . . .

Irrigation, water! Life here is water! Coming from four hundred miles away. Coming in concrete pipes. Flowing down ditches . . . Water company scout-cars roaring round the valley, spying, reporting unlucky people who have allowed water to get away from them . . .

I regain sanity through a simple thing. I like the land. Why not be on it? These Swedes and Mexicans are good people. I like them and get along with them . . .

I shall become a sane individual again out in this valley. I almost begin to think what a picture it would make . . .   **ERIC KNIGHT**, *to a friend*

1939
. . . I had the experience Sat. night which confused and upset me and left me with a feeling of spiritual nausea.   **TENNESSEE WILLIAMS**

1942
This afternoon we went up to the grandstands to look at the visitors. There were not so many people today. The Negroes are coming down here in increasing numbers. Peter Ray, a well known dancer who used to perform with Duke Ellington's band, came to see Mornii and the other jive boys, and he drew a great crowd by his dancing exhibition. He is now at the Town Club. The jitterbug craze is still strong with the young kids and for them nothing else exists. Most of them are from S. F. Last night at the dance they were all dressed up in their draped pants and bright shirts. These boys are really extrovert and many of them speak the special jitterbug language with the facial expressions which they copy from the Negroes. They are not too popular with the majority of the Nisei girls who are more conservative . . .

Walt Gordon, Jr.. the well known Negro football player at Cal, was also here today visiting Bobby O. and Joan N. Melvin Stewart introduced me to him. Melvin is also a Negro. He is now working in the Post Office, but plans to go into social work. He graduated from State with me and then worked as a redcap with the Santa Fe railroad for a couple of years before getting his present Civil Service job. When he saw all the Negroes around he said, "You know who are your real friends now. A lot of us are behind any movements that will fight this thing because we have had to face a lot ourselves and so are opposed to anything so un-American. The trouble with the Negroes is that we have been so involved in our problems that we didn't see the danger of this war hysteria against the Japanese soon enough. It's so impersonal with us, but when we actually see you people in camp, we go out mad as anything and want to do something about this great injustice because we know you Nisei are just as loyal as we are. The color of the skin is no indication of loyalty-we can testify to that."   **CHARLES KIKUCHI**

JUNE 15

1846

SONOMA

To all persons, citizens of Sonoma, requesting them to remain at peace, and to follow their rightful occupations without fear of molestation.

The Commander in Chief of the Troops assembled at the Fortress of Sonoma gives his inviolable pledge to all persons in California not found under arms that they shall not be disturbed in their persons, their property or social relations one to another by men under his command . . .

He further declares that he believes that a Government to be prosperous and happyfying [sic] in its tendency must originate with its people who are friendly to its existence. That its Citizens are its Guardians, its officers are its Servants, and its Glory their reward.   *President* **WILLIAM B. IDE**,

in an open letter proclaiming the Bear Flag Republic

1937

. . . I have to unfortunately report to you that at the Stendahl Gallery No. 445, the panel painting "Whitish" was cut from the frame with a razor blade; luckily I had a photograph which I had copied in order to send it to all art journals and newspapers, so that if it appears in the trade everyone knows about it. But of course I hope that the police, whom I will inform tomorrow, will find it first so as to use the opportunity to do a little publicity: that Kandinsky's pictures are so valuable that someone would steal them. The same thing happened to Klee and I got the picture back . . .

art dealer **GALKA SCHEYER**, *to Wassily Kandinsky*

1945

Last week I saw an advertisement in one of the San Francisco newspapers which described the attractions of 'a historic old ranch home now transformed into a luxury hotel situated in a beautiful valley in easy reach of San Francisco'. What a delightful escape, I thought, from the pressures of the Conference! ...

Last Saturday we all set forth by car in a holiday spirit to savour the delights of old-style ranch life in California as advertised to include 'gourmet meals, horseback riding and music in an exclusive atmosphere.' It seemed an eminently suitable setting for this little group of overworked and fastidious *conferenciers* ...

Once in the entrance hall we found ourselves in the midst of an animated crowd, but what was unexpected was that all the men were sailors and young sailors at that, while the women were equally young and some strikingly luscious. This throng, exchanging jokes, playful slaps on bottoms and swigs out of beer cans, filtered off from time to time in pairs to mount the noble staircase leading to the rooms above. Our diplomatic quintet stood together waiting for guidance among the jostling throng and were soon the objects of remarks. 'Who the hell are those old guys?' Finally, seeing that no one was coming to our rescue we set off up the stairs, luggage in hand to inspect our rooms. Mounting floor by floor we found all the bedrooms in a state of active and noisy occupation ...

Norman seemingly not in the least disconcerted sank with a sigh into the only available chair and addressed himself to the evening paper. The other members of our party were less philosophical. Hume and Jean appearing in the doorway rounded sharply on me. 'Why had I lured them into this brothel? Was this my idea of a joke?' ...

The night was an uneasy one for me. I was kept restlessly awake by the beery hoots of laughter and the moans and murmurs of passion from the next room. Norman settled into his bed and slept peaceably with his deaf ear uppermost ...

By mutual agreement for which no words were needed our party left the ranch before luncheon and returned to San Francisco. On the way back in the car the French Ambassador raised the possibility that one of the assiduous gossip writers of the San Francisco press might learn where we had spent the week-end and he asked what effect this would be likely to have on the prestige of our respective delegations and indeed on our own reputations. My own colleagues reassured him by saying that in the event of publicity the episode could be attributed to my misleading them owing to my innate folly and vicious proclivities. This seemed to satisfy him.

CHARLES RITCHIE

JUNE 16

1942

I'm fascinated. Our work is very good. It's not literature. But the wrestling with sheer craft, the calculations in a mosaic of exposition [are] bracing.

THORNTON WILDER, *on working with Alfred Hitchcock*

1963

Summer is a-coming in and I am off to the mountains, first Giant Forest and then a donkey trip with my daughters from Tuolumne Meadows

KENNETH REXROTH

1982

The next day, Sunday, I visited [Rexroth] after saying Mass in a local church. He looked good and was anticipating another hour in the sun, or watching another hummingbird play before him (as he had done on Sat.). Evidently his heart began to show signs of fluttering in the later p.m. An e.k.g. machine was ordered for an electrocardiogram. About 7:00 P.M. it arrived. He was hooked-up to it. Between 7:15–7:30 he began to experience a massive heart attack. Craig, the male nurse, attempted to revive him by pounding on his chest. Nothing happened. However, the electrocardiogram machine kept on registering peculiar signs, and eventually blew a fuse of sorts. To say the least, from these events Kenneth himself would have written a most interesting chapter of his autobiographical novel . . .

He probably would say that the damn machine couldn't handle this spiritual overflow. All in keeping with the Rexroth way of life and death . . .

FR. ALBERTO HUERTA, SJ

JUNE 17

1579

BEE IT KNOWN VNTO ALL MEN BY THESE PRESENTS IVNE 17 1579
BY THE GRACE OF GOD AND IN THE NAME OF HERR MAIESTY
QVEEN ELIZABETH OF ENGLAND AND HERR SVCCESSORS FOR-
EVER I TAKE POSSESSION OF THIS KINGDOME WHOSE KING AND
PEOPLE FREELY RESIGNE THEIR RIGHT AND TITLE IN THE WHOLE
LAND VNTO HERR MAIESTIES KEEPEING NOW NAMED BY ME AN
TO BEE KNOWNE VNTO ALL MEN AS NOVA ALBION.

SIR FRANCIS DRAKE

privateer, slave trader, global circumnavigator

1907

SAN FRANCISCO REDIVIVUS!

"Come, Let Us Consider." regarding our beloved city.
DEAR SIR AND MADAM:
. . . Many tremendous things have happened in our beloved city of San
Francisco during the last twelve-month. In spite of everything, her promise is greater than ever before. Who that beholds the wonderful sight
of those splendid buildings arising with such rapidity as if an Aladdin
were directing some Genie-of-the-lamp to do his bidding, can fail to be
bewildered? . . .

We want to go back to the old days and hear the much pleasanter voices
of the hackmen and runners for the hotels, who used to call merrily, "What
Cheer?" till we all smiled as we came in . . . We want it made known to all
the world that San Francisco is in fact a place of security and protection for
the homes, the women and the children.

pioneer, writer **ELLA STERLING CUMMINS,**

in an "An Open letter to all San Franciscans and Californians"

1979

On my last night in LA I dined with Joan Didion and her husband John
Gregory Dunne at their house in Pacific Palisades. His-and-hers twin Toyo-
tas stood nose to nose in the driveway. Mexican food was served. Both writers unashamedly thrive in Los Angeles. Dunne's excellent long article about
California ["Eureka"] in *New West* for January 1, 1979 is an unbroken paean,
while even Didion's famously mordant title essay in *Slouching Towards Bethlehem* is written more from fascination than from fear.

Both writers make their money from writing movies and use the money to buy time in which to write their books—a system pioneered by William Faulkner. Both writers know in advance that scripting the remake of *A Star is Born* for Barbara Streisand must inevitably entail a certain literary contribution by Ms Streisand herself. They know exactly what the difference is between compromise and capitulation. If two people so intelligent can live in Los Angeles on their own terms, then the place has become civilised in spite of itself. I enjoyed their company very much and did my best not to let them know that I had swallowed a habanero. They probably thought my muffled sobs were due to homesickness.

At midnight Hector and Alphonse fetched me away up through the hills to Mulholland Drive. From a look-out high on the ridge I could see all the way down the coast to Balboa and inland to the Sierra Madre. Turning around, I could see the whole of the San Fernando Valley. It was all one sea of light. This is where the first space voyagers will come from. When our children leave the Earth and sail away into relative time, they will have the confidence of naivety. They will have forgotten what it is like not to get anything you want just by reaching out. In a way the Angelenos have already quit America.   **CLIVE JAMES**

1993
FRESNO

. . . Do keep your wagon wheels greased and ready to roll. In the meantime, TNB [Take No Bribes].   *poet* **WILMA ELIZABETH MCDANIEL**

JUNE 18

1894
I feel so glad I put on my terracotta robe and a 'coiffure.' Reporter from the Call seeks to interview me on the [below] theme, in vain.
CHARLOTTE PERKINS GILMAN, *on hearing that
her ex-husband had married her friend*

1966
Ballantine and Random are pushing me toward some kind of non-fiction book on the Right Wing. I've been resisting it for several months, but now that the nutcracker has started to close I'm getting more interested. I'm

beginning to think that there might be a good book in the Right Wing vis-à-vis the fate of California. It is really a microcosm of American history. The destruction of California is a logical climax to the Westward Movement. The redwoods, the freeways, the dope laws, race riots, water pollution, smog, the FSM, and now Governor Reagan—the whole thing is as logical as mathematics. California is the end, in every way, of Lincoln's idea that America was "the last best hope of man." Here is where the sins of the fathers and forefathers are being visited on the sons, who in turn visit them on the land and each other. For 100 years the bunglers and rapists had an escape valve; they could always move west, to something new. But now they have come to the end, and they have to live with whatever they can make of it. The story has all the elements of a tragic parable. California is the ultimate flower of the American Dream, a nightmare of failed possibilities . . . .

Books are too slow. Only old men should write them. But since I already have a contract for another non-fiction book I think it should be on the most pertinent subject I can find. Right now the above paragraph strikes me as a possibility, both for a book and an article—and possibly a grant of some kind. If you have any ideas along these lines, send word.

Thanks,   HUNTER S. THOMPSON, *to Carey McWilliams*

JUNE 19

1849

IMPERIAL COUNTY

Cariso Creek was reached at last by the advance guard, and after satisfying their thirst they filled up their canteens and hastened back to assist the others, a small cup of water to each sufferer with the assurance of plenty more near at hand, was welcome news indeed. Hunger is dreadful, but extreme thirst is fearful. On reaching the creek my thirst was so great that I drank six pint cups of water, one after the other, before I could stop, then I had to lay down—nearly fainted away—but in an hour or so began to feel hungry, put our last beans to cooking and two of my messmates went back some eight miles to where one of our pack mules gave out and returned with some mule meat . . .

At Cariso Creek we found on our arrival an original character, a real, down east Yankee. He had been there several days when we arrived, trying to recruit his two broken down horses. He appeared in good spirits, taking it easy. He had some two pounds of mule's liver left in the provision line, and that was tainted; he said he managed to get along, and had been feasting on rawhide soup for several days. I asked him where he got the rawhide. "Oh," says he, "plenty of horses and mules have died in this vicinity and the dry atmosphere preserves the hides while the rest of the carcass disappears. I take the hides so found and they make very good soup by boiling them well," or to use his own words, "the gol darned soup would be very good if I had plenty of seasoning to put in." *pioneer* **HARVEY WOOD**

1856

MY DEAR ANGIE No doubt you will feel very anxious about me, when you read of the state of things existing here. We look upon tomorrow as big with the fate of this unfortunate city. I cannot be frightened but many can neither eat, nor sleep, they say the law and order people will plunder and burn the city, and there is no knowing what will become of the women, and children, I assure you it looks very like war, to go through our streets in the evening and see thousands [of] bayonets glimmering in the moonlight . . .

We are to have an opening party next week if we do not all get killed. I have got me a white muslin and Emily wears her lemon silk. You may think I speak rather slightly but you can get familiar with any thing . . .

Mother **MARY JANE MEGQUIER**,
boarding house owner, to her daughter

1964

Alan Swallow came to Los Angeles for the Publishing Conference . . . He was the only panelist who did not talk about money. He talked about the writers he had loved and published because he had loved them . . .

We gathered afterwards for an evening of talk to which he had invited the writers he publishes . . . how I dislike the snobbish attitude of the East about a "little publisher out West" . . . **ANAÏS NIN**

JUNE 20

1928

I was in Avalon when Dr. G. said it might be necessary to have an operation performed upon Dolly. That struck terror to my soul. But I could not believe it would have to be. Nevertheless it did have to be. I knew it ten days ago. When I saw Dolly, I was reassured because she seemed well and strong and confident. She went to the Good Samaritan Hospital in L.A. on June 18. I left her there . . .

She was bright, cheerful, cool, game as a thoroughbred. Pride overcame my fears for a little. Then I saw her moved down the hall and into the elevator to go to the ward upstairs to take ether. She said, "I'm all right." Somehow I got over that first hour, or through it. When the second began, the minutes dragged. I paced the gloomy hall. My mind whirled, yet outwardly I appeared calm. But I could not sit or stand still . . . When Dr. G. came down, it was about time to save me from collapse. He reported that the operation had been imperatively necessary and that it had been successful.

Something caved in in me, but I could thank God . . .

ZANE GREY

1978

Muzzletoff! Happy New Year (Rosh Hashannah). And yesterday our favorite, Isaac Singer, wins the Nobel Prize. What a wonderful succession of events.

HENRY MILLER, *to a friend*

1980

Id love more news of Chelsea Victoria—what a marvelous name! How did you come by it? Was she conceived in Victoria Station . . . ?

Best regards, Decca   JESSICA MITFORD, *to Hillary Rodham Clinton*

JUNE 21

1938

SISKIYOU COUNTY TO YOSEMITE

Wakened at 5:30—dragged weary bones out, dressed, closed baggage, was ready shortly before six, and we were off again "on the dot"—at six o'clock. So out of Klamath, the lake's end, and a thread of silver river in the desert—and immediately the desert, sage brush, and bare, naked hills, great-molded, craterous, cuprous, glaciated, blasted—a demonic heath with reaches of great pine, and volcanic glaciation, cuprous, fiendish, desert, blasted—the ruins of old settlers' homesteads, ghost towns and the bleak little facades of long forgotten post-offices lit luridly by blazing morning sun . . . and then Mount Shasta omnipresent— Mount Shasta all the time—always Mt. Shasta—and at last the town named Weed (with a divine felicity)—and breakfast at Weed at 7:45—and the morning bus from Portland and the tired people tumbling out and in for breakfast.

. . . and over an enormous viaduct across a flat and marshy land and herons flying and then the far-flung filling stations, hot dog stores, 3 little pigs, and Bar-B-Q's of a California town and then across the Sacramento into town—the town immediate and houses now and mighty palms and trees and people walking and the state house with its gold-leaf dome and spaghetti at the first Greek's that we found . . . .

. . . a sense of the imminent terrific and at length the valley of the Yosemite, roads forking darkly, but the perfect size—and now a smell of smoke and of gigantic tentings and enormous trees and gigantic cliff walls, night black all around and above the sky-bowl of starred night and Curry's Lodge and smoky gaiety and wonder—hundreds of young faces and voices—the offices, buildings, stores, the dance floor crowded with its weary hundreds, and the hundreds of tents and cabins and the discovery of the life and the immensity of all and 1200 little shopgirls and stenogs and maids and school-teachers and boys—all, God bless their little lives, necking, dancing, kissing, feeling, and embracing in the giant darkness of the giant redwood trees all laying and getting laid tonight—and the sound of the dark gigantic fall of water— so to bed!

novelist **THOMAS WOLFE**

1942

Lots of visitors as usual. Many of them probably came out of curiosity to look at us and the camp. Makes one feel like being either in a zoo or a prison. The person who owns the property across the highway in front of the main gate has opened up a very profitable enterprise. He has a 15 cent parking lot!

CHARLES KIKUCHI

1966

Thank you for the reviews of [Richard Fariña's] book. It doesn't look as if hardly any of them even read what they were reviewing, the bastards. God. I know it's a lousy racket, the pay's bad, there aren't enough other reviewers on the staff usually, too many books being published to begin with, not to mention deadlines. But is that still any excuse for not reading? letting your head get so brutalized by all the media that you forget, imperceptibly, how to read at all?

. . . Got the Modern Library dust jacket. Pretty sharp, that Art Nouveau typeface—- it fits. Colors, even in rough, look good. When does it come out?

THOMAS PYNCHON

JUNE 22

1938

KERN

Woke at 7:00 after sound sleep—water falling—girls' voices, etc.—Breakfast and good one at cafeteria—after that visited waterfalls, took photographs, talked to people, visited swell hotel, sent postcards, etc., and then on way out—by the South Wawona entrance—then beautiful rockrim drive down through wooded Sierras to foothills the brilliant leafage of scrub pine—then the hay—bright gold of wooded hogbacks—then the hay-gold plain and hay-gold heat—a crowded country road—and Clovis—lunch there—then the ride up to the mountains again—the same approach as the day before—by haygold hogbacks—then cuprous masses—then forested peaks—then marvelous and precipitous ride upward and the great view back across the vast tangle of the Sierras.

Then General Grant [National Park] and the great trees—the pretty little girls—then the 30 mile drive along the ridge to the Sequoia [National Park]— and General Sherman [Tree]—and the giant trees —then straight through to other entrance, then down terrifically the terrific winding road—the tortured view of the eleven ranges—the vertebrae of the Sierras—then the lowlands and sheer hogback—no bends and Visalia—then by dark straight down the valley—to Bakersfield—then East and desertwards across the Te-hachapi range—the vertical brightness of enormous cement plants—and now at 1:30 in Mohave at desert edge—and tomorrow across the desert at 8:00 o'clock—and so to bed—and about 365 miles today.

At Bakersfield:

Enormous electric sign—Frosted Milkshakes—a Drive Inn—And Girls in white sailor pantys serving drinks—I drank Frosted Lime . . .

THOMAS WOLFE

1941

HOLLOW HILLS FARM, MONTEREY, CALIFORNIA

Dear Carlo,

We had a very pleasant visit yesterday from Henry Miller at luncheon. He drove up from Hollywood . . . Henry is going to see the Jeffers today. He says he is tired of his trip and thinking of giving it up and living out here in California which he likes a great deal . . . .

Tuesday I am going up to San Francisco to see CABIN IN THE SKY and CITIZEN CANE [sic] . . . I'm glad I'm a lyric poet. It might be interesting to search for new rhymes for moon and June as the old ones have been worn out . . .

I hear the lunch bell, so,

Sincerely, Langston   **LANGSTON HUGHES**, *to Carl Van Vechten*

1946

We landed at the airport of Los Angeles, breathing fresh air after the stifling atmosphere over the desert.

I felt happy. I believe, in every sensitive person born in the Northern climate, there lives a longing for the South where the human race originated. The prospect of living among palm trees like Robinson Crusoe in our children's books, among flowers which were in blossom all year around, in an even climate, just as near to the sea as to the mountains whose outlines reminded me of Greece—seemed fabulous.

One could browse among old books in bookshops of the street around the corner, some open late in the evening. A few blocks further I came to Pershing Square, shaded by palm trees, where every seat was taken on the long benches which criss-crossed it. In the center reformers and fanatics made speeches just as in Hyde Park and were surrounded by people who had a good time joking about what they heard . . .

A part of the Spanish population still lived in the museum area. Since they take life easier, these people are being slowly driven out by hard-working Americans. In the afternoons and on holidays one could see them lying on the green lawns in front of the museum, enjoying the sunshine, in light dresses. They formed a considerable proportion of the visitors to the museum and were never in a hurry, for which reason art probably penetrated deeper into their minds than into that of the casual American visitor, who does not give the seed of his impressions time to grow . . .

curator **WILLIAM R. VALENTINER**

JUNE 23

1938

Up at 7 o'clock in hotel at Mohave—and already the room hot and stuffy and the wind that had promised a desert storm the night before was still and the sun already hot and mucoid on the incredibly dirty and besplattered window panes and a moment's look of hot, tarred roof and a dirty ventilator in the restaurant below and [no] moving life but the freight cars of the S.P. r.r.—and a slow freight clicking past and weariness so up and shaved and dressed and snapped the zipper and downstairs and the white-cream Ford awaiting and the two others in the back—and to the cafe for breakfast—eggs and pancakes, sausages, most hearty—and a company of r.r. men—So out of town at 8:10 and headed straight into the desert-and so straight across the Mohave at high speed for four hours to Barstow—so in full flight now the desert yet more desert-blazing heat—102 inside the filling station—the dejected old man and his wife—and so the desert mountains, crateric, lavic and volcanic . . . and Needles at last in blazing heat and the pleasant station and hotel and Fred Harvey all aircooled, and a good luncheon . . .

THOMAS WOLFE

1968

INCARCERATION BEGINS, JUNE 23, 1967—"D" DAY.

. . . I guess in our situation "D" should stand for defeat. Except it's all been such a trip—Bus, Pranksters, Faye, kids, everybody in that courtroom doing the courtroom zonk blah blah blah then suddenly very fast and efficient we're standing up and the judge is finished and (and here it gets weird) moving out of that same old stiff agonizing courtroom posture (here we start to come out of the zonk) walking through the double doors only this time everybody is turning left toward the elevator except Page and me (here we begin to believe it) hustled away from our people too fast for attempted farewells (yep, now we believe it) upstairs prints photos clothes "B Tank, boys." Ka-slash! Door slides open. Ka-slam! shut . . .   *novelist, jailbird* KEN KESEY

JUNE 24

1847

For a Californian to ride 100 miles a day is quite common, nor does it appear to require any extraordinary effort. 100 miles a day are as frequently driven by them as fifty by the people in the United States, in truth with them it is but an ordinary day's ride, but which is generally performed by two or three horses. Their great exploits with the lasso in catching wild horses and cattle are astonishing . . .

They will, when on full gallop stop and pick up a lasso from the ground, or even a piece of money, without either halting or dismounting. They never walk even the shortest distance. They are never on foot, only when entering a house, at which time they will take a lasso, made of hair, one end of which is fastened to the neck of the horse and the other end held by them . . .

I saw a game played by these Spaniards. I saw a cock (or as the Yankees say, a rooster) was buried in the sand save his head only. The Spaniards rode by in turns on a full gallop, trying at the same time to pick up the cock, several being successful and none falling from the horse. These horses are much better trained for the saddle than ours. They endure fatigue much more than the American horses. **HENRY STANDAGE**

1940

The radio is off its top, even crazier than back east. One whirl of the dial and you want to jump out the window. All day every day they sell GOD here, and I mean sell him, along with used car, soap and dainties for milady. Also Swing mixed with news of Disaster in Europe on the scale that you know. So I can't listen to the radio. I'm invited to the home of Mrs. William Wyler to a swimming party. Sounds ducky, isn't it? I'm going, mainly because Wyler is a nice intelligent sort of man and I'll play a little pool. But his house is full of refugees, most of whom, God help me, I hate. That is, most of them in Hollywood. . . .

I must find some way to live that does not involve this Paradise. I hope I will. I have some new ideas; we'll see. Be careful of money. For lack of it can ruin your life. Cagney, who is a millionaire, at least, says in an answer to every implied criticism of Hollywood in the industry;—"There's always Wednesday!" *director, novelist* **ELIA KAZAN**

1976

NAPA

Yesterday Mike and Arlene saw two hours of rushes [from *Apocalypse Now*], and when they called to ask us if we would like anything from the city, Arlene said she thought the acting was kind of tentative. Francis went into a tailspin. He felt totally defeated. He has spent $7 million, and months of grueling production, and they didn't say, "Hey, you've got some fantastic stuff there." He really got into a black depression. As I see it, Francis has ninety hours of film, and no chunk can give you an idea of what fifteen minutes' worth of moments he is going to select from it. What you finally see on the screen does not give the slightest clue of what was left out. For someone to just look at an arbitrary piece is meaningless. Francis felt hopeless and scared. We slept outside on the lawn. It was a beautiful night, so clear with stars. Francis tossed and turned most of the night, having nightmares. We woke up at dawn; there was a crescent of new moon rising near the horizon in the pinkish light. Francis said he had had a dream about how to finish the script, but now that he was awake it wasn't really any good. Francis talked to Brando on the phone yesterday.   **ELEANOR COPPOLA**

JUNE 25

1869

Mr. Editor . . . To know the greatness of our state one must travel its length and breadth, visit its mountains and valleys, hills and plains. California embraces all climates; it has regions of perpetual summer, and Sierras where eternal winter reigns; fields ever bright with perennial green, and forests always glowing in Autumnal beauty . . .

I think I have seen no prettier place in California for a home than Oroville. It is a mining town, but surrounded by land fit for agriculture, which argues well for the continued prosperity of the place . . .

There are very few colored people living here. They all speak in terms of highest praise of Rev. Mr. Bates' the Methodist Minister, who is without prejudice regarding color. God has some true and good men left on this earth, and when we see one taking public opinion, throwing it on one side, when it comes in contact with duty it keeps our faith in humanity. The local paper is what I call an itemized journal, having two columns of small items in each week's issue, the collecting of which must employ the brain of one man. I suppose it is a good paper, and answers the people for an advertizing medium . . .   **JENNIE CARTER**

1931

I planted an acre of potatoes and, as none of them has come up, I am inclined to think that they were planted upside down and are probably making their way slowly to the Antipodes . . .   **EDGAR RICE BURROUGHS**

JUNE 26

1888

It is whispered that San Francisco is already growing jealous of this Southern city, and as for San Diego—that it goes off into a convulsive fit at the mere mention of the name. These are rumors, however, that I do not altogether credit, and merely give them for what they are worth. I know that Marion and I are quite happy to be back here again; that we greeted the mountains, and the orange groves, and the vineyards, and the brisk, busy streets with a smile of true affection, and we confided to each other in the midst of our twelve bundles, that there was no place like Los Angeles. **HARRIET HARPER**

1930

If you asked me, I would say I loved Hollywood. Then I would reflect and have to admit that Hollywood is the most loathsome place on the map but that, never going near it, I enjoy being out here.

My days follow each other in a regular procession. I get up, swim, breakfast, work till two, swim again, work till seven, swim for the third time, then dinner and the day is over. When I get a summons from the studio, I motor over there, stay there a couple of hours and come back. Add incessant sunshine, and it's really rather jolly. It is only occasionally that one feels as if one were serving a term on Devil's Island . . .

It's odd how soon one comes to look on every minute as wasted that is given to earning one's salary . . .   **P. G. WODEHOUSE**

1945

The Charter of the United Nations which you have just signed is a solid structure upon which we can build a better world. History will honor you for it. Between the victory in Europe and the final victory, in this most destructive of all wars, you have won a victory against war itself . . . With this Charter the world can begin to look forward to the time when all worthy human beings may be permitted to live decently as free people . . .

If we fail to use it, we shall betray all those who have died so that we might meet here in freedom and safety to create it. If we seek to use it selfishly—for the advantage of any one nation or any small group of nations—we shall be equally guilty of that betrayal.   *President* **HARRY TRUMAN**

1945

I congratulated President Truman at the end of his speech, while the audience accorded him standing applause and he made a gesture of appreciation, opening his arms wide toward the audience . . .

I then said: I hereby declare the United Nations Conference on International Organization adjourned . . . —with a single heavy rap of the gavel . . .

The band played the Star Spangled Banner, and then it seemed as if school was over and everybody was going home for vacation. . . .

Secretary of State **EDWARD R. STETTINIUS**

JUNE 27

1921

Well—the building stands. Your home.

It is yours for what it has cost you. It is mine for what it has cost me.

And it is for all mankind according to all its cost in all its bearings.

Can we not pronounce benediction upon it, now, absolving the building at least from rancor and false witness?

Whatever its birth pangs it will take its place as your contribution and mine to the vexed life of our time. What future it will have?—who can say?

Faithfully yours,

maimed as it is –   **FRANK LLOYD WRIGHT**,

to client Aline Barnsdall

1973

. . . the *Tonight Show* is an all-American institution. At one go, Python will be seen by the few aficionados in New York and San Francisco, and also by the Mormons in Salt Lake City, the tobacco farmers of Louisiana and the potato growers of Idaho . . . To make things more nerve-wracking, it was to be recorded as a live show, with no stops or retakes, for the tape had to be ready an hour or so after recording to the various parts of the States for transmission the next evening.

A great air of unreality. Here was Python going out to its greatest audience ever, and to us it was no more than a hastily organized cabaret. We were totally unknown to the audience, and felt like new boys at school. At 6.00 the recording started. This week Joey Bishop, one of F Sinatra and D Martin's buddies, was hosting the show as regular host Johnny Carson was on holiday. Bishop was on good form, fluent and funny. When it came to our spot he produced our two latest LPs and tried, quite amusingly, to explain the crossed-out Beethoven cover. All good publicity . . . **MICHAEL PALIN**

1991

OJAI, THATCHER ROAD

. . . I've been coming to this house for twenty-seven years I came here as a teenager with Dan. I took my first mescaline and LSD in this house. I came here after my car accident to heal. I came here when my mother died. I came here for my fortieth birthday, for my honeymoon night with Lloyd . . .

This place hasn't changed much for the twenty-seven years that I've been coming . . . This morning I walked through the groves. So many of the avocado groves were devasted by the freeze this year. Entire old orchards are dead. Some of the larger trees are sprouting new leaves again. Tonight will be full moon and I'll walk to the Japanese gardens next door. The estate is owned by some millionaire couple who come up on holidays only. Hollywood money, I'm told. On New Year's Eve Lloyd and Shanta and I went to see the full moon reflected in the carp pond and Shanta fell in. It was very cold and we did not want to have to [go] in that murky water to pull her out. She finally galumphed her way out. Wet puppy. I think she was admiring the reflection of the moon when she fell in. I made a drawing of just that.

LOUISE STEINMAN

2012

On the bus, rumbling toward LA . . . The thing is, lately, when I tour with Steely Dan, the venues also seem to be shrinking. Of course, I'm being disingenuous. Mike, Boz and I are pretty old now and so is most of our audience. Tonight, though, the crowd looked so geriatric I was tempted to start calling out bingo numbers . . . *Steely Dan co-founder, essayist* **DONALD FAGEN**

JUNE 28

1941

We met the Border Patrol and they didn't like me, because I hadn't had my last extension confirmed (whereas of course Ben [Britten] has). So we had to empty all our suitcases and find papers etc and I had to go to the police station and answer endless questions, and then had to call on someone else in San Bernardino, and so on. But they were all amiable and I just have to let them know when I get my confirmation . . .   *tenor* **PETER PEARS**

1993

First day of jury duty. I had heard they were calling panels for the Menendez brothers' trial, but I didn't necessarily believe it because I thought that case had been settled a long time ago. Even I knew that Lyle and Erik Menendez were the Beverly Hills teenagers who had shotgunned their parents to death in their home because they were greedy for their inheritance. When Erik Menendez walked into the courtroom, my blood went cold . . .

juror **HAZEL THORNTON**

JUNE 29

1937

Bought a paper on the way out to Santa Monica. the bodies have been found. Bodies being those of three Inglewood girls, ages 7,8, and 9, missing a couple of days. The police with some clews are now searching out what the paper describes as a "Mexican-looking, maniac degenerate".

Near Ventura, Cole driving about 42, a cop waves us to the road side. Asks to see Cole's license and looks piercingly at me. Edward produces his press card. Cop says "Who's that in the back seat?" Edward: she's a member of our party.—another overhaul from the cop's gimlet eyes. "O.K." says he. And explains he's "working on this Inglewood thing" and couldn't get a good look at me as we drove by. Of course I was dressed in my usual faded blue shirt and pants, but the real trouble was I had just lit up my pipe for the first time in months, and he saw it clamped in my jaw as we went by . . .

CHARIS WILSON

1940

My own belief is that pictures needn't hurt a writer, but that they probably will. If he could merely work for them they would teach him a lot, particularly about concision and the necessity for building a story before trying to sell it. But he rarely stops there. Having as a rule little critical sense, he begins to believe in them, talk of the screen as a "great medium," and so on, and that sinks him. Pictures are entertainment if they entertain you, but to allow them any validity beyond that one night is to be silly . . . .

[It] isn't so much that he can't give up the pool, and the three servants, and the genuflections at Ciro's, as that after being paid such sums his own work no longer excites him. With luck, his novel may pay him $10,000, $25,000 if he sells it to pictures. But it will take him six months, perhaps a year, to write, and what are such buttons to a shot who could make $50,000 in the same space of time, working for pictures? His own work ceases to seem real.

And they become silly. They drink, they collect first editions, they believe the reviews about "sparkling dialogue," they become incorporated institutions, managed by agents. For myself, I'm a lucky case. I work for them now and then, rather cynically, I am afraid, and not any too successfully, though they pay me fairly well when they do send for me. The rest of the time I manage to make a living without them, and I hope retain my own ideas of what my work should be like. Also, my taste is to live simply, and see the few friends that I care about, and call that a life. But: if a writer becomes convinced that he has no important talent, and enjoys working for pictures, why not? Nunnally Johnson puts himself in that category. For him, I confess, I have complete respect . . . .   *novelist, essayist* **JAMES M. CAIN,**
to Edmund Wilson

1968

Dear Ms. Kael,

My children (adult) read Pauline Kael too. So when Roxie . . . brought in the letter with your name on it they were consumed with curiosity. Did I really know you? What in God's name would you be writing to me about? I hope you won't mind that I confessed to them that this was a romance that had been going on for some years now. You usually wrote me, I explained, in care of a cigar store mail drop in Burbank, and why you should have been so rash as to write me at home was completely beyond my understanding. I asked them not to tell their mother, who would either break into tears or laughter, I couldn't guess which. It's not often that an aging father finds an opportunity to bring a ray of sinful sunshine into his children's lives.

screenwriter **NUNNALLY JOHNSON,**

acknowledging a letter from Kael

1987

. . . [Yesterday's] marvellous gay parade . . . really is the best day of the year—everybody is so nice to each other—even I realize that I am a look-snob and am very nice to the uglies, as the beauties are to me! Also, I like the way the lesbians are at last standing up for themselves in great numbers, and now almost half the audience & marchers are dykes. They are so sweet really: my awkwardness around them makes me realize how they must feel around me . . .

Every now and again I have Sensational Safe Sex. (Not often enough.) . . . I think by the end of this year I'll have a new book completed. Round the end of '88 maybe I'll xerox it up in about 10 copies & send you one. It will be called The Man with Night Sweats, as I probably told you. I am just finishing a poem about an otter's genitals. (Really.)

My sick friends are exemplary. There do seem an awful lot of them to visit, and some of them are so weak you can't stay long—but they are on the whole so brave, so cheerful, so courteous—almost as if they are afraid of making you feel bad. I'm sure I'd bitch all the time—disagreeable old woman that I am. The most difficult one to deal with is my dear feisty Charlie—my love of 2 years ago—he is blind in one eye now and the other eye is going. I don't know how he can stand it. He is 30. Still, we (I think I speak for San Francisco) have got out of our state of shock (I think) and are trying to be practical in helping people. Of course, none of us can be confident that we won't get it ourselves, but there's no point in dwelling on our fear. 'If it be now, 'tis not to come,' etc . . .

It has been wonderfully overcast lately I can see the hummingbirds giving blowjobs (actually they are catheterizing them) to the fuchsias from my windows. My yard has been so good this year & I have done very little work on it: the rewards of age, they call it. You wither up, the young laugh at you, you write nonsense, you dabble in your shit & require a nurse to clean your piss off the furniture, you live in a shroud of your own mucous, but AT LEAST YOU HAVE A GOOD GARDEN. In that case you will have the richest old age of all.   **THOM GUNN**

JUNE 30

1930

CARMEL

Dear Mother,

I had a jolly time yesterday, tramping up and down the beach. Then I sat in a throne-like place on a rock that was out in the ocean. I didn't leave until a huge breaker came and splashed over me.

In the afternoon I hiked around the town until now I know it pretty well. I walked a mile or so to the San Carlos Mission and the Carmel River. When I got back in town I went to Edward Weston's studio and made friends with him. A man who gave me a ride near Morro Bay had told me about him. I saw a large number of his photographs. He is a very broad-minded man.

Love from Everett

I slept among the pines last night. Write to General Delivery, Carmel.

EVERETT RUESS

1938

And now the sun is shining and the birds, 50 different kinds, are singing in the trees outside my window, and the woods are green and beautiful. It is a good day in which to finish the first book . . .

There is more noise in the house than out here, even with the washing machine going. So I'll stay out [on the porch deck] and work through it if I can. It isn't very long after all. My head aches today I don't know why. But I'll finish and I hope I'll have the new part ready by tomorrow. It would be good to have a few days off. I think I'll take them. Carol is right. Why should I rush? October and November and December will be enough to get finished. Maybe I'll take the time off. I'll see. It would be good for me. And now to finish Book One. It occurs to me that I'll finish Book Two by the end of July and then two months for Book Three. And now Book One is done. And I am going to take Friday, Saturday, Sunday, and Monday off. I feel a little daring doing this but I think it will be better if I do. I'm getting a tenseness and a weariness. I must get fresh. This will be the last until the 5th.

JOHN STEINBECK

1942

I am working on various shifts of the 4th Interceptor Command and find it is very important work and keeps me on my toes. I don't suppose the censor will let me tell you all about it but it is connected with aeroplane work and wonderfully carried out. They treat us well too, give us a meal and transportation. I am quite proud of the work and am glad I am strong enough to do the work . . .

Bless you sweetheart—I wish I could answer a letter from you! Love from your Mother.   *defense worker* **RUTH WOLFFE MERRITT**

1990

I do my food review every month for California, and my book review for Mademoiselle, and a pretty flabby job of trying to keep this journal up to date. I take notes and dick around with possible scenes for a novel, but I don't feel like writing much else. Certainly not a long sustained piece of fiction. I can't really remember how you do it. But I just remembered the other day a weekend I spent with my family at our cabin in Bolinas when I was seven or eight and my older brother was nine or ten. He had this huge report on birds due in school and hadn't even started it, but he had tons of bird books around and binder paper and everything. He was just too overwhelmed, though. And I remember my dad sitting down with him at the dining table and putting his hands sternly on my brother's shoulders and saying quietly, patiently, "Bird by bird, buddy; just take it bird by bird." That is maybe the best writing advice I have ever heard.   *essayist, novelist* **ANNE LAMOTT**

JULY 1

1927

I start the new month with a new love! I am not surprised. F. and I were forecast to have this experience—at least once.

She came to be photographed again. From the last time I have one extraordinary negative. She bent over forward until her body was flat against her legs. I made a back view of her swelling buttocks which tapered to the ankles like an inverted vase, her arms forming handles at the base. Of course it is a thing I can never show to a mixed crowd. I would be considered indecent. How sad when my only thought was the exquisite form. But most persons will only see an ass! . . .

We drove to Pasadena. We drank. We kissed. She was an artist with those lips . . .   EDWARD WESTON

1955

Just to give you the terrible news that —as far as anybody knows—since he left no note & his body was not found—Weldon [Kees] threw himself off the Golden Gate Bridge last week . . .

Isn't it awful, this world we live in?   KENNETH REXROTH

JULY 2

1895

SAN FRANCISCO, JULY 2.

One thing—a surprisingly pleasant one I have nearly forgotten. Wednesday morning I stepped into the elevator. "Good morning, sir," said the man with a heartiness that struck me, so I returned him the same. As we went down he suddenly burst out: "Well, sure I'd like to live as you do, sir, and look so smiling and happy every morning. It's a pleasure to see your face." This embarrassed me so completely that all I could say was to exclaim as he reached the bottom, "Is that true? Why that's delightful."

Curiously enough, only the evening before at dinner Frank had been quoting Stevenson's lines about, "If I have faltered more or less in my great task of happiness," and we had all admired their beauty and their ethics. Well, I do not always feel happy; I do hope I generally seem so; and certainly in San Francisco the cup was full this time.   *novelist* **OWEN WISTER**

1927

One reason I'm keeping this diary, as Mother insists on calling it, is because I *have* grown, in so many ways besides inches and vocabulary. I'd like to see if I have the mentality to write what I *want* to write—what I think. I doubt it. Damn it—what's my idea in forever playing to an invisible audience? Or not an audience so much as an observer? Sometimes, in those rare moments of companionship that flicker between people I meet and me, I almost say what I want to, and then as I say the words in my mind, something utterly different comes out of my mouth and is twisted into a meaning I don't recognize—hate—sneer at. Well, I shall see—maybe—and this book will be amusing, even if it doesn't say what it's supposed to—maybe. **M. F. K. FISHER**

1969

[Outfielder Steve Hovley] was standing by the clubhouse man's tobacco shelf opening up a can of snuff. (Just wanted to try it, he said later.) Joe Schultz walked by wearing nothing but a towel around his waist and hollered out, "Hey, men, look who's dipping into the snuff." Then he grabbed a paperback book out of Hovley's pocket. It was Dostoyevsky's *The Possessed*. Schultz held the book up in the air and said, "Hey, men, look at this! What the shit kind of name is this?"

By this time there was a group of guys around him looking at the book like a group of monkeys might inspect a bright red rubber ball. Schultz read off the back cover—a sentence anyway—until he got to the word "nihilism." "Hey, Hy," Schultz said to Hy Zimmerman, "what the hell does 'nihilism' mean?"

"That's when you don't believe in nothing," Zimmerman said. Whereupon Schultz, shaking his head and laughing, flung the book back at Hovley, hitched up his towel and strode amid much laughter.

If Hovley weren't 9 for 20 (.450) since he was called up I'd figure him to be back in Rochester in a matter of days.

Afterward Hovley said that this was, of course, anti-intellectualism at work, but that he didn't mind since he counted himself as anti-intellectual too—that is, if by "intellectual" we meant the academic community. Academic people bore him, Hovley said, and that while he wouldn't choose to spend all his free time with Joe Schultz, he rather enjoyed the company of players. **JIM BOUTON**

JULY 3

1769

July 3, 1769. Hail Jesus, Mary, Joseph! Reverend Father Professor and President Fray Francisco Palou. My very dear friend . . .

Thanks be to God, I arrived here the day before yesterday, July 1st, at this Port of San Diego. It is beautiful to behold, and does not belie its reputation. Here I met all who had set up before me whether by sea or by land; but not the dead. Here I am with my companions Father Crespi, Vizcaino . . . and all in good health, thank God. Here also are the two boats. The San Carlos is minus its crew, as all the sailors died of scurvy. *Father* **JUNÍPERO SERRA**

1872

Dear Diary,

Yesterday, I received a letter from one of my canvas customers—a tailor from Reno, Nevada by the name of Jacob Davis. It was very poorly spelled, but I still could read it. Here it is:

"The secratt of them Pents is the Rivits that I put in those Pockets and I found the demand so Large that I cannot make them up fast enough. My nabors are getting jealouse of my Sucess and unless I secure it by the Patent Papers (which I cannot aford the fee) it will soon become a general thing. Everybode will make them up and thare will be no money in it. Therefore Gentlemen, I wish to make you a Proposition that you should take out the Latters Patent in my name as I am the inventor of it."

What do you think, Diary? I think Jacob is a genius! Now, when rushers stuff that heavy and damaging ore into their pockets, they won't break! I must find time to write a letter back to him. Of course, I will agree. Adieu!

manufacturer **LEVI STRAUSS**

JULY 4

1847

Independence. This day was celebrated by the troops at Pueblo de Los Angeles . . . A short address by Col. Stevenson and the name of Fort Moore given to the fort at Ciudad de Los Angeles . . . An offer made to the Spaniards to have the Declaration &c. read in their own language, if desired; not read . . .

HENRY STANDAGE

1868

SAN FRANCISCO

The patriotism of this city is great, if "star spangled banners" are any evidence of love of country . . . after reflecting upon the subject, I have come to the conclusion that there is very little patriotism in California, and that all this display is a farce . . .

O! for a Lincoln at the head of this nation, and a Starr King in this city . . . An Anglo Saxon editor of this city, told me a year ago, in our home at Mud Hill, that he was fearful our people had not the energy to elevate themselves. Is it true? Are we quietly submitting to insult and neglect, deprived of rights of place and position, without raising a note of indignation?

JENNIE CARTER

1933

So at last I landed in Hollywood! Rodriguez met me at the station—he looks exactly like Zangara the would-be assassin of Roosevelt. He is native of Guatemala, and one can even discover some sing-song element in his dashing English. He was with his wife (second, I suspect, for in the course of conversation he mentioned his 11-year-old son). His wife had a dog in her arms. They drove me to this hotel which is situated on the Hollywood Boulevard, corner of Highland St.. Half-a-mile up Highland St. is the Hollywood Bowl. I walked up after Rodriguez went and came upon this imitation-antique amphitheatre. The moon and Jupiter shone down on this auditorium around which so many petty passions raged. . . .

He is very brilliant, very self-assertive and, it seems to me, without nerves. I am seeing him tomorrow morning—we'll rearrange the programs—he is enthusiastic over the fanfare idea, he is writing the program notes, and I am delighted with this . . .

My room is fine, but it has a superfluous bed. Three dollars a day, no weekly rate. Rodriguez said to the manager that the Hollywood Bowl Association will take care of the bill. I don't bank on it, however. . . .

musician, encyclopedist **NICHOLAS SLONIMSKY,**

on José Rodríguez

1976

Dear Noel Young:

Although I have managed to write something like thirty-two books, I'm still unable to do an outline about what I intend to write. Things take on different shapes and meanings as they develop, and for me there is no telling what changes might take place . . . I want to ring in the long dead figures of the life-long prisoners in the cells of Alcatraz. I spent much time there during the Indian occupation of the island and even have a photograph of myself locked in one of the cells. (I'll try to find it to send you.)

I want to write as well of the Chinese immigrants who were held prisoner by the thousands on Angel Island (which I've written a little about). The collapsing buildings are still there on Angel Island, and I visit them from time to time with Chinese-American friends and students of mine, and we seek to read (and are trying to preserve) the poetry which was scratched through the years on the stone of the now crumbling walls . . .

The experiences of individual women prisoners whom I served time with in Santa Rita will (I believe) be the framework, the main structure, within which the Alcatraz, Angel Island, and also Japanese internment camp imprisonment, stories will be interwoven. I think this is the way it will be, but again I cannot foresee what may take place. As a total thing, I see it as if entirely surrounded by walls, and through the barred windows of these various places the people of whom I write (including myself) will catch glimpses every now and then of the America outside.

Sincerely **KAY BOYLE,** *on day of the Bicentennial*

JULY 5

1867

Mr. Editor:— I have been a reader of your excellent paper for some time, and thank you for your efforts on behalf of our people . . . [If you] think my scribbling any account, I will write for you. **JENNIE CARTER**

1872

TUOLUMNE COUNTY

Dear Diary,

I have written a letter in return to Davis. The two of us will meet up here in San Francisco, and then file the patent as quick as a thunderbolt comes down from the sky. I am so privileged to file the patent with him, but I have to admit, that tailor does not know how smart he is. Once we start producing these enhanced trousers, they will sell like hotcakes on a bitingly cold winter day. And more money means more to donate to charity!

LEVI STRAUSS

1938

Yesterday was the Fourth of July. Today, here we are. This probably adds up to something or other, but I'm not quite sure what; isn't very important, however you look at it. . . .

[Two] of our more important hotels are in a veritable fever of anticipation over the arrival here this month of our great and good President, Mr. Franklin D. Roosevelt.

These befuddled hostelries are the Palace and the Mark Hopkins. The Palace has a presidential suite ($35 per day). It's the only presidential suite west of Chicago. The Mark has no presidential suite, but has Manager George Smith, a member of the State Democratic Committee. This fact is supposed to be important, politics being what they are these days.

Neither hotel has received any reservations yet, but both are watchfully waiting for them, both filled with near-optimism, both a little worried that they'll miss out on a great publicity and prestige bet . . .

On clear days, when Treasure Island is plainly discernible from the mainland, we look somewhat dolefully at the palm trees which have magically arisen on its surface. We don't like to believe that this is a concession to the Easterner's idea of California, an idea planted and nurtured by the Chamber of Commerce of Southern California. Come, all ye fogs!

HERB CAEN, *in his first daily column*

JULY 6

1871

YOSEMITE

Dear Emerson,

I remember that some of your party remarked the silence of our woods & the absence of birds. Well, ere you were half way down the hill a gush of the richest forest song that ever tingled human soul came in grand confidence from the whole grove choir of trees, birds, & flies. When you went away I walked to the top of the ridge commanding a view of the arterial grooves of the Fresnoe, to calm, & when I returned to the grove near Samoset I was welcomed by five or six birds. The magnificent pileated woodpecker eighteen inches in length came right up to me & turned round & round as if anxious that I should know all his gestures & notes & observe the color & polish of every feather. A little brown specky titmouse was building a house near the ground beneath a flake of Sequoia bark & she allowed me to remain within five feet of her building without ceasing her work only pausing an instant now & then to look at me . . .

In a few days I start for the high Sierra East of Yosemite & I would willingly walk all the way to your Concord if so I could have you for a companion— the indians & hot plains would be nothing[.] In particular I want to study a certain pinetree at different elevations, & the lavas of Mono . . .

Since I cannot have yourself I want your photograph

Ever Yours   JOHN MUIR

1941

The ocean bathing (I'm afraid this must make your mouths water, poor dears) is lovely, with surfing, but the latter isn't nearly as good as Cornwall was . . .

I'd give anything for a good Kipper! The Pacific is full of battleships & what-not, & the air is full of aeroplanes—San Diego, the big naval base, is near here—& one sees as many uniforms about almost as in England. I know it (this apparent American indifference) must seem infuriating to you all, but Roosevelt is being very smart. You see this is such an enormous country, & takes such a long time to move—Europe seems so far off from the Middle-West or West—Roosevelt is just moving a little ahead of public opinion all the time, & that is gradually swinging round to realisation that something's got to be done . . .

I expect you get as sick of News-commentators as we do. Now, we hardly ever listen to the wireless—one always seems to hear what news there may be sooner or later, & it's no use going all of a flap every five minutes with hysterical news revues . . .   *composer* **BENJAMIN BRITTEN**

JULY 7

1898

In the afternoon we attended the "literary exercises" in a crowded hall. These consisted of a plentiful supply of bad music, choruses, solos and orchestral overtures, all alike being refrains and varieties of the Star Spangled Banner: a welcoming speech from the Irish mayor and an oration from an Irish orator, a glowing tribute to the "Liberty, Independence and Free Institutions" of America. The celebration concluded with a recitation of the Declaration of Independence by some well-known elocutionist. The note of the whole thing was the unique character of American Institutions—the "only Democracy of the World"—the Americans being the chosen people who had, by their own greatness of soul, discovered freedom, and who were now to carry it to other races (notably to the Cubans). The Declaration of Independence was received with deafening applause as if this declaration had been made yesterday and sealed by the blood of the present generation. . . .

The Mayor [James D. Phelan] is a decent little fellow: one of the wealthiest of San Francisco's citizens, an Irishman by extraction whose father was fortunate enough to speculate in the right acre of ground and to have his title approved of by the courts. The great Phelan is a dapper little person; ambitious and public-spirited, but without any special distinction of body or soul . . .   *social reformer* **BEATRICE WEBB**

1902

. . . Signed a petition or protest against putting "mezcla" (cement?) on the edge of the sidewalk in place of the wood that is there now. It is too expensive and there is no need for such expense at the present time . . .

DON JUAN BAUTISTA BANDINI

1918

After more or less delay, I decided to go out to my uncle's dairy for the summer, and there I am now—and have been for almost a week. Something tells me I shan't read or write much this summer, although I did compose one arsenic poem on the milk route. My day's schedule runs something as follows: 3:30 A.M. get up; 4:00 A.M., milk; 5:00 A.M., bottle milk; 6:00 A.M., deliver milk; 8:00 A.M., eat breakfast; 8:30 A.M., wash bottles; 10:00 A.M., clean milking shed; 10:30 A.M., clean cow yard; 12:00, eat dinner; 12:00 to 3:00 P.M., do miscellaneous jobs and sleep; 3:00 P.M., milk; 4:30, bottle milk; 5:15, deliver milk; 7:30, eat supper; 8:30, go to bed. Now I know why Burns was a poor farmer. The only way I can keep from becoming utterly bovine is to recite poetry and compose arsenic while I am working. I am getting some great material for the latter. I am also collecting material for a sonnet-sequence on hog raising . . . **poet YVOR WINTERS**

1934

Please, dear kid, believe what I say about how much I like you. If you want me to say it over and over and more and more, just act like you don't believe it in the next letter you write me . . .

Two tons of love to you,

Write soon,

Wish I could kiss you! Do you?

LANGSTON HUGHES, *to modern dancer Sylvia Chen*

2018

On April 15, 1991, my family came to the United States as refugees from the Soviet Union, which was then teetering on the verge of collapse. I was eight going on nine, and after my initial excitement (candy bars! supermarkets!) wore off, I was struck by panic. The prospect of learning English from scratch paralyzed me. We settled in what was—and still is—the de facto Russian neighborhood of Los Angeles, and I was enrolled in a public school that was struggling to accommodate a growing population of displaced Soviet children. The first months were difficult, to say the least, but with the help of my dedicated if somewhat bewildered teachers, I made a go of it. My third grade teacher wisely paired each new student with a classroom buddy: another émigré who had arrived a bit earlier and could serve as a translator. It was the half-blind leading the blind, but the system worked. And my classroom buddy, Igor, is one of my very best friends to this day.

I could say a lot more about my experience, but the topic of this post is a book, a very funny book, to which I returned last week, on a whim. I first discovered it two decades ago, in a rusty rotating rack at the back of my tenth grade English classroom. The book is titled *The Education of H*Y*M*A*N K*A*P*L*A*N* (1937), and it recounts the linguistic misadventures of the titular hero, a hopeless but indomitable student of English

. . . Kaplan's creator, Leonard Q. Ross, knew his subject inside out. Ross's real name was Leo Rosten (1908–1997), and he himself was an immigrant from the former Russian Empire, who grew up speaking both Yiddish and English. He is also the author of another of my favorite books, *The Joys of Yiddish* (1968).

I feel close both to the wonderfully accomplished Rosten and to the brilliantly bumbling Kaplan. They remind me that my own immigrant childhood is a gift, not a hindrance—and that my adopted country can, when it tries, become a warm and welcoming home to those huddled masses yearning for a better life. Just some thoughts that occurred to me on the 4th of July, and that I'm posting on my birthday, as I mark my 27th year in America.

writer, editor, translator **BORIS DRALYUK**

JULY 8

1845

MONTEREY

[California] is fast coming into notice. It must in time join the Origon as an independent Nation or belong to Eng. or U.S. . . . the new Settlers at the Origon are runing down C. while I am runing it up. They publish in Am. papers, we have no timber, no rain, have to send to the O. even for flour . . . I should like to have you shake off your apathy and idleness, come forth into the field, and write for the Country you intend to live. You are a good writer, know well the country, its people and recources, whether it will grow hemp, Cotten, wheat or corn, what fruit wild or cultivated, know the soil, climate, rivers and Bays . . .

. . . bring forward the country in its best light, write [everything] you know respecting English agents or Consul or her subjects, all you know respecting they or the [Hudson's Bay Company] agents, trading, smuggling in C., aiding revolution, acting for or counteracting the supreme or local Gov't in any way . . .

Do not let the new Settlers in [Oregon] cry down [California]. Awake, slumber not forever . . .

THOMAS O. LARKIN, *American consul,*
exhorting editorial writer John Marsh to puff California

1940

We have moved into a rather magnificent roomy house in a hilly landscape strikingly similar to Tuscany. I have what I wanted—the light; the always refreshing dry warmth; the spaciousness compared with Princeton; the holm oak, eucalyptus, cedar, and palm vegetation; the walks by the ocean which we can reach by car in a few minutes. There are some good friends here, first of all the Walters and Franks, besides our two eldest children, and life might be enjoyable were it not that our spirits are too oppressed for pleasure—and for work also, as I discovered after some initial attempts.   **THOMAS MANN**

1946

I garden, irrigate, prune from 9 to 10:30 a.m., all of which must heal my wounds . . . Finally, my poor feet have calmed down . . .

GABRIELA MISTRAL

1974

"California dreaming is becoming a reality," is a line from a Mamas and the Papas song of a few years ago, but what a dreadful surreal reality it is: foglike and dangerous, with the subtle and terrible manifestations of evil rising up like rocks in the gloom. I wish I was somewhere else. Disneyland, maybe? The last sane place here? Forever to take Mr. Toad's Wild Ride and never get off?   *novelist* **PHILIP K. DICK**

JULY 9

1944

I hope these horrible robot bombs haven't done you any damage or robbed you of too much well-earned rest. In their present state of development I imagine they cannot play a decisive part in war. But the possibilities they open up for the future are really blood-curdling. One can be safe in betting that, within ten years, there will be rockets, or jet-propelled flying bombs, carrying several tons of phosphorus or explosives, capable of flying any distance up to five thousand miles, and travelling along a radio beam precisely to their destination. Five thousand launching stations, firing off twenty robots apiece—and that would be the end of any metropolis in the world. And of course the logic of technology and the inner necessities of power politics are such that that is what governments will think it right and reasonable to prepare for. They may talk about leagues and security; but meanwhile they will be engaged in intensive research on, and manufacture of, these long-range robot bombs. And the whole history of war is there to show that the possession of large stocks of efficient armament constitutes an almost compulsive temptation to use them . . .   **ALDOUS HUXLEY**

1976

When I think about last night (note—Mitch and I drove up to the observatory and got stoned to experience the Laserium), I am just so impressed. I really feel I experience more than just a light show. It was so in tune with the images I felt they carried me to new extremes. It's funny how things can change so quickly . . . For the most part, I've given up the idea of renouncing the automobile while I'm in L.A. The entire lifestyle is centered around its use and in order to enjoy L.A. it's necessary to utilize the medium of the city. Namely, the car.   **AARON PALEY**

JULY 10

1945

The Conference at San Francisco suffered from inadequate preparation and lack of fundamental agreement among the Big Three; from an unfortunate Press which praised it beyond all limit at its commencement which paved the way for subsequent disillusionment both in England and in this country.

The finished Charter is a product of these weaknesses —but it is also the product of the hope, and even more, the realization that humanity can ill afford another war.

In practice, I doubt that it will prove effective in the sense of its elaborate mechanics being frequently employed or vitally decisive in determining war or peace.

It is, however, a bridge between Russia and the Western world and makes possible discussion and a personal relationship which can do much to ease mutual suspicion.   **JOHN FITZGERALD KENNEDY,**
covering the founding of the United Nations
for Hearst Newspapers

1951

A writer discloses himself on a single page, sometimes in a single paragraph.

novelist **RAYMOND CHANDLER**

1972

We ran, and we won in fifty of the fifty-eight counties. We didn't try to violate the law. We obeyed the law and we beat 'em man for man, woman for woman, and child for child. We were tough.

mayor, legislator **WILLIE BROWN, JR.**

JULY 11

1847

Bull fighting again commenced today in good earnest. Quite dangerous to be in town. Some horses gored by the bulls in the combat. 2 men considerably hurt and Cap. Davis' little boy thrown about 20 feet by a bull although not much hurt. The bull broke out of the enclosures and fight continued till late in the evening. Gen Peko took quite an active part today. He was very richly attired as was also many others.   **HENRY STANDAGE**

1953

The diary serves as a safety valve for the rebellions . . . I rebelled mostly in the diary . . . .   **ANAÏS NIN**

1961

I have too long put off sending you a message about *Newsday*. As a newspaper, it is beautifully affirmative about life. It is sweet, keen, strong and quiveringly alive. It is in terrific contrast to the *Los Angeles Times*. Sometimes when I ask myself, "What in the hell is wrong with this paper?", I find myself answering, "Somehow it seems to try to love people and life and can't quite make it."   *poet, film critic* **CARL SANDBURG**

JULY 12

1864

KINGS CANYON

. . . We started early in the morning and rode twenty-five miles before noon. The trail went down, down, down all the time—we sank five thousand feet in that twenty-five miles. Most of the way the trail led through magnificent forests. The giant sequoias, or Big Trees, were abundant; they occurred for several miles along the trail—hundreds of them from fifteen to twenty-five feet in diameter.

At twenty-five miles we struck a pleasant ranch, in a little valley, where we stopped all the afternoon. It was a nice place, and we got two very nice meals—the first square meals for some time and we did them ample justice.

WILLIAM H. BREWER

1940

1403 NORTH LAUREL AVENUE

HOLLYWOOD, CALIFORNIA

Dearest Scottie:

. . . Max Perkins writes me that Jane and three classmates are coming here and want to see something of the movies. I don't know who to introduce them to except Shirley Temple with whom I spent the day yesterday. (Her mother was there so it was all right.) She really is a sweet little girl and reminds me of you at 11½ when you hadn't succumbed to the wiles of Fred Astaire, lovey dovey and the radio crooners. But I told her mother it wouldn't be long now. I don't know whether she's going to do my picture not . . .

I think it's very modern to be taking dramatic criticism though it reminds me vaguely of the school for Roxy ushers. It seems a trifle detached from drama itself. I suppose the thing's to get really removed from the subject, and the final removal would be a school for teaching critics of teachers of dramatic criticism.

Isn't the world a lousy place? . . .

F. SCOTT FITZGERALD

1956

I just can't afford to live here. There's nothing for me to write about. To write about a place you have to love it or hate it or do both by turns, which is usually the way you love a woman. But a sense of vacuity and boredom—that is fatal.

I send you large amounts of love and I know damn well I sound like a bitter and disappointed man. I guess I am at that. I was the first writer to write about Southern California at all realistically, as the UCLA librarian [Lawrence Clark Powell] admitted when asking [successfully] for my original manuscripts for the Special Collections of their library. Now half the writers in the country piddle around in the smog . . .

RAYMOND CHANDLER

JULY 13

1937

1315 ANGELO DRIVE

BEVERLY HILLS CAL.

The way we work is, we map out a scene together, then I go home and write the dialogue, merely indicating business, and he takes what I have done and puts it into screen play shape. Thus relieving me of all that 'truck shot' 'wipe dissolve' stuff!   **P. G. WODEHOUSE**

1937

The film was to be shown at the Los Angeles Philharmonic Auditorium [just across 5th Street from] Pershing Square, gardens where the bums clustered in the twilight under subtropical boscage. . . . Outside the hall neon lights shone: HEMINGWAY AUTHOR- SPANISH EARTH.

novelist **ANTHONY POWELL**

1937

Last night I went to see the Joris Ivens film,—*Spanish Earth*, at the Philharmonic. Some of it is . . . very vivid. The music was annoying,—it kept drowning out the soundtrack. An immense crowd. Ernest Hemingway spoke,—or rather read a paper. Very large fellow,—lame. Stood before the stand with his feet spread far apart. He got them together, once, but then he turned . . . so they spread apart again. After finishing the paper he turned abruptly and walked off stage. Curious how many faces you come to recognize at these meetings,—gets to be a family affair almost.   **CAREY MCWILLIAMS**

1980

We see photographs of Salvadoran men and women lying dead in the Arizonan desert, and these photographs rebuke us for our cynicism and ennui. Forget, for the moment, that these Salvadorans were coming to us illegally. After all, millions came to us "illegally" in the 19th century, fleeing the oppression of legal systems they disagreed with or which kept them suppressed. Let us not be hard of heart. Let us not be Pharisees and say to ourselves: those Salvadorans who died in the desert, dreaming of America, were illegal and so we will close our hearts to them . . . .

Putting aside legalisms, eschewing hardness of heart, those simple peasant people who died in the desert, searching for America. We, after all, possess America, don't we? And we are bored with it, aren't we? Or at least we seem to be bored with it—bored by that vast and lavish dream that would draw unprotected simple men and women into a landscape filled with terror and destruction.

And so they died in the desert, seeking America, just as did Irish peasants more than a hundred years ago . . . who left their ships after an unspeakably terrible transatlantic voyage, lay down on the ground of America, on the very seashore itself, kissed the sandy earth and died, their America lasting only for the minutes it took them to die. Legal or not, those Salvadorans died Americans! They had better American dreams than many of us have. They knew what we have forgotten—that America is worth everything, if it is worth anything at all. With what ferocious and fearsome honesty do those dehydrated and sunblistered bodies speak to us. Were we worth their quest? Had they reached us, would they have reached a promised land?

historian, columnist **KEVIN STARR**

JULY 14

1929

891 POST ST., SAN FRANCISCO

I'm glad you like *The Maltese Falcon.* I'm sorry you think the to-bed and the homosexual parts of it should be changed. I should like to leave them as they are, especially since you say they "would be all right perhaps in an ordinary novel." It seems to me that the only thing that can be said

against their use in a detective novel is that nobody has tried it yet. I'd like
to try it . . .   **DASHIELL HAMMETT**

1935

. . . it's never cold so it's never hot so it's full with a great and little emptiness—
the emptiness of sick people . . . BUT 1 miraculous ocean!!!

poet **E.E. CUMMINGS**, *to Ezra Pound*

JULY 15

1864

SAN FRANCISCO, CALIF.

Dear Dan:

. . . Steve & I have moved our lodgings. Steve did not tell his folks he had
moved, & the other day his father went to our room, & finding it locked, he
hunted up the old landlady & asked her where those young men were. She
didn't know who he was, & she got her gun off without mincing matters.
Said she—"They are gone, thank God—& I hope I may never see them again.
I did not know anything about them, or they never should have entered this
house. Do you know, Sir, (dropping her voice to a ghastly confidential tone,)
they were a couple of desperate characters from Washoe—gamblers & murderers of the very worst description! . . .

"They always had women running to their room—sometimes in broad
daylight—bless you, they didn't care. They had no respect for God, man, or
the devil. Yes, Sir, they are gone, & the good God was kind to me when He
sent them away!"

There, now—what in the hell is the use of wearing away a lifetime in
building up a good name, if it is to be blown away at a breath by an ignorant
foreigner who is ignorant of the pleasant little customs that adorn & beautify a state of high civilization?

The old man told Steve all about it in his dry, unsmiling way, & Steve
laughed himself sick over it . . . .

Yr old friend

Sam   **MARK TWAIN**

1926

Do you know that boy I raved to you about, Gary Cooper? Well I raved so much about him to Mr. Goldwyn, Mrs. Goldwyn, Frances Marion and our casting agent—and in fact to anyone who would listen to me—that Mr. Goldwyn finally wired to camp and asked our manager to sign him up under a five year contract. I was happy that he did this. Of course, this only makes the rift between us wider because he wouldn't have a thought for me since he is now on the road to bigger things, but I am happy anyway and I shall always cherish the thought that I helped him.   **VALERIA BELLETTI**

JULY 16

1891

Conversed concerning the appropriation of water in the San Gabriel Canyon for purposes of power.   *attorney* **HENRY O'MELVENY**

1975

Jim [Jones] asked how many are looking forward to living in the promised land . . .

I got home at 11.45.

I made popcorn. I ate it and a piece of toast and jam, reading Edmund Wilson.   **EDITH ROLLER**

JULY 17

1961

Last Saturday night went for the first time in my life to the Hollywood Bowl, the guest of Mr. and Mrs. Andre Kostelanitz [sic], taking with me as fellow guests Lilla Perry and Betty Peterman. It was a kind of a Grand Canyon of an audience, every seat taken, twenty thousand people, to hear an all-Gershwin program. A master of ceremonies named Cassidy at the intermission, before reporting coming events, suddenly was saying, "We have present with us this evening a man who has become a legend in his own time, Carl Sandburg." On the instant a spotlight played on me and I stood up and stretched my right arm to this announcer and then to the twenty thousand innocent people assembled. So there we are, "A legend in our own time." And what you and I have to say is, "Jesus, it could be worse!"

CARL SANDBURG, *to his wife*

1988

Have you seen the quilt yet? If it has yet to come to NY, you might devote an hour or two to it when it does. It is very moving, you will probably see panels for several lost friends, from Liberace to some attractive bartender—but you will be impressed by the solidarity, and by the feelings expressed which tend to a gentle almost teasing wit rather than solemnity.   **THOM GUNN**

JULY 18

1940

1403 NORTH LAUREL AVENUE,

HOLLYWOOD, CALIFORNIA

Dearest Scottie:

. . . you see how difficult it was to get a job this summer. So let's see what Vassar's got. The first thing that occurs to me is Spanish, which is simply bound to be of enormous value in the next ten years. Every junior-high-school child in California gets a taste of it and could beat you out of a job in South America if we expand that way. It is enough like French so that you have few alphabetical troubles, is pronounced as written, and has a fairly interesting literature of its own. I mean it's not like studying Bulgarian or Chippewa or some strange dialect in which no one had ever had anything to say. Don't you think this would be a much wiser move than the Greek and Latin culture?

I wonder if you've read anything this summer—I mean any one good book like *The Brothers Karamazov* or *Ten Days That Shook the World* or *Renan's Life of Christ.* You never speak of your reading except the excerpts you do in college, the little short bits that they must perforce give you. I know you have read a few of the books I gave you last summer—then I have heard nothing from you on the subject. Have you ever, for example, read *Pere Goriot* or *Crime and Punishment* or even *The Doll's House* or *St. Matthew* or

Sons and Lovers? A good style simply doesn't form unless you absorb half a dozen top-flight authors every year. Or rather it forms but, instead of being a subconscious amalgam of all that you have admired, it is simply a reflection of the last writer you have read, a watered-down journalese.

With dearest love,

Daddy   F. SCOTT FITZGERALD

JULY 19

1870

Hauled dung all day to smoke out the grasshoppers.

pioneer, gunrunner HENRY DALTON

1935

I am taking the broad highway running along the east levee of the Sacramento River, heading toward the capital city.

Behind is Mount Diablo, the lone sentinel of these perceptions, sinking beneath the horizon.

Kain-tuck is also there, behind the horizon, and it is hardest to think of that. And there too are Solomon, Wimbledon Common, the embankment of the Thames at Twickenham, and a breeze from Cornwall over the water.

composer HARRY PARTCH

JULY 20

1918

The [San Francisco] *Bulletin* is dead. Funeral early in 1919. No flowers. Only members of the family will be present at the interment.

journalist, ghostwriter ROSE WILDER LANE

1941

1392 HULL LANE

ALTADENA, CALIFORNIA

[The dancer-ethnographer Katharane Mershon] said to me off-hand, "You ought to see a bit of California while you are out here."

"Oh, that would be fine!" I crackled and gleamed at the idea. So I saw California! At first, I thought it was just to give me some pleasure, but I soon found out it was the gleeful malice of a Californiac taking revenge upon a poor defenseless Florida Fiend.

She fried me in the deserts, looking at poppies, succulents (cactus, to you and everybody else except Californiacs), Joshua trees, kiln dried lizards and lupin bushes. Just look at those wild lilacs! Observe that chaparrel! Don't miss that juniper . . .

From San Diego up, we looked at every wave on the Pacific, lizards, bushes, prune and orange groves, date palms, eucalyptus, gullies with and without water that these Californiacs call rivers, asphalt pits where the remains of prehistoric animals had been found . . .

Then there was barracuda and shark meat, abalones, beaches full of people in dark sun glasses, Hollywood, and slacks with hips in them all swearing to God and other responsible characters that they sure look pretty, and most of them lying and unrepentant. Man! I saw Southern California . . . .

"Now, I shall take you to see Northern California—the best part of the state," my fiendish friend gloated. "Ah, the mountains!!

"But, I don't care too much about mountains," I murmured through the alkali in my mouth . . .

So we went north. We drove over rocky ridges and stopped on ledges miles up in the air and gazed upon the Pacific. Redwood forests, Golden Gates, cable cars, missions, gaps, gullies, San Simeon-with-William Randolph Hearst, Monterey-with-history. Carmel-with-artists and atmosphere, Big Sur and Santa Barbara, Bay Bridges and Giant Sequoia, Alcatraz, wharves, Capitol buildings, mountains that didn't have sense enough to know it was summer and time to take off their winter clothes . . .

I mean to write to the Florida Chamber of Commerce and get them to trick a gang of Californiacs to Florida and let me be the guide. It is going to be good, and I wouldn't fool you. From Key West to the Perdido river they are going to see every orange tree, rattlesnake, gopher, cougar, palm tree, sand pile, beach mango tree, sapodilla, kumquat, alligator, tourist trap, celery patch, bean field, strawberry, lake, jook, gulf, ocean and river in between, and if their constitutions sort of wear away, it will be unfortunate, but one of the hazards of war.

But California is nice. Buen nice! Of course they lie about the California climate a little more than we do about ours, but you don't hold that against them. They have to, to rank up with us. But at that this California is a swell state, especially from Santa Barbara on north . . . it seems that California does wear its hips a bit high. I mean all those mountains. Too much of the state is standing up on edge. To my notion, land is supposed to lie down and be walked on—not rearing up, staring you in the face. It is too biggity and imposing. But on the whole, California will do for a lovely state until God can make up something better . . .

novelist, essayist **ZORA NEALE HURSTON**

1961

Can I help it if my hair is short? Damn everyone who makes cracks at it . . . I feel like hell. **WANDA COLEMAN**

JULY 21

1937

You know those two wall fixtures the ornamental blacksmith put up? Well, the damn things shorted and blew Walt Stewart out through the front door and smashed down a lot of Ed Rowe's hollyhocks—and Walt is mad and so is Ed and Walt says if we don't get them fixed he is going to yank them off and throw them away.

Now Mr. Goelz, you know I would hate to have Walt do anything like that because it leaves big holes in the wall, and anyhow we haven't got anything else to put up in their place unless we cut the bottoms out of some cans and nail them over the holes and Fred don't think that would work because it wouldn't be authentic.

So I ask you, Mr. Goelz, what am I going to do unless you bring your tools and a keg of Schlitz and come up and fix those two fixtures before Walt gets too mad and starts swearing right in the chapel. If you can't get Schlitz, most any good kind of beer will do that there is a kick in.

H. V. "VEE" SMITH, *Civilian Conservation Corps superintendent, in charge of city boys restoring La Purísima Mission*

1939

At WPA headquarters, 12th and Santee streets, a handful of "white collar" project workers struck. Of 100 writers project employees, 22 left for two hours and lounged quietly in front of the building . . .

journalist **MACK JOHNSON**,
in the Los Angeles Daily News

2021

How about something like,

The United States' most precious and overlooked resource is stories, the stories of all the people who live far beyond the spotlight, rural people, indigenous people, elderly people who hold memories of the past that will soon vanish, people who struggled, people who witnessed, people who experimented, people who migrated or stayed home as their home metamorphosed into something unfamiliar. The idea of sending waves of writers out to connect to these stories and maybe preserve them, as the oral historians of the Federal Writers Program did, is gorgeous and would save innumerable stories from vanishing for good, the stories of who we really are. It may as well prompt new kinds of storytelling from the writers, who I imagine moving like threaded needles through the patchwork of this nation to stitch the fragments together and make them stronger.

essayist, critic, biographer **REBECCA SOLNIT**, *to the editor,*
about the 21st Century Federal Writers' Project Act

JULY 22

1850

TRINITY COUNTY

It is said that misery makes strange bedfellows—so does California. I had one the other night. Now don't blush—but it is a fact—I was fairly caught. I slept in the open air on the ground. Towards morning I was awakened by something pricking my side. Supposing it to be an ant or bug of some kind, half-asleep, I brushed it hastily away and turned over and went to sleep again. A little after daylight, I awoke, and throwing off the clothes, there lay snugly nestled by my side a large scorpion. Whether it was him that stung me or something else, I cannot tell, but I felt no inconvenience from it, and

they are very poisonous. I soon made beef of him and have thoroughly shook
and examined by blankets ever since on retiring . . .

ALONZO DELANO

1944

HAMMER FIELD

FRESNO, CALIFORNIA

Dear Mom, Well, things are going fine. My pilot and I have gotten in most of
our time for this month, and are now taking things a little easier. By the way,
I never got my barracks bag. Did you send it? Tell Pop I'll have a picture made
just as soon as I get a chance. It is really hot out here, but the officer's pool
is right across the street, full of pretty nurses, so I don't mind too much. I've
been going with one, (an ex-Billy Rose bubble-dancer!!?) named Nan Ross,
and she's really treating me swell. (She's only 26?!!) I am in love with Gwen,
but I don't think anything will ever come of it, because she is inclined to be
a little snotty (excuse the expression) when she doesn't have everything she
wants (which is plenty) and who wants a wife like that? . . .

If it were not so hot out here the climate would be wonderful . . .

That's about the way it is, Mom, just like you told me. I love you all, so I'll
be back one of these days, and we'll all be happy again.

All my love,

Jim

JAMES DICKEY

JULY 23

1943

New York makes you hard and grubby, California relaxes you too much.
Reading back through my journal to the summer I was here before, Laguna
Beach in 1939, just before the war broke out in Europe—those far-away
days . . .

During that summer I was care-taker on a chicken-ranch while the
owners were away. For days I would forget to feed the chickens, life was so
dreamy, then I would make up for it by feeding them too much. About half
of them died, fell on their backs with their feet sticking rigidly up, and I left
the ranch in disgrace for New Mexico . . .

TENNESSEE WILLIAMS, *to his publisher*

1966

MT. HARKNESS

Do I seem to write only of the surfaces of things? Yet, it seems to me that only surfaces are of ultimate importance—the touch of a child's hand in yours, the taste of an apple, the embrace of friend or lover, sunlight on rock and leaf, music, the feel of a girl's skin on the inside of her thigh, the bark of a tree, the plunge of clear water, the face of the wind.

ED ABBEY

JULY 24

1855

The idea of liberty in the United States is truly curious . . . Certain people have no liberty at all. It is denied by the courts to every person of color . . . But there is the great liberty of any white man to buy a human being in order to arbitrarily hang him or burn him alive. This happens in states where slavery is tolerated and the vilest despotism runs wild. This, in the center of the nation that calls itself a "model republic."

journalist FRANCISCO P. RAMÍREZ

1949

We spent this afternoon driving around the hills & the beach. L.A. is a weird town. For its size (much larger in area than New York) it's got a very small central section. The rest is residential poor like Coney [Island], middle-class like Flatbush, tony like Westchester—but the surroundings—high hills, almost mountains –are quite terrific. And the beach is beautiful—in places like the Riviera—other places like Asbury Park.

novelist, essayist NORMAN MAILER

JULY 25

1942

During the evacuation we did a lot of work with the Japanese. Since then I have done some in re library and art service for the camps, and Marie

[Rexroth] donated her vacation as Public Health Nurse for Tanforan, the concentration camp nearest SF.   **KENNETH REXROTH**

1950

... I don't want to conclude this letter without mentioning the great danger which the American nationalism might provoke. Will it not finally degenerate into anti-Semitism? We have seen such things.

composer **ARNOLD SCHOENBERG**, *to Aaron Copland*

JULY 26

1958

By traveling on the road to Sausalito, San Francisco then Big Sur, I see how much the earth still surrounds us. Willow Road juts out in my memory. Mission San Rafael Archangel. Redwood Highway. Where man is going now, who knows. The earth no longer need be his home. Maybe this means the end of the old world. And man, on the minutest of planets may and can range thru all of space. To the very frontiers, limits, barriers of outer worlds. Lucky Drive. End construction project. With what frightening speed we move ahead ...   *diarist* **JOHN WIENERS**

2004

And even more than my—these days near obsessional—devouring of words, la salvación está en esto: my feverish *scratch scratch scratching* of rust-colored, fat, felt-tip pen. ¡He aquí! Con este acto puedo—*tengo* que—expiar, extirpar la angustia. Mitigar. Paliar. What else to do?

SUSANA CHÁVEZ-SILVERMAN

JULY 27

1846

The bustle of preparation is active in the squadron. Commander Du Pont received orders last evening to have the Cyane ready for sea in twenty-four hours. She has tripped this afternoon, and is off for San Diego, though it has

been given out on shore that she is bound elsewhere, but this is a war strata-
gem. She has on board Col. Frémont and a hundred and fifty of his riflemen.
The wind is fresh, and they are by this time cleverly sea-sick, and lying about
the deck in a spirit of resignation that would satisfy the non-resistant principles of a Quaker. Two or three resolute old women might tumble the whole
of them into the sea.

The colonel is a man of small stature, of slender but wiry formation, and
with a countenance indicative of decision and firmness. This is the fifth time
he has crossed the continent in connection with his scientific purposes. His
enterprises are full of hardship, peril, and the wildest romance. To sleep
under the open heaven, and depend on one's rifle for food, is coming about
as near the primitive state of the hunter as a civilized man can well get; and
yet this life, in his case, is adorned with the triumphs of science. The colonel
and his band are to land at San Diego, secure horses, and advance upon the
position of Gen. Castro, at los Angeles. "War's great events lie so in Fortune's
scale, That oft a feather's weight may kick the beam."

writer, clergyman **WALTER COLTON**

1890

When my awful story, "The Yellow Wallpaper," comes out, you must try &
read it. Walter says he has read it FOUR times and thinks it the most ghastly
tale he ever read. Says it beats Poe, and Doré! But that's only a husband's
opinion.

I read the thing to three women here however, and I never saw such
squirms! Daylight too. It's a simple tale, but highly unpleasant.

I don't know yet where it will be. If none of the big things will take it I
need to try the *New York Ledger*. Have you that in its new form? Kipling and
Stevenson etc. etc. write for that now, so I guess I can.

CHARLOTTE PERKINS GILMAN

1933

This place is not at all what I expected. It isn't very fantastic, just a desert
got up to look like Asbury Park. And so far I've bumped into none of the
things I expected and was prepared for by reports and plays like *Once in a
Life Time*. The studio I am working [for], Columbia, is a highly organized
and very practical business place. Five minutes after I arrived I was given
an assignment, a picture called BLIND DATE and I have been working nine
hours a day on it since then with a full day on Saturday. **NATHANAEL WEST**

1955

Finished *Paradise Lost* this morning. Neither so hard to read nor so forbidding as some say. There are a few good twists on Genesis. "O hell, what do mine eyes with grief behold?" Working with an old Singlejack miner, who can sense The vein and cleavage In the very guts of the rock, can Blast granite, build Switchbacks that last for years Under the beat of snow, thaw, mulehooves. What use, Milton, a silly story . . .   *poet* **GARY SNYDER**

JULY 28

1862

TO ORION CLEMENS

AURORA, CALIF./NEV. TERR.

Can't someone up there . . . find a way to start a bookstore . . . ?

Yr Bro,

Sam.   **MARK TWAIN**

1864

Thursday, July 28, we were up at dawn and went to Owens River . . . The Sierra Nevada catches all the rains and clouds from the west—to the east are deserts—so, of course, this valley sees but little rain, but where streams come down from the Sierra they spread out and great meadows of green grass occur. Tens of thousands of the starving cattle of the state have been driven in here this year, and there is feed for twice as many more . . .

Here is a fact that you cannot realize. The Californian deserts are clothed in vegetation—peculiar shrubs, which grow one to five feet high, belonging to several genera, but known under the common names of "sagebrush" and "greasewood" . . . When it dries they cease to put forth much fresh foliage or add much new wood, but they do not die—their vitality seems suspended. A drought of several years may elapse, and when, at last, the rains come, they revive into life again! Marvels of vegetation, some of these species will stand a tropical heat and a winter's frosts; the drought of years does not kill them, and yet the land may be flooded and be for two months a swamp, and still they do not die.   **WILLIAM H. BREWER**

1972

Last night we went to Henry Miller's home. He limps and he is in pain, but he hesitates to undergo surgery. His mood was good . . . Of course we both carry in our minds images from the past. I always see him dynamic, walking forever all through Paris, joyous. He always sees me as I was, lively, a dancer . . .

Henry's Japanese ex-wife was there. She never loved him; for this I dislike her . . . On one wall the shelves are filled with the translations of his books in fifteen or twenty languages.   **ANAÏS NIN**

JULY 29

1941

Everyone out here of course is terrified of the Japanese & there is a terrific prejudice against the poor wretched Japs who have settled down and become perfectly respectable citizens. There are terrific 'goings-on' in 'defense preparations' round here—but of course San Diego is the biggest naval base on this coast . . .

We've just re-discovered the poetry of George Crabbe (all about Suffolk!) & are very excited—maybe an opera one day—

. . . We have made two excursions to Los Angeles—horrible place—the real 'Auspuff' of America!   **PETER PEARS**, *beginning to mull Peter Grimes with partner Benjamin Britten*

1989

Laurent [de Brunhoff, son of the original creators] edited out the cannibals in the 1981 Babar's Anniversary Volume, having been approached in the 1960s by his Random House editor, Toni Morrison, who protested similar stereotypes in Laurent's own *Babar's Picnic* in 1949.

I'm not sure that this retrospective editing is such a good idea. As Dr. Johnson said about prudish eighteenth-century editors of Shakespeare, 'If phraseology is to be changed as words grow uncouth by disuse, or gross by vulgarity, the history of every language will be lost.' If that was the way either of the de Brunhoffs saw things, then leave them be. Next thing you know, Jacobin elephants will be complaining that de Brunhoff stereotyped their kind as monarchists, thus ignoring the long tradition of republicanism for which elephants are justly renowned.

journalist, contrarian **ALEXANDER COCKBURN**

JULY 30

1769

We proceeded for four hours on a good road, with the exception of two very steep hills. We halted in a very large valley where there was much pasture and water. Here we had to construct a bridge to cross the gully. I consider this a good place for a mission.   *Governor, explorer* **GASPAR DE PORTOLÁ**

1769

We left Los Ojitos, where there was another earthquake of no great violence, at half-past six in the morning. We crossed the plain in a northerly direction, steadily approaching the mountains. We ascended some hills which were quite rugged and high, afterwards we descended to a very extensive and pleasant valley where there was an abundance of water, part of it running in deep ditches, part of it standing so as to form marshes. This valley must be nearly three leagues in width and very much more in length. We pitched our camp near a ditch of running water, its banks covered with watercress and cumin. We gave this place the name of Valle de San Miguel. It is, perhaps, about four leagues from Los Ojitos. In the afternoon we felt another earthquake.

engineer, cartographer, cosmographer **MIGUEL COSTANSÓ**

JULY 31

1868

. . . Why, for instance, is this magazine called "The Overland Monthly"? It would perhaps be easier to say why it was not called by some of the thousand other titles suggested. I might explain how "Pacific Monthly" is hackneyed, mild in suggestion, and at best but a feeble echo of the Boston

"Atlantic" . . . "California,"— honest and direct enough—is yet too local to attract any but a small number of readers . . .

The bear who adorns the cover . . . is crossing the track of the Pacific Railroad, and has paused a moment to look at the coming engine of civilization and progress—which moves like a good many other engines of civilization and progress with a prodigious shrieking and puffing—and apparently recognizes his rival and his doom. . . . Look at him well, for he is passing away. Fifty years and he will be as extinct as the dodo or dinornis . . .

BRET HARTE, *editor's letter,*
debut issue of the Overland Monthly

1876
Earthquakes occur fairly frequently, usually in August.
Archduke LUDWIG LOUIS SALVATOR

1879
. . . In the spring, if all is well, we return to California . . .
ROBERT LOUIS STEVENSON

AUGUST 1

1852

Ice and frost this morning. Four miles to Red Lake. This is . . . the head of Salmon Trout, or Carson River. It is a small lake and is within one mi. of the summit of the Sierra Nevada. From this lake to the summit the ascent is very great, some places being almost perpendicular . . . Four mi. from the summit we cross a small creek, a tributary of the Sacramento At this creek we stop to noon. Here we help inter a young man who died last night of bilious fever. He was from Michigan. His name was Joseph Ricker. His parents reside in the state of Maine. Here we ascend another ridge of this mt . . .

forty-niner **WILLIAM KILGORE** —
Joan Didion's great-great-grandfather

1875

. . . At the base of the fall there is a beautiful pool. Standing on the rocks on the margin of this pool, right opposite the fall, a most perfect unbroken circular rainbow is visible. Sometimes it is a double circular rainbow. The cliff more than six hundred feet high; the wavy, billowy, gauzy veil reaching from top to bottom; the glorious crown, woven by the sun for this beautiful veiled bride—those who read must put these together and form a picture for themselves by the plastic power of the imagination. Some of the young men took a swim in the pool and a shower-bath under the fall. I would have joined them, but I had just come out of the Merced River. After enjoying this exquisite fall until after sunset, we returned to camp. On our way back, amongst the loose rocks on the stream margin, we found and killed another rattlesnake. This is the fourth we have killed.

professor, geologist, conservationist **JOSEPH LECONTE**,
at Bridalveil Fall in Yosemite

1925

This tooth in itself is sufficient to prove beyond doubt that the bear was a Grizzly . . .   *professor, mammalogist* **CLINTON HART MERRIAM,**
after the shooting of the last known California grizzly

1932

I am in California for the health of one of the family. We are seeing the Olympics of course—not Hollywood of course. I suppose you know some of your athletes over here for the games.

I wish I knew more of ours. Our professors spend a lot of time resenting athletics in college. But athletics, as I mean to tell them someday in verse, are nearer the arts than scholarship ever thought of being.

Ever yours,   *poet* **ROBERT FROST,** *to*
British novelist Hugh Walpole

1942

This is a strange and curious place . . .   **WILLIAM FAULKNER,** *to his agent*

AUGUST 2

1769

We halted not very far from the river, which we named Porciúncula. Here we felt three consecutive earthquakes in the afternoon and night. We must have traveled about three leagues today. This plain where the river runs is very extensive. It has good land for planting all kinds of grain and seeds, and is the most suitable site of all that we have seen for a mission, for it has all the requisites for a large settlement. As soon as we arrived about eight heathen from a good village came to visit us; they live in this delightful place among the trees on the river. They presented us with some baskets of pinole made from seeds of sage and other grasses. Their chief brought some strings of beads made of shells, and they threw us three handfuls of them. Some of the old men were smoking pipes well made of baked clay and they puffed at us three mouthfuls of smoke. We gave them a little tobacco and glass beads, and they went away well pleased.   **FRAY JUAN CRESPI**

1846

FORT SACRAMENTO

NEW HELVETIA

This is to certify that having been made a Prisoner by the residents of California in arms asserting the Independence of California, I, in consideration of being set at liberty, hereby most solemnly pledge my sacred word of honor, not to take up arms against the United States of North America or the Residents of California. That I will not furnish supplies, carry communications or in any way assist any person or persons who may be opposed to the United States of North America or the above named residents of California . . . understanding distinctly that if this pledge is not faithfully performed my life is forfeited wherever I may be found.

And hereunto I affix my hand and seal.

statesman **GEN. MARIANO VALLEJO**

1886

. . . the Donner family and party . . . consisted of about one hundred persons en route for California . . . who were overtaken by one of those terrible snow storms when near Donner Lake. There were many children among them, all of whom perished, with most of the men. Some of the women were saved and this little lake at the top of the mountains receives its name from the fidelity of Mrs. Donner, who chose to die with her husband rather than escape with the children and leave him to perish alone. When spring came and the snows began to melt, the corpse of the husband was found tenderly cared for by her hands while she had perished alone . . .

It is at this point the waters divide, some going east to a desert grave and others to water the great Sacremento Valley . . . we are now in that part of the Sierras known as the gold bearing mountains of America, where so many have both lost and gained wealth . . . the red soil has been left uncovered and every mark of vegetation destroyed which may require ages to replace. Farms in these lovely valleys have been completely ruined by the debris which has been cast upon them by this process of mining, which legislation has failed to check, and as we descend to the valley we find the once clear and sparkling brooks fresh from the mountains now turbulent streams of muddy water . . .

We reach Oakland at 10:30 p.m., board the ferry, cross the bay, and are now in San Francisco. We have, after nine days travel, landed on the golden shore . . .

travel writer **SUE A. SANDERS**,

visiting from Illinois

1959

. . . Aunt Frieda had a wonderful cold chicken lunch, string beans, potato salad, tomato and lettuce salad, hot rolls, fresh pineapple, coffee cake and tea ready for us yesterday when we came. Both she and Uncle Walter are handsome, fun, and so young in spirit. They have a little green Eden of a house, surrounded by pink and red and white oleander bushes, with two avocado trees loaded down with (alas) not-yet-ripe fruit, a peach tree, a guava tree, a persimmon tree, a fig tree and others.

Aunt Frieda has had some wonderful adventures and is a great storyteller. Ted gets on magnificently with Walter; we simply love them both. It is amazing how Frieda resembles daddy . . .   *poet* SYLVIA PLATH

AUGUST 3

1769

On our way we met the entire population of an Indian village engaged in harvesting seeds on the plain. In the afternoon there were other earthquakes; the frequency of them amazed us . . .   MIGUEL COSTANSÓ

1769

At half-past six we left the camp and forded the Porciúncula River, which runs down from the valley, flowing through it from the mountains into the plain. After crossing the river we entered a large vineyard of wild grapes and an infinity of rosebushes in full bloom. All the soil is black and loamy, and is capable of producing every kind of grain and fruit which may be planted. We went west, continually over good land well covered with grass. After traveling about half a league we came to the village of this region, the people of which, on seeing us, came out into the road. As they drew near us they began to howl like wolves; they greeted us and wished to give us seeds, but as we had nothing at hand in which to carry them we did not accept them. Seeing this, they threw some handfuls of them on the ground and the rest in the air . . .

We judge that in the mountains that run to the west in front of us there are some volcanoes, for there are many signs on the road which stretches between the Porciúncula River and the Spring of the Alders, for the explorers saw some large marshes of a certain substance like pitch; they were boiling and bubbling . . .   FRAY JUAN CRESPI

1940

Lord, how I hate the good . . . I like [the] good but it must be with salt and pepper, a small onion and a bay leaf.

French chef, broadcaster **JULIA CHILD**

2022

On the one hand, human suffering. On the other hand, BETTER JOURNAL ENTRIES!!!!   **SAMIA SAAD**

AUGUST 4

1852

From our log cabin, Indian Bar

We have lived through so much of excitement for the last three weeks, dear M., that I almost shrink from relating the gloomy events that have marked their flight. But if I leave out the darker shades of our mountain life, the picture will be very incomplete. In the short space of twenty-four days we have had murders, fearful accidents, bloody deaths, a mob, whippings, a hanging, an attempt at suicide, and a fatal duel . . .

[Only] think of such a shrinking, timid, frail thing as I *used* to be "long time ago" not only living right in the midst of them, but almost compelled to hear, if not see, the whole. I think I may without vanity affirm that I have "seen the elephant" . . .   *newspaper correspondent* **LOUISE CLAPPE**, *aka "Dame Shirley"*

1920

The reason I stay here is because this summer climate is without exception the finest I have ever known. Sky, mountains, the sea, light, temperature and a sensuous wind combine to make it perfect. 88 to go at noon. Cool winds 23¢, a blanket at night—and every night. No flies, no mosquitoes, no gnats, ants, cockroaches or bugs of any kind. Name me a better summer world with—of course—the exception of Baltimore.

novelist **JOHN FANTE**, *to H. L. Mencken*

1942

Toby told me confidentially that the visiting system is going to be changed. It will be announced soon. The plan is to have visitors stay in the social hall on one side of the table with us on the other, just like in Prison! No more cakes, pies, or fruit will be allowed in the Center. It is so unnecessary . . . How simply the minds of some people do function!

CHARLES KIKUCHI

AUGUST 5

1949

. . . In this fourth year of drought everything is horribly parched, the stream is dry, the oaks losing their leaves, even the pine trees unhappy. A few more seasons of this kind of thing, and the whole of southern California will have gone back to the coyotes. Which might be quite a good thing, perhaps.

ALDOUS HUXLEY, to Anita Loos

1954

From the very first moment of setting foot in the [YMCA] this summer, [I] could tell that something had changed. There was a kind of furtiveness everywhere: people were quiet, there was no loud talk of any kind, and everyone walked with eyes almost painfully (and certainly maidenly) downcast. Perhaps there was an explanation for the surface dullness in the set of "House Rules" that old Pruneface handed me—saying in effect that since they wanted to establish a "Christian atmosphere" here in this Y, that absolutely no one would ever be allowed up on the residence floors . . . and that even among residents there would be no visiting after 11:30, and that if anyone were caught loitering in the halls or toilets he would be asked to give up his residence . . . I don't see why they didn't simply say "we're trying to get rid of the homos here," and let it go at that. And they certainly seem to have succeeded.

SAMUEL STEWARD

1958

LOWER RAE LAKE

. . . California—so much . . .

GARY SNYDER

1974

[I] am the victim of my books, and spent several days in San Francisco and Palo Alto, revisiting some of the more painful scenes of my life, in the hope that mad California will hurt me into prose again. She will. I have a rather grim story in the planning stage, and my trip will help to flesh it out. San Francisco was rather fun, though it's becoming overbuilt and has more skyscrapers sticking out of its poor bones than a chicken has feathers. I enjoyed the Bay scenes, though, and the crowds where you could see any kind of persons and feel a certain fraternity with them . . .

ROSS MACDONALD, *to Eudora Welty*

2020

. . . Lately, some of the reading I have been doing about real estate, especially in California and especially at just this point in our history, has left me anxious on your behalf about the risks that I fear you face . . .

Why are prices so high in California? The prices are not to be explained by supply and demand as we have known it in the past, as Mom and I knew it, for example, when we bought our Pasadena house in 1986. Then, we were bidding against other individual buyers. Now, you two are bidding against investment bankers capitalized not just by American but also by foreign capital . . .

Confidence that real estate in any area will basically at least retain its value rests on an assumption that the future will be in basic regards like the past. *But what if this ceases to be true in a given region?* What if California itself begins to become undesirable to almost uninhabitable over the next generation? The Camp Fire in Northern California left San Francisco with air quality worse than that of New Delhi and more than wiped out the positive effect of everything else that California did in 2018 to reduce emissions and mitigate global warming. Nobody's house burned down in San Francisco, but everybody's sense there about the future changed on the day when because of the smoke, it was as if the sun never came up . . .

So, it would seem highly imprudent to sink a very large chunk of all your available capital, counting not just your own but everything that your parents' can spare, to buy in at what might just be the very top of the California real estate market and then be stuck with a colossal debt as property value in the state—and surely much else along the way—starts to really go to hell because of a factor independent of supply and demand. This is why, as you know too well, I keep trying to push you toward waiting until you can move into Mom's Pasadena house . . .

JACK MILES

AUGUST 6

1837

Perfecto Hugo Reid, native of Great Britain, Roman Catholic, resident of the City of Our Lady of the Angels, appears before your Lordship in the best legal manner to state: that during the term of three years he has lived in the above-mentioned city, engaged in business, et cetera, has benefited society in every way possible, and finding himself ready to enter into the state of matrimony with a native daughter of this country, respectfully requests and entreats your permission to contract this marriage . . .

immigrant columnist **HUGO REID**

1936

To all of us—both to those of us oldsters who have been in and out of the theatre of the past and have seen that old theatre languish and all but perish . . . and likewise to those younger ones among us who have striven to equip and train themselves . . . to all of us, the energy and vision, the imagination and devotion you have brought to your task as administrator of the National Federal Theatre Project have been an inspiration.

SAN FRANCISCO'S FEDERAL THEATRE PROJECT,
in a scroll presented to Hallie Flanagan

1952

The town is a horror of ugliness, flat as your hand and crawling with cars. Nobody dreams of walking anywhere and shops and houses are miles apart.

The sudden change is a bit bewildering, and I shall be glad to get over the first few days. One feels a little like the new boy at school but it is all amusingly new, though exactly like one had expected really. I think I have already persuaded them that a beard for Cassius is not a good plan.

actor **JOHN GIELGUD,** *to his mother*

2021

More bad news. I find out from my sister that four family members in Texas, including my 79-year-old grandmother, are unvaccinated and have all contracted the coronavirus. I am distraught.

I wish I could find a way to get vaccine-hesitant Black people to believe that COVID-19 vaccines are not a Tuskegee experiment, the infamous study in which the United States Public Health Service knowingly kept syphilis diagnoses and treatments from its hundreds of Black subjects for decades. My unvaccinated family members have all brought it up as a reason they don't want the shot. Yes, the Tuskegee experiment was a race-driven atrocity that America has yet to properly reckon with. But this is not that.

director, screenwriter, actor **ESPIE RANDOLPH III**

AUGUST 7

1932

Got a good rub down in morning and had steak. Went to stadium, warmed up, another hot rub. Ran second in the relay. We got 1st place and broke Olympic and World Record.   *sprinter* **EVELYN OJEDA**, *nee* **FURTSCH**

1993

PETROLIA

. . . I often think of Baudrillard careening through landscapes that only time and an expert guide can help one comprehend. Europeans love to repeat that silly line of the expatriate Gertrude Stein about Oakland, 'When you get there, there's no there there.' Of course Oakland is there, invisible or uninteresting only to those for whom America can be shrunk to a handful of cities genteelly advertised as being on the beaten track . . .

Often American intellectuals slide into a native version of the same snobbery, believing that thinking, writing or political work can only be conducted in a handful of metropolitan or campus habitats.

What would a Baudrillard or kindred transient make of Watsonville, maybe pulling off Highway 1, looking for a gas stop, heading east on Airport Boulevard, past Hector's, down Freedom Boulevard, along Main, out through some broccoli fields at the south end of town and then without further ado back on 1 with Castroville, artichoke heart of the world, next up on the route map . . .

The glazed tourist's eye might, even at a speed never dropping below 30 mph, pick out a few of the insignia of local drama: a church without a steeple, some of the south end of Main missing altogether. Watsonville got hit pretty bad in the earthquake of 1989.

But even at a walking pace it's hard to decipher the main streets and side alleys without detour and patient investigation. Take those snug-looking, single-story Maybeck houses. How many families are crammed in them? Two? Three? More? And the broccoli cutters, a raggedy line of figures in the middle distance. You can't tell anything about them at that range, unless through their old cars, sometimes their homes parked nearer at hand. How much are they making? Where are they from?

.... There are no closed horizons. At the other end of Main Street is Michoacán, whence so many of the workers came; is Irapuato whither so many of the jobs finally went ...

The fingers of the world economy shape and reshape its destinies. The town's polar attraction shifts from the southward pull of Salinas, to the valley of silicon an hour's drive north ...   **ALEXANDER COCKBURN**

AUGUST 8

1919

MISS JULIA MORGAN, MERCHANTS EXCHANGE BLDG
SAN FRANCISCO CALIF
    WOULD LIKE TO HAVE MISS MORGAN COME TO RANCH WHENEVER CONVENIENT WE ARE EXPECTING HER

journalism tycoon **WILLIAM RANDOLPH HEARST**

1934

CARMEL, CAL.,

Dear Maxim,

.... Ella Winter, when I last saw her ten days ago in Carmel, did not want her name used on the script—although it is copyrighted in our joint names. The Red Scare in Carmel and the vicious rumors put out concerning my associations with whites there and the fact that the Steffens home was branded as a nest of Reds and a meeting place for Negroes and Whites, etc. etc. prompted this move on her part. After all she does have to live there and send her kid to a school headed by a Legionnaire and get her milk from a dairyman who declared he was just waiting for the day when he could get behind a machine gun and drag all the members of the JRC John Reed Club out in Ocean Avenue and shoot 'em. And lots of good citizens visiting the City Council and urging them to do something about the Steffens ...

And not a hall to meet in any more as the landlords are all threatened with destruction of property if they rent to us. And a great frothing at the mouth from the New Dealers when Steffy issued from his sickbed a statement to the press, saying among other things, "Let them come and get me. Let them send me to jail. I'd rather go there than to the White House. It's more honorable!" . . . .

. . . most of the happenings and situations in the play come directly from the things we ourselves saw in the Valley last fall, or from what the participants, both growers and strikers, told us. The play follows the strike almost exactly. We hope it is dramatic as well as historical and true . . .

LANGSTON HUGHES, *to his agent, Maxim Lieber*

AUGUST 9

1945

Dear Kids

I started to write you a letter last night, but it's a good thing I didn't, because I was too depressed. I haven't heard anything definite from Yank or Robie yet, but our division schedule is being speeded up and we'll be leaving this camp on the 17th of this month. All this happened yesterday, a day of mixed blessings, which also brought the first Atomic Bomb and Russia's entrance into the war . . .

God grant that this may be the last day of war.

Love,   poet **ANTHONY HECHT**, *to his parents*

1952

Brando is a funny, intense, egocentric boy of 27, with a flat nose and bullet head, huge arms and shoulders, and yet giving the effect of a lean Greenwich Village college boy. He is very nervous indeed and mutters his lines and rehearses by himself all day long. Very deferential to me, and dragged me off to record two speeches of Antony on his machine . . . He tells me he owns a cattle ranch, and after two more years filming, will be financially secure altogether!!

The parties are grand, but clumsy—awful food, too much drink, rather noisy and the weirdest mixture of clothes, women in beach clothes or full evening dress and the men in every crazy variety of sports clothes. But it is not difficult to pick out the people one wants to talk to, and the rest of the guests don't seem to trouble one or expect one to trouble about them.

JOHN GIELGUD, *to his mother*

1987

To Walnut Creek for Ewa's wedding, then the reception in the park in Danville. When I first came to Berkeley in 1960 with Janka and the children, and Alfred Tarski drove us around to show us the area, the countryside began to the east of the Berkeley Hills—chestnut orchards in the valleys; higher up, straw-colored slopes punctuated by black oaks throughout most of the year. Now the city is everywhere: streets and houses covered with green foliage, lawns, tennis courts, swimming pools, parks. Also, the metro, which runs aboveground here, has been extended all the way from San Francisco. I'm not sure that I'm so much in favor of conservation and against development. Those were quite desolate landscapes, with their dry grass and wiry oaks. Because the climate here is different from Berkeley's, the ocean fog doesn't reach this far, the sky is always blue, everything is parched . . .

Well then, it has been given to me to see in one lifetime the end of the countryside. What happened here is a pattern for the entire planet, not that it has to look the same everywhere, but a clear pattern is developing, if only with regard to population density. So, housing tracts are scattered over a great distance, preserving relics of the countryside, but already maintained artificially: irrigation, trees, space set aside for sports. Farming is kept separate, but there are no more hamlets.   *poet* **CZESLAW MILOSZ**,

Nobel laureate in Literature

AUGUST 10

1846

My Friends: Farewell! I take leave of you, I abandon the country of my birth, my family, property and everything that a man holds most dear . . .

rancher, Californio **ANDRÉS PICO**

1939

YOU AND YOUR FRIENDS
ARE INVITED TO THE
PREMIERE
WEST COAST SHOWING
OF
PICASSO'S

MASTERPIECE
GUERNICA
AND 63 RELATED PAINTINGS
AND DRAWINGS . . .

DAILY FROM 10 a.m. to 10 p.m.
AT THE
STENDAHL ART GALLERIES
3006 WILSHIRE BOULEVARD
LOS ANGELES CALIFORNIA
ENTRANCE FOR PREMIERE
TWO-FIFTY
(plus tax)
General Admission—Aug. 11th to 21st, 100.
Students 25 c (plus tax)

BENEFIT SPANISH ORPHANS
Under Auspices of
MOTION PICTURE ARTISTS' COMMITTEE
Hillside 7361 for Reservations   *gallerist* **EARL STENDAHL**

1949

Lunch at the Farmers' Market with the [Stravinskys], Christopher Isherwood, and the Huxleys, the latter cooing to each other today like newly-
weds, or oldlyweds making up after a spat. Owing to its extensive variety of
salads, seeds (Aldous eats quantities of sunflower seeds, for his eyes), nuts,
health foods, exotic fruit (Milton: "The savory pulp they chew, and in the
rind"), the restaurant is a Huxleyan haunt. Most of the other tables are held
down by drugstore cowboys, movie stars, Central European refugees, and—
to judge by the awed glances in our direction—Aldine and Igorian disciples.
All are vegetarians, for the nonce, and all nibble at their greens like pastur-
ing cows . . .

   I would exchange some, if less than half, of my kingdom for a peek at the
pictures these two observers draw of I.S. . . .

                    writer, conductor, amanuensis **ROBERT CRAFT**

2021

My mother's concern for her own mother's deteriorating health grows. I am
increasingly worried about my own mother's health, which has also taken a

turn for the worse. In this moment, we are able to connect. My grandmother begins breathing too shallowly and is taken to the hospital.

Racial distrust in America runs so deep that people in my family thought it was logical to risk getting a deadly virus rather than trust a physician's recommendation to get a vaccine. Old wounds remain unhealed. A cycle that is unending.   **ESPIE RANDOLPH III**

AUGUST 11

1935

SERA CAMP, INGOT

The flotsam and jetsam of my beloved California is gathered here—it is a state camp (admitting those with established California residence)—and, dispassionately, I say that it flottles and jettles with better manners than the riffraff of our Eastern hinterland.

My first hour in camp I am asked by three men if I care to read, and offering to lend me books, and at my first meal I am continually being asked what I wish.

In Stockton they refused to admit that I was a California resident, while in Redding they refused to admit I wasn't.

Ingot is thirty miles northeast of Redding. A little brook washes its rocky bed through the camp. The water runs in and about clusters of sweet cold cress. Across the brook there is a little flat corralled by towering mountains. A group of trees is growing there, with just now reddening apples weighting its boughs. The men have built a rustic bridge over the creek, leading to the flat. The apples beckon . . .

HARRY PARTCH

1945

TO ALBERT ERSKINE

201 SOUTH BENTLEY AVENUE LOS ANGELES

. . . Unbelievably, my health changed suddenly for the better. My doctor in desperation gave me penicillin, and everything that has troubled me all these years—except, as I said to him, my state of mind about the European situation—cleared up as by miracle almost overnight. I am in a delicious state of well being, though still being filled up twice a week with vitamines and calciums and so on. The only troublesome thing, my hair is turning dark, and shortly I shall not be able to recognize myself any more . . .

This if you please when I had finally despaired, and was ready—not ready, but trying to be—to die. It seems strange now, but it was real then and is still real, but in the past . . .   **KATHERINE ANNE PORTER**

1961

. . . At the moment, I am hung up in a small town in California, with trouble with the transmission of my car, and great difficulty in getting the repair work done as the mechanics quite naturally feel that they have first responsibility to take care of the farm vehicles that are broken down, which are needed for the harvests which are now coming in. The town is loaded with Mexican agricultural workers, and their lot does not appear to me to be a very happy one, though I judge it is some better out here than with the ones which work the East Coast from Florida up north.

. . . Well, I must trot off to see if anything is being done about my car, which I rather doubt. I suppose if I stomped and hollered this would move faster, but I can't really believe that whether I get to San Francisco a few days sooner really matters that much.

As ever,   *publisher* **JAMES LAUGHLIN**, *to Thomas Merton*

AUGUST 12

1959

TO: JAMES HARRIS

BROCKWAY HOTEL

BROCKWAY, CALIFORNIA

Dear Mr. Harris, My husband asks me to write you a few lines to explain why he decided against undertaking the writing of the script for LOLITA. The day Mr. Kubrick and you came to talk things over with him he felt quite enthusiastic about the approach to the script-writing which had been evolved in that conversation. But as the negotiations dragged on, somehow the pattern became upset, and he began to feel more and more that the thing could not be managed (at least, in so far as he was concerned) along the lines that had been suggested. A particular stumbling block became to him the idea of having the two main protagonists married with an adult relative's blessing.

He hoped that a few days of quiet thought devoted to the matter amidst the Sierra pines, in complete solitude, might trigger his imagination into finding an artistic solution which would help him to harmonize your needs with his own vision of the book. But unfortunately nothing came of it. We both enjoyed very much meeting Mr. Kubrick and seeing you again. My husband was very pleasantly impressed by the way you two had read, and saw, the book, and has no doubts that the picture you eventually make of LOLITA will be artistic and excellent in every respect. We both send you our best regards.

Sincerely,   *editor, translator* **VERA NABOKOV**

2021

My grandmother's kidneys are failing. This is one COVID-19 side effect among a host of other symptoms she's experiencing. My heart hurts.

I'm not judging the vaccine hesitant. I was one of them for many months. But I did get the jab. Why? Because white people began to colonize it. No matter how widely the vaccines were distributed in communities of color, it seemed to me there were always some white people showing up and waiting in other people's lines to get their hands on it.   **ESPIE RANDOLPH III**

AUGUST 13

1866

San Francisco—Home again. No—not home again—in prison again—and all the wild sense of freedom gone. The city seems so cramped, & so dreary with toil & care & business anxiety. God help me. I wish I were at sea again!

MARK TWAIN

1937

Scandal about [actor] Henry Daniell and wife. Apparently they go down to Los Angeles and either (a) indulge in or (b) witness orgies—probably both. Though don't you think there's something rather pleasantly domestic about a husband and wife sitting side by side with their eyes glued to peepholes, watching the baser elements whoop it up? All it needs is the kiddies at their peepholes. And what I want to know is—where are these orgies? I feel I've been missing something.   **P. G. WODEHOUSE**

AUGUST 14

1882
BERKELEY

. . . I go to Harvard with a mixture of trembling and impudence that will doubtless be charming to witness when I arrive. Doubtless I shall blunder through a year in some fashion, and I shall hope at all events can make no enemies, unless it be by my ugly face and my Californian barbarity.

philosopher JOSIAH ROYCE

1955
Lunch with Gore. I guess he's still wondering what I think of *Messiah*, his novel. Well, I don't. I'm bored and stuck fast. He asks quite often about my journal and talks apprehensively about the famous one Anaïs Nin is keeping—seventy volumes already!—in which he believes he figures most unfavorably. I believe he really thinks about "posterity" and its "verdict"— just like a nineteenth-century writer! And I don't know whether to admire this, or feel touched by it, or just regard him as a conceited idiot.

CHRISTOPHER ISHERWOOD

1963
Imagine! Clifford Odets dying!

playwright CLIFFORD ODETS, *to Elia Kazan and Jean Renoir,*
on his Cedars of Lebanon Hospital deathbed,
while Rae Sal Kipen gives birth nearby
to your editor

AUGUST 15

1850
When the city has no work in which to employ the chain gang, the Recorder shall, by means of notices conspicuously posted, notify the public that such a number of prisoners will be auctioned off to the highest bidder for private service . . .   LOS ANGELES CITY COUNCIL MINUTES

2021

My grandmother feels better and is no longer contagious. She decides she wants to come home rather than remain at the hospital. My mother's symptoms are waning, and she's feeling better. I'm overjoyed. If we can get them both out of the woods and then get them vaccinated, maybe this whole nightmare will be over. I feel hope.

Black vaccination hesitancy has valid roots in our health care system. But if that distrust creates so much fear that we die when we don't have to, our Black lives won't matter much at all.   **ESPIE RANDOLPH III**

AUGUST 16

1935

Jesus, I just this instant heard that Will Rogers was killed; I was doing an original script which I hoped to sell to Fox for him—

DON MARQUIS, *upon Rogers' fatal crash in Alaska*

1940

Dear Ma and Pa:

The past week has been more like the old days. I've been almost as busy as during the old days in New York. The difference is that here I manage to get my quota of sleep and exercise. There is a Ping-Pong table at the Laughtons, and spending a Sunday at home is the equivalent of going to a resort . . .

broadcaster, screenwriter **NORMAN CORWIN**

2010

PESCADERO, CALIFORNIA

Pescadero is only 45 minutes from Facebook's offices on Page Mill Road in Palo Alto. But it feels a century removed. It's a coastal California farming town, about a mile inland from the crashing waves of the Pacific Ocean. We're here for our annual family pilgrimage to Duarte's Tavern. Artichoke and green-chile soup, sourdough bread, dungeness crab and olallie-berry pie.

The coastal fog burns off, and the sun peers through. On our way home, we stop by Harley Farms Goat Dairy. The goats are in the pens so we try free samples. On the wall is Mark Doty's poem, *Pescadero* . . .

The little goats like my mouth and fingers, and one stands up against the wire fence, and taps on the fence board a hoof made blacker by the dirt of the field, pushes her mouth forward to my mouth, so that I can see the smallish squared seeds of her teeth, and the bristle-whiskers.

Another clipping on the wall, about "Pie Ranch." It's a working farm down the coast that promotes sustainable agricultural practices and educates young people. I recognize the name of the founder. My best friend in 4th Grade. I haven't spoken with him since 1982. It feels like a rare moment of re-connection that doesn't involve the internet. I send him a message on Facebook. He doesn't remember me.

Driving back over the Santa Cruz Mountains in my father-in-law's car, we listen to the soundtrack to *Oklahoma*, which my daughter loves. "All the cattle are standing like statues . . . " She's developing an early fondness for show-tunes, much to my wife's chagrin. I think of Neil Young, and my college roommate, who used to shower for hours while listening to "After the Gold Rush." Neil lives somewhere up here in La Honda with the last hippie holdouts.   *filmmaker* **JESSE MOSS**

AUGUST 17

1892

ST. HELENA

You asked me what books would be useful to you—I'm assuming that you've repented your sacrilegious attitude toward literature . . . There is a little book entitled (I think) simply "English Composition." It is by Prof. John Nichol—elementary, in a few places erroneous, but on the whole rather better than the ruck of books on the same subject.

Read those of Landor's "Imaginary Conversations" which relate to literature.

Read Longinus, Herbert Spencer on Style, Pope's "Essay on Criticism" (don't groan—the detractors of Pope are not always to have things their own way), Lucian on the writing of history—though you need not write history . . . Read Burke "On the Sublime and Beautiful."

Read—but that will do at present. And as you read don't forget that the rules of the literary art are deduced from the work of the masters who wrote in ignorance of them or in unconsciousness of them . . . Doubtless you have read many—perhaps most—of these things, but to read them with a view to profit *as a writer* may be different . . .

I wish you would write some little thing and send it me for examination. I shall not judge it harshly, for this I *know*: the good writer (supposing him to be born to the trade) is not made by reading, but by observing and experiencing. You have lived so little, seen so little, that your range will necessarily be narrow, but within its lines I know no reason why you should not do good work. But it is all conjectural—you may fail. Would it hurt if I should tell you that I thought you had failed? Your absolute and complete failure would not affect in the slightest my admiration of your intellect. I have always half suspected that it is only second rate minds, and minds below the second rate, that hold their cleverness by so precarious a tenure that they can detach it for display in words.   **AMBROSE BIERCE**, *to his niece*

1935

Human life consists in mutual service. No grief, pain, misfortune, or "broken heart," is excuse for cutting off one's life while any power of service remains. But when all usefulness is over, when one is assured of an unavoidable and imminent death, it is the simplest of human rights to choose a quick and easy death in place of a slow and horrible one. I have preferred chloroform over cancer.   **CHARLOTTE PERKINS GILMAN**, *her suicide note*

1938

Corinne phoned good-bye. Feel quite a gap. Don't know what to think yet.

philosopher **MARSHALL MCLUHAN**,
researching at the Huntington,
courting his wife-to-be

1946

If Howard Hughes intends to continue producing pictures like *The Outlaw*, his studio had better do something about research.

At any moment now I am expecting to walk into a theater to see Ulysses S. Grant attacking the Maginot Line, or Lydia Pinkham doing the Salome dance with the head of Senator Bilbo.

To anyone with the slightest knowledge of Western history, this most recent display of Western lore is painful, to say the least.

If I were a relative of either Pat Garrett or Doc Holliday, I'd sure sue somebody . . .

writer **LOUIS L'AMOUR**

2021

I find out that my sister has jumped in her car and driven the five hours from Dallas to my mom's small town to see our mom. When she arrives, she finds that my mother has returned to her teaching job after testing negative. When she gets home from work, my mom FaceTimes my father, my brother and my nephew so they can talk to my grandmother.

Amid the chatter and fuss, quietly, peacefully my grandmother passes away.   **ESPIE RANDOLPH III**

AUGUST 18

1936

Worked with Billy Wilder, who paces constantly, has over-extravagant ideas, but is stimulating. He has the blasé quality I have missed sadly in dear Frank Partos. He has humor—a kind of humor that sparks with mine . . .

screenwriter **CHARLES BRACKETT,**
on meeting his frequent collaborator

1942

The movies were scheduled for eight o'clock and the place was not supposed to be open until 7:30, but the 1500 people were in line by 6:35. It extended all the way down past the postoffice in three columns. The shows are given every Monday, Tuesday, Friday, and Saturday night with 1500 people attending each showing. Only the first 7 or 800 to get in can see the picture very well. This week a lot of blankets were put up against the windows to darken the place and two loudspeakers have been installed on the girders crossing the large room.

The Issei are as bad as the kids when it comes to pushing and crowding in. They just come and plop down on any space that is even left slightly open. And they take their shoes off! . . .

This week Abbott and Costello in "Hold That Ghost" was playing. The audience really seemed to enjoy the picture, but I thought it was a bit corny. But why should I be an old wet blanket?

The film scheduled for next week was "Citizen Kane" but Yoshio K. told me that he had to cancel it upon the request of Mr. Thompson of the Rec. Department, who claimed that the picture would be too deep for 80% of the audience and he thought that comedies should be shown.

CHARLES KIKUCHI

2004

Don't be evil. We believe strongly that in the long term, we will be better served—as shareholders and in all other ways—by a company that does good things for the world even if we forgo some short term gains. This is an important aspect of our culture and is broadly shared within the company.

Google users trust our systems to help them with important decisions: medical, financial and many others. Our search results are the best we know how to produce. They are unbiased and objective, and we do not accept payment for them or for inclusion or more frequent updating. We also display advertising, which we work hard to make relevant, and we label it clearly. This is similar to a well-run newspaper, where the advertisements are clear and the articles are not influenced by the advertisers' payments. We believe it is important for everyone to have access to the best information and research, not only to the information people pay for you to see.

co-founder **ERIC SCHMIDT**,
quoting Gmail creator Paul Buchheit
in Google's IPO prospectus

AUGUST 19

1942

. . . Life is going on much the same as usual here with occasional excursions into Hollywood—to concerts that Barbirolli conducts at the Bowl, and to see odd people that are, have been, or may be useful to any of us. It is an extraordinary place—absolutely mad, and really horrible. I can't really attempt to describe it, because it has no relation to any other place on earth. It actually isn't a place by itself but a suburb of Los Angeles, which is the ugliest and most sprawling city on earth. The chief features of Hollywood are that the things that one worries about so much don't matter a damn— money, time, distance, behaviour, clothes (especially for men). It is completely unreal . . .

One house we stayed in was built like a boat, with a moat round it,—in the middle of all the other houses—which anyhow are any and every style from a native-mud-hut to an Indian temple—via Pagoda & Spanish villas . . .

The driving is mad—I saw a wonderful little argument between 2 cars the one on the right wanting to go left, across the other which wouldn't give

way. After blowing its horn madly for about 1 minute (they were both travelling about 45 down a main Boulevard), it started to swerve madly about—
like this [diagram] until finally it just barged into the side of the other, &
there was an awful crash—just because neither would give way!

BENJAMIN BRITTEN, *to his sister*

1948

How I long to surrender! How easy it would be to convince myself of the
plausibility of my parents' life!   **SUSAN SONTAG**

1962

6233 MULHOLLAND, LOS ANGELES 28, CAL.

To Dr Humphry Osmond

[It] seems worth trying at least to do something to mitigate the current organized insanity. How fabulously well-organized the insanity is was borne
in upon me the other day at the local North American Aviation plant, where
I went to have a look at the Apollo moon-shot capsule and the latest plane-
to-ground missiles, which can turn at right angles, skim along the ground,
shoot perpendicularly up into the air to avoid interception and finally be
guided, warhead and all, to whatever orphanage or old people's home may
have been selected as the target. All this concentrated knowledge, genius,
hard work and devotion, not to mention all those incalculable billions of
dollars, poured forth in the service of vast collective paranoias—and meanwhile our three billions of mainly hungry people are to become six billions
in less than forty years and, like parasites, are threatening to destroy their
planetary host and, with their host, themselves.

ALDOUS HUXLEY

2010

ENCINITAS, CALIFORNIA

Visiting old friends in Encinitas, a little surfer town north of San Diego. Jerry's a civil rights lawyer. His "Free Mumia" bumper-sticker stands out on the
palm-lined cul-de-sac. They have chickens in the back yard and Christian
neighbors. Jerry plays Bruce Springsteen all morning. I try to like Bruce, but
can't. Jerry's the biggest book lover I know. I marvel at his ability to read, to
concentrate, amidst the chaos around him: kids, a menagerie of animals,
300 pending cases. He finds the fragments of time, where most of us would
fail to even look. I remember him on my last visit, on the elliptical in his
living room, watching a "Great Courses" history lecture. He sent me a book
about the murder of Fred Hampton months ago. I haven't read it . . .

Later, we take the Avocado Highway east to Escondido, for a vegetarian potluck at La Milpa, an organic farm. I feel like I've stepped into a time-warp, like a Grateful Dead show at Frost Amphitheater. There's even a VW bus parked in the field. Only in California. I ask Jerry if the bus is a prop. My daughter runs through the corn. I imagine her remembering this event, as a fragment of a memory, years from now. It reminds me so much of my own half-remembered early 70s childhood.

The kids are asleep. We stay up and talk Wiki Leaks, "Collateral Murder," and *Behind the Green Door*, the "classic" Marilyn Chambers porn film, which I saw in 1982. My friend Seth Godfrey claimed to have found a VHS copy of the film in a field behind an adult bookstore, a field that is now the new Facebook Offices in Palo Alto.   **JESSE MOSS**

AUGUST 20

1922

YOSEMITE, CAL

Didnt know it was Sunday until next day. Climbing all day from the Carlin Inn to Yosemite. The big trees—Pride of California and Fallen Giant. That hiker we picked up is with us. His talk. His character. Helen & I quarrel about her refusing to put the top down. At Yosemite I get out & walk. Yosemite. El Capitan. The Inn. The village. The stream. The people. The cafeteria. The fakery. We see it all. Decide to motor to Wawona. The fierce climb. Last view of Valley. The shadowy forrest. The broken down Chevrolet & family. It gets dark. The girl & boy with the donkey. The thrill of beauty. Car insulation threatens to burn. Helen strikes wheel & knocks air tube lose. We limp into Wawona. $11 for room for 1 night with breakfast. That dinner! Dancing. We sit in the car & look at the stars.   **THEODORE DREISER**

1976

. . . we saw some high-resolution pictures from Mars the other day when some of the scientists involved were having a show, and you wouldn't be-lieve them. Twenty-six shades of gray, from velvet black to creamy white, and detail so clear and clean you could see the crests on the dunes, and tell the direction of the prevailing wind. From 240 million miles away. That's the place you should travel to . . .

WALLACE STEGNER, *to Ansel and Virginia Adams*

AUGUST 21

1919

Dear Mr. Hearst:
. . . On receipt of your telegram, I started the working layout of the central building and have most of the structural questions solved . . .

JULIA MORGAN

2008

. . . un coyote, te lo juro, about three feet from me. Not running, not walking. Un poco como yo iba, ese southwestern ícono . . .

de cuando en cuando, their howls cut through, rise above the muffled roar de la 210E freeway extension. I can hear them after dark, when the winds change pero la rush hour traffic hasn't died down del todo. Los high-pitched howls drift in, a mournful, choral overlay to the *whoosh whoosh* de la 210, por la ventanita de la master bathroom . . .

SUSANA CHÁVEZ-SILVERMAN

2013

Dear Diary
Just got to San Francisco for a concert. Should be fun, it'll be my crowd: fifteen thousand gay guys and the fat gal pals they dance with . . .

comedian **JOAN RIVERS**

AUGUST 22

1859

San Pedro. The point—the beach—the hill!

writer, lawyer, merchant seaman **RICHARD HENRY DANA**

1944

KING GEORGE HOTEL

My Darling Love,
I've been in Frisco since noon, and it is now six, and for hours and days I have been aching for you so badly. But today especially. We would have loved to discover Frisco together, for it is a city you would love—little crowded streets that go up hills so steep you have to climb little terrace stairway sidewalks.

I did I suppose what every serviceman does first here, I went up to the top of Telegraph Hill and gazed across the harbor and I looked at all the modernistic little houses that squat next to the shanties and tenements tumbling down the hill. The sun was shining in the park on the top of Telegraph Hill . . .   **NORMAN MAILER**

AUGUST 23

1769

The 23rd of August, we proceeded for four hours and a half, part of the way along the beach. We halted in a town of eighty houses and the number of natives that we saw was about four hundred. Much running water and pasture. They made us a present of great quantities of fish, and the first thing they entreat, all along this channel, is that they be permitted to dance; this we conceded so as not to displease them.   **GASPAR DE PORTOLÁ**

1934

Why can't this thing be established upon a national scale [to] employ the services of trained observers and interpreters of the American scene?

HUGH HARLAN,
to WPA head to Harry Hopkins,
proposing what became the Federal Writers' Project

1950

Very sick—constant nausea and vomiting—life is horrible—O death, sweet death, why do you tarry so?   **JAIME DE ANGULO,** *to Ezra Pound,*
his last letter

1965

. . . I really miss him as a person now—do you know what I mean, he's not so much 'The Baby' or 'my baby' any more, he's a real living part of me now, you know he's Julian and everything and I can't wait to see him, I miss him more than I've ever done before—I think it's been a slow process my feeling like a real father! I hope all this is clear and understandable. I spend hours in dressing rooms and things thinking about the times I've wasted not being with him—and playing with him—you know I keep thinking of those stupid bastard times when I keep reading bloody newspapers and other shit whilst he's in the room with me and I've decided it's ALL WRONG! . . .

I'll go now 'cause I'm bringing myself down thinking about what a thoughtless bastard I seem to be—and it's only sort of three o'clock in the afternoon, and it seems the wrong time of day to feel so emotional—I really feel like crying—its stupid—and I'm choking up now as I'm writing—I don't know what's the matter with me—it's not the tour that's so different from other tours—I mean having lots of laughs (you know the type hee! hee!) but in between the laughs there is such a drop . . .   *songwriter, Beatle, poet*

JOHN LENNON, *to his wife Cynthia*

1980

I just got back from Disneyland with Marylou. I rode Thunder Mountain with some guy from Huntington Beach named Bunga Cowabunga!—(His real name was Howard!)   **COLLEEN JAURRETCHE**

AUGUST 24

1937

TO SAXE COMMINS

LAFAYETTE, CONTRA COSTA COUNTY

Dear Saxe,

. . . All the building trades are trying to get a general strike on out here. So there you are. They find fourteen dollars a day not enough for plasterers! And so life goes. In a way I envy you. But I feel we must have a home and in the country. For city life kills Gene . . .

Our love always,

P.S. Gene says to suggest to Bennett and Donald that a several volume collection of best works by Nobel Prize Winners should certainly be a fine bet. Each winner, of course, to be represented by one piece of writing. The one for which he, or she, probably got the prize. If the Pulitzer Prize Book was a success, the above should sell a million.   *actress, former Miss California*

CARLOTTA MONTEREY O'NEILL

1966

You remember all the ruckus about the Mayor's Committee on the Arts here which the Artists Liberation Front was formed to raise voice against, etc?

Well, surprise, I just got a letter from the Mayor asking me to join the Committee (Rexroth behind this I think) . . . Now, as the major tactician of the Movement, what would you advise me?? Join or refuse . . . shall I now play cultural commissar or still leave the field to Waxwroth?

. . . My only achievement is lying on the beach at Bixby . . .

luf,

Larry

poet, painter, columnist, D-Day veteran
LAWRENCE FERLINGHETTI, *to Allen Ginsberg*

AUGUST 25

1929

Met Bobby Jones and had a chat with him about Peachtree Street. I know nothing about the game, but he strikes me as being a man that would be mighty discouraging to play against. There was 6,000 watching him play golf. Shows you the advancement that game has made. Why, six years ago there wasn't fifty pair of misfit knee breeches in this whole State, and ten years ago there wasn't 6,000 folks in Los Angeles that would lie to you about anything but real estate.

The Zep lands here tomorrow. We was the only town that would go out and get a hitch rack to tie the thing to.

WILL ROGERS

1969

I swam out through the deep rise and fall of the water, pale rose and blue in the late light, and lay floating on my back, watching the people crowded along the rails. They were not fishing, I wonder what sort of party had chartered the boat. They were not drinking or shouting or singing either, but were unusually quiet. I swam back, over the kelp beds, on my back—the easiest way to get through them. You can pull yourself along by the kelp faster than you can swim and your body is high in the water, out of the tangle. There were schools of anchovies about and the dark, paleontological looking pelicans were diving around me like rockets. It is wonderful to float in the lift of the evening sea . . .   **KENNETH REXROTH**

AUGUST 26

1903

It was really cold and I soon put on my coat. San Antonio de Padua—is the mission here, some 6 miles from Jolon. It is in a bad state to tumbling down now . . . It is an extremely picturesque old building and I enjoyed every second of the time I spent there sketching and photoing.

JOSEPH JACINTO "JO" MORA,

artist, pictorial cartographer

1966

Dear Mom:

Right now I am in the middle of one of the biggest writing jags of my life . . . The whole situation here is chaotic and under terrible pressure. I am up until dawn every night, beating these rotten keys. And no rest in sight until at least the first of the year, if then. This is a nerve-wracking period. There is real money just around the corner, but turning that corner is going to be hard as hell. It is going to take an incredible amount of good pages in an incredibly short space of time. Sandy is getting depressed with the constant urgency of things. There is not a moment to relax. I couldn't handle this pace if I thought it was anything but a temporary thing. But if the book goes big, in hardback as well as paper, I'll be able to relax for a while.

Love—

Hunter   HUNTER S. THOMPSON

AUGUST 27

1954

. . . an announcement in the papers of the reversal of the guilty-of-treason verdict of Sergeant Provoo of Berkeley. Reason: the prosecution had introduced "irrelevant testimony" regarding defendant's homosexuality. Did I feel the world shift just a little under my feet at that moment?

SAMUEL STEWARD

2012

Today it is official, I guess, that I am old . . .

I saw Sandy Koufax pitch from the dugout boxes, saw that rising fastball and the 12 to 6 curve ball that was impossible to hit. I personally remember my team winning five gonfalons and was curbside at every Laker parade since 1980. I sold programs at the Memorial Coliseum as a kid and saw every Ram home game for over thirty years. I went to UCLA when the village was all Mediterranean pink and Coach John Wooden made me think the Bruins would always win every game. I drove an Impala when it was new and tasted a chubby champ handed to me by a car hop at Harvey's broiler when boys put Butch wax in their pompadours to make them stiff. I was at Disneyland when it opened and remember running on the spongy asphalt down Main Street and once rode the Matterhorn behind Walt Disney. I parked cars in the 60's and had my hands on all the grand muscle cars when they had that new car smell. Oh man.

. . . When transistor radios were introduced it seemed this was the greatest technological advance ever, especially when I heard Vin Scully announce a game like the greatest poet who ever lived. Last week, I listened to him on my iPhone . . .

Above all else, in my adult life I owe the Los Angeles Public Library almost everything. When I started to work as a librarian I was able to compare dirty old Central to being a janitor, a salesman, a ticket broker, a newspaper drudge and a parking lot attendant and I felt like a King. When I started I sat at a reference desk with rotary phones that were connected to a switchboard operator, put periodical requests into Lampson tubes, searched a card catalog and met the most interesting people in my life, including the mother of my daughter. From that desk I have seen the world turn and things happen that I could never have dreamed . . .

While I might groan when I stand and get up too many times in the night to whiz and can't see fine print too well or need a pinch runner in softball I am still filled with hope for tomorrow, for a new adventure that might surprise me almost as much as falling in love in the Autumn of my years, which already happened once. So, today I am old but I still don't need no rocking chair.   *map librarian* **GLEN CREASON**

AUGUST 28

1929

The Zep, in taking off here in Los Angeles, just missed spoiling a great trip and killing everybody by missing a high tension line surrounding the field. Towns bury their dead but they never bury their electric lines . . . There is one sure fire recipe for a pilot in a strange town, that don't know where the field is located. Locate a high tension line, follow it till it crosses another higher tension one. There is almost sure to be a field there. If not, follow it till it comes to an intersection of three or more lines and there will be located the city's municipal field. It's as sure as the sure fire method of locating a speakeasy by following the town's leading citizens.   **WILL ROGERS**

1989

SAN FRANCISCO CHRONICLE

Dear Editor:

Thanks to the efforts of an organization called NIMBY (Not in My Backyard), the solution to the homeless problem in Marin Country has been postponed until after Christmas. What a sensible decision! Now we will be able to work on our Christmas gift list of family and friends without having our attention diverted by less pressing matters.

Had I been a member of NIMBY, however, I would have urged that the postponement of the homeless question be in effect until the first of the year. The week after Christmas is inevitably a time when innumerable demands are made on those of us who celebrate the holidays in the true Christmas spirit— demands such as disposing of the mountain of discarded wrappings and boxes under the Christmas tree, and the writing of thank-you letters to friends and relatives for their presents, and the tiresome necessity of driving to various shops to exchange the gifts for articles more to our liking, etc., etc . . . .

Sincerely   **KAY BOYLE**

2022

. . . The world has exposed itself to be obviously exactly what I thought it was when I virulently turned against it all those years ago as a studied sociopath. Look around. Read the news for two seconds . . . Civilization is full of consuming strife, now collapsing in on itself like a fucked up flan in the cupboard.

And now I have two television projects I'm pitching around Hollywood. First one about the first Latina to have a robot boyfriend in East L.A. The second show about a Chicago bank robbing Latino family who piss off a

Chechen mob boss, so they end up in Witness Protection in Carpenteria, CA. Never been this far along in Hollywood with shows I've created, or co-created, and I have to say, I hate this world. I love spending my day thinking about story (characters, plot, scenes, dialogue, etc..) but I hate hate loathe despise wanna pluck out my eyeball with a rusty spoon rage against the Hollywood pitch process. I've a bank robber's take-what-I-want mentality now forced to parade my hat-in-hand hobo slash mendicant performance around tinseltown. Fucking unbecoming the begging. Humiliating . . .

. . . drought dazed, fire fatigued, prison pummeled California . . . I think that's why the lush Welsh countryside calls for me to retire there with my stories and sea swims and gales and warm fish pie everyday. I could podcast from there. Hide again. In the greenest green fields ever conceived. It's mad Edenic.

And my Rosie is like pre-fall Eve. She leaves me the loveliest phone messages. Dylan Thomas poetry and James Joyce letters dance fiercer in my ear with her Welsh dialect . . . Calls all the local mountains by their original names. Can name all the indigenous plants and fauna on our strolls.

Weird to equate indigenous with someone so utterly pale skinned. Skin almost Swedish albino. And me, skin so dark that all those white evangelical fathers in our mega-church in the San Fernando Valley told their daughters in the 70s not to date me since I was obviously Mexican . . .

Indigenous. White ass Rosie in Wales hates the British. But she loves me . . . My intellect weaned on Protestant English milk. Cut my literary teeth on *Robinson Crusoe, Jane Eyre, Wuthering Heights,* pasty white shit like *Great Expectations.* And my Irish American stepmother made sure I knew Joyce (also her middle name). But it was dad who instilled in me my love of Greek and Roman literature, along with 19th century theologians and British preachers. Even my post-prison life was a soft landing because of my white education . . . I'm white AF, as the kids say.

So yeah, Rosie's indigenous. In her way. My DNA test that came back 49.8% Native American. Indigenous AF . . .

It's like I'm a two-striped flag. Only two colors. White. And rich deep San Fernando Valley tan. A weird ass transplant flag I hope to fly over Rosie's Welsh farmhouse very soon.   *writer, former bank robber* **JOE LOYA**

AUGUST 29

1915

You know I have never cared for cities but San Francisco is simply the most beautiful thing.

writer **LAURA INGALLS WILDER**,
to her husband, Almanzo

1936

American Fascism will get nowhere without a dictator. Somewhere he exists; somewhere in the murky valleys of politics lurks the American Hitler. Soon or late, he will appear. Let us pray that when he comes, he will have the mark of the beast set on his brow, so we shall know him.

screenwriter **PHILIP DUNNE**

1969

I had gone into this dress shop and inside it was freaky everywhere. Mirrors and silver shining areas and sales people with long hair and the clothes were all "groovy," fancy with gimmicks in imitation of our spontaneous fantasy of dress. The place was loud with earblast rock and I stood there feeling paranoid watching the rich kids from Brentwood and Beverly Hills buy "our" clothes for $40 a dress. I got out of there fast . . .   **LIZA WILLIAMS**

1989

It's Sam's birthday today. He is one year old, my little walking dude. . . .

I still look at him and think, Where did you come from, little boy? How did you find your way? I've been thinking about his birth all day, of walking to the drive-in with Pammy, of the male doctor at Kaiser who said the baby was flat. . . .

Pammy asked a nurse if I could get a Valium or something, and they looked at her like she was Jim Morrison. I thought about the ride over to Mount Zion in her car, which is this twenty-year-old Mercedes of her late mother's that we used to drive around in high school. I was bellowing "Fuuuuuuuuuuck" at the top of my lungs. I kept remembering today the blood Pammy said looked like just a little crankcase oil down the back of my dress, of Carol, the angelic but no-nonsense resident who delivered Sam, and the nurses who'd read my books, and how deeply and quickly Pammy and Steve and I bonded with all of them. . . .

I can remember the feel of the sheets, warm from the dryer, on my body, and how hard I was shivering, and what despair I was feeling, and then Sam was born, purple as an eggplant, with his umbilical cord wrapped around his neck, but alive. The mystery of this still leaves me scratching my head, that a baby was made in my body, grew on my milk, and lives here in the house with the kitty and me. . . .

When I held Sam alone for the first time, after Steve and Pammy had gone home the night that he was born, I was nursing him and feeling really spiritual, thinking, Please, please, God, help him be someone who feels compassion, who feels God's presence loose in the world, who doesn't give up on peace and justice and mercy for everyone. And then one second later I was begging, Okay, skip all that shit, forget it—just please, please let him outlive me. He's in for it now, big-time, for all kinds of crazy shit. There are times when he experiences bad things, pain or fear or hurt feelings, and he clings to me like a wet cat, like a cat you're trying to bathe in the sink who tries to climb onto your head . . .

I don't know what to make of it all. But, as I was writing this just now, Sam went into the living room closet, played a little song on the guitar, and then, just this second, peered around from behind the closet door, babbling absolutely incoherently, grinning at me like some like crazy old Indian holy man.

ANNE LAMOTT

AUGUST 30

1910

From 8 A.M. to 4 P.M. in a carriage going up Mt. Wilson. Several dangerous turns in the road, at one of which we all had to get out. Road so narrow that there is no chance for teams to pass. Outer wheels within a foot of the edge (and death) for a large part of the way.

astronomer **EDWARD CHARLES PICKERING**

1915

This valley contains towns, railroads, State and County highways, and many highly improved homes and farms. The district is rapidly growing and values advancing, and it is necessary for the proper protection of these areas that these floods should be controlled.

engineer, hydrographer **JOSEPH BARLOW LIPPINCOTT**

AUGUST 31

1928

. . . all but the tree prints Bender took were purchased by children of eighteen years or younger.

My faith in the new generation of Americans is maintained . . .

The important and only vital question is, how much greater, finer, am I than I was yesterday? Have I fulfilled my possibilities, made the most of my potentialities?

What a marvellous world if all would,— could hold this attitude toward life.   **EDWARD WESTON**

1935

ROOSEVELT HOTEL,

HOLLYWOOD BLVD., HOLLYWOOD-

11:45 in Morning

Got here day before yesterday—called up Sayres and in evening went with Mrs. S. to Trocadero, Beverly Brown Derby, back to Trocadero, dining until 2 or 3 o'clock-so home to Sayre apt.—met S.—talked till daylight-home to hotel-talked to old woman with fishing rod on st.—she said wonderful things about Utah—but forget what so home to bed—Gertrude Sayre phoned promptly at 12 o'clock to remind me of date at M.G.M . . . .

[Sets] of Western mining towns, French Villages, ancient fortresses, ships, small town streets, villages in Greece, etc. saw Warner Baxter and Frank Morgan making pictures, saw Tarzan of the Apes set, met Clark Gable and Miss Jean Harlow, Miss Una Merkle, various directors, writers, etc.—met Humphrey Cobb, so back to Oppenheimer's office—and with Gertrude in her car to Dorthy [sic] Parker's home in Beverly Hills—so drinking with Miss Parker, her husband, Allen, and a beautiful young woman named Muriel King—scene designer from N.Y.—Joel Sayre came in—and finally late departed for Gloria Stuart's and husband's house—Sayre had made some remarks so I offered to fight him—good-naturedly but willingly enough— so dinner at Miss Stuart's—Sayre and I still half friendly but truculent—so departed with Gertrude Sayre and Joel Sayre in their car along shore road above Santa Monica—singing-and Sayre fell asleep so home to hotel—good night and to bed—Sat. A.M.—am on my way to R.K.O. studios to lunch with Joel Sayre—he phoned me about 45 mins. ago.   **THOMAS WOLFE**

1935

I have some amazing and fantastic stories to tell you [about] this moving picture world, as well. I have met the famous stars, directors, producers, writers etc., I've seen them at work—this is simply incredible—in the midst of all the false and unreal world, the technical, building, working world is simply amazing in its skill and knowledge. Good God! I could write a magnificent book even about this place if I lived here a year. They want me to stay, have offered me a job, and mentioned huge sums, but perhaps I shall resist.

THOMAS WOLFE, *to Maxwell Perkins*

SEPTEMBER 1

1933

I cannot thank you too much or often for your kindness to Helen. She seems to have been overwhelmingly impressed by the superiority of Eastern people in general to the Californians; and I do not doubt that her impression is correct. Out here, we have been afflicted with the riff-raff of America—as well as of several other continents. **CLARK ASHTON SMITH**, *to H. P. Lovecraft*

1956

Girls are what boys want, young men get, and old men think about. I have long intended to counsel with you on this matter as a father should, and will delay it no longer . . .

Let us assume you are at a dancing party, and a girl strikes your fancy . . . at some moment during the dance when the music is soft and languorous, draw your lips close to her left year and whisper—distinctly but not so loudly that others can overhear—a sequence of lewd and obscene words. Do not weave them into a sentence, and if inadvertently you do, in no circumstances allow the sentence to conclude with a question mark. Far better the short, simple, sturdy words in artful arrangement, and nothing more . . .

If she turns away from you and runs across the floor to her mother's arms, chattering away and pointing at you, put her down for a prude, and turn your eyes otherwise . . . The number who turn away from you may be considerable, but in them you have lost nothing. If, however, among all that company of girls, just one continues to dance with you—oh my boy, my boy!

Your mother and I send our blessings. Cherish us in your heart and honor us by your conduct. **DALTON TRUMBO**, *to his son*

1977

Well, it's been quite a vacation! But I can hardly wait to get back to the soot and smell of Los Angeles. The camper is giving us a lot of trouble so we're spending the night in the enthralling city of Eureka!

COLLEEN JAURRETCHE

SEPTEMBER 2

1860

My Dear Bessie: I thought I would send you a letter, that you could read yourself—at least a part of it. But here and there I propose to write in the usual manner, as I find the printing style comes rather awkwardly in a rolling ship. Mamma will read these parts to you. We have seen a good many sea-birds. Many have followed the ship day after day. I used to feed them with crumbs. But now it has got to be warm weather, the birds have left us. They [were] about as big as chickens—they were all over speckled—and they would sometimes, during a calm, keep behind the ship, fluttering about in the water, with a mighty cackling, and whenever anything was thrown overboard they would hurry to get it. But they never would light on the ship—they kept all the time flying or else resting themselves by floating on the water like ducks in a pond. These birds have no home, unless it is some wild rocks in the middle of the ocean. They never see any orchards, and have a taste of the apples & cherries, like your gay little friend in Pittsfield Robin Red Breast Esq.

— I could tell you a good many more things about the sea, but I must defer the rest till I get home.

I hope you are a good girl; and give Mama no trouble. Do you help Mama keep house? That little bag you made for me, I use very often, and think of you every time.

I suppose you have had a good many walks on the hill, and picked the strawberries.

I hope you take good care of little FANNY and that when you go on the hill, you go this way:

[freehand drawing of two figures climbing a steep hill]

that is to say, hand in hand.

By-by

Papa.

novelist, poet, common sailor HERMAN MELVILLE,
mailed from San Francisco on arrival

1942

Sometimes here I begin to doubt myself. [Director Anatole] Litvak says, as I spoke of films: "Did it ever occur to you that you're all wrong and we in Hollywood are all right?" And, you know, that almost gets you. For a fatal moment I believed him. And then, of course, I believed what only any man can believe—his own reason. I cannot believe that this town, its manifestations, its puny films, can be right.   **ERIC KNIGHT**, *to his wife*

SEPTEMBER 3

1939

Carol is typing now and the book is beginning to seem real to me. Also Carol got the title last night "The Grapes of Wrath." I think that is a wonderful title. Must query Elizabeth, but will use it any way until I am forbidden. The looks of it—marvelous title. The book has being at last. I think really that a good month will finish it. Middle of October anyway, which is six weeks. No mail again but requests. Young man wants to talk, wants to be a writer. What could I tell him? Not a writer myself yet. But the story is having a reality finally. I said that before but I am stunned with the fact. I think I never really believe I will finish a book until it is finished. And Carol's draft is going to be the final. Let them pay for retyping if they want. We'll put it in shape so it is readable with ease. I just hope it is good. Now to work . . .

     JOHN STEINBECK

1962

Visit with Henry Miller in Los Angeles . . . He looked more than ever like a Buddhist monk, with the same jolliness. He had a picture of a Buddha on his wall as if this were his model. He was the same Henry with the scrutinizing eyes and mellow voice.

He talked about his children. He loved them more than anyone (as Eve wrote me). He had not slept the night before because Val, his sixteen-year-old daughter, still had not come home at four A.M . . . His son had broken his ankle surf-boarding. They both came in. They looked like a million other teen-agers. I could not have said: these are Henry's children.

"Success, oh Anaïs, success does not mean anything. The only thing which means anything are the few special letters one gets a year, a personal response."

He was unchanged, modest, unaffected, naïve, no ego showing. The Henry who wants to be thought a saint . . .

He said he was not done with writing, but that the world did not give him time now. He was on his way to a writers' conference . . .   **ANAÏS NIN**

1969

. . . the hawks that I had feared shot who had prospected for nests in the eucalyptus in both front and rear of the house suddenly appeared in the sky crying their high pitched cries in considerable excitement. The reason was obvious when I looked up. There were three—the young hawks of this year. They were teaching their child the joys of soaring.   **KENNETH REXROTH**

1977

Right now I'm on a TWA Boeing 707 to L.A.X. from San Fran. It's amazing! I feel as if I'm in a ride at Disneyland or something! 30,000 feet and Parallel with the Stars!

It's so beautiful! I'd forgotten the thrill of a jet at takeoff, the rumbling and roaring, the inertia, and then airborne! I'll be able to see all the little hamlets beneath me and the stars next to me! I love it!

COLLEEN JAURRETCHE

SEPTEMBER 4

1857

. . . Emily has exchanged calls with the American ladies she knows here; there are not many of them. Since she does not speak Spanish, few of the Californian ladies have called.   *Judge* **BENJAMIN HAYES**

1911

Sitting alone in the customs office,
How could my heart not ache?
Had my family not been poor,
I would not have traveled far away from home.
It was my elder brother who urged me
To embark on a voyage to this shore.
The black devil here is unjust-
He forces the Chinese to clean the floor.

Two meals a day are provided,
But I wonder, when will I be homeward bound?

*"**LEE**," from Toishan District*

1915

It is fairyland.

LAURA INGALLS WILDER,
visiting San Francisco for the Panama-Pacific Exposition

1922

I thought of stopping off at Yosemite Valley but feel—oh damn scenery . . .

novelist, poet **D. H. LAWRENCE**

1939

TO BLANCHE KNOPF

HOLLOW HILLS FARM, JAMESBURG ROUTE,

MONTEREY, CALIFORNIA

I have settled down in a charming little Mexican house on the side of a hill above the pear orchard here on this beautiful farm in the Carmel Valley to finish my book. The house is entirely my own for work, and as remote and quiet a place as one would want to find, so I shall not be interrupted. I am sorry the manuscript is not ready to send you now, as I had hoped it would be, but it is going along splendidly and is two-thirds finished, so a month more of steady work should get it done. However, my difficulty at the moment is this: having turned down all lectures for this fall and put aside everything else in order to get the book done, my sources of income have temporarily ceased and I find myself with an eviction warning from my New York landlord if I do not come through with the August rent. Which is bad enough, but not quite as bad being unable to employ a typist to assist me in the preparation of a final draft some five hundred pages—which I shall shortly have ready to have recopied. So, much as I dislike to do it at this stage of the game, I am writing to ask you if it would be possible to now allow me an advance of $200.00 on the book, at the moment tentatively entitled THE BIG SEA and which, barring an act of God, will be ready for you in October . . .

LANGSTON HUGHES

1981

Not a big day. Met with Al Haig——the world is still exploding. The French ambassador to Beirut was gunned down by terrorists doing the Syrians' work.

Met with Jim Watt. He's taking a lot of abuse from environmental extremists but he's absolutely right. People are ecology too and they can't forage for food and live in caves.

Saw a film on Begin, a kind of character study. He'll be here Wed.

Had a pleasant evening with a stack of horse and western magazines.

actor, President **RONALD REAGAN**

SEPTEMBER 5

1876

On arriving at the point of junction at Lang Station the entire working force of the road—some 4,000 strong—was seen drawn up in battle array. Swarms of Chinese and scores of teams and drivers formed a working display such as is seldom seen. The secret of rapid railroad building was apparent at a glance. The spot selected for the ceremony was on a broad and beautiful plain surrounded by undulating hills on the one side and the rugged peaks and deep gorges of the San Fernando mountains on the other. The scene was one worthy of the painter's pencil, but by some strange oversight, no photographer was present and the picture presented will live only in the memories of those whose good fortune it was to be present . . .

The spike is of solid San Gabriel gold . . . Col. Crocker said, 'Gentlemen of Los Angeles and San Francisco, it has been deemed best on this occasion that the last spike to be driven should be of gold, that most precious of metals . . . This wedding of Los Angeles with San Francisco is not a ceremony consecrated by the hands of wedlock, but by the bands of steel. The speaker hopes to live to see the time when these beautiful valleys through which we passed today will be filled with a happy and prosperous people, enjoying every facility for comfort, happiness and education. Gentlemen, I am no public speaker, but I can drive a spike!'   **THE LOS ANGELES STAR**

1895

ST. HELENA

It . . . is impossible yet to know the nature and extent of my injuries. They are serious enough at the best. Whether my kneecap is broken or not the swollen condition of the leg prevents us from determining. If so it is likely that I shall have a stiff leg as a bequest (I scorn to say legacy) of the incident. One arm is useless at present, and the other can do nothing of greater utility than write to you. Doubtless I shall remain in bed a long time, but I have an excellent physician (who abstains, mostly, from advice) and the best of care. So you need not worry about doing anything for me.

I must exculpate the bicycle—the accident was, as usual, the fault of the rider . . .   AMBROSE BIERCE

1939

It is 104 here today but the papers in this godawful hellhole proclaim "Angelenos Suffer No Discomfort." That would be too bad. I hope the sons of bitches burn up.   JAMES THURBER, *to the* New Yorker *office manager*

1966

MT. HARKNESS FIRE LOOKOUT

Home in a stone tower: fire lookout. All around me spread the drab-green coniferous forests of Northern California. West stands the plug-dome volcano of Lassen Peak, northwest the shining Fuji-like form of Shasta, fourteen-thousand feet high and eighty miles away.

Finished Desert Solitaire two weeks ago; shipped it off to Congdon. No reply yet. One chapter, "Water," to appear in Harper's this fall. A good book? Yes. My best so far. Everything about it pleases me, except the more egregious errors on technical details—it's a solid book. No waste, no excess, except certain obviously superfluous passages I inserted deliberately for the editors to remove. (They've got to earn their salaries, right?)

Bound for Death Valley in October. Will finally get started on the novel—but which one? Not sure yet.

The big issues in my life at present: . . . writing a good solid novel; fulfilling my obligation to McGraw-Hill (still owe them a book on the welfare mess) . . . and finally, ideally, reaching a clear understanding of and with myself. Ah! But that job seems too much! Too difficult! Impossible! . . .

ED ABBEY

SEPTEMBER 6

1922

Well, here I am in America—San Francisco very pleasant, and not at all overwhelming, except rather expensive: in fact, very, according to my mere European idea. We have a room here for $7. a day, but eat out quite moderately. . . . It is sunny and nice, and we've gone an automobile trip round the city. There is still a bit of Bret Harte-R.L. Stevenson unfinished 'West' about it: not much. Terrible the noise of iron all the while, breaks my head: and the black, glossy streets with steel rails in ribbons like the path of death itself. Terrifying, that is. But night, with great masses and bunches of light, and lights splashing and starring and running up and down and round about, bewildering, beautiful too, a sort of never-stop Hades. I went to a cinema and with jazz orchestra and a huge and voluminous organ . . .

We leave Friday night for Taos. I simply daren't stop off at Yosemite or Grand Cañon: feel I might drop dead if any more stupendousness assails me . . .   **D. H. LAWRENCE**

1961
America to resume underground atom tests, after third Russian explosion.
Bye now.   **CHRISTOPHER ISHERWOOD**

SEPTEMBER 7
1945
I inquired as to whether his [Russia's] government had given any thought to a person who would take the position of secretary general. [Ambassador to the U.S. Andrei Gromyko] said he had not given this matter a thought.

He volunteered however that if the constituent assembly were held in the United States this autumn, and we were not in a position to select in London the permanent secretary general, he would be very happy to see Alger Hiss appointed temporary secretary generals he had a very high regard for Alger Hiss, particularly for his fairness and impartiality . . .
Secretary of State **EDWARD R. STETTINIUS**

1948
160 ALPINE TERRACE

SAN FRANCISCO

Last night I took Carolyn to the S.F. Hospital to give birth, at 12:49 this A.M., to a female. Both are well. —7 lbs. 3 ozs.

Life is fine, I awakening, so pure, so pure. . . .

I love all—sex—yes, all: all, sex. Anyway I can get it I need it, want it shall *have* it—now . . .   **NEAL CASSADY,** *to Allen Ginsberg*

1989

So anyway, I had a baby last week . . .

Both the nurses who were taking care of me had read my books and were treating me like I was Princess Di. The doctor was a woman and I fell in love with her, and I felt really for the first time that things were going to be okay. Perhaps there was a fifty-fifty chance that I would actually give birth to a live baby . . .

Finally, finally, Sam slid out, and they put him on my chest for a bit and then cleaned him up, and then Pammy and Steve held him because I was too hurt and out of it. . . .

I felt like my heart was going to break from all the mixed-up feelings and because I couldn't even really take care of my baby. Finally the fever went away, just as the doctor finished stitching me up, and hope came back into me, hope and tremendous feelings of buoyancy and joy. They took us all to my room, Sam and Pammy and Steve and me, and I nursed the baby for the first time. None of us could take our eyes off him. He was the most beautiful thing I had ever seen. He was like moonlight.   ANNE LAMOTT

1991

Francis turned an old barn into a rehearsal stage and is here working with the cast of *Bram Stoker's Dracula*. Fourteen actors and crew members have been staying with us in the house and two guest cottages. My attention has been on details such as dry towels, the constantly ringing phone and dinner preparations. I am surrounded by people coming and going and have begun to feel hungry to be alone, but at the same time I am relishing the creative energy and the entertaining company around me . . .

I could hear Tom Waits talking to his daughter on the phone in the hall about a homework paper she was writing on the topic of friendship. The pasta water began boiling and as Francis put the spaghetti in, I went out on the porch to light candles and invite everyone to come to the table . . .

As the last light faded from the garden, Francis and I went back into the kitchen where he cooked the veal and I sauteed zucchini. We brought out platters and passed them family style.

We all remained at the table in the candlelight sipping grappa and espresso. Polite conversation had fallen away long before. Tony Hopkins and Gary Oldman gave imitations of Richard Burton, Marlon Brando and Jack Nicholson. Explosions of laughter burst across the porch and into the trees, seeming to rustle the leaves in the darkness.   ELEANOR COPPOLA

1991

We rehearse all day. Francis is totally at ease surrounded by a phalanx of assistants, technicians, choreographer, dancers, musicians—in fact the bigger the extended family, the better he seems to enjoy himself. He seems determined to throw every possibility and option up in the air and see where and how they land. At one point there are so many versions and variations of a single scene, that it feels like direction by committee. Quite often I feel I am invisibly loaded with flying custard pies . . .

Rehearse the Renfield Lunatic Asylum scenes with Tom Waits, who is exceptionally open and easy to work with. We compare notes on being parents. He says his two girls get 'outta hand—you know how it is, so I say, "That's it, Time Out time," which means they have to sit awhile in the same place and regather their forces before the festivities can continue.' But the way he inflects and words this, you half expect him to start singing THE 'Ballad of Time Out', in those trademark vocals.

I discover that the desk in the corner of the studio, alongside the props table crammed with artefacts and reference books, is the one used by Don Corleone in that for ever shuttered study where Brando dispensed his 'justice'. Outside the barn doors, to the left of the car park, stands the boat that took Martin Sheen upriver in *Apocalypse Now*.

. . . Beer chased down by shots of tequila is the preferred entertainment and lays most people out, with Gary literally blacking out. We heave him into the back of Tom's Cadillac and to bed.   *actor* **RICHARD E. GRANT**

SEPTEMBER 8

1849

Still on our way down the river. At 10 enterd the Slues, where the river is divided into several chanels. This is emphatcally the Musketoes batle ground & the man that comes off with a whole hide may be counted luckey.

forty-niner **HIRAM DWIGHT PIERCE**

1955

Santa Barbara surrounded by flames. Last night all roads going north were closed. Today one at least is said to be open.

ALDOUS HUXLEY

SEPTEMBER 9

1907

MARTINEZ, CALIFORNIA

Dear Mr. President
I am anxious that the Yosemite National Park may be saved from all sorts of commercialism and marks of man's work other than the roads, hotels etc required to make its wonders and blessings available. For as far as I have seen there is not in all the wonderful Sierra, or indeed in the world another so grand and wonderful and useful a block of Nature's mountain handiwork. There is now under consideration, as doubtless you well know, an application of San Francisco Supervisors for the use of Hetch Hetchy Valley and Lake Eleanor as storage reservoirs for a City water supply . . .

The few promoters of the present scheme are not unknown around the boundaries of the Park, for they have been trying to break through for years. However able they may be as capitalists, engineers, lawyers or even philanthropists, none of the statements they have made descriptive of Hetch Hetchy dammed or undammed are true, but they all show forth the proud sort of confidence that comes of a good sound substantial irrefragable ignorance.

For example the capitalist, Mr. James D. Phelan, says there are a thousand places in the Sierra equally beautiful as Hetch Hetchy, it is inaccessible nine months of the year, and is an unlivable place, the other three months because of mosquitoes . On the contrary there is not another of its kind in all the Park excepting Yosemite . . .

The first forest reserve was in Eden and though its boundaries were drawn by the Lord, and angels set to guard it, even that most moderate reservation was attacked. I pray therefore that the people of California be granted time to be heard before this reservoir question is decided: for I believe that as soon as light is cast upon it, nine tenths or more of even the citizens of San Francisco would be opposed to it . . .

Faithfully and devotedly yours   **JOHN MUIR**, *to Theodore Roosevelt*
trying, ultimately in vain, to preserve Hetch Hetchy Valley

1945

We've just come back from ten days of camping out in the Sierra and down at Big Sur, and my loins are blistered from nuding on the deserted beach by Thurso's Landing, which isn't called Thurso's on the map; also my tail is blistered from riding a stiff-legged horse up into the Santa Lucia Mountains behind Big Sur, which are really something, when you pop out onto the ridge two thousand feet above that incredible coastline and look down on waves that have rolled in from Japan and redwoods that were growing there before the Shoguns, and headlands that have been wearing away ever since the coast range first poked its snout out of the sea . . .

Yrs, Wally

WALLACE STEGNER,
to Stanford colleague Richard Scowcroft

1947

ROCKPORT, CALIFORNIA

Tuesday, September 9 (Admission Day)

For years this project has been in the back of my mind. The section roughly from Rockport to the mouth of the Eel is the only uncivilized coast left in continental United States where there is no paved road or no road at all. The reasons are pretty obvious: steep, irregular mountains, heavy rainfall in the winter, and consequently deep forests and dense brush. Almost no one (except the "queer") sees any point in battling the difficulties . . .

Were there a constant, concentrated, and valuable natural resource a road would of course be built. But logs aren't such. Sawmills are set up only for a few months or a few years, depending on the supply and the price. The settlements they engender disappear, and aren't reestablished for fifty years, if ever . . .

With my forty-five pound pack on my back, it's that "up and down" ingredient of the present route that gets me . . . I can see the road to Usal taking flight up to the ridge ahead of me. First it goes across and through a creek, as though to get a fresh drink before the ascent . . .

Up the road goes for about twenty-five miles. (The scientifically inclined might say that the map shows the ascent to be about a mile and a half, but maps are only half-emotional. The only true picture of the effort involved is twenty-five miles.)

At the top is a sign: "Danger-bear traps on this place."

Only one car passes me—going my way—all day. And I was fondly gazing at the ocean when it passed. I wasn't even noticed. In the evening, after walking the seven miles from the junction with State 1 to Usal, I camp by a little creek with the tallest alders I ever saw. The creek is swift, running over rocks. Each rock has a clump of watercress against its upper part. I eat several bales of the cress before making a fire, getting supper, and bedding down.

HARRY PARTCH

2011

The day after the attacks, I was driving near my house when another driver abruptly pulled out of his driveway directly in front of me. I did not respond as I normally do, with cursing and exasperated hand gesturing. I simply braked, sighed and let him take the lead. At the next intersection, we pulled up to the stop sign abreast of each other. He was turning right, and I was continuing straight ahead.

We turned toward each other. "I'm sorry," he mouthed, offering a penitent look. I nodded, mouthed "OK," and drove off, wondering about the origins of the alien that suddenly inhabited my body.

writer **ELLEN ALPERSTEIN**

2018

The last time I looked upon Admission Day as an important holiday for our dear Golden state was probably back in Sister Leocritia's grade 4 classroom at St. Helen school back when electricity was new.

While September 9 is an extremely important day in California history, the holiday has assumed a rather jejune reputation since no one gets out of school or stays home from work that day. It is a legal observance but businesses and government offices do not close . . . sigh.

Yet, the event involves some of the most complicated and contentious political skirmishes in the history of the United States . . . The truth is the residents of California were very dissatisfied with the colonial governments of Spain and later Mexico who mostly ignored the far-off colonies and provided little stimulus to commerce, agriculture, and culture. The Californios were so unhappy with the do-nothing governments they even seriously considered offering England a shot at making them part of the empire as a protectorate . . .   **GLEN CREASON**

SEPTEMBER 10

1849

MONTEREY

Mr. WOZENCRAFT submitted the following, which was considered and adopted: Resolved, That a Committee of three be appointed to receive

proposals for the printing of the proceedings of this Convention in Spanish and English . . .   **JOHN ROSS BROWNE**, *in his "Report of the debates*
in the Convention of California, on the formation
of the state constitution"

1860

People are very kind. But it isn't New England. I wonder why I came.

Unitarian minister **THOMAS STARR KING**

1973

I'm riding into that future and frankly I don't know if I'm wearing the fabled helm of Mambrino on my head or if I'm wearing a barber's basin. I guess we wear what we want to wear and we fight what we want to fight. Maybe I see dragons where there are only windmills. But something tells me the dragons are for real and if I shatter a lance or two on a whirling blade, maybe I'll catch a dragon in the bargain.

So I'm asking you to take a chance and ride with me against the windmills and against the dragons, too. To make the quality of life in San Francisco what it should be, to help our city set an example, to set the style, to show the rest of the country what a city can really be. To prove that Miami's vote was a step backwards and that San Francisco's was two steps forward.

Yesterday, my esteemed colleague on the Board said we cannot live on hope alone. I know that, but I strongly feel the important thing is not that we cannot live on hope alone, but that life is not worth living without it. If the story of Don Quixote means anything, it means that the spirit of life is just as important as its substance. What others may see as a barber's basin, you and I know is that glittering, legendary helmet.

shopkeeper, activist, supervisor **HARVEY MILK**,
the day after his inauguration

1983

Today I read Joan Didion and discovered a woman I could love to listen to. Mostly men live in my bookshelves; only the panting of Anaïs Nin and the yearnings of Sylvia Plath have so arrested my attention. Daddy says I never write—probably true.   **COLLEEN JAURRETCHE**, *aspiring writer*

2018

I fooled around with a blurb that was itself epistolary. Here's more or less what it would have looked like:

"Kipen, you need a blurb from me for your LA Letters book? Happy to do it, I've been trapped on the shitter for days with the thing. What do you want it to say? That it's a feast, a banquet—or is this whole communique getting way too peristaltic?"   *novelist* **JONATHAN LETHEM**, *to the editor*

SEPTEMBER 11

1935

SAN FRANCISCO

Dear Max: This is a fascinating and wonderful city—we can be proud of it— They are trying to get me to stay but I am leaving today and will see you in a few days—Feel fine, but do you think I will be able to work again?

THOMAS WOLFE, *to Maxwell Perkins*

1947

USAL BEACH

. . . The mountains on each side of this little cove are steep and forbidding, even though the tops are forested. The beach is desolate, lonely, and I love it. It has the blackest sand I ever saw. Clean but black.

I had thought that fresh water might be a problem, but there are a dozen little springs in the cliffs around me. None of them really run, this dry time of year, but I can get a canful of drips in an hour or two. Some of them stop running when the sun hits them, start again at night . . .

Haven't seen a soul down here in twenty-four hours . . . No one is around the fishers' huts, though they seem well kept, and one has a nice little vegetable garden. I knocked and halloed, but such souls as may have been around probably saw me coming. There is evidence of the army or navy, some kind of amphibious craft being abandoned in front of the huts.

A few wisps of fog are coming in this afternoon, partially obscuring the north mountain occasionally. But I refuse to put on my clothes as long as I make a shadow in the sand . . .   **HARRY PARTCH**

1952

We are now at the killing of Caesar, a very messy proceeding—the daggers spout mock blood which splashes over clothes and faces, and then they want to photograph the scene again from another angle and everyone has to wash and change and make up all over again, making endless delays on to the already tedious procedure.

The nicest Hollywood gag I have heard so far happened the other day, when the live pigeons were sitting patiently all day on the plinths and columns of the Forum. They are apparently clipped so that they can't fly about, but one daring bird was bold enough to flutter to the pavement, where he was strutting about. The cowboy character who looks after the animals noticed him and went over and was heard to remark severely 'Now get back up there. Go on, didn't you hear me? Don't you want to work tomorrow?'

JOHN GIELGUD, to his mother

SEPTEMBER 12

1923

. . . saw eclipse yesterday—very impressive—also 7 destroyers on rocks— depressive Los A silly—much motoring, me rather tired and vague with it . . .

D. H. LAWRENCE

1938

Things get no more peaceful. Today Hitler is to make his war or peace speech. That may toss the world into a mess. Apparently the whole world is jittery about it. All armies mobilized. It might be a shambles by tomorrow. And it might recede for a while. Can't tell . . .

I must untighten my jaw. Too many things are happening. Must be calm and not disgusted. But it is hard because I have been working too long on this book, longer than on anything in my life. If this book is bad, I'm going to be terribly disappointed. Today Ma meets the ladies committee and it must have some charm. It must. It can't flop because here is the great contrast. Here is the tremendous contrast. It must be charming. And I am late getting started today. Jaw is too tight.

JOHN STEINBECK

1961

ABOVE BIXBY CANYON

I am up here in the golden fields at the top of Big Sur, on one of the highest hills, over the ocean, the long wheat grass is gold-yellow up here, its tares blow in the wind, I sit cross-legged, naked under the hot sun.

Homer the Dog has made himself some shade under a bush, he is full of tares and burrs, and the flies bother him, he's panting . . . It's early afternoon—a high noon—way down below, westward, the blue-gray sea fading into a vague horizon of clouds; a car creeps like an ant on the highway. I think I could wander this way the rest of my life—a small knapsack, sneakers, an old Navy CPO shirt, khaki pants, a small knife, a bottle opener, a nail clipper, a pencil & pad, a book, all I have . . . So to India one day.

The wind blows thru me, over the hills.   **LAWRENCE FERLINGHETTI**

1993

Last week I was screaming at the top of my lungs, louder than I ever have, "I USED TO PLAY HANDBALL! I WAS IN THE FUCKING SCHOOL CHORUS!" It was so painful to remember who I used to be.   **AMY ASBURY**

SEPTEMBER 13

2004

Home from San Quentin. leading a writing workshop for 8 guys who wrote soulful sad stories.

where to begin. the tour of the yard . . . the stacks of bodies, the sleeping men in orange jumpsuits on their cots. trying to get some rest in the cacophony. the casualness (they didn't inspect my bag, in which I had my Swiss army knife and my cell phone) and then the heavy metal door to Death Row . . .

Steve & Dana's house is utter chaos but also very serene . . . in the morning, Dana proposes a walk on the hill behind the house. You have to understand, her house is on the grounds of the prison. You can hear the loudspeakers. You drive through the gate to get there. I keep thinking of the houses near Auschwitz.

We stop at the house of a young mom with three kids, a woman named Terry. Her husband is the only locksmith in San Quentin. Her older boy asks questions about the prison. She tells him that the men there made bad choices in life but they are not bad people. On the top of the hill she points out the exercise facility on the roof, covered with chain link mesh—for the Death Row inmates. "Their feet never touch the ground." She points out the new "fish" in the yard, just reeled in, new inmates, not assigned yet.

Terry (the locksmith's wife) says that when there are executions everyone "feels bad." it's terrible, she says. her 7 year old asks questions . . .

why they live there: they pay $600 rent and their son goes to a great school in Larkspur and there are wonderful parks in Marin. and that's the decision they had to make in order to live in the Bay Area. they make the decision for their kids and they live within spitting distance of Death Row.

she can't not think about it . . .

Henry writes about crying in the sweat lodge, a visitation by his Yurok grandmother. Kenny and Steve and Jomon all write about the visiting room, the focal point of their week. Kenny—a talk with his father about revenge; Steve, preparing to meet his wife . . . the way he dresses, makes sure he smells good. the intensity of that circumscribed space . . .

I'm reading Tracy Kidder and finishing Mark Salzman and thinking about San Quentin.   **LOUISE STEINMAN**

2016

Dear Los Angeles

We met many years ago when we were both young and we had stars in our eyes and wanted to make a beautiful oasis, a beautiful place. There weren't a lot of rules, there weren't a lot of spotlights, and there weren't a lot of people watching. There was a lot of freedom for a creative person to explore ideas, make things. Anywhere else in the world, I would have had difficulty taking the route that you afforded me. Together we all want to help, to address our collective experience and some of the challenges still confronting us. We've been good partners and we are stronger for it. Let's continue taking care of each other.   *architect* **FRANK GEHRY**

2021

ALPINE COUNTY

Wildfires have no morality. They do not skip a house because sensitive and wonderful children live there, or because the owner is a talented oil painter and all her life work is stored inside. They do not overlook temporary homes where talented individuals live, nor do they spare dream homes, that are in the process of being built . . .

In the deepest sense, we have nothing, yet possess everything: or at least all that is hidden in this present moment. The future is unwritten in my mind: there is no way for us to see what will happen next. Just as the sad little bear who has come through my yard hangs his head, looking for his mother in this changed landscape, I look around for the familiar and find it vanished. The road ahead has become clouded with blowing smoke, hiding the future, reminding me of my impermanence, and at the same time, filling me with gratitude.   *writer* **LISA GAVON**

SEPTEMBER 14

1910

I didn't mean to cry today —I meant to show you how brave I could be, —but not to see your dear eyes—not to feel your lips against my throat— the intolerable pain I am to feel through endless months, came over me like a flood.

UNA KUSTER,
to her future husband, Robinson Jeffers

1930

Our weather here now is the golden, azure, Indian-summery kind, with a mellow warmth that pervades one's being like an elixir. I, too, still work out of doors as much as possible. Probably the mountain scenery was a stimulant to my writing—but it was so tremendous that it temporarily altered and confused my sense of values. Mere words didn't seem to stand up in the presence of those peaks and cliffs.   **CLARK ASHTON SMITH**

1934

I sit here. I have nothing to do. I have had nothing to do for days. I have had nothing to do since I came here. No one opens my office door. No one hints what might be expected of me to earn my handsome salary. No one knows I'm here, or gives a good Goddamn . . .

I would go home as a final gesture except that I won't be licked by damned idiocy. I shall now stay here and rot in my beautiful office. My cadaver shall begin to smell. They will think it is just the normal smell of a completed film somewhere. Then, years later, another writer shall be given my office. He'll find my skeleton here, sitting amid a welter of pay checks I shall never cash . . .

[You] wouldn't believe that a place could be like this. The sham and the indescribable beauty.

That's the real hell of it. It should be the most marvellous place in the world. You can't picture it, because California has never told the truth to the world even about California . . .

When you arrive here, you don't come to the Los Angeles station. They drive out and meet the train at Pasadena. You are whisked into a gorgeous Cadillac. That's showmanship! After that you can rot in your office unknown and unsung . . .

I know that out of all this hodge-podge there must come something. There are men here who know and who long and who desire. They are slowly beginning to outnumber the pants-pressers. Some day they will break through—the total pressure will be too great for the soft surface. And then watch the films. Just as the sun-dried soil of this parched land springs miraculously to bounteous return the moment water touches it, so from the manure and dirt that are these now-reigning moguls will burst marvellous film-growth. The soil is arid and barren now. It needs only the water that courageous men can bring.   **ERIC KNIGHT**, *to a friend*

1966

Mt. Harkness

. . . My philosophy, I guess, insofar as I still have one, would fall under some such heading as Romantic Naturalism.

Fourteen days since I took my wife and sweetheart (yes, both!) to Reno and the bus depot. Today, this afternoon, this hour, I am in a blue funk of loneliness and boredom—strange childish terror of being alone, with nothing to do. A kind of panic and horror grips me I can easily understand why solitary confinement is the cruelest of all tortures, easily sufficient to drive a man mad . . .   **ED ABBEY**

SEPTEMBER 15

1969

On the bus to the airport to the hotel in San Diego it was a dark and tired time, and all you could see was the lighted of ends cigarettes. It was quiet, except for a few mumbled conversations . . .

Jim Owens: "Hey, are you going to use names in that thing you're writing?"

"Once in a while."

"Christ, be careful" . . .

My wife suggested that I might save some money at the Astroworld after she left if I had a roommate. She had noticed that Tommy Davis was living at the hotel alone and thought maybe he would like to save some money too. So I asked him. He said he'd think about it.

Even though we're friends, there was this moment of awkwardness. Maybe Tommy Davis doesn't want to room with anybody. Maybe he doesn't want to room with me, but wouldn't mind a different white guy. And he might have wondered if I was trying to prove something. I wondered if he wondered. The tiny tension was there. Too bad.

I think I should explain here that I too have gone through a difficult learning process. When I was in high school I was certain —with all the snobbish certainty of youth—that I would never let my daughter marry a Negro, nor would I like to live next door to a Negro family. What I know now is that life is a lot more complicated than that.   JIM BOUTON

2018

Canvassing in Lancaster today with Charlotte. We're talking to a doughy white woman at the door of her garage. (she said she'll vote for Katie Hill). She looks us both over and says, "you two look like you only eat one pea apiece."   LOUISE STEINMAN

SEPTEMBER 16

1860

PACIFIC OCEAN

My Dear Malcolm . . . The other day we saw a whale-ship; and I got into a boat and sailed over the ocean in it to the whale-ship, and stayed there about an hour. They had eight or ten of the "wild people" aboard. The Captain of the whale-ship had hired them at one of the islands called Roratonga. He wanted them to help pull in the whale-boat when they hunt the whale . . .

When we get to San—Francisco, I shall put this letter in the post office there, and you will get it in about 25 days afterwards. It will go in a steamer to a place called Panama, on the Isthmus of Darien (get out your map, & find it) then it will cross the Isthmus by rail road to Aspinwall or Chagres on the Gulf of Mexico; there, another steamer will take it, which steamer, after touching at Havanna in Cuba for coals, will go direct to New York; and there, it will go to the Post Office, and so, get to Pittsfield.

I hope that, when it arrives, it will find you well, and all the family. And I hope that you have called to mind what I said to you about your behaviour previous to my going away. I hope that you have been obedient to your mother, and helped her all you could, & saved her trouble. Now is the time to show what you are—whether you are a good, honorable boy, or a good-for-nothing one. Any boy, of your age, who disobeys his mother, or worries her, or is disrespectful to her—such a boy is a poor shabby fellow; and if you know any such boys, you ought to cut their acquaintance . . .

The picture which I have of you & the rest, I look at sometimes, till the faces almost seem real.—Now, my Dear Boy, good bye, & God bless you

Your affectionate father

H Melville

I enclose a little baby flying-fish's wing for Fanny   **HERMAN MELVILLE**

1878

BERKELEY, ALAMEDA CO. CAL.

PRES. GILMAN,

Dear Sir

. . . I instruct the 3d & 4th Classes in Rhetoric, Composition, & Literature. The classes are attentive, and at moments quite bright: but their wants are very elementary, and the supplying of the same more of a strain on the patience than on the intellect . . .

These lectures will strain all my resources in the directions of brevity, clearness, and original work, and I look forward to the undertaking with no little interest. If I succeed, I shall do myself much more good than I shall in the class. Even if I make no success of it, the students may yet carry off a trifle of logic, or at least a few bits of useful terminology; and the effort will at all events do me no harm . . .

I doubt if capital Philosophy is destined to succeed well in California, or Literary Criticism, either. If I want to continue my worship at these two altars, I must make a pilgrimage . . .

Very Truly Yours   **JOSIAH ROYCE**

1932

I am afraid I am a coward. I am sorry for everything. If I had done this a long time ago, it would have saved a lot of pain.

PEG ENTWISTLE, *before leaping from the Hollywood sign*

1940

I started to work this morning . . . got all my notes in order for the book on eating. I don't want to write it particularly, but I want to write. It is like having the itch. Now that I have started to work again, I am easier, as if I have put ointment on my mind.   **M. F. K. FISHER**

SEPTEMBER 17

1923

LOS ANGELES

. . . Here I've been in California eighteen days. The time slips by quickly.—It is a loose, easy, rather foolish world here. But also, a great deal of falseness is also left out.—It's not so bad, in some ways . . .   D. H. LAWRENCE

on the same day

LOS ANGELES

. . . I think, this day week, I shall go down to Mexico. Perhaps I shall find a little ranch there. Put a new peg in the world, a new navel, a new centre. Esperamos! We're hardly beginning yet. America's awfully foolish and empty. But perhaps, if it went through a great convulsion, it would be the place. . . .   D. H. LAWRENCE

1940

. . . In the evening Fay [Wray] and I went to the house of Dolores del Rio in Bel Air. We were to have dinner with her and Orson Welles, her light of love. She is a typically Mexican woman, charming, feminine, chatting lightly, and feeling about anything that catches her eyes. We drove to a restaurant where Welles joined us later, tired with work [on *Citizen Kane*]. He was very gracious and articulate, as usual, in fact articulate enough to be very glib. I did not mind this. In fact he is a sort of biological sport, stemming out of Lord Byron through Oscar Wilde, I should say. But he has a peculiarly American audacity. Of other people he said just what he thought of them, with scorn and derision; with us he was deferential, once referring to me as "in the foremost ranks of the talents of the world."

I liked best when he suddenly said of himself, "I have a touch of rhinestones in my blood," meaning he is part-charlatan . . . .

I found that I disagreed with everything Welles said and I like him in spite of that. He is a very octopus of evil, but for all that there is a good side to him, a sense, for instance of humble people. A communion of intelligence is possible with him; finally, too, he also is in opposition to the values around him, even though they may finally swallow him up.   CLIFFORD ODETS

1969

SAN FRANCISCO

It was great coming back to Candlestick Park. I hadn't been there since the World Series of 1962. The odor of the clubhouse was strangely familiar, and I remembered where all the guys had their lockers and the table in the middle of the room loaded with ten dozen baseballs for us to autograph.

This was my rookie year and I remember Whitey Ford hurt his arm and I was going to have to pitch the seventh game, except that it rained for five days in a row and Ralph Terry was able to come back and win the final game 1–0 when Willie McCovey hit a screaming line drive off him and Bobby Richardson caught it for the final out. And I remember the police escorts we had wherever we went, sirens screaming. Great year for a rookie.

"It was a terrible year," Tommy Davis said. "The Dodgers should have been in that Series, not the Giants."

Except that they lost to them in a playoff. Can't be a great year for everybody, I guess . . .   JIM BOUTON

SEPTEMBER 18

1913

Imagine that I ride to the laboratory every morning on horseback! Could you conceive of that in France? In the evening we have to close the henhouse carefully because of "coyotes," a sort of wolf-fox. In the mountains which we see from our window one still occasionally finds "pumas" . . .

Does it surprise you that I am not in a great hurry to leave this country where I can combine my love of life in the wilderness and my wish to cultivate literature?   JAIME DE ANGULO

1944

Our hegira was fairly hot and hectic, but much fun. Every time I come west I swear I'll never go back east. This time maybe the swearing gets somewhere . . . .

We found a desert terrapin in the Mojave Desert that made the trip complete for Page. He is not a housebroke terrapin, I just discovered. The house here, apart from the Southern Pacific which runs through the back yard like a banshee every hour, is really fine. Hibiscus trees and palm trees and eucalyptus trees and pine trees and a thousand flowering shrubs, a nice sweep of lawn, a view of the Pacific seventy feet away through the pines . . .

WALLACE STEGNER

1969

. . . I would enjoy having a Jefferson Airplane platter the jacket of which has been inscribed by all the members of the combo. I now own Surrealistic Pillow, Bless its Pointed Little Head, Jefferson Airplane Takes Off, and Crown of Creation. I think you have several more titles; if you can lay hands on one for me, I will appreciate it. And please tell Miss Slick that even if I did not enjoy her singing (I do!), nevertheless she would be an asset to any group just through her smile.   ROBERT A. HEINLEIN, *to Paul Kantner*

1987

The days of the Pope's visit to America and our West Coast. I preferred watching it all on television. Many people, very many, did the same, with the result that the crowds were smaller than expected . . .

The Pope in Hollywood: he has come to the lions' den, and unaware that they are ready to rip him to pieces, he recommends that they start eating vegetable cutlets instead of their bloody cuisine. A marvelous text. It makes one think that it is possible to address the most spoiled community and to move or convince some members . . .

The Pope in San Francisco: the same thing; the courage to proclaim the Word in the city of the loosest mores, in the capital of homosexuality, in a city that would be expected to turn a deaf ear. St. Paul in Corinth? The speech at the Dolores Mission was a masterpiece of balanced construction. About St. Francis, the patron saint of the city, and his spirit of love. Then a homily about the Prodigal Son and the Father's love for every sinful son. Followed by quotations from St. Paul, the enemy of homosexuals, but actually about something else, about his, Paul's, own transgressions that show he is the lowest of all sinners.

The greatness of John Paul II and his missionary journeys. For intellectuals it is repetition to the point of boredom of the same thing in a huge number of words. They forget, however, that millions of people are hearing the simplest truths for the first time. And John Paul II's mind embraced those millions like children who need him most in his role as teacher.

CZESLAW MILOSZ

SEPTEMBER 19

1932

MONROVIA

I have no interest in the Hollywood Punch and Judy show either way, for or against it. I don't want to have to see it or to have to refuse to see it.

ROBERT FROST, *to Louis Untermeyer*

1964

NORTHRIDGE

. . . I hope to get going on some new stuff now that I'm out in the California sun. Houghton Mifflin will do the novel you and I talked about at Don Hall's. It seems to be developing pretty well, though I know nothing of the writing of novels . . .

Jim   **JAMES DICKEY**, *at work on* Deliverance

1965

Eureka!

OCTAVIA E. BUTLER

SEPTEMBER 20

1863

GENESEE VALLEY, PLUMAS COUNTY.

. . . Camptonville, a miserable, dilapidated town, but very picturesquely located, with immense hydraulic diggings about. The amount of soil sluiced away in this way seems incredible. Bluffs sixty to a hundred feet thick have been washed away for hundreds of acres together. But they were not rich, the gold has "stopped" . . .   **WILLIAM H. BREWER**

1925

. . . Miss Marion, Mr. King and a special title writer are retitling Stella Dallas so that it will be ready to be previewed tomorrow night at Pasadena. We had one preview of it at San Bernardino last week . . . However, this doesn't mean much because most of the people of San Bernardino are ranchers and their opinions count for naught . . .

The weather here is glorious, but awfully dry. We haven't had a bit of rain since about the 10th of June. One day is just like the other, hence you can never start a conversation with "Isn't this awful weather we're having?" which you must admit is quite a drawback in making new friends, especially with the opposite sex. When I meet a new fellow, all I can say is "Aren't the stars bright tonight!" or some other such dumb remark—and that ends it. You just have to talk about other things or appear stupid . . .

VALERIA BELLETTI, *to a childhood friend*

1934

My position has become untenable here. The people with whom I'm staying can scarcely scrape their bread together, and I can't impose on them much longer.   *poet, novelist* MAXWELL BODENHEIM,

to his wife, from Hollywood

SEPTEMBER 21

1884

[A] man that understands the printing business from the bottom up and all the way through, so as to be able to take full charge of the paper . . . We know such a man is hard to get . . . Perhaps Will can attend to it?

miner, businessman GEORGE HEARST, *to his wife, Phoebe,*

with regard to their wastrel son

1938

VAN NUYS

Dear Bill—

I put in an exhibit at the University library which would interest you: "Printers of Los Angeles"-75 items by about 8 or 10 printers. The Public Library has asked to have it during their Book Fair in November, but my real joy in that occasion will be in putting in an exhibit of my own Steinbeck collection & giving a talk about it. I am doing a background map of Monterey County, annotating the books, etc. I like such things. They lead people to read . . .

LAWRENCE CLARK POWELL

1915

Dear Manly,

... OH I saw the Carnation milk cows being milked with a milking machine. And it milked them clean and the cows did not object in the least. The men in charge took your address and if you get any literature be sure and save it, for this machine is surely a success ...   **LAURA INGALLS WILDER**

SEPTEMBER 22

1849

The novelty of being safely moored in harbour prevented me from sleeping last night. Going on deck this morning, I was much struck with the strange appearance of everything around us—high hills covered with a low green herbage, tents pitched here and there, the men around them differently employed, some washing, some cooking &c &c. These are persons just arrived, and waiting for conveyances to the mines ...

The harbour looks beautiful, It is thought there are upwards of 300 vessels here ...

forty-niner **ANNE WILLSON BOOTH**

1851

LONG BAR

EL DORADO CO. CAL

I wrote you a long letter by the last mail from Sacramento informing you of my fall from Proprietor of one of the finest Hotels in town to a common digger in the ground now you may think this a great fall but I do not ...

It is now two years scince I arrived in this country and I have not made my pile ...

You may prehaps conclude that I have [been] entirely weaned from home and [its] associations by my puting [off] the time of starting so often and so far ahead but I know you would rather have me absent a little longer and come home with somthing than come now with what I have, just think to have it said that Lush come home with out making any thing and those Mutton headed B—- Boys made a pile, You would be ashamed of me and I am sure I should be ashamed of my self so I am bound to have the pile if possible. I should like to [see] little Lottie and have her call me "Uncle Lush" just to see how it would sound. Well, well, Poco tempo—I have run out of news . . .   *forty-niner, later Wisconsin governor* **LUCIUS FAIRCHILD**

1888

. . . It is rather singular that it should be reserved for San Diego to boast the largest and perhaps the finest hotel in the world, but such is the case . . . It is an immense hostelry, prominently poised, and no matter where you are in San Diego, if you look toward the bay you look also upon this huge hotel . . .

I sat on the very edge of the blue brocaded chair and stared dumbly and doubtfully around me . . . Certainly there could be no more visible voluble proof of the ambitious aims of the San Diegans than this right royal hostelry . . .

We have gathered the daintiest of sea shells at Pacific Beach, and we have been several times to Tia Juana, the chosen site of the future American Monte Carlo . . .

But there is one fatal lack in San Diego, and that is its water supply. Water rates are high and the quantity is limited. There are few gardens, hedges, trees, no park save the one small bit of green that is called the Plaza . . . the effete Eastern people, with luxurious homes and many servants to do their bidding, come here and crowd into a three-room cottage, becoming themselves maids of all work . . .

Now that the great flume is near completion it is to be hoped that gardens will spring up, that trees will be planted, that something may be done to beautify and make lovely this spot, favored of the gods.

San Diego has many points of peculiar interest to the tourist. It was the primal point of civilization of the whole Western slope. Here the first mission was established in 1769 . . . The mission has long been a crumbling ruin . . . and all that is visually left of this first love's labor of Father Junipero are a few crumbling stones, fast dropping, one from another.

HARRIET HARPER,
visiting the Hotel Del

1916

At the Summit of the Cajon Pass our troubles ended.

EDGAR RICE BURROUGHS

SEPTEMBER 23

1915

I am very tired this morning after my trip seeing the Santa Clara Valley yesterday. I started at 8:30 in the morning, rode for half an hour on the streetcar and then one and one half hours on the train . . .

The trip took us clear around the valley so that I saw all parts of it. It is a beautiful place to look at if one likes to see very intensive orchard raising and handling. The bottom of the valley is as level as a floor and the foothills rising to mountains completely surround it except for the side open to the bay and the ocean breezes. It was very, very hot in the sun but cool in the shade and with a cool breeze blowing. Most of the valley is in orchard and the trees are of course set with mathematical precision . . .

It looked ugly to me, someway, to see the men working in the hot sun letting the water into the ditches so it would run around the feet of the tree while the tree itself and all its leaves were loaded with dust from the plowing. They did look as though they wanted a drink so much . . .

LAURA INGALLS WILDER

1947

DAVIS CREEK

I meet Roy Crockett and his wife and baby, and have coffee, cake, and ice cream (and talk about Schoenberg and the atonal scale, at Crockett's prompting) on what is described by some maps of California as the "Westernmost Point in Continental United States."

It is perhaps a matter of incidental interest that I have also seen maps of Oregon that give the same information in regard to Cape Blanco, and maps of Washington indubitably the same in regard to Cape Flattery, on the Olympic peninsula.

Well, they could all be right, I suppose. Perhaps the "Westernmost Point in Continental United States" ends in a westernly dead heat—Blanco, Mendocino, and Flattery.

But mapmakers might be more specific. That is: "One of Three Westernmost Points in Continental United States," but this would be ambiguous, and it would remove the fascination of the one "mostest." . . .

HARRY PARTCH

1990

KINGFISHER FLAT

DAVENPORT, CALIFORNIA

Autumn Equinox, 1990

For the aged poet, confrontation with his correspondence of fifty years back does not betoken an occasion of euphoric retrospection . . . The care a poem requires would daunt the resourcefulness of the most gung-ho correspondent, for whom language is provisional, and revision is forgone, or at least minimized.

There are rare exceptions like D.H. Lawrence, a virtuoso of immediacy, whose first drafts and published correspondence seem to presuppose a common denominator, eliminating the gross distinction in genre. The blaze, the vibration of immediacy, breaks out of the naked language, envelops the syntax and, in effect, dissolves the differences in mode . . .

poet **WILLIAM EVERSON**

SEPTEMBER 24

1846

Believe the bearer [Juan Flaco, who rode from L.A. to S.F. in 52 hours]

ARCHIBALD GILLESPIE,
to Commodore Robert F. Stockton

1879

[CARMEL VALLEY]

Here is another curious start in my life. I am living at an angora goat ranche, in the Coast Line Mountains, eighteen miles from Monterey. I was camping out, but got so sick that the two rancheros took me in and tended me. One is an old bear hunter, seventy-two years old, and a captain from the Mexican war; the other a pilgrim and one who was out with the bear flag and under Frémont when California was taken by the States . . .

ROBERT LOUIS STEVENSON

1923

Los Angeles, 24

. . . California is a queer place—in a way, it has turned its back on the world, and looks into the void Pacific. It is absolutely selfish, very empty, but not false, and at least, not full of false effort. I don't want to live here, but a stay here rather amuses me. It's sort of crazy-sensible . . . I'll send you an address as soon as I get one. I'm glad to be going south. America exhausts the springs of one's soul.—I suppose that's what it exists for. It lives to see all real spontaneity expire . . .   **D. H. LAWRENCE**, *upon visiting an ostrich farm*

1969

I went up to SF to a brain storm—a special commission called by MIT to discuss—exhaustively—the reform of their humanities division and the teaching of humanities generally. The emphasis was on dynamic interpersonal relationships and the fostering of creativity. It was very good for my self esteem to get away from this provincial backwater where the faculty think Montessori is something with cheese and tomato sauce and associate with my intellectual equals.   **KENNETH REXROTH**

SEPTEMBER 25

1864

My Dear Mother & Sister

. . . I have engaged to write for the new literary paper—the "Californian"—same pay I used to receive on the "Golden Era"—one article a week, fifty dollars a month. I quit the "Era," long ago. It wasn't high-toned enough. I thought that whether I was a literary "jackleg" or not, I wouldn't class myself with that style of people, anyhow. The "Californian" circulates among the highest class of the community . . .

Been down to San José (generally pronounced Sanno*zay*—emphasis on last syllable)—today—50 miles from here, by Railroad. Town of 6,000 inhabitants, buried in flowers & shrubbery . . .   **MARK TWAIN**

1991

I think that people who keep notebooks and jot down their thoughts are jerk-offs. I am only doing this because somebody suggested I do it, so you see, I'm not even an original jerk-off. But this somehow makes it easier. I just let it roll. Like a hot turd down a hill.

I don't know what to do about the racetrack. I think it's burning out for me. I was standing around at Hollywood Park today, inter-track betting, 13 races from Fairplex Park. After the 7th race I am $72 ahead. So? Will it take some of those white hairs out of my eyebrows? Will it make an opera singer out of me?   CHARLES BUKOWSKI

SEPTEMBER 26

1925

Do you remember when Thomas Ince suddenly died on a yacht party? Well, Marion Davies, Hearst, Charlie Chaplin and a number of others were on that party and according to the wild rumors around the lots, it is said that Hearst became very much incensed over the attention Charlie was paying Marion—after a few drinks, they got quarreling about it and Hearst either shot at or threw something at Charlie. Charlie ducked and Ince got the blow and died a few hours after.

I don't know how true this tale is—but I've heard it from a number of people and they all seem to believe it. I can't really say that I believe it because I know how ready people are to talk and I usually give anyone the benefit of the doubt until I'm positive . . .

Am going to a beach party tonight—we are going to build a big fire on the beach and have supper there. This seems to be quite a popular diversion for the "younger set" in Hollywood. I've never been to one before so I'm looking forward to having a good time.

Sunday morning Nancy and I are going on a hike with the Sierra Hiking Club. We leave at six in the morning and there will be about 100 in the party and we will ride in busses to the mountains . . .

                                                         VALERIA BELLETTI

1964

NORTHRIDGE, CALIFORNIA

Dear Don:

Welcome home! Please forgive my not writing, but I have been travelling about a good deal, and have only just now settled in California in a little house with a dusty swimming pool near the school I'm teaching at this year.

Things look good, and the future also, for at least a few years. I'll be here this year, then take a few months off to do some movie writing . . .

. . . I also almost got killed again in a canoing accident in North Georgia on the greatest river in the world, the Chatooga (not the Chattahoochee or the Chattanooga), swam a good bit, read some things I'd always wanted to read, and geared up for the next struggle, which was (and is) California. How are things with you? Write and let me know when you can; the address below is firm.

Yours, Jim

P.S. Houghton Mifflin will do the novel, *Deliverance.*

JAMES DICKEY, *to Donald Hall*

2018

MAMMOTH LAKES

We cruise-controlled. We barely escaped. We crossed the divide. We were stiff sore bedraggled. The grocery stores on 395 were all closed. Lloyd forgot the delicious sandwiches he'd made in the morning and packed for our lunch. We ate dismal soggy focaccia in Olancha.

Dinner in the room of the lodge. Cheese and crackers. Hummus, pear, a bottle of rose between the 2 of us. PBS on my Ipad, more Kavanaugh shenanigans. Sweaty night. No good sleep. Kept waking to dark thoughts.

We checked out a canoe this morning. bright light. We drifted. Shadows on water. Raptors in the trees. Ducks on a floating bonsai garden. Great blue heron. Dusky grey against the scree in palette of Sierra pastels. Lloyd looking, snapping photos, sizing up. We find a rhythm to move forward. A new practice of navigation . . .

At ease with quiet. Flutter of mallards and coots. Last bronze blush on the granite. The waterfall as if frozen across the lake . . .

LOUISE STEINMAN

SEPTEMBER 27

1927

San Diego can rightfully claim a great credit in the flight. But you can't beat Los Angeles. They had to get in on it somehow. They claim they raised the pigs that the ham sandwiches were made from that Lindy took to Paris . . .

P. S.—In five years this town will have grown till it reaches Tijuana, Mexico . . .   *essayist, critic, novelist* **EDMUND WILSON**

2007

. . . las montañas San Gabriel. A la izquierda, chaparral still slightly charred from the wildfires hace ya cuatro años . . .   **SUSANA CHÁVEZ-SILVERMAN**

SEPTEMBER 28

1857

Henry killed a very large hawk. George knew some one who said California hawks were fine eating. Reel believes in experimenting (I do not), but the hawk was cooked, that is all.   *traveler* **HELEN CARPENTER**,

with no further elaboration

1915

I love a ride on the streetcars at night and to get to the ferry station we go through the famous Barbary Coast. Most of the buildings on the street are closed and dark now, but a little nearer the station is what they call the "waterfront," where every building on the street is a saloon. Gillette says the sailors come ashore there with all their pay from a six-months' voyage and they have to have some place to get rid of their money. He says that if they have not managed to spend it all by two or three o'clock in the morning someone will obligingly hit them over the head with a piece of gas pipe and take it away from them.   **LAURA INGALLS WILDER**

2020

I do a BBC radio show in half an hour on the fires. Then Mary and I are evacuating. I'm too tired to head down to LA so we have rented a room in Bodega Bay for three days till the smoke clears. I don't think our house is in any danger, but Mary's sanity is. We can see the hills burning on the southern horizon.   *former California poet laureate* **DANA GIOIA**

SEPTEMBER 29

1858

Before sunrise of the 29th he was lying in the bushes at San Francisco, in front of the Congress frigate, waiting for the early market boat to come on shore, and he delivered my dispatches to Commodore Stockton before 7 o'clock. **ARCHIBALD GILLESPIE**,

on courier Juan Flaco's 52-hour L.A.-to-S.F. ride

1929

. . . We are travelling across the Californian desert in Mr. Schwab's [railway] car, & we have stopped for 2 hours at this oasis. We have left the train for a bath in the hotel, & as it is so nice & cool I will write you a few of the things it is wiser not to dictate.

Hearst was most interesting to meet, & I got to like him—a grave simple child, with no doubt a nasty temper—playing with the most costly toys. A vast income always overspent: Ceaseless building and collecting & not vy discriminatingly works of art: two magnificent establishments, two charming wives; complete indifference to public opinion, . . .

At Los Angeles (hard g) we passed into the domain of Marion Davies; & all were charmed by her . . . We lunched frequently at her bungalow in the film works—a little Italian chapel sort of building vy elegant where Hearst spends the day directing his newspapers on the telephone, & wrestling with his private [chancellor of the Exchequer]—a harassed functionary who is constantly compelled to find money & threatens resignation daily.

We made gt friends with Charlie Chaplin. You cd not help liking him. The boys were fascinated by him. He is a marvelous comedian—bolshy in politics—delightful in conversation. He acted his new film for us in a wonderful way. It is to be his gt attempt to prove that the silent drama or pantomime is superior to the new talkies. Certainly if pathos & wit still count for anything it ought to win an easy victory . . .

We went on Sunday in a yacht to Catalina Island 25 miles away. We had only one hour there. People go there for weeks and months without catching a swordfish—so they all said it was quite useless my going out in the fishing boat wh had been provided. However I went out & of course I caught a monster in 20 minutes! . . .

Prime Minister **WINSTON CHURCHILL**, *to Lady Churchill*

1933

Have already succeeded in selling one or two of them on the idea. These moguls are hard to pin down for more than a few minutes talk—however I have joined Hillcrest and am making progress between the drive and the approach shot.   *anti-Nazi spymaster* **LEON LEWIS**

1943

BEVERLY GLEN

Dear Bill—

. . . I've put off answering your last letter in the day-to-day hope I'd have a final report to make. Now I have & I hasten it to you. I have been appointed head librarian at UCLA . . .

How does it sound to you, pal? As good as it does to me? I hope so. Because I'm goddam well set-up, yes sir! What a two months! Northwestern wanted me badly & at the last moment, its President telephoned me an offer of $7500 plus all moving expenses. It was hard to turn down—but I did—& day before yesterday I signed the deal with Pres. Sproul. My salary at UCLA will be $6000—a cool thousand more than the incumbent has been receiving. It looks like I've arrived. I'm gladdest for Fay-for the respite from hard work it'll mean for her. Goddam this paper! It won't take ink.

For the next three months I'll probably go into a defense plant my brother is running; making life preservers & sleeping bags for the army. As a laborer @ 1.00 an hour. I want a change from libraries. I'll take the job if it doesn't entail being "frozen" in it.

It's been a hell of a strain for 2 months, but I've thrived on it. Never felt more brimful o' piss 'n vinegar. I was near you & Edwa two weeks ago. Made a quick round trip to Berkeley on the Owl. Wanted to stop over, but knew you'd be swamped with work, & besides had to get back close to campus for the denouement.

It's a rags-to-riches story that has the campus agog. Never before has anyone jumped from the bottom rank in a department (Librarian, junior grade) to the top spot in one lewd leap. The point is, the young men in the faculty are greatly encouraged. Powell has broken ground for them.

It means that I can put into practice much of my philosophy of books & people. Etc. For example, in the Clark Library I am going to commence a collection of western fine printing—Grabhorn, Ritchie, etc. And in the Univ. Lib. a collection of every book printed in Los Angeles. And poetry man, poetry! Everything. I am going to make the library a throbbing heart. Dead books will live. Young men & women students & faculty will enter a living atmosphere, not a mausoleum.

It means that I stay in the land I love, where my roots go deepest, the land whose hills & weather I know & love. And to live amidst my friends here & up the coast. Wow!

In Berkeley I crossed your hot spoor. In Creed's Bookstore near Sather Gate . . .

I wrote to you of hearing Elgar's violin concerto (Menuhin) here in my study one night. How it moved me! Have you ever heard it? Of course, nothing can equal the solemn tympani opening of Beethoven's violin concerto. I write always to music. Ambition is to own a big automatic machine, that I can program & let her buck.

In the mad world I live my rich & secret life. I grieve, sorrow, rejoice, exalt—all things experience—& know I am keenly, vividly alive, in the prime years of my life—& that unless I channel my life in writing all the other triumphs are naught. Whether or not I publish doesn't matter now. To write is everything. I write . . .

1,000,000 greetings
Larry   **LAWRENCE CLARK POWELL,** *to William Everson*

SEPTEMBER 30

1879

Gentlemen of Stockton: I am very much pleased to be back in your city once more, not having beheld it since twenty-five years ago. . . . I passed through your city several times when I was on this coast before. The only untoward event of to-day was the news which I gained from a gentleman whom I met, that he had known me at Knight's Ferry in 1849. I did not come west of the Rockies till 1852, so I am sorry to think that some one must have been personating me there. However, I am very glad to meet you all to-day, and if anyone hereafter says that he met me in Stockton in 1879, I shall have the pleasure of not being able to deny it.   **ULYSSES S. GRANT**

1912

The old town don't look the same. By the old town we mean Los Angeles. But not looking the same is a habit with this little pueblo. . . . It's got so that a person can't reasonably spend a two weeks vacation and come back here without the aid of guide book.

cartoon artist, Krazy Kat creator **GEORGE HERRIMAN**

2018

And now onto the Promised Land—Colusa County!

retiring Gov. **EDMUND G. BROWN, JR.**

OCTOBER 1

1869

We have been camped in Calafornia at last . . . There was a death in the camp on the 30th, an infant, 10 months old, of Mrs. Collins. They are from Arkansas. It was a pretty corpse. They buried it near the station under a tree. Poor little child, it is now at rest.

We bought some nice apples, onions, and potatoes from a gentleman that is just from Los Angeles in Calafornia. He gives a favorable report of that country. *traveler* **HARRIET BUNYARD**

1935

I am glad to be here and take part in the dedication of this great statue. It is good to see you all. You are doing a splendid piece of work.

President **FRANKLIN DELANO ROOSEVELT**, *unveiling the CCC'S*
"Iron Mike" statue in Griffith Park

1935

I am getting sick and tired of these people on the W.P.A, and local 84 relief rolls being called chiselers and cheats. It doesn't do any good to call these people names, because they are just like the rest of us. They don't drink any more than the rest of us, they don't lie any more, they're no lazier than the rest of us—they're pretty much a cross section of the American people . . . We are coming to the day when we are going to have decent houses for the poor, when there is genuine and real security for everybody . . .

I have learned something in these three and a half years. I have taken a look at a lot of these public servants. I have seen these technical fellows working for three or four thousand a year—not working seven hours a day but working fifteen hours a day. I have seen these fellows in the Army engineer corps. The motivation can't be money—they don't get very much . . .

I am proud of having worked for the Government. It has been a great experience for me. I have signed my name to about $6,000,000,000 in the last three and a half years . . . If we have made mistakes we have made them in the interests of the people that were broke.

When this thing is all over and I am out of the Government the things I am going to regret are the things I have failed to do for the unemployed . . .

Every night when you went home and after you got home and remembered there was a telegram you didn't answer, the fact that you failed to answer the telegram and the telephone call may have resulted in somebody not eating. That is the kind of a job I have had for the last three and a half years, and still have.

When it is all over, the thing I am going to be proudest of are the people all over America, public officials, volunteers, paid workers, thousands of people of all political and religious faiths who joined in this enterprise of taking care of people in need. It has been a great thing. I am not ashamed of one of them and I hope when I am through they are not going to be ashamed of me . . .   *WPA leader, presidential advisor* **HARRY HOPKINS**

1960

I love you more than I have ever loved anything or anyone in my life. If you think a marriage license will make me love you more—or give you any more security than you have now—we might as well go ahead and get one . . .

I have still not decided if San Francisco is good or bad. Whether it is or not, I'm hitting the streets Monday in search of a job. My fortune now rests at $9; if you have any money, please send it along . . .

I would give at least four of my fingers to be able to wake up right now at 107 Thompson, with you beside me, quite naked, and face an evening of love and indolence. The past six months have been so good that I will be forever spoiled. Never before in my life have I felt so happy that I wanted nothing to change . . .

For god's sake, have a little faith in me, and be strong enough to stay as lonely and frustrated as I am until we can be together. Write instantly.

Love, Hunter   **HUNTER S. THOMPSON**,
                                         to his eventual first wife, Sandy

1987

Yesterday the fog lifted around noon; now it's hot again. Toward evening a trip to San Jose to attend a seminar on the hundredth anniversary of the birth of Robinson Jeffers. A marshy, boring plain, no longer under cultivation; factories. An enormous new complex of Japanese-American automotive plants. Approaching San Jose, there's the hump of a mountain, almost unreal in the light of the setting sun, a pink-colored specter. I left the freeway to get a sandwich in Milpitas; many newly constructed streets, entire neighborhoods. The seminar is at San Jose State University. I don't quite realize that I have fallen into a lions' den, that is, into the company of "specialists on insect legs"—English professors for the most part who devour and digest Jeffers while dutifully idolizing him at the same time . . .

Unfortunately, I have a feeling that no one understands what I want to say. I read my poem "To Robinson Jeffers," where my opposition is clearly demonstrated, I think. But I, who defended Jeffers's greatness when no one in the universities studied him, appear to be only his enemy, or envious of him. This performance doesn't reflect badly on me; it is only a tactical error; what I thought was obvious, the audience perceived as abracadabra. It is curious, after all, that Jeffers, who was held in contempt until recently is now making a comeback as the representative of a Nature that deserves to awaken ecological passions. Stas and his daughter drove up from Los Gatos for the lecture. Stas begs me not to die yet, because so few of us from our class at the Zygmunt August High School are still alive. Returned to Berkeley around midnight.   **CZESLAW MILOSZ**

OCTOBER 2

1879

MONTEREY

My dear Sir,
The more I see of America, the more I find of the old country from which you and I both come. One of the most pleasant incidents that I have yet met with, as an Englishman and a man of letters, was the kind present you made me today. Addison on the Pacific coast, and in an old edition—there could scarce be anything more homely . . .   **ROBERT LOUIS STEVENSON**

1934

I'm trying to like California. I wish I could put on paper what it's like. The countryside, dusty pepper trees, rolling hills, serrated mountains, is all curiously divided into planes. I couldn't see why at first, but I suddenly solved it the other night. It's the lack of rains. It's so dry here all is dust. The dust lies at the end of the day hovering over the land. The light hits the dust clouds, and gives that curious hazy separation to the planes of distance . . .

I try to rationalize this whole country, and excuse it. If the people are nuts, it is because after the flat middle lands this is Heaven to them. If they strew the place with the ostentatious vulgarity of palm trees, it's because they still can't believe in the miracle of landing in a land where palms will grow. If their houses are cheap-jack, it is because they're afraid of earthquakes which crumble brick and stone buildings. If they dress like fools, it's because this is the tropics in a way, and anyhow our own sane clothes are about as foolish as could be conceived for such living conditions. So the women wear pants and shorts, and everyone lives in a sort of cheap-jack fugitiveness as if all this would vanish suddenly and they'd have to live back on earth again. A temporary feeling everywhere—waiting for what? Earthquakes, some sectarian Domesday, the collapse of the motion picture industry, the millennium? I don't know. I only know that I believe in film, and must stick to that as long as I can.   **ERIC KNIGHT**, *to a friend*

1934

. . . California's a great place right now. You can look out the window and watch the profit system crumble . . . .

novelist **JOHN DOS PASSOS**, *to a critic*

1937

At eight o'clock in the morning by motorboat to work. Was made up outside. Sat around the whole day and was not used. Long walk with George and a drive to Big Bear, where we found a sweet restaurant. An English lady who brought us wonderful tea told us without charge her entire life story.

dancer **VERA ZORINA**, *with George Balanchine,*
filming The Goldwyn Follies

OCTOBER 3

1849

It is said there were four deaths in one single encampment during yesterday, but little notice is taken of these occurrences. The immediate companions of the deceased procure a coffin and quietly inter the remains without any farther ado. There was a very sudden death on shore yesterday evening; that of a man who started to go to the Post Office from the beach, and fell dead instantly. I did not hear what cause was assigned. Many are becoming disgusted with the place and are making preparations to leave it. A resolution I think very nonsensical; for who could expect to find a second Paradise in California?   **ANNE WILLSON BOOTH**

1931

You are quite right in thinking that my law work will interfere with what writing I do. The clash between the two is becoming very difficult to manage. I fear that I shall soon write like a lawyer and argue like a writer.

CAREY MCWILLIAMS, *to Mary Austin*

1939

PLEASE ANSWER ABOUT TUITION MONEY STOP YOU HAVE NO IDEA HOW MUCH A HUNDRED DOLLARS MEANS NOW

F. SCOTT FITZGERALD, *to his agent*

1962

Dear César:

I hope you have fully recuperated from the meeting last Sunday and are ready to roll on ahead . . . However, I shall wait for your commands, General. So give me the word on the next line of tactic. The troops are restless . . .

Also I want to know if you will lend me your station wagon. It makes me sick of the time I have lost because of my junkie cars, yet I hate to get in debt for a better car when I'm not sure where my next month's check is coming from.

If you can lend it to me, let me know, and I can go after it. I will take out the insurance on it, if you will let me, and as soon as I can I shall get another car. The CSO car burns too much oil and is very unpredictable. I'm going to cut this short now. Please write and let me know the next plan of action.

Sinceramente,
Dolores
Viva La Causa   **DOLORES HUERTA**

1991

SAN FRANCISCO

Out here in one of the centers where the plague rages without cease, a kind of numbness has descended on all of us; we seem to be unable any longer to react . . . My master's thesis many years ago was written on the mutability cantos of Spenser, and it always rather comforted me to remember that the closing lines were those selected to be graven on the tombstone of Joseph Conrad: "Sleep after toyle, porte after stormie seas, / Ease after warre, death after life doth greatlie please."   **SAMUEL STEWARD**

OCTOBER 4

1915

Went to a movie theater last night that cost $600,000. Seats 4,000 people. Largest in U.S. . . .

The more I see of how Rose works the better satisfied I am to raise chickens. I intend to do some writing that will count, but I would not be driven by the work as she is and I do not see how she can stand it.

Lovingly, Bessie   **LAURA INGALLS WILDER**

1938

And now all of the foolishness and the self-indulgence is over. Now there can be no lost days and no lost time. Straight through to the finish now without loss. It must be that way. And I shall do it. Shall gather all my will together and go on. That is settled. The disintegration lately has been terrible. It can't go on. I have done that amount before and I can again. In fact, at the beginning of each day now I shall again put down the pages to be done and then they will get done. My laziness is overwhelming. I must knock it over. Don't feel right about it if I don't, and I think after this good rest it will be all right. I have the energy now. All I need is the force to go ahead. There isn't an awful lot more. But it must move slowly and truly on and on until the finish and this time there must be no hesitation. This work diary is complete thus far. Must make it final. And now the time has come. There have been delays and rests and squirms. And now such things are over. What do I care if criticism is adverse? The book must go on to a conclusion this time. I remember the drive of the other days. And this must be a drive to the end. And now I'll read a little of the early diary and then plunge in. This time it is a GO signal and a real one. I've been looking back over this diary and, by God, the pressures were bad the whole damned time. There wasn't a bit that wasn't under pressure and now the pressure is removed and I'm still having trouble. It would be funny if my book was no good at all and if I had been kidding myself. Now forget the end and just go gradually to work. So long, diary . . .   **JOHN STEINBECK**

1969

Today was cool! First of all it was about 75 degrees which always puts everyone in a good mood. Agnes, Peaches and I left at 12:30 to go to Grant Avenue (I told Mommy Ghirardelli Square). First we just walked up the avenue looking at all the beautiful people and the far out stores. I can really dig the stuff down there! Anyways, we went to a store and all bought grapes and went down the avenue passing them out to people. Some people think that they have to give you something in return which isn't really right. We were just in a charitable mood, but we got things like beer and incense in return. Anyway, since that worked so well, we went and got a loaf of bread and artichoke hearts and went to Washington Square to pass them out. It's a cool way to meet people! Agnes had the bread, I had grapes and Peaches the artichokes. Everyone was really nice and thought it was a cool idea we had . . .

NIKKI LASTRETO

OCTOBER 5

1852

WEAVERVILLE

Since my last letter the Indian Chiefs from the South Fork have come in and sued for peace and the people have had so much business on hand that mining has been neglected.

King 'Tulas' was accompanied by eight warriors and a large crowd assembled to hear him . . . He promised to eat no more mules if he could be allowed to come on to the river and fish, and said 'he was glad to see we had such good houses and plenty of blankets and he would come over this winter and live with us.'

The Treaty was drawn up and signed and afterwards we had a war dance . . . There must have been at least a thousand persons present. The Indians dressed in all their finery with their bows and arrows came bounding into the ring and were received with thundering applause . . .

The Indians went back very pleased with their visit and I don't think it will be their fault if the Treaty is broken, as the wrong in most all cases is first on the side of the whites. The poor Indians have been treated with great cruelty, I always thought, by our forefathers at home, but they have been killed off in this State like some wild animals, without the slightest cause and driven to actual starvation . . .

While we were in the midst of the Treaty a man by the name of Holt, who started to go to Shasta, was found shot about 2 miles from town. Suspicion immediately fell on an Irishman: Michael Grant, who was seen in company with him close by the spot where he was found. He was arrested and from the facts which soon came out, the sovereign people: i.e. a mob, held a meeting and resolved to take him . . .

A wagon on which he was standing was driven out from under which caused his death by strangulation. He had a Catholic Priest to attend on him, which he said was a great consolation and died perfectly resigned to his lot. He was about 25 years of age.

Although no one has the slightest doubt as to his guilt and I think he suffered justly, yet I say Heaven preserve me from falling into the hands of an excited people . . .

Write me every month and if you don't like these blood-thirsty letters say so and I will gloss it over.   FRANKLIN A. BUCK

1956

I slept late and had few appointments, the most important being to take Fray pony riding . . . the trade notices on *Ten Commandments* came out today, too, and were really fabulous . . .   CHARLTON HESTON

1961

It was very thoughtful of you to send me a book explaining James Joyce's "Ulysses." All I need now is another book explaining this study by Stuart Gilbert who, if memory serves, painted the celebrated picture of George Washington which hangs in the Metropolitan Museum. I realize that there is some two hundred years' difference in their ages, but any man who can explain Joyce must be very old and very wise.

You disappeared rather mysteriously the other night, but I attribute this to your life of crime in the movies.

writer, actor, broadcaster GROUCHO MARX,

to Peter Lorre

OCTOBER 6

1911

Auburn is nothing but a cage, and with little gilding on the bars at that.

CLARK ASHTON SMITH, *to George Sterling*

1956

Cecil Blount DeMille's *The Ten Commandments* was previewed this week for a company of two hundred and sixty-three archangels in a temple of strawberry meringue especially built for the occasion on the Paramount back lot. Y. Frank Freeman led vespers with a reading from the letter of "a Protestant church leader" to the effect that "The first century had its Apostle Paul, the thirteenth century had St. Francis, the sixteenth had Martin Luther and the twentieth has Cecil B. DeMille."

After heaping portions of the Sacred Host had been served up in a rich sauce with seconds for everybody, de Mille himself, clad in the rosette of the Order of the Holy Sepulcher, appeared among them on a Technicolor screen to explain his affection for the Almighty. The picture was then revealed.

DALTON TRUMBO

OCTOBER 7

1851

. . . If I should give you a month of Sundays, you would never guess what we use in lieu of a bookcase, so I will put you out of your misery by informing you instantly that it is nothing more nor less than a candle-box which contains the library, consisting of a Bible and prayerbook, Shakespeare, Spenser, Coleridge, Shelley, Keats, Lowell's Fable for Critics, Walton's Complete Angler, and some Spanish books, —spiritual instead of material lights, you see . . .

How would you like to winter in such an abode? in a place where there are no newspapers, no churches, lectures, concerts, or theaters; no fresh books; no shopping, calling, nor gossiping little tea-drinkings; no parties, no balls, no picnics, no tableaus, no charades, no latest fashions, no daily mail (we have an express once a month), no promenades, no rides or drives; no vegetables but potatoes and onions, no milk, no eggs, no *nothing*? Now, I expect to be very happy here. This strange, odd life fascinates me . . .

In good sooth, I fancy that nature intended me for an Arab or some other nomadic barbarian, and by mistake my soul got packed up in a Christianized set of bones and muscles. How I shall ever be able to content myself to live in a decent, proper, well-behaved house, where toilet-tables are toilet-tables, and not an ingenious combination of trunk and claretcases, where lanterns are not broken bottles, bookcases not candle-boxes, and trunks not wash-stands, but every article of furniture, instead of being a makeshift, is its own useful and elegantly finished self, I am sure I do not know. However, when too much appalled at the humdrummish prospect, I console myself with the beautiful promises, that "sufficient unto the day is the evil thereof," and "as thy days, so shall thy strength be," and trust that when it is again my lot to live amid the refinements and luxuries of civilization, I shall endure them with becoming philosophy and fortitude.   **LOUISA CLAPPE**

2010

3:40 A.M. Alarm #1 goes off.

3:45 A.M. Alarm #2 goes off.

Happy Nobel Prize in Literature day! It's so early my body hurts. I drag myself into the living room: couch, laptop, streaming from Sweden. The tech is way better this year than last year. The new laureate is, as everyone now knows, Mario Vargas Llosa, who I haven't read but whose name I at least recognize. I spend the predawn hours researching him—significant, yes, problematic, also yes—so I can write a newsy story. There's a long profile of him from 1997 in the *LA Times* archives. It's a great piece, but it throws two things about newspapers into sad relief: how few stories our international reporters get to write about cultural figures now, and how little space there is for all stories today. The Vargas Llosa piece is twice as long as the features I write. I have plenty of time to contemplate this, because after the sun is up, I discover that someone else is writing the Nobel story after all.

11:00 A.M. Our newsroom is made up of vast rows of desks under bright lights, like those in *All the President's Men* and *The Wire* . . . The furniture and typing machines have changed, but the architecture remains the same. Tour groups come through—mostly teenagers and retirees—to look at journalists in action, which can't be all that exciting. The one exception is the test kitchen, which has a big glass window overlooking sleek new counters, large stoves and white-jacketed chefs. The book section, where I sit, is between the test kitchen and the elevators, so the tour groups bunch up nearby. They whisper about our fantastic stacks of books with envy and wonder (at least, that what I'd like to think they're whispering).   **CAROLYN KELLOGG**

OCTOBER 8

1542

Came to the mainland in a large Bay . . . named it "Bahía de los Fumos" [Bay of Smokes] on account of the many dark billows seen there . . . engaged in intercourse with some Indians captured in a canoe . . . The bay is 35 degrees latitude; it is an excellent harbor and the country is good with many plains and groves of trees.   *explorer* JUAN RODRÍGUEZ CABRILLO

2010

Press preview at the Huntington Library. Henry Huntington leveraged businesses in trains, real estate, and utilities to become one of Southern California's earliest tycoons. Later in his life, not necessarily in this order, he retired, collected rare books, and married Arabella, an art lover who was the richest woman in America (and also his uncle's widow). Their home and estate in San Marino, south of Pasadena, is now the Huntington Library, Art Gallery, and Botanical Garden. It's hard to imagine, wandering through it, what it was like to live in the house and to own so much land. Huntington built his library to house a collection that includes a Gutenberg Bible and a very early complete, gorgeously illuminated manuscript of Chaucer's *The Canterbury Tales*, both of which are on display.

Which makes the preview interesting: It's the unveiling of a new Charles Bukowski exhibit just down the hall.

The not-so-staid-after-all Huntington has been acquiring the papers of twentieth-century writers: Its collection now includes Christopher Isherwood, Jack London, W. H. Auden, and Octavia Butler.

I have mixed feelings about Bukowski, but how I feel isn't what matters when I meet Linda Lee Bukowski, his widow. The event had mostly wound down: The ham-on-rye sandwiches, set outside in the returned fall heat, had been snapped up by other journalists. Linda stood inside the lobby, talking to two Huntington staffers, one of whom vouched for me as I approached, saying I was from the *LA Times*. Linda responded with a wry comment about my former editor there, David L. Ulin.

That's because Ulin wrote in the *Times* that Bukowski was "a hit-or-miss talent, capable of his own brand of small epiphany but often stultifyingly banal." As far as I know, Ulin's opinion hasn't changed, but I try to tell Linda that if she met him, she'd like him. Diminutive and with delicate bone structure, she bounces energetically and raises her fists. "Maybe after I give him a punch in the nose," she laughs.   CAROLYN KELLOGG

2016

My city. My city. I am drawn to this perch at a particular moment of day, I can see a shaft of light straight below me through the spine of Central library out through to Hope St. on the other side, the street where I was born. Hope Street.

I sit still and let all the stories from Gordon Davidson's funeral at Leo Baeck wash through me. Rabbi Lerman's spirit was there too, waiting to take Gordon to a play in Heaven. "Angels in America,"—Gordon just walks into the play. He already has a role, everyone knows who he is, the Moses of L.A. theater. Moses with a grin . . .

In the shadow of the tallest building, U.S. Bank Tower, the "other" target of 9/11. The cause of all the bomb threats called into the library in the months years after 9/11. All of us having to trundle out of the building, sometimes the only place you'd see someone who works on LL4, the History Dept stacks, everyone jovial. And the night when we hosted a Chilean novelist and the alarm sounded, we all had to move out of the post-lecture reception in the courtyard out onto 5th Street, leaving our keys and wallets behind, so we were there for some half hour until the library security officer walked over to me and, motioning to our Chilean guest novelist, said, "could I talk to your visitor?" Yes of course and I walked with them and the officer asked Alberto, "do you have any known enemies? Anyone who would want to hurt you?" and he rolled his eyes and said, "All I can tell you is that Gabriel García Marquez hates my novels," and I watched as the security officer wrote it down. We were all looking for evidence in those days.

LOUISE STEINMAN

OCTOBER 9

1850

MONTEREY

My dear Mother,

. . . The tracts I have, or will, read and then distribute, if possible, but I don't know how, as Mr. Willey had an immense number of tracts and could not get rid of them; and a number of prayerbooks which I had, I placed in a store to be given away, or sold for almost nothing, and I see they are still there . . .

I did not say anything to Uncle about the Padre [state Constitutional

Convention chaplain Ramírez de Arrellano] . . . He is not popular, here, because he talks too plainly to the people. Many of them think him heretical. His sermon on Sunday morning was on the abuse of the Sacraments. "Many persons," he says, "to save the trouble of repenting as often as they sin, leave the Sacraments until their last hour, in order to do away at one blow with all their offences." . . .

I have a thousand dollars here put away, and 6 or 700 due me in San Luis. I would invest it at 5 or 6, or perhaps 8 or 10, per cent a month, if I was where i could watch it, but there is so much rascality that I will not trust everybody . . . .   **WILLIAM RICH HUTTON**

1976
dear Howard: -

Your talk before the college English teachers of California was a tremendous success. To my great astonishment, I got a standing ovation, something that's never happened to me before! It was all due to your words on silence and "making the familiar strange."

The wonderful thing about living is that there is a possibility of learning something new practically every day. Yesterday, I learned that when a squirrel hibernates, its heart beats 3 times a minute, while in non-hibernating periods the heart-beat is 364 per minute. I am very much impressed by this.

In haste, but with much love-   **KAY BOYLE,** *to Howard Nemerov*

OCTOBER 10

1870

GEOLOGICAL EXPLORATION OF THE 40TH PARALLEL,

CHICO, CAL.

General,

I have the honor to report that since the date of my last communication I reached Mt. Shasta, and spent the entire month surveying and studying the complicated geology of the Butte itself, and the country lying between it and our former work. The labor has been extremely severe. Our camps were frequently up to 11,000 feet above sea level, and, on one occasion, over 14,000 ft. We completely upset the ideas of Humboldt and of Fremont . . . and have made the somewhat startling discovery of immense existing glaciers. This is the more surprising when we consider that Whitney, Brewer, Dana, and Frémont all visited the peak without observing this; and that Whitney, Dana and Agassiz have all published the statement that no true glaciers exist in the United States.

May I ask that this be kept private until my return?

geologist, mountaineer **CLARENCE KING**

1940

Mr. Hitler is a skyrocket whose fuse has already been lighted. He is a one-chance rocket. Soon he must fall and come to earth, fulfilling the nature of the rocket by spluttering to death in the dark. This does not mean he will not do great damage before he dies, probably by his own hand.

CLIFFORD ODETS

1997

BIG SUR

There's extra dense fog this late afternoon driving through Big Sur. Highway 1 is moving extra slow and a few folks honk at our bus but most are cool though because they know it's a safety thing. Especially when you have hairpin turns and massive cliffs. A dude in a VW Cabriolet almost just killed himself. He went around our bus near a curve when out of the blue another car came from the other direction around that curve. Luckily for the Cabriolet there was a turnout on the other side of the road and he swerved over there just in time. He let the other car pass and then quickly stepped on the gas to pass our bus as fast as he could. This was a mistake he could not make twice. . . .

poet, regional historian **MIKE SONKSEN**

2010

. . . [My] alarm is set for 5:15 A.M. The National Book Award finalists will be announced the next morning, and I'm going to be up just as soon as they slip the early notice under my e-mail door.

CAROLYN KELLOGG

OCTOBER 11

1849

They say I have acted wisely in remaining on board the ship, there being on shore no place half as comfortable. Capt. Hugg seems to be entirely disgusted with the country, and says, if it were not for the gold, he would vote for its entire obliteration from the map of the civilized world.

ANNE WILLSON BOOTH

1944

CAMP CALLAN HOSPITAL, SAN DIEGO

Dear Folks

October Fool! You thought I'd be at Camp Cooke now, as previously advertised, didn't you? Ha, ha! Well you're wrong-wrong as hell. I'm back at Callan. It is a long and relatively uneventful story. I took off on my cruise of the Pacific and environs; altogether we made four landings, securing, against almost no opposition except cactus, small portions of the California Coast and adjacent island. It will doubtless give you great satisfaction to know that these strategic spots are in safe hands . . .

Then the barracks bags didn't arrive. They contained the tents and blankets and additional warm clothes. In fact, they didn't arrive till very late that night, by which time I had contracted quite a cold. To break it off, they took me to the hospital at Callan (because it is much nearer to where I was than Cooke) where the doctor pronounced me in great danger of living. I subsist on a diet of liquids and sulfur drugs. I must admit I don't feel too good, but my temperature has gone down to about 99 so I guess it's not too serious any more. Write same old address Camp Callan Hospital.

Love,

Tony

ANTHONY HECHT

OCTOBER 12

1918

The better people here are alive and interested . . .

painter **STANTON MACDONALD-WRIGHT,**

to Alfred Stieglitz

1947

We can already see the first signs of terrorism, talebearing, political inquisition, and suspension of law, all of which are excused by an alleged state of *emergency*. As a German. I can only say that is the way it began among us, too.

THOMAS MANN

1955

I MC'd a reading at the 6 Gallery last Friday. Allen Ginsberg read a terrific poem—a real jeremiad of unbelievable volume—"This is what you have done to my generation." When he finished the audience of 250 stood and clapped & cheered and wept . . .

Love

K R & family   **KENNETH REXROTH,**

after hosting the first public reading of Howl

1955

HOLLYWOOD 46, CALIFORNIA

Dear Marcus and Mrs. Winslow:

I have nothing of Jim's—nothing to touch or look at except the dried mud that clung to my shoes—mud from the farm that grew him—and a single kernel of seed corn from your barn. I have nothing more than this and I want nothing more. There is no need to touch something he touched when I can still feel his hand on me . . .

He spoke my words and played my scenes better than any other actor of our time or of our memory could have done. I feel that there are other gifts to come from him—gifts for all of us. His influence did not stop with his breathing. It walks with us and will profoundly affect the way we look at things. From Jimmy I have already learned the value of a minute. He loved his minutes and I shall now love mine . . .

I write from the depths of my appreciation—to Jimmy for having touched my life and opened my eyes—to you for having grown him all those young years and for having given him your love—to you for being big enough and humane enough to let me come into your grief as a stranger and go away a friend.

When I drove away the sky at the horizon was yellowing with twilight and the trees stood clean against it. The banks of flowers covering the grave were muted and grayed by the coming of evening and had yielded up their color to the sunset. I thought—here's where he belongs—with this big darkening sky and this air that is thirst-quenching as mountain water and this century of family around him and the cornfield crowding the meadow where his presence will be marked. But he's not in the meadow. He's out there in the corn. He's hunting the winter's rabbit and the summer's catfish. He has a hand on little Mark's shoulder and a sudden kiss for you. And he has my laughter echoing his own at the great big jokes he saw and showed to me—

and he's here, living and vivid and unforgettable forever, far too mischievous to lie down long.

My love and gratitude, to you and young Mark,

Rebel Without a Cause *screenwriter* **STEWART STERN,**

to James Dean's parents

1957

DENUNCIATION (inspired by [my] presence at a party in Berkeley, California, October 12, 1957):

"I say, oh you young fuddie-duddies, you young fogies, you prematurely middle-aged! Where are the gray flannel suits to go with your gray flannel mouths? You crumb-eaters! You knuckle-gnawers! You cappuccino drinkers! What right have YOU to be so wise, so dull, so blase and jaded, so conservative, so timid, so morose and defensive? at your age! So bored with protest, so disdainful of revolt, so tired tired tired of the straight and angry statement! What have you done to EARN your indifference?

"I say, hurrah for Ginsberg, hurrah for Rexroth, hurrah for Kerouac, hurrah for Miller and Jeffers and Mailer and Abbey and Williams and Dean Moriarty!"   **EDWARD ABBEY**

OCTOBER 13

1849

MONTEREY

TO THE PEOPLE OF CALIFORNIA. The undersigned, Delegates to a Convention authorized to form a Constitution for the State of California, having to the best of their ability discharged the high trust committed to them, respectfully submit the accompanying plan of government for your approval . . .

Although born in different climes, coming from different States, imbued with local feelings, and educated perhaps with predilections for peculiar institutions, laws and customs, the delegates assembled in Convention, as Californians, and carried on their deliberations in a spirit of amity, compromise, and mutual concession for the public weal . . .

Let every qualified voter go early to the polls, and give his free vote at the election appointed to be held on Tuesday, the 13th day of November next, not only that a full and fair expression of the public voice may be had, for or against a constitution intended to secure the peace, happiness and prosperity of the whole people, but that their numerical and political strength may be made manifest, and the whole world see by what majority of freemen California, the bright star of the West, claims a place in the diadem of that glorious Republic, formed by the union of thirty-one sovereign States.

JOSEPH ARAM,
CHARLES T. BOTTS,
ELAM BROWN,
JOSE ANTO. CARRILLO,
JOSE M. COVARRUBIAS,
ELISHA O. CROSBY,
LEWIS DENT,
MANUEL DOMINGUEZ,
K. H. DIMMICK,
A. J. ELLIS,
STEPHEN G. FOSTER,
PABLO DE LA GUERRA,
EDWARD GILBERT,
WILLIAM M. GWIN,
JULIAN HANKS,
HENRY HILL,
J. D. HOPPE,
JOSEPH HOBSON,
H. W. HALLECK,
L. W. HASTINGS,
J. McH. HOLLINSWORTH,
JAMES McHALL JONES,
THOMAS O. LARKIN,
FRANCIS J. LIPPITT,
BENJAMIN S. LIPPINCOTT,
M. M. McCARVER,
JOHN McDOUGAL,
BENJAMIN F. MOORE,
MYRON NORTON,
P. ORD,
MIGUEL DE PEDRORENA,
RODMAN M. PRICE,
ANTONIO M. PICO,

JACINTO RODRIGUEZ,
HUGH REID,
J. A. SUTTER,
JACOB R. SNYDER,
WINFIELD S. SHERWOOD,
WILLIAM C. SHANNON,
PEDRO SANSEVAINE,
ABEL STEARNS,
W. M. STEUART,
R. SEMPLE,
HENRY A. TEFFT,
M. G. VALLEJO,
THOMAS L. VERMEULE,
JOEL P. WALKER,
O. M. WOZENCRAFT . . .

And then, on motion of Mr. McCARVER, the Convention adjourned *sine die* . . .   **JOHN ROSS BROWNE**

1955

I GREET YOU AT THE BEGINNING OF A GREAT CAREER [stop] WHEN DO I GET MANUSCRIPT OF "HOWL"? [stop]

LAWRENCE FERLINGHETTI, *City Lights Bookstore*

OCTOBER 14

1915

Rose and I went over to Berkeley to hear Fritz Kreisler, the Austrian, play the violin. This you know meant a trip across the bay, which is always such a pleasure, then a streetcar ride through Oakland, for this time we landed at the Oakland pier, then a walk across the campus or college grounds to the Greek Theater . . . The music was the most beautiful I have ever heard.

We sat for two hours, almost without breathing, listening to it. The seats were crowded and all we could see of the people was a dark blur and all the white faces . . .

First we looked at the kangaroos and wallabies. They are in a wire yard between the Australian and New Zealand Buildings . . . From Australia we went to France, which is just across the street . . . There are wonderful old tapestries, each of which covers an entire wall . . . Some of them were made in Brussels, the capital in Belgium, that the Germans have now . . .

There is one little long room. As we came to the archway opening into it and looked down we saw on each side large paintings of battle scenes where the French and Germans were fighting in the old war . . .

From France we saw Belgium, which is an annex of the French Building and filled with what poor Belgium could gather up from the wreck . . . After we saw Belgium we went to the Food Products Building, got a couple of Scotch scones and then went to the East Indian tea room in the same building and got some tea and cakes to eat with the scones . . .

Lovingly,
Bessie   **LAURA INGALLS WILDER**

1915

Mama Bess is getting fat . . . Perhaps it is the Scotch scones. They are very delicious, crumbly, hot cakes, spread thick with butter and jam. She eats two of them without a quiver. Once she ate three. Afterward she said she felt queer, and wondered if she had eaten something. It may be the scones . . .

ROSE WILDER LANE

2020

Voted today! I won't reveal who for, but my voting method of choice was biking to the local library to drop it off. Actions speak louder than words. They take a lot of health precautions, which mom said were a little extreme, but I don't think so at all, given that most of the staff and visitors fall into the high risk category. It was sad to be at the library again. It used to be my place. I'd always visit the side bookstore whenever I told mom I was "out with friends." She's still saying I need to be more social, but it's not as bad as it was before. At least I am allowed to read my New Yorkers again. It didn't feel good for my way of life to be so attacked a few weeks ago:

"For fuck's sake! You're *eighteen*! You need to be hanging out with people your own age! Stop reading that shit!" . . .   **SAMIA SAAD**

OCTOBER 15

1863

. . . It is a desolate country. Of all those streams shown on the map of the estate, I don't think there are three in existence. & these three are mere threads, used over & over & over again, so valuable that a man's eyes will sparkle when he points them out to you. They are coaxed to the mills and made to wash gold again & again by ingenious contrivances and what finally gets away is seized upon by China-men and made the most of by their pains-taking industry.

Well—I visited Princeton, Mt Ophir & Green Gulch yesterday. The mills were in excellent order, the mining very bad; the men in charge very good, the whole aspect of the country detestable . . .

landscape architect, writer **FREDERICK LAW OLMSTED**

1973

Re:

Your November issue, "On the Scene" section on Mr. Hunter S. Thompson as the creator of Gonzo Journalism, which you say he both created and named . . . Well, sir, I beg to take issue with you. And with anyone else who says that. In point of fact, Doctor Duke and I—the world famous Doctor Gonzo—together we both, hand in hand, sought out the teachings and curative powers of the world famous Savage [Robert] Henry, the Scag Baron of Las Vegas, and in point of fact the term *and* methodology of reporting crucial events under fire and drugs, which are of course essential to any good writing in this age of confusion—all this I say came from out of the mouth of our teacher who is also known by the name of Owl . . .

lawyer **OSCAR "ZETA" ACOSTA**, *to Hugh Hefner*

OCTOBER 16

1860

SAN FRANCISCO

In a few days I shall be at sea again, and as I want to see what I can while here, you may imagine I have not much idle time. I have just written to your father, and slip this little note in, just to say that your letter received here was very interesting to me, and merits a longer & more communicative reply than I shall be able to make. Indeed, as I write by night (rather unusual for me) and my eyes feel tired, all I can add here is, that I hope you are a good enough Christian in this matter of correspondence to be willing cheerfully to give much and receive little.

Thine   **HERMAN MELVILLE**, *to his wife's cousin*

1937

Preparations for my next picture *Shanghai Deadline* have not quite reached what I might call the 'Hell—Let's Shoot It' stage and consequently there are numerous story conferences, at which tremendous attention to the minutest detail of dialogue and characterization is paid by all concerned, and advance scripts marked 'Revised Temporary Final' are issued to the principals. It never pays, however, to *read* these scripts as the entire story is invariably rewritten on the set, the dialogue improvised by the players, and the characterization moulded by the Director in accordance with his day-to-day moods, whims and fancies . . .   *actor* **GEORGE SANDERS**, *to his father*

1944

FRESNO, CALIFORNIA

Dear Pop,

. . . you have such a vague knowledge of this particular situation that I cannot help but feel that you are totally unqualified to pass competent judgement upon it. The girl in question is of excellent character, and of the highest moral grade, the daughter-in-law of the former commanding officer of this post . . . I have never been happier, and do not believe I could call this existence sin if I were the Archbishop of Canterbury or the Pope of Rome.

You seem to think that in my reaching the age of 21 I have used my new-found "freedom" for an orgiaic display of atheism and free love. Nothing could be further from the truth . . . As for religion, I have been a somewhat apathetic atheist since I was 13 or 14. I doubt if I ever really believed. I make no great show of this, for by now I have learned caution in these matters, but I feel that I can no longer profess to believe in something in which I do not, especially in the presence of my own family.

Love, Jim   **JAMES DICKEY**, *to his father*

OCTOBER 17

1932

SAN QUENTIN PRISON

My dear Comrade Stalin:

Just three weeks from today (November 7th) marks the Fifteenth Anniversary of the Russian Proletarian Revolution, beyond any question the greatest happening in the whole history of the world so far as the working class is concerned. It is my desire that you should know that I, along with millions of other revolutionary workers the world over will rejoice with you and your brave comrades all over the USSR and particularly in Moscow . . .

[My] dear 84-year-old Mother . . . will be in Moscow on November 7th, 1932, in the continued interest of the working class fight for my freedom from the Dungeons of American Capitalist Imperialism. All Hail to the Russian Revolution and the Dictatorship of the Proletariat. I'm for it hook, line and sinker, without equivocation or reservation. Please accept my warm personal regards and best wishes,

I am

Comradely yours,

labor leader, convicted Preparedness Day bomber

TOM MOONEY, *31921.*

1936

Pusher: "You pack 15 boxes a day OR ELSE."
Camper: "I been wuking here for 2 years, an I ain't had no one tell me I loafs on the job . . . I ain't gonna pack 15 boxes because I ain't gonna put rotten grapes in these boxes to ship . . . so OR ELSE to you and like it. I ain't gonna quit . . . so what's your other OR ELSE?"

TOM COLLINS,

Weedpatch migrant labor camp manager

1951

. . . An old acquaintance of mine, James Agee, many years the movie reviewer on *Time* and latterly engaged in doing a script for John Huston on *The African Queen*, is also on the beach and occupying a room in Dotty's house (no romantic connection; he spends his time drooling over some unseen dame Dotty calls The Pink Worm). Parker says Agee consumed three bottles of scotch unaided last Friday. I didn't get Agee's closing quotations on Parker's consumption. They both exist in a fog of crapulous laundry, stale cigarette smoke, and dirty dishes, sans furniture or cleanliness; one suspects they wet their beds. All this, added to an absolutely manic pitch of fear out here on everyone's part that he's about to get about to be jugged by the FBI—and people *are* being so jugged and blacklisted—makes for a Hollywood that is nothing like any I ever knew, a combination of boom town gone bust and Germany in 1935. By Monday I was in such a dreary frame of mind I was strongly tempted to cry frig to my various assignments [and] jump the east-bound plane . . .   *essayist, reluctant screenwriter* **S. J. PERELMAN**

1962

I want you to know this is a literary family. Tony came home from school the other day with a composition entitled "Why I Must Not Talk in Class," for me to read and sign. His father, on the other hand, is sending you *his* compositions for you to read . . . unless some crook with excellent taste has rifled the envelope looking for first edition material that he can sell as hot goods to the Huntington Library.

The pieces are from a book to be called *Overkill and Megalove* which World Publishing has scheduled for spring publication, always allowing that there will be any paper or people by then. Tell me frankly what you think and why you believe they are great . . .

Fuck the New York Yankees.

NORMAN CORWIN, *to lyricist E.Y. "Yip" Harburg*

OCTOBER 18

1852

Monday October 18th. A cold, foggy morning; not the least hope of landing. We are sadly disappointed. A vessel passed just before our bows this morning. The Captain is very much concerned; the fog is so dense we may be close to shore and yet he knows not which way to turn, in case during the night we have drifted inside those fearful rocks. He has, however, turned the ship's head to sea. We have just had a glimpse of our longed-for haven and now are to turn from it again. It is like showcasing food to a starving man and then taking it away; this seems hardest of all to bear. Before night; the fog has dispersed enough to enable the Captain to see we are free of land. We have been sailing towards the sea some hours. Now the Captain has ordered the ship around again and during the night we shall sail gently towards shore.

traveler **LUCY KENDALL HERRICK**

1930

There is no Los Angeles face. Almost any other great city will have an imaginable characteristic physiognomy . . . The Los Angeles picture, nevertheless, would be a very remarkable thing—-namely, the truest conceivable representation of the whole American face, urban, big town, little town, all together.

columnist **GARET GARRETT**

1934

TO SYLVIA CHEN (LEYDA)
Dearest Sylvia,
CARMEL, CAL.

I got all your letters and was mighty glad to hear from you each time. Carmel was pretty exciting for a while (California has turned Hitler on us since the general strike was broken), but I am still about. I stayed away from Carmel about a month (not wishing to be tarred and feathered) . . .

Don't be nobody else-cause I don't want nobody else—but you.

Love and—kisses.

XXXXXX

These are the kisses

XXXXXX

Lang

LANGSTON HUGHES

1946

Today I topped all the foolish things I've ever done by getting up from my sickbed and going to the Frank Sinatra show with Joan and Opal. I never saw such bedlam anywhere, thousands of bobby soxers screaming and pushing. Finally, they broke a plate glass door, cutting one girl and we were swept inside and viewed the voice, fashion show and all.

WILMA ELIZABETH MCDANIEL

1973

I visited Henry Miller after serious surgery, fourteen hours and eight hours on separate days. He was so weak and frail. He is blind in his right eye from being too long on the operating table. He does not hear well. When he asked to have the pillows removed so he could slide into bed and rest, I felt almost as if he was going to curl up and sleep forever . . .

I don't want to live as Miller has, limping, in pain, not able to travel and now for the second time undergoing major surgery. Henry once so healthy, joyous, lively. Tireless walker, hearty eater.

But let the sun shine on a beautiful autumn day, let me have a morning free of engagements when I can work on Volume Six and I am light again. Stay alive, Anaïs Nin.   **ANAÏS NIN**

OCTOBER 19

1963

6 p.m. Well, it hasn't taken long to fall in love with San Francisco . . . The three great wonders of San Francisco are a) the roller-coaster gradients of Nob Hill, b) the Chinese quarter, and c) a magnificent stucco building (described by Mr. Sommer as being of papier-mache, which it just might have been) called the Palace of Fine Arts. It seems that the lower dockside areas of the port near Fisherman's Quay used to be a bit homicidal in the early days, so the richer tycoons moved their families to the comparative safety of Nob Hill—just as the King of Naples moved up from the harbor during times of crisis. Sommer said that the ridge rises to 906 ft. and can have a gradient of 25° or 30°. It is prodigious. The brakes of his taxi are reset every day and renewed every month . . .

China Town must be the only China Town outside China which is not a phony for tourists. To begin with, it houses 22,000 Chinese . . . San Francisco has several exotic colonies, apart from the Chinese. For one thing the Beatniks began here (contemporaries of Mort Sahl) and there is a restaurant where the entertainment is by males dressed as females . . .

[The] Palace of Fine Arts was built for the 1915 Exhibition. It is a terrific, exuberant yet not incorrect Corinthian building centered around a rotunda on a lake with duck and gulls and geese on it. It is partly chocolate and partly white, a sort of very late Roman extravaganza, and it is coming to bits . . . It is a sort of imperial dream by Cecil B. de Mille in lath and plaster. I discovered that its actual materials were chicken wire, horsehair, gypsum and hemp . . .

It is literally true that in all of America which we have seen so far we have not come across a single entire nude male in a public place . . . In fiery Naples, for fear of inflaming the passions, they wear rather large scrolls, like sporrans. In America no form of leaf is sufficient. A swirl of stone drapery has to be wafted across the loins. Does this mean that Americans are even more virile than Neapolitans? Or has the censorship of females extended so far as emasculation? (In San Francisco I should have thought not.) . . .

novelist **T. H. WHITE**

1991

I drove to the studio this morning to visit the set. Inside a huge stage at Columbia Studios a grand Victorian mansion had been built. I loved seeing the furnishings, all the rich silks and brocades in a perfect harmony of muted color. Francis took my hand and said, "Come see this." He led me to the bedroom to look at the large round headboard for Lucy's bed with its carved bat designs and thick tassels.

The room opened onto a terrace overlooking the garden. We walked down two flights of wide stone steps to a fountain and a pond with water lilies blooming. Beyond, I could see the entrance to the crypt and a hill with family gravestones. There was a rose arbor and a maze of high hedges. Francis said, "All this garden is built in the pit of the stage where Esther Williams' swimming pool once was." **ELEANOR COPPOLA**

OCTOBER 20

1846

U.S. SHIP PORTSMOUTH ANCHERAGE

YERBA BUENA COVE

BAY OF SAN FRANCISCO

COAST OF CALIFORNIA

My Dear Mother,

It is with great pleasure that I seize upon an opportunity to write to you . . . I shall proceed to give you an account of the grand drama that has been acted in California since our anchoring in this Bay on the 1st of June last, to wit: On the 14th of June a revolution broke out on the part of the Americans & other Foreign residents against the Californian government & a party of 34 men surprised & took the interior town fortress of Sonoma making Gen. Don Mariano Guadalupe Vallejo & his brother Don Salvadore Vallejo & Col. Don Victor Prudon all distinguished Mexican army officers prisoners & hoisted a flag of their own manufacture of this fashion. A white field with

a reborder on the lower edge a Grizzly bear in the center with a star in the
upper corner . . .   **JOHN ELLIOTT MONTGOMERY**, *to his mother,*
shortly before his disappearance

1852

What a change does a few hours effect in our feelings! Since dinner the fog
has gradually dispersed and we are safe by the dreaded rocks. At half past
five P.M. a pilot boat approached us; we watched it most anxiously. We saw
it discharge a pilot at a neighboring vessel and then it came to us. One of
the men, not a pilot but one who was familiar with the coast, then boarded
us and we began to realize that our journey was at an end. This evening
closes the voyage and with it my journal. Joys and sorrows, hopes and disap-
pointments are the lot of human beings, but with my parting breath I would
exclaim against a voyage around Cape Horn. Our landing took place on the
morning of the 20th of October, 1852—137 days at sea.

LUCY KENDALL HERRICK

1865

You are in trouble, & in debt—so am I. I am utterly miserable—so are you.
Perhaps your religion will sustain you, will feed you—I place no depen-
dence in mine. Our religions are alike, though, in one respect—neither can
make a man happy when he is out of luck. If I do not get out of debt in 3
months,—pistols or poison for one—exit *me*. {There's a text for a sermon on
Self-Murder—Proceed.}
   . . . P. S. You had better shove this in the stove—for if we strike a bargain
I don't want any absurd "literary remains" & "unpublished letters of Mark
Twain" published after I am planted.

MARK TWAIN, *to his brother and sister*

1915

I am writing the life of Henry Ford now, and he was telling me yesterday that
he is building a farm tractor now that sells for $200 and weighs only 1,500
pounds . . . it would be better than a team of horses for lots of the farm work,
because it would not cost any more, and when it was not working it would
not be eating . . .   **ROSE WILDER LANE**

OCTOBER 21

1940

Had dinner upstairs with Luther and Sylvia, after this going for a walk down
Hollywood Boulevard. They told me of a scene that happened in Ciro's nightclub here the other night. [Anatole] Litvak, director, and [Paulette] God-
dard, actress, were drunk there together. They have been sleeping together,
in public, for weeks. Drunk at Ciro's, sitting at a ringside table, he took out
her breasts and kissed them passionately. They were stopped by the help but
later continued the same thing on the dance floor. For this the management
banished them to the outer sanctum of the bar. There A. Litvak suddenly
disappeared, finally was discovered under the bouffant skirt of Miss God-
dard on his knees, kissing the "eagerly sought triangular spot" with the bliss-
ful unawareness of a baby at a bottle.

For my part, I told Sylvia, I would rather be like Litvak than lead a life of
wooden caution.

A warm feeling came to me when I began to think about the trio play this
evening. I hope to come to it again with real excitement. Part of the theme of
this play is about how the men of our country irresponsibly wait for the voice
and strong arm of authority to bring them to life, etc. So comes fascism to a
whole race of people. Danger ahead—I see it all over, even in myself. Nothing stands for authority and I wait for its voice! There is something in men
in the world over today that welcomes dictatorship; the children are seeking
for the father to arrange their lives for them!

CLIFFORD ODETS, *quoting Havelock Ellis*
and at work on Clash by Night

1961

. . . [Don't] send any books to Big Sur. Hang onto them until I give a new
word. I have been evicted . . .

HUNTER S. THOMPSON, *to William Kennedy,*
after caretaking what would become the Esalen Institute

1963

. . . Our Chinese lunch again ended with pastries that contained printed
prophesies. Carol's said, You will be fortunate in everything you put your
hands to. Mine said, This is the month that indicates your greatest success . . .

During the broadcast I had to answer questions put to me over the telephone by listeners. I thought this an excellent variant from the English
method. The taxi drivers of S. F. are charming and friendly, and on the whole

I believe this is the happiest city we have visited. Carol has gone off to have dinner with a friend who lives here, so now is my chance to go out on the town.   **T. H. WHITE**

OCTOBER 22

1929

I have been ousted from school again. The head of the Physical Ed. Dept. and I came to blows the other day. We saw the principal about it but he was too thick to see my side. He told me to get out and find another school. I have a number of teachers backing me so there is some possibility of my getting back . . . If I get back in school I will have to be very careful about my actions. The whole outfit think I am a rotten rebel from Russia. I will have to go about very quietly for a long period . . . .

I am doubtful of any talent, so whatever I choose to be, will be accomplished only by long study and work. I fear it will be forced and mechanical. Architecture interests me but not in the sense painting and sculptoring does. I became acquainted with Rivera's work through a number of Communist meetings I attended after being ousted from school last year. He has a painting in the Museum now. Perhaps you have seen it, Dia de Flores . . .

As to what I would like to be. It is difficult to say. An Artist of some kind. If nothing else I shall always study the Arts. People have always frightened and bored me consequently I have been within my own shell and have not accomplished anything materially. In fact to talk in a group I was so frightened that I could not think logically. I am gradually overcoming it now. I am taking American Literature, Contemporary Literature, Clay Modeling and the life class. We are very fortunate in that this is the only school in the city that have models. Altho it is difficult to have a nude and get by the board, [Manual Arts High art teacher Frederick Schwankavsky, who also mentored Philip Guston] is brave enough to have them.   **JACKSON POLLOCK**

1942

OJAI

I got "A" on an English theme which Mr. Barnes read to the class, because they begged him to read it after he had read the first paragraph out loud to make a correction on it. If you would like I'll send it to you to read. It is about a cat. I think that my writing is O.K. I hope that the fact that you miss me does not influence your judgment. If you want me to be a spoiled brat, then just let me come home. That would be admitting defeat, and I am going to prove that I am just as much a man as any boy here. It is beautiful here, I wish you all could see it. Marion would love to paint the mountains. Meemaw would love the restfulness of the Los Padre Forests all around us, and I'm sure that you would enjoy the perfect climate here. Joe would like the city of Ojai. Now don't get the idea again that just because I am homesick I want to come home. I am just not that kind of a man, who would run away from something that was difficult to get used to. I have made some good friends and some bad enemies here . .

Love, Phil   **PHILIP K. DICK**

2003

It's hard to convey the tranquility and normalcy of these neighborhoods— the skateboarding kids, the Pizza Huts, the garage sales—while still presenting a truthful picture of their crime problems.

In fact, what many people in Los Angeles think of as this city's "bad neighborhoods" are in many ways indistinguishable from those with milder reputations. They brim with aspiration and middle-class comfort, even as they distill every kind of despair. I pass blocks of graffiti on Slauson Avenue in the morning before stopping in at the bright new Western Avenue Starbucks, inevitably full of well-dressed commuters listening to cutting-edge blues. This is just northwest of where the 1992 riots broke out, and the area is now booming, construction everywhere: a new Gigante grocery store, a new Subway sandwich shop.

But just across the street is the permanent swap meet where a shootout broke out recently amid a crowd in daylight.   *journalist* **JILL LEOVY**

OCTOBER 23

1849

There is quite an excitement in the harbour this morning, this being the day on which the poor, unfortunate men are to be executed on board the war vessels. Boats are plying about in all directions, filled with persons anxious to witness the horrible scene. The surrounding hills are thronged with spectators, as well as the different vessels lying near those selected for the performance of the sad deed. At 12 o'clock, we heard the firing of a gun, which signified that one had paid the penalty of his crime.

ANNE WILLSON BOOTH

1940

2000 words today and all good.   F. SCOTT FITZGERALD

1963

This is a brief picture of our day. We got up at 8 a.m. I was interviewed at 9 a.m. by a newspaper. At 9:30 I recorded a broadcast by telephone, a broadcast I never did get around to hearing and so far as I know nor did anybody else. At 10 we took a taxi with a colored driver who drove us the long distance to Watts Towers . . .

1) We had a long conversation with the Negro cabdriver. His most interesting contribution to the integration argument was this. It is useless, said he, to put white and colored children together at high school level. It must be done long before the age of puberty, at kindergarten level in fact, so that they may grow up getting used to each other . . . .

2) Watts Tower is an extraordinary fantasy built single-handed by an eccentric tile setter called Simon Rodia, by birth an Italian. It is reminiscent of the architecture of Gaudi in Spain. It is made of steel rods, mesh, mortar, broken tiles, cups, dishes, bottles, seashells, bed frames and the reversed prints in concrete of tools, hands, corncobs, baskets and the implements of a tile setter. He took 33 years to erect its astonishing spires, with no architect, engineer or even scaffolding. The towers are about 100 ft. high and all he had to get up them was themselves as they grew and a window washer's belt and bucket. He was forty years old when he started. When he had finished, he simply went away, nobody knows why. I believe he is still living. Asked in 1959 why he would not even talk about the Tower, he replied, "If your mother dies and you have loved her very much, maybe you don't speak of her." . . .

Bureaucratic efforts have been made to tear down this strange spout of American genius, as being unsafe, but I am glad to say they have been thwarted. It was finished in 1954. It stands in the Negro quarter.

3) How can I write about Los Angeles when I have been giving out or taking in all day? It is a vast city, the largest in America for area, which has grown outwards instead of up. The poorer quarters lie forever and forever athwart its endless and rather featureless plain—7,000,000 people of which the driver claimed that 3,000,000 were colored—adorned with all the advertisements in the world. The rich, and there are thousands and thousands of them, have withdrawn to Beverly Hills above its fringes and live there

sumptuously in rather Chinese-looking cliff dwellings. They think nothing of bulldozing a mountain or two to landscape a garden, drive or garage . . .

We drove past the mementos of Hollywood's greatness, the footprints in concrete, the film stars' portraits set in the pavements, the crazy cinema called Grauman's Chinese Theatre—all of them matters which will one day be touchingly romantic with a different romance from the one they started with . . .   **T. H. WHITE**

1981

Dearest Maya,

. . . The appalling business of Kathy Boudin. As I'm sure you realize, her papa Leonard & ma Jean are old, old friends of ours. K. was one of Dink's best friends when they were aged 17 (Dink) & 14 (Kathy). I can hardly express the total horror of it all. Both WICKED and STUPID, is all I can say. Kathy has managed in one deft moment to rehabilitate the discredited FBI, possibly ensure passage of the "terrorist" bill which would re-establish HUAC in a new & more palatable form, plus senselessly murdering the three people. Apparently one of the cops was a well-liked black policeman, only one in Rockland County . . . .

Kathy & co. have evidently completely lost touch with reality as any of us know it. On top of all she's got a one-year-old babe that nobody (her parents etc) knew about. Madness reigns.

At the risk of boring you I must just tell one thing about Kathy—this was ages ago, she'd have been about 16. We got an appeal letter. Not the usual scruffy mimeo job of those days—no, it was hand-typed on Leonard's office stationery, obviously by one of his secretaries, starting "Dear Bob & Decca." The appeal, which was for an organization called "The Second American Revolution," asked for contributions for a fund needing $200,000. Bob said "I bet the first American revolution didn't cost anything like that."

Well—that's OK, maybe, at age 16—but THIRTY-EIGHT??? which she now is. What happened to her noggin in the meantime? Next time I heard of her was in the Spock trial. Kathy (we are now in 1968, she's out of college, graduated with highest honors) was living in Cleveland where she became great friends with the Spocks. When Dr. S. was indicted, K. said "There's only one lawyer worth having & that's my father." So Spock, who didn't know many lawyers, got Leonard . . . Sorry to inflict all this on you but I must say I've been in a state of semishock over it all . . . .

JESSICA MITFORD, *to Maya Angelou,*
about family friend and SLA member Kathy Boudin

OCTOBER 24

1871

There has been a Chinese massacre . . . a most disgraceful affair, the like of which is fortunately not on American records. Some members of different Chinese secret societies fought over the possession of a woman . . .

A few Celestials were taken to jail in consequence. The disturbance was thought to have ended and the jailbirds were taken the next day before the police court for preliminary hearing . . . .

No sooner had the court set the day for trial than the Mongolians repaired to their own quarters, where a new fight ensued, which soon attracted a multitude of Mexicans and Americans from that vicinity . . . .

The heathens fought desperately and an officer, Robert Thompson, who attempted to quell the riot, was killed and his deputy, Bilderain, was wounded, which naturally roused the boundless anger of the white mob . . .

One of the heathens ventured into the street and was at once caught by his pursuers . . . and hanged to the doorway of a corral amid the abjurations of the enraged spectators. Having tasted the blood of the almond-eyed stranger, the combined mob of Americans and Spaniards now largely reinforced, began the real massacre. As the beleaguered heathen had barricaded doors and windows, a crowd of hoodlums in desperate frenzy climbed upon the roofs, broke holes through and shot the inmates, males, females, young and old . . . .

When quiet was restored, there were eighteen bodies found dangling in mid air, some from window casings, some from lamp posts, while one or two had actually been tied to the seat of farm wagons and others to awnings, among these the body of a child!   FRANK LECOUVREUR

1933

Dear Father and Mother,
. . . Mrs. Dixon and I went to Berkeley to hear Rockwell Kent. We enjoyed seeing the cuts and paintings shown very large on a screen . . .

EVERETT RUESS, *after an outing*
with painter Maynard Dixon's wife, Dorothea Lange

1937

LAFAYETTE / CONTRA COSTA COUNTY / CALIFORNIA
This last Stock Market crash actually laid me low. Building a home, at this time, is no joke. Plasterers demanding $13.00 a day— for 6 hours work!— This man [organizer Harry] Bridges ought to be deported— or shot!— It is

the Labour Agitator who keeps the Racket going. The workers are trapped—
&, of course, will suffer like hell this Winter for all people will stop building,
etc. —At least, out here. One simply can not pay what they are demanding.
And they are so damned impudent. . . .

The bright side of life for me is that Gene is feeling so much better.—
And that we sold our Sea Island home. Here we have a splendid climate, no
negroes, sand flies, hookworms or mosquitoes. All of which I dislike— in
quantity. Also, we have friends here— people we can talk with. And Gene
adores the football. California has a grand team . . .

As I sit here & write I can't help but wish that you were here. Lovely
sun,— fresh breeze, beautiful rolling hills enclosing a long valley, with Mt.
Diablo at the end. The garden is so lovely . . .

CARLOTTA MONTEREY O'NEILL

OCTOBER 25

1908

I anxiously await Saturdays so that I can see your little letters, my love.
All week I've been waiting to see if you show up, from my cell through the
window on the alley, which is the third window . . .

When you all pass by the third window on the alley, stop if only for a
half minute so that I can see you well. My dear: I feel that you are feeling
a bit of pain. Would some of my kisses where you hurt make it well? I
would give them so tenderly that you would feel no discomfort. I know,
my life, I understand that you miss me as much as I miss you. But what
can be done? More than the tyrants, it is our friends who are keeping us
in jail, because their laziness, their indolence, their lack of initiative has
tied them up, and they do nothing. I believe that they love us and have us
in their hearts; but this isn't enough to rescue us. What's needed is that
they work in an effective manner for our liberation, and they're not doing
that. Everyone comes forth in manifesting their sympathy for us and de-
ploring our situation. We are devoting ourselves to putting an end to the
tyrant in Mexico and nobody will lift an arm to stop the tyrant's henchmen. There is much that could be done in our favor, but little or nothing
is being done, and nothing, of course, is being gained. There should be
a commission that is constantly after the press so that something could

appear favorable to the prisoners, as much in the local press as that outside of California . . .

Goodbye my love, look closely and you'll see that it is our friends who
are keeping us prisoner through their apathy. Receive my immense love and
adoration, you, the only woman who makes my heart beat. What I've told
you isn't a reproach for you, my angel. You're doing everything you can, and
I thank you from my soul. If you don't win in this struggle against despotism
and do not rescue your Ricardo who loves and adores you, it won't have been
for lack of effort on your part. With all my soul, your Ricardo kisses you
tenderly.   *social reformer* **RICARDO FLORES MAGÓN**,

to his beloved

1920

Work on *An American Tragedy* & letters. Helen collects $35.00 from Metro
& gives it to me. Wonderful session in evening—after dinner at Petitfils.
Helen has a streak of perversion in her. Makes me promise never to teach
any other girl to osculate my penus as she does!   **THEODORE DREISER**

1935

NEAR SLATE'S HOT SPRINGS

On the very face of the next cliff north of this one are Slate's hot sulphur
springs.

The original owner, who gave the springs his name, is long since dead,
and the present owner has leased the property to the state for a highway
construction camp.

Twin bathtubs stand on a little platform fully exposed to the great sun
and Pacific, and to anyone who wants to look down from the tops of adjacent
cliffs.

But he can't look intimately without glasses, the country is so immense.

There is a little trail—a miniature Bright Angel—leading from the flat to
the baths, halfway down the cliff . . .

Because the water is too hot for bathing as it comes from the spring, a
cooling barrel is provided between the two tubs. The bather fills his tub with
hot water from the trough, then dips as much cold water from the cooling
barrel as he wants and refills it from the trough for the next bather.

The baths are free to what little public is present . . .

HARRY PARTCH, *at what would become Esalen*

1977

Today I talked to Prince Charles of England! Correction, I didn't talk to him, he talked to me! I was at the Broadway and he shook my hand and complimented me on my "Star Wars" shirt!

COLLEEN JAURRETCHE

OCTOBER 26

1849

Mr. Booth tore down the state rooms to night, and will have the lumber taken ashore to morrow so as to commence our little cottage on Monday morning.

ANNE WILLSON BOOTH

1866

MEADOW LAKE

to J. T. Goodman, Editor

Our circus is coming. Sound the hewgag.

MARK TWAIN

1935

These San and Santed hills-these swerving piles of earth, rock, and redwood behind me, they are called Saint Lucy!

I would like to know the Indian names for this land, although it is useless to try to change them, since Californians are sublimely doped with the tradition of the people they hot-tailed out of here in the 1840s.

California! Land of oncoming Los-es and Las-es, Sans and Santas, Virgins, Conceptions, and Angels! . . .

Ah, the glorious conquistadores!

Their imaginations ran the gamut from Saint John to Saint John.

HARRY PARTCH

1938

Today should be a day of joy because I could finish today—just the walk to the barn, the new people and the ending and that's all. But I seem to have contracted an influenza of the stomach or something. Anyway I am so dizzy I can hardly see the page. This makes it difficult to work. On the other hand, it might get worse. I might be in for a siege. Can't afford to take that chance. I must go on. If I can finish today I don't much care what happens afterwards.

Wish—if it was inevitable, that it could have held off one more day. My fault really for having muffed on Monday oddly enough. I feel better—sitting here. I wish I were done. Best way is just to get down to the lines. I wonder if this flu could be simple and complete exhaustion. I don't know. But I do know that I'll have to start at it now and, course, anything I do will be that much nearer the end.

Finished this day—and I hope to God it's good.   JOHN STEINBECK

1963

My friend, the forest ranger, decided I had been working too hard and needed diversion. "I'm going to take you to visit the oldest things on the planet. As we drove north from Los Angeles, I assumed we were going to the redwoods . . .

. . . It seemed as though we had landed in a spaceship on another planet, the planet Mars. Out of great expanses of bare, white, bone-colored rock grew a few scattered trees, nothing else. The trees were short, stunted, twisted and gnarled, only a few green needles, a symbol of strength and defiance. The forester said they were bristlecone pines, the oldest known living things. Methuselah, the eldest, is 4,600 years old. Many were growing here when the Egyptians were building the Pyramids. He explained these trees are the only plants that can survive here, exposed to high winds, growing on very poor rocky soil with very little rainfall. They have been able to survive by allowing most of the tree to die so that a small part may live on in equilibrium with the harsh environment. They grow incredibly slowly, in one hundred years only one inch. Their twisted roots have been almost completely exposed by four hundred years of erosion. Many of the pines had been sculptured into objects of powerful beauty by wind-blown sand, by ice and by fire . . .   ANAÏS NIN

OCTOBER 27

1869

MUD HILL

Mr. Editor:-"What of the night?" Is there one ray of hope for California? It seems Democracy is again triumphant. When will truth prevail? Is it possible that intelligent people will be gulled by lying politicians, and men have the highest offices in the State, who, a few years ago, cursed the Government, cursed the Flag, rejoiced over every Union defeat, and went about with saddened faces when the telegraph heralded a defeat to the Confederacy? I am astonished that all this boldness (electing such men to our offices of Government) should occur so soon after great struggle, before the tears are dry for the departed heroes, who willingly went to death that the old flag might wave over a whole country with all its stars entire. There are some who can never forget those near and dear to us, who so bravely died, and never can we be reconciled to traitors, for let them talk ever so boldly of "our flag," we can look back only a few years, and then they styled it "the old rag." I wonder where consistency has fled! It surely is not with the Democratic party in California.

Mr. Editor, will we not awake one of these days and hear that the welcome cry of the Fifteenth Amendment is an established fact? Shall we not see our men walking boldly up to the polls by that Act, saying, "I am a man in God's image, and a free man with his privileges. After all this, then may the women talk of their rights, and press the matter if they so desire."

Semper Fidelis   JENNIE CARTER

1921

ALTURAS

Here I am, living with an Achumawi family. Yes, there are pitch tones in the language, undoubtedly. And the devil of a language it is, with the verbal stem lost out of sight in a mass of affixes, pronominal and otherwise.

. . . perhaps it is because I am but a tyro, but it usually takes me some 10 or 20 questions, before I disentangle the stem I want. My informant can't for the life of him say "table" or "knife" but must hurl at me a string of consonants meaning perhaps "bring the knife here and cut this meat." You know how it is! . . .

There is no gender according to sex. There is a dual and plural in all three persons.

It is quite a living language. There are about 500 or more Indians speaking it. Nothing else is heard inside the house; even the younger generation use it among themselves.   JAIME DE ANGULO

1934

I still have my fine office, I still have my emptiness: but I think it fairly well established by now that I am "not quite the man for the job". For it is all a process of wearing down. It seems they expect you to come here with the ember of revolt glowing somewhere. They smile and wait for it to get dampened in the application of non-resistance blankets. They seem to say: "We will let this fellow make his protestations for his soul's sake, and then, having made them, he can get to work". But if you won't let revolt die, then you're not the "man for the job". If desire goes on burning fiercely, you are an outcast.   ERIC KNIGHT, *to a friend*

OCTOBER 28

1878

"He loved his fellows, and their love was sweet. Plant daisies at his head and at his feet."   RICHARD REALF, *poet, abolitionist, in his suicide note*

1930

I like the place. I think California scenery is the most loathsome on earth,—a cross between Coney Island and the Riviera, but by sticking in one's garden all the time and shutting one's eyes when one goes out, it is possible to get by.
                                                        P. G. WODEHOUSE

2021

We are at the beginning of the next chapter for the internet, and it's the next chapter for our company too . . . We call this the metaverse, and it will touch every product we build . . .

In this future, you will be able to teleport instantly as a hologram to be at the office without a commute, at a concert with friends, or in your parents' living room to catch up . . . Think about how many physical things you have today that could just be holograms in the future . . . We believe the metaverse can enable better social experiences than anything that exists today . . .

To reflect who we are and the future we hope to build, I'm proud to share that our company is now Meta . . . I used to study Classics, and the word "meta" comes from the Greek word meaning "beyond". For me, it symbolizes that there is always more to build, and there is always a next chapter to the story. Ours is a story that started in a dorm room and grew beyond anything we imagined . . .

If this is the future you want to see, I hope you'll join us. The future is going to be beyond anything we can imagine.   MARK ZUCKERBERG

OCTOBER 29

1969

LO

professor **LEONARD KLEINROCK,**
inaugurating the Internet in UCLA's Boelter Hall

2001

Yesterday morning at approximately 9:30 am PST, a smallish rumbling earthquake hit Los Angeles and woke me from a drooling slumber. It was the first earthquake I've ever been awake or sober enough to experience, and like any other natural disaster frightened me into rabid cable news channel surfing and knuckle gnawing for the rest of the afternoon.

Rounding out the list of phobias that render me a paralyzed, shivering goose bump—fear of heights, rodents, spiders, and hairy toes to name just a few—is a mammoth anxiety over potential natural disasters, thoroughly aggravated in my youth by my older brother's daily tortuous threat: "Do what I say or the tornado will come and get you."

Tornado season in Tennessee starts in mid-March and continues through July, sometimes hiccuping into the latter part of September. When thunderstorms aren't uprooting forests or rearranging acres of farmland, the South often suffers hailstorms, flashfloods and torrentially ghoulish winds during this season. Rarely is there a week not littered with severe thunderstorm warnings blinking in red Helvetica across the bottom of "Days of Our Lives" . . .

18 years later and over 1000 miles from any weather conducive to tornado formation, I've got earthquakes to worry about and no siren-ific warnings or radar screens to issue me into the tub and into safety. I wonder how long I can stand under a doorframe before passing out.

blogger **HEATHER B. ARMSTRONG,** *aka "Dooce"*

2007

. . . as I head down the Thompson Creek trail esta mañana, iPodless, tuning in, instead, to a chirpy sky just beginning to clear of post-fire smoke and ash— por apocalíptico que parezca, just the "typical" Califas fall conflagration—I *do* know one thing for sure. Si el Bruce was born to run, yo nací para escribir.   **SUSANA CHÁVEZ-SILVERMAN**

2020

. . . our pool man has not shown up this week . . . I phoned Joel Moreno to inquire when he might next be coming and found his phone out of service. My immediate fear was that this quiet, intelligent, skillful, and knowledgeable Hispanic gentleman may have been deported. Kitty weakly objected, "But he has a son at Tustin High School." But we both know that the savage Stephen Miller/Donald Trump manhunt has never been slowed by a consideration like that one. A regime of matchless cruelty . . .   JACK MILES

OCTOBER 30

1894

. . . the doctor devoted his eloquence to G. and me, and made, for our information, a scathing exposition of the "frightful corruption" in every department of the Californian state . . .

They next inveighed against all monopolies—the South Pacific Company in particular—by which, they said, the entire country was held in bondage, and which appears to be an egregious *bete noire* to every Californian not connected with it.

This seemed to us a great mistake on their part, for most of the development and prosperity of California appears to be owing to this and other companies; the facilities for travel in every direction, the magnificent hotels attracting visitors from all parts, the opening out of the beauty of the country, the vast bathing establishments, and the rapid rise of towns on every picturesque spot—in short, they seemed to us great benefactors.

traveler WINEFRED, LADY HOWARD OF GLOSSOP

1916

You ask when we expect to return. Have rented this house until June 4 and shall probably stay the limit. To my surprise I like it here very much. I do not know when I have been more contented. We have a very pretty little place with many flowers and trees, and a good lawn . . . The children are playing out in front now with no wraps, and wearing sox . . .

There are oodles of writers here, too . . . If I could establish a colony of human beings, it would be a nice place to live permanently.

EDGAR RICE BURROUGHS, *to his editor*

1938

. . . whatever you may say about 'unproductive' WPA projects, the Writers' Projects (not only here but everywhere in the country), have been producing work that needed to be done, that makes a genuine contribution, that does and will stimulate much else in the way of literature in the days to come.

JOSEPH HENRY JACKSON,
San Francisco Chronicle book critic

OCTOBER 31

1927

Five people killed in plane yesterday and it is headlined today in every paper. Saturday in Los Angeles at one grade crossing seven were killed and six wounded and the papers didn't even publish the names.

It looks like the only way you can get any publicity on your death is to be killed in a plane. It's no novelty to be killed in an auto any more.

WILL ROGERS

1933

Ansel Adams waxed very enthusiastic about my black and white work . . . He is going to trade me one of his photographs for one of my prints. The photograph I chose is of a mysterious lake at Kaweah Gap . . .

On Thursday I have a sitting with Dorothea Lange, who wants to make some photographic studies . . .

The children had a Halloween parade down Polk Street tonight. They were having a gay time with much excitement.

Love to all,

EVERETT RUESS

1990

All afternoon I have asked myself if it was true, did the developer of Compound Q really call me and say that my case sounded interesting, that negative viremia was remarkable at this point? Is it really true that we are on the right track at long last, able to suppress the virus and forestall illness? Are we rounding the corner on treatment, approaching the long-hoped-for "chronic" status for HIV disease? (The doorbell just rang, and I went down to greet a group of giggling trick-or-treaters—neighborhood children costumed as witches, ghouls, and skeletons. Luckily I had laid in a supply of mini candy bars!)

I feel lucky to be in the midst of this promising treatment. I recall last year, when Robert Pittman was quoted in the papers as saying that we were all going to be able to dance in the streets very soon. He was one of the original Compound Q patients in the Project Inform treatment program, and he was unequivocally enthusiastic about what Q had done for him. How many years have we waited for a real breakthrough, for some real shining light of hope? I've been living and breathing this subject for so long that I lose sight of just how remarkable this is. It will be possible to live with HIV infection and not be overwhelmed by it. It is possible to retard the progress of the infection. It is possible to postpone becoming ill. And it is possible to live amidst this tragedy . . .   **PAUL REED**

NOVEMBER 1

1849

. . . the schooner came near running down a craft of Chilians. It was amusing to see their fright. Some fell on their knees, and commenced counting their beads.

ANNE WILLSON BOOTH

1919

Enroute from Salt Lake to Los Angeles. Awaken at dawn in berth with Helen. I insist on rutting here. She protests but kisses me & lets me . . .

The Orange Groves. Helen & I on the back platform. Her joy and beauty. We reach Los Ange. 7 P.M. Helen's efficiency. Phones. The incident of the boys. We get off at the wrong corner. Finally reach the Stillwell at length & Grand Ave. Room 523. The nice service. We dress & go to a restaurant in Spring Street. Not much. Then back to hotel & spend a delicious night together. I am crazy about her.

THEODORE DREISER

NOVEMBER 2

1942

. . . lang's secretary called to say that shooting was starting and I was '*invited, more than invited*'. The first scene lang shot was one [co-screenwriter John Wexley] and I had cut; the heroine is arguing with her aunt about her wedding dress—she wants a deeper decollete. The heroine is cast with a fifth-rate English actress, a smooth doll with no character. The lord of the lens is sitting beside his camera, unapproachable, while beside me a german refugee doctor waits to give him his vitamin injections. Lang, of course, gives me an unconvincing wave and says half-audibly, 'hi, brecht! You'll be getting a script tomorrow!'

BERTOLT BRECHT

1973

He says Bill I believe this is killing me
As a smile ran away from his face
Well I'm sure that I could be a movie star
If I could get out of this place
Oh, la-la-la de-de da
La-la de-de da da-da
Now Paul is a real estate novelist . . .   *songwriter* **BILLY JOEL,**
                                    during a six-month gig at a Wilshire Boulevard piano bar

NOVEMBER 3

1888

. . . oh! who can describe the real estate agent of Southern California! And
what would California be without him? Notice him as he leans at his office
door, with a flower in his button hole, while over his suave and seductive
countenance ripple ravishing dreams of carloads of Eastern tourists wishing
to buy lots.   **HARRIET HARPER**

1942

I have now to go and vote. I hope Governor Olsen and Will Rogers will be
elected.   **GALKA SCHEYER**

1952

We came out here almost two years ago & are glad we did. I was around
San Francisco many years ago & loved it. New York got to be too much of a
struggle, at least for me, and one that availeth close to naught. Mostly got
tired of all the dirt and darkness . . . and seeing so many people turning sad
and/or crazy. Some of it had to do with the fact that we were living, if you can
call it that, during the last winter there, in a loft on the lower East Side, poor
as hell, with a kerosene stove that only heated about a thirtieth of the room.
We damn near froze.   *poet, painter, critic, novelist* **WELDON KEES,**
                                            to Malcolm Cowley

1957

HALF MOON BAY

The stink of acres and acres of rotting artichokes. Groves of eucalyptus, Monterey pine, redwoods, oaks, gray lichen-splotched boulders, meadows of tough short tawny grass—the golden hills! . . .

Man is not an alien in this world, not at all. He is as much a child of it as the lion and the ant. Nevertheless, it is true that the natural world does not return our love, that it is indifferent to our ideas and that, after all, the heartbreaking beauty will remain when there are no hearts to break for it. (Gulls on the shore, the sough of wind among mountain aspens, the red-tailed hawk soaring over the silence of the desert.. . .)

[Wallace] Stegner: has most distinguished-looking bags under his eyes.

We will now hear a few words from GAWD: "Friends. Are you tired, confused, uncertain about the meaning of life?" **ED ABBEY**

NOVEMBER 4

1892

I cut down a eucalyptus tree sixty feet high and made a pole and began laboriously to worm its point down through the bottom of the shaft. The process would have discouraged anyone not possessing the sublime faith that we possessed that a few inches or a few more feet at the most would tap for us incalculable wealth.

Suddenly gas spewed out and oil flooded the shaft to a depth of ten or fifteen feet in a few moments . . . *oil magnate* **E. L. DOHENY**

1894

. . . G. was told such tales of numerous bears, "grizzly" and "black," seen lately tramping through the forests, that he could not resist the hope of shooting one . . . **WINEFRED, LADY HOWARD OF GLOSSOP**

1951

PASADENA, CALIFORNIA

My thoughts are full of this southern California world I see below me and about me. It is easy to ridicule it, as Aldous Huxley and so many other intellectuals have done—but it is silly, and a form of self-condemnation, to do so. These are ordinary human beings: several million of them. The things that brought them here, and hold them here, are deeply human phenomena . . .

I feel great anxiety for these people, because I do not think they know what they are in for. In its mortal dependence on two liquids, oil and water, which no individual can easily produce by his own energy, even together with family and friends, the life of this area only shares the fragile quality of all life in the great urban concentrations of the motor age. But here the life-lines of supply seem to me particularly tenuous and vital. That is especially true of water, which they now have to bring from hundreds of miles, and will soon have to bring from thousands of miles, away. But equally disturbing to me is the utter dependence on the costly, uneconomical gadget called the automobile, for practically every process of life from birth and education, through shopping, work and recreation, even courtship, to the final function of burial.. . .

Here, it is easy to see that when man is given . . . freedom both from political restraint and from want, the effect is to render him childlike in many respects: funloving, quick to laughter and enthusiasm. unanalytical, unintellectual, outwardly expansive, preoccupied with physical beauty and prowess, given to sudden and unthinking seizures of aggressiveness, driven constantly to protect his status in the group by an eager conformism—yet not unhappy. In this sense, southern California together with all that tendency of American life which it typifies, is childhood without the promise of maturity . . .

It is not meant as an offense to the great achievements of the Latin cultural world if I say that there will take place here something like a "latinization" of political life. Southern California will become politically, as it already is climatically, a Latin American country . . .   **GEORGE F. KENNAN**

1952
My radio review is going good—people like it. Wish it paid me some money.
KENNETH REXROTH

1956
One of Ginsberg's poems was called *Howl*. It was a great, long, desperate wail, a struggle to make poetry out of all the objects, surroundings and people he had known. At times, it reached a kind of American surrealism, a bitter irony; it had a savage power. At moments, it did seem like the howling of animals. It reminded me of Artaud's mad conference at the Sorbonne.

Then a man in the audience challenged Ginsberg in a stupid way. "Why must you write about the slums? Isn't enough that we have them?"

Ginsberg was in a frenzy of anger. He proceeded to take off all his clothes, throwing each piece to the audience. My friend Ingrid received the soiled jockey shorts. He provoked and challenged the man to come and expose his feelings and his real self as nakedly as he had. "Come and stand here, stand naked before the people. I dare you! The poet always stands naked before the world."

The man in the packed audience tried to leave. Ginsberg said: "Now let someone dare to insult a man who offers what he feels nakedly before everyone . . . " The way he did it was so violent and direct, it had so much meaning in terms of all our fears of unveiling ourselves. The man in the audience was booed and hissed until he left. People began to throw his clothes back to Ginsberg. But he sat at ease on the couch and showed no signs of dressing again . . . The two poets went on reading for hours. I left, thinking it was like a new surrealism born of the Brooklyn gutter and supermarkets.

ANAÏS NIN

NOVEMBER 5

1926

AMBASSADOR HOTEL

This place is a genuine horror. If I described it literally I'd be set down as the damnedest liar ever heard of. Architecturally it is inconceivable, and the people all seem to be imbeciles. The movie folk, by comparison, are enlightened and civilized . . .   *newspaperman, essayist, editor* **H. L. MENCKEN,**

to his wife, Sara

1934

BEVERLY WILSHIRE

BEVERLY HILLS, CALIFORNIA

I went back on the booze pretty heavily until Saturday night—neglecting studio, dignity, and so on. And was I sick Sunday and today! This morning I showed up at M.G.M. for the first time since last Tuesday and squared myself, but didn't get much work done, since the publicity department took up most of my time, what with photographs, interviews and the like.

I'm still surprised at the fuss the *Thin Man* made out here. People bring the Joan Crawfords and Gables over to meet me instead of the usual vice versa! Hot-cha!

. . . I love you something awful and days are years till I see you again! And . . . I'm not going to be an actor and don't pay any attention to the publicity the studio is sending out on me: I gave 'em a free hand and they've gone pretty nutty . . .

I love you and miss you and love you and miss you and not much else.

DASHIELL HAMMETT, *to Lillian Hellman*

1940

SLEEPING LATE STOP STUFF ON DINING ROOM TABLE HOORAY FOR ROOSEVELT AFFECTION SCOTT   F. SCOTT FITZGERALD,

to his amanuensis, Frances Kroll (Ring)

1960

Dear John [Huston],

I have it on good authority that the Freud family does not approve of anyone making a picture of the life of Freud– so I wouldn't want to be a part of it, first because of his great contribution to humanity and secondly, my personal regard for his work. Thank you for offering me the part of 'Annie O' and I wish you the best in this and all other endeavors.

Yours   *actress* MARILYN MONROE

1986

. . . this weekend was spent in Los Angeles, where I continued to hang out with Gary Larson, the cartoonist I'm writing the profile of for the *New York Times* magazine. Larson was giving a talk at UCLA, so I thought this might provide an excellent opportunity for me to look at him from another angle: in a setting outside the privacy of his home in Seattle, which is where the previous weekend was spent . . .

So what do I do? I pull an Al Young; that is, I land at Burbank Airport, rent a Chevy Nova, drive around looking for the first motel that looms in view, and end up at a place called the Bali Hai out in Sepulveda in Van Nuys, It's $30 a night, but it also turns out to be a low dive; a rendezvous joint for hookers and their johns and their pimps and male prostitutes and probably dope traffic too . . .

It always feels like Nathanael West's *Day of the Locust* whenever I'm in L.A . . . But there was a rather remarkable thing that happened after I packed up and left Santa Monica for Hollywood. No sooner have I driven the couple of miles up the Coast Highway to Sunset than my attention is drawn to a hitchhiker right there at the intersection with her thumb out, looking every bit like one of the students I teach at Uncle Charlie's Summer Camp (as the kids call UC Santa Cruz)

. . . it's almost one in the morning. I pack up, as you might've guessed, and sleep like concrete, rise at 5, shower, jam down the elevator, settle my bills, hop in the Nova, remember to get gas before I get back to the rental site, dash into a 7–11 out near the Burbank Airport for coffee, which I snap a lid onto for drinking while I finish up my papers on the plane, but it's too close to take-off time, which is 6:53 a.m., so I end up leaving the coffee at the ticket counter, make the jet by the skin of my minty teeth, land in San Jose and hour later, find my Tercel, stuff my belongings inside it, motor to Santa Cruz and on it rolls like a dream. **AL YOUNG**

NOVEMBER 6

1894

. . . I went by train to Santa Monica, the whole way through a valley of the most exquisite gardens and groves of every imaginable fruit tree, all so covered and loaded with fruit that one wondered how the branches could sustain such weight, especially the enormous "grapefruit," or pomelo, of which you often see from forty to fifty hanging on one small delicate-looking branch. Sparkling streams irrigate this lovely valley, which is bordered by low, but most graceful hills.

In less than an hour the blue Pacific came into sight, and we arrived at the pretty little sea-bathing town of Santa Monica, picturesquely perched on cliffs with brilliant gardens, and in front the wonderful golden sands that everywhere stretch along this coast, up which come rolling emerald-green waves breaking into lovely clouds of snowy foam. Sea-bathing here, as everywhere in these favoured climes, goes on the whole year round.

The train runs on straight for a mile or two, on to a huge "mole" which projects a long distance into the sea, whence daily steamers start for various points of the coast. After an hour's enjoyment of the sunny sea and delicious breeze, I returned by train to Santa Monica, where it was enchanting to wander along the sands, hard and firm as a board, picking up exquisite shells and watching the great shining green waves. But all at once, without the slightest warning, waves, sea, and cliffs were absolutely obliterated from sight by the densest and wettest of seafogs . . .

I was told that consumption, resulting from neglected colds, was very prevalent here, and no wonder, with these sudden and violent changes of temperature; one moment you are inhaling the warmest and driest of airs, the next the coldest and dampest of vapours!

I never heard anywhere such incessant and racking coughing as everywhere in the trains and hotels of California!

WINEFRED, LADY HOWARD OF GLOSSOP

1933

The writers here at Carmel who have read [sections of *The Ways of White Folks*] seem to think that they would make an interesting and provocative collection . . . The new magazine ESQUIRE has bought one . . .

The weather here at Carmel is great. It is still warm enough to swim. I don't think I'll be coming East this winter. I like it too well out this way. And I'm really getting some work done . . .

LANGSTON HUGHES, *to Blanche Knopf*

2002

So the landlord came by last week and suddenly realized that the secure building we're all paying to live in isn't necessarily a traditionally "secure" building. In fact, the secure building we're all paying to live in happens to be the same secure building several homeless people are using as a home base of sorts, stashing mismatched Reebok tennis shoes, foam pads and oversized panties in the corners of the secure roof space.

Why she suddenly realized just now that this secure building isn't really a secure building is gobstopping, because I know of at least four tenants who have complained to her specifically that the secure building we're all paying to live in lacks a certain sense of, I don't know, security.

HEATHER B. ARMSTRONG

NOVEMBER 7

1918

They are ringing the school bell and tooting horns—it must be PEACE—God, but I am excited. If you were here I would jump on top of you and pound you in an ecstasy of joy. How is that for sadism? Oh, darling, don't worry about where you will be it will all work out, and maybe you won't have to cohabit with maids and putas! Wouldn't that be glorious?

JAIME DE ANGULO

1919

Her interest in all things seductive. Licks my P & A—cant let my Roger alone. Always getting it out & feeling it. Comes off with me now very quickly. Didn't at first. We dress. I start keeping these notes.

THEODORE DREISER

1961

TO MATTHEW HUXLEY

6233 MULHOLLAND HIGHWAY, L.A. 28, CAL.

. . . We are in the midst here of the most ghastly fire, compared to which what happened last May was no more than a Guy Fawkes day display. If this drought continues, Los Angeles is really done for—or at least so it seems under existing circumstances. One may be forced to move somewhere a little damper. Ever your affectionate,   **ALDOUS HUXLEY**

NOVEMBER 8

1852

Sacramento City has been nearly consumed. The Dr. has had all his instruments and a good deal of clothing burned, loss not exceeding $300. It really seems as though it was not right for us to come to California & lose so much. I do not think that we shall be as well off as at home.

traveler **MARY STUART BAILEY**

2008

Earl Ofari Hutchinson's column today urged Rick Caruso to run for mayor, saying "you can beat Tony [Villaraigosa] because there are legions of voters fed up with his media grandstanding and self-serving, it's-all-about-me ca-reerism." Oh well, not going to happen . . .

Assembly members Curren Price and Mike Davis are atop the list of possible candidates to fill Mark Ridley-Thomas's seat in the state Senate, but other names mentioned include Herb and Fabian Wesson and Speaker Karen Bass . . .   KEVIN RODERICK

NOVEMBER 9

1894

Near Salton, at the lowest depth (265 feet below sea) a lake 30 miles long by 10 wide, and only 4 feet deep, has been formed by the river Colorado, so late as 1891. What a paradise for skaters! Were it not in torrid zone! . . .

Soon after . . . we looked our last (I trust not for ever!) on that lovely land, where, the whole year round, you can eat freshly-gathered oranges, lemons, limes, strawberries, guavas; and for a lesser portion, innumerable other de-licious fruits!   WINEFRED, LADY HOWARD OF GLOSSOP

1927

Well, I have my Ticket and Destination—but not Train-time as yet . . . town at 2:25 and up to Dr. Tholen. He had received his analysis from the Clinical Laboratory with the verdict "malignant" . . . He is a real nice man and a good workman, and I came away with much respect for him, and in entire resig-nation, as I always have for anything that can't be helped . . . Came down to 6th and Spring, and trotted around four blocks to get some sweetpeas for my home folks . . .   CHARLES FLETCHER LUMMIS

2007

The oil spilled totaled 58,000 gallons. Now the Oiled Wildlife Care experts are on the scene in the Presidio, and Baker Beach is closed. The National Park Service says the beach is closed to keep people safe. The oil can make us sick too, albeit given that we don't have feathers, less so. I don't believe them. I believe they want to keep us from seeing the carnage the dead birds washing ashore.   *writer* LESLIE CAROL ROBERTS

NOVEMBER 10

1869

The largest cheese ever made in the world, was made on one of these dairy ranches. It was made during the late war, and weighed four thousand pounds. It was sold in San Francisco at fifty cents a pound, for the benefit of the "Sanitary Fund." The butter, as well as the cheese, is manufactured by steam power. In this business, fortunes may be made or lost in a single year. Little things cannot be done in California; it must be great things or nothing.   *newspaperman, traveler* **HARVEY RICE**

1918

SANTA ROSA

Yours of November 8th received. Although I have some eight thousand visitors each year not one in fifty of whom I can meet personally, yet I shall be very glad to have you come sometime when convenient to you, and will guarantee that you will be treated with the consideration which is so well due you. Come anytime but if you want to see the Places in full working order July is the best time; but that is too far away.

Your son seems to be a genius too. Full specifications were not given however regarding the new fruit tree wanted. I should specify a white fig of excellent quality which will bear the year around and also it should bear a few oranges, bananas and ice-creams at the proper seasons. I am like him, I like figs and think them about the best fruit that ever grew. We could not very properly make the figs as large as cocoanuts for they would probably in falling from the tree be mush instead of figs when they arrived.

P.S. You will not find so many cranks to the square yard in this end of the state as there are there.

horticulturalist **LUTHER BURBANK**, *to Upton Sinclair*

1926

I've decided that you were—peculiarly—wrong in assuming that I think you lovelier now because I don't see you as often as I did. You are lovelier. If it were a glandular delusion, it would work the other way round . . . I love you more when I'm with you than when I'm away; and more when I'm touching you than when I'm merely looking at you and most of all when I'm tasting you—but that's not happened often enough to be talked about very much. So you must be actually improving; perhaps the doubtless considerable spiritual benefits of being loved by me are showing themselves physically . . .

I love you, dear animal.

Hammett
DASHIELL HAMMETT,
to one rumored model for Brigid O'Shaughnessy

NOVEMBER 11

1919

Armistice Day . . . Today baby & I wake in our room at 338 Alvarado. Every day sunshine here. I had a dream last night that I got off the train & that it started without me but I ran after it & with difficulty made it. Helen & I indulge in a delightful round, as usual. She has the most teasing methods. Talks all the time & tortures me into an orgasm by her sweet brutalities & descriptions. Up at 9:30 & go to the little restaurant in 7th St near Alvarado . . .

Later baby & I get to playing in bed. Her beauty just knocks me. It is unbelievable—a dream of fair women. She looks like an angel or a classic figure & yet is sensuality to the core. We indulge in a long suck & then I put her on her knees. A wild finish. Return to my work. The poems & flowers here seem in no wise affected by the sharp coolness which begins at about five. A wonderful climate. We go downtown at 6:30 to the B. & M. cafeteria . . .

Home at 11 & Helen & I talk in bed until 3. Another delicious round with her. Has the full forward, lavender lids & bluish white eye lids of the sex extremist. Uses the most coaxing & grossly enervating words of any girl I know. (Theo & Helen are between the sheets & no one sees what they are doing. No one, No one. Oh—oh—no one. Theo is between Helen's thighs—Helen's soft white thighs. Theo is fucking Helens cunt. Yes—he is—yes—yes—oh. Theo is fucking her and Helen is taking it—giving herself to him—her belly—her tittys—her thighs—oh—oh). So on to orgasm.   **THEODORE DREISER**

1950

Dear Norris,

When the Smiths finally are able to move, the McChesneys will move upstairs, and we will move into their place . . . It is a few steps from a beach on the bay, the house is surrounded by eucalyptus trees, and it's about a half-hour drive from downtown SF. I am wild to get back to painting, have a lot of writing projects lined up, must be at this publicity work . . . but for a while we are doomed to life in a rather expensive motel where, at least, Ann is able to cook. After a while, restaurants lose their charm, if any . . .

We went back to Los Angeles for a time, when we learned of the apartment difficulties—mostly to hear (Kid) Ory . . . I think I may have written you that we were lucky to have the guidance of Nesuhi Ertegun & his wife through the mazes of LA jazz activities; Nesuhi is the son of the former Turkish ambassador to the US and runs the Jazz Man Record Shop in Hollywood—a beautiful place that looks more like an interior decorator's office than what it is—and who issues Jazz Man records . . .

It is white jazz at its most intelligent—and Rushton is a bit better than that. (Rushton, by the way, is a Yale man, the black sheep of a "good" family, who bears a spookily-close resemblance to Chester Morris (the movie star); he's enormously witty.) Ory is one of the most nervous characters I've come up against: a peasant with worries, rubs his face & eyes until you wonder how his skin takes it; all those gestures which from a distance look joyous are only (possibly) nervous tics . . .

All of which has nothing to do with the fact that he is one of the great men of our time, along with Matisse and Schweitzer and Proust, and is playing breathtakingly. He and his boys are fed to the teeth with LA, and will probably be up here pretty soon, if their contract at Lyman's (on Vine St in Hollywood, where they now play) is not picked up again . . .

California seems, if not to hold its own, to debase itself less frenetically than the East Coast. At least my central nervous system has responded to it rather nicely. And the jazz, some of the painting, the landscape, the temperature, have it all over the E. seaboard . . . **WELDON KEES**

1968

Eleven-forty they take me out give me my clothes whistle and harp put me in this room with a bench and one other Short-timer, gray-pated mahogany-hued old dude of sixty years or so. "Oh, am I one Ready Freddy. Am I ever!" He's pacing around the little room picking up and putting back down and picking back up one of those old-fashioned footrest shoeshine kits . . .

I'm alone on the bench, sipping what's left of his cup of coffee, spoon still sticking out. The plastic bag his suit was in hangs from the conduit; his blues are right where he left them, on the floor. Ghost clothes. I'm ready too. This stationery is finished both sides. "Kesey! Ken E.—" "On my way!"

KEN KESEY

NOVEMBER 12

1833

Soon after dark the air appeared to be completely thickened with meteors falling towards the earth, some of which would explode in the air and others would be dashed to pieces on the ground, frightening our horses so much that it required the most active vigilance of the whole company to keep them together. This was altogether a mystery to some of the men who probably had never before seen or heard of anything of the kind, but after an explanation from Capt. Walker, they were satisfied that no danger need be apprehended from the falling of the stars, as they were termed.

fur trapper **ZENAS LEONARD**

1948

6005 CAMINO DE LA COSTA

LA JOLLA, CALIFORNIA

We had lovely weather all the way to San Francisco and back. It rained the night we stayed at Carmel but was fine again in the morning. Carmel, which I suppose you know, is a very cute place, but has a slightly unreal look as though it had been constructed on MGM's back lot. It has been compared to La Jolla and does resemble it in the lack of billboards and other ugly things, but the resemblance stops there. I really think it is more attractive than La Jolla, and has the advantage of not being near a large city. La Jolla is full of tired old men and tired old money; Carmel seems a more middle-class sort of place. If you ever go to Santa Barbara, stop at the Biltmore Montecito. There is really a hotel. San Francisco I liked, but its hotels stink. The Fairmont has a magnificent lobby and that's all. The Mark [Hopkins] has a beautiful grill room (and the sky lounge, of course) but its food is exorbitant, its lobby has no trace of style, and the place is full of chisel-eyed characters who look if they were afraid they might not smile at a producer . . .

The thing I love about S.F. is its go to hell attitude. The narrow streets are lined with NO PARKING AT ANY TIME signs and also lined with parked automobiles which look as if they had been there all day. For the first time in my life I saw a lady traffic cop, a real cop too, complete with nickel star and whistle. I saw one other cop. He was driving around with a piece of chalk on the end of a long stick and about once a block he took a swipe at some rear tire, just to keep his hand in. The taxi drivers are wonderful too. They obey no laws but those of gravity and we even had one who passes street cars on the left, an offense for which you would probably get ninety days in Los Angeles . . .

RAYMOND CHANDLER

NOVEMBER 13

1939

The 1ˢᵗ cloudy day we have had. I did no work. Went to the Bohemian Club with Joseph Jackson and John Terrell. It is far from a Bohemian club.

SHERWOOD ANDERSON

1970

We've been back home only about ten days, and most of that time I've been shoveling out from under the accumulated pile of mail, including a good many books by former students here. It is getting so that I do very little other reading. But one such opportunity that I thoroughly enjoyed was *The Hidden Wound*. I read it with the deepest sort of respect, not only for its prose, which is as usual eloquent and even elegant, in the way an equation is said to be elegant, but for its qualities of wisdom and dignity—I guess the combination really is what Ed Abbey says it is; nobility. You take care, hear? You're a great man . . .

I think the book is absolutely great. In my enthusiasm for The Hidden Wound I have not yet got to the latest book of poems. I have to admit it—I read prose with more comfort and probably with more discrimination than I read poetry. I will read your poems because they're yours, but I read The Hidden Wound because after trying two paragraphs I couldn't help myself. I suspect that when I read the poems I will find the same integrity I find in the prose, and many of the same convictions. I thought I understood why you had made the decision to stay on the farm in Kentucky, I understand a little better now. If anyone tries to woo you away, as I did, send him to me and I will talk him out of it. You belong right where you are . . .

WALLACE STEGNER, *to Wendell Berry*

1973

WARD KIMBALL
8910 ARDENDALE AVE.
SAN GABRIEL, CALIF. 91775
WALT DISNEY PRODUCTIONS
Dear Will Finn:
. . . I take it that you are shot in the ass to become an animator . . . becoming an animator is a growth process that involves basic curiosities for all things, because man, animation is just not making things move, it is THINKING, THINKING, THINKING! You can't know enough about everything. Curiosity is the key word. See everything! Do everything! Find out what makes everything tick. How does it work? What motivated this— What motivated

that. Learn from others, BUT DON'T COPY THEM! Try to retain your individualism while learning the basic rules. Don't become dogmatic because you're going to change your mind about what you like and what you dislike hundreds of times before you're thirty! . . .

Go see the "Yellow Submarine" if you have not already done so. Go see "Fritz the Cat" and if it requires parental guidance, then bring your old man! See everything, as I said above. Go to film festivals. Be a Laurel and Hardy fan. Study Buster Keaton. Study their timing and how they stage a gag or a comedy situation.

Of course, Hanna Barbera are pretty crude compared to Disney's. But this is a problem of economics. H&B are filling a need and it is a business just like selling washing machines. We all can't be part of an organization such as Disney's . .

Blah! Blah! Blah! If you find that you don't at first like this reply to your seeming knowledgeable letter, put it aside and read it again at a later date, and you will see that hidden between the lines is a lot of good advice, even though the writing is crude, to say the least!   *animator* **WARD KIMBALL**

1985

Dear Audre,
The tour was probably one of the best things that could have happened to me . . . I was very pleasantly surprised by the response of audiences everywhere I went. I was ready to pack up and move to Boston and Manhattan. (That is a joke.) . . .

It's hard for us strong Black women types to admit we're fucking falling apart at the seams as you must well know. Out of all this madness, and I really do believe I was mad, I've come to some decisions that are as scary as hell, but at the same time are exciting.

I informed the women at the Health Center that I am leaving effective January 1st . . .

It means I'll have to give up things like my weekly lobster or crab and I definitely can't afford to hang out in the bars and drink, but it also means I get to take that shot. I've never had the opportunity to write full time and that has me jumping up and down.

Given how fast I usually work when I write, I don't see any reason why I can't do a novel in a year as well as a book of poems. It means I finally get to see how good I really am or how bad.

Right now, I'm so pumped up from the excitement that my confidence is soaring, but still have the other voice that says "what if?" . . .   **PAT PARKER**

NOVEMBER 14

1931

While Vic and T were blasting this joint, having lots of laughs and FEELING good, enjoying each other's fine company, we were standing in this great big lot in front of some cars. Just then, two big healthy dicks (detectives, that is) come from behind a car, man, nonchalantly, and say to us, "We'll take the roach, boys." Vic and I said nothing. So one dick stayed with me until I went into the club and did my last show. He enjoyed it, too. Because when he and I were on our way down to the police station, he and I had a heart-to-heart talk. The first words that he said to me were, "Armstrong, I'm a big fan of yours and so is my family. We catch your programs every night over the radio."   *trumpeter, singer, memoirist* **LOUIS ARMSTRONG**,
about to serve nine days in jail and then leave town

1950

I have never found it difficult to be interested in more than one thing at the same time.   **WELDON KEES**

1969

Spent last Sunday in that small grass thing called a park next to the County Museum. That's a park, I suppose, because it has grass, and it has the La Brea tar pits, carefully enclosed in wire mesh so we can't become fossils, and cement statues of saber-mouth tigers and their babies, and a place guarded by police dogs where what look to be students sift through mud looking for more fossils. The museum is having a Van Gogh exhibition. The waiting line to get in stretches about two blocks long. I asked the guard if that was usual, such a long line. "He had a very tragic life, you know," the guard said, "and he painted all those pictures in so few years . . . "   **LIZA WILLiAMS**

2008

. . . i'm going to try to freelance—just finished a piece for nyt—until things get better. everything, incl university teaching, very backed up right now. have spoken to dana [NEA Chair Gioia] abt starting a website which will be a long shot.

bc this recession likely to last three years at least, i'm considering what will happen if things DONT work out financially.. . . thanks to the idiots at the times, i'm realizing i may be moving my family back into my mom's basement at some pt—really dont want to do that, but LA has become a very expensive place to live . . .   *journalist* **SCOTT TIMBERG** *(1969–2019)*,
to the editor

NOVEMBER 15

1602

In this bay the general, with his men, went ashore. After they had gone more than three leagues along it a number of Indians appeared with their bows and arrows, and although signs of peace were made to them, they did not dare to approach, excepting a very old Indian woman who appeared to be more than one hundred and fifty years old and who approached weeping. The general cajoled her and gave her some beads and something to eat. This Indian woman, from extreme age, had wrinkles on her belly which looked like a blacksmith's bellows, and the navel protruded bigger than a gourd. Seeing this kind treatment the Indians came peaceably and took us to their *rancherias* . . .

They had pots in which they cooked their food, and the women were dressed in skins of animals. The general would not allow any soldier to enter their *rancherias*; and, it being already late, he returned to the frigate, many Indians accompanying him to the beach . . .

I do not state, lest I should be tiresome, how many times the Indians came to our camps with skins of martens and other things. Until the next day, when we set sail, they remained on the beach shouting. This port was given the name of San Diego.   *explorer* **SEBASTIÁN VIZCAÍNO**

1879

MONTEREY, CALIFORNIA

It is the history of our kindnesses that alone makes this world tolerable. If it were not for that, for the effect of kind words, kind looks, kind letters, multiplying, spreading, making one happy through another and bringing forth benefits, some thirty, some fifty, some a thousandfold, I should be tempted to think our life a practical jest in the worst possible spirit . . .

today it is *mucho frio*, as we Spaniards say; and I had no other means of keeping warm for my work. I have done a good spell, 9 and a half foolscap pages . . . My trouble is that I am all too ambitious just now . . . A novel whereof 85 out of, say, 140 are pretty well nigh done. A short story of 50 pp., which shall be finished tomorrow, or I'll know the reason why . . . The [unfinished] novel is called *A Vendetta in the West* . . . I see I am in a grasping, dismal humour, and should, as we Americans put it, quit writing. In truth, I am so haunted by anxieties that one or other is sure to come up in all that I write.

I will send you herewith a Monterey paper where the works of R.L.S. appear . . . The paper is the marrow of the place . . .

ROBERT LOUIS STEVENSON

1916

BIG SUR

. . . How far away I am! Sometimes I come almost to forget the existence of
the outside world. Imagine, sometimes I pass weeks together without seeing
a soul alive. The mail, which comes from time to time, passed from hand to
hand by neighbors ("neighbors" who live five or 10 miles one from another)
brings me a bunch of newspapers already two or three weeks old. I read them
bit by bit—for example this evening I read the one of 14 October! Never have
I read the daily news with such a philosophical calm: why heat myself up
this evening about the electoral campaign, when I know that, right now, the
president has already been elected a week. I wonder who it is. I won't know
for at least a good week . . .   JAIME DE ANGULO

2007

I saw the ruins . . . The Witch Creek fire has also destroyed much of the
irrigation infrastructure throughout the Ramona valley, melting plastic
and aluminum piping and knocking out the big generators that pump
water over the mountains from the Colorado River . . . On the road to
Ramona, an electronic billboard flashes an urgent warning: 'do not use
the water' . . .

In the 1930s, my older sister cantered her Indian pony through my parents' avocado 'ranchito' in Bostonia, ten miles south of Ramona, and the
little house my father built with its knotty-pine walls has survived every
fire. Otherwise, little of my childhood Bostonia remains. The Barker family's
1880s general store, the irrigation ditches, the country-western dancehall,
the gas station that sold cigarettes to 12-year-olds, the Fryes' hardware store,
the lemons and the pomegranates: all vanished in a whirlwind of 'growth'.
What remains are ageing tract homes, auto body shops, intractable meth-
amphetamine addiction, and long lines of tail lights headed out towards the
brave new suburbs . . .

I can easily visualise the impending apocalypse: more view homes on the
graves of trees, the art-deco Ramona Theater bulldozed for a Home Depot,
the Turkey Inn turned into a Starbucks, a Cineplex where Judy Van der
Veer's home used to be. I suppose the realist view is that our fire problem
will ultimately be solved by burning all the fuel and then paving the ashes. In
Southern California, catastrophic fire only fertilises more sprawl.

I pop the big question to Tom. 'Can you really get this ranch up and
running again, or will some home developer make you an offer you can't
refuse?'

Tom furrows his eyebrows for a moment, then smiles. 'Do you know the etymology of the word "avocado"?'

'*Aguacate* in Spanish,' I mumble.

'Yes, but the Nahuatl original is *ahuacatl*—balls.'

writer, scholar, cultural historian **MIKE DAVIS**

NOVEMBER 16

1853

PALM SPRINGS

The Indian guide conducted us to "*Pozo hondo*", or Deep Well, a deep excavation in the clay made by the Indians to obtain water . . . We encamped, and before the mules were satisfied with water, it was exhausted. It oozed in through the clay very slowly, but appeared to be abundant; about twenty buckets full were obtained in the course of the night.

geoscientist **WILLIAM PHIPPS BLAKE**

1863

My last letter left me at Low Divide, the region of the principal copper mines of Del Norte County . . .

From there I walked to Crescent City, sixteen miles. I descended from these barren hills, and soon a marvelous change in the vegetation came on the scene. I passed through a forest, called everywhere "The Redwoods," a forest of redwood timber—and such forests the world probably does not show elsewhere . . .

A reliable gentleman, Doctor Mason, told me that once caught in a storm he with his four companions sought shelter in one of these hollows. They built a fire, and the five men with their five horses passed the night in this novel shelter! I fully believe the story . . .

There are two species of the genus: one only in the Sierra, the other only near the sea—both of them grand wonders of the vegetable world. The amount of timber in one of these trees is almost incredible. A man will build a house and barn from one of them, fence a field, probably, in addition, and leave an immense mass of brush and logs as useless.

These forests have almost an oppressive effect upon the mind. A deep silence reigns; almost the only sound is that of some torrent coming down from the mountains, or the distant roar of the surf breaking upon the shore of the Pacific.

A restless genius who has seen much of the world and of adventure, but is yet poor, has conceived the idea of a speculation in one of these trees, which is rather novel. There is a large tree near Trinidad so near the water that he proposes to build a large boat of it and launch it—cut from a single tree, like a canoe, but modeled like a schooner. He says he can have a boat of twenty-four or twenty-five foot beam, and eighty to one hundred feet long, and have the sides, the bottom, and floor of the grand saloon of the natural wood, the interior being dug out of the solid tree . . .   **WILLIAM H. BREWER**

1906

. . . Hunt sent me over a wonderfully handsome color elevation of the Southwest Museum to-day. If we build it on these very lines it would be the handsomest Museum in the world . . .

Kroeber [the anthropologist Alfred, father of Ursula K[roeber] LeGuin] rather won my heart this morning . . . he is so frank and young a lad that one can't get as disgusted with him as one does with the 60-year-old incompetency that can't fall out of the back end of a wagon. His lecture is to-morrow night and I hope we can get an audience for him.

CHARLES FLETCHER LUMMIS

1969

. . . I am going crazy and can't stand the post office job any longer. I have one of two choices—stay in the post office and go crazy (I have been there eleven years) or stay out here and play at writer and starve. I've decided to starve . . .

CHARLES BUKOWSKI, *to an editor*

NOVEMBER 17

1940

Just now T. and I went out from the warm lighted study and the whuddering firelight of the living room to the porch and watched a half rainbow grow and die against the hills . . .

It's long since I wrote here. There are days when I want to, but I am too content—and other days my spirit is too black. Today, after a weekend of company and, just now, a highball, I am verbose but uninspired—and today . . .

My heart is heavy, thinking of my friends in France and of England so hard pressed. I can hardly bear to think of anything at all these days, and dwell resolutely on the growth of a kitten or an acacia tree and the progression of clouds in a winter sky.   **M. F. K. FISHER**

1998

At the end of the day I stopped and pondered: What did i accomplish today except for filling up the e-mail in-boxes of my CEOs and running up my bill on several long-distance and cellular phone carriers? But it is the nature of the beast . . .   *venture capitalist* **RUSS SIEGELMAN**

2018

. . . shabbat service at the Fire House this morning; there were four, count 'em, four rabbis, and all of them were women. Actually one visiting rabbi as well, and his gorgeous family, his red-haired daughter fell asleep as we sang nigun. Those wordless tunes with which we all connected, the chazzan (also a rabbi) lead us through the melodies and we found our harmonies, in this smokey time, we cleared our lungs by singing together.   **LOUISE STEINMAN**

NOVEMBER 18

1939

FRESNO

This is another big fruit and vegetable center. The climate wonderful. I wrote many letters. Did a piece for the San Francisco Chronicle. In the p.m. went out to a park to watch the Brooklyn baseball tryout. In the evening to watch the movie [*Stanley and Livingstone*]. The African scenes good—the acting rotten.   **SHERWOOD ANDERSON**

1952

. . . Southern California talks of itself as the Southland, and is hardly even a part of the Union–– when you mail letters to the rest of the country you drop them into a post-office-slot marked *The States* . . .

poet critic, novelist **RANDALL JARRELL,**

to John Crowe Ransom

1998

I took two plans off my stack at random and, believe it or not, they were nearly identical business propositions! Both companies plan to become the leader in the "next great Internet play"—being an e-commerce portal. A sure reason not to invest in a company is that you have seen dozens of the same plan. I won't be investing in a new e-commerce portal . . .

By 6:30 I'm home for dinner. Max and Jake eat slices of Max's birthday cake while I eat lasagna. After dinner Max and Jake help me build a fire, and we sit on the couch with Beth, roughhousing and listening to Max playacting as a helicopter pilot. By 8 they are in the shower, by 9 in bed. I tuck Max in, say happy birthday, and give him a good-night kiss. It is the most satisfying moment of the day.   **RUSS SIEGELMAN**

2013

Someday I may do the decades behind the desk at "dear dirty" [L.A. Public Library] justice but on this oddball anniversary I will just give twenty things I learned . . .

6. When you least expect it something great will happen but pretty girls/boys don't want you, they want the reference book.

7. No matter what people say when they leave, you will never hear from them again . . .

9. Call in sick at random and go to Disneyland or the race track or lay in bed half the day. No one will really notice or suffer that you were not there that day . . .

11. Try like hell to be kind to patrons, it is not their fault they are really are clueless about a lot of simple stuff . . .

17. Tell co-workers they are good, especially if they are good . . .

20. Say something ridiculous to a patron or co-worker every shift.
                                                        GLEN CREASON

NOVEMBER 19

1862

I shall deliver at Acapulco or at a place indicated by the government, all the rifles I am able to acquire . . .   **HENRY DALTON**, *to Benito Juarez*

1894

1267 WEBSTER ST., OAKLAND

Dear John Muir,

For the fruit of your land and the fruit of your brain, I thank you. For this last, I cannot say how much I thank you, nor how glad I am to see you in covers. I began to think I should never behold that Book with the eyes of the flesh . . . I supposed your pubs. send you the press notices, but I enclose one chanced upon in a paper sent me by my friend Miss Carpentier. If you already have it send this back. It is hardly the kind of "criticism" I would like to see, for while the reviewer tells what the book is about, and gives you credit for understanding your subject, he says not a word about the consummate beauty of your work. I don't believe the man could tell a bird-carol from a steam-whistle, or note the difference between one of the poor abortive little hills of the East, and the infinite heights of which you sing, for your book is a song, a grand song!

Love to all your family and yourself.

Your old-time friend,

P. S. No, I cannot have [San Francisco Free Librarian] Mr. Cheney's place. I am "disqualified by sex."   **INA COOLBRITH**

1933

We are trying, out here, to work up an intensive campaign for Scottsboro Funds, and for interest in the general problems of the Negro in the South. The remoteness of this part of the world to all that is amazing . . .

LANGSTON HUGHES, *to Countee Cullen*

1941

. . . In the afternoon they took us on a big driving tour along the coast. Landscape of incomparable beauty, reminiscent of the French Riviera. We are happy and hope you will come soon.

Hugs from your child Teddie   **THEODOR ADORNO**, *to his parents*

NOVEMBER 20

1784

The cattle are increasing in such manner, that it is necessary in the case of several owners to give them additional lands; they have asked me for some sitios which I have granted provisionally, namely to Juan José Domínguez who was a soldier in the presidio of San Diego and who at this moment has four herds of mares and about 200 head of cattle on the river below San Gabriel, to Manuel Nieto for similar reason that of la Zanja on the highway from said Mission along by the oak tree, and to the son of the widow Ignacio Carrillo that on the deep creek contiguous to the foregoing . . .

soldier, explorer, governor **PEDRO FAGES**,

making land grants

1936

FEDERAL WRITERS PROJECTS

751 SOUTH FIGUEROA ST.

LOS ANGELES, CALIF.

HENRY G. ALSBERG, DIRECTOR FEDERAL WRITERS PROJECTS, WPA

1734 NEW YORK AVENUE, NW

WASHINGTON, D. C.

Dear Mr. Alsberg:

Herewith are the Table of Contents and wordage breakdown for the Los Angeles County Guide.

It may be well to call our Guide the Los Angeles County Guide rather than the Los Angeles Metropolitan Area Guide in order to avoid the possibility of arousing the jealousies of large and important cities, such as Long Beach and Pasadena, which are in the Los Angeles metropolitan area but do not care to be known as a part of Los Angeles. The far-flung regions of the county we shall cover in tours, as you suggest.

Very truly   **HUGH HARLAN**

1969

Proclamation to the Great White Father and All His People

We, the native Americans, re-claim the land known as Alcatraz Island in the name of all American Indians by right of discovery.

We wish to be fair and honorable in our dealings with the Caucasian inhabitants of this land, and hereby offer the following treaty:

We will purchase said Alcatraz Island for twenty-four dollars ($24) in glass beads and red cloth, a precedent set by the white man's purchase of a similar island about 300 years ago. We know that $24 in trade goods for these 16 acres is more than was paid when Manhattan Island was sold, but we know that land values have risen over the years. Our offer of $1.24 per acre is greater than the 47¢ per acre that the white men are now paying the California Indians for their land. We will give to the inhabitants of this island a portion of that land for their own, to be held in trust by the American Indian Affairs and by the bureau of Caucasian Affairs to hold in perpetuity—for as long as the sun shall rise and the rivers go down to the sea. We will further guide the inhabitants in the proper way of living. We will offer them our religion, our education, our life-ways, in order to help them achieve our level of civilization and thus raise them and all their white brothers up from their savage and unhappy state . . .

We feel that this so-called Alcatraz Island is more than suitable for an Indian Reservation, as determined by the white man's own standards. By this we mean that this place resembles most Indian reservations in that:

1. It is isolated from modern facilities, and without adequate means of transportation.
2. It has no fresh running water.
3. It has inadequate sanitation facilities.
4. There are no oil or mineral rights.
5. There is no industry and so unemployment is very great.
6. There are no health care facilities.
7. The soil is rocky and non-productive; and the land does not support game.
8. There are no educational facilities.
9. The population has always exceeded the land base.
10. The population has always been held as prisoners and kept dependent upon others.

Further, it would be fitting and symbolic that ships from all over the world, entering the Golden Gate, would first see Indian land, and thus be reminded of the true history of this nation . .

The Alcatraz Proclamation,

attributed to **ADAM FORTUNATE EAGLE**

NOVEMBER 21

1852

My heart is heavy at the thought of departing forever from this place. I like this wild and barbarous life: I leave it with regret. The solemn fir trees, 'whose slender tops are close against the sky' here, the watching hills, and the calmly beautiful river, seem to gaze sorrowfully at me, as I stand in the moonlighted midnight, to bid them farewell. Beloved, unconventional wood-life; divine Nature, into whose benign eyes I never looked, whose many voices, gay and glad, I never heard, in the artificial heart of the busy world,—I quit your serene teachings for a restless and troubled future. Yes, Molly, smile if you will at my folly; but I go from the mountains with a deep heart sorrow. I look kindly to this existence, which to you seems so sordid and mean. Here, at least, I have been contented. The 'thistle-seed,' as you call me, sent abroad its roots right lovingly into this barren soil, and gained an unwonted strength in what seemed to you such unfavorable surroundings. You would hardly recognize the feeble and half-dying invalid, who drooped languidly out of sight, as night shut down between your straining gaze and the good ship Manilla, as she wafted her far away from her Atlantic home, in the person of your now perfectly healthy sister.

LOUISA CLAPPE, *upon leaving California,*
and with it her muse, forever

1969

I had to go out to Pitzer College in Claremont to give a reading. I read some of my columns to the somber stare of the students . . . "But what about your political commitments?" they asked . . . they had me flummoxed. They seemed to want me to write "up against the wall" instead of anything lyrical in celebration of humanity and its capacities.

"What do you do?" I asked in return. They had a problem, it seems. Everything was too good, they complained. If they wanted to change something at Pitzer, they had only to go to the administration and the administration changed it . . . What they wanted was something to fight, all the other campuses were in turmoil, protesting, fighting, trying to make changes, and there at Pitzer it didn't take a fight or a boycott, it was all negotiable. Well, tough shit, too bloody bad, there they were in an optimum situation, able to get the kind of education they wanted and they were frustrated by not having a fashionable enemy . . .

As I was leaving, the student who was walking with me to the car said, "You know, I think the faculty here is more hip than the students."

LIZA WILLIAMS

1995

The end of a week of night shoots in a gravel quarry in a place called Antelope Valley. Not a bleeding antelope in sight—they clearly have the right idea. This place is possibly the closest I'll ever get to hell. The wind whips up the sand and gravel something fierce. Of course, according to sod's law as applied to film, the more disgusting and unpleasant the location, the better the rushes! The movie [*Mojave Moon*] looks wonderful, thank God!

ALFRED MOLINA

2002

The movers will be here in about an hour, and the only things left to pack are the computers, the cds and everything in the storage unit downstairs, which just so happens to be the same storage unit to which we can't find the key, which at first seemed like a total disaster, because in a situation like this, when you need to get into that storage unit more than any other time you've needed to get into that storage unit, it could be a total disaster. But when you think about the larger scheme of life, like getting to drive up the coast to Seattle to spend Thanksgiving with your brother and his 5-yr old daughter who likes to take Mr. Potato Head and put the body parts into all the wrong places because "that's what Picasso would do," and then drive to Utah, arriving triumphantly with liquor cabinet in tow and the funniest dog in the world who will unsuspectingly get to experience cold weather for the first time, who cares about the damn key to the storage unit.

HEATHER B. ARMSTRONG

NOVEMBER 22

1964

Sorry to hear you've joined the club but it can be whipped . . . Keep punching.

JOHN WAYNE, *to Nat King Cole,*
on their shared cancer diagnoses

1976

You are perhaps not planning the definitive in-depth biography of him (it's a little soon for that anyway, I suppose) but rather an appreciative study. Thornton's homosexuality, his sense of guilt (and the New England Puritanism which kept him from ever describing a sexual scene in his novels [consider especially *Theophilus North*]) were a lifelong burden to him. Just how much freedom he allowed himself I honestly don't know, save in matters touching my own association with him. I don't know the names of his particular friends, and I doubt whether anything at all can be documented; his delicacy (or self-protection or whatever it was) made him write even his intimate letters mostly "between the lines." Eventually, I suppose, someone will come along, and will pull the deepest secrets out of Thornton's stories . . . The only thing I could do would be to hasten the process, and since you put the matter to my conscience, I suppose I would have to say no . . .

SAMUEL STEWARD,
on his relationship with Thornton Wilder

NOVEMBER 23

1854

AMADOR COUNTY

Clear, cool & pleasant Morning cloudy and a light shower of rain—"Thanksgiving day" with us . . . Our hens have been busy laying at the rate of three eggs a day lately, so by saving up the eggs and having a bottle or so of brandy we made out to get up a tiptop egg-nog—nearly a bucket full—It was a glorious drink and did honour to the occasion—Afternoon George & myself made up a dozen or so of mince pies and baked them . . .   **ALFRED DOTEN**

1919

Los Angeles. Helen sets clock for 7:30—but at 6:30 wake & in the dawn indulge in one of the loveliest rounds ever—she lying on her side one arm up. We laugh & dress and at 8 leave for Pacific Station En route to Santa Catalina. Down town on West 1st street. Breakfast in a Cafeteria Quick Lunch—a new proposition to me—Get our own steak & waffles. Then to Station & take 3 car trolley to San Pedro. The mountains in the distance—small towns—Cattle, oil wells etc. Arrive at San Pedro at 10 A.M. & take boat for Santa Catalina. Helen looks too sweet in her light grey gorgette & grey hat. Seats on side of boat . . . .

See perch & sea goldfish in their native haunts. The diver after Abalone Shells. Back to dock. Aeroplane takes passengers at 1.00 per minute for a 10-minute flight. Then onto boat again. The blue sea. Rainbow. A whale . . .

We come home and go straight to bed. Very tired but before long we pull a heavy screw, finally getting down on the floor on pillows to avoid the squeaking of the bed . . .

Wants her beauty eaten by a big rough brute.   **THEODORE DREISER**

1941

. . . the journey from Los Angeles station to our motel (a group of cabins for automobile drivers, each consisting of two very nicely furnished rooms and bathroom, kitchen and garage) takes a good hour by car. Los Angeles is 30 miles or so more from the sea, while the places around where we are now living still extend past Hollywood—to Santa Monica, Brentwood Heights, Pacific Palisades—in hollows that approach the sea and line the coast itself. The beauty of the region is so incomparable that even such a hardboiled European as myself can only surrender to it.

. . . best of all are the incredibly intense, in no way reproducible colors; a drive along the ocean around sunset is one of the most extraordinary impressions that my—by no means highly responsive—eyes have ever had. All the red, blue and violet activity found there would appear laughable on any illustration, but it is overwhelming if one sees the real thing. As well as this, the more southern style of architecture, a certain reduction of advertising and one or two other factors combine to form something that is almost like a cultural landscape: one actually has the feeling that this part of the world is inhabited by humanoid beings, not only by gasoline stations and hot dogs. The entire wider vicinity here is somewhere between city and country . . .

THEODOR ADORNO, *to his parents*

1974

Neither of us has any illusions of "romance rekindled" and all that. There is no need for such fantasy . . .

I can come down to SF, or perhaps you, with or without companions, can drive up here. In SF I always stay at the ole Clifto (which I've known for 50 years through thick and thin . . . it's now on top, but has not always been!!!) . . .

A while ago I was trying to tell why I had stopped writing (writing as such . . . as a job . . .), and my sister who is my confidante said, "But you are still doing reviews and introductions and and and . . ." and I said that it was the way a snake moves and writhes until the sun sets after its death. She did not like that, and it was indeed rather brutal, but true . . .

M. F. K. FISHER, *to Southern California bookman Jake Zeitlin*

NOVEMBER 24

1793

... the coast took a direction S. 67 E., sixteen miles to the north point of a deep bay, off which lie two or three small rocks; this point, which I called Point Dume, bore N. 59 W ... this being a very conspicuous promontory, I named after Father Vincente [Dumetz] ...

According to the Spanish charts, I at first supposed this bay to be that which is there called the bay of St. Pedro but I was afterwards informed that this conjecture was ill founded. I had also been given to understand that a very advantageous settlement is established on a fertile spot somewhere in this neighbourhood within sight of the ocean, though at the distance of some miles from the coast, called Pueblo de los Angelos, 'the country town of the angels,' formed in the year 1781. This establishment was looked for in all directions, but nothing was perceived that indicated either habitations or inhabitants.   *explorer* **GEORGE VANCOUVER**,

christening Point Dume

1904

OUT WEST

A MAGAZINE OF THE OLD PACIFIC AND THE NEW

EDITOR'S OFFICE

LOS ANGELES, CAL.

Dear Mrs. Austin: ...

When you use Spanish names, it is your business as a decent woman, and as a writer, to have them right. What would you think of yourself if, as a Californian, writing of California, you described seasons as they are in New England? What would you think of yourself if you made your stage-setting in Inyo county and described the landscape such as the people of the northeast of Maine are familiar with, and as no one ever saw in California? Now you happen to know about these things, and therefore realize the iniquity it would be to misrepresent them. It is an equal iniquity—and I mean that word—to misrepresent other things just as characteristic, just as easy to learn and just as necessary to the picture. Don't fill yourself with that Chautauqua idiocy about leaving it to the dreadful scientists to know anything. It won't hurt you any more than it hurts other people to be right ...

CHARLES FLETCHER LUMMIS, *to Mary Austin*

1925

Among the many things we have done to arouse the hostility and antagonism of Mexicans has been our treatment of them in our fiction, where they
are nearly always portrayed as heartless scoundrels. I believe that a policy of
consideration and fairness toward our sister republic in our literature would
do much to lessen this hostility . . .

EDGAR RICE BURROUGHS

1961

. . . I was in L.A. for a week, most of the time digging Forest Lawn (as you
teen-agers say), making pre-need arrangements etc. The pre-needery was
rather bliss. I was accompanied by a Forest Lawn aficionado, head of the
English Dept of the Immaculate Heart (Catholic girls) College.

Our story: his mother, my sister (for I was his aunt for the nonce) was
dying of the usual. Cancer. We had to go through all this because I was
dying to see the Slumber Rooms, Casket Display Room and all. So, through
them we went. After much consideration, we turned from the $145 casket
(honestly it was a bit frightful looking) and our choice was between one at
$675 and another at $995. We decided on the $675 one—I suggesting that it
would suit Mother's complexion better (it was a dull beige).

After we finally got out, my companion, a bit green about the gills, made
a dive for the nearest phone booth, muttering to me: "Excuse me, I just want
to call Mother to make sure she's feeling OK." That's what I like to see, someone who can really identify in a dramatic role . . .

Oh yes another nice thing about F. Lawn. Among the multiplicity of final
resting places (all named things like Brotherly Love, Garden of Memories,
etc) is one called Patriots' Hall. I asked the man if one had to be a citizen to
finally rest there, he said oh no, not a bit necessary. (I mean the Final Resting
Place salesman said all this.) So I said, Well, I should think you'd at least ask
for some sort of loyalty oath, after all it's supposed to be for Patriots? He said
absolutely not, as long as you've got the money to pay for the site, all would
be OK . . .   **JESSICA MITFORD**

1997

We headed to Haight Street to get some CDs at Amoeba. I could hardly
concentrate in the massive store because of the echo of hundreds of people
thumbing through CDs and records. Rows and rows of people searching for
the perfect beat. I held off buying anything and we left to get a drink . . .

Right after a quick one we went east on Vallejo and right on Columbus to hit Jack Kerouac Alley to merge into City Lights bookstore. On the third floor in the poetry room, a reading had just finished. Older literary types were sipping wine. I recognized Lawrence Ferlinghetti in the corner in a pair of well worn khakis and a T-shirt decorated with a jazz saxophonist in action. For a moment I sat there and watched from the other side of the room . . . Ferlinghetti walked across the room to pour more wine. I didn't say anything this time, I was even satisfied just seeing him.

Yesterday I was at a poetry workshop taught by Amiri Baraka at the La Pena Cultural Center off Shattuck in Oakland. Baraka asked all the attendants questions that demanded answers: "Why do you write?" "For whom do you write?" "What do you hope to say?" . . .

He left me with a lot to think about. The moment especially made me think of a line from one of his poems: "Organize your shit as rightly burning." Seeing literary giants like Ferlinghetti and Baraka up close in a 24-hour period made me think about organizing my reality. I got a lot of work to do.

MIKE SONKSEN

NOVEMBER 25

1940

Los Angeles denies the existence of slums. But go across the river to South Gless Street. You'll find a woman and her nine children living in a four-room house, every room of which leaks when it rains. Rain drips down into the faces of the children as they sleep. It lays all day long in puddles on the floor. Because of defective plumbing, the family uses a gallon tin can for sanitary purposes, disposing of the contents in the back yard.

Across the street sewer gas leaks into the kitchen where eleven people eat three meals a day and three children sleep at night.

Over on Pecan Street is a two-room shack owned by a loan association which has fought low cost housing for Los Angeles. There is no inside plumbing; there are holes in the roof through which you can see the sky . . .

THEODORE DREISER, *to Edward G. Robinson*

1970

. . . the further I get into this wretched profession the clearer is that I am doing very little consciously beyond some clerk routine—assembling, expediting— and that either (a) there is some Extra-Personal Source, or (b) readers are the ones who do most of the work . . .

Hope you're having a good year. The university thing these days must be something of a hassle, but also, I would guess, a tremendous source of hope. I know I ain't up to it, but I'm glad there are people who are . . .

THOMAS PYNCHON, *to Arthur Mizener*

NOVEMBER 26

1857

In the evening went to a dancing party—saw everybody—tried to dance and couldn't—very much annoyed, came home incontinently—went to bed and spent a restless night.   BRET HARTE

1934

18904 MALIBU RD.,

PACIFIC PALISADES, CALIFORNIA

I haven't a single bit of news beyond what I told you over the phone except that I still love you very much please and would ask that you might find it possible to return my affections if it so happens you could do it without too much trouble . . .

Alfred's been bothering me with pleas that we bring "The Big Knockover" out between covers with a foreword saying it was written long ago and we don't think much of it, but there it is. He claims he's being hounded by my public—the rats!—and I love you very much, but I don't think I'll let him do it.

Now—still loving you very much—I'm off for another crack at the thin man sequel, on which I'm pretty cold at the time, but will probably be high-pressured by Hunt Stromberg into the wildest enthusiasm before long.

I love you very much.

Dash   DASHIELL HAMMETT

1949

. . . We showed an enormously improved picture to an audience which responded beautifully, giving lots of spontaneous applause at the end. I sat next to Bill Holden, who wore glasses and kept his head down, and still was recognized . . .

I thought with amusement what a surprise it would have been to Mr. and Mrs. Brackett of 605 N. Broadway, Saratoga Springs, New York, could they have been told that 57 years after the arrival of their matutinal son he would be celebrating on the other side of the continent a pleasant event in a medium of which they'd never heard.

CHARLES BRACKETT, *finishing* Sunset Boulevard

NOVEMBER 27

1602

. . . On the 27th of the month, and before casting anchor in a very good cove which was found, a multitude of Indians came out in canoes of cedar and pine, made of planks very well joined and caulked, each one with eight oars and with fourteen or fifteen Indians, who looked like galley-slaves. They came along side without the least fear and came on board our ships, mooring their own. They showed great pleasure at seeing us, telling us by signs that we must land, and guided us like pilots to the anchorage . . . Many Indians were on the beach, and the women treated us to roasted sardines and a small fruit like sweet potatoes.   *Father* **ANTONIO DE LA ASCENSIÓN**

1826

Cattle skulls in rows on each side of the road conveying the Idea that we were approaching an immense slaughter yard . . .

trailblazer **JEDEDIAH SMITH**

1958

Sweet letter from you this morning to cheer up Thanksgiving, which is a complete holiday here like Christmas in England. Not a shop open or a car in the streets, but glorious weather after a filthy fog last night, and a horrid drive to and from Sacramento (88 miles) and a dreary, po-faced party for Callas . . . .

JOHN GIELGUD

2007

Today a ring of slime. No slugs visible. 55 degrees at 7:45 a.m. No sign of the oil spill as I walk down the dunes to the beach. They have cleared out the ice grass on the dune-hill behind my house, cut down some trees. They are restoring this to the native habitat, which will be a rolling carpet of silvery green, low-lying plants that flower in the spring . . . it crosses my mind: I am a non-native species and that status cannot, will not change.

LESLIE CAROL ROBERTS

NOVEMBER 28

1826

My party arrived and I had my things put into the room which I occupied. The Corporal who was called Commandant came to me and after a few preparatory compliments observed that the best thing I could do with my guns would be to put them in his charge where they would be safe . . . strangers visiting you will be constantly handling them they being a kind with which they are unacquainted. I thanked him for his kindness and gave him the arms though I knew he was influenced by a motive very different from the one assigned.   **JEDEDIAH SMITH**

1850

. . . in the distance distinctly to be seen are the Farollones, three small islands . . . Pilot brought us two or three California papers. Before I retired for the night went on deck for a peep and to appearance the land was over our ship's deck we were anchored so close to it. It is at least 6 or 800 feet high, frightful looking enough a mass of barren rock on the side of the Island which is called Virgin Id.   *pioneer* **CAROLINE STODDARD**

1939

FIGUEROA HOTEL

The place is filled with fussy upper middle-class old women, perhaps sent out here by their children to be rid of them.   **SHERWOOD ANDERSON**

NOVEMBER 29

1935

Banana Center, Central Park, El-Lay

This became Pershing Square in the war-mad days, but it is still Central Park to me . . .

"May I speak to you?"

"Surely."

"Have you been saved?"

"I'm sorry, but your subject doesn't interest me."

The young man bows and walks away, and I mentally collapse from astonishment. Such passivity before pagan resistance is unlike evangelical votaries.

Endless, endless movement.

Loitering figures—lingering, lurking.

Some have been heard to say that no respectable person would allow himself to be seen in the park after dark. Huh! I walk about under the thousand shadows of the bamboo and banana trees with utter unconcern.

HARRY PARTCH

1947

To my way of thinking, the Breen office is narrowing our range of properties down to where we can either make a musical or a comedy. It is becoming more and more apparent that each story we do faces the same problem—we might offend some vocal minority. As you know, the Breen office condemned *John Loves Mary* in toto. You have seen the play and you know there is nothing in it that is immoral . . . .

The Breen office is good in many ways, but somewhere along the line we should get together and try to find out exactly what we can make and cannot make. The Breen office today goes by a production code that was written in 1930. Many important events have taken place since the code was written. Is it possible that the code is dated? Certainly a reexamination is due. The industry today is feeling the box-office slump with bowed heads and long faces, but yet I notice that *Body and Soul* and *Gentleman's Agreement* are both doing stand-out business. I understand that both these pictures had quite a job of getting past the Breen office. Certainly *Body and Soul* is cluttered with gangsters and henchmen and their kept women. It is also good box-office because it has guts and vitality. The story we are trying to tell in *Key Largo* is a moral one and certainly there is no better way to point a moral than to use a gangster as a symbol of everything that we are trying to avoid going back to . . .

This piling up of continuous censorship is what is making all our pictures empty, and running along with a competent mediocrity. We could never have made *Odd Man Out* in this country, or *Shoeshine*, or *Open City*, or many other outstanding films . . .

You've got to help us. This is serious.

writer, producer **JERRY WALD**, *to a Warner Bros. colleague*

2021

not sure anyone has heard but, I resigned from Twitter

CEO **JACK DORSEY**

NOVEMBER 30

1849

Yesterday 29th was Thanksgiving Day. There was service in all the churches but very few of the stores were closed—all are so intent on making money that they have time for nothing else . . .

MARGARET DEWITT

1866

. . . They had just struck a rich place in the mine, and I saw chunks of quartz as large as a child's head, which were plastered nearly all over with gleaming leaves and plates of the purest gold . . . The thing that touches a traveler's heart nearest, is to come drearily into a strange place and find himself at home in a good hotel. I found such in Grass Valley . . .

MARK TWAIN

1943

. . . I am being sued by the motor scooter company as I refuse to pay them for the scooter after it proved a Jonah. I had signed an un-read contract that held me responsible for the entire sum even with scooter returned. The sheriff has been sieging my Santa Monica apt. trying to serve papers on me but I have successfully evaded him so far. He hasn't tracked me to Pasadena yet. I intend to return at midnight, pack up and be out before daybreak. I understand that if he doesn't touch me with the papers I can escape the suit.

TENNESSEE WILLIAMS

2007

. . . native-to-the-southwest plantas: la salvia. Always my homecoming scent. The soft dryness of mimosa-powdery dust bajo los eucaliptos y pinos . . .

SUSANA CHÁVEZ-SILVERMAN

DECEMBER 1

1939

Eleanor with a fever but going it all day. I did not know she had a fever until we had gone off to dine with Teddy and Helen Dreiser. The old boy in fine form but intent on defending Stalinism. We saw the beautiful new Union Station here, one of the most beautiful buildings I have seen in America.

SHERWOOD ANDERSON

1964

I am listening to Hester's transistor, trying to follow events at Cal, where another big uprising is apparently developing. In October the students uprose and refused to obey or whatever, whereupon a police car was brought onto the campus to haul away one of the chief offenders. I forget who he was or how he offended, if I ever knew, but he had a Jewish name and I was therefore inclined to take his side, at least in my mind. So also were hundreds of students, who prevented the police car from driving away, by the simple expedient of surrounding it and refusing to move, and camping that way for several days, thus frustrating the police, disrupting the campus, and horrifying the bourgeoisie. This boy is now a leader of the present demonstration, I believe, and another boy named Mario Savio, from New York, a philosophy student who is most eloquent and rational and does not believe in combing his hair. I like most about him the fact that when he is interviewed on TV, as he was this evening, he does not look into the camera but actually addresses the person he is addressing, as if the person mattered.

novelist **MARK HARRIS**

DECEMBER 2

1920

We would, all of us, like to be somebody in this great, indifferent, cruel swirl . . .   THEODORE DREISER

1964

There is a time when the operation of the machine becomes so odious, makes you so sick at heart, that you can't take part! You can't even passively take part! And you've got to put your bodies upon the gears and upon the wheels . . . upon the levers, upon all the apparatus, and you've got to make it stop.   *activist* MARIO SAVIO

DECEMBER 3

1879

It is a pity in one sense, one sense, for I believe that the class of work I might yet give out is better and more real and solid than people fancy. But death is no bad friend; a few aches and gasps, and we are done . . .

ROBERT LOUIS STEVENSON

1946

A long talk with a Dr. Hortense Powdermaker, who is working on a study of Hollywood from a purely anthropological point of view. At 4:30 Zoltan Korda and Aldous Huxley arrived, without the copy of the script they'd promised . . .

I've met Huxley before, but let me restate him again: tall, elegant, in an utterly careless way, quite beautiful of feature despite the one silvered eye and utterly beyond my power to like. Helplessly aloof from one . . . Frankly, I detest this writer, whose work I worship . . . Jokingly I say, "I expect the best thing since Euripides from you." He smirks, and I realize that this goes into his experience as a comic saying of a Hollywood producer . . .

CHARLES BRACKETT

1950

I'll be staying out till middle or late January, working on a script with John Huston, *The African Queen*, from novel by C.S. Forester. If everything works out right, it could be a wonderful movie . . . The work is a great deal of fun:

treating it fundamentally as high comedy with deeply ribald overtones, and trying to blend extraordinary things—poetry, mysticism, realism, romance, tragedy, with the comedy . . .

I haven't read a book, heard any music to speak of, or seen a movie or but one play, since I have been out here. For the present, I don't miss them either. I see a lot of people and like most of them. Compared with most of the intellectual literary acquaintances I avoid in New York (who are—wrongly— my image of New York) they are mostly very warmhearted, outgoing, kind, happy, and unpretentious—the nicest kind of company I can imagine . . .

novelist, screenwriter, film critic, **JAMES AGEE,**

to his old teacher and friend Father Flye

1958

San Francisco was a bit of a disappointment, except for the Saturday night when I went on the town with my friend from the reception desk and the bars were simply fabulous—people squashed together in milling hordes of jeans and manch, packages galore, and I finished up at 4 a.m. with a rather bashful teacher from Santa Barbara with a very handy property and a beige corduroy SUIT. So that was quite an evening, though I was a little the worse for wear next day, especially as I had two shows!   **JOHN GIELGUD**

1967

Hello, Dear,

Thank you for telling me to go to "Bonnie & Clyde", I liked it very much. Thanksgiving was heaven. I had Don staying with me, and also a splendid man from Los Angeles whom I'd met a few weeks before, a rather sexy University professor, of all the outlandish occupations. And then Don's ex-lover and Cecil Beaton's ex-lover, who are lovers for the moment, came over, and we had lots of dexamyl and beer and turkey and apricot wine and grass. Waves of sheer love pulsed around and one by one we collapsed on the floor in sheer wiped-outness. It was all terribly happy, and one did feel that one was giving veritable thanks for something or other, though maybe it was only for being part of the warp and woof of life itself. (A homosexual dog, by the way, could colloquially be called a warped woof.) . . .

There are some very splendid songs around. Of course the Eggman song (which is about a crisis of identity?), and its lovely flipside, the best of Hello Songs. And the Stones 'We Love You.' And have you come across the Bee Gees' "Every Christian Lion-Hearted Man" and the Small Faces' "Itchykoo Park" (some fabulous electric orgasmic sounds) . . .

I was sorry Proposition P (the peace proposition) lost in the election here. I was asked to be one of its "independent sponsors" and said yes. I thought I would be in the list of famous writers, along with Isherwood and people, but actually I was in the list of local homosexuals (in an advt in the local San Francisco "homophile" magazine)." I was rather pleased by that!

Isherwood came to see me the other day. Very nice to talk with him after all these years. One interesting thing. He was saying how attractive Auden used to be, & "For years we used to screw like weasels," he added offhandedly. Somehow it was so obvious I never thought of that. Also, the talentless John Rechy has a new "novel" coming out, which contains unkind caricatures of Isherwood, his lover Gavin Lambert, and his ex-lover . . .

Well, that's the end of this piece of paper, I think.

Love to both,

x x x x x x x

The Walrus   THOM GUNN

DECEMBER 4

1939

The most remarkable thing here is the [Ross-Loos] medical clinic where I found the best and most intelligent medical treatment and advice I have ever experienced.   SHERWOOD ANDERSON

1952

Patsy and I and friends of hers went to Disneyland yesterday. It was simply divine and I *longed* for you to have been there. You get in to a little launch on Jungle River and glide away past, crocodiles, gorillas, giant butterflies etc., and the divine young man at the helm (in very tight white ducks and jersey and a peaked cap) does a commentary of wonderful camp—now steady here, folks, it's dangerous here—over the rapids, shooting off a pistol at intervals as a huge hippo rears its head into the boat, and rubber arrows go flying past, mad life-size clockwork (I suppose) animals and natives. I can't tell you what fun. Then we went on two *mad* rides—the Snow White one with shrieking witches and sound effects, pitch dark passages, sailing through walls that open and close behind you, figures leaping out as you pass—and another Peter Pan, in which you go up a slope in a small boat through opening windows and appear to fly over London, model Big Ben and all, and descend at a hair-raising angle passing Hook and Smee and the Pirate Ship all posed and shaking their fists from the deck below—and a ridiculous mining train with the driver and guards in ten gallon hats (and jeans) puffing through caves and deserts and descending to a brilliant cavern of jewels and waterfalls. It really was a hilarious afternoon. And it is 85 degrees here in the daytime!, hotter than the South of France. So it is all rather fun but a bit exhausting too. The *pace*, and the cars and the mad ladies and sexy looking boys on every corner. If I ever do a picture here again you *must* come out. You would simply adore it.   **JOHN GIELGUD,** *to his partner*

DECEMBER 5

1850

. . . we walked to Portsmith Square and here what we saw defies description. The largest buildings are occupied by gamblers in large saloons, which as we passed by, we saw filled with men and boys—tables covered with gold and silver in piles, beautiful music in most of them, and of course a bar, and shocking as it may appear a woman sometimes attending them, as we saw in our walk the most frightful set of desperadoes of every country. It is said there are seven thousand convicts from Sydney N.S.W. who help swell the list of vagabonds. Every week, or night rather, there are one or two shot in these gambling establishments. The wonder might be, that more do not fall victims in these horrible places.   **CAROLINE STODDARD**

1896

As for the newspapers I think you must not be impatient. They will not hurt you. A *man* can only hurt himself.   *poet, frontiersman* **JOAQUIN MILLER,**

to author Yone Noguchi

1907

ORLAND, GLENN COUNTY

. . . it is raining really raining . . . People laugh at us old farmers when we are so interested in the weather, but a rain sometimes means the difference be-tween profit and loss in a year's work . . . It may mean the lives of many little lambs saved and I know you'll be glad of that.

PETER RUSS PETERSON

1932

Selznick is the big noise; he is young, massive, well-educated, and with tremendous vitality . . . I saw Selznick in his office with Cooper, another member of the executive. He was the man who did "Chang" and "Four Feathers". They want me to do a horror picture for them . . .

novelist, screenwriter **EDGAR WALLACE,**

taking his first meeting on King Kong

1934

I am now an authority on torture. I have been railroaded into this magnificent office now more than three months. I have undergone the humiliation of not even being considered or given anything to do . . .

Why, why, why, did they do this? Why have they brought me here to pay me fat money for sitting here? . . .

Last night the bankers came out here. The studio threw a big luncheon. Stepin Fetchit and Bill Robinson (Negroes both) tap-danced for the bankers . . .   **ERIC KNIGHT,** *to a friend*

DECEMBER 6

1846

. . . off we put in search of adventure . . . .

[The] Enemy fired on us. The balls whistled about most infernally for a while . . . and, we found they had made a stand in front of a Ranchereo. This was called St Pasqual. At this time a fellow came dashing by . . . presenting with his hat &c a most Mexican look—when bang went a dragoon pistol . . .

[Another] dragoon who happened to be near—drew his sabre and was about cutting the man down when I yelled out to him to stop as the man was one of Gallespies party—by this time we were very much disordered . . . Capt Moor however ordered the charge to be continued and it was in the most hurly burly manner . . .

[The] Enemy . . . rallied and came at us like devils with their lances . . . the devils got around me, and like to have fixed my flint—but I got off by . . . drawing an empty pistol—this answered the purposes of a loaded one . . .

[Upon] the whole we suffered most terribly in this action—in all 35 men killed and wounded . . . This was an action where decidedly more courage than conduct was showed The first charge was a mistake on the part of Capt Johnston, the 2d on the part of Capt Moor . . .

All that day was engaged in dressing the wounded.

JOHN S. GRIFFIN, MD,
at the Battle of San Pascual

1942

I watched a friend last night who had invited me to his home for supper, stop at seven grocery stores to find batter and found none. The street lamps are hooded from above here, wardens patrol the streets for cracks in window shades, etc. There are barrage balloons along the coast, and searchlights (and of course, A.A. batteries [anti-aircraft, not Duracell] hidden) in all sorts of unexpected places throughout the city: in all the canyons, and now and then on the playgrounds of schools. They expect a bombing here. But nobody is afraid of it . . .

There is something here for an anthropologist's notebook. This is one of the richest towns in the country. As it exists today, its economy and geography was fixed and invented by the automobile. Therefore, the automobile invented it. The automobile (for a time, anyway) is as dead as the mastodon. Therefore the town which the automobile created, is dying. I think that a detached and impartial spectator could watch here what some superman in a superheated diving-bell could have watched at the beginning of the ice age, say: a doomed way of life and its seething inhabitants all saying: Why, Jack Frost simply cant do this to us. It's not so. That's not ice we see; that's not cold we feel. We've got to be warm. We cant live otherwise.

WILLIAM FAULKNER, *to his stepson*

DECEMBER 7

1860

In Camp at Los Angeles.

Well, we are in camp. It is a cold rainy night, but I can hardly realize the fact that you at home are blowing your fingers in the cold, and possibly sleighing, while I am sitting here in a tent, without fire, and sleeping on the ground in blankets, in this month . . .

The houses are but one story, mostly built of adobe or sun-burnt brick, with very thick walls and flat roofs. They are so low because of earthquakes, and the style is Mexican. The inhabitants are a mixture of old Spanish, Indian, American, and German Jews; the last two have come in lately. The language of the natives is Spanish, and I have commenced learning it. The only thing they appear to excel in is riding, and certainly I have never seen such riders.

Here is a great plain, or rather a gentle slope, from the Pacific to the mountains . . . all that is wanted naturally to make it a paradise is water, more water. Apples, pears, plums, figs, olives, lemons, oranges, and "the finest grapes in the world," so the books say . . .

The effect of the pepper, fig, olive, and palm trees in the foreground, with the snow in the distance, is very unusual . . .

WILLIAM H. BREWER

1941

Pearl Harbor. We are at war! Jesus Christ, the Japs bombed Hawaii and the entire fleet has been sunk. I just can't believe it. I don't know what in the hell is going to happen to us, but we will all be called into the Army right away. Wang . . . is worried about his relatives as the radio says there are riots in Los Angeles, and they think it is sabotage. I can't believe that any Nisei would do anything like that . . .

I think of the Japs coming to bomb us, but I will go and fight even if I think I am a coward and I don't believe in wars . . . I am selfish about it. I think not of California and America, but I wonder what is going to happen to the Nisei and to our parents. They may lock up the aliens. How can one think of the future?

. . . The next five years will determine the future of the Nisei. They are now at the crossroads. Will they be able to take it or will they go under? If we are ever going to prove our Americanism, this is the time. The Anti-Jap feeling is bound to rise to hysterical heights, and it is most likely that the Nisei will be included as Japs. I wanted to go to San Francisco tonight, but Pierre says I am crazy. He says it's best we stick on campus. In any event, we can't remain on the fence, and a positive approach must be taken if we are to have a place in fulfilling the Promise of America . . .   **CHARLES KIKUCHI**

1989

Today is the memorial service for a good friend of mine. He died, of course, of the Big A. We'll all gather in some all-purpose room somewhere and there under the fluorescent lights we'll mark the occasion of his passing, with little ceremony or ritual.

There's something about seeing, actually viewing a corpse that brings home the fact of death. I think: "closure." a Californian would say, which is ironic, since it's been more or less Californians who have eliminated funerals from the cultural scene . . . .

[Sitting] in the Sinai Memorial Chapel in San Francisco, listening to an elderly tenor sing a pure, haunting kaddish. I thought about this: What happens to all that energy of grief when people have no way to give it voice? Where does it go?   *writer* **FENTON JOHNSON**

DECEMBER 8

1941

Sixteenth Year of Showa

A bolt out of the blue sky, like water in [a] one's sleeping ear, unimaginably fearful, cruel this reality—indescribably waves of strong shock and fear over my entire body; if I try to stop it, it becomes even stronger and overcomes me!

"At present, Japanese airplanes are bombing Hawaii's Pearl Harbor!"

I heard those words from a young waiter at the Chinese restaurant, Sankohro, in Los Angeles. Unimaginable that it was winter; it was a warm Sunday, around eleven o'clock . . .

My chest is pounding! . . . Ordinarily delicious dishes of food are all bitter and tasteless. I taste strange saliva in my mouth.

My two daughters, Yoko, age twelve, and Sachiko, age ten, ate so fast it was difficult to see where they swallowed it and hurriedly went out to buy a special edition of newspapers being announced on sale in the street.

Looking at the newspaper they brought back, in large bold letters that appeared two inches square, "WAR . . . ," I involuntarily gasped! I had been completely mentally unprepared and felt as though I had been hit with a sledge hammer. Blood rushed to my face, and breathing became difficult, and in inverse proportion, my feet inside my shoes, starting from the toes, started to get cold as ice. I looked down, covering both cheeks, and tried to organize my confused mind . . .

On the way home, Japanese we met all had worried faces drained of blood. What should we do?   **AOKI HISA**

1963

6233 MULHOLLAND HIGHWAY

LOS ANGELES 28, CALIFORNIA

... 'I am going to give him a shot of LSD, he asked for it.' The doctor had a moment of agitation because you know very well the uneasiness about this drug in the medical mind. Then he said, 'All right, at this point what is the difference.' Whatever he had said, no 'authority,' not even an army of authorities could have stopped me then. I went into Aldous' room with the vial of LSD and prepared a syringe. The doctor asked me if I wanted him to give him the shot—maybe because he saw that my hands were trembling. His asking me that made me conscious of my hands, and I said, 'No I must do this.' I quieted myself, and when I gave him the shot my hands were very firm ...

I had been warned in the morning that there might be some up-setting convulsions towards the end, or some sort of contraction of the lungs, and noises. People had been trying to prepare me for some horrible physical reaction that would probably occur. None of this happened, actually the ceasing of the breathing was not a drama at all, because it was done so slowly, so gently, like a piece of music just finishing in a *sempre piu piano dolcement* ...

All five people in the room said that this was the most serene, the most beautiful death. Both doctors and the nurse said they had never seen a person in similar physical condition going off so completely without pain and without struggle ...   *musician, therapist, memoirist* **LAURA HUXLEY**,
to Aldous's brother Julian

DECEMBER 9

1941

Berkeley. Holy Christ! San Francisco last night was like nothing I ever saw before and everybody was saying that the Japs are going to get it in the ass. I ran into Jimmy Hong up on Grant Avenue, and he says I'm not allowed to screw Chinese girls anymore. Angelo, too, he says, because he is a Wop. Jimmy was kidding; and he will give me some kind of a badge which says that I am a Chinese as he says some of the Japanese boys from U. C. got beat up. I didn't hear anything about that. Kenny told me it was true when I got back, and he said that all of the students are going to be restricted to campus. A lot of them want to get the hell out of here and go home . . .

I think Pop would praise Japan; but he is not going to blow up anything. It may be dangerous for him in the barber shop with all those Mare Island guys coming in. I told Alice to tell Mom to have Pop's Navy discharge framed and put on the wall next to the barber license and take that Buddha statue the hell out of there. Alice says the Army should put me in charge of patriotism because I am suspicious of my own father. I did not mean it that way; but it is true, I don't trust the Issei. If just one of them sabotaged something, what hell there would be to pay . . .   **CHARLES KIKUCHI**

1948

There is a magnificent view from the windows of this ward. On one side the Ocean and the Beach—On the other the narrows of the Golden Gate and the Bridge. Can you imagine a better setting for a prostate cancer?!

I imagine that you are lonely. So am I. It doesn't matter how many friends we have—some of us are always lonely. Look at Blaise Cendrars. What a life! What hasn't he done? He has been everywhere, he has known everybody . . . and he is always lonely. His daughter came thru Big Sur a couple of months ago and told Henry Miller that her father was writing sixteen books! (I suppose if he still had his right hand he'd write thirty-two books at the same time.) . . .   **JAIME DE ANGULO,** *to Ezra Pound*

1964

This is the story. Bob has been lawyer for the Free Speech Movement right along. On Thurs. night, the night of the big sit-in at Sproul Hall, he got a call from his clients asking to confer. So he went over after dinner . . .

[The] D.A. had him arrested forthwith. He was booked in the basement of Sproul Hall (where they had set up a full-scale booking procedure, fingerprints, photos, the works) and eventually was taken to Santa Rita Prison farm along with the other 860 arrested. There he was given a bad time, put in a solitary cell with stone floor and nowhere to sit, so he stood for about 3 hours. Meanwhile I was going quietly bonkers as our British cousins say. I had been called at 4 a.m. to say he was arrested, but natch I thought he'd be out at once. He wasn't released till 11:30 Friday. He is livid, as you might think, planning massive false arrest suits against all concerned.

However the dear boy rather thrives on this sort of thing. The whole free speech fight has been simply thrilling. I guess you've followed it in the NY papers. It's a new and marvellous development, much like the sit-ins of 1960.

Bob is very much the hero of students and faculty members, it's all been terrific. This wknd, we are going to L.A. for a few days, at the invitation of our newfound friend Julie Andrews. She said she would show a Disneyland if we would show her Forest Lawn, so that's the deal . . . .

ps. At one point the cops in Sproul Hall started locking up the johns, presumably to discourage students with weak blads. So some of the men students took the doors off by the hinges, and they had what you might call a shit-in. Bob said he met Joan Baez in one of the johns.

Also, the other night Bob addressed the 860 defendants at a mass meeting, starting off with "Fellow Jailbirds." He got a standing ovation. They simply adore him.   JESSICA MITFORD

1964

. . . this generation has stood up and continued to speak plainly of truth. 'When you go in, go in with love in your heart,' Joan Baez said. Those words and Mario's eloquent speech remain the only rhetoric of these ten weeks that history will remember. Literature, poetry and history are not made by the smooth jowl and a blue suit. They are made with sweat and passion and dedication to truth and honor.

San Francisco Chronicle *music critic, broadcaster,*
Rolling Stone *and Monterey Jazz Festival co-founder*
RALPH J. GLEASON

DECEMBER 10

1826

There was five Inds. brought to the mission by two other Inds, who act as constables, or overseers, and sentenced to be whiped for not going to work when ordered.

Each received from 12 to 14 lashes on their bare posteriors; they were all old men, say from 50 to 60 years of age, the commandant standing by with his sword to see that the Ind. who flogged them done his duty. Things in other respects similar to the last sabbath.

frontiersman HARRISON ROGERS

1846

10th Sergt [John] Cox died this morning his wound on the left side, just above the crista of the Illeum—he had singultus [hiccups] for several hours before death . . .

On the evening of the 10th we were grazing our animals at the foot of the hill near our camp when we saw the Mexicans driving a band of wild horses towards us . . . we were prepared. We waited a few moments so as to entice some of the rascals in gun shot if possible . . . the drove of wild horses were turned . . . One mule however . . . was so imprudent as to come within gun shot, forty balls I was told struck him, yet he did not fall . . .

JOHN S. GRIFFIN, MD

1941

Max has been appointed an air warden!

THEODOR ADORNO, *to his parents*

2004

The Fillmore is a tough gig to play. It's a huge cube, which is ideal for absorbing the noise of rock-and-roll, but not so easy for throwaway lines. They have filled the room with round tables so it's more like a bar mitzvah or a Hollywood Ratfuck (a rubber-chicken charity dinner) than the nicely laid-out theaters we are used to. It's also beastly cold. Ancient psychedelic posters look down on us everywhere . . .

actor, composer, lyricist, Python **ERIC IDLE**

2020

JOSHUA TREE

We are so glad to land here, after dark, on a washboard road. Lights shining like a wayside inn, fire purring (pellets) a la Cocteau's Sleeping Beauty. We pour mezcal, clink, dance to Robert Wyatt and Llasa de Sela, kiss slowly and deeply. Drink wine. Lloyd crashes on the couch. I distribute our reading material throughout the house, NY Sunday Times in the bathroom, Polish poetry in the living room. Make green tea . . .

Wake to desert sun. **LOUISE STEINMAN**

DECEMBER 11

1906

. . . I put my new invention into effect this morning and the two Library Guides went to work. They stand by the elevator and pick up the lost patrons that come in and don't know what they want nor where to find it and tell them both things . . .   **CHARLES FLETCHER LUMMIS**

1946

OAKLAND

I am very well and in good spirits and hope that the *pneuma* will continue to blow and keep us both off the rocks. Any way, He knows best . . .

Domincan priest **VICTOR WHITE**,
to his friend and collaborator Carl G. Jung

1946

SAN FRANCISCO

. . . Amplitude and plenitude of California life, openness and hospitality . . . .

I must tell about [my family] so that they should be expressed and should not die out without their goodness, their enjoyments, and their pathos being put on record. They were the first people after the pioneers who . . . had loved fresh and futile California . . .

They had been the Americans, the frank, the free, the first, the adventurous, who had lived in the society that Jefferson had said was something new under the sun . . . falling below them in my character in some respects, I must make up for it by concentrating [on] my literary ability, not merely to tell about them, but to bring their virtues into my writing, make my writing exemplify their virtues . . . .

. . . We walked out and tried the grill, where we found exactly the same menu at considerably lower prices—revolting but rather pretty mural in soft pinks, blues, and greens, of (of course) the early days in the West: prospectors, big railroad men, etc., soaring through the air to California . . .

EDMUND WILSON

2004

It's a beautiful sunny day in San Francisco with clear blue skies and fresh air and I am absolutely cream crackered after last night's show . . . Four Seasons is totally fab, from their comfortable cottony beds to their deep-water baths. I have a high suite looking out over the Moscone Convention Center and across the bay. My wife has thoughtfully left her bathrobe behind so I can still smell her.

I lunch alone at the Yank Sing at Stevenson Place. The most fabulous dim sum in town. You see, I really do like Chinese. I am now totally committed to dining solo. The great thing about eating by yourself is you don't have to talk to anyone. The train of thought can go by without stopping at anyone else's station . . .

There was a heartrending moment at the signing last night when a lady called Wendy tells me her husband died on Wednesday, but she had to come to see me. She says she is very glad she did. I am touched and saddened by her loss, but I am also very glad she had the courage to come. The laughter has done her good . . .

I'm not going to lecture you about laughter and tears, but when George [Harrison] lay dead and we were all sitting there very gloomy consuming Kleenex, his son, Dahni, said "Come on, Dad wouldn't have wanted this." And I said, "Yeah, he wasn't all he was cracked up to be," and we all laughed, because it was one of George's favorite lines from Python. Laughter can be such a wonderful release. Saying the unsayable at these moments can work really well.

When George was stabbed by an intruder in early 2000 . . . Tania and I immediately jumped on a plane and flew to stay with him and [Hawthorne High School graduate] Olivia at their home in Oxfordshire . . .

"I thought I was dead, Eric," he said.

Carried out to the ambulance, covered in blood, he said to his appalled house managers, who had just started working for him, "So, what do you think of the job so far?"   ERIC IDLE

DECEMBER 12
1906
It has rained steadily for several days. Last Sunday there was a real storm that lasted through Monday morning. Houses trembled, and traffic was stopped in the burnt part of the city where they are busy rebuilding, because of the ruined walls that the wind managed to demolish. Nature certainly seems unrelenting toward this poor city, yet nothing discourages the inhabitants. There is as much business as before, and already a great part is rebuilt. The

most pessimistic say that in fifteen years San Francisco will be bigger than it was before the catastrophe.   JAIME DE ANGULO

1938

Saturday night I was greatly exhilarated by the Fire Sequence. It was one of the biggest thrills I have had out of making pictures——first, because of the scene itself, and second, because of the frightening but exciting knowledge that *Gone With the Wind* was finally in work. Myron rolled in just exactly too late, arriving about a minute and a half after the last building had fallen and burned and after the shots were completed. With him were Larry Olivier and Vivien Leigh. Shhhhh: she's the Scarlett dark horse, and looks damned good. (Not for anybody's ears but your own: it's narrowed down to Paulette, Jean Arthur, Joan Bennett, and Vivien Leigh. We're making final tests this week, and I do frantically hope that you'll be home in time to sit in on the final decision . . . At least when I am lynched I want you to be able to shout sincerely that I did the best I could.)

                                        producer **DAVID O. SELZNICK**, *to his wife*

1969

And so perhaps this marks the end of an era. The gravestone—a face straight from central casting, long hair, wild hypnotically staring eyes, the king of "love" called Jesus and Satan and God. And what can we say, we look at that picture, we read the pathetic details of the murder, the senseless, useless, misdirected antagonism toward a world that they know, somehow, has cheated them of reason. Or My Lai, and *Life* magazine with pictures of the dead and the about to die, the eyes again, terror, despair, I want to cry . . .

I am sick, made sick, sickened, nauseated, helpless, and almost without hope. Yesterday while shopping for a gift I glanced at the bare arm of the saleslady who was wrapping it for me. On her arm was a tattooed number. I am sick, we are all sick.   LIZA WILLIAMS

1990

I was reading through Samuel Pepys' diaries—he lived in London at the time of the plague—the "Black Death" of 1655 . . . What's remarkable about his diaries is his attitude toward death, his supposition that it may come at any time, and is handed out by a capricious and not necessarily merciful God (an attitude much closer to that of the ancient Greeks than to that of contemporary Americans) . . .

A week before [my lover] died, I turned to him in the courtyard of the Picasso Museum, under a dusk-deep sapphire sky and said, "I'm so lucky." And it was as if the time allotted to him to teach this lesson, the time allotted to me to learn it had been consumed, and there was nothing left but the facts of things to play out. At the risk of being sententious I say: Think on these things, and what they mean to you. All relationships are mortal, it's just that most of the time we're too "well-wadded with stupidity," as George Eliot would have it, or needing a gun pointed to our heads, as Flannery O'Connor would have it, and we avoid thinking about it. And then it happens, and it's over. There's no door more unquestionable, more unanswering than death.

FENTON JOHNSON

DECEMBER 13

1963

Personally, I was very pro-Kennedy; but I was still amazed at how much I minded. And, in this quite largely anti-Kennedy town, which has so little to unite it, it was amazing how much everybody minded. People just sat listening to the radio in their cars and sobbing. We were all in love with him, without knowing it.   **CHRISTOPHER ISHERWOOD**

1976

Back from a weekend in San Francisco. Drove there by the coast route, stopping to see San Simeon, an important pilgrimage for me, since *Citizen Kane* was the crucial artistic experience of my life and San Simeon was in many ways its inspiration. The place is awe inspiring, not just because of the mountainous setting (one might be in a sun-baked part of the Scottish Highlands) but because the incredible eclectic jumble of styles and tastes—the façade of the Casa Grande, for instance, which contains bits of Far Eastern temples, medieval monasteries and Ronda Cathedral—does hang together, does achieve an unvulgar unity, thanks to the extraordinary talent of Julia Morgan, the architect who planned it all with Hearst. The swimming-pools—the indoor even more than the outdoor—have a genuine antique splendour.

In a sense San Simeon is a humble creation. When Louis XIV builds a monument to himself at Versailles, everything about it must be of his time, reflecting his era and its aesthetic. Whereas Hearst collects from all periods and places and builds a monument not so much to himself as to the history of civilisation. I buy from the gift shop an ashtray in the shape of a foot, with the following inscription: 'I get a kick out of the Hearst Castle at San Simeon', which I propose to send to Orson . . .

In San Francisco one superb French meal at L'Etoile, and a sad lunch with Bob Kaufman, my old friend, the former Beat poet who, hooked alternatively on alcohol and amphetamines, fell into a virtually complete silence that lasted from J.F.K.'s assassination to the end of the Vietnam War. His wife Eileen had assured me that he was now recovered and off dope and drink. That he is off stimulants I can believe; but he looks like a man struck by lightning—not an inept image, because Eileen tells me that he had massive doses of ECT in a state mental institution. These have turned him into a zombie. He speaks little, and then only as if we were living a decade ago. 'How are the Beatles coming along?" he asks me. Moreover, he's extremely deaf. I cannot possibly write about this shattered man. He used to be a demonic lord of mischief and misrule . . .   KENNETH TYNAN

1980

Yoko Ono asked that at 11:00 am today, ten minutes of peace and silence be offered for John. I just finished my praying for him. Those were beautifully calm, peaceful few minutes. I could feel a sense of union with the John fans that I know were praying all over the world. In Central Park ½ million people were expected. In Griffith Park there was a gathering also. I'd like to do something loving in his memory. I guess just remembering him always is the most I can do.

It's been a sad week on radio and television stations. Everyone was shocked. There is a certain pleasure, though, in seeing that he was loved by so many. I still feel tranquil from praying. Now I feel like he's really dead. Almost like he's buried (he was cremated).

God bless John Lennon

[entry bears wax seal]   COLLEEN JAURRETCHE

DECEMBER 14

1850

I now learned of the death, a few days before, of my very dear friend, George Matlock, with whom I had crossed the plains, and who had been instrumental in saving my life . . . alas! alas! the inexpressible loss and sorrow of his widow and family when the story of his death reaches them in their far distant Iowa home.   *pioneer* JOHN BIDWELL

1931

I met Diego! I stood beside a stone block, stepped out as he lumbered downstairs into Ralph's courtyard on Jessop Place— and he took me clear off my feet in an embrace. I photographed Diego again, his new wife—Frieda [sic]— too: she is in sharp contrast to Lupe, petite—a little doll alongside Diego, but a doll in size only, for she is strong and quite beautiful, shows very little of her father's German blood. Dressed in native costume even to huaraches, she causes much excitement on the streets of San Francisco. People stop in their tracks to look in wonder. We ate at a little Italian restaurant where many of the artists gather, recalled the old days in Mexico, with promises of meeting soon again in Carmel.   **EDWARD WESTON**

DECEMBER 15

1775

I make no excuses for announcing to your Excellency the tragic news I have just received of the total destruction of the San Diego Mission, and of the death of the senior of its two religious ministers, called Father Fray Lewis Jayme, at the hand of the rebellious gentiles and of the Christian neophyte . . . The gentiles came together from 40 rancherias . . . and set fire to the church . . . On the morning following that sad night, [Father Fustér] withdrew . . . They carried the dead on the shoulders of those Christian Indians who had remained loyal . . .

. . . if ever the Indians, whether they be gentile or Christian, killed me, they should be forgiven . . . As to the murderer, let him live, in order that he should be saved—which is the very purpose of our coming here, and the reason which justifies it. Give him to understand, after a moderate amount of punishment, that he is being pardoned in accordance with our law, which commands us to forgive injuries; and let us prepare him, not for death, but for eternal life.   *Father* JUNÍPERO SERRA

1866

My Friends and Fellow-Citizens: I have been treated with extreme kindness and cordiality by San Francisco, and I wish to return my sincerest thanks and acknowledgments. I have also been treated with marked and unusual generosity, forbearance and good-fellowship, by my ancient comrades, my brethren of the Press—a thing which has peculiarly touched me, because long experience in the service has taught me that we of the Press are slow to praise but quick to censure each other . . .

[California] stands in the centre of the grand highway of the nations; she stands midway between the Old World and the New, and both shall pay her tribute . . . Half the world stands ready to lay its contributions at her feet! Has any other State so brilliant a future? Has any other city a future like San Francisco?

This straggling town shall be a vast metropolis; this sparsely populated land shall become a crowded hive of busy men; your waste places shall blossom like the rose, and your deserted hills and valleys shall yield bread and wine for unnumbered thousands; railroads shall be spread hither and thither and carry the invigorating blood of commerce to regions that are languishing now; mills and workshops, yea, and factories shall spring up everywhere, and mines that have neither name nor place to-day shall dazzle the world with their affluence. The time is drawing on apace when the clouds shall pass away from your firmament, and a splendid prosperity shall descend like a glory upon the whole land!

I am bidding the old city and my old friends a kind, but not a sad farewell, for I know that when I see this home again, the changes that will have been wrought upon it will suggest no sentiment of sadness; its estate will be brighter, happier and prouder a hundred fold than it is this day. This is its destiny, and in all sincerity I can say, So mote it be!

MARK TWAIN, *taking leave of California,*
never to return

1906

I was an eager, thirsty, hungry little kid—and one day, at the library, I drew out a volume on Pizarro of Peru . . . you praised me for reading books of that nature. Proud! If you only knew how proud your words made me . . . You were a goddess to me.   JACK LONDON,
to poet, editor and Oakland city librarian Ina Coolbrith

1939

We went down in the afternoon and that evening saw *Grapes* at Twentieth-Century. Zanuck has more than kept his word. He has a hard, straight picture in which the actors are submerged so completely that it looks and feels like a documentary film and certainly it has a hard, truthful ring. No punches were pulled—in fact, with descriptive matter removed, it is a harsher thing than the book, by far. It seems unbelievable but it is true. The next afternoon we went to see *Mice* and it is a beautiful job. Here Milestone has done a curious lyrical thing. It hangs together and is underplayed. You will like it. It opens the 22nd of December in Hollywood. As for *Grapes*, it opens sometime in January. There is so much hell being raised in this state that Zanuck will not release it simultaneously. He'll open in N.Y. and move gradually west, letting the publicity precede it. He even, to find out, issued a statement that it would never be shown in California and got a ton of mail, literally, in protest the next day. He has hired attorneys to fight any local censorship and is trying to get Thomas Benton for the posters. All this is far beyond our hopes . . .

I can't tell you what all this means to me, in happiness and energy. I was washed up and now I'm alive again, with work to be done and worth doing.

JOHN STEINBECK, *to his agent*

1940
. . . I am still in bed—this time the result of 25 years of cigarettes. You have got two beautiful bad examples of parents. Just do everything we didn't do and you will be perfectly safe. But be sweet to your mother . . . the insane are always mere guests on earth, total strangers carrying around broken decalogues that they cannot read.   **F. SCOTT FITZGERALD**, *to his daughter*

1957
I am fifty-two years old, and I have three children who shall soon require expensive education. I have perhaps ten years of peak work capacity remaining to me. During these ten years, in addition to educating the children, I must somehow accumulate enough reserve capital to provide for Cleo and me in old age. Otherwise I shall become a public charge . . .

In order to keep this madhouse going, I awaken each morning between 3 and 5 a.m., although rarely as late as five. I work steadily until about one. Then I take a half-hour nap. Work steadily until 7 or 7:30 p.m. After that I take three stiff belts of whiskey to uncoil on, eat dinner, and go to bed. This schedule is absolutely unfailing, Saturdays and Sundays included. I was never a social person, but I am much less so now than formerly. I dread going out because it means drinking and lowered vitality for tomorrow. We do, however, go out perhaps once a month. Certain people are angry with me for turning down simple dinner invitations on the plea of work. It is getting to be assumed that either I am (a) getting snobbish, or (b) crazed for money. I cannot help these impressions, and I don't give a damn about them. I am doing not what is pleasing to me to do, but what I must and am determined to do.   **DALTON TRUMBO**, *to a fellow blacklistee*

DECEMBER 16

1969

Dear Brothers and Sisters . . .

We moved onto Alcatraz Island because we feel that Indian people need a Cultural Center of their own. For several decades, Indian people have not had enough control of training their young people. And without a cultural center of their own, we are afraid that the old Indian ways may be lost. We believe that the only way to keep them alive is for Indian people to do it themselves.

While it was a small group which moved onto the island, we want all Indian people to join with us. More Indian people from throughout the country are coming to the island every day. We are issuing this call in an attempt to unify all our Indian Brothers behind a common cause.

We realize that there are more problems in Indian communities besides having our culture taken away. We have water problems, land problems, "social" problems, job opportunity problems, and many others.

And as Vice President Agnew said at the annual convention of the National Congress of American Indians in October of this year, now is the time for Indian leadership . . .

We hope to reinforce the traditional Indian way of life by building a Cultural Center on Alcatraz Island. We hope to build a college, a religious and spiritual center, a museum, a center of ecology, and a training school . . .

We have made no attempts at starting a hard and fast formal organization. We have elected spokesmen because someone has had to be a spokesman. We feel that all Indian people should be present or represented at the outset of a formal national Indian organization . . .

We hope to see you on December 23rd.   **INDIANS OF ALL TRIBES**

1985

Finnila's Steam Baths on Upper Market in the Castro is closing forever on December 31. Such a San Francisco landmark. I went today for my last steam bath and massage (an hour massage is $14) and there was an even more re-markable cast of characters in the women's public steam than I'd seen ever before. Besides the usual Russian women soaping their enormous breasts, there were two small Japanese women slathered in cucumber and a manic woman with one arm carrying on a fantastic monologue about married men.

LOUISE STEINMAN

DECEMBER 17

1927

. . . today on the beach a mile below here, at Venice, I found myself talking literature, Spengler, Kant, Descartes and Aquinas. He turned out to be one of the best scholars I've ever met . . .   **HART CRANE**, *to a friend*

1930

Your article is excellent. You are a graceful, witty and intelligent writer.

editor **WELFORD BEATON**, *to James Dalton Trumbo,*
his first acceptance

1940

Not dead. Nor down with flu–– as is half Los Angeles. But merely entangled in that unprofitable thing known as the show business–– going out to Holly-wood or Beverly Hills or Hollywood every morning and not getting back to the hotel until 12 or 1 or 2 o'clock at night–– since those remote districts are from where I live just about like going from Harlem to Philadelphia–– and in this charming democracy of ours there seems to be no place for Negroes to live in Hollywood even if they do work out there occasionally . . .

I do not enjoy this collective way of writing very much as I feel that when too many people are involved in the preparation of scripts, the material loses whatever individual flavor and distinction it might otherwise possess. That is probably what was the matter with ZERO HOUR. After everybody got their paragraph in, it was simply a depersonalized un-human editorial, well-meant but with none of the blood of life or the passion of mankind in it. I do not think plays, or even skits can be written by eight or ten people with various ways of feeling and looking at things.

LANGSTON HUGHES, *to his agent*

1950

... why Joan and I didn't live Happily Ever After; Very simple, we were given no chance.

You see, as I drank the last Blood-Brother beer—I remember deciding in all seriousness that it was definitely the last one—2 plainclothesmen approached, asked if I was Neal C and promptly hauled me away . . . to be held in jail charged with suspicion of Burglary! Of my poolhall hangout yet. Because the charge had a superficial plausibility, since I racked balls there a couple of times and knew the layout—I knew a lot of fearful moments before Capt. of Dicks admitted he knew I was clear all along, and released me finally weeks later.

Joan had disappeared completely!

NEAL CASSADY, *in the infamous "Joan letter"*
to Jack Kerouac that helped inspire On the Road

DECEMBER 18

1858

And you, imbecile Californians! You are responsible for the lamentable acts we are witnessing. We are tired of saying: 'Open your eyes, now is the time to assert your rights and interests.' It is shameful, but necessary to admit that you are the sarcasm of humanity. When the time comes to vote, the first of your rights, you go about the streets in the carriages of [Democratic] candidates, and you will not cast your votes unless you are paid for them . . . You are cowardly and stupid, inspiring nothing but disdain . . . You might as well renounce once and for any and all noble sentiments and prepare to cast upon yourselves the yoke of slavery.   FRANCISCO P. RAMÍREZ

1953

Kenneth Anger said to me, "You are a magical person." He was to capture in his film that luminosity that made my entrance into the party so startling . . . the common error of the contemporary artist was made: the chaotic material of the unconscious was reproduced without its pattern of meaning, like the worlds before birth, unformed, shedding no light on our true nightmares.   **ANAÏS NIN**

DECEMBER 19

1926

MILLIONS ARE TO BE GRABBED OUT HERE AND YOUR ONLY COM-
PETITION IS IDIOTS STOP DON'T LET THIS GET AROUND

screenwriter **HERMAN MANKIEWICZ**, *in his mythic,*

please-not-apocryphal telegram to Ben Hecht

1939

They're quarreling (out here in the movie world) as to which of 84 directors are entitled to the honor of filming that world's masterpiece—*Gone With the Wind*. T.S. Stribling's Trilogy—the source of most of it [—] is never mentioned.   **THEODORE DREISER**, *to H. L. Mencken*

1941

BERKELEY

All kinds of rumors and I am worried. There is no way to have a normal life, and I can't be a student anymore. But I don't want to leave the campus. Talked to Shibs and he says there will be a report on the Nisei on campus and that we should all write up everything that happens. I don't think I would be very good at it; but I might give it a trial. All the so-called intellectuals like Shibs, Kenny, and Jimmy Sakoda say that we should document everything. They are so cold and impersonal, and I don't know what good that will do if any violence starts.

There have been houses stoned in Placer County, and some of the newspapers are raising hell and making all kinds of wild statements about even the Nisei. Kenny showed me a lot of clippings, and it is very dangerous. Yet, I feel that we are so helpless. Who in the hell is going to worry about the Nisei when we are at war? Maybe the thing to do is to get into the Army. Wang says they will need the Nisei for interpreters. That's one thing I won't qualify for. I think that the Nisei should forget all things Japanese and not attract that kind of attention to ourselves. We must wave the old flag like the very first patriot. I think the Nisei are loyal, but we may be too short for the

Army, and I refuse to be a messboy. There is a lot of hysteria going on. Went to Vallejo and the family does not know what to do . . .

Mariko is talking of going East as the hysteria against Japs gets stronger. She says that the Japs are going to invade California; and she is convinced of it, and she says she is going to get a Chinese card too. She asked me to get a few more from Jimmy Hong for the family. I don't think things are that bad.

CHARLES KIKUCHI

1948

There are so many books and plays and stories I have to read—Here are just a few . . .

Diary of a Writer—Dostoyevsky
Against the Grain—Huysmans
The Disciple—Paul Bourget
Sanin—Mikhail Artsybashev
Johnny Got His Gun—Dalton Trumbo . . .   SUSAN SONTAG

1968

We have encountered, in our declining years, the rise of the director to a position from which I think it will be impossible to topple him. His ascendancy has been accompanied by the simultaneous arrival of a new school of young critics who have no idea of how movies are made and rely almost exclusively upon the French auteurist school to tell them. The prospect is so depressing that I, who have never leched to direct, am going to take over *Johnny Got His Gun,* not merely to assure that my contribution as its writer must then be recognized, but to make certain that if it is fucked up by muddle-headed direction, I, for a change, shall be in charge of the fucking.

DALTON TRUMBO

DECEMBER 20

1913

FLAGSTAFF NO GOOD FOR OUR PURPOSE. HAVE PROCEEDED TO CALIFORNIA. WANT AUTHORITY TO RENT BARN IN A PLACE CALLED HOLLYWOOD FOR $75 A MONTH. REGARDS TO SAM.

CECIL B. DEMILLE,
to Jesse Lasky and Samuel Goldwyn in New York

1969

Dear Melvin, This is the Zodiac speaking. I wish you a happy Christmass. The one thing I ask of you is this, please help me. I cannot reach out for help because of this thing in me wont let me. I am finding it extreamly dificult to hold it in check I am afraid I will loose control again and take my nineth & posible tenth victom. Please help me I am drownding. At the moment the children are safe from the bomb because it is so massive to dig in & the triger mech requires much work to get it adjusted just right. But if I hold back too long from no nine I will loose all controol of my self & set the bomb up. Please help me I can not remain in control for much longer.

ZODIAC, to district attorney Melvin Belli

2004

I come swinging in from Phoenix, riding shotgun on the bus with 'Lish for the last two hours of a 15,750-mile journey. We float down the l-10, cross over to the 134, past the sign for Occidental College (Terry Gilliam's alma mater), coming on home from Pasadena. It all begins to feel familiar. Odd that this should now feel like home, but it does.

It is a wonderful sight to see my tour bus outside my own front gate at last.

Tania and Wee (our Thai wonder woman) come to the door bleary-eyed. The Greedy Bastard is home.

ERIC IDLE

DECEMBER 21

1864

And now comes the curse of God on the land—two years no rain falls, and famine with her grim reality compels the surrender of lands rendered tenantless of hoofs & horns already. The old spell is broken & Southern California will now be regenerated. The few stout hopeful hearts who have found courage to stand out for years hoping for a change will be rewarded. The great and splendid Estates will be broken up into small farms & thrifty industrious farmers and associations of them will take the place of the brigands who have made Santa Barbara, Los Angeles and San Bernardino Counties infamous.

scientist BENJAMIN SILLIMAN

1976

Dinner at Christopher Isherwood's with Gore Vidal and Tony Richardson. Asked by me to name the twentieth-century figures whose letters and/or journals he would be most excited to read, Christopher says E.M. Forster (many of whose letters he received); and later adds, to my delight, that if there were anything unpublished by Cocteau, that would come a close second . . .

I congratulate Christopher, whose new book I've seen reviewed but have not yet read (although it's on order at the Brentwood Bookshop), on contributing to the literature of testimony—i.e. eye-witness accounts of significant events which I suspect will prove to be the most lasting of our time . . .

KENNETH TYNAN

2016

MR. TIMOTHY SLOAN CEO

WELLS FARGO

420 MONTGOMERY STREET

SAN FRANCISCO, CA 94104

Dear Mr. Sloan,

As a customer of your bank, I reject the notion of my money helping to support your investment in the Dakota Access Pipeline (DAPL), an inherently dangerous and unjust oil pipeline that threatens air and water quality in many states and violates sacred lands of the Standing Rock Sioux Tribe . . .

I ask that Wells Fargo withdraw its financial support of DAPL until a full scale environmental Impact Statement is completed and the outstanding issues with Standing Rock Sioux Tribe are resolved to the Tribe's full satisfaction. Until then, I am withdrawing my money from your bank.

Sincerely   *actress, activist, memoirist* **JANE FONDA**

DECEMBER 22

1939

. . . There are not many real Spaniards here, but large numbers of Mexicans. I have one Spaniard in my seminar—his father is a wine merchant, and Franco stole 1,000,000 bottles of sherry from him, so he has correct sentiments on Spain . . .

I have a great deal of work here, most of it too elementary to be interesting. [His wife] Peter has so much to do that she is worn out—arranging for John and Kate, driving the car (everything here is 20 miles off), and spending hours a day on our permits to stay in this country, to get which we have to go to Mexico. The red tape has driven us both to the edge of insanity.

They assure us that it will rain soon—hitherto we have had endless sunny days—2 days ago the temperature was 84. One gets to long for wet and cold . . .

Conrad is the joy of our lives—partly by his merits, partly because he doesn't know there is a war. He is very intelligent—he knows endless poems and stories by heart, and has a vast vocabulary. We love him and he loves the cat and the cat loves her dinner. Love is not the reward of services rendered . . .   *philosopher* **BERTRAND RUSSELL**, *to a friend*

1942

[To Pascal Covici, Viking Press]
414 SHRADER STREET, SAN FRANCISCO
Dear Pasquale
I am very grateful for your interest and for your trouble with the New York [Office of Wartime Information] people. You will find, I'm afraid, that very little can be done in my case. The OWI is a big-scale Federal Writer's Project, honey-combed with the same type of bureaucrats who have been wallowing in the public trough since the Republic first got up steam and started on its spooky and misty voyage in 1776.

This is hardly a complaint. I was simply naive. I did want to help. I felt I had something to give my country. I was angry about Nazis and Fascists and Japs. The year before I made a lot of money—about thirteen thousand dollars. I could have gone back to Hollywood and made more. But no—the cold fire of hatred burned against the enemy and I wanted do what I could until they drafted me. And so I came to San Francisco and asked for work. The OWI gave me a blank to fill out; what have you done? What have you written?

I put it all down. Books, short stories, radio work. They studied this (or they didn't, I don't know which) and quickly put me to work at a type of writing I had never done. I asked for a chance to do feature work. They were very sympathetic. They would try to find a place for me. They are still trying. They can't imagine where I would fit in the feature department. They feel that, having had no experience in radio newswriting, I am better qualified to be a newswriter.

This is hardly logical. But it is policy. Now I have been here these months and I have done a good job. I am told I am the best newscast writer in the organization. This is no achievement. Any ass can do it. But there are more asses who can't.   JOHN FANTE

1949

Christopher Isherwood wrote me a superb letter about *Sunset [Boulevard]*, with which I plan to combat Billy's childlike resistance to retaking the questioning scene. Christopher points out, in highly literate English, why it's wrong—that the detectives seem to have read the end of the script.

CHARLES BRACKETT

DECEMBER 23

1849

The world's age never knew such an era as this. No sagacity could have predicted it; no human intellect can foretell its result. It is difficult to say which predominates here: mud, men or gold.

forty-niner WILLIAM SMITH JEWETT

1994

Marsha's party. As promised, there are uninteresting people. Familiar types. Jog-bike-hot-tub-massage-eat-meditate-fuck-flyaround-the-world-California-people. Big house and not a book anywhere. Some guys in a corner played video games. I got a beer and joined them intending to kibitz, but there was no conversation. They made little grunts when the video motorcycle went off the road or smashed into something. I made grunts, too, but didn't feel accepted by the group. Couldn't grunt right. After about twenty minutes, I asked if I could try the game. The guy at the controls gave them to me and left the room. The others followed him. I pretended to be absorbed, like a Jog-bike-hot-tub-kind-of-guy, though nobody watched me.

novelist LEONARD MICHAELS

2021

Everything Didion wrote was an elegy. Years ago, I wrote yet another piece about her—a review of *Where I Was From*, I think, her homesick poison-pen letter to California. A few days later, a card comes in the mail. All I remember of it now is her saying, now that she'd had a good review in the *San Francisco Chronicle*, her family would finally know she'd really made it.

I put the card in a safe place and, of course, lost it. But, as Didion might've asked, is any place really safe?

Editor on Joan Didion's death,
to Dorany Pineda

DECEMBER 24

1926

FAIRMONT HOTEL

SAN FRANCISCO

CHRISTMAS EVE

Darling,

Here I am in California at last! . . . San Francisco is really divine. We motored out to Burlingame to lunch, everything green and fresh and roses out! The streets are steep like Edinburgh and Chinatown right in the middle of everything. There's a Rock just outside the town by the Golden Gate covered with seals! They're so sweet. I sail at four o'clock this afternoon. It's now 9:00 a.m. which means about 5 p.m. in England if you've had your Christmas dinner I expect you're all lying about stuffed . . .

Be a good Snig and don't have too many nightmares about shipwrecks, this is not the Typhoon season! Hugs and kisses, Snoop

playwright **NOËL COWARD**

1932

Ibañez [author of *The Four Horsemen of the Apocalypse*] arrived in Los Angeles. We became his host. Of course he would wish to visit the studios? Not at all, but the Missions, ah, yes, the Missions! But whom in this Land of Celebrities did he wish to meet? Only two persons—"Carlos" (Charlie Chaplin) and Upton Sinclair! It is the same with all distinguished authors. Sometimes they may omit the name Chaplin, but never Sinclair.

Script editor, publisher **ROB WAGNER**

DECEMBER 25

1857

What the d—l am I to do with myself!—the simplest pleasures fail to please me.   BRET HARTE

1871

Book-making frightens me because it demands so much artificialness and retrograding. . . . Moreover, I find that though I have a few thoughts entangled in the fibers of my mind, I possess no words into which I can shape them. . . . These mountain fires that glow in one's blood are free to all, but I cannot find the chemistry that may press them unimpaired into booksellers' bricks. True, I can proclaim that moonshine is glorious, and sunshine more glorious, that winds rage, and waters roar. . . . This is about the limit of what I feel capable of doing for the public. But for my few friends I can do more because they already know the mountain harmonies and can catch the tones I gather for them, though written in a few harsh and gravelly sentences.

JOHN MUIR

1884

. . . the people say there are "very few flowers just now" & then they proceed to idly snip off for you, your two hands full!—Los Angeles is just as rubbishy, barbaric, huddled, gay colored, as ever—the most un-American place in America . . .   HELEN HUNT JACKSON, *to Charles Dudley Warner*

1941

A special edition of the Japanese-language newspaper came out saying Issei (first-generation Japanese) will turn in all shortwave radios and cameras to the police by 11:00 p.m., Monday. It was in last night's English newspaper. The one at our house is a radio with both shortwave and normal listening, so we called the radio shop and had the shortwave portion removed . . .

Sewing instructor Mrs. M dropped by. She said, "For twelve years, I sewed only American things, but in the end, Americans are Americans, and we are Japanese. Since the war started, Americans ask me if everything is okay, but not one said Merry Christmas to me."   AOKI HISA

1969

You may have wondered how I found time to write so many reviews back in October and November. Simple: I never attended classes or did my homework.   *rock critic* LESTER BANGS, *to Greil Marcus*

DECEMBER 26

1932

CARMEL

On my way up here I saw a coyote on the Malibu estate, a group of beautiful egrets at Point Mugu, and an owl of some kind. I was just waking from a pleasant sleep in a haystack near Salinas when I saw the owl, perched like a carved block of wood, atop a derrick. The morning sun poked through a cloud and a level beam shone in the old bird's eyes. He turned his head around and about, then flew soundlessly off. The next moment, when I was contemplating the Pacific, the farmer drove up in a truck, to pitch away my haystack. He was quite good natured about finding me.   **EVERETT RUESS**

1936

But come what may—we'll find a way through this thing—for we are the American people.   **ROBERT HARDIE**,
Weedpatch migrant labor camp manager

1937

Don't think that I am a "convert" or 'revolutionist." I am not a CP member. I have worked fairly closely with them locally because they seemed to be the only people doing any work . . . I have never joined the Party because I have known that I could not work satisfactorily within its requirements . . .

CAREY MCWILLIAMS, *to Louis Adamic*

DECEMBER 27

1863

There is an enormous preponderance of males in the population—in some counties there are, on the average, eight men to one woman! Even in this city there are 20,000 more men than women. As a consequence, the natural increase of the population is far less than in a population normally constituted. The women, what there are of them, are prolific and fruitful to a satisfactory degree— there is no complaint on that score—it is their lack of numbers from which the population suffers . . .

This is not only the great seaport of the state, but of the western coast of America—there is not another good harbor between Cape Horn and the

Bering Straits, and this is not only a good one, but one of the very finest in the world—so this place must ever be of necessity the commercial metropolis of the Pacific—the New York of an immense region, not only of this state, but the center of commerce for the whole coast—all parts must pay tribute to it. Capitalists seeing this, invest their money here. They make it elsewhere in the state, perhaps—in mines or trade—but invest it here. Huge buildings have gone up this year, built with money made in Washoe, but invested here . . .

The city abounds in fine mansions, substantial buildings, palatial hotels, and all the accompaniments of a large city—the only thing strange is that it has grown in fifteen years.

It is the best-governed city in the United States—there is less rowdyism than in any other city I know of in America. This will surprise you . . . it is not perfect, but compared with New York City it is as far ahead of that, as that is ahead of the Fiji Islands . . .   **WILLIAM H. BREWER**

1998

. . . for the first time since he was diagnosed, Frankie was acutely, excitedly and happily aware of Christmas. Like any normal child, he chatted incessantly about Santa, Rudolph, the Grinch and other seasonal characters. He sang carols and other holiday songs and eagerly helped decorate our Christmas tree . . .

The very next morning, in predawn darkness, Uncle Joe called to tell me Aunt Hope had suffered a diabetic seizure and cardiac arrest during the night . . .

. . . Frankie was the biggest surprise . . . He was curious, as any small child is when first facing the reality of death. He was full of questions, like where heaven is and whether Aunt Hope would ever return from living there with Jesus. But he was also caring.

. . . even amid the sadness of family tragedy, I became more confident than ever that Frankie will continue to overcome his autism. Not just because he has family, therapists, teachers and classmates who support him, but because he has a special new angel watching over him—an angel named, so very aptly, Hope.   *newspaperman* **FRANK DEL OLMO**

DECEMBER 28

1847

Denton with his cane kept knocking pieces off the large rocks used as fire-irons on which to place the wood. Something bright attracted his attention, and picking up pieces of the rock he examined them closely; then turning to my mother he said: Mrs. Reed, this is gold. My mother replied that she wished it were bread. Denton knocked more chips from the rocks, and he hunted in the ashes for the shining particles until he had gathered about a teaspoonful. This he tied in a small piece of buckskin and placed in his pocket saying, "If we ever get away from here I am coming back for more."

VIRGINIA REED,
remembering the find of John Denton, who never made it out

1930

The audience now is unlimited and eclectic. Radio brings to us one moment the swooning harmonies of Cesar Franck, and the next moment the frisky vulgarities of true jazz. Radio knows no boundary lines of taste. All music is "good music" in radio. . . .

Thus the function of the broadcaster is to be completely and unreservedly open and ready for every musical expression—from the austerities of modal counterpoint to the whinings of boop-boop-a-doop. The broadcaster must regard each as equally important, because, sociologically and philosophically, they *are* equally important.

broadcaster, Hollywood Bowl programmer **JOSÉ RODRÍGUEZ**

1941

Dear Jim,
. . San Francisco is in a state of psychological siege; contrary to opinion in NY, the West Coast, with the exception, for some reason, of Seattle, has always dreaded a Japanese war, and, behind its blustering chauvinism and race prejudice, has a very healthy respect for the Japanese navy. In the last weeks the city has prepared itself for a large scale air raid . . .

A few pursuit planes loaded with incendiaries will finish SF. A large section of the public still thinks it isn't going to happen, but I know of no responsible person who doesn't expect it to happen pretty quick . . .

People seem to take an invasion attempt for granted, and expect our yellow brothers to wage a war of literal extermination against California. I sometimes wonder if this isn't guilt. The prejudice against orientals in California has always sickened me. Maybe the constituents of Senator Johnson realize they are being called to a terrible accounting for the Oriental Exclusion Act . . .   **KENNETH REXROTH**, *to James Laughlin*

2011
Met Kay at an erotic poetry open reading (her idea). There were around thirty people there, and about half of them read something. Kay read a piece she had written about some of her past relationship experiences. I read one of Rexroth's more erotic love poems and a couple of his translations from Petronius . . .   *author, Rexroth archivist, serial personal-ad answerer* **KEN KNABB**

DECEMBER 29
1941
During the morning hours, it rained on and off, and even the clear part of the sky was fairly dark. Husband went to clear up the school association office. Our house radio was inspected by the police and passed; the camera was put in police storage . . . Today I had a reason to visit Mr K.'s home, but in the streetcar and on the street, I was subjected to continuous unfriendly looks.   **AOKI HISA**

1946
BERKELEY

My address is 2918 Wheeler, as before . . . The day before Christmas I began work at Creed's Book Store near the campus on Telegraph Ave.—a crowded dusty place stacked ceiling high with all manner of stuff, good, bad, and atrocious, and finished out the week. My work has been mostly alphabetizing the various sections which have been in huge disorder. I hope eventually to get in some binding and pick up that aspect of bookmaking while I have to stay in the city. I am going to try at the University of California Press, as I'd rather work there than any place else I know of.

                                                          WILLIAM EVERSON

1973
To: Ansel Adams
. . . one reason why I don't respond to your portraits as much as to your big magnificent natural scenes is that I don't respond to any photographic portraits much. That goes for Karsh, certainly, and now I find it goes for Strand, good as he is. I guess I want a more distorting medium for portraits. Most of us need to be distorted before we become interesting. Nature doesn't.

God bless, take care, read good books, practice charity. We'll all need it in 1974. I am about to start trying to put a new novel on the page beginning after New Year, and I am all quivers and quakes. It's like starting out to swim across Lake Superior in winter.

Buss your lovely blue-eyed bride for us. Some angel blood got into her veins, probably by sinister means. Yours, Wally   **WALLACE STEGNER**

1986

I requested two songs from KROQ tonight: "Changes" by Bowie, "Ever Fallen in Love" by the Fine Young Cannibals. The first because I haven't heard it in a while, and the second because they'll probably play it anyway. I'm still waiting . . .   **CAROLYN KELLOGG**

DECEMBER 30

1938

Signs of decay multiply. One eye is now useless. My teeth are growing thinner and hearing is impaired, and my feet are so tender that walking is a painful "process of falling," as Dr. Holmes called it. But [what] can a man of seventy-eight expect but growing disability? The worst of it is I have no one to help me now, no one to share the daily burden of maintaining this house and garden. My daughters have leaned so long on Daddy that they regard me as an everlasting prop. I have tried to arrange matters so that they can carry on if I meet with an accident, but it is very hard to bring myself to it. Sorting papers and the use of my eyes in reading letters is now a wearisome business, and I do not feel able to have it done. Looking ahead is dismal business now . . .   **HAMLIN GARLAND**

1940

TO MAXIM LIEBER

HOLLOW HILLS FARM,

MONTEREY, CALIFORNIA,

Dear Maxim,

. . . How did MEET THE PEOPLE fare at the hands of the Broadway critics? If it flops I see no cullud show in Hollywood . . . no more show business for me—only literature . . .

Sincerely,   **LANGSTON HUGHES**

1941

This job here at the studio is not the end of things for me. It is a means.

ZORA NEALE HURSTON

1950

. . . You have got to realize that I am too old to be impressed by my own name in print. I *must* make at least an appreciable portion of my income as a writer, or stop writing. If I am to go on writing I must get out of the city. I can no longer work here at all. Also, the flat is not suitable for the baby—and of course within a year San Francisco will be obliterated . . .

KENNETH REXROTH,

who would stay in San Francisco for another 18 years

DECEMBER 31

1846

Thursday 31th last of the year may we with Gods help spend the Comeing year better than the past which we purpose to do if Almighty God will deliver us from our present dredful situation which is our prayer if the will of God sees it fitting for us Amen morning fair now Cloudy wind E by S for three days past freezing hard every night looks like another snow storm snow storms are dredful to us, snow very deep Crust on the snow

PATRICK BREEN

1846

The mountains at a distance covered with snow, the grass and wild oats springing up most luxuriently, and in a short time we will have fine pasturage . . .

I visited the place where we passed three very anxious days, every thing just as we left it, except poor Sergt Coxs grave the wolves had scratched down to the body, and eaten off part of his feet. The Californians I do not think had had any hand in it. We received report today that the Mexicans & a party of Indians had attacked the Indians about Warner's Ranch and killed some thirty of them. These Indians are our friends, and have most certainly been encouraged to take up arms in our favour and I should think ought to be supported . . .

JOHN S. GRIFFIN, MD

1962

6233 MULHOLLAND,

L.A. 28, CAL.

. . . tomorrow we start a new year. Will the few scores of people who decide the world's immediate fate permit it to be a tolerably good year? And will the impersonal forces which determine our long-range destiny permit themselves to be controlled for man's benefit—and shall we even attempt to control them? It remains to be seen.   **ALDOUS HUXLEY**

1975

I strolled downtown Powell Street, looking at the old calendar leaves strewn about in what is said to be a custom observed nowhere else.   **HERB CAEN**

1975

[It is] doubtless easier to feel that God is the only refuge when you don't have any human being to love and be loved by. But I do . . .

CHRISTOPHER ISHERWOOD

1983

Throwing the entire calendar out the window is considered bad form, and somebody could get hoit.   **HERB CAEN**, *again*

2004

The craziness is receding but no clarity is taking its place.

I look for resolution and find none . . .

I realized today for the first time that my memory of this day a year ago is a memory that does not involve John. This day a year ago was December 31, 2003. John did not see this day a year ago . . .

I think about swimming with him into the cave at Portuguese Bend, about the swell of clear water, the way it changed, the swiftness and power it gained as it narrowed through the rocks at the base of the point. The tide had to be just right . . .   *writer* **JOAN DIDION**

AFTER THE END

Three days after a person has been buried the soul comes up out of the grave in the evening. Between the third and fifth day it wanders about the world visiting the places it used to frequent in life. On the fifth day after death the soul returns to the grave to oversee the destruction of its property before leaving for Similaqsa, the Land of the Dead. The soul goes first to Point Conception, which is a wild and stormy place . . .

There are many poppies growing there in the ravine and the soul quickly picks two of these and inserts them in each eyesocket and so is able to see again immediately. When the soul finally gets to Similaqsa it is given eyes made of blue abalone. After leaving the ravine the soul comes to La Tonadora, the woman who stings with her tail. She kills any living person who comes by, but merely annoys the soul who passes safely.

Just beyond this woman lies a body of water that separates this world from the next, with a bridge that the soul must cross to reach Similaqsa. The souls of murderers and poisoners and other evil people never reach the bridge, but are turned to stone from the neck down. They remain there on the near shore forever, moving their eyes and watching other souls pass . . . Once the soul has crossed the bridge it is safe in Similaqsa . . .

Souls live in Similaqsa forever and never get old. It is packed full of souls. They harvest islay, sweet islay, and there is no end of it . . .

THE SOUL'S JOURNEY TO SIMILAQSA (CHUMASH)

CONTRIBUTORS

ABBEY, EDWARD Author of *The Monkey Wrench Gang* and *Desert Solitaire*, teller of truths, scalawag of heroic proportions. Quoted from *Confessions of a Barbarian: Selections from the Journals of Edward Abbey*, edited by David Petersen (Boulder: Johnson Books, 2003).

ABBEY, HARVEY Lassen Peak park ranger.

ACOSTA, OSCAR "ZETA" Chicano lawyer, activist, memoirist, novelist. Author of *Autobiography of a Brown Buffalo* and the un-squashable *Revolt of the Cockroach People*. Inspiration for the Samoan lawyer, Dr. Gonzo, in Hunter S. Thompson's *Fear and Loathing in Las Vegas*. Also immortalized in Thompson's *Rolling Stone* article about the Chicano movement, "Strange Rumblings in Aztlan." Like Ambrose Bierce before him, disappeared in Mexico. Quoted from *Oscar "Zeta" Acosta: The Uncollected Works*, edited by Ilan Stavans (Houston: Arte Público, 1996).

ADAMIC, LOUIS Pioneering immigrant author of, among others, *Dynamite: The Story of Class Violence in America* and *The Truth about Los Angeles*. Lived for a time in a pilothouse at the mouth of San Pedro Bay. Quoted from *Laughing in the Jungle: The Autobiography of an Immigrant in America* (New York: Harper & Brothers, 1932).

ADORNO, THEODOR Refugee philosopher. Wrote *The Psychological Technique of* [L.A.-based preacher] *Martin Luther Thomas' Radio Addresses,* and most of *Minima Moralia,* while exiled on the Westside. Quoted from *Letters to His Parents: 1939–1951* (Malden, Mass.: Polity Press, 2006).

AGEE, JAMES Film and book critic, author of *A Death in the Family* and *Let Us Now Praise Famous Men*. Screenwriter of *The African Queen* and *The Night of the Hunter*. Visited Los Angeles periodically in the forties and fifties to interview filmmakers for *Time* magazine and work on screenplays, both produced and un-. These included one for Chaplin about the Little Tramp after a nuclear apocalypse, and *African Queen* for John Huston, whose demands for both revisions and tennis games helped give Agee a heart attack. Quoted from *Letters of James Agee to Father Flye* (New York: Melville House, 2014).

ALPERSTEIN, ELLEN   Los Angeles journalist, blogger, and longtime contributor to laobserved.com, where this entry first appeared. By gracious permission of the author.

ANDERSON, SHERWOOD   Short-story writer, ex-businessman. Major influence on Faulkner, Edmund Wilson, and many others, best known for the connected stories in *Winesburg, Ohio*. A successful copywriter and business owner until he walked out of his office one day, never to return. Whether decision or nervous breakdown, it worked out. Quoted from *The Sherwood Anderson Diaries, 1936–1941* (Athens: University of Georgia Press, 1987).

APTED, MICHAEL   Civilized, versatile British director for almost five decades. Documentarian behind the incomparable *Up* series. Also reeled off *Coal Miner's Daughter, Continental Divide,* and *Gorky Park* in just three years—arguably as good a run as anybody since Peter Bogdanovich made *Targets, The Last Picture Show, What's Up, Doc,* and *Paper Moon.* Quoted from *Inside Stories: Diaries of British Film-makers at Work* (London: British Film Institute, 1996).

ARMSTRONG, HEATHER B.   Blogger known as Dooce, one of the first to make a living at it. Posts from dooce.com appear here by gracious permission of the author.

ARMSTRONG, LOUIS   Pioneering jazz trumpeter, vocalist, American, giant. Quoted from *Pops: A Life of Louis Armstrong* (New York: Houghton Mifflin Harcourt, 2009).

ASBURY, AMY   Memoirist, published in *The Sunset Strip Diaries* (Los Angeles: Estep & Fitzgerald Literary Publishing, 2011).

AYRES, WILLIAM ORVILLE   San Francisco pioneer, honorable abstainer from the Vigilance Committee.

BABITZ, EVE   The Colette of L.A. Novelist, essayist, feuilletonist. In a blithe, forgotten, somehow never-anthologized introduction to a Chronicle Books anthology called *Los Angeles Stories*, she wrote, "Whenever I was at the Stravinskys' home when I was growing up, there were always these wonderful Europeans thrilled to be in a place with no war and flowers, silken nights filled with night-blooming jasmine. . . . Not people like Nathanael West who . . . took one look at L.A. and decided that the city was a metaphor for apocalyptic chaos. People who had really been in apocalyptic chaos took one look at L.A. and decided that they wanted to go on a picnic." Quoted from *Eve's Hollywood* (New York: New York Review Books, 2015).

BAILEY, MARY STUART   Pioneer, journal-keeper.

BAKER, ISAAC W.   San Francisco pioneer. Quoted from *A Year of Mud and Gold: San Francisco in Letters and Diaries, 1849–1850* (Lincoln: University of Nebraska Press, 1999).

BANDINI, DON JUAN BAUTISTA   Long-lived diarist, descendant of Californios. As with Don Pío Pico, the world he was born into bore little resemblance to the one he departed. Quoted from the diary of Juan Bautista Bandini, Huntington Library, San Marino, Calif.

BANGS, LESTER Escondido-born, El Cajon–bred, revelatory rock critic for *Rolling Stone* and *Creem*, memorably played by Philip Seymour Hoffman in *Almost Famous*. Quoted from *Let it Blurt: The Life and Times of Lester Bangs, America's Greatest Rock Critic* (New York: Broadway Books, 2000).

BEATON, CECIL British designer, fashion photographer, *and* war photographer. A three-time Oscar winner—twice for costume design and once for the art direction of *My Fair Lady*. Also a rare winner of the coveted IBDOT: the Oscar, the Tony, and the International Best Dressed list. Quoted from *The Wandering Years: 1922–39 (Cecil Beaton's Diaries #1)* (London: Sapere Books, 2018) and *The Parting Years: 1963–74 (Cecil Beaton's Diaries #6)* (London: Sapere Books, 2018).

BEATON, WELFORD Editor of the *Hollywood Spectator*. Rescued Dalton Trumbo from the slush pile and a truly miserable bread factory job. Quoted from *Dalton Trumbo: Blacklisted Hollywood Radical* (Lexington: University Press of Kentucky, 2015).

BEHAN, BRENDAN Playwright, author of *Borstal Boy*. The letter quoted is viewable in the Dublin Writers Museum.

BELLETTI, VALERIA Secretary to Samuel Goldwyn and other studio heads, lovingly delivered from obscurity by film historian Cari Beauchamp. Quotations from *Adventures of a Hollywood Secretary: Her Private Letters from Inside the Studios of the 1920s*, used by kind permission of the editors, Cari Beauchamp and Margery Baragona (Berkeley: University of California Press, 2006).

BELLOW, SAUL Nobel Prize–winning Canadian-born novelist and essayist. Word-sozzled, life-hungry, Bellow's semi-autobiographical Jewish antiheroes crashed the country club of American literature. They chiseled and loved, they humped and swore, and they did it in a vernacular that owed a leg-breaking debt to Yiddish and borrowed from Greek and Latin to pay it back. His National Book Award–winning 1953 novel *The Adventures of Augie March* helped inaugurate the continuing golden age of American immigrant fiction. In the words of Martin Amis, *Augie March* "isn't written in English; its job is to make you feel how beautiful American is, with its jazzy verbs . . . *Augie March*, finally, is the Great American Novel because of its fantastic inclusiveness, its pluralism, its qualmless promiscuity. In these pages the highest and lowest mingle and hobnob in the vast democracy of Bellow's prose." *Augie* landed in the lap of early-fifties American literature with the impact of a cherry bomb. As Bellow's friend Philip Roth once said, "The backbone of 20th century American literature has been provided by two novelists—William Faulkner and Saul Bellow. Together they are the Melville, Hawthorne, and Twain of the 20th century." Quoted from *Saul Bellow: Letters*, edited by Benjamin Taylor (New York: Penguin Publishing Group, 2010).

BENÉT, STEPHEN VINCENT Yale-educated author of *The Devil and Daniel Webster* and *Western Star*, a long narrative poem about Manifest Destiny that won the Pulitzer Prize before Benét could finish it. He never did. Quotations from *Selected Letters of Stephen Vincent Benét*, edited by Charles A. Fenton (New Haven, Conn.: Yale University Press, 1960).

BERTENSSON, SERGEI   Filmmaking factotum. Quoted from *My First Time in Hollywood*, edited by Cari Beauchamp (Los Angeles: Asahina & Wallace, 2015).

BIDWELL, JOHN   Emigrant, politician, founder of Chico. Quoted from *In Camp & Cabin* (New York: Citadel Press, 1962).

BIERCE, AMBROSE   Famously bitter journalist, polemicist, lexicographer, master of short fiction. Author of, among others, the great short story "Occurrence at Owl Creek Bridge" and also "Moxon's Master," which appeared in the *San Francisco Examiner*, probably marking the first appearance in literature of a robot. Bierce wrote for both William Randolph Hearst and the forgotten satirical weekly *The Wasp*, a defunct San Francisco city magazine just waiting for the right anthologist to come along and pick its bones. His cynically aphoristic *Devil's Dictionary* still convulses undergraduates to this day. Carey McWilliams (q.v.) wrote a biography of him that somebody should absolutely reprint. Bierce disappeared into Mexico during the revolution, where his disagreeableness surely made him the last of his many enemies. Quoted from *The Letters of Ambrose Bierce* (New York: Riverrun Press, 1967).

BIGLER, HENRY W.   Pioneer, present at the discovery of gold at Coloma on the American River. The only member of Sutter's sawmill crew whose original diary, albeit sketchy, survives. Quoted from *Journals of Forty-niners: Salt Lake to Los Angeles: with Diaries and Contemporary Records of Sheldon Young, James S. Brown, Jacob Y. Stover, Charles C. Rich, Addison Pratt, Howard Egan, Henry W. Bigler, and Others* (Glendale, Calif: Arthur H. Clark, 1954).

BLAKE, WILLIAM PHIPPS   American geologist, mining consultant, chemist, Yale professor.

BLOCH, ERNEST   Swiss American composer, Berkeley professor. Quoted from *Music and Politics in San Francisco: From the 1906 Quake to the Second World War* (Berkeley: University of California Press, 2012).

BODENHEIM, MAXWELL   Impressive Depression-era American novelist and poet, heroically resurrected by critic Jason Boog in his fine, impassioned book *The Deep End: The Literary Scene in the Great Depression and Today*. Quoted from *Maxwell Bodenheim* (New York: Twayne Publishers, 1970).

BOOTH, ANNE WILLSON   Pioneer, pungent diarist. Quoted from *A Year of Mud and Gold: San Francisco in Letters and Diaries, 1849–1850* (Lincoln: University of Nebraska Press, 1999).

BOOTH, EDMUND   Deaf journalist, voice for the hearing-impaired, gold miner. Quoted from *Edmund Booth (1810–1905) Forty-niner: The Life Story of a Deaf Pioneer, Including Portions of His Autobiographical Notes and Gold Rush Diary, and Selections from Family Letters and Reminiscences* (San Joaquin Pioneer and Historical Society, 1953).

BOUTON, JIM   Knuckleball pitcher, chewing-gum entrepreneur, ballpark preservationist, writer. Author of *Ball Four* and its cruelly forgotten sequel, *I'm Glad You Didn't Take It Personally*. Whether *Ball Four* robbed America of its heroes or, as many think, actually helped to emancipate exploited players from their former indentured servitude, his funny, well-observed diaries made readers out of more than a few Little Leaguers who grew up to be writers. I'm one. Quoted from *Ball Four: My Life and Hard Times Throwing the Knuckleball in the Big Leagues*, edited by Leonard Shecter (New York: World Books, 1970).

BOYLE, KAY   Novelist, educator, activist. Blacklisted out of her posting as a foreign correspondent for the less-than-brave *New Yorker* magazine. Won *two* O. Henry awards for her short fiction. Quoted from *Kay Boyle: A Twentieth-Century Life in Letters* (Chicago: University of Illinois Press, 2015).

BRACKETT, CHARLES   Screenwriter-producer, longtime writing partner of Billy Wilder's earlier, less raunchy comedies. Quoted from *"It's the Pictures That Got Small": Charles Brackett on Billy Wilder and Hollywood's Golden Age*, edited by Anthony Slide. (New York: Columbia University Press, 2015). Used by permission.

BRADBURY, RAY   Author of *Fahrenheit 451* and *The Martian Chronicles*; screenwriter of *Moby Dick*. Descended from a seventeenth-century Salem woman tried for witchcraft, Bradbury and his parents motored across the country to Los Angeles in 1934, with young Ray piling out of their jalopy at every stop to plunder the local library in search of L. Frank Baum's *Oz* books. Two years later, Bradbury experienced a rite of passage once familiar to most science-fiction readers: the realization that he was not alone. At a secondhand bookstore in Hollywood, he discovered a handbill promoting meetings of the Los Angeles Science Fiction Society. Thrilled, he joined a weekly Thursday-night conclave that would grow to attract such science-fiction legends as Robert A. Heinlein (q.v.), Leigh Brackett, and the future founder of Scientology, L. Ron Hubbard. Bradbury wrote *Fahrenheit 451* on a rental typewriter in the basement of UCLA's Lawrence Clark Powell Library, one invaluable dime at a time. Quoted from *The Bradbury Chronicles: The Life of Ray Bradbury* by Sam Weller (New York: William Morrow, 2005).

BRECHT, BERTOLT   Author of, among other plays, *Galileo, Mother Courage*, and the perennially prophetic *Resistible Rise of Arturo Ui*. Fled Europe for Santa Monica. After World War II, fled Joseph McCarthy for Europe again. Quoted from *Bertolt Brecht Journals, 1934–1955* (London: Methuen, 1993).

BREED, CLARA E.   San Diego children's librarian who opposed Japanese internment and kept up a gently reassuring correspondence with all her old regulars. Quoted from *Dear Miss Breed: True Stories of the Japanese American Incarceration During World War II and the Librarian who Made a Difference* (New York: Scholastic, 2006).

BREEN, PATRICK   Donner Party diarist.

BREWER, WILLIAM H.   Botanist on the first California Geological Survey; first chair of agriculture at Yale. Quoted from *Up and Down California in 1860–1864: The Journal of William H. Brewer* (New Haven: Yale University Press, 1930).

BRITTEN, BENJAMIN   British composer of *Peter and the Wolf, The Young Person's Guide to the Orchestra*, and *Peter Grimes*—the last-named inspired by his discovery of George Crabbe's poems in a maddeningly unspecified Los Angeles bookstore. At the time, he was staying with Peter Pears at the Escondido home of a patron, working against the imminent world premiere in L.A. of his first string quartet. Published in *Letters from a Life: Selected Diaries and Letters of Benjamin Britten*, edited by Philip Reed and Donald Mitchell (Berkeley: University of California Press, 1991).

BROOKS, VAN WYCK   Distinguished critic, historian, biographer of Twain and Thoreau. Won a Pulitzer Prize for *The Flowering of New England 1815–1865*. Quoted from *The Van Wyck Brooks-Lewis Mumford Letters: The Record of a Literary Friendship, 1921–1963* (New York: Dutton, 1970).

BROWN, GOV. EDMUND G., JR.   Governor, mayor, governor again. Plenty of Californians were sorry to see him go. Quoted in final bill-signing postscript.

BROWN, WILLIE JR.   Natty, flamboyant politician, self-christened "Ayatollah of the Assembly," later Mayor of San Francisco. Quoted from *Basic Brown: My Life and Our Times* (New York: Simon & Schuster, 2008).

BROWNE, JOHN ROSS   Dublin-born writer, artist and, in his capacity as official reporter, the James Madison of the Constitutional Convention of California. Quoted from his "Report of the debates in the Convention of California, on the formation of the state constitution."

BRYANT, EDWIN   Newspaper editor, second alcalde of San Francisco. Quoted from his *What I Saw in California: Being the Journal of a Tour by the Emigrant Route and South Pass of the Rocky Mountains, Across the Continent of North America, the Great Desert Basin, and Through California in the Years 1846, 1847* (New York: Appleton, 1849).

BUCK, FRANKLIN A.   Yankee trader in the gold rush, to quote the title of his published letters to his sister. "A good-natured, good-hearted man," per Gary Kamiya, the never-wrong, never-infelicitous San Francisco author of *Cool Gray City of Love: 49 Views of San Francisco*. Quoted from *A Yankee Trader in the Gold Rush: The Letters of Franklin A. Buck* (Boston: Houghton Mifflin, 1930).

BUKOWSKI, CHARLES   Poet, novelist, and "Notes of a Dirty Old Man" columnist for the *Los Angeles Free Press*. Quoted from *Screams from the Balcony: Selected Letters, 1960–1970* (Santa Rosa, Calif.: Black Sparrow Press, 1993).

BULL, DEBORAH   British dancer, writer, member of the House of Lords. Quoted from *Dancing Away: A Covent Garden Diary* (London: Methuen, 1999).

BUNYARD, HARRIET   Diarist, who at 19 crossed the plains from Texas to El Monte in 1868. Quoted from the unfortunately titled *Ho for California! Women's Overland Diaries from the Huntington Library* (San Marino: Huntington Library, 1980).

BURBANK, LUTHER   Once incredibly famous Santa Rosa horticulturalist. Developed upwards of 800 new plants including the spineless cactus, a couple of which I've worked for. Quoted from *Upton Sinclair: California Socialist, Celebrity Intellectual* (Lincoln: University of Nebraska Press, 2013).

BURMAN, JENNY   Erstwhile author of the Echo Park blog "Chicken Corner." Quoted by gracious permission of the author.

BURNETT, PETER   Bank president, bad businessman, genocidal governor.

BURROUGHS, EDGAR RICE Imaginatively gifted and lavishly prolific novelist, creator of *Tarzan of the Apes* and *Princess of Mars*, founder of Tarzana. He introduces his novel "At the Earth's Core" with a metafictional SOS from the imperiled hero to his creator, in effect screaming, "Dad, get me out of this!"—all via a subsonic radio transmission to Burroughs' eventual hero, Jason Gridley—of Tarzana! All quotations from Edgar Rice Burroughs © 1975, 2017 Edgar Rice Burroughs, Inc. All rights reserved. Trademarks TARZAN® and Edgar Rice Burroughs® owned by Edgar Rice Burroughs, Inc. and used by permission.

BUTLER, OCTAVIA E. MacArthur-winning author of, among other works, *Kindred* and *Parable of the Sower*. Born and raised in Pasadena, which appears in disguised form in some of her work. Labored in solitude until she found camaraderie among other science fiction and fantasy writers, including Harlan Ellison. Years after her death from a fall, her reputation continues to rise. Octavia E. Butler papers, The Huntington Library, San Marino, Calif.

CABRILLO, JUAN RODRÍGUEZ Iberian mariner, explorer. Died of gangrene after a fall suffered while rescuing his men from a skirmish with the Tongva, though you have to wonder what the Tongva version of the story was.

CAEN, HERB San Francisco columnist, man about town. For readers who didn't grow up on him, encountering him today is a revelation. He banged out every day what newspaper columnists today win Pulitzers for trying to emulate twice a week. Originally published in the *San Francisco Chronicle*, July 5, 1938.

CAGE, JOHN Composer, musician, Joycean. Born in Los Angeles. His mother wrote about society and classical music for the *Los Angeles Times* back when they were often the same thing. Studied under Arnold Schoenberg. His experimental "silent" sonata, "4'33"," was the first of his pioneering works to be influenced by random chance. Absquatulate. Returned to L.A. late in life for a production of *Rolywholyover*, his Joyce-inspired "composition for museum." Quoted from *The Selected Letters of John Cage*, edited by Laura Kuhn (Middletown, Conn.: Wesleyan University Press, 2016).

CAIN, JAMES M. Novelist, author of, among others, *The Postman Always Rings Twice, Double Indemnity, Mildred Pierce*. Managed to write classic crime novels without ever once creating a detective. Quoted from *James M. Cain and the American Authors' Authority* (Austin: University of Texas Press, 2014).

CALDWELL, ERSKINE Novelist, reluctant screenwriter, author of *Tobacco Road*. Quoted from *Erskine Caldwell: Selected Letters, 1929–1955* (Jefferson, N.C., and London: McFarland & Company, 1999).

CALVINO, ITALO Author of *Invisible Cities* and *If on a Winter's Night a Traveler*. Taught at UCLA for a semester. Did not go native. Quoted from *Hermit in Paris: Autobiographical Writings* (New York: Pantheon, 2003).

CAMPBELL, JULIA Student at UCLA. Quoted from class diaries by gracious permission.

CARPENTER, HELEN Pioneer, witty journal-keeper. Quoted from *Women and Indians on the Frontier, 1825–1915* (Albuquerque: University of New Mexico Press, 1984).

CARTER, JENNIE   California and journalistic pioneer. From her home in Nevada County, Carter wrote an opinionated, often funny, patriotic column for an anti-segregation San Francisco newspaper, *The Elevator*. Quoted from *Jennie Carter: A Black Journalist of the Early West*, edited by Eric Gardner (Jackson: University Press of Mississippi, 2007).

CASSADY, NEAL   Writer, brakeman, muse. The model for Dean Moriarty in *On the Road*, he inspired not only Jack Kerouac but frequent pen pal Allen Ginsberg—and, through them, a generation. Quoted from *As Ever: The Collected Correspondence of Allen Ginsberg & Neal Cassady* (Berkeley: Creative Arts Book Company, 1977).

CATHER, WILLA   Canonical American author of novels including *My Ántonia*, *Death Comes for the Archbishop*, and *The Song of the Lark*. Stayed in Long Beach and commuted to Pasadena to care for her ailing mother. Not predisposed to love the place, and didn't. Quoted from *The Selected Letters of Willa Cather* (New York: Alfred A. Knopf, 2013).

CHA, STEPH   Gifted Van Nuys–born author of the Los Angeles Times Book Prize and California Book Award winning *Your House Will Pay*. Also author of reliably incisive book reviews and the Juniper Song detective novels. Quoted from "When we were quarantined," *Los Angeles Times*, June 20, 2020.

CHANDLER, RAYMOND   Author of *The Big Sleep*, creator of detective Philip Marlowe, co-screenwriter of *Strangers on a Train*. There are no great writers without contradictions. Chandler was a pulp hack who could conjugate Latin verbs, a born prose stylist who managed the office of a Los Angeles oil company for 20 years before publishing his first story, a reluctant scenarist who wrote "Double Indemnity" for Billy Wilder and "Strangers on a Train" for Alfred Hitchcock—and a cynic who tried to shoot himself in the shower after his wife died. The only thing Chandler did consistently was write well, and when he wasn't writing well, he was writing brilliantly. Chandler was always there at the end of a sentence with the perfect noun from nowhere. It's there in 1940, when he writes that "the English civilian population is the least hysterical in the world. They can take an awful pounding and still keep on planting lobelias." It's still there in 1958, a year before he died: "No man grows old as long as he can create. You may die in the midst of it—so may I, who am older than you are—but you don't die of lethargy." Directly or indirectly, Chandler has colored Angelenos' perceptions of their city more than any other writer. Quoted from *Selected Letters of Raymond Chandler*, edited by Frank MacShane (New York: Columbia University Press, 1981).

CHÁVEZ, CÉSAR   Co-founder of the United Farm Workers. Wielding the power of the hunger strike and the boycott, he fought for and won the first binding farm-worker contracts ever negotiated in California. Apprenticed and flourished as a community organizer in Boyle Heights alongside Fred Ross, under the auspices of Saul Alinsky. Born in Yuma, he is buried at the National Chávez Center in Tehachapi, in the mountains that divide the state he did so much to unite. Quoted from *The Crusades of Cesar Chavez: A Biography*, by Miriam Pawel (New York: Bloomsbury, 2014).

CHÁVEZ-SILVERMAN, SUSANA Los Angeles–born Spanglish writer, scholar; author also of *Killer Crónicas*. Quoted from *Scenes from la Cuenca de Los Angeles y Otros Natural Disasters* (Madison, Wisc.: University of Wisconsin Press, 2010).

CHEEVER, JOHN Novelist and short-story writer, author of the *Wapshot* novels, *Bullet Park*, and *Falconer*. Passed through L.A. en route to Manila in 1945 for the Signal Corps. Returned periodically, staying at the home of his friend John Weaver (q.v.). Published in *Glad Tidings: A Friendship in Letters. The Correspondence of John Cheever and John D. Weaver, 1945–1982* (New York: HarperCollins, 1993).

CHILD, JULIA French chef from Pasadena, author of *Mastering the Art of French Cooking*, and a natural broadcaster. No TV producer ever had to tell Julia Child to be herself. What many still don't realize about her famous, fondly mocked voice is that she speaks with the classic, characteristically flutey, fast-disappearing Pasadena accent. Quoted from *Appetite for Life: The Biography of Julia Child* (New York: Knopf Doubleday, 2012).

CHURCHILL, WINSTON British politician, author, even a novelist. As prime minister, rallied his countrymen to victory in World War II. Turfed out soon after. Awarded the Nobel Prize in literature for his history of the war. Visited L.A. a month before the 1929 Crash. Met Hearst, Chaplin, and a swordfish, to the latter's cost. Published in *Speaking for Themselves: The Personal Letters of Winston and Clementine Churchill*, edited by Baroness Mary Soames (née Mary Spencer Churchill (New York: Doubleday, 1998).

CLAPPE, LOUISE, AKA "DAME SHIRLEY" Proper Massachusetts lady who accompanied her husband to Plumas County in the California goldfields, whence she sent delightful, widely published letters home to her sister.

CLUGSTON, GINA Founder/Publisher/Editor of Sierra News Online. Quoted from "Exact Center Of California Has Its Balance Restored," *Sierra News Online*, May 22, 2017.

COCKBURN, ALEXANDER Anglo-Irish-Hibernio-American political journalist and press critic. For years, wrote the endlessly educational Press Clips column for the *Village Voice*. Latterly and proudly a columnist concurrently for the *Wall Street Journal* and Northern California's *Anderson Valley Advertiser*. Uncle of Olivia Wilde, if that's what it takes for people to rediscover him. Quoted from *The Golden Age Is in Us: Journeys and Encounters* (New York: Verso Books, 1996).

COHN, RABBI ELKAN Early San Francisco clergyman.

COLEMAN, WANDA Beloved, occasionally fearsome doyenne of the L.A. poetry scene for decades. Fugitive from TV soap opera writing. Author of the National Book Award–nominated *Mercurochrome*. Quoted from *The Riot Inside Me: More Trials & Tremors* (Boston: David R. Godine, 2005) and from her letter to Truong Tran, originally published in Rain Taxi, online edition, Fall 2006, https://www.rain taxi.com/letters-truong-tran-and-wanda-coleman/.

COLLINS, TOM Migrant worker camp manager and principal source for *The Grapes of Wrath*, which Steinbeck dedicated to him. Quoted from *Prologue: The*

Journal of the National Archives Winter 2008, Vol. 40, No. 4 (United States: National Archives and Records Service).

COLTON, WALTER   Author, Monterey alcalde, co-publisher of the state's first newspaper, *The Californian*.

COOKE, ALISTAIR   Broadcaster and author, best known for his long-running, only partly catalogued BBC Radio essays explaining the ways of Americans to the British. Returned to L.A. frequently to visit friends and file observations for the Beeb, including the one quoted here, about the night he saw RFK shot. *Letter from America* scripts © Cooke Americas, RLLP.

COOLBRITH, INA   California poet, librarian, heroine. A niece of Mormon founder Joseph Smith, Coolbrith lived as a teenager in Los Angeles before a broken marriage chased her to the Bay Area. There she fell among writers, among them Bret Harte and Charles Warren Stoddard, with both of whom she co-edited the *Overland Monthly*. Mark Twain, Ambrose Bierce, and even Alfred, Lord Tennyson, sang her praises, but the depredations of sexism and its attendant family caretaking reduced her to penury, even librarianship. As the overworked Oakland City librarian, she initiated the young Jack London and Isadora Duncan into the mysteries of the stacks. For years she worked on a personal history of California literature but lost the manuscript to the fires of 1906. Eventually she became the first poet laureate not only of California, but of any state in the country.

COPPOLA, ELEANOR   Writer-director of *Paris Can Wait*. Eloquent diarist of, among other experiences, her screenwriter-director husband Francis's descent into genius on the set of *Apocalypse Now*. Quoted from *Notes on a Life* (New York: Nan A. Talese, 2008).

CORWIN, NORMAN   Radio man, Oscar-nominated screenwriter of *Lust for Life*, centenarian. Author of *On a Note of Triumph*, the all-star broadcast tribute to America heard coast-to-coast on V-E Day—the most listened-to radio drama in American history. Also screenwriter of *Lust for Life*, quoted from *Norman Corwin's Letters*, edited by A. J. Langguth (New York: Barricade Books, 1994).

COSTANSÓ, MIGUEL   Catalan cartographer and cosmographer. Quoted from *The Portolá Expedition of 1769–1770: Diary of Miguel Costansó* (Berkeley: University of California Press, 1911).

COWARD, NOËL   Playwright, actor, songwriter. Returned to California periodically to see friends and perform for films and on stage. Quoted from *The Noël Coward Diaries*, edited by Graham Payn and Sheridan Morley (New York: Little, Brown, 1982).

CRAFT, ROBERT   Boswell to, er, Igor Stravinsky's Johnson. Quoted from *Dialogues and a Diary*, by himself and Stravinsky (New York: Doubleday, 1963).

CRANE, HART   Poet. Stayed in Southern California over the winter from 1927 to 1928 visiting family and acting as companion to a wealthy Altadenan. Seen with Chaplin, gay-bashed in San Pedro. Quoted from *The Letters of Hart Crane, 1916–1932*, edited by Brom Weber (Berkeley and Los Angeles: University of California Press, 1965).

CREASON, GLEN   Erstwhile map librarian at the Los Angeles Central Library. Quoted by gracious permission of the author.

CREELEY, ROBERT   American poet, identified with the Black Mountain School. Quoted from *The Selected Letters of Robert Creeley* (Oakland: University of California Press, 2020).

CRESPI, FRAY JUAN   Expedition chaplain. Quoted from *Fray Juan Crespi, Missionary Explorer on the Pacific Coast 1769–1774*, edited by Herbert Eugene Bolton (Berkeley: University of California Press, 1927).

CROWE, CAMERON   Writer-director, music journalist. Went from freelancing on spec for *Rolling Stone* while still in high school to writing and directing the modern classics, *Say Anything* and *Jerry Maguire*, and the semi-autobiographical *Almost Famous*. Also edited a book of his conversations with Billy Wilder, whose influence on his work is unmistakable. Quoted from *Becoming Almost Famous: My Back Pages in Music, Writing, and Life* by Ben Fong-Torres (San Francisco: Backbeat Books, 2006).

CUMMINS, ELLA STERLING   Pioneer, writer, historian from Mormon Island, California.

CUMMINGS, E. E.   American poet. Accepted Eric Knight's entreaties to visit. Stayed two months and angled for Hollywood money, to no avail. Quoted from *Selected Letters of e. e. cummings* (New York: Harcourt, 1969).

DALTON, HENRY   Rancher and newspaper publisher. Quoted from the papers of Henry Dalton, Huntington Library, San Marino, Calif.

DANA, RICHARD HENRY   Author of the first bestseller about California, *Two Years Before the Mast*, an account of his hitch as a midshipman up and down the Pacific Coast. Most editions contain his shorter account of a return visit twenty years later, when he found the state utterly transformed. Quoted from *Two Years Before the Mast* (New York: Library of America, 2005).

DAVIS, MIKE   Fontana-born writer, activist, social historian. Reading Davis's *City of Quartz* today is a very different experience from when Verso first published it in 1990. Back then, reading Davis felt like discovering some long-lost teacher's edition of Los Angeles. He knew where the bodies were buried and precisely who had buried them. He knew all this because he'd read seemingly everything in Christendom, and with total photographic recall—from pulp novels barely even in print the first time around to enough critical theory to put the "hork" into Horkheimer and Adorno. Davis gave us a deeper revisionist history of L.A. than anybody since Carey McWilliams, but his masterpiece also helps us know what it felt like to live in L.A., specifically in 1990, and smell a riot coming. Without the warning shot heard in *City of Quartz*, we might just be living in the future Davis predicted. The book may just be that rare thing: a self-averting prophecy. Quoted from *Global Suburbs: Urban Sprawl from the Rio Grande to Rio de Janeiro* (London: Routledge, 2015).

DE ANGULO, JAIME   Spanish linguist, ethnographer, poet, KPFA broadcaster. Author of *Indian Tales* and *Indians in Overalls*. Quoted from *The Old Coyote of Big Sur: The Life of Jaime de Angulo* (Berkeley: Stonegarden Press, 1995).

DE BEAUVOIR, SIMONE   Author and groundbreaking feminist. Toured America, including California. Liked what she saw. Quoted from *America Day by Day* (Berkeley: University of California Press, 2000).

DE LA ASCENSIÓN, FATHER ANTONIO   Missionary, diarist of the Vizcaíno Expedition. Quoted from *Spanish Exploration in the Southwest, 1542–1706*, edited by Herbert Eugene Bolton (New York: Charles Scribner's Sons, 1916).

DELANO, ALONZO   Redoubtable Gold Rush newspaperman.

DEL OLMO, FRANK   Longtime *L.A. Times* editor and columnist, well-remembered for a continuing series about his autistic son. Inspiration to a generation of journalists. There's a school named after him on First Street. It's not enough. Quoted from *Frank Del Olmo: Commentaries on His Times* (Los Angeles: Los Angeles Times Books, 2004).

DE MILLE, AGNES   Dancer, choreographer, UCLA English major. Niece of the director Cecil B. De Mille (see below*)* and granddaughter of the great California social economist Henry George, who wrote the eerily prophetic essay "What the Railroad Will Bring Us." Quoted from *No Intermissions: The Life of Agnes de Mille*, by Carol Easton (Boston: Little, Brown, 1996).

DEMILLE, CECIL B.   Longtime Hollywood director, not only of both silent *and* sound versions of *The Ten Commandments*, but also the Oscar-winning *The Greatest Show on Earth*—according to Steven Spielberg, the formative experience of his moviegoing childhood. Uncle of modern dance pioneer Agnes de Mille (see above). Quoted from *Dark History of Hollywood: A Century of Greed, Corruption, and Scandal Behind the Movies* (London: Amber Books, 2017).

DEWITT, MARGARET   Gold Rush pioneer. Quoted from *A Year of Mud and Gold: San Francisco in Letters and Diaries, 1849–1850* (Lincoln: University of Nebraska Press, 1999).

DICK, PHILIP K.   Massively influential science fiction writer. Where Jules Verne predicted inventions, Dick foresaw entire societies. He didn't just *anticipate* such modern amenities as robotic pets and Prozac, he imagined a future alienated enough to want them—a future that doesn't look as comfortably like science fiction as it used to. The screenwriters Hampton Fancher and David Webb Peoples transplanted Dick's 1968 novel *Do Androids Dream of Electric Sheep?*—set in San Francisco—into 2021 Los Angeles to create the classic film *Blade Runner*. When he died of stroke-related heart failure at fifty-three (weeks after pronouncing himself thrilled with a rough cut of *Blade Runner*), he was living in Orange County, lured there a few years earlier by an admiring academic at Fullerton to donate his archive and original sci-fi pulps to the library. Maybe Dick wrote so convincingly of marginalized alternate worlds in part because he worked in two of them: the cultish shadowlands of pre–*Star Wars* science fiction, and the literary Siberia that is writing for the East Coast from California. Quoted from *The Exegesis of Philip K. Dick*, edited by Pamela Jackson and Jonathan Lethem (Boston: Houghton Mifflin Harcourt, 2011).

DICKEY, JAMES   Poet, rakehell, author of several collections and the novel *Deliverance*. Taught for a year on the faculty of Cal State Northridge, where he wrote one or two great California poems. Quoted from *Crux: The Letters of James Dickey* (New York: Alfred A. Knopf, 1999).

DIDION, JOAN   Sacramento-born essayist, novelist, screenwriter. The story of modern American cultural criticism is, as much as anything, the story of three California girls who went east: Pauline Kael, Susan Sontag, and Joan Didion. Of the three, only Didion ever publicly copped to that inconsolable condition, homesickness for California. It's a sorrowful ache, California homesickness, unrelieved by the many ethnic restaurants, expat bars, and benevolent associations that make homesickness *in* California for someplace else so much easier to bear. Didion knows what it's like to pine for redwoods. Her last California book, *Where I Was From*, painted an impressionistic panorama of the state to which her ancestors emigrated a century and a half ago—forking away en route from a couple of families with whom they'd shared much of the trail, the Reeds and the Donners. The Donner Party haunts *Where I Was From*, standing in throughout for California's entire bloody understory. Quoted from *The Year of Magical Thinking* (New York: Knopf Doubleday Publishing Group, 2007).

DOHENY, E. L.   Oil millionaire. With his partner Charles Canfield, struck a gusher at the corner of Patton and West State Streets near Echo Park, inaugurating L.A.'s black gold rush. Homeowners rushed to sink wells in their backyards, but Doheny cornered much of the market and became ludicrously wealthy. Later implicated in the Teapot Dome scandal. Quoted from *Hearst's: A Magazine with a Mission* (New York: International Magazine Company, 1919).

DORSEY, JACK   Co-founder of Twitter, who more and more looks like he took the world's richest man to the cleaners.

DOS PASSOS, JOHN   Novelist, epoch-making author of the *USA Trilogy*. Visited California awhile to work unsatisfyingly with Josef von Sternberg and make mock. Quoted from *The Fourteenth Chronicle: Letters and Diaries of John Dos Passos*, edited by Townsend Ludington (Boston: Gambit, 1973).

DOTEN, ALFRED   Still-enjoyable Gold Rush newspaperman.

DRALYUK, BORIS   Ukrainian American author of *My Hollywood and Other Poems*, translator, Fairfax High grad, erstwhile editor of the *L.A. Review of Books*. Quoted from "O Kaplans, My Kaplans!", personal blog, July 7, 2018.

DRAKE, SIR FRANCIS   Sixteenth-century British explorer who sailed up the California coast and made brief landfall, probably near Tomales Bay.

DREISER, THEODORE   Author of *Sister Carrie, An American Tragedy*, and essays including the amusing *Hollywood: Its Morals and Manners* (https://archive.org/details/hollywood_morals_manners_1208_librivox). Lived here lustily in the twenties with his beloved bride, Helen, while starting *American Tragedy*. Returned in the late thirties. Suffered a fatal heart attack on December 28, 1945, after driving to the beach to watch the sunset. Buried at Forest Lawn. Quoted from *The American Diaries, 1902–1926*, edited by Thomas P. Riggio and James L. W. West III (Philadelphia: University of Pennsylvania Press, 1982).

DUNNE, JOHN GREGORY   Journalist, essayist, screenwriter, novelist. The quint-essential writer you don't appreciate until he's gone. Someday, somebody should collect in one place all of Dunne's short California pieces, today mostly scattered through the books *Quintana & Friends* and *Crooning.* Moved here with his wife, Joan Didion, in 1964 and stayed almost a quarter century, writing for such publications as the *Saturday Evening Post, Esquire,* the *Atlantic* and *New York* magazine. Somehow he made every take on a story seem incomplete until his, and every one afterward anti-climactic. Quoted from *Monster: Living off the Big Screen* (New York: Random House, 1997).

DUNNE, PHILIP   Well-regarded screenwriter, liberal, son of "Mr. Dooley" columnist Finley Peter Dunne. Quoted from *The Best of Rob Wagner's* Script, edited by Anthony Slide (Lanham, Md.: Scarecrow Press, 1985).

EARHART, AMELIA   The first woman to fly across the Atlantic solo, she later took off from Oakland on a round-the-world flight, never to be seen again.

EINSTEIN, ALBERT   Physicist, discoverer of the theory of special relativity. *Time* magazine's "Man of the Century" for his involvement in the two most important cataclysms of the twentieth: the splitting of the atom, to which his discoveries led, and the rise of Nazi Germany, from which, as a Jew, he sought refuge in America. He also spent a term at Caltech. Quoted from *A Lone Traveler: Einstein in California,* by William M. Kramer and Margaret Leslie Davis (Los Angeles: Skirball Cultural Center, 2004).

ELIOT, T. S.   Poet, author of, among others, "The Wasteland" and the *Four Quartets.* He traveled to America briefly as a guest lecturer at, among other campuses, Pomona. Quoted from *The Letters of T. S. Eliot,* vol. 6, edited by Valerie Eliot and Hugh Haffenden (London, Faber & Faber, 2016).

EMERSON, RALPH WALDO   Before Emerson, America had little literary expression that didn't slavishly copy from European models. He combined informal yet sermon-cadenced sentences—intended always for an imagined reader he once called "the unknown friend" —with a syntax so peculiar that one might sooner diagram a hurricane.

ENTWISTLE, PEG   Actress who leapt to her death from the Hollywood sign.

EVERSON, WILLIAM   Poet, critic, hand-press printer. Also known as Brother Antoninus. Along with Thomas Merton, America's most renowned poet-monk.

FAGEN, DONALD   Musician, half of Steely Dan, savvy film music critic for the sadly short-lived *Premiere* magazine. His song "My Old School" contains the line "California tumbles into the sea/That'll be the day I go back to Annandale." If the sea rises any higher, he might want to start pricing flights. Quoted from *Eminent Hipsters* (New York: Penguin Publishing Group, 2014).

FAGES, PEDRO   Soldier, explorer, early governor of Alta California.

FAIRCHILD, LUCIUS   California pioneer who later became governor of Wisconsin.

FANTE, JOHN   Author of, among other novels, *Ask the Dust* and *Wait Until Spring, Bandini.* Discovering Fante is like tasting garlic for the first time. Quoted from *John*

Fante: Selected Letters, 1932–1981, edited by Seamus Cooney (Santa Rosa, Calif.: Black Sparrow Press, 1991).

FARIÑA, RICHARD   Novelist, essayist, author of *Been Down So Long It Looks Like Up to Me.* Went to Cornell with Thomas Pynchon, whose novel *Gravity's Rainbow* is dedicated to him.

FARRELL, MIKE   Actor, activist. Outstanding as the sweet, sincere B. J. Hunnicutt on the TV series *M*A*S*H,* especially the "Hanky Panky" and "The Joker Is Wild" episodes. Quoted from *Of Mule and Man* (New York: Akashic Books, 2009).

FAULKNER, WILLIAM   Nobel Prize–winning author of, among other novels, *Absalom, Absalom!, The Sound and the Fury,* and *As I Lay Dying.* Co-adapted *The Big Sleep* and *To Have and Have Not* for Howard Hawks. Reputedly asked the studio if he could work from home, then took a favorable answer as permission to return to Mississippi. Wrote one great short story about L.A., "Golden Land." Quoted from *Selected Letters of William Faulkner,* edited by Joseph Blotner (New York: Random House, 1977).

FERLINGHETTI, LAWRENCE   Poet and founder of San Francisco publisher and bookstore City Lights. Quoted from *Writing Across the Landscape: Travel Journals 1950–2010,* edited by Giada Diano and Matthew Gleeson (New York: Liveright, 2015). Used by generous permission of the author.

FERRELO, BARTOLOMÉ   Mariner, promoted from chief pilot to captain on the death of Juan Cabrillo off Santa Barbara.

FEUCHTWANGER, LION   Historical novelist, playwright, fugitive from Nazi Germany. His Pacific Palisades house, the Villa Aurora, became a kind of clubhouse for European refugees. Now it serves as an artists' residence. Feuchtwanger's prophetic 1933 novel *The Oppermanns* is a classic cautionary tale of fascism on the rise.

FINCH, CHARLES   An L.A.–based, too-little-known mystery novelist and Balakian Prize winner for Excellence in Book Reviewing. Quoted from "When we were quarantined," *Los Angeles Times,* June 20, 2020.

FISHER, M. F. K.   Essayist, cook, novelist, author of *Consider the Oyster* and *How to Cook a Wolf.* Like her friend and admirer Julia Child, Fisher grew up surrounded by citrus groves—in Whittier, a few miles southeast of Child's native Pasadena. Her erudite father ran the local newspaper with every good small-town editor's mix of intelligence, boosterism, and cheerful overqualification. Early culinary influences included a grandmother who regarded all flavor as sinful and an aunt who steamed fresh mussels in seaweed on their weekend jaunts to Laguna. She wrote about the pleasures of the table with all the sensuous urgency of someone for whom other pleasures came less often and rarely lasted long. Lovers came and went, and she ruthlessly considered her own talent second rank, but happiness was always just a good meal away. Quoted from *M. F. K. Fisher: A Life in Letters: Correspondence 1929-1991,* compiled by Marsha Moran, Patrick Moran, and Norah K. Barr (Berkeley: Counterpoint Press, 1998).

FITZGERALD, F. SCOTT   Author of *The Great Gatsby, Tender Is the Night,* and *The Last Tycoon,* among others. If you want your child to be a writer, go bankrupt.

Failing that, at least suffer a severe financial reversal, obliging your son or daughter to endure the social opprobrium of changed schools and dropped friendships. Do all this, and you may yet join the impecunious fraternity of writers' parents that includes John Shakespeare, John Joyce, John Clemens, John Dickens, John Ernst Steinbeck—and F. Scott Fitzgerald's father, Edward. (You might also want to consider changing your name to John.) Scott Fitzgerald's early literary successes made him and his charming, mercurial wife, Zelda, celebrities of the Jazz Age, a term he coined. Fitzgerald relocated in 1937 to write screenplays for Hollywood, where he began his novel *The Last Tycoon* (1941). Tragically, his end came before the book's did. Several chapters shy of finishing, Fitzgerald died of a heart attack in the apartment of his Hollywood companion, columnist Sheilah Graham, while listening to Beethoven's *Eroica* and reading the *Princeton Alumni Magazine*. Quoted from *The Letters of F. Scott Fitzgerald*, edited by Andrew Turnbull (New York: Charles Scribner's Sons, 1961).

FLANAGAN, HALLIE   Founding director of the Federal Theatre Project. Under her leadership, as many as a million Americans saw their first play and, in almost all cases, not their last. Quoted from *Furious Improvisation: How the WPA and a Cast of Thousands Made High Art Out of Desperate Times* (New York: Walker, 2008).

FLEMING, THOMAS C.   Pioneering African American newspaperman, mostly in Oakland. Got his start working for the Bay Area offices of the Federal Writers' Project. Found at http://www.sfmuseum.org/sunreporter/fleming16.html.

FONDA, JANE   Religions have grown up around people with less interesting lives than Jane Fonda's. She's had a ringside seat for some of the twentieth century's epic achievements and atrocities. With his customary infallibility, Randy Newman nailed it: "Every once in a while I'll think that Jane Fonda's life would make a tremendous opera. . . . You could pick any part of her life: growing up with a movie star, Henry Fonda—fantastic for music; then becoming a movie star, with that walk of hers in 'Walk on the Wild Side'—fantastic for music; then Roger Vadim's 'Barbarella,' and all that exploitation shit; and then all of a sudden she's in Vietnam, she's married to [antiwar activist turned California legislator Tom] Hayden, she's in 'Klute,' and then enormous success independently with her exercise thing and she makes millions of dollars—and then she's with Ted Turner! I've known her briefly, and she's also the best-looking person I was ever up close to. And she probably hasn't changed. There's tons of different music you could write for her! It's one in a million. Someone will do it someday: Citizen Jane." Quoted from *My Life So Far*, by Jane Fonda (New York: Random House, 2003).

FONT, PEDRO   Franciscan missionary. Quoted from *Font's Complete Diary: A Chronicle of the Founding of San Francisco*, edited by Herbert Eugene Bolton (Berkeley: University of California Press, 1933).

FORSTER, E.M.   British author of, among others, the towering novels *A Passage to India* and *Howard's End;* a priceless collection of short fiction, *The Celestial Omnibus and Other Stories;* and the endlessly useful *Aspects of the Novel*. The last-named contains a crucial distinction: "The king died and then the queen died is a story. The king died, and then queen died of grief is a plot." Twenty times nominated for the

Nobel Prize, he should be better known for the E. M. Forster award, which his great friend Christopher Isherwood endowed using the proceeds Forster's suppressed novel *Maurice*. It comes with a U.S. residency for a promising youngish writer from the U.K. Everybody from Seamus Heaney to Ian McEwan to David Mitchell has won it. Essentially, almost all the great British authors of the last 40 years have traipsed in their twenties around America—and, inevitably, California—on E. M. Forster's dime, often recording their impressions in print.

FORTUNATE EAGLE, ADAM   Witty, eloquent, Native American activist behind the 1969–71 occupation of Alcatraz.

FOSTER, STEPHEN CLARK   Los Angeles has a weak-mayor system, and Angelenos prefer them that way. You could call Stephen Foster a lot of things, though— vigilante, murderer, Yalie—but "weak" didn't really enter into it. Still, think of the millions saved in liability costs if more mayors would kindly take a sabbatical before committing their felonies. Such was the case with Foster, a machine politician who abdicated the mayoralty just long enough to lead the lynch mob that strung up Dirty Dave Brown for murder. His responsibility as a private citizen thus fulfilled, his constituents voted him back in office two weeks later. Electing Foster got to be something of a habit with Los Angeles voters. In addition to a term apiece as a city councilman and state senator, he was elected mayor as many as four times, depending how you count the term he served before cityhood and his post-vigilante reelection. He declined to write his memoirs after leaving office, preferring to serve as county supervisor for *another* four terms. Quoted in *Eternity Street: Violence and Justice in Frontier Los Angeles*, by John Mack Faragher New York: Norton, 2015).

FOWLES, JOHN   Author of, among others, *The Collector* (whose dubious film adaptation occasioned his skeptical visit to L.A.*)* and *The French Lieutenant's Woman*. Quoted from *The Journals, Volume I: 1949–1965* by John Fowles, edited by Charles Drazin (New York, Alfred A. Knopf, 2005).

FRANCIS, KAY   Actress, star of *Trouble in Paradise*. Quoted from *Kay Francis: A Passionate Life and Career* (London: McFarland & Company, 2006).

FRANKAU, GILBERT   Author, poet, verse novelist. Quoted from *My Unsentimental Journey* (London, Hutchinson & Co., 1926).

FRÉMONT, JESSIE BENTON   Writer, editor, ghostwriter. Co-author of several books either with or for her husband, John C. Frémont (q.v., below). His marriage to Jessie Benton turned out to be the best of all the many shortcuts he ever took. She promoted him even better than he could promote himself. Mostly because of her, when people heard of California before the Gold Rush, they thought of John. As much as anything, that's why there's more stuff in California named after him than anybody else who wasn't a president—which he almost was. There's a makeable case for their expedition reports as the first American bestsellers—and she pretty much ghostwrote all of them. Quoted from *The Letters of Jessie Benton Frémont*, edited by Pamela Lee Herr and Mary Lee Spence (Champaign: University of Illinois Press, 1992).

FRÉMONT, JOHN C.   Pathfinder, presidential candidate, enigma. A young man in a hurry, Frémont somehow managed to be both ahead of and behind his time. In 1856, four years before Abraham Lincoln, Frémont ran for president on the first-ever Republican ticket. In 1861 he emancipated every slave in Missouri, a year and a half before Lincoln accomplished the same on a national scale. Yet Lewis and Clark's Western explorations beat Frémont's by four decades. In retrospect, Frémont was cursed: he came in first when it paid to be second, and second when it paid to be first. Born in Georgia, he came into the world illegitimate and went out of it insolvent. In between, he served as governor of pre-statehood California for all of six weeks, and as one of her first two senators for all of twenty-one working days. (If the term-limits movement ever needs a patron saint, Frémont is definitely the man to beat.) He returned east to write his expeditionary journals with his wife, the equally intriguing Jessie Benton Frémont (q.v., above). Most historians make her out to be the brains of the operation. He was the outdoorsman and scientist who could discern the hydrology of a landscape just by looking at it; she, the eloquent mythologizer and apologist for her husband's tail-chasing—both other women's and his own. A psychologist might further suggest that Frémont, whose father died when the boy was four, showed the frequent indiscipline of the fatherless child. Distractable, given to bouts of grandiosity, forever testing the leash and then vowing amends, Frémont did his best with a birthright that was problematic for more than merely heraldic reasons. Frémont was rash, heedless of the lives he disrupted, altogether consumed by the need to do or see or know something that nobody else ever had. Nations need such men, but not forever.

FROST, ROBERT   Major American poet, born in San Francisco, known for "Mending Wall," "The Road Not Taken," "The Gift Outright," and many others. Quoted from *The Letters of Robert Frost: Volume 3, 1929–1936* (Cambridge, Mass.: Harvard University Press, 2021).

FROST, WILL   Short-lived San Francisco newspaperman, father of Robert Frost.

FUJIMOTO, GEORGE   Internee, rancher. Assigned to Military Intelligence Service Language School, where he took intensive language training in Japanese. Served in occupied Japan, where he visited his parents' families. Later a rancher back in Riverside.

GALEANO, EDUARDO   Uruguayan journalist and man of letters, author of *The Open Veins of Latin America* and the *Memory of Fire* trilogy, whose third volume, *Century of the Wind*, contains vignettes about L.A. figures including Bertolt Brecht, Carmen Miranda, Rita Hayworth, and Marilyn Monroe. Quoted from *Looking North: writings from Spanish America on the US, 1800 to the present*, edited by John J. Hassett and Braulio Muñoz (Tucson: University of Arizona Press, 2012).

GARCETTI, ERIC   Proudly half-Jewish, half-Latino, half-Italian former mayor of Los Angeles. Former city councilman, son of the photographer and former city attorney Gil Garcetti. The entry here was originally published in *Slate* and later included in *The Slate Diaries*, edited by Jodi Kantor, Cyrus Krohn, and Judith Shulevitz, with an introduction by Michael Kinsley (New York: Perseus Book Group, 2000). Copyright 2000 by Michael Kinsley. Reprinted by permission of Public Affairs, a member of the Perseus Book Group.

GARLAND, HAMLIN   Glum Midwestern Pulitzer-winning author of *A Son of the Middle Border.* Retired here. Hated every minute. Quoted from *Hamlin Garland's Diaries,* edited by Donald Pizer (San Marino, Calif.: Huntington Library Press, 1968).

GARRETT, GARET   Isolationist, anti-New Deal newspaper columnist. Quoted from "Los Angeles in Fact and Dream," *The Saturday Evening Post,* in *What They Say About the Angels* (Pasadena: Val Trefz Press, 1942).

GEHRY, FRANK   L.A. architect, renowned for his early use of humble materials like plywood and chain link, later for such city-defining buildings as the Guggenheim Museum Bilbao and Disney Hall.

GAVON, LISA   Knowledgeable Alpine County historian, blogger.

GIELGUD, JOHN   Distinguished British actor on stage and latterly in films, including his early turn as Cassius in *Julius Caesar, Arthur* with Dudley Moore, and Peter Greenaway's *The Tempest.* Quoted from *Sir John Gielgud: A Life in Letters,* edited by Richard Mangan (New York: Arcade, 2004).

GILLESPIE, ARCHIBALD   American officer in the Mexican-American War.

GILMAN, CHARLOTTE PERKINS   Writer and feminist, known best for her short story "The Yellow Wallpaper," written in California but published in the *New England Magazine.* Correspondence quoted from *The Selected Letters of Charlotte Perkins Gilman,* edited by Denise D. Knight and Jennifer S. Tuttle (Tuscaloosa: University of Alabama Press, 2009).

GINSBERG, ALLEN   Poet, author of "Howl." Active mostly in his native New York and the Bay Area, but visited family near Los Angeles in the 1950s, most memorably for a 1956 reading/disrobing. Quoted from his *Journals Mid-Fifties, 1954–1958,* edited by Gordon Ball (New York: HarperCollins, 1995).

GIOIA, DANA   Poet, critic, broadcaster, NEA chairman. Award-winning author of, among others, the poetry collections *Daily Horoscope, The Gods of Winter, Interrogations at Noon, Pity the Beautiful,* and *Meet Me at the Lighthouse.* Also the essay collection *Can Poetry Matter?,* which grew out of an *Atlantic* essay that touched off a national conversation. As California poet laureate, he hosted readings in all fifty-eight counties.

GLEASON, RALPH J.   Essayist, Emmy-nominated broadcaster, *San Francisco Chronicle* music critic. Co-founded *Rolling Stone* magazine and the Monterey Jazz Festival. Grammy-nominated for liner notes on albums by Lenny Bruce, Miles Davis, and Duke Ellington. The very model of a modern critic: he heard the early sounds that others missed and artfully shared them with his readers.

GLICKMAN, HARRIET   Concerned Encino mother who suggested Charles M. Schulz create a black Peanuts character. He took her up on it. Her son Paul is now a news editor at KPCC in Pasadena.

GOLD, JONATHAN   Writer, most influentially for the *LA Weekly* and *Los Angeles Times.* Author of *Counter Intelligence: Where to Eat in the Real Los Angeles.* The first food critic to win the Pulitzer Prize, and—with apologies to Eloise Klein Healy, Luis J. Rodriguez, and Robin Coste Lewis—the everlasting poet laureate of modern

Los Angeles. Before most people had ever heard of Zankou Chicken, Gold (Beverly Hills High '78) unforgettably called their beloved garlic puree "a fierce, blinding-white paste . . . whose powerful aroma can stay in your head—also your car—for days." Nobody has ever used the second person as intimately as Gold did. He just assumed that you, too, knew and loved L.A.—and somehow, if only while you read his reviews, you did. With him gone, who's the glue now? Especially after the passing of Vin Scully, who else could ever mean so much to so many different Angelenos? George Takei? Kareem? Seriously, who?

GOLDMAN, "RED" EMMA   Anarchist, lecturer, almost tarred and feathered one night in San Diego.

GORDON-CUMMING, CONSTANCE FREDERICA   Scottish painter and a travel writer, as she put it, from the *Hebrides to the Himalayas*. Quoted from *Granite Crags of California* (London: William Blackwood And Sons, 1886).

GRAFF, EDWARD   1906 San Francisco Earthquake survivor.

GRANT, RICHARD E.   Sleek-haired, combustible British actor, pleasantly reminiscent of Ray Milland, familiar from *Withnail & I* and *How to Get Ahead in Advertising*. In Los Angeles long enough to shoot the canonical Southern California pictures *The Player* and *L.A. Story*, among others. Quoted from *With Nails: The Film Diaries of Richard E. Grant* (Woodstock and New York, N.Y.: The Overlook Press, 1998).

GRANT, ULYSSES S.   Storekeeper, general, president of the United States. Stationed in California, he drank his way out of the army in 1854. It didn't take.

GREY, ZANE   Western novelist of *Riders of the Purple Sage* and many, many others, long resident on Catalina. Quoted from *Dolly and Zane Grey: Letters from a Marriage* (Reno: University of Nevada Press, 2008).

GRIFFIN, JOHN S., MD   Military physician turned early settler. Griffin Avenue in Lincoln Heights is named for him. Quoted from *A Doctor Comes to California: The Diary of John S. Griffin, Assistant Surgeon with Kearny's Dragoons, 1846–1847* (San Francisco: California Historical Society, 1943).

GRIFFITH, GRIFFITH J.   Journalist, industrialist, philanthropist, would-be uxoricide. Shortly before his death, Tolstoy actually answered Griffith's letter as follows: "Dear sir: Thank you heartily for sending your book. I have only looked through it and I think it is a book that is most necessary in our time. I will read it with the greatest attention and will then express to you my more thorough opinion on it." Quoted from the *Los Angeles Herald*, vol. 33, no. 91, 1910.

GUNN, THOM   Poet, professor, backyard gardener. With family roots in a Scottish village by the delightful name of Echt, Gunn was born English in 1929 to a journalist father and, as if that weren't bad enough, an ex-journalist mother. He came to the Bay Area in 1954 and stayed, writing poetry, teaching at Berkeley, and eventually winning a MacArthur Fellowship in 1993. He also earned the sadly discontinued PEN West prize for *The Man with Night Sweats*, his collection about love and friendship in the time of AIDS. "In trying to write in both free verse and metre," he once wrote, "I think I am different from a lot of my contemporaries. There are things I can do in the one form that I can't do in the other, and I wouldn't gladly relinquish either." Reading him can make a reader sorry that conning poetry by heart has fallen out of fashion. Quoted from *The Letters of Thom Gunn* (New York: Farrar, Straus & Giroux, 2022).

GUTHRIE, WOODY Folksinger-songwriter. Born Woodrow Wilson Guthrie, he wrote America's folk national anthem, "This Land Is Your Land," but also hundreds of other tunes just as good. The composer he most recalls may be Mozart, with whom he shared a boundless immaturity—he once dried a dish with the nearest soiled diaper that came to hand—and a graphomaniacally prodigious rate of production. Fellow tunesmith Pete Seeger once said, "I can't stand [Woody] when he is around, but I miss him when he's gone." Him and America both. (Found at https://www.loc.gov/resource/afc1940004.afc1940004_007/?sp=2&st=text.)

HALDEMAN, H. R. L.A.-born ad exec turned White House chief of staff under President Nixon. Afterward, served 18 months in Lompoc testing sewage, presumably drawing on prior work experience. Quoted from *The Haldeman Diaries: Inside the Nixon White House* (New York: G. P. Putnam's Sons, 1994).

HALEY, BILL Rock-and-roll pioneer, recorded "Rock Around the Clock" with his band, the Comets. Quoted from *Bill Haley—The Father of Rock and Roll: The Rise of Bill Haley* (Norderstedt: Books on Demand, 2016).

HAMMETT, DASHIELL Author of *The Maltese Falcon* and other brilliant American crime fiction. His was a style like nobody else's—certainly not that of his perennial yokemate in publicist's hyperbole, Raymond Chandler. A Hammett sentence is stingy with ornamentation, suspicious of sentiment but by no means immune to it, and facetious down to its very serifs. As one might expect of a guy who never named his most frequent alter ego—the San Francisco detective agency operative called, by default, the Continental Op—Hammett guarded his emotional life as if it were a flight risk. He wrote most of his letters either to his two beloved girls, to his wife—from whom he separated after the birth of their second daughter, but with whom he kept up a healthy, affectionate correspondence—or to his lovers. These chiefly included the playwright Lillian Hellman, whom he'd met during one of his periodic bouts of screenwriting. But he seemed happiest when thousands of miles away from any of them, stationed with a U.S. Army company in the Aleutian Islands after volunteering for World War II at the age of forty-eight. There he edited the base's paper, turning a bunch of jarheads into journalists—some of them for life. Hammett returned to L.A. over the years to visit his daughters and grandchildren, by generous permission of one of whom these letters are gratefully excerpted. He died in 1961. Once interned in federal prison for contempt of Congress, he was interred at his request in Arlington National Cemetery for service to his country. Quoted from *Selected Letters of Dashiell Hammett, 1921–1960*, edited by Richard Layman with Julie M. Rivett (Berkeley: Counterpoint Press, 2001).

HARDIE, ROBERT Migrant labor camp manager whose words " . . . we'll find a way through this thing—for we are the American people"— ought to ring a bell for any reader of *The Grapes of Wrath*.

HARLAN, HUGH   Los Angeles newspaperman who dropped a line to his old Grinnell College classmate Harry Hopkins suggesting the rudiments of what became the Federal Writers' Project. Later started his own local paper in Topanga Canyon.

HARPER, HARRIET   Paid a six-month visit to California with another young woman and privately printed an account of their travels. Quoted from her *Letters from California* (Portland, Maine, B. Thurston & Co., 1888).

HARRIS, MARK   Novelist, English professor at Berkeley, and author of, among others, the great baseball novel *Bang the Drum Slowly.*

HARTE, BRET   Popular yarn-spinner of the 1850s remembered for "The Outcasts of Poker Flat" and other short stories, mostly about rascals with visions of gold and hookers with hearts of it. Suffers by comparisons to Mark Twain, but who wouldn't?

HASTREITER, KIM   Editor, publisher, and co-founder of the magazine *Paper.* Surely a very nice person, but *so* New York. Quoted from "A Week in Culture: Kim Hastreiter, Editor," *Paris Review*, April 6, 2011.

HAWTHORNE, JULIAN   Journalist, son of the writer Nathaniel Hawthorne. Convicted of mail fraud, later a crusader for the abolition of penal imprisonment.

HAYES, BENJAMIN   Lawyer, judge, memoirist of the city's early years, and, like many a frontier judge before and after him, among the most learned men in town. He had arrived in Los Angeles via the Mormon Trail through San Bernardino with all the saddlebags full of lawbooks that two mules could carry. As a judge, a year before the U.S. Supreme Court got the *Dred Scott* decision wrong, Hayes got the *Biddy Mason* decision—effectively the same case—dead right. Quoted from *Pioneer Notes from the Diaries of Judge Benjamin Hayes: 1849–1875*, edited and published by Marjorie Tisdale Wolcott (Los Angeles: privately printed, 1929).

HAYES, EMILY   Wife and partner of jurist Benjamin Hayes. Quoted from *Pioneer Notes from the Diaries of Judge Benjamin Hayes: 1849–1875*, edited and published by Marjorie Tisdale Wolcott (Los Angeles: privately printed, 1929).

HEARST, GEORGE   Miner, businessman, politician. His son William Randolph Hearst, like his cinematic alter ego Charles Foster Kane, thought "it would be fun to run a newspaper."

HEARST, WILLIAM RANDOLPH   Publishing tycoon, opinion-maker, amateur architect. Quoted by gracious permission of the family.

HECHT, ANTHONY   Award-winning American poet, stationed for a time in California, whose wartime experiences would haunt his life and work. Quoted from *The Selected Letters of Anthony Hecht* (Baltimore: Johns Hopkins University Press, 2013).

HEINLEIN, ROBERT A.   Science-fiction novelist, latterly a resident of Bonny Doon in Santa Cruz County. Author of, among others, *Stranger in a Strange Land* and *Starship Troopers*. His first short story, "Life-Line," appeared in the landmark July 1939 number of *Astounding*, which many believe inaugurated the Golden Age of Science Fiction. Quoted from *The Heinlein Letters: Volume III* (Houston: The Virginia Edition Publishing, 2012).

HERRICK, LUCY KENDALL   Pioneer whose 1852 travel journal appeared as *Voyage to California: Written at Sea.*

HERRIMAN, GEORGE   Pioneering newspaper cartoonist behind the *Krazy Kat* comic strip. Herriman lived most of his life between downtown L.A. and the Hollywood Hills, though few noted it at the time. (Nobody realized Herriman was Creole, either, and he took pains to keep it that way.) Beloved for both his wordplay and his draftsmanship by everybody from T. S. Eliot to Stan Lee, Herriman worked out his racial ambivalence in the anarchic continuing saga of an immortal black-and-white cat and his unrequited love for a brick-throwing mouse, Ignatz. Quoted from the *Los Angeles Herald*, 1912.

HESTON, CHARLTON   Fine actor, star of *The Ten Commandments, The Omega Man, Will Penny,* and *Planet of the Apes.* Quoted from *The Actor's Life: Journals, 1956–1976,* edited by Hollis Alpert (New York: E. P. Dutton, 1978).

HILLMAN, BRENDA   Pulitzer-nominated Bay Area–based poet and translator. Quoted from *The Writer's Journal: 40 Contemporary Authors and Their Journals* (New York: Delta, 1997).

HIMES, CHESTER   Novelist, essayist, ex-con. His *If He Hollers Let Him Go* remains foundational to L.A. fiction, but Himes is more widely remembered for his Harlem-set detective novels. If only the reality behind L.A.'s World War II–era promises hadn't wounded him so deeply, the NYPD's Coffin Ed Johnson and Gravedigger Jones might by rights have worked for the LAPD. His essay "Zoot Suit Riots Are Race Riots" is a model of cross-racial empathy. Quoted from *Chester B. Himes: A Biography* (New York: W. W. Norton, 2017).

HISA, AOKI   Wife, mother, World War II internee, writer. Quoted from *White Road of Thorns,* edited by Mary Y. Nakamura. (Los Angeles: Xlibris, 2015).

HOPKINS, HARRY   New Deal administrator, statesman, FDR confidante. Almost as much as FDR, he helped lick the Depression and win a world war—all while suffering from excruciating stomach cancer. Churchill called Hopkins "a crumbling lighthouse from which there shone the beams that led great fleets to harbour."

HOPPER, JAMES   Unsung journalist, novelist, 1906 earthquake survivor, for a time head of the Federal Writers' Project in California.

HOWARD OF GLOSSOP, LADY WINEFRED   Witty British diarist in the 1890s on the *other* Grand Tour—of America.

HUERTA, FR. ALBERTO, SJ   Jesuit and friend of Kenneth Rexroth, with him at his deathbed.

HUERTA, DOLORES   Co-founder with César Chávez of the United Farm Workers. Quoted from *A Dolores Huerta Reader,* edited by Mario T. Garcia (Albuquerque: University of New Mexico Press, 2008).

HUGHES, LANGSTON   Poet, vital contributor to the Harlem Renaissance. In and out of Hollywood before World War II working on songs and sketches for liberal revues. Was picketed at a Pasadena Hotel by the evangelist Aimee Semple McPherson and her congregants until police ungently escorted him out of a potentially lucrative book luncheon. Quoted from *Selected Letters of Langston Hughes*, edited by Arnold Rampersad, David Roessel, and Christa Fratantoro (New York: Alfred A. Knopf, 2015).

HURSTON, ZORA NEALE   Author of the epochal novel *Their Eyes Were Watching God*, with its ageless opening line, "Ships at a distance have every man's wish on board." Born in Notsaluga, Alabama, raised in the all-black town of Eatonville, Florida, Hurston wanted to write great literature about African American lives, and succeeded. Came to Hollywood in 1941 as a story consultant for Paramount. Lived in West Adams, almost across the street from the William Andrews Clark mansion, now home to some of the UCLA Library's rarest archives—but not hers, alas. Quoted from *Wrapped in Rainbows: The Life of Zora Neale Hurston*, by Valerie Boyd (New York: Charles Scribner's Sons, 2003).

HUXLEY, ALDOUS   British author of *Brave New World, After Many a Summer Dies the Swan*, and *The Doors of Perception*. Relocated to Los Angeles originally for eye treatment and eventually for enlightenment, chemical and otherwise. Quoted from *Selected Letters of Aldous Huxley*, edited by James Sexton (Chicago: Ivan R. Dee, 2007).

HUXLEY, LAURA   Author, psychotherapist, musician, and wife of Aldous (see above).

HYDE, DOUGLAS   First president of the Republic of Ireland, devoted scholar of the Irish tongue. Also answered to the name An Craoibhín Aoibhinn.

IDE, WILLIAM B.   Leader of the Bear Flag Revolt and the 25-day California Republic—a good idea but flawed in execution, at least last time.

IDLE, ERIC   Writer, lyricist, performer, Python. Long resident in Southern California. Quoted from his *The Greedy Bastard Diary: A Comic Tour of America* (New York: HarperCollins, 2005).

IKEDA, TOMOKO   Japanese American schoolgirl, internee. Quoted courtesy of the Japanese American National Museum (File number 2000.378).

IMMEN, LORAINE   Elocutionist and clubwoman. Visited California in the winter and spring of 1896. Quoted from *Letters of Travel in California, in the Winter and Spring of 1896* (Grand Rapids, Mich.: privately published, 1896).

ISHERWOOD, CHRISTOPHER   Author of *The Berlin Stories* and *A Single Man*, screenwriter of *Frankenstein: The True Story*, pioneering chronicler of gay life. Even a cursory reading of his work discloses a master stylist whose understandable importance to gay literature, California literature, and the literature of pre-World War II Germany tends to obscure his contribution to literature, full stop. He caught Los Angeles as few ever have. Quoted from the three volumes of his *Diaries* (New York: Harper, 1996, 2010, 2012); and *The Animals: Love Letters Between Christopher Isherwood and Don Bachardy* (New York: Farrar, Straus & Giroux, 2014). All edited and introduced by Katherine Bucknell.

JACKSON, GEORGE   Armed robber who landed in Soledad Prison, blossomed as a writer, fell in love with Angela Davis, and died in his last escape attempt. Quoted from *Soledad Brother: The Prison Letters of George Jackson* (New York: Lawrence Hill Books, 1994).

JACKSON, HELEN HUNT   She brought more people to California than the Super Chief. Still in print after all these years, Jackson's 1884 novel *Ramona* tells the story of an illegitimate biracial orphan and her doomed romance with the dashing Indian Alessandro. Jackson wrote it mainly to protest America's genocidal treatment of its indigenous population, but hundreds of thousands promptly clasped it to their bosom as a wisteria-scented lament for California's bygone adobe days. Legions of those readers bought tickets—by no means all of them round-trip—to see "Ramona country" for themselves, thereby only hastening the demise of the dubious Mission paradise the author mourned. Quoted from *The Indian Reform Letters of Helen Hunt Jackson, 1879–1885*, edited by Valerie Sherer Mathes (Norman, Okla.: University of Oklahoma Press, 1998).

JACKSON, JOSEPH HENRY   Print and radio book critic. He reviewed a book every morning in the *San Francisco Chronicle* for decades and, like his opposite number at the *Los Angeles Times*, Robert Kirsch, read himself into an early grave. Originally published in the *San Francisco Chronicle*, July 5, 1938.

JAMES, CLIVE   Critic, poet, essayist, translator, polymath. After being diagnosed with the cancer that would kill him, he taught himself Italian so he could translate the *Divine Comedy*. In the best sense, an armchair hero. Quoted from *Flying Visits* (London: Jonathan Cape Ltd., 1984).

JAMES, HENRY   Great Anglo-American novelist, essayist and critic, brother of William, (q.v., below). Lousy playwright. Author of *The Portrait of a Lady*, *The Ambassadors*, *Daisy Miller*, *The Wings of the Dove*, *The Turn of the Screw*, *The Aspern Papers*, and scores of short stories, including the everlastingly brilliant "The Figure in the Carpet."

JAMES, WILLIAM   American pragmatist philosopher, essayist, author of *Varieties of Religious Experience*. Brother of Henry, (q.v., above).

JARRELL, RANDALL   Poet, critic, novelist. Lived in L.A. in the twenties with his paternal grandparents. Quoted from *Randall Jarrell's Letters: An Autobiographical and Literary Selection*, edited by Mary Jarrell (Boston: Houghton Mifflin, 1985).

JAURRETCHE, COLLEEN   Author, professor, Joycean. (Quoted by gracious permission of the missus.)

JEFFERS, ROBINSON   "The great poet of the American West Coast," per California poet laureate Dana Gioia. Went to Occidental, where he wooed his beloved Una away from her husband and cribbed the idea for his dramatic Tor House from "El Alisal," the arroyo-stone house of writer Charles Lummis (q.v.). Quoted from *The Collected Letters of Robinson Jeffers, with Selected Letters of Una Jeffers: Volume One, 1890–1930*, edited by James Karman (Palo Alto: Stanford University Press, 2009).

JEFFERS, UNA KUSTER   Muse, mainstay, and wife of the above. Also an Angelena, until she and Jeffers fled scandal to Carmel. Quoted from *The Collected Letters of Robinson Jeffers, with Selected Letters of Una Jeffers: Volume One, 1890–1930*, edited by James Karman (Palo Alto: Stanford University Press, 2009).

JOBS, STEVE   Syrian American founder of Apple, winner of the Presidential Medal of Freedom.

JOEL, BILLY   The ultimate New York pop star wrote his best song about an L.A. piano bar. Sorry.

JOHNSON, FENTON   Novelist, essayist, author of *Keeping Faith: A Skeptic's Journey.*

JOHNSON, MACK   Reporter for the crusading publisher Manchester Boddy's *Los Angeles Daily News.* Deeper knowledge of him awaits a long-overdue history of L.A. journalism's very good bad old days.

JOHNSON, NUNNALLY   Screenwriter-producer best known for *The Grapes of Wrath.* Quoted from *The Letters of Nunnally Johnson*, edited by Dorris Johnson and Ellen Leventhal (New York: Alfred A. Knopf, 1981).

JOYCE, JAMES   Author of *Dubliners, Ulysses*, and *Finnegans Wake.* Never visited California, but it's my book. Quoted from *Finnegans Wake* (New York: Viking Press, 1939).

KAEL, PAULINE   Petaluma-born film critic. Kael got her start writing program notes for the UC Theatre in Berkeley and then reviewing on air at KPFA. She wound up at the *New Yorker* for a quarter-century run that changed the nature of American criticism well outside her chosen field. She had the best job in the world because, as a notoriously eccentric critic, she could make careers but never break them. If she raved about a filmmaker, he was well and truly launched. If she panned one, well, that was just Pauline for you. Kael had perhaps the two faculties any great critic needs: a minute attentiveness to her own unpredictable artistic responses, and utter deafness to anyone else's. Quoted from *Pauline Kael: A Life in the Dark* (New York: Penguin Group, 2011).

KAHLO, FRIDA   Mexican surrealist painter, frequently of brilliant self-portraits. Even if you hate the word "iconic," what else to call a woman whose likeness may well account for an appreciable fraction of her country's gross national product? Quoted from *Frida in America: The Creative Awakening of a Great Artist* (New York: St. Martin's Press, 2020).

KAZAN, ELIA   Stage and film director of *On the Waterfront, East of Eden*, and *A Face in the Crowd.* Quoted from *The Selected Letters of Elia Kazan*, edited by Albert J. Devlin with Marlene J. Devlin (New York: Alfred A. Knopf, 2014).

KAZIN, ALFRED   Son of immigrants, literary critic, and memoirist. His first book, *On Native Grounds: An Interpretation of Modern American Prose Literature*, all but reoriented the study of U.S. literature. The audiobook of his memoir *A Walker in the City* makes an ideal companion for urban pedestrians everywhere. Quoted from *A Lifetime Burning in Every Moment: From the Journals of Alfred Kazin* (New York: HarperCollins, 1996).

KEES, WELDON   American poet, painter, literary critic, novelist, playwright, jazz pianist, short story writer, and filmmaker. Not a seismologist or a polo player, that we know of. He left his car in a parking lot beside the Golden Gate Bridge in 1955 and disappeared. Quoted from *Weldon Kees and the Midcentury Generation: Letters, 1935–1955* (Lincoln: University of Nebraska Press, 2003).

KELLOGG, CAROLYN   Book critic and editor. Kellogg worked at the *Los Angeles Times*, and did a job not commonly thought to be all that creative, i.e., assigning and editing book coverage. But she found young, raw writers and somehow turned them into cogent, graceful critics. Her matchmaking skills between reviewer and material were impeccable. The indicator species for literary culture, and quite possibly American daily journalism, is book coverage. Kellogg kept it alive and lively. Quoted by gracious permission.

KENNAN, GEORGE F.   Author, historian, architect of America's Cold War "containment policy." A sometime diplomat, though you wouldn't know it from the California entries in his diary. Quoted from *Sketches from a Life* (New York: W.W. Norton, 2000).

KENNEDY, JOHN FITZGERALD   War hero, journalist, senator, president. Thomas Pynchon unflatteringly attributed Kennedy's foreign policy to his "role model James Bond," but, as Christopher Isherwood writes in these pages, "We were all in love with [JFK] without knowing it."

KENNEDY, ROBERT FITZGERALD   Lawyer, senator, winner of the California presidential primary on the night he died.

KEROUAC, JACK   Author of *On the Road* and *The Dharma Bums*. Rode a northbound freight through L.A., stopping just long enough to get thoroughly depressed. Quoted from *Windblown World: The Journals of Jack Kerouac 1947–1954*, edited by Douglas Brinkley (New York: Viking, 2004).

KESEY, KEN   Novelist, jailbird, Prankster. Kesey's exuberant novels *Sometimes a Great Notion* and *One Flew Over the Cuckoo's Nest* championed individualism under attack from the forces of conformity, and he wrote them both before he turned thirty. Both books grew out of his experiences as an orderly in the Menlo Park Veterans Affairs Medical Center, where he had worked to put himself through a Stegner Fellowship at Stanford. Kesey also used to pick up walking-around money by participating in medical experiments, ingesting such hallucinogens as psilocybin, mescaline, and LSD. He wound up extolling their mind-altering properties as a founding member of the extended counterculture family known as the Merry Pranksters. Even Tom Wolfe, who immortalized the Pranksters, not always kindly, in his 1968 book *The Electric Kool-Aid Acid Test*, called Kesey "one of the most important American writers of the second half of the 20th century." Quoted from *Kesey's Jail Journal: Cut the M************ Loose* (New York: Viking, 2003).

KESSLER, COUNT HARRY   Diplomat, aristocrat, patron of the arts.

KIKUCHI, CHARLES   Berkeley graduate student in social work, internee, peace activist. His diary—idealistic, heartbreaking, occasionally very funny—provides one of the best-written accounts of life under America's World War II internment policy. He later raised two children with his wife, a dancer in the Martha Graham company, and died in the Soviet Union on a peace march. Quoted from *The Kikuchi*

Diary: Chronicle from an American Concentration Camp: The Tanforan Journals of Charles Kikuchi (Chicago: University of Illinois Press, 1992).

KILGORE, WILLIAM   Pioneer, great-great-grandfather of Joan Didion. Quoted from Didion's *Where I Was From* (New York: Knopf, 2003).

KIMBALL, WARD   Disney animator, L.A. Zoo frequenter for ideas, and one of Walt's revered Nine Old Men. Quoted from *The Life and Times of Ward Kimball: Maverick of Disney Animation* (Jackson: University Press of Mississippi, 2019).

KING, BILLIE JEAN   Long Beach–raised tennis star, activist, minority owner of the Dodgers. The handsome new Long Beach Main Public Library is named for her.

KING, CLARENCE   Geologist, author, mountaineer. First director of the United States Geological Survey. In his private life, under an assumed name, he fell in love with a formerly enslaved woman to whom he claimed *he* was black, too. Their common-law marriage produced five children and the deathbed confession that he'd been white all along. Several physical features including Clarence King Lake at Shastina bear his name, but his five children never did.

KING, THOMAS STARR   Minister, orator, abolitionist. For a long time the most admired man in California, credited by Lincoln with keeping California in the Union.

KIPLING, RUDYARD   Novelist, poet, imperialist, genius. Author of, among others, *The Jungle Book*, *Kim*, and the novella *The Man Who Would Be King*. The first English-language writer awarded the Nobel Prize—partly, per the Swedish Academy, for his "virility of ideas."

KIRBY, GEORGIANA   Santa Cruz County pioneer.

KLEINROCK, LEONARD   Professor at UCLA, sender of the first message via the Internet. It was supposed to read "log in," but a system crash abbreviated it to "lo." The biblical connotation puts modern AI-generated attempts at humor to shame.

KNABB, KEN   Writer, translator, and a benefactor to Kenneth Rexroth (q.v.) fans everywhere with his indispensable website, the Bureau of Public Secrets (bopsecrets.org).

KNIGHT, ERIC   This Yorkshire-born screen- (and brilliant letter-) writer of the 1930s, after almost losing his sanity doing thankless hackwork for the studios, walked away one day and built a farmhouse with his bare hands in what's now the San Fernando Valley. His equilibrium gradually restored, he started writing again and wound up turning out an unsung classic noir, *You Play the Black and the Red Comes Up*, and another novel that became one of the most beloved kids' movies of all time. Indeed, few realize that the Yorkshire-born title character was really based on Toots, his lovable best friend from Northridge. (We know her better as Lassie.) Knight also wrote acclaimed patriotic documentaries for Frank Capra before dying tragically in a World War II plane crash. Quoted from *Down but Not Quite Out in Hollow-Weird: A Documentary in Letters of Eric Knight*, by Geoff Gehman (Lanham, Md.: Scarecrow Press, 1988), and *Portrait of a Flying Yorkshireman: Letters from Eric*

Knight in the United States to Paul Rotha in England, edited by Paul Rotha (London: Chapman & Hall, 1952).

LALAMI, LAILA   Gifted Moroccan American novelist, essayist, and UC Riverside professor of creative writing. Pulitzer Prize and National Book Award finalist for *The Moor's Account* and *The Other Americans*, respectively. Quoted from "When we were quarantined," *Los Angeles Times*, June 20, 2020.

LAMOTT, ANNE   Novelist, essayist, memoirist. Lamott's voice on the page has what most other writers would kill for: instant reader rapport. Blessed with a shaggy, truthful charm, she's still best known for her two books of instruction: *Operating Instructions: A Journal of My Son's First Year* and *Bird by Bird: Some Instructions on Writing and Life*. In them she's pioneered a genre describable as how-not-to, or maybe how-to-if-you-absolutely-can't-help-it. Self-deprecating to a fault—to a methodology, even—she recounts her missteps and neuroses until readers buck up in spite of themselves. If she can do it, we think, how hard can it be? With self-concealing skill, Lamott makes making life look hard look easy. In reality, Lamott's on record in *Bird by Bird* as revealing the best trade secret she knows: "shitty first drafts." Quoted from *Operating Instructions: A Journal of My Son's First Year* (New York: Knopf Doubleday Publishing Group, 2005).

L'AMOUR, LOUIS   Beloved prolific author, primarily of westerns, including the influential *Hondo*, and some early L.A. crime fiction. Lived and wrote in Southern California later in life, finally coming to rest at Forest Lawn. Quoted from *The Best of Rob Wagner's* Script, edited by Anthony Slide (Lanham, Md.: Scarecrow Press, 1985).

LANE, ROSE WILDER   Journalist, daughter of Laura Ingalls Wilder, uncredited co-writer if not ghostwriter of *Little House in the Big Woods*, *Farmer Boy*, and other Little House books. Quoted from *West from Home: Letters of Laura Ingalls Wilder, San Francisco, 1915* (New York: Scholastic, 1999).

LARKIN, THOMAS O.   American consul to Alta California, businessman, likely a spy for the U.S. government.

LASTRETO, NIKKI   Good Catholic girl, later cannabis CEO.

LAUGHLIN, JAMES   Publisher, founder of New Directions, poet.

LAWRENCE, D. H.   Groundbreakingly frank British novelist. Author of *Women in Love*, *Lady Chatterley's Lover*, *The Rainbow*, many others. Cruised through California during his New Mexico years. The subject of Geoff Dyer's terrific reluctant biography, *Out of Sheer Rage*. Quoted by Carey McWilliams in "Tides West," his books column for *Westways*. the magazine of the Automobile Club of Southern California.

LECONTE, JOSEPH   Scientist, professor, polymath. Long at UC Berkeley, where the physics building bore his name until 2020. Died of a heart attack in Yosemite.

LECOUVREUR, FRANK   Prussian immigrant, later a county clerk, surveyor, and businessman. Quoted from *From East Prussia to the Golden Gate*, translated by Julius C. Behnke (New York & Los Angeles: Angelina Book Concern, 1906).

"LEE" FROM TOISHAN DISTRICT   Angel Island prisoner, poet. Found at https://www.aiisf.org/poems-and-inscriptions.

LENNON, JOHN   Musician, poet, Beatle. A regular visitor to California for concerts and solo recording sessions. Quoted from *John*, by Cynthia Lennon (New York: Crown/Archetype, 2010).

LEONARD, ZENAS   Fur trapper, mountain man, author of, what else, *Narrative of the Adventures of Zenas Leonard.*

LEOVY, JILL   Author of *Ghettoside*, formerly of the *Los Angeles Times*. Inaugurated the paper's acclaimed murder blog, memorializing each new murder victim in the city. Diary entry originally published in *Slate*, later included in *The Slate Diaries*, edited by Jodi Kantor, Cyrus Krohn, and Judith Shulevitz and with an introduction by Michael Kinsley (New York: Perseus Book Group, 2000). Copyright 2000 by Michael Kinsley. Reprinted by permission of Public Affairs, a member of the Perseus Book Group.

LEPUCKI, EDEN   Novelist, teacher. California and science fiction are both where, famously, the future happens first. Lepucki's debut novel *California* doesn't try to predict the future—she just exaggerates the present to imply a point: that families, cults, gated communities, and the entire First World are closed, inbred systems obliged to overcome their selfishness or bleed out.

LETHEM, JONATHAN   Fiction writer, essayist. Author of *Motherless Brooklyn*, *The Arrest*, and *The Fortress of Solitude*. Along with Dinaw Mengistu's *The Beautiful Things That Heaven Bears*, *The Fortress of Solitude* is among the very best novels yet about gentrification. Born in 1964, Lethem is the bookstore geek who actually made good, the unkempt kid cataloguing first editions at Moe's in Berkeley whose own firsts now adorn the shelves he once straightened. An upstanding literary citizen too, always ready with an introduction or appreciation, even at the cost of time for his own work.

LEWIS, LEON   L.A.–based Jewish lawyer turned spymaster against the Nazis. Overlooked until scholar Steven J. Ross uncovered his spy ring's papers in Cal State Northridge's Oviatt Library and wrote *Hitler in Los Angeles: How Jews Foiled Nazi Plots Against Hollywood and America.*

LINDBERGH, ANNE MORROW   Writer, aviatrix, and wife of Charles Lindbergh (q.v., below), the first man to fly across the Atlantic. Her memoirs, especially of losing her kidnapped child, have offered solace to generations of readers. Quoted from *Bring Me a Unicorn: Diaries and Letters of Anne Morrow Lindbergh, 1922–1928* (San Diego: Harcourt Brace Jovanovich, 1993).

LINDBERGH, CHARLES   Aviator, the original "America Firster." Played footsie with Nazis, transferring his isolationism out of the cockpit and into American foreign policy with near-disastrous results.

LIPPINCOTT, JOSEPH BARLOW   The dark lord of California water politics, a hydraulic engineer implicated in both the draining of the Owens and flooding of the Hetch Hetchy valleys. Quoted from Joseph Barlow Lippincott Papers. UCR Library Special Collections & University Archives.

LONDON, CHARMIAN KITTREDGE   Writer, rancher, and second wife of Jack London.

LONDON, JACK   Oakland-born writer, former oyster patrolman. Author of, among others, *The Call of the Wild, Martin Eden, The People of the Abyss,* and the short story "To Build a Fire," which ends with perhaps the cruelest perspective shift in all of American literature. His novel *The Sea Wolf* begins on a ferry crossing San Francisco Bay, with his alter ego reading an article he's written for a newly arrived magazine—until another boat broadsides the ferry and hurls him overboard. Signed his letters "Yours for the Revolution." Quoted from *The Letters of Jack London: Vol. 3: 1913–1916,* edited by Earle Labor, Robert C. Leitz, and Milo Shepherd (Palo Alto: Stanford University Press, 1988).

LOPEZ, STEVE   Newspaper columnist, novelist. Maybe Northern Californians get Southern California better than the natives do. First there was Joan Didion, blowing south out of Sacramento like some neurasthenic tule fog, writing the books that color how we see Los Angeles even today. Now Angelenos have Steve Lopez, a bread-truck driver's son from Pittsburg, California, whose city-side column may be the best thing to appear in the *Times* since Nixon's hometown op-ed page demanded his impeachment. Quoted from "Column: 50 years later, RFK busboy still waits on someone to follow in Kennedy's footsteps," *Los Angeles Times,* June 2, 2018.

LOWRY, MALCOLM   Author of *Under the Volcano.* Met his wife here and worked on *Under the Volcano* at the Normandie Hotel—later a cannabis hostel, now a boutique hostelry with the storied Cassell's Hamburgers grilling again on the ground floor. Quoted from *Selected Letters of Malcolm Lowry,* edited by Harvey Breit and Margerie Bonner Lowry (Philadelphia: Lippincott, 1965).

LOYA, JOE   East Los-born bank robber turned effortlessly fluent, funny writer whose books include *The Man Who Outgrew His Prison Cell: Confessions of a Bank Robber.* Quoted by gracious permission of the author.

LUGO, JOSÉ DEL CARMEN   Californio landowner, militiaman, justice of the peace. Owned a lot of San Bernardino until the California Land Act of 1851. One of his descendants was your editor's physical therapist.

LUMMIS, CHARLES FLETCHER   Newspaperman, city librarian, archaeologist, and founder of the Southwest Museum. Also a booster, self-promoter, windbag, and rapscallion. Diaries in the Charles Fletcher Lummis Papers, 1850–1929. Braun Research Library Collection, Autry Museum of the American West; MS.1.

MACDONALD, ROSS   Author of *The Chill,* the surprisingly contemporary *Black Money,* and other fine novels featuring detective Lew Archer. Quoted from *Meanwhile There Are Letters: The Correspondence of Eudora Welty and Ross Macdonald,* edited by Suzanne Marrs and Tom Nolan (New York: Arcade, 2015).

MACDONALD-WRIGHT, STANTON   American painter, co-founder of Synchromism. He grew up in Pacific Palisades, went to New York, then had the good sense to come home. Much of his work survives, including glorious murals for Santa Monica's main library and city hall. Also served with distinction from 1935 to 1943 as director of the Southern California division of the WPA's Federal Art Project

MAGÓN, RICARDO FLORES   Mexican revolutionary and journalist. Briefly resided on Red Hill in Echo Park while on the lam from the Mexican government. Did time as a guest of the local constabulary. Quoted from *Dreams of Freedom: A Ricardo Flores Magón Reader,* edited by Chaz Bufe and Mitchell Cowen Verter (Oakland, Calif.: AK Press, 2005).

MAILER, NORMAN   Novelist, journalist, filmmaker, author of *The Naked and the Dead* and *The Armies of the Night*—and a Palm Springs-set Hollywood novel, *The Deer Park.* Covered the 1960 Democratic Convention at the Sports Arena, where JFK won the nomination. Returned on book tours, granting voluble interviews to journalists including this one. Quoted from *Selected Letters of Norman Mailer,* edited by J. Michael Lennon (New York: Random House, 2014).

MANKIEWICZ, HERMAN   Co-author with Orson Welles of *Citizen Kane.* Pauline Kael credited him with writing half the great comedies of the 1930s, which was pushing it, but not by much.

MANN, THOMAS   Nobel Prize-winning German author of *The Magic Mountain, Buddenbrooks,* and *Doktor Faustus.* Fled Hitler for Pacific Palisades, where the modernist home he built now houses a cultural center dedicated to democracy. Quoted from *Letters of Thomas Mann, 1889–1955,* selected and translated by Richard and Clara Winston (New York: Alfred A. Knopf, 1971).

MARCHESSEAULT, DAMIEN   Mayor of Los Angeles. Wrote the note quoted here and then fatally shot himself in City Hall. *Los Angeles Semi-Weekly News,* January 21, 1868.

MARCUS, GREIL   Groundbreaking Bay Area-based cultural critic. Author of *Mystery Train: Images of America in Rock 'n' Roll Music* and *Lipstick Traces: A Secret History of the 20th Century,* plus the rest of a shelf long enough to reach into the soul of the country.

MARQUIS, DON   Created the immortal newspaper adventures of archy, a typing-impaired cockroach, and mehitabel, an alley cat. Came to L.A. to write scripts. Hated it. Wrote a novel about it, *Off the Arm.* Went home. Quoted from *Selected Letters of Don Marquis,* edited by William McCollum, Jr. (Stafford, Va.: Northwoods Press, 1982).

MARX, GROUCHO   Comedian and star, with his brothers, of, among others, *Animal Crackers, Horsefeathers,* and the immortal *Duck Soup.* Quoted from *The Groucho Letters* (New York: Simon and Schuster, 1987).

MASUMOTO, DAVID MAS   Indispensable author and peach farmer, author of *Epitaph for a Peach.* Quoted from *The Writer's Journal: 40 Contemporary Authors and Their Journals* (New York: Delta, 1997).

MATISSE, HENRI   Titanically great French painter, sculptor, and cut-out artist.

MCCOY, ESTHER   Architecture critic, author of the indispensable *Five California Architects.* In Reyner Banham's words, "No one can write about architecture in California without acknowledging her as the mother of us all." Quoted from *Piecing*

Together Los Angeles: An Esther McCoy Reader, edited and with an essay by Susan Morgan (Valencia, Calif.: East of Borneo Books, 2012).

MCDANIEL, WILMA ELIZABETH   Oklahoma emigrant and talented "Dust Bowl Poet" of the Central Valley.

MCLUHAN, MARSHALL   Public intellectual, professor, philosopher, futurist. Courted his future wife, Corinne, while living in Pasadena and researching the Elizabethan pamphleteer Thomas Nashe at the Huntington Library. Quoted from *Letters of Marshall McLuhan,* edited by Matie Molinaro, Corinne McLuhan, and William Toye (New York, Oxford University Press, 1987).

MCWILLIAMS, CAREY   Historian, journalist, activist, author of *Southern California: An Island on the Land* and *California: The Great Exception.* McWilliams reported and editorialized on California's most important battles for social justice of the last century. He also helped organize committees that won several of them. Other fights, such as the one to get the government to admit its mistake in interning Japanese Americans during World War II, were won only after his death. A contagiously jovial writer, McWilliams found the stupidity of politicians not only unconscionable but also risible. His merry takeouts on California's water wars and ecology have left writers as varied as Robert Towne, Kevin Starr, and Mike Davis in his debt. His diaries are preserved in the UCLA Library Special Collections, Charles E. Young Research Library, and published here by gracious permission of his scholar granddaughter.

MEGQUIER, MARY JANE   Gold Rush businesswoman in San Francisco. Made a mint providing housekeeping services to slovenly miners.

MELVILLE, HERMAN   Author of *Moby-Dick* and other novels—which is a little like saying "God, the author of all creation, et cetera." At the end of Chapter 27, Melville invokes the idealistic, long-forgotten one-world philosopher Anacharsis Clootz to describe the multiethnic crew of the Pequod (and, indirectly, the planet we all share, or try to). It's where Melville refers to Ahab's men as "Anacharsis Clootz deputation from all the isles of the sea, and all the ends of the earth." Quoted from *The Letters of Herman Melville* (New Haven: Yale University Press, 1960).

MENCKEN, H. L.   Newspaperman and author of a series of gleeful ragbags titled *Prejudices,* the much-revised landmark *The American Language,* and even a youthful translation of Ibsen. Mencken's biliously quotable prose is the culmination of all the Twain and Wilde that Mencken ingested from childhood—Twain for sand, Wilde for silk—*and* the disappointment he must have felt when nobody else measured up. He said such wonderful things as "A horse-laugh is worth ten thousand syllogisms. It is not only more effective; it is also vastly more intelligent." Enjoyed his brief reporting visit here like a mountain lion enjoys a mule deer. Quoted from *Mencken and Sara: A Life in Letters: The Private Correspondence of H. L. Mencken and Sara Haardt,* edited by Marion Elizabeth Rodgers (New York: McGraw-Hill, 1987).

MERRIAM, CLINTON HART   Scientist, co-founder of the National Geographic Society.

MERRITT, RUTH WOLFFE   Douglas Aircraft worker here in World War II. Quotation published by gracious permission of her granddaughter-in-law.

MERTON, THOMAS   Inspirational Trappist monk, author of a never-out-of-print spiritual autobiography, *The Seven Storey Mountain.*

MICHAELS, LEONARD   Fiction writer, essayist. A published diary is the most forgiving of genres. Write badly and the reader thinks, "Well, he must have been half-asleep at the time." But write well and it's, "To think he must have been half-asleep at the time!" People assume the diarist can do better, but few fault him for neglecting to. Whenever Michaels' published diaries flirt with navel-gazing, his honesty and healthy self-suspicion pull him back to the journal-keeper's true north: daily life, its desolations and consolations, the diurnal medicine of picking oneself up by getting it all down. Also author of the deathlessly titled *I Would Have Saved Them If I Could* and the novel *The Men's Club*—and co-editor of an invaluable, still-consulted anthology of California writing, *West of the West: Imagining California.* Quoted from *Time Out of Mind: The Diaries of Leonard Michaels, 1961–1995* (New York: Riverhead Books, 1999).

MILES, JACK   Author of *God: A Biography* and other books, former *L.A. Times* books editor. Quoted from *A Friendship in Twilight: Lockdown Conversations on Death and Life,* co-written with Mark C. Taylorn (New York: Columbia University Press, 2022).

MILK, HARVEY   Castro Street camera shop owner turned happy warrior and organizer for gay rights, eventually a San Francisco County supervisor. The subject of Dustin Ray Black's Oscar-winning film, and a national hero.

MILLER, HENRY   Author of *Tropic of Cancer, The Cosmological Eye,* and *The Air-Conditioned Nightmare.* Relocated from the cliffs of Big Sur to the bluffs of Pacific Palisades to spend his last years there. Quoted from *Letters by Henry Miller to Hoki Tokuda Miller,* edited by Joyce Howard (New York: Freundlich Books, 1986).

MILLER, JOAQUIN   Writer, "Poet of the Sierras" [sic], he spent his last years in an Oakland cabin on the grounds of what is now the park that bears his name.

MILLIKAN, ROBERT   Caltech president, Nobel laureate for measuring the charge of an electron, and eventual anticommunist informer for the FBI. Quoted from "The Creation of LA's 'Most Recognizable and Beloved' Building," by Hadley Meares, posted at https://la.curbed.com/2014/12/17/10011026/the-creation-of-las-most-reco gnizable-and-beloved-building-1 (2014).

MILOSZ, CZESLAW   Nobel prize–winning poet, Berkeley professor, exile. With its customary verbal inertness, the Nobel committee praised Milosz as a writer "who with uncompromising clear-sightedness voices man's exposed condition in a world of severe conflicts." Milosz captured the spirit of the occasion much better in his Nobel lecture, which should be read by anybody who at first finds Milosz's work forbidding or granite-hewn. It begins: "My presence here, on this tribune, should be an argument for all those who praise life's God-given, marvelously complex, unpredictability" (www.nobel.se/literature/laureates/1980/milosz-lecture.html). Perhaps Milosz's greatest vindication came when the totalitarian regime that cost him a writer's dearest birthright—the daily company of his mother tongue—staggered in the early 1980s and collapsed at decade's end. He made his first visit home after thirty years in 1981 and he received a hero's welcome from dissident and future president Lech Walesa, the man who helped reclaim Poland from its Soviet puppet regime. Milosz said, "I told [Walesa] that I considered him my leader. He said that he had gone to jail because of my poetry."

MINGUS, CHARLES   Pathbreaking black-Chinese-German–Native American jazz composer and musician. Raised in Watts playing classical cello, then found the double bass and jazz. Quoted from his memoir *Beneath the Underdog: His World as Composed by Mingus* (New York: Alfred A. Knopf, 1971).

MISTRAL, GABRIELA   Nobel Prize–winning Chilean poet. Even after the award, she remained mostly untranslated into English and worked for a time at the Chilean consulate in Los Angeles.

MITFORD, JESSICA   Author, journalist, activist. She was "Decca" to friends, of which there were many on both sides of the Atlantic. One of the lavishly gifted and occasionally scandalous Mitford sisters, she moved to San Francisco in the forties and became an eloquent muckraking journalist, most notably in *The American Way of Death*, which took a power mower to Forest Lawn. Quoted from *Decca: The Letters of Jessica Mitford*, edited by Peter Y. Sussman (London: Phoenix, 2007).

MOLINA, ALFRED   Commendably versatile British actor of stage and screen whose hundreds of roles include Diego Rivera, Doc Ock, and a swarthy native at the beginning of *Raiders of the Lost Ark*. Quoted from *Inside Stories: Diaries of British Film-makers at Work* (London: British Film Institute, 1996).

MONROE, MARILYN   Actress, star of *Some Like It Hot* and *The Misfits*. Quoted from *Marilyn Monroe Day by Day*, by Carl Rollyson (Lanham, Md.: Rowman & Littlefield, 2014).

MONTGOMERY, JOHN ELLIOTT   Ship's clerk of the USS *Portsmouth* who preserved the original Bear Flag. Souvenir of the short-lived Bear Flag Revolt, the flag ultimately went up in the 1906 San Francisco Earthquake.

MOONEY, TOM   Labor leader and accused Preparedness Day bomber, a crime for which he was railroaded and later pardoned.

MOORE, ERNEST CARROLL   Co-founder of UCLA. Quoted from *UCLA: The First Century*, by Marina Dundjerski (Los Angeles: Third Millennium Publishing, 2011).

MORA, JOSEPH JACINTO "JO"   Monterey-based painter and cartographer, frequently at the same time.

MORGAN, JULIA   Trailblazing San Francisco-born architect of Hearst Castle and the Asilomar conference center in Pacific Grove, among seven hundred others. Despite all the lovely but sturdy fixtures in her work, she never recognized a locked door she couldn't bust open or a glass ceiling she couldn't break. Quoted from *San Simeon Revisited: Correspondence between Architect Julia Morgan and William Randolph Hearst*. (San Luis Obispo, Calif.: Library Associates, California Polytechnic State University, 1987).

MOSS, JESSE   Emmy-winning documentarian of *The Overnighters* and *Boys' State*, among others. Quoted from "A Week in Culture: Jesse Moss, filmmaker," *Paris Review*, September 8, 2010, and from "A Week in Culture: Jesse Moss, Part 2," *Paris Review*, September 9, 2010.

MOTLEY, WILLARD F.   African American author of the social-protest novel *Knock on Any Door*, adapted into the Humphrey Bogart film. Later resident in Mexico. Nephew of the artist Archibald Motley. Didn't stay long, but plenty of journalists have stayed longer and seen less. Quoted from *The Diaries of Willard Motley* (Ames: Iowa State University Press, 1979).

MUIR, JOHN   Writer, naturalist. It's irresistible to see the five days Ralph Waldo Emerson and John Muir spent together in the Sierra as a passing of the torch. At the time, Muir was an unpublished thirty-three-year-old mill hand, Emerson a tubercular sixty-eight-year-old essayist-lecturer of international reputation. Originally too shy to approach Emerson in person, Muir left a note at the cabin where his hero was lodging with his family. Once they met, the friendship was immediate, and they spent several days tramping and camping together. Muir's own account of their parting on the trail, written in 1901 for the book *Our National Parks*, reads like an acolyte's prostration before his prophet: "Emerson lingered in the rear of the train, and when he reached the top of the ridge, after all the rest of the party were over and out of sight, he turned his horse, took off his hat and waved me a last good-bye. . . . Emerson was still with me in spirit, though I never again saw him in the flesh." There had been California writers before Muir, just as there had been American writers before Emerson, but not until Muir met his model on that mountaintop did he find his own voice. His first published essay, "Yosemite Glaciers," appeared just seven months after Emerson left him that day on the trail. Quoted from *John Muir in Southern California*, by Elizabeth Pomeroy (Pasadena: The Castle Press, 1999).

MUSK, ELON   Businessman, industrialist, car salesman.

NABOKOV, VERA   Editor and translator of her novelist husband, Vladimir (see below). Subject of the biography *Vera (Mrs. Vladimir Nabokov)*, by Stacy Schiff, who has also written the lives of Ben Franklin, Sam Adams, Antoine de Saint-Exupéry, and Cleopatra.

NABOKOV, VLADIMIR   Russian-born author of *Lolita*, *Pnin*, and *Pale Fire*. Nabokov's prose is beautiful, and therefore funny, in ways that no native English speaker would think to write. He knew English from lessons and books, but his arrival in the United States in 1940 may have marked his first real opportunity to hear English spoken badly. The evidence suggests that he found the sound intoxicating. Always oblique yet never obscure, Nabokov's sounds like English on the morning of its birth, with every word equally available to him, and all ruts of habit gone smooth. In 1960, he took a rented villa at 2088 Mandeville Canyon in Los Angeles to work on a screenplay of *Lolita* for the young director Stanley Kubrick. Not much of Nabokov's work remains in the finished film, but he liked the unorthodox screenplay he wrote enough to publish it later. He got sole screen credit, but graciously spoke well of Kubrick's version. According to biographer Brian Boyd, "He and Vera would have been ready to settle permanently in 'charming semitropical' California if their son had not been singing in Milan." In 1963, the Academy of Motion Picture Arts and Sciences nominated him in the Best Adapted Screenplay category. Alas, there's no indication that he returned to Los Angeles for the Oscar ceremony. Nabokov lost to Horton Foote for *To Kill a Mockingbird*. Quoted from *Dear Bunny, Dear Volodya: The Nabokov-Wilson Letters, 1940–1971*, edited, annotated, and with an introductory essay by Simon Karlinsky (New York: Harper & Row, 1979).

NASH, OGDEN   Poet and wit. Came for the movies, missed his family too much to stay long. Quoted from *Loving Letters of Ogden Nash*, edited by Linell Nash Smith (Boston: Little, Brown, 1990).

NAZIMOVA, ALLA   Ukrainian-born actress, latterly founder of the Garden of Allah Hotel on Sunset Boulevard—a kind of 24-hour Algonquin Roundtable, only with a swimming pool, better writers, and a more frolicsome male-to-female ratio. Quoted from *Nazimova: A Biography* (New York: Alfred A. Knopf, 1997).

NICOLSON, HAROLD   Diplomat, hugely prolific writer, and diarist. Devoted but mercifully gay husband of Vita Sackville-West. Quoted from *Harold Nicolson: Diaries and Letters, 1930–1939* (New York: Collins, 1966).

NIN, ANAÏS   Frenchwoman of letters, author of *Delta of Venus*. Led parallel lives with her husband in New York and her longtime paramour in Sierra Madre. Quoted from *The Diaries of Anaïs Nin*, vols. 6 and 7, edited by Gunther Stuhlmann (New York: Harcourt Brace Jovanovich, 1976, 1980).

NISHIDA, J. W.   Jailed communist bookseller. Quoted from *Gentle Rebel: Letters of Eugene V. Debs*, edited by J. Robert Constantine (Champaign: University of Illinois Press, 1995).

ODETS, CLIFFORD   Pioneering playwright and screenwriter of American social drama. Author of plays including *Waiting for Lefty, Awake and Sing!, Golden Boy*, and several films, among them *Sweet Smell of Success* and *The Big Knife*, from his play about compromise in Hollywood. In 1940 he kept his only journal, which he himself called "the daily diary, often naïve, sometimes crude, occasionally pompous, prejudiced, mannered, unfair, even conceited and arrogant." He left out "delightful." Quoted from *The Time Is Ripe: The 1940 Journal of Clifford Odets*, with an introduction by his son, Walt Whitman Odets (New York: Grove Press, 1988).

OJEDA, EVELYN   Gold medalist in the 1932 Olympic Games. Quoted in Andrew Bell, "Female Gold Medalist From 1932 Olympics Turns 100" (*USA Today*, April 17, 2014).

OLDER, FREMONT   San Francisco newspaperman, long in the fight for good government and prisoner's rights, among many other causes. After years of crusading to free alleged Preparedness Day bomber Tom Mooney, Governor Culbert Olson pardoned Mooney a mere eight days after Older's death.

OLMSTED, FREDERICK LAW   Writer and landscape architect whose designs include the Main Quad and master plan at Stanford, the master plan at Cal, and some park in Manhattan.

O'MELVENY, HENRY   Lawyer, city father, founder of O'Melveny & Myers. Quoted from *History of the Law Firm of O'Melveny & Myers*, by William W. Clary (Los Angeles: privately printed, 1966).

O'NEILL, CARLOTTA MONTEREY   Actress, former Miss California, wife of Nobel Prize–winning playwright Eugene O'Neill.

PALEY, AARON   Urbanist, photographer. He created CicLAvia, the quarterly Sunday happening during which all automobile traffic is banished from some of L.A.'s most traffic-choked boulevards. Every three months or so, Angelenos now reclaim their streets on foot, on bicycles, on rickshaws, you name it. The result has fairly transformed the way a lot of L.A. thinks of itself. Quoted by gracious permission.

PALIN, MICHAEL   Author, actor, Python, screenwriter of *A Fish Called Wanda*. Has slithered into Los Angeles whenever his career obliged him, including for the Pythons' triumphant stand at the Hollywood Bowl. Quoted from his *Diaries, 1969–1979: The Python Years* (New York: Thomas Dunne Books, 2007).

PARKER, PAT   Poet, feminist, lesbian, gay-rights activist. Author of *Womanslaughter*, about her sister's murder, and co-author of *Sister Love: The Letters of Audre Lorde and Pat Parker 1974–1989*. Quoted from *Sister Love* (Dover, FL: A Midsummer Night's Press, 2018).

PARTCH, HARRY   Avant-garde composer and designer of hard-to-reproduce musical instruments, alum of the Federal Writers' Project as writer *and* editor. Dropped out of USC to compose. Ushering for the L.A. Philharmonic helped him keep body and soul together. Among all American composers, arguably the best writer, though John Adams comes close. (Among American writers, nobody composes worth a damn.) Quoted from *Bitter Music: Collected Journals, Essays, Introductions, and Librettos*, edited by Thomas McGeary (Champaign: University of Illinois Press, 2000).

PATTON, GEORGE S., SR.   Attorney, father of General George S. Patton, Jr., "Son-in-law of" pioneer Don Benito Wilson. Quoted from *General Patton: A Soldier's Life*, by Stanley P. Hirshson (New York: HarperCollins, 2002).

PEARS, PETER   Opera singer, partner of the composer Benjamin Britten. Quoted from *The Travel Diaries of Peter Pears, 1936–1978*, edited by Philip Reed (London: Boydell & Brewer, 1999).

PERCIVAL, OLIVE   Admired writer, regional historian, botanist. Olive Percival Papers (Collection 119). UCLA Library Special Collections, Charles E. Young Research Library.

PERELMAN, S. J.   Dyspeptic writer, satirist, screenwriter. He and Nathanael West married sisters and lived here in the thirties. Later visited Southern California periodically to write scripts, including his Oscar-nominated adaptation with Dorothy Parker of *Around the World in 80 Days*. Served as writer-in-residence in sadly knishless Santa Barbara. Quoted from *Don't Tread on Me: The Selected Letters of S. J. Perelman*, edited by Prudence Crowther (New York: Viking, 1986).

PETERSON, PETER RUSS   Glenn County farmer.

PICKERING, EDWARD CHARLES   American astronomer. Quoted from "Edward Charles Pickering's Diary of a Trip to Pasadena to Attend a Meeting of Solar Union,≈August 1910." Edited by Howard Plotkin, Southern California Quarterly, Spring 1978.

PICO, ANDRÉS   Californio rancher from the illustrious Pico family. Led the Mexican side to victory in the battle of San Pascual. Later a California state senator and assemblyman.

PICO, ANTONIO MARÍA   *Also* a Californio rancher from the illustrious Pico family (see above). Politician, signer of the California Constitution. Cast his ballot in the 1860 Electoral College for Abraham Lincoln.

PIERCE, HIRAM DWIGHT   Mariposa County argonaut. Quoted from Letters of Hiram Dwight Pierce, Huntington Library, San Marino, Calif.

PLATH, SYLVIA   American poet (*Ariel*) and autobiographical novelist (*The Bell Jar*). If only Sylvia Plath could have married Leonard Woolf, and Virginia Woolf could have married Ted Hughes, maybe everybody would have lived happily ever after. Plath visited California on a road trip to see her aunt in Pasadena, where her bountiful garden made a strong impression—though not as strong as an ornery bear she met in Yellowstone. Quoted from *Letters Home: Correspondence 1950–1963*, edited by Aurelia Schober Plath (New York: Harper & Row, 1975).

POCHODA, IVY   Edgar-nominated L.A.–based author of *These Women* and other novels. Quoted from "When we were quarantined," *Los Angeles Times*, June 20, 2020.

POLLOCK, JACKSON   Abstract expressionist action painter and, along with Philip Guston, a distinguished alumnus of Frederick J. Schwankovsky's third-period art class at L.A.'s Manual Arts High School. Quoted from *American Letters: 1927–1947, Jackson Pollock and Family* (Malden, Mass.: Polity Press, 2011).

PORTER, KATHERINE ANNE   American short-story writer, novelist, journalist, and activist. Author of *Pale Horse, Pale Rider, Ship of Fools*, and her *Collected Stories*, which won the National Book Award *and* the Pulitzer Prize. Quoted from *Letters of Katherine Anne Porter* (New York: Atlantic Monthly Press, 1990).

PORTOLÁ, GASPAR DE   Explorer of 1769 California. Quoted from *The Official Account of the Portolá Expedition of 1769–1770*, edited by Frederick J. Teggart (Berkeley: University of California Press, 1909).

POWELL, ANTHONY   British novelist, author of the towering *A Dance to the Music of Time* dodecalogy. Summoned briefly from England to Hollywood as a consultant on *A Yank at Oxford*. Quoted from *To Keep the Ball Rolling: The Memoirs of Anthony Powell* (New York: Penguin, 1984).

POWELL, LAWRENCE CLARK   Librarian, author, essayist on the literature of California and the West. LCP, as those few people busy as he was abbreviated him, arrived in California in 1910, when his pomologist father went to work for Sunkist.

Powell, as he liked to say, "learned to read in the Carnegie Library of South Pasadena and learned to work in Los Angeles' Central Library." He went to Oxy with the poet Robinson Jeffers and the printer Ward Ritchie and picked up pocket money playing hot jazz on the Dollar Line boats between San Diego and San Francisco, but his ultimate career was never in much doubt. Like his friend, the great L.A. bookseller Jake Zeitlin, Powell was fired from his first professional bookstore job and found his calling as founding dean of UCLA's School of Library Science, whose majestic first library bears his name. Upon his retirement at sixty he took up his pen, concentrating at last on the novels, essays, and memoirs that an unfortunate talent for administration had hitherto consigned to his life's margins. A joy in books suffuses every page in such works as *California Classics*, *The Blue Train*, and *Ocian in View*—his harrowingly beautiful memoir of the 1956 Malibu brushfire that spared his house, and the 1978 blaze that finally took a priceless personal library from him. His California literature–besotted essay collection *Books in My Baggage* landed on the Chronicle Western Hundred list of twentieth-century books west of the Rockies. Quoted from *Take Hold Upon the Future: Letters on Writers and Writing, 1938–1946* (Lanham, Md.: Scarecrow Press, 1994).

PREUSS, CHARLES   Surveyor, amateur photographer on three of Frémont's five expeditions. Like the Donner Party, he had to eat his friends, but at least they were quadrupeds. Good grouchy company.

PRINZE, FREDDIE   Gifted comic actor of the 1970s who died absurdly young by his own hand. Even online today, the laughs on an episode of his sitcom *Chico and the Man*—about an irascible Jewish body-shop owner on the Eastside of L.A. and his scapegrace mechanic—easily outnumber the cringes.

PYNCHON, THOMAS   American writer, born May 8, 1937, in Glen Cove, Long Island. Between the 1960s and the 1980s, spent some time in California, where three of his novels are set. Others range all over the globe and throughout history, often in the same book. Many pit a plucky heroine or poor, priapic, paranoid schnook against some merciless bureaucratic conspiracy. The voice in his occasional nonfiction is postdoctoral yet cheerfully sophomoric, sad yet undespairing. It's also an instrument tuned and retuned in more than half a century of occasional essays, reviews, and liner notes—forming one of the great uncollected anthologies in American letters. In fiction or nonfiction, Pynchon's underlying verbal music stays ever recognizable, unique as a great reed player's embouchure. He remains our archpoet of death from above, comedy from below and sex from all sides, ringing endless fresh variations on the same two questions: What happened to the country we wanted? And can its original promise ever be redeemed? No one rivals Pynchon's range of language, his elasticity of syntax, his signature mix of dirty jokes, dread, and shining decency. As announced in 2022, his research notes and manuscripts will be archived and partially exhibited at the Huntington Library. In truth, the entire Huntington—with its deep holdings in American and world history, science, Californiana, and literature—already *is* a Thomas Pynchon exhibition. (Letters quoted from the Stephen Michael Tomaske Collection of Thomas Pynchon, Huntington Library, San Marino, Calif., by gracious permission.)

RAMÍREZ, FRANCISCO P.   Pioneering prodigy of bilingual Los Angeles journalism, lovingly resurrected in Paul Bryan Gray's *A Clamor for Equality: Emergence* *and Exile of Californio Activist Francisco P. Ramírez* (Lubbock: Texas Tech University Press, 2012). Translations by Gray and me.

RAND, AYN   Novelist, philosopher, author of *The Fountainhead* and *Atlas Shrugged*. Founder of Objectivism, a branch of social Darwinism. Quoted from *The Journals of Ayn Rand* (New York: Penguin Publishing Group, 1999).

RANDOLPH, ESPIE, III   Director, screenwriter, actor, eloquent COVID diarist. Quoted by gracious permission of the author.

REAGAN, RONALD   President, actor. Quoted from *The Reagan Diaries*, edited by Douglas Brinkley (New York: HarperCollins, 2007).

REALF, RICHARD   British-born poet, abolitionist, soldier. No less an arbiter than Ambrose Bierce took pride in having "published his work and paid him for it, when nobody else would have it; repeatedly pointed out its greatness . . ."

REED, JAMES   Donner Party diarist.

REED, PAUL   Unflinching memoirist of the AIDS crisis. Quoted from *The Q Journal: A Treatment Diary* (Berkeley: Celestial Arts, 1991).

REED, VIRGINIA   Donner Party memoirist.

REID, HUGO   Early Scottish settler, author in the *Los Angeles Star* of the "Indian Letters," calling attention to wretched conditions for Native Americans in post-statehood L.A. Quoted from the *Los Angeles Star*, 1852.

REXROTH, KENNETH   San Francisco-, Sierra-, and ultimately Santa Barbara-based poet, critic, translator, radio commentator. Also the author of the terrific, still-unpublished "Camping in the Western Sierra" during his time with the Federal Writers' Project. Rexroth had a prodigious breadth of learning, a hungry attention to the natural world, a contempt for warmongering, and a profound, occasionally overlapping love of women. He grew up in the Midwest, but California worked a mighty transformation in him. The poet Robert Hass has written that Rexroth's first book, *In What Hour*, seems "to have invented the culture of the West Coast." His poem "Requiem for the Spanish Dead" contains these terrifying lines:

> I see the unwritten books, the unrecorded experiments,
> The unpainted pictures, the interrupted lives,
> Lowered into the graves with the red flags over them.
> I see the quick gray brains broken and clotted with blood . . .

Rexroth's fury at war's waste here seems as fresh as ever, the ink gone wet again, like stigmata. Published by permission of the Kenneth Rexroth Trust. With thanks to the Bureau of Public Secrets, Berkeley, 2017.

REYNOLDS, RYAN   Actor, known for *Buried* and *Deadpool*, among others. Witty tweeter, too.

RICE, HARVEY   Ohio newspaper publisher, father-in-law of Orange County patriarch James Irvine I. Stayed a week at his son-in-law's Rancho San Joaquin. Quoted from his *Letters from the Pacific Slope* (New York: Appleton, 1870).

RIDE, SALLY   Physicist, first American woman astronaut. Grew up in Encino, then took a BS in physics and a BA in English literature at Stanford. Spent 343 hours in space over multiple missions. Returned safely to Earth and continued her career as a physicist.

RITCHIE, CHARLES   Prolific Canadian diplomat. Among the funniest and least diplomatic diarists ever to visit California. Quoted from *The Siren Years: A Canadian Diplomat Abroad, 1937–1945* (New York: Macmillan, 1974).

RIVERS, JOAN   Self-deprecating, insult-reliant, pioneering comedian. Quoted from her *Diary of a Mad Diva* (New York: Berkley, 2014).

ROBERTS, FREDERICK MADISON   Assemblyman, integrationist, Son of the American Revolution. Roberts was the first African American ever elected to statewide office this side of the Mississippi. But even before his trailblazing victory in 1918, one family secret had long since guaranteed his place in history. Carved on that other Mt. Rushmore, as it turns out—the one in South Dakota, alongside George Washington, Abraham Lincoln, and Theodore Roosevelt—is the face of Frederick Madison Roberts's great-grandfather, Thomas Jefferson. Roberts served in the state legislature for 16 years, eventually winning from his colleagues the unofficial honorific of "Dean of the Assembly." Finally unseated, back in Los Angeles year-round, Roberts devoted himself to family and civic life. The man who'd regularly written his wife, Pearl, warm, apologetic letters from Sacramento—"My heart just dropped when I found I couldn't leave tonight. . . . A big hug and kisses for both my baby darlings"—had come home. In 1952, as Pearl described it in an oral-history interview, Fred "was backing the car out of the driveway, and another car came speeding by and crashed into him. . . . He passed the following day." At least one important echo still reverberates between Thomas Jefferson and Frederick Roberts: each believed in the power of the West to redefine America. The closest Roberts ever came to admitting his birthright—something that other Founding Fathers' descendants have spent their lives dining out on—comes down to us in a rare surviving exercise of wit. When Roberts wasn't using official Capitol stationery, almost every letter he wrote bore the address of his now long-demolished L.A. home: a handsome two-story affair, once filled with music and talk of politics late into the night, located at 350 East *Jefferson* Boulevard.

ROBERTS, LESLIE CAROL   Widely published writer, professor, environmentalist. Author of *Here is Where I Walk: Episodes from a Life in the Forest* and *The Entire Earth and Sky: Views on Antarctica*. Quoted from *Here is Where I Walk* (Reno: University of Nevada Press, 2019).

ROBERTS COMMISSION   Presidential body convened to investigate any possible espionage that may have resulted in Pearl Harbor's vulnerability to attack. Quoted from the *REPORT OF THE COMMISSION APPOINTED BY THE PRESIDENT OF THE UNITED STATES TO INVESTIGATE AND REPORT THE FACTS RELATING TO THE ATTACK MADE BY JAPANESE ARMED FORCES UPON PEARL HARBOR IN THE TERRITORY OF HAWAII ON DECEMBER 7, 1941* (Washington, D.C., Government Printing Office, 1946).

RODDENBERRY, GENE   Beloved creator of *Star Trek*, former LAPD patrolman. "Star Trek" Collection, UCLA Library Special Collections, Charles E. Young Research Library.

RODERICK, KEVIN   Newspaperman, founding editor of LAObserved.com. Quoted by gracious permission.

RODRÍGUEZ, JOSÉ   Guatemalan American classical music impresario. Went to high school in L.A. Studied music and found a mentor in the editor Rob Wagner, the editor of a magazine in the 1920s and 1930s called *Script*, which some East-Coast-centric readers called a West Coast version of the *New Yorker*. Rodríguez wrote mostly about music and wound up programming both the Hollywood Bowl and the L.A. Philharmonic. He also became a host and music director for local radio stations, especially KFI, driven by a democratic, leveling, thoroughly Angeleno vision for the potential of radio. Quoted from *The Best of Rob Wagner's* Script, edited by Anthony Slide (Lanham, Md.: Scarecrow Press, 1985).

ROGERS, HARRISON   Member of the Jedediah Smith expedition through California. Quoted from *The Ashley-Smith Explorations and Discovery of a Central Route to the Pacific 1822–1829*, edited by Harrison Clifford Dale (Cleveland: Arthur H. Clark, 1918).

ROGERS, WILL   Humorist, entertainer, and newspaper columnist. Lovingly published at willrogers.com/writings.

ROLLER, EDITH   Jonestown victim.

ROOSEVELT, ELEANOR   First Lady of the United States, shoulder to shoulder with her husband, Franklin (see below), in the White House from 1932 to 1945. Peace advocate and social activist. Visited Los Angeles several times on goodwill tours to benefit the less fortunate. Champion of the New Deal, which paved roads and built bridges that Californians still drive every day. Naming the WPA's First Street Bridge in L.A. after her wouldn't be a bad idea. "My Day," *The Eleanor Roosevelt Papers Digital Edition* (2017), https://www2.gwu.edu/~erpapers/myday/displaydoc.cfm?_y=1946&_f=md000295.

ROOSEVELT, FRANKLIN DELANO   President, New Dealer, national savior. On May 6, 1935, President Roosevelt signed legislation authorizing the Works Progress Administration—and with it, for any reader or writer, one of the enduring glories of his administration, the Federal Writers' Project. The project wound up creating American Guides, a series of travel books to 48 states, many cities and counties, and any number of deserts, rivers, and other wonders, books expressly created to "hold up a mirror to America." John Steinbeck navigated by the guides to write *Travels with Charley*, where he called them "the most comprehensive account of the United States ever got together." The FWP was one of a whole Scrabble rack of acronyms that came out of the New Deal, thanks to the most effective monogram of them all: FDR.

ROOSEVELT, THEODORE   President of the United States, uncle of the above. The fatal shooting of President William McKinley on September 6, 1901, may well be the only political assassination in history that actually worked out for the best. In McKinley's place, we got the indefatigable Teddy Roosevelt. It's startling to realize just how many strains in contemporary American political thought trace their origins, under different names, to TR. His unprecedented efforts to conserve the country's natural resources, inspired by his friend John Muir (q.v.), we now recognize as federal environmentalism in embryo. His trustbusting of Big Oil, Big Sugar, and Big Coal could come straight out of an Occupy platform. Roosevelt's overall progressive agenda looks uncannily like what people used to call modern liberalism, until the stigma attached to that word now has us calling it progressivism all over again. Quoted from a *Compilation of the Messages and Speeches of Theodore Roosevelt*, vol. 1, edited by Albert Henry Lewis (New York and Washington: Bureau of National Literature and Art, 1906).

RUESS, EVERETT   Free-spirited young man who left L.A. and wandered into the California wilderness, never to be seen again. Quoted from *Everett Ruess: A Vagabond for Beauty*, by W. L. Rusho (Salt Lake City: Gibbs Smith, 1983).

ROYCE, JOSIAH   Harvard philosopher and historian born in Grass Valley, the son of Sarah (see below). Author of *California: A Study of American Character: From the Conquest in 1846 to the Second Vigilance Committee in San Francisco*, much beloved of California scholars, much despised by John C. Frémont, who, Royce argued, "possessed all the attributes of genius except ability."

ROYCE, SARAH   Writer, teacher, pioneer, mother of Josiah (see above). Author, at her son's urging, of an enjoyable memoir titled *A Frontier Lady: Recollections of the Gold Rush and Early California*.

RUÍZ DE RODRÍGUEZ, DOÑA BERNARDA   Uncredited contributor and compromise broker for the Treaty of Cahuenga, which ended the Mexican-American War. Quoted in "In a State of Peace and Tranquility," by Hadley Meares, https://www .kcet.org/history-society/in-a-state-of-peace-and-tranquility-campo-de-cahuenga -and-the-birth-of-american.

RULAND, JIM   Novelist, critic, booklength journalist, noted for his eclectic choice of subjects. Quoted from *The Elegant Variation*.

RUSSELL, BERTRAND   British philosopher, pacifist, anti-nuclear campaigner. Taught at UCLA for a term. Like most professors, he left few traces of his sojourn. Someday someone will compile a roster of all the distinguished visiting faculty to grace California campuses over the years, and what they said and did here. The list isn't short. The talent is phenomenal. Quoted from *The Selected Letters of Bertrand Russell, Volume 2: The Public Years, 1914–1970*, edited by Nicholas Griffin (New York: Routledge, 2001).

SAAD, SAMIA   UCLA undergraduate, believe it or not. See also under Acknowledgments.

SACKVILLE-WEST, VITA   British novelist, poet, gardener, and the inspiration for Virginia Woolf's *Orlando*. Quoted from *The Letters of Vita Sackville-West to Virginia Woolf* (Berkeley: Cleis Press, 2004).

SAITO, SANDIE   Japanese American schoolgirl and internee. Quoted at http://ddr .densho.org/ddr-janm-1-10/.

SALVATOR, LUDWIG LOUIS   Archduke of Austria, son of the Duke of Tuscany. Visited Los Angeles in the winter of 1876, not long after the city was linked directly by rail to the East. While most of the ballyhooers in town were falling all over themselves comparing L.A. to Italy, an actual Italian princeling visited L.A. and, without resorting to cheap comparisons, saw that it was good. Quoted from his *Los Angeles in the Sunny Seventies: A Flower from the Golden Land*, translated by Marguerite Eyer Wilbur (Los Angeles: Bruce McCallister and Jake Zeitlin, 1929).

SALZMAN, ED   Oakland Tribune newspaperman whose stories about industrial encroachment on San Francisco Bay inspired Esther Gulick, Kay Kerr, and Sylvia McLaughlin to found the organization that did, indeed, Save the Bay. Found at http://www.sfmuseum.org/sunreporter/fleming16.html.

SANDBURG, CARL   American poet, Lincoln biographer, pioneering film critic. Sandburg went to Hollywood in 1960 for a year and a half to work on the script for *The Greatest Story Ever Told*, which fell well short of becoming the greatest movie ever made but paid the best-loved poet in America $125,000. Quoted from *The Letters of Carl Sandburg*, edited by Herbert Mitgang (New York: Harcourt Brace & World, 1968).

SANDERS, GEORGE   Urbane, insinuating British actor, familiar from *Rebecca, All About of Eve*, and scores more. Quoted from his *Memoirs of a Professional Cad* (New York: Putnam, 1960).

SANDERS, SUE A.   Traveler, correspondent. Quoted from her *Journey to, on and from the "Golden Shore"* (Delavan, Ill.: Times Printing Office, 1887).

SAROYAN, WILLIAM   Fine if self-infatuated Armenian American writer, son of immigrants. By his twenties, he had romanticized a deprived childhood into the best-selling short-story collections *The Daring Young Man on the Flying Trapeze* and *My Name Is Aram*. Within a few years he added a similarly beloved semiautobiographical novel, *The Human Comedy* and, in 1939, a play set in a San Francisco waterfront saloon, *The Time of Your Life*, which won the Pulitzer Prize. There's a little bit of William Saroyan in every fine writer, but aggressive therapy can usually keep it in remission. Quoted from *The Best of Rob Wagner's* Script, edited by Anthony Slide (Lanham, Md.: Scarecrow Press, 1985).

SARVAS, MARK   Novelist, teacher, author of *Memento Park* and *Harry, Revised*, formerly a blogger of distinction at The Elegant Variation, which took its name from a literary term meaning the substitution of one word or phrase for another for the sake of variety. (Examples include "the high court" for "the Supreme Court," and, of course, "the Golden State" for "California.") Quoted by gracious permission of the author.

SAVIO, MARIO   Student leader, free-speech activist, orator. Savio grew up Sicilian in Queens, an altar boy and physics prodigy. He had a paralyzing stammer, which made his later leadership in the Free Speech Movement not so much ironic as deeply personal. Savio loved free speech as maybe only someone denied it since childhood could. Fired with the idealism of his work in Mississippi during the Freedom Summer of 1964, he resisted the cult of personality with which journalists kept trying to saddle him. Thanks to the pitiless Darwinism of YouTube, Savio's legacy primarily rests on his brief, astonishingly extemporaneous "bodies upon the gears" speech, delivered right before the Free Speech Movement's climactic sit-in on December 2, 1964. In his justly celebrated speech that day, Savio gives ragged but eloquent voice to the rage and especially the pain of a cohort that, in the words of a John Updike poem, did not yet know it was a generation.

SCHEYER, GALKA   Refugee, educator, pioneering art dealer for, among others, the European painters of the Blue Four group—Wassily Kandinsky, Lyonel Feininger, Paul Klee, and Alexej von Jawlensky. Also a client of architect Richard Neutra. Quoted from *Galka E. Scheyer and the Blue Four: Correspondence 1924–1945*, edited by Isabel Wünsche (Salenstein, Switzerland: Benteli Verlags, 2006).

SCHINDLER, RUDOLF   Architect of landmark L.A. buildings, including his namesake house on Kings Road. Quoted from *Vienna to Los Angeles: Two Journeys: Letters Between R. M. Schindler and Richard Neutra + Letters of Louis Sullivan to R. M. Schindler*, by Esther McCoy (Santa Monica: Arts + Architecture Press, 1978).

SCHLIEMANN, HEINRICH   German businessman-archaeologist who discovered the ruins of ancient Troy in modern-day Turkey. Years before, he'd developed his interest in excavation as a none too scrupulous mining investor. The gold fields he once visited are now, like Troy, ghost towns too.

SCHMIDT, ERIC   Successful businessman, engineer, Google co-founder, philanthropist. Just how successful? Search me.

SCHOENBERG, ARNOLD   Modernist "serial music" composer of, among others, *Moses und Aron* and *Verklärkte Nacht*. A fairly acclimated refugee here, like his occasional tennis partner Stravinsky. When they were on the outs, the Brentwood Country Mart wasn't big enough for both of them. He taught at UCLA, where the music building once christened after him now shares its name with another great musical Angeleno, Herb Alpert. Quoted from *Schoenberg Remembered: Diaries and Recollections*, by Dika Newlin (New York: Pendragon, 1980).

SEABORG, GLENN T.   Nobel Prize–winning physicist, co-discoverer of plutonium. Grew up in Southern California. "Glenn Theodore Seaborg Diaries, 1927–1946," Box 951575, UCLA Library Special Collections, Charles E. Young Research Library.

SELZNICK, DAVID O.   Producer. *Gone With the Wind* had sixteen co-writers and several directors, but not a single co-producer. His memos are marvels of perspicacity and megalomania. Quoted from *Memo from David O. Selznick*, edited by Rudy Behlmer and Roger Ebert (New York: Grove Press, 1972).

SERRA, FATHER JUNÍPERO   Franciscan padre, saint, father of the California mission system. Let's just say his reputation hasn't worn well.

SHAW, GEORGE BERNARD   Anglo-Irish playwright and essayist. Wrote more plays than Sousa wrote marches, but with Shaw you can actually tell them apart, and several are brilliant: the class-struggle comedy of *Pygmalion*, the drawing-room metaphysics of *Man and Superman*, and *Heartbreak House*, with its strikingly modern, all-but-apocalyptic finale. Quoted from *George Bernard Shaw: Collected Letters, 1926–1950* (New York: Viking, 1988).

SHELLHORN, RUTH   A celebrated landscape architect whose projects included, often frustratingly for her, Disneyland. "Ruth Patricia Shellhorn papers, 1909–2006," UCLA Library Special Collections, Charles E. Young Research Library.

SIEGELMAN, RUSS   Venture capitalist, nonprofiteer. Originally published in the *Paris Review.*

SILLIMAN, BENJAMIN   Yale-educated scientist, the first to distill petroleum. Quoted in *What They Say About the Angels*, Pasadena: Val Trefz Press, 1942.

SIMONIN, LOUIS LAURENT   French geologist, journalist, travel writer.

SINCLAIR, JOHN   Donner Party diarist.

SIRHAN, SIRHAN   Assassin of Robert F. Kennedy, at the time a student at Pasadena City College. Quoted from his published notebooks, including in *RFK Must Die* by Robert Blair Kaiser (Woodstock and New York, N.Y.: Overlook Press, 2008).

SLONIMSKY, NICHOLAS   Longtime editor of *Baker's Dictionary of Musicians.* Lived to be 101, updating his invaluable compendium right to the end. Quoted from *Dear Dorothy: Letters from Nicolas Slonimsky to Dorothy Adlow*, edited by Electra Slonimsky Rourke (Rochester, N.Y.: University of Rochester Press, 2012).

SMITH, CLARK ASHTON   Placer County horror writer, based in Auburn, a friend and colleague of H. P. Lovecraft. Quoted from *Selected Letters of Clark Ashton Smith* (Sauk City, Wis.: Arkham House, 2003).

SMITH, H. V. "VEE"   As a superintendent for the Civilian Conservation Corps, he oversaw the WPA's restoration of La Purísima Mission in Lompoc by a bunch of unemployed city boys who'd never seen stars before.

SMITH, JEDEDIAH   Explorer, cartographer. Furrier too—especially after months on the trail without a razor. Finally killed by Native Americans. Quoted from *The Travels of Jedediah Smith: A Documentary Outline. Including the Journal of the Great American Pathfinder*, edited by Maurice Sullivan (Santa Ana, Calif.: Fine Arts Press, 1934).

SNYDER, GARY   Poet, essayist, environmentalist, and Buddhist. Born in San Francisco, long resident somewhere up a mountain above Nevada City, Snyder's work ranges from the poetry of *Mountains and Rivers Without End* to the essays in *The Practice of the Wild*—to his Pulitzer Prize–winning *Turtle Island*, which combines both. Only carelessly grouped with his friends Ginsberg, Kerouac, and Ferlinghetti, in truth Snyder was never a Beatnik, more like a Beatific. He may be California's last sage—a compliment at which he'd probably laugh and ask, "What good is a sage, except to brew tea from?" We'll take a pot. Quoted from *The High Sierra of California* (Berkeley: Heyday Books, 2016).

SOLNIT, REBECCA   Essayist, critic, magpie. Rebecca Solnit has the wide-foraging mind of a great essayist and the West-besotted soul of the recording secretary for your local historical society. In such books as *River of Shadows: Eadweard Muybridge and the Technological Wild West, A Field Guide to Getting Lost, Orwell's Roses*, and *Hollow City*—her fierce requiem for a vanishing San Francisco—she raises free association to a fine art, finding patterns and following ideas with a ravenous curiosity. A San Franciscan, she's who Susan Sontag (q.v., below) might have become if Sontag had never forsaken California for Manhattan—only better. Quoted by gracious permission.

SONKSEN, MIKE   Third-generation L.A. poet, teacher, performer, essayist, lay historian. Author of *I Am Alive in Los Angeles!* and *Letters to My City.* Quoted by gracious permission of the author.

SONTAG, SUSAN   Critic, essayist, novelist, author of *Against Interpretation, Illness as Metaphor,* and *The Volcano Lover.* Consummate New Yorker, but also the sweetheart of North Hollywood High. Ungraciously, she all but apologized for selling her papers to UCLA instead of New York. She wrote only once about her San Fernando Valley youth, an essay about her teenage pilgrimage to meet Thomas Mann at home in Pacific Palisades. "Papers of Susan Sontag," UCLA Library Special Collections, Charles E. Young Research Library.

SPALDING, WILLIAM ANDREW   Los Angeles newspaperman. Quoted from *William Andrew Spalding: Los Angeles Newspaperman,* edited by Robert V. Hine (San Marino, Calif.: The Huntington Library Press, 1961).

SPECKTOR, MATTHEW   Underappreciated novelist, screenwriter, essayist, culture critic. Author of the novels *That Summertime Sound* and *American Dream Machine* and a sublime book of nonfiction, *Always Crashing in the Same Car: On Art, Crisis, and Los Angeles, California.* Quoted by gracious permission of the author.

SPENDER, STEPHEN   British poet, contemporary of Christopher Isherwood and W. H. Auden. Stopped for tea with the Hollywood Raj and wrote his libretto *The Rake's Progress* in nine days on Stravinsky's couch. Quoted from his *Journals 1939–1983,* edited by John Goldsmith (London: Faber and Faber, 1985).

STANDAGE, HENRY   Member of the Mormon Battalion in the Mexican-American War. Quoted from *The March of the Mormon Battalion from Council Bluffs to California Taken from the Journal of Henry Standage,* by Frank Alfred Golder with Thomas A. Bailey and J. Lyman Smith (New York: The Century Co., 1928).

STARR, KEVIN   California historian. His was ebullient, nuanced, interdisciplinary history of the grandest kind, drawing parallels and distinctions where perhaps no one ever thought to see them before. Starr was a born storyteller, mining a rich seam of anecdotal coal to animate complex, enigmatic figures in California history. Such a brilliant historian could also prove an occasionally divisive figure. To those fundamentally decent but still skittish folks who dominate local historical societies, Starr was a corking good storyteller, but did he have to dwell so much on minorities, women, and gays? To academic historians he was a prodigious researcher, but also a Jesuit-educated generalist who served unapologetically in the U.S. Army, and who wrote unfashionable Francis Parkman–style narrative history. It's stereotypes like these, of course, that keep those of us who love California from loving each other with equal ardor. If only by example, Starr's omnivorous, benevolent curiosity may just suggest a way around these fortifications. Originally published in *The San Francisco Examiner.*

STEFFENS, LINCOLN   An indefatigable investigative journalist, Steffens was born in San Francisco and died in Carmel. In between, he raked more muck than any crusading California journalist except perhaps Carey McWilliams. His book *The Shame of the Cities* changed profoundly the way America thought about urban poverty. Quoted from *Lincoln Steffens: Portrait of a Great American Journalist* (New York: Simon and Schuster, 2013).

STEGNER, WALLACE   Novelist, environmentalist, teacher. Winner of the National Book Award *and* the Pulitzer Prize—the latter for his delightfully cranky novel *Angle of Repose*, which was partly set at Stanford, partly in the Sierra Nevada of the 1850s. Also author of *Beyond the Hundredth Meridian*, which topped the Chronicle Western Hundred for twentieth-century nonfiction. Stegner helped inaugurate the storied writing fellowships at Stanford that bear his name. Without its graduates, *Dear California* might be considerably thinner. Bill McKibben once observed that Wendell Berry studied with Stegner in a seminar that also included Edward Abbey, Larry McMurtry, and Ken Kesey—"as much literary firepower as may have ever slouched in the same classroom." (Not to mention Tillie Olsen and, a year or so later, Ernest J. Gaines.) Stegner also godfathered the modern environmental movement with his essay known as "The Wilderness Letter"—at least as influential a California letter as any in this book. Quoted from *The Selected Letters of Wallace Stegner* (Berkeley: Counterpoint, 2007).

STEIN, GERTRUDE   Novelist, playwright, librettist, art collector. Born in Oakland, though don't go looking for any plaques. Lived most of her life in Paris with her partner, Alice B. Toklas, in an apartment whose walls all but sagged under the weight of many a young painter's masterpieces. Quoted from *The Letters of Gertrude Stein and Thornton Wilder* (New Haven: Yale University Press, 1996).

STEINBECK, JOHN   Novelist, foreign correspondent, environmentalist, thrice-Oscar-nominated screenwriter. Nobel Prize-winning author of, among others, *The Grapes of Wrath* and *Travels with Charley*—especially its Lonesome Harry chapter, which is basically a whole MFA program in four pages. The knock on Steinbeck has always been that he's too sentimental and his symbolism so apparent that—heaven forfend!—even a high school student can appreciate it. The worst offender here has to be the *New York Times*, which ran a hit piece on Steinbeck the day he was to receive the Nobel Prize for Literature. And what were Steinbeck's crimes? For one, he was political. Though his fiction could be surprisingly nuanced on the subject of unionism, Steinbeck made no secret of his sympathies for workers over their bosses. For another, people make a habit of reading Steinbeck without the *Times* telling them to. Steinbeck still has what critic Jay Parini referred to as "actual voluntary readers." Finally, Steinbeck was a Californian—from New York's perspective, a not-one-of-me. But don't believe a Californian with a chip on his shoulder. Believe Chicago-born Saul Bellow, who lobbied for Steinbeck's Nobel years before he got his own. Should we feel sorry for Steinbeck, still stuck in the critical doghouse after all these years? No, only for those who put him there. They can't possibly know what they're missing. Quoted from *Steinbeck: A Life in Letters*, edited by Elaine Steinbeck and Robert Wallsten (New York: Viking Press, 1975).

STEINMAN, LOUISE   Writer, dancer, founding curator of the Los Angeles Central Library's long-running "Aloud" series of public conversations. Author of *The Crooked Mirror: A Memoir of Polish-Jewish Reconciliation* and *The Souvenir: A Daughter Discovers Her Father's War*. Quoted by gracious permission.

STENDAHL, EARL   Gallerist, chocolatier. It's just possible that no one now alive visited Stendahl's modest but elegant L.A. art gallery for the unveiling of the most important painting of the twentieth century, Picasso's *Guernica*—brought to town by European exiles like Fritz Lang and art dealer Galka Scheyer (and New York exiles like Dorothy Parker) as a fundraiser for Spanish Civil War orphans. Quoted by gracious permission.

STERN, STEWART   Author, twice Oscar-nominated screenwriter—but not for his most enduring contribution to American culture, *Rebel Without a Cause*.

STETTINIUS, EDWARD R.   American secretary of state who presided over the 1945 United Nations Conference in San Francisco. Everyone expected the UN itself to wind up in San Francisco—until John D. Rockefeller made an offer of free land on the East Side of New York that the organization couldn't refuse. You have to wonder how much more effective the UN might have been all these years if only it had spurned Manhattan for someplace more . . . pacific.

STEVENSON, ROBERT LOUIS   Scottish novelist, poet, travel writer, the author of *The Strange Case of Dr Jekyll and Mr Hyde*, *A Child's Garden of Verses*, and *Treasure Island*—whose setting many insist he modeled on his own sometime home of Monterey. Argentine fabulist Jorge Luis Borges often called Stevenson's his favorite English-language prose.

STEWARD, SAMUEL   Poet, novelist, professor, body artist for the Hell's Angels. His prodigious "Stud File" included everyone from Rudolph Valentino to Thornton Wilder. Also a subject of sex researcher Alfred Kinsey and close friend and correspondent of Gertrude Stein. Kevin Bacon should just give up. Quoted from *Secret Historian: The Life and Times of Samuel Steward, Professor, Tattoo Artist, and Sexual Renegade* (New York: Farrar, Straus & Giroux, 2010).

STODDARD, CAROLINE   San Francisco pioneer.

STRAIGHT, SUSAN   Novelist, essayist, and educator, mentored by the great screenwriter-journalist Bill Bowers. Author of National Book Award–nominated *Highwire Moon*, her retelling of the Evangeline story set on both sides of the California-Mexico border. As head of the UC Riverside Creative Writing program, she herself has nurtured more first-generation authors than anyone in California, and maybe out of it. Quoted from "When we were quarantined," *Los Angeles Times*, June 20, 2020.

STRAUSS, LEVI   German-Jewish businessman who gave us blue jeans—or, as they're happily called in Spanish, *bluyines*.

SUTTER, JOHANN AUGUSTUS   Swiss immigrant who established a fort in present-day Sacramento and, during the waning days of the Mexican-American War, commissioned a sawmill on the South Fork of the American River. If he hadn't, American history itself might have forked a different way.

SWAIN, DANIEL   It is now illegal in the state of California to write a newspaper weather story without quoting this UCLA climate scientist and blogger, sometimes referred to as "The Young Swain." Quoted from Twitter, January 19, 2021.

TAPE, MARY   Activist and plaintiff in the desegregation case *Tape v. Hurley*, where the California Supreme Court ruled that San Francisco schools had to admit her daughter, Mary.

THOMAS, DYLAN   Welsh poet, author of "Do Not Go Gentle into That Good Night," *A Child's Christmas in Wales*, and the story collection *Adventures in the Skin Trade*—the little-remarked titular precursor to William Goldman's classic screenwriter's-eye-view of Hollywood, *Adventures in the Screen Trade*. Lurched through California on the American tour immortalized by Peter DeVries and Julius J. Epstein, respectively, in the novel and film *Reuben, Reuben*. Quoted from *Dylan Thomas: The Collected Letters*, edited by Paul Ferris (London: J. M. Dent & Sons, 2000).

THOMPSON, HUNTER S.   Journalist, political columnist, author of *Fear and Loathing in Las Vegas* and *Fear and Loathing on the Campaign Trail*. For the hard-living or the famous, somebody's always ready to spin suicide into a cautionary tale. It's too easy to forget what a brilliant writer Thompson was. The signature Thompson speedball combines grandiosity, paranoia, and pure poetry. He wrote about his nemeses, especially Nixon, with an invigorating lack of gentility. Met Oscar "Zeta" Acosta (q.v.), the inspiration for Dr. Gonzo in *Fear and Loathing in Las Vegas*, while reporting his firsthand account of the Chicano Movement and Moratorium. Quoted from *The Proud Highway: Saga of a Desperate Southern Gentleman, 1955–1967, The Fear and Loathing Letters, Volume One*, edited by Douglas Brinkley (New York: Random House, 1997).

THOMSON, DAVID   British film critic and novelist, long resident in San Francisco. His idiosyncratic, imperishable *Biographical Dictionary of Film* will outlive us all. Quoted from *Los Angeles Times*, April 15, 2020.

THORNTON, HAZEL   Juror, diarist. Quoted from *Hung Jury: The Diary of a Menendez Juror* (Philadelphia: Temple University Press, 1995).

THURBER, JAMES   Writer and cartoonist, long at the *New Yorker*, author of *My World and Welcome to It* and the short story "The Secret Life of Walter Mitty." Thurber didn't hate L.A. as much as he let on. He hated it more. Quoted from *The Thurber Letters: The Wit, Wisdom, and Surprising Life of James Thurber*, edited by Helen Thurber and Edward Weeks (Boston: Little, Brown, 1981).

TIMBERG, SCOTT   Journalist, musician, cultural omnivore, on-again-off-again lover of L.A., perpetual enthusiast. Author of *Culture Crash: The Killing of the Creative Class*. To paraphrase A. J. Liebling, Timberg wrote about music better than any other literary journalist, and about literature better than any other music journalist. Possessed of a Stakhanovite work ethic, he left behind more words than friends, but it was close.

TÓIBÍN, COLM   Irish author who wrote "Tales from the L.A. River" as part of a series of pandemic stories commissioned by the *New York Times*. Tóibín has won everything from the Booker Prize to, back in 1995, the E. M. Forster award. Quoted from "Tales from the L.A. River," *New York Times*, July 7, 2020.

TRUMAN, HARRY   The unlikely thirty-third American president, whose plainspoken, sometimes truculent manner inspired a one-man-show titled *Give 'Em Hell*,

Harry. Hell is precisely what he gave Hiroshima in 1945; afterward, he claimed never to have lost a night's sleep over it. Most American GIs in the Pacific, spared a bloody invasion, thanked God for Truman's decision. Bombing Nagasaki three days later, though, when the Japanese still barely knew what had hit them, looks, in retrospect, ever more unforgivable. Quoted from his San Francisco address at the closing of the United Nations Conference, June 26, 1945.

TRUMBO, DALTON   Screenwriter, novelist, and the man who broke the blacklist. Author of the antiwar classic *Johnny Got His Gun.* In *Spartacus*, Trumbo has Kirk Douglas shout "I am Spartacus!" to reclaim his identity—just as Trumbo was reclaiming his own, by securing screen credit after a decade on the blacklist. Quoted from the canonical *Additional Dialogue: Letters of Dalton Trumbo, 1942–1962*, edited by Helen Manfull (New York: M. Evans and Company, 1970).

TURNER, PATRICK   Corona del Mar student, whose suicide note decrying a modern high school's relentless emphasis on success has gone sadly unheeded. Quoted from news reports.

TWAIN, MARK   Writer and humorist, as if that weren't redundant. Author of, among others, *The Adventures of Huckleberry Finn* and *The Adventures of Tom Sawyer.* To call Twain "the Lincoln of our literature," as his friend William Dean Howells did after attending Twain's funeral, was a great compliment—and Lincoln doesn't fare too badly by the comparison, either. Sometime in 1866, probably in his lodgings at the Occidental Hotel near Sutter and Montgomery, Twain put a pistol to his head. That day in San Francisco, he couldn't know that he was holding the future of American literature at gunpoint. Twain saw as clearly as anybody that as Americans we're all on this raft together, afloat between oceans, crewed by oarsmen of more than one color, tippy as hell but not aground, not yet. Quoted from *Mark Twain's Letters, Volume 1: 1853–1866* (Berkeley: University of California Press, 1975).

TYNAN, KENNETH   Critic and author of *Oh, Calcutta!* Alongside Laurence Olivier, the presiding intelligence behind the birth of Britain's National Theatre. Latterly, critic at large for the *New Yorker.* Moved to Southern California and wrote trenchant profiles of everyone from Louise Brooks to Johnny Carson for the *New Yorker.* Called himself "a climatic émigré" and died of emphysema in Santa Monica. His daughter Roxana runs the Los Angeles Alliance for a New Economy. Quoted from *Diaries of Kenneth Tynan*, edited by John Lahr (New York: Bloomsbury, 2001).

VALENTINER, WILLIAM R.   Pivotal curator of the Los Angeles County Museum of Art during its pre–Wilshire Boulevard, Exposition Park era. Quoted from *The Passionate Eye: The Life of William R. Valentiner* (Detroit: Wayne State University Press, 1979).

VALLEJO, MARIANO   General, politician, rancher. Eventually, elder statesman and consensus *menschissimo* of the Californios. Quoted from his 1846 parole document.

VANCOUVER, GEORGE   British explorer of the Pacific Coast. Named Point Dume after his friend Francisco Dumetz, a Franciscan padre. Quoted from *Captain George Vancouver* (London: G. G. and J. Robinson, 1798).

VANDEVENTER, PRIVATE JAMES CHARLES   Soldier, son, brother. Quoted by gracious permission of the family.

VENEGAS, DOLORES   Mother. Quoted from *Letters Home: Mexican Exile Correspondence from Los Angeles, 1927–1932*, by María Teresa Venegas (self-published, 2012). Department of Archives and Special Collection, William H. Hannon Library, Loyola Marymount University.

VENEGAS, JOSÉ MIGUEL   Son. Quoted from *Letters Home: Mexican Exile Correspondence from Los Angeles, 1927–1932*, by María Teresa Venegas (self-published, 2012). Department of Archives and Special Collection, William H. Hannon Library, Loyola Marymount University.

VIZCAÍNO, SEBASTIÁN   Soldier, explorer, merchant. The sixteenth century was pretty sleepy in Alta California as far as exploration was concerned, but Vizcaíno's expedition managed to christen—in some cases, literally—San Diego Bay, Point Conception, the Santa Lucia Mountains, Point Lobos, Carmel River, *and* Monterey Bay. They might have done even more, but half his crew died of scurvy or starvation.

WAGNER, ROB   This 1930s Angeleno edited *Script*, the magazine some called a West Coast *New Yorker*, and published everybody from Chaplin to the unsung L.A. classical music writer Jose Rodríguez (q.v.). Quoted from *The Best of Rob Wagner's Script*, edited by Anthony Slide (Lanham, Md.: Scarecrow Press, 1985).

WALD, JERRY   Writer, producer, some say model for Sammy Glick, the amoral studio striver in Budd Schulberg's great Hollywood novel, *What Makes Sammy Run?* Quoted from *Inside Warner Bros. (1935–1951)*, edited by Rudy Behlmer (London: Weidenfeld and Nicolson, 1986).

WALKER, ALICE   Pulitzer-winning author of *The Color Purple*. At least as important to American literature, she found an out-of-print, closed-stacks copy of *Their Eyes Were Watching God* and wrote the article "In Search of Zora Neale Hurston" for *Ms.* magazine, triggering the modern Hurston revival. Quoted from *Gathering Blossoms Under Fire: The Journals of Alice Walker* (New York: Simon and Schuster, 2022).

WALLACE, EDGAR   Prolific novelist, today best known for conceiving, with Merian C. Cooper, the idea for *King Kong*. Four days after confiding to his diary that he again felt "quite gay and bright now," he died in L.A. of double pneumonia. Quoted from his *My Hollywood Diary: The Last Work of Edgar Wallace* (London: Hutchinson & Co., 1932).

WATERS, ALICE   Chef, proprietrix of Chez Panisse, godmother of the California culinary revolution. Quoted from "Alice Waters's Open Letter to the Obamas," *Gourmet*, "Food Politics," January 15, 2009, http://www.gourmet.com.s3-website-us-east-1.amazonaws.com/foodpolitics/2009/01/alice-waters-letter-to-barack-obama.html.

WAUGH, EVELYN   Author of *The Loved One, Brideshead Revisited, Scoop*, and the *Sword of Honour* trilogy. Visited Los Angeles in 1947, essentially to keep *Brideshead* from being made into a movie, and succeeded beyond his fondest dreams: he came away with the material for *The Loved One*, his merciless dissection of Forest Lawn, and, by extension, the embalmed lives of the expats around him. Quoted from *The Diaries of Evelyn Waugh*, edited by Michael Davie (Boston: Little, Brown, 1976).

WAXMAN, AL   Columnist and editor of the *Eastside Journal* in Boyle Heights; uncle of Congressman Henry Waxman. Quoted in *Southern California: An Island on the Land* by Carey McWilliams (New York: Duell, Sloan, & Pearce, 1946).

WAYNE, JOHN   American actor, frequently for director John Ford, and an Oscar winner for *True Grit*. Joan Didion wrote admiringly of him in her classic essay "John Wayne: A Love Story." Quoted from *John Wayne: The Life and Legend* (New York: Simon and Schuster, 2015).

WEBB, BEATRICE   British social reformer and quite funny diarist. Quoted from *The Diary of Beatrice Webb* (London: Virago, 1982).

WELCH, LEW   Much-admired poet of the San Francisco Renaissance who disappeared in Big Sur in 1971, presumed dead by suicide. Some prefer to believe he opened a bar in Mexico with Weldon Kees. Widely quoted final note, e.g., https://www.theunion.com/news/local-news/lew-welch-went-southwest/article_9a85e618-9e09-55e7-a91e-3ab52ac443cd.html.

WEST, NATHANAEL   Author of the novella *Miss Lonelyhearts* and the great Hollywood novel *The Day of the Locust*. Found L.A. a nice place to write about, but he didn't want to live here—until he did. His unexpected happy marriage might well have wound up spoiling him for satire, but the couple perished in a car crash that same year, just a day after the death of his friend and admirer F. Scott Fitzgerald. Quoted from *Nathanael West: Novels and Other Writings*, edited by Sacvan Bercovitch (New York: Library of America, 1997).

WESTON, EDWARD   Celebrated photographer best known for his Western landscapes and nudes. After a lot of tomcatting around, he shacked up with his beloved Charis Wilson (q.v.), eventually a distinguished author in her own right, and helped redefine modernist photography. Diaries published in *The Daybooks of Edward Weston; Two Volumes in One: I. Mexico, II. California*, edited by Nancy Newhall (New York: Aperture, 1991).

WHALE, JAMES   Gifted British director of *Frankenstein*, *The Invisible Man* and *Bride of Frankenstein*, long resident in Los Angeles. His life was dramatized in the film *Gods and Monsters*, based on Christopher Bram's novel *Father of Frankenstein*. Widely quoted, e.g., https://www.arkansasonline.com/news/2018/mar/02/ods-and-monsters-20180302/.

WHITE, T. H.   Highly influential author of *The Once and Future King*, an adaptation of Arthurian legend that's inspired everything from *Camelot* to *Harry Potter*. Born in Bombay and died in Piraeus, in between an Englishman. Quoted from *America at Last: The American Journal of T.H. White* (New York: Putnam, 1965).

WHITE, VICTOR   Theologian, philosopher, and the California-based Dominican priest to whom the psychologist Carl Jung wrote some of his profoundest letters—until White happened to pan one of his books, and the friendship dissolved. Quoted from *The Jung-White Letters* (London: Routledge, 2007).

WIENERS, JOHN   Poet of the San Francisco Renaissance. Quoted from *Stars Seen in Person: Selected Journals* (San Francisco: City Lights Books, 2015).

WILD, HELEN   Invaluable diarist of the 1906 San Francisco earthquake.

WILDE, OSCAR   Irish author of *The Importance of Being Earnest*, among other plays; *The Picture of Dorian Gray*, among other fiction; the letter "De Profundis," and "The Ballad of Reading Gaol," among other poems. Martyred for his homosexuality by the British courts.

WILDER, THORNTON   Author of a great play, *Our Town*; a great screenplay, *Shadow of a Doubt*; and a great novel, *The Bridge at San Luis Rey*. How many writers can say as much? Some lesser work too, but still, that's quite a trifecta. Quoted from *The Thornton Wilder Encyclopedia* (Lanham, Md.: Rowman & Littlefield, 2022).

WILDER, LAURA INGALLS   Author of *Little House on the Prairie*, *Farmer Boy*, and other beloved, underrated books about her childhood homesteading on the South Dakota plains. Quoted from *The Selected Letters of Laura Ingalls Wilder*, edited by William Anderson (New York: HarperCollins, 2016).

WILLIAMS, LIZA   Sadly under-remembered, coolly neurasthenic columnist for the *Los Angeles Free Press*. Quoted from *Up the City of Angels* (New York: G. P. Putnam's Sons, 1971).

WILLIAMS, TENNESSEE   Playwright, author of *A Streetcar Named Desire* and *The Glass Menagerie*, the latter more or less begun in Santa Monica during an otherwise unproductive—albeit highly sociable—screenwriting stint. Earlier, deflowered in Laguna Beach, to his mortification. Quoted from *The Selected Letters of Tennessee Williams, Volume 1, 1920–1945*, edited by Albert J. Devlin and Nancy M. Tischler (New York: New Directions, 2000).

WILLIS, ELLEN   National Book Critics Circle Award–winning critic, feminist, anti-anti-Semite, and political essayist. Did graduate work in comp lit at Cal before serving as the first-ever pop music critic at the *New Yorker*. Author of, among others, *Questions Freshmen Ask: A Guide for College Girls*, *No More Nice Girls: Countercultural Essays*, and *Out of the Vinyl Deeps: Ellen Willis on Rock Music*.

WILSON, CHARIS   Author, model, diarist, once the wife and muse of photographer Edward Weston (q.v.). "Charis Wilson journal, letters and notes documenting the Whitman trip with Edward Weston, 1936–2009," Huntington Library, San Marino, California.

WILSON, EDMUND   Critic, historian, essayist, man of letters. Like Mencken and too many other great American critics, he soon gave up on American fiction—except his own—and pursued other curiosities. The rest of his career consistently altered the world's understanding of whatever caught his fancy, from the history of Communism to the Dead Sea Scrolls. Quoted from his *The Twenties: From Notebooks and Diaries of the Period*, edited by Leon Edel (New York: Farrar, Straus & Giroux, 1975).

WILSON, WOODROW   President of the United States. Celebrated for his worst achievement, winning World War I, and ridiculed for one of his best, trying to bring about world peace. Wilson's best biography is A. Scott Berg's, his weirdest by Sigmund Freud. According to biographer (and Pacific Palisades High grad) Berg, Woodrow Wilson was seen actually *clicking his heels* aboard the presidential sleeping car on the morning after his second wedding night. Most of us picture Wilson as a picklepuss, a hypocrite who ran on a peace platform and within months took us to war, a racist who threw a black civil-rights activist out of the Oval Office, a sap who bet his presidency on a gossamer sand castle called the League of Nations and lost. How to reconcile that Wilson with the virile, adoring husband who wrote from the road to his doomed first wife, "I am madly in love with you.... Are you prepared for the storm of love making with which you will be assailed?" He was whisked through California in 1911 just long enough to give an anti-corporate speech to the since-disappeared Jefferson Club in L.A. and, wistfully, to look up an old flame. A year later, though, the California vote made all the difference, putting him over the top in his first presidential election. Quoted from *A Day of Dedication: The Essential Writings and Speeches of Woodrow Wilson*, edited by Albert Fried (New York: Macmillan, 1965).

WINTERS, YVOR   Revered poet and professor. Quoted from *Selected Letters of Yvor Winters*, edited by R. L. Barth (Athens, Oh.: Swallow Press, 2000).

WISTER, OWEN   Author of the Western classic *The Virginian*, famously misremembered for the line "Smile when you say that." The actual line is "When you say that, smile." Which is better? You decide. Quoted from *Owen Wister Out West: His Journals and Letters* (Chicago: University of Chicago Press, 1958).

WODEHOUSE, P. G.   Comic author of the Jeeves and Wooster novels. Wodehouse passed through California just long enough to write the Hollywood-set novel *Laughing Gas*, nine short stories, and many mostly unused scenes for reputedly unmemorable movies. He also cleared $104,000 and complained about it in an *L.A. Times* interview, thus killing the golden goose for himself, and likely not a few other screenwriters too. Quoted from *A Life in Letters*, edited by Sophie Ratcliffe (New York: W. W. Norton & Co., 2013).

WOLFE, THOMAS   Author of the novels *You Can't Go Home Again* and *Look Homeward, Angel*, among others, and of the immortally titled short story "Only the Dead Know Brooklyn." Along with Hemingway and Fitzgerald, a third thoroughbred in the stable of famed Scribner's editor Maxwell Perkins. Quoted from *A Western Journal: A Daily Log of the Great Parks Trip, June 20–July 2, 1938* (Pittsburgh: University of Pittsburgh Press, 1980).

WONG AH SO   Chinese immigrant, forced into prostitution in San Francisco. Her dutiful self-abnegation as her letter begins makes her ultimate hopes for the future all the more moving. Quoted from *Unbound Voices: A Documentary of Chinese Women in San Francisco* (Berkeley: University of California Press, 1999).

WOODS, REV. JAMES   The first Presbyterian pastor in L.A. Lasted less than a year. Diaries published in *The Reverend James Woods, Recollections of Pioneer Work in California* (San Francisco: Joseph Winterburn & Co., 1878).

WOOLLCOTT, ALEXANDER   Waspish actor and wit. Quoted from *The Letters of Alexander Woollcott*, edited by Beatrice Kaufman and Joseph Hennessey (New York: Viking Press, 1944).

WRIGHT, FRANK LLOYD   Architect of Hollyhock House, La Miniatura, and other landmark buildings in California and around the country. His reputation has aged better than his buildings, as anyone over six feet tall can tell you. Quoted in *What They Say About the Angels* (Pasadena: Val Trefz Press, 1942).

WRIGHT, WILLARD HUNTINGTON   Born in Virginia but raised in Santa Monica, by the time he was twenty-one he was already literary editor of the *L.A. Times.* Wrote the bestselling Philo Vance detective novels under the pseudonym S. S. Van Dine.

X   Pioneering L.A. punk band fronted by Exene Cervenka and John Doe, later featuring uncrowned California poet laureate Dave Alvin. Quoted lyrics Published by Concord Music Publishing.

YEATS, WILLIAM BUTLER   Nobel Prize–winning Irish poet. Quoted from *W.B. Yeats, 1865–1939* (London: Palgrave Macmillan, 1989).

YOUNG, AL   Poet, novelist, screenwriter, journalist, and professor. Served as California poet laureate from 2005 to 2008. Quoted from *The Writer's Journal: 40 Contemporary Authors and Their Journals* (New York: Delta, 1997).

YU, CHARLES   Author of the National Book Award–winning novel *Interior Chinatown* and some much-admired science fiction stories. Has also written acclaimed television, including early episodes of *Westworld*. Quoted from "When we were quarantined," *Los Angeles Times*, June 20, 2020.

YUEN, SANG   Restaurant owner, anti-discrimination activist.

ZEVON, WARREN   Singer-songwriter, addict-lothario, poet-wastrel, *genius.* Quoted from *I'll Sleep When I'm Dead: The Dirty Life and Times of Warren Zevon* (New York: HarperCollins, 2008).

ZODIAC   Serial killer, *San Francisco Chronicle* subscriber. Quoted from letter to attorney D.A. Melvin Belli.

ZORINA, VERA   Dancer on stage and film, a muse of the choreographer George Balanchine. Quoted from her *Zorina* (New York: Farrar, Straus & Giroux, 1986).

ZUCKERBERG, MARK   Businessman, philanthropist. Like half the world, the last entry in this book belongs to him.

ACKNOWLEDGMENTS

The great California publisher Malcolm Margolin of Heyday Books once told me that I'd taken—as a well-meaning twice-a-week book critic who got three hundred new books in the mail a week—a vow of perpetual apology. In editing *Dear California*, with all the inevitable lapses and omissions that such a task entails, the opportunities for guilt are even greater.

To make matters chancier still, as someone who's not above sheepishly glancing at the acknowledgments of my friends' books in search of my own name, I know that the next couple-three pages count. I've worked on *Dear California* for four years, and I daresay the acknowledgments below will leave somebody out—surely cause for relief in certain cases, but maybe knocking a nose or two out of joint elsewhere. I apologize to anybody who might look at these acknowledgments and find their own contributions unfairly missing. Whether below or not, numberless souls have helped me bring this book in for a landing. I so, so, thank you all.

Speaking of thanks, have you noticed that everything good in the world comes from either librarians or their patrons? From the day I first ransacked the endless-seeming shelves of the mighty UCLA library system as a high school student, right up to my current dependence, bordering on the chemical, as a member of the faculty, it has hardly ever failed me. I thank its dedicated full-time staff for never deaccessioning all the books that I never knew I needed until I did.

In the spirit of crosstown comity, I also thank USC's Los Angeles Institute for the Humanities, which has given me a sense of unearned legitimacy for more than a dozen years now. The friendships I've made or deepened at LAIH have nourished this book in ways beyond counting. Hats off to its ringmasters over the years, Louise Steinman, Allison Engel, Steve Ross, Leo Braudy, and Clifford Johnson—and to Louise especially, for introducing me to the one book I'll never finish reading. Oh, and to Catherine Quinlan of the USC Libraries, graceful sitter in the Ronald and Valerie Sugar Dean's Chair, for courtesies and cookies of many kinds.

The same goes for countless California repositories and their stewards from Calexico all the way up to Hilt, and from the Bancroft Library at UC Berkeley on down to the most underfunded local historical society. Writing a research-based book during a lockdown is not for the faint of heart. I didn't get to see nearly as many of you in person as I would have liked, but that's a pandemic for you. I look forward to visiting you all now, book in hand, so you can break my heart by showing me all the great stuff I left out.

At my home away from home, the Huntington Library, I gratefully genuflect toward President Karen Lawrence; curator of Literary Collections Karla Nielsen; retired curator of Western American History Peter Blodgett; curator of Graphic Arts and Social History Dave Mihaly; Christopher Adde, wizardly keeper of the library; retired Collections curator Sue Hodson; and Natalie Russell, Sue's deserving inheritor. All have made the creation of this book both possible and congenial.

And to all the stalwart librarians of the Los Angeles Public Library, a deep and lifelong bow.

And, less directly but just as indispensably . . .

To the Sycamore Street book group, for all the truly stupendous food, California savvy, good books, and conviviality you've brought into my life.

To the bookstores of Southern California, which have nourished me for as long as I've known how to read. If I'd bought every book I ever browsed among your shelves, there'd be even more of you left. I wish I had.

To this region's reporters, critics, and editors, past and present, under good management and bad, who never stop teaching me how to write. You're forever in my heart, and in my driveway.

To three bosses who gave me the most fulfilling work I've ever known: Paul Wilner, Dana Gioia, and Bruce Beiderwell. If I could see you all in one room, I would levitate with joy.

To Kevin Starr, who taught me a lot of what I know about California, and Jeffrey Lustig, the founder of the California Studies Association, who introduced me to Kevin and so much more. I picture them both, strolling the strand at Carey McWilliams's favorite beauty spot, Point Sal, north of Santa Barbara, the only state park closed for repairs all but permanently. Save me a towel, guys.

To the staff of Libros Schmibros, the nonprofit lending library we've built over the years—shelve this one under "gratitude."

To all the people in all the permissions departments who cut us some slack, a huge thank-you. I know you were only looking out for the rights of two groups I revere: authors and publishers. Sorry for all the guilt trips.

For Teresa Carpenter, in whose slushy footsteps I walk. Her book *New York Diaries* does the impossible: it makes New York almost as interesting as Los Angeles.

To my undergraduate assistant, permissions whiz, and sounding board, Samia Saad, who—amazingly—fetishizes old back issues of the *New Yorker* and appears to believe that literary publishing is still a sacred calling. With enough like her, maybe it can be again.

To Rick Prelinger's Internet Archive and the librarians behind Hathi-Trust, who aren't Google Books.

To everyone who's worked so hard in Congress to make the 21st Century Federal Writers' Project Act a reality: Representative Ted Lieu, Leah Uhrig, former representative Steve Israel, Andrea Riccio, Denise Bode, Lucia Alonzo, Emily Green, Jim Fallows, and so many more—especially, of course, my enduring consigliere and erstwhile dedicatee, Colleen Jaurretche. Until we can fully reinvent a contemporary, coast-to-coast Federal Writers' Project, everybody, please accept this chronicle full of California voices as a modest down payment.

To my agent and friend, Sandy Dijkstra, and to her whole team, especially Elise Capron, Andrea Cavallaro, Jill Marr, and Thao Le. They may rep bigger authors, but none more grateful.

To my editor, Kate Wahl, for winkling *Dear California* out of me, and to the whole Redwood/Stanford University Press team and Newgen team. Maybe one day I'll actually meet you. Let's do it again sometime. *The California Dictionary of Quotations*, anyone?

Needless to say, and yet impossible not to, *none* of these people are responsible for this book's innumerable omissions. To attempt any kind of selectivity nowadays—even my value-neutral selection of all the heroes and reprobates in this book—is to wear a kick-me sign the size of a Jumbotron. My *Dear California* is not anyone else's *Dear California*; it won't even be *my Dear California* by tomorrow morning. Just since I submitted the final manuscript last week, I've already come across a few irresistible new diaries and letters juicy enough, had I included them, to lose some unwary small-town acquisitions librarian her job. Too late, alas, too late. Such are the agonies of editing a book as hypothetically endless as *Dear California*. It's bad enough wearing a kick-me sign without regularly wanting to kick *myself.*

But enough self-flagellation. It has been the slaphappy privilege of a lifetime, however undeserved, to spend four years effectively reading California's diaries and mail. The trick now will be training myself to stop.

And one final thank-you: to all the diarists, correspondents, and their families included here, this book is the party I wish I could throw for you. At the risk of winding up in the second edition, please write me a letter and let me know how you liked it.

Oh, and to Californians everywhere: I'd love it if you'd at least consider sharing a personal or family diary entry or a letter with me at DearCA@sup .org. The preceding pointillist history of the Golden State has more blind spots than a Camry with a busted mirror. Let's fill them in together . . .

INDEX

Page numbers beginning with 447 refer to contributor biographies.

CREDITS

pp. 132, 294, 353 from *Screams from the Balcony: Selected Letters, 1960–1970* by Charles Bukowski, edited by Seamus Cooney, copyright © 1993 by Charles Bukowski. Reprinted by permission of HarperCollins Publishers. **Deborah Bull:** Excerpt from *Dancing Away: A Covent Garden Diary* (London: Methuen, 1999). **Edgar Burroughs:** All quotes printed from Edgar Rice Burroughs © 1975, 2017 Edgar Rice Burroughs, Inc. All rights reserved. Trademarks TARZAN* and Edgar Rice Burroughs* owned by Edgar Rice Burroughs, Inc. and used by permission. **Octavia Butler:** Various quotes by Octavia Butler, copyright © by Octavia E. Butler. Reprinted by permission of Writers House LLC acting as agent for the Estate. **Herb Caen:** Excerpt originally published in the *San Francisco Chronicle*, July 5, 1938. **John Cage:** Letters from John Cage to Pauline Schindler. Reprinted by permission of the John Cage Trust. **Erskine Caldwell:** From *Erskine Caldwell: Selected Letters, 1929–1955* © 2012 [1999] Erskine Caldwell. Edited by Robert L. McDonald by permission of McFarland & Company, Inc., Box 611, Jefferson N.C. 28640. www.mcfarlandbooks.com. **Italo Calvino:** Excerpts from *Hermit in Paris: Autobiographical Writings* by Italo Calvino, translated from the Italian by Martin McLaughlin, copyright © 2003 by the Estate of Italo Calvino. English translation copyright © 2003 by Jonathan Cape. Reprinted by permission of Houghton Mifflin Harcourt Publishing Company. All rights reserved. **Neal Cassady:** Excerpts from *As Ever: The Collected Correspondence of Allen Ginsberg & Neal Cassady* (Berkeley: Creative Arts Book Company, 1977). **Willa Cather:** Excerpt(s) from THE SELECTED LETTERS OF WILLA CATHER by Willa Cather, letters copyright © 2013 by The Willa Cather Literary Trust. Introduction, annotation, commentary and compilation copyright © 2013 by Andrew Jewell and Janis Stout. Used by permission of Alfred A. Knopf, an imprint of the Knopf Doubleday Publishing Group, a division of Penguin Random House LLC. All rights reserved. **Steph Cha:** Excerpt from "When we were quarantined" (*Los Angeles Times*, June 20, 2020). Reprinted by permission of the *Los Angeles Times*. **Raymond Chandler:** Excerpt from *Selected Letters of Raymond Chandler* by Raymond Chandler, edited by Frank McShane (New York: Columbia University Press, 1981), copyright © 1981 by College Trustees, Ltd.; introduction, selection, editorial matter copyright © 1981 by Frank McShane. Reprinted by permission of the Estate of the author c/o Rogers, Coleridge & White Ltd., 20 Powis Mews, London, W11 1JN. **César Chávez:** Excerpts from the writings of César Chávez, TM/© 2018 the César Chávez Foundation www.chavezfoundation.org. Reprinted by permission of the César Chávez Foundation. **Susana Chávez-Silverman:** Excerpt from *Killer Crónicas* by Susana Chávez-Silverman. Reprinted by gracious permission of the author. **John Cheever:** Excerpts from *Glad Tidings: A Friendship in Letters, The Correspondence of John Cheever and John D. Weaver, 1945–1982* by John Cheever and John D. Weaver (New York: HarperCollins Publishers, 1993). Reprinted by permission of Harold Ober Associates Incorporated. **Julia Child:** Excerpt(s) from APPETITE FOR LIFE by Noel Riley Fitch, copyright © 1997 by Noel Riley Fitch. Used by permission of Doubleday, an imprint of the Knopf Doubleday Publishing Group, a division of Penguin Random House LLC. All rights reserved. **Winston Churchill:** 427 words from a letter from Winston S. Churchill to Clementine Churchill dated September 29, 1929, copyright © The Estate of Winston S. Churchill. Reproduced with permission of Curtis Brown, London on behalf of The Estate of Winston S. Churchill. **Alexander Cockburn:** Excerpts from *The Golden Age Is in Us: Journeys and Encounters* (New York: Verso Books, 1996). Reprinted by permission of Verso Books. **Wanda Coleman:** Quoted from letter to Truong Tran, originally published in Rain Taxi, online edition Fall 2006, https://www.raintaxi.com/letters–truong-tran-and-wanda-coleman/, and from *The Riot Inside of Me: More Trial & Tremors* by Wanda Coleman, copyright © 2005 by Wanda Coleman. Reprinted with the permission of Black Sparrow Books, an imprint of David R. Godine, Publisher. **Alistair Cooke:** Quotes by Alistair Cooke © Cooke Americas, RLLP. Reprinted by permission of the Alistair Cooke Estate. **Eleanor Coppola:** Excerpts from *Notes on a Life* by Eleanor Coppola, copyright © 2008 by Eleanor Coppola. Used by permission of Nan A. Talese, an imprint of the Knopf Doubleday Publishing Group, a division of Penguin Random House LLC. All rights reserved. **Norman Corwin:** Letters by Norman Corwin housed in the Norman Corwin Collection. Reprinted by permission of the Thousand Oaks Library Foundation. **Noël Coward:** Excerpt from *The Noël Coward Diaries* edited by Graham Payn and Sheridan Morley, copyright 1982 by NC Aventales AG. Reprinted by permission of Alan Brodie Representation Ltd., www.alanbrodie.com. **Robert Craft:** Excerpt from *Dialogues and a Diary*, by himself and Igor Stravinsky (New York: Doubleday, 1963). **Glen Creason:** Diary entries by Glen Creason. Reprinted by permission of the author. **Robert Creeley:** Excerpt from *The Selected Letters of Robert Creeley* (Oakland: University of California Press, 2020). Reprinted by permission of University of California Press. **Cameron Crowe:** Excerpt from *Becoming Almost Famous: My Back Pages in Music, Writing, and Life* by Ben Fong-Torres (San Francisco: Backbeat Books, 2006). **Mike Davis:** Excerpt from "Diary: California Burns" by Mike Davis (*London Review of Books*, November 15, 2007). **Simone de Beauvoir:** Excerpt from *Letters to Sarte* by Simone de Beauvoir, translated by Quintin Hoare, published by Vintage, an imprint of Penguin Random House UK, copyright © 1992. Reprinted by permission of The Random House Group Limited. **Frank del Olmo:** "Perspective on Autism: Facing Loss by Keeping Hope" by Frank del Olmo (*Los Angeles Times*, December 27, 1998). Reprinted by permission of the *Los Angeles Times*. **Philip K. Dick:** *The Exegesis Of Philip K. Dick*, Edited by Pamela Jackson and Jonathan Lethem. Copyright © 2011 by Laura Coelho, Christopher Dick and Isa Hackett. Used by permission of HarperCollins Publishers. **James Dickey:** Excerpt(s) from CRUX: THE LETTERS OF JAMES DICKEY by James Dickey, Letters copyright (c) 1999 by the Estate of James L. Dickey III; Matthew J. Bruccoli, Literary Personal Representative*. Used by permission of Alfred A. Knopf, an imprint of the Knopf Doubleday Publishing Group, a division of Penguin Random House LLC. All rights reserved. **Joan Didion:** Excerpt(s) from THE YEAR OF MAGICAL THINKING by Joan Didion, copyright © 2007 by Joan Didion. Used by permission of Vintage Books, an imprint of the Knopf Doubleday Publishing Group, a division of Penguin Random House LLC. All rights reserved. **John Dos Passos:** Writings by John Dos Passos. Reprinted by permission of Lucy Dos Passos Coggin. **Boris Dralyuk:** Excerpt from "O Kaplans, My Kaplans!" *Los Angeles Review of Books*, posted online on July 7, 2018. Reprinted by gracious permission of the author. **Philip Dunne:** Quotes from Philip Dunne from *Script Magazine*. Reprinted by permission. **Theodore Drei-**

tions, and Librettos. Copyright 1991 Board of Trustees of the University of Illinois. Used with permission of the University of Illinois Press. **George S. Patton:** Excerpt from *General Patton: A Soldier's Life* by Stanley P. Hirshson, copyright © 2002 by Stanley P. Hirshson. Reprinted by permission of HarperCollins Publishers. **S. J. Perelman:** Excerpts from *Don't Tread on Me: The Selected Letters of S. J. Perelman,* edited by Prudence Crowther. Reprinted by permission of Harold Ober Associates Incorporated. **Sylvia Plath:** *Letters Home by Sylvia Plath: Correspondence 1950–1963,* Selected and Edited with Commentary by Aurelia Schober Plath. Copyright (c) 1975 by Aurelia Schober Plath. Used by permission of HarperCollins Publishers. **Ivy Pochoda:** Excerpt from "When we were quarantined" (*Los Angeles Times,* June 20, 2020). Reprinted by gracious permission of the author. **Katherine Anne Porter:** Katherine Anne Porter, excerpts from *Letters of Katherine Anne Porter,* selected and edited by Isabel Bayley (Atlantic Monthly Press, 1990). Compilation copyright © 1990 by Isabel Bayley. Reprinted with the permission of The Permissions Company, LLC, on behalf of the Katherine Anne Porter Literary Trust at the University of Maryland Libraries. All rights reserved. **Lawrence Clark Powell:** By gracious permission of UCLA and the family. **Thomas Pynchon:** Letters quoted from the Stephen Michael Tomaske Collection of Thomas Pynchon, Huntington Library, San Marino, Calif., by gracious permission. **Ayn Rand:** Excerpt(s) from THE JOURNALS OF AYN RAND by Ayn Rand, edited by David Harriman, copyright © 1997 by Ayn Rand. Used by permission of Dutton, an imprint of Penguin Publishing Group, a division of Penguin Random House LLC. All rights reserved. **Ronald Reagan:** Excerpts from *The Reagan Diaries* by Ronald Reagan, edited by Douglas Brinkley, copyright © 2007 by The Ronald Reagan Presidential Library Foundation. Reprinted courtesy of HarperCollins Publishers. **Kenneth Rexroth:** Excerpt from a *San Francisco Chronicle* column by Kenneth Rexroth. Reprinted by permission of the Kenneth Rexroth Trust. **Charles Ritchie:** Excerpts from *The Siren Years: A Canadian Diplomat Abroad, 1937–1945* (New York: Macmillan, 1974). **Joan Rivers:** Excerpts from *Diary of a Mad Diva* by Joan Rivers, copyright © 2014 by CCF Productions, Inc. Reprinted by permission of Berkley, an imprint of Penguin Publishing Group, a division of Penguin Random House LLC. All rights reserved. **Leslie Carol Roberts:** *Here is Where I Walk: Episodes From a Life in the Forest* by Leslie Carol Roberts. Copyright © 2019 by University of Nevada Press. All rights reserved. Reproduced with the permission of the University of Nevada Press. **Vita Sackville-West:** Excerpt from *The Letters of Vita Sackville-West to Virginia Woolf* (Berkeley: Cleis Press, 2004). **Sandie Saito:** Excerpts from letters between Sandie Saito and Molly Wilson archived at Densho: The Japanese American Legacy Project, www.densho.org. Reprinted by permission. **Carl Sandburg:** Excerpts from *The Letters of Carl Sandburg,* copyright © 1968 by Lillian Steichen Sandburg. Reprinted by permission of Houghton Mifflin Harcourt Publishing Company. All rights reserved. **George Sanders:** Excerpt from *Memoirs of a Professional Cad* (New York: Putnam, 1960). **William Saroyan:** Quotes from William Saroyan from *Script Magazine.* Reprinted by permission. **David O. Selznick:** Two memos. Reprinted by permission of Daniel Selznick. **Ruth Shellhorn:** Excerpt from the Ruth Patricia Shellhorn Papers (Collection 1757), UCLA Library Special Collections, Charles E. Young Research Library, University of California, Los Angeles. Reprinted by permission. **Nicolas Slonimsky:** Excerpts from *Dear Dorothy: Letters from Nicolas Slonimsky to Dorothy Adlow,* edited by Electra Slonimsky Yourke. Reprinted by permission of Boydell & Brewer, Inc., University of Rochester Press. **Gary Snyder:** Excerpts from *The High Sierra of California* (Berkeley: Heyday Books, 2016). **Susan Sontag:** Excerpts from "1948" and "1949" from *Reborn: Journals and Notebooks, 1947–1963* by Susan Sontag, edited by David Rieff, copyright © 2008 by The Estate of Susan Sontag. Reprinted by permission of Farrar, Straus & Giroux. **Stephen Spender:** Reproduced with permission of Curtis Brown Group Ltd, London on behalf of the Beneficiaries of The Estate of Stephen Spender. Copyright © Stephen Spender. **John Steinbeck:** Excerpts from a letter by John Steinbeck to Robert Ballou dated February 11, 1933, and excerpts from a letter by John Steinbeck to Elizabeth Otis dated December 15, 1939, from *Steinbeck: A Life in Letters* by John Steinbeck, edited by Elaine Steinbeck and Robert Wallsten, copyright © 1952 by John Steinbeck, copyright © 1969 by The Estate of John Steinbeck, copyright © 1975 by Elaine Steinbeck and Robert Wallsten. Reprinted by permission of Viking Books, an imprint of Penguin Publishing Group, a division of Penguin Random House LLC. All rights reserved. **Samuel Steward:** Excerpts from *Secret Historian: The Life and Times of Samuel Steward, Professor, Tattoo Artist, and Sexual Renegade* (New York: Farrar, Straus & Giroux, 2010). **Susan Straight:** Excerpt from "When we were quarantined" (*Los Angeles Times,* June 20, 2020). Reprinted by gracious permission of the author. **Hunter S. Thompson:** Excerpts from *The Proud Highway: Saga of a Desperate Southern Gentleman, 1955–1967, The Fear and Loathing Letters, Volume One,* edited by Douglas Brinkley (New York: Random House, 1997). **David Thomson:** Excerpt from "When we were quarantined" (*Los Angeles Times,* June 20, 2020). Reprinted by gracious permission of the author. **Hazel Thornton:** Excerpts from *Hung Jury: The Diary of a Menendez Juror.* Reprinted by permission of the author. **James Thurber:** Two excerpts from James Thurber's correspondence with the *New Yorker,* copyright © 1939 by James Thurber. Reprinted by arrangement with Rosemary A. Thurber and the Barbara Hogenson Agency, Inc. **Colm Tóibín:** Excerpt from "Tales from the L.A. River," *New York Times,* July 7, 2020. **Dalton Trumbo:** Excerpts from *Additional Dialogue: Letters of Dalton Trumbo 1942–1962* by Dalton Trumbo. Reprinted by permission. **Kenneth Tynan:** Excerpts from the diaries of Kenneth Tynan. Reprinted by permission. **William R. Valentiner:** Reprinted from Sterne, Margaret. "Distress in the East: A New Life in the West, 1945–1954" from *The Passionate Eye: The Life of William R. Valentiner.* Copyright © 1980 Wayne State University Press, with the permission of Wayne State University Press. **James Charles Vandeventer:** Quoted by gracious permission of the family. **Dolores Venegas:** Excerpts from letters published in *Letters Home: Mexican Exile Correspondence from Los Angeles 1927–1932.* Reprinted by permission. **José Miguel Venegas:** Excerpts from letters published in *Letters Home: Mexican Exile Correspondence from Los Angeles 1927–1932.* Reprinted by permission. **Rob Wagner:** Quotes from Rob Wagner from *Script Magazine.* Reprinted by permission. **Jerry Wald:** Excerpt from *Inside Warner Bros. (1935–1951),* edited by Rudy Behlmer (London: Weidenfeld and Nicolson, 1986). **Alice Walker:** Excerpt from *Gathering Blossoms Under Fire: The Journals of Alice Walker* (New York: Simon and